I0729531

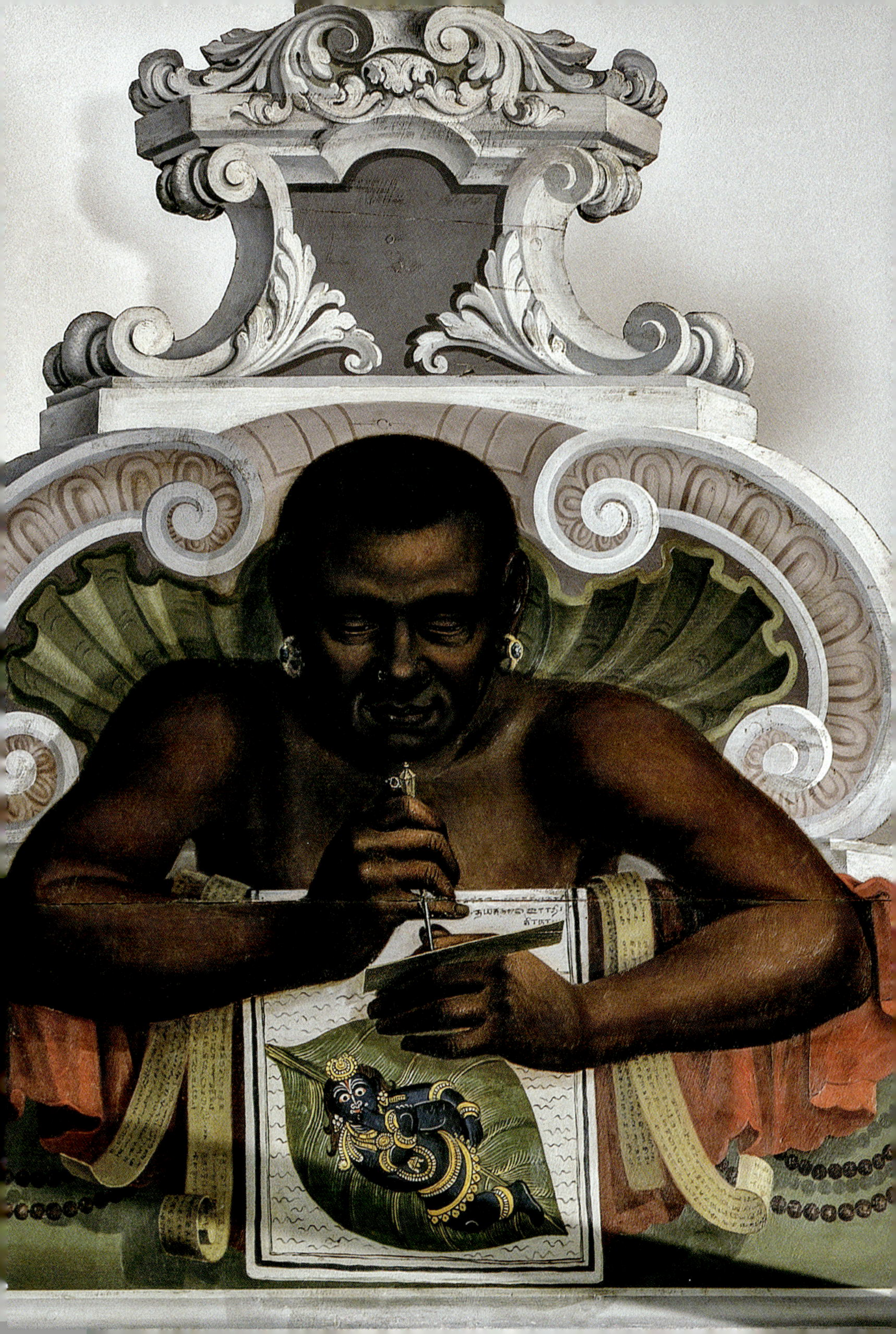

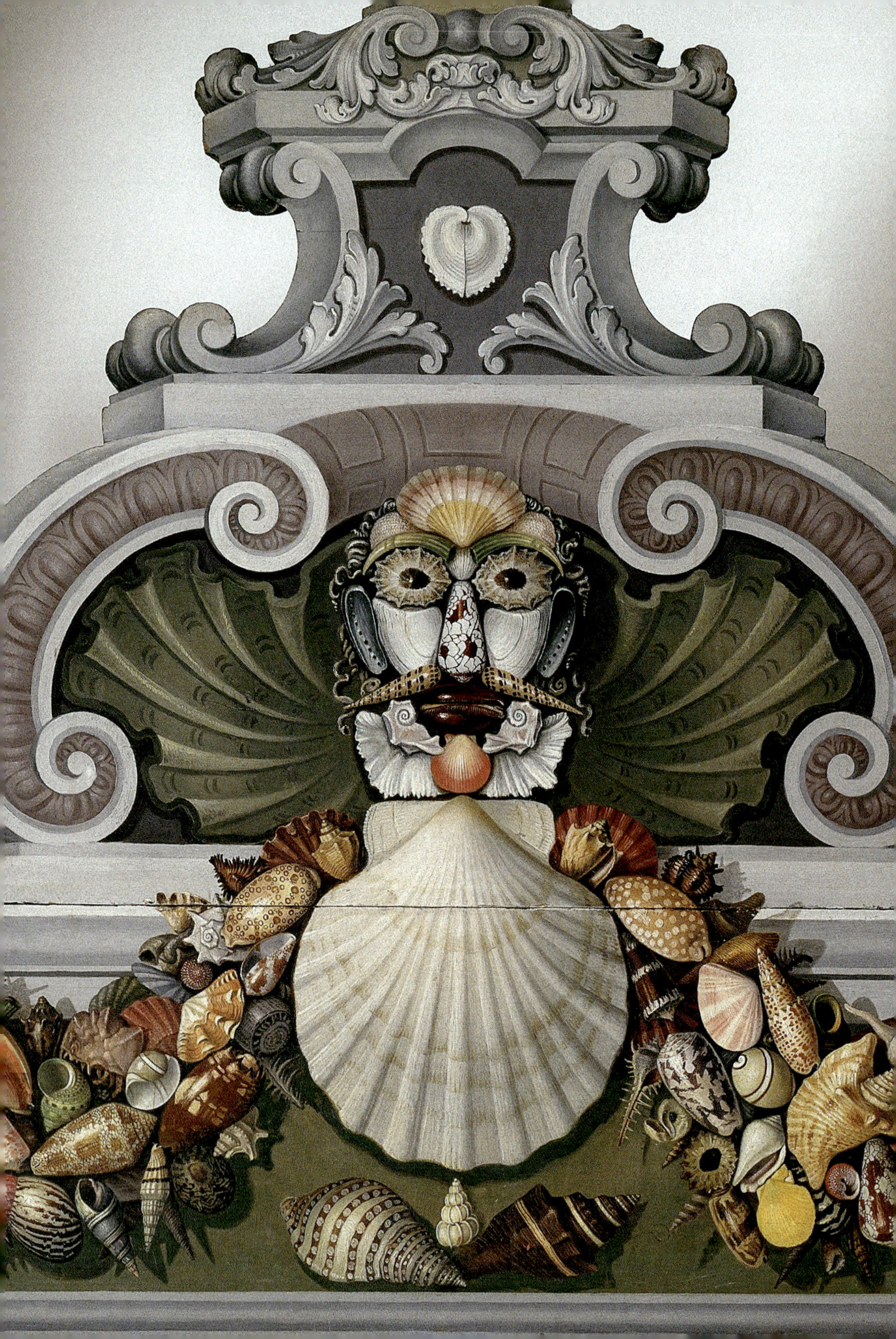

Massimo Listri

CABINET OF CURIOSITIES

DAS BUCH DER WUNDERKAMMERN
CABINETS DES MERVEILLES

Introduction by Antonio Paolucci
Catalogue by Giulia Carciotto

TASCHEN

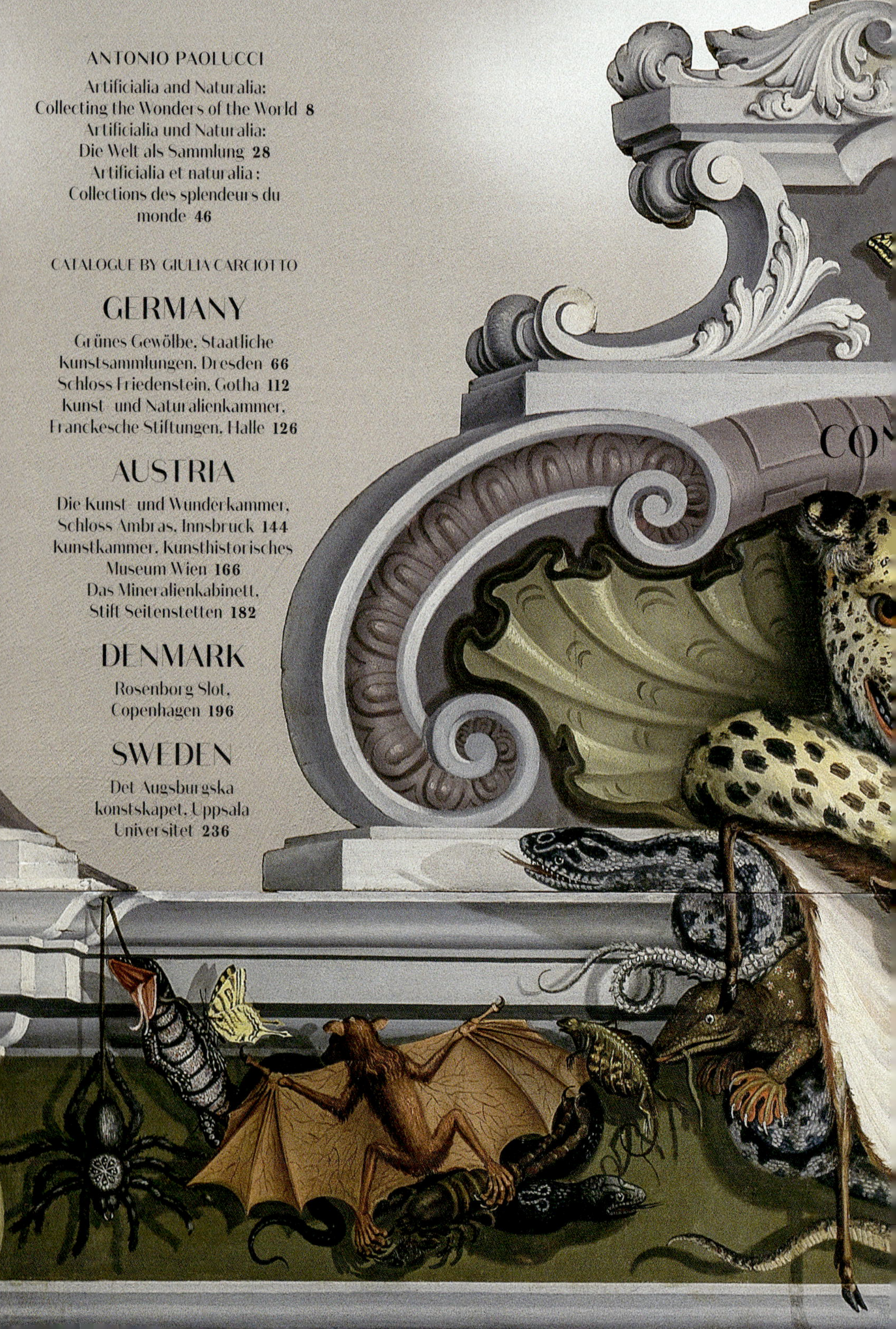

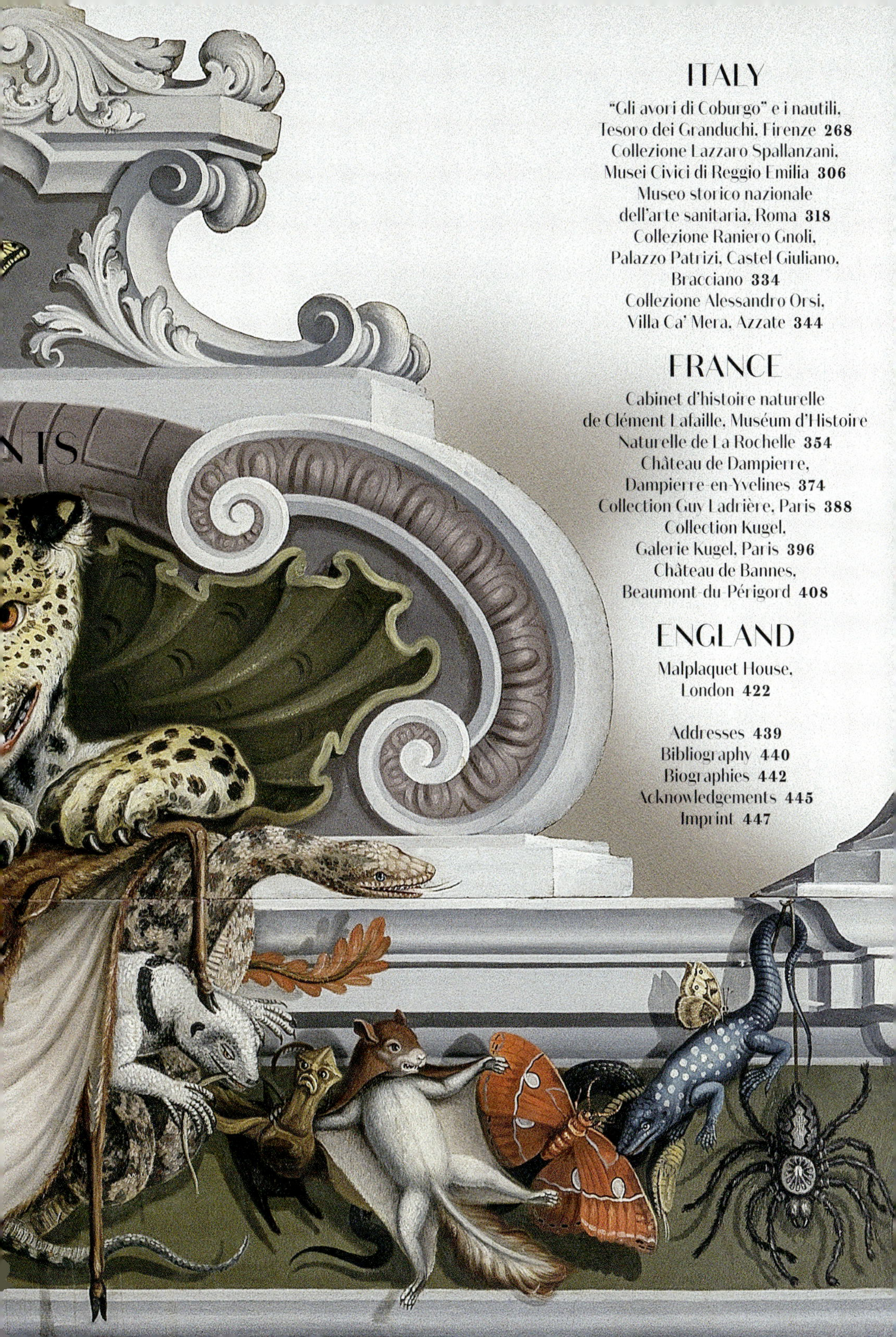

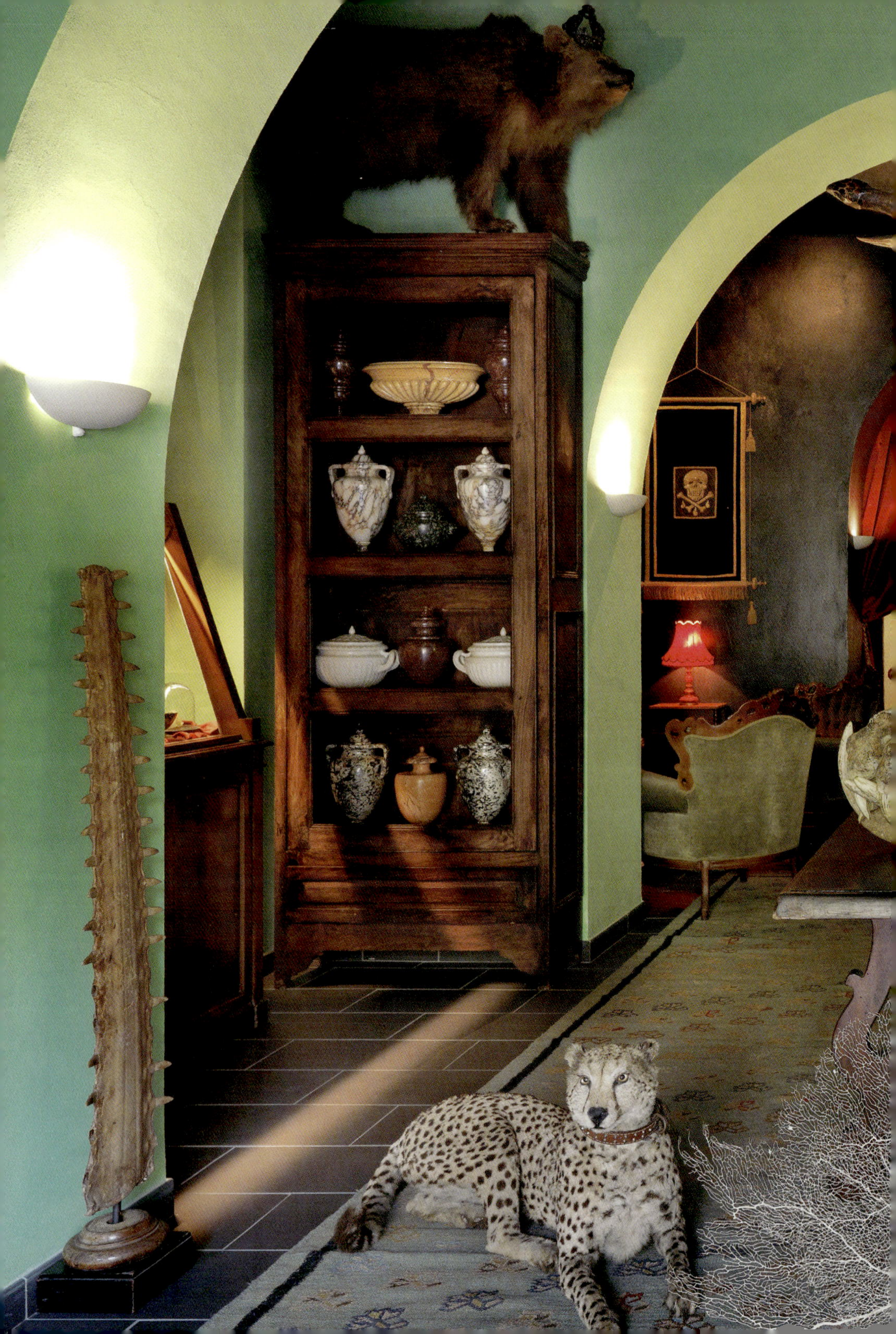

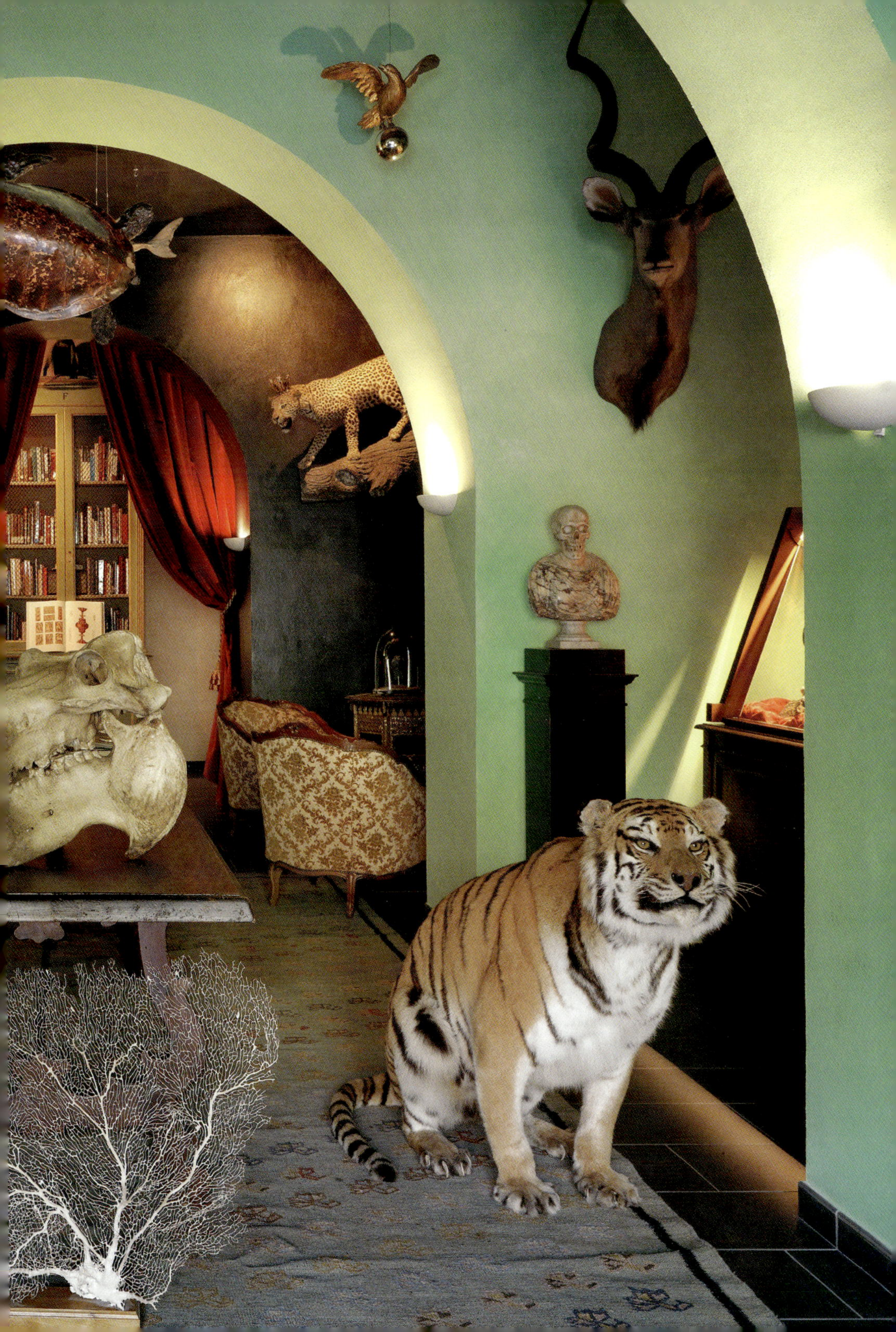

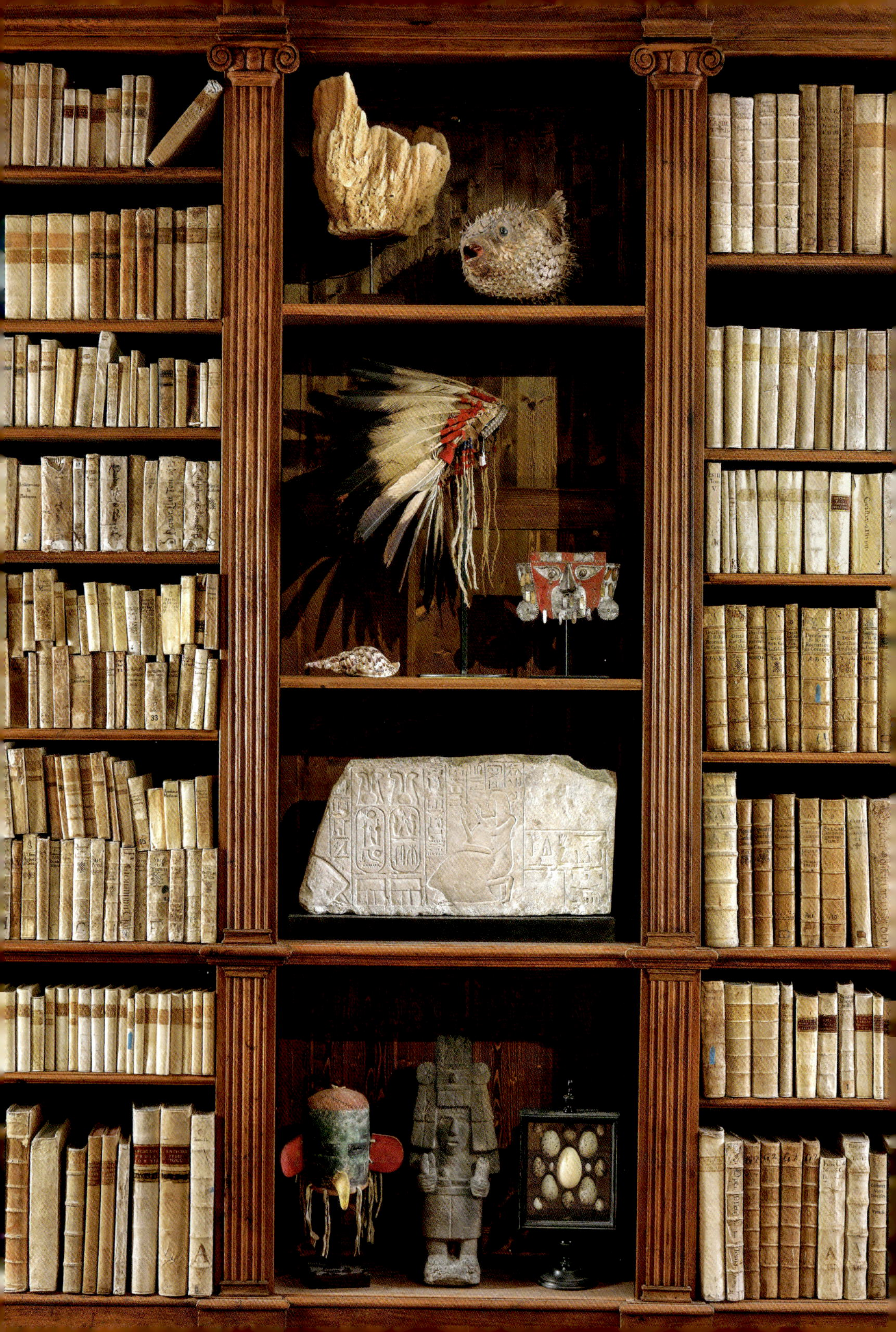

Artificialia and Naturalia: Collecting the Wonders of the World

Antonio Paolucci

The cabinet of curiosities is synonymous with delight and surprise, with marvels and rare objects, but is also the mirror and representation of the world in its entirety (see ill. pp. 16–17). Just as Tommaso Campanella (1568–1639) intended for his ideal museum, almost if not quite everything can be represented in a cabinet of curiosities: visual arts and scientific instruments, astrology and medicine, zoology and botany, gemmology and metallurgy, as well as alchemy and the more esoteric sciences (see ill. p. 25).

This is how the philosopher, theologian and utopian Campanella described his "imaginary museum" in his *Città del Sole* (*City of the Sun*) of 1602 (see ill. p. 10). He conceived a building designed and organised to be a temple to the arts and the sum of human knowledge, which would be subdivided in circles: "Inside the first circle are all the mathematical figures. On the outside of the building is a map of the whole world, with a table for every country, describing its rituals, customs and laws, and with our alphabet displayed above theirs. Within the second circle are all the precious and non-precious stones, and minerals and metals, real and painted. Outside this circle are the wines, oils and various liquors, with their properties, origin and qualities described; also vessels filled with different liquids, from 100–300 years old, which can cure almost all diseases. Inside the third circle are illustrations of all the various types of herbs and trees in the world [...], with their properties described together with their similarities with the celestial bodies, metals and the human body, as well as their medicinal use. On the outside of this circle are depictions of all kinds of fish, rivers, lakes and seas, combined with their characteristics and mode of existence [...]. Inside the fourth circle are illustrations of all the various types of birds with their distinctive traits, sizes and habits, and amongst them the phoenix is very much true to life". Campanella's account continues, referring to examples of all living species, until it reaches the sixth and final circle, where are to be found "all the mechanical arts, together with a catalogue of the various equipment and the different manners in which each is used around the world." Alongside all these examples of human genius in the fields of technical and scientific achievements are some of the most notable figures from earlier periods: "Moses, Osiris, Zeus, Mercury, Mohammed and many others, and, in pride of place, Jesus Christ with his 12 Apostles, whom they respect above all men; also Caesar, Alexander, Pyrrhus and all the Romans". Campanella's imaginary museum also includes the technical advances made in the Far East, because in China "cannons and also the printed word were invented before we knew them".[1] The kind of imagination which, in 1602, inspired Campanella's prose, is the same impetus that generated the culture of the cabinet of curiosities, a phenomenon that spread throughout Italy at this time as well as through the rest of Europe.

The Uffizi Gallery was itself created as a cabinet of curiosities, that is to say a place of wonders. It was originally the Magistrates' Palace, as built by Giorgio Vasari "on the river, almost in the air"; in 1581 Grand Duke Francesco I de' Medici transformed the top floor of the palace into a gallery to house the crown jewels (see ill. p. 13). Bernardo Buontalenti's Tribune has always been both the physical and the symbolic centre of the Uffizi (see ill. pp. 60–61). It was here that the most valuable treasures of the Medici dynasty were kept in order to elicit the curiosity and wonder of the family's distinguished visitors and guests. Francesco Bocchi provided this description of the Tribune in 1591, in *Le bellezze della città di Firenze* (The Beauties of the City of Florence): "At the heart of the Gallery is a dome, called by everyone 'the Tribuna', divided so that it has eight sides and with a diameter of 10 *braccia*, designed by Bernardo Buontalenti and which is most beautiful".[2] The Tribune contained masterpieces of Graeco-Roman statuary (the "Medici" *Venus*, the *Sleeping Eros*), paintings by great masters (Andrea del Sarto, Pontormo, Leonardo da Vinci, Raphael's *Portrait of Leo X*) and small bronzes by Giambologna, but it was some of the other items that impressed Bocchi the most. These included a head of Julius Caesar "made of precious stone, which is blue, and most beautiful in its artifice", and which was beyond all comparison in "the value of its extraordinary manufacture"; a "mound of pearls and jewels" made by Grand Duke Francesco himself; and a turned ivory globe incorporating six ovals of pure ivory with the portraits of the Duke of Bavaria, his wife and children. These objects fascinated Bocchi every bit as much as the vault made of mother of pearl, or the meteorological, astronomical and astrological information conveyed by the lantern and the rotating weather vane suspended from the ceiling.

Over the course of the centuries the Uffizi Gallery lost the defining quality of being a journey through a series of wonders for which it had been known at the time of the Medici. This resulted from the development, in the 18th and 19th century, of modern methods of museology which aimed to classify art on more instructive chronological grounds, or according to school, iconography, style or technique.

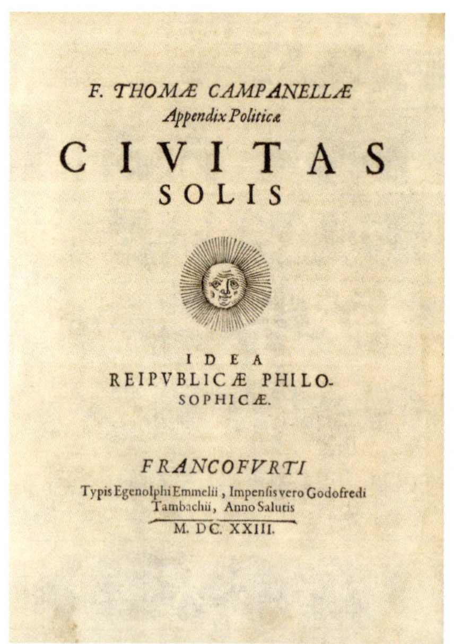

The original layout of the Uffizi cabinet of curiosities can only be reconstructed from early documents. For example, among the masterpieces by Caravaggio displayed in the museum today, alongside the *Sacrifice of Isaac* there appeared the *Head of the Medusa*, a *rotella* (in the terminology of the time) or round painted shield used on ceremonial occasions (see ill. p. 21). This was a gift from Cardinal Francesco Maria del Monte (the Grand Duke's ambassador to the Pope and a sophisticated intellectual, also a friend and patron of Caravaggio) to Ferdinando I de' Medici, presented on 7 September 1598 and noted as such by the armourer Antonio Maria Bianchi. The *Medusa* today appears in the section of the Uffizi dedicated to the masters of 17th-century Naturalism, including Gherardo delle Notti, Manfredi, Stomer and Ribera, among others. At the end of the 16th century the armoury of the cabinet of curiosities was housed in three rooms of the current Uffizi Gallery. The inventories of the time are filled with flashes of pikes, spears, swords (including the legendary sword reputed to have belonged to Charlemagne), helmets, shields and horses' crownpieces. There were bows and arrows, light shields bristling with steel spikes, spears that converted into guns, arquebuses, culverins and springalds. In addition, there were weapons and instruments of war from several parts of the world: Turkish scimitars and "Indian-style" daggers, German gorgets and blades from Milan, Burgundy armlets and "Hungarian-style" helmets. And in amongst all these instruments of warfare, in this extraordinary museum filled with examples of formal beauty and technical excellence, was Caravaggio's *Medusa*. The *rotella* must be imagined in its original location, where it was expressly designed to have a powerful theatrical effect.

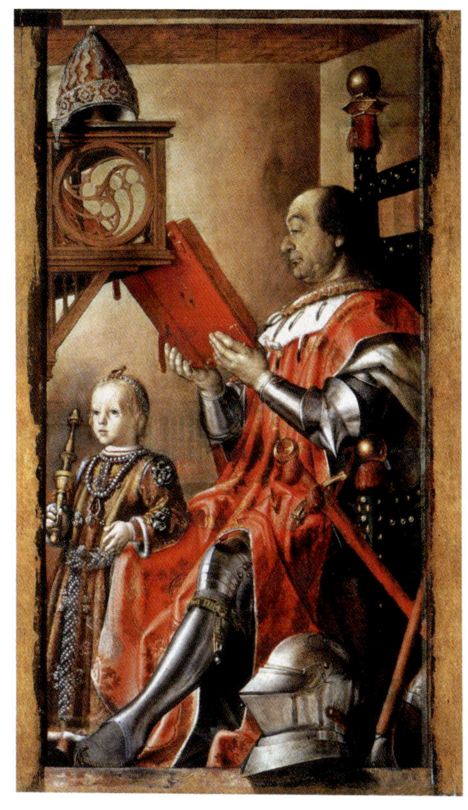

Page 8
Theatrum Mundi
Arezzo, Luca Cableri Collection

Tommaso Campanella
Title-page of / Titelblatt von / Page de titre de Civitas solis, Frankfurt am Main, 1623
Göttingen, Niedersächsische Staats- und Universitätsbibliothek

Pedro Berruguete
Federico da Montefeltro with his Son Guidobaldo / Federico da Montefeltro mit seinem Sohn Guidobaldo / Federico da Montefeltro et son fils Guidobaldo,
c. 1476/77
Oil on panel, 138.5 x 82.5 cm / 54½ x 32½ in.
Urbino, Palazzo Ducale, Galleria Nazionale delle Marche

Within the glittering scenario that unfolds from the inventory of the armoury, this forest of cruelty and death evoked by the endless ranks of weapons in every conceivable shape and for every possible use, there appears a wooden horse dressed in red and blue ("with edging of worked and gilded iron plate of a blue colour, attached with brass links and clasps, with red and yellow decoration at the bottom of the border, lined with red cloth", according to the inventory) seated on which was a mannequin of an oriental warrior, clad in gold and steel armour and wearing a turban "embellished with gold in the shape of a peacock's eye".[3] In one hand the knight held a spear and in the other (here is the *coup de théâtre*!) "a shield adorned with the painted head of Medusa, covered with snakes, as depicted by Caravaggio". If we try to imagine Caravaggio's *Medusa* in the armoury of the Uffizi, as it offset the beautiful but terrifying suit of horse armour given to the Grand Duke by the Persian Shah Abbas the Great, we may allow our imagination to take flight, and so understand the words of the poet Giambattista Marino written after his visit to the Uffizi in 1601:

> *What enemy would not turn into cold marble*
> *Upon beholding on your shield, my lord,*
> *The fierce and cruel Gorgon*
> *So hideously adorned*
> *With a mane of writhing vipers*
> *For all to see in their wretchedness and horror?*[4]

Now it all falls into place. The poet's Mannerist hyperbole is a reflection of the same hyperbole as employed by the person who supervised the layout of the collection, who succeeded in transforming Caravaggio's *Medusa* into the symbolic heart of the armoury in the Medici cabinet of curiosities.

The cabinet of curiosities of the Mannerist and Baroque periods originated in the Italian Renaissance *studiolo*, a central part in the life of a humanist intellectual but also the defining feature of a court, a space that was intended to reflect and illustrate the artistic, historical and philosophical interests of the lord, almost as a concrete representation of his spiritual self (see ills. pp. 11, 15). The *studiolo* was a secret and private place, a repository for the rare and outstanding objects collected and cherished by its owner; these may include archaeological finds, rare metals, precious and semi-precious stones, gold artefacts, books, scientific instruments, favourite paintings and sculptures, along with *exotica* and *naturalia* (see p. 18). Contemporary literary accounts and other documents feature descriptions of the most famous Italian *studioli*, whose treasures have almost always become dispersed in the course of time through either dynastic succession or political events.[5] Among the most noteworthy are the *studioli* of Leonello and Borso d'Este in the Palazzo Belfiore, near Ferrara, and the Palazzo Ducale in Urbino, with its beautiful wooden intarsia by Botticelli and Benedetto da Mariano, and Flemish paintings by Justus van

Gent and Pedro Berruguete (see ill. p. 11). "Beyond the library there is a little room set aside for study […] with wooden chairs with arm-rests and a table in the centre, their inlay and intarsia work all accomplished with the utmost care and attention. Wood veneer covers the floor and also the walls to the height of a man or else a little higher to the ceiling; the surface is divided into square niches, each containing the portrait of a famous writer from the past or present." The painters who produced these works came from far away, because "Federico was most passionate about the matter of painting, and when he could not find a suitable master painter in Italy he went as far even as Flanders to find an excellent artist, and invited him to Urbino, where he commissioned him to make many beautiful paintings,

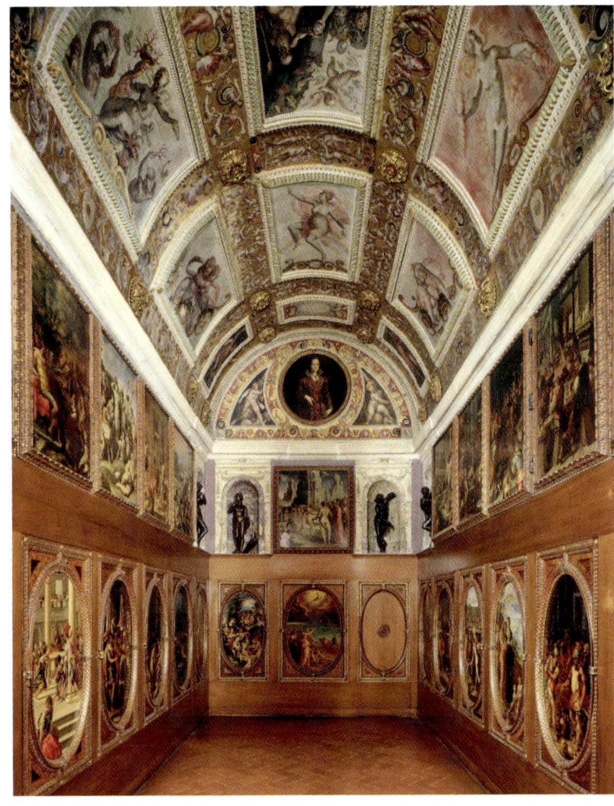

Giorgio Vasari
Studiolo of Francesco I de' Medici / Studierzimmer von Francesco I. de' Medici / Cabinet de travail de François Ier de Médicis, 16th century
Florence, Palazzo Vecchio

which he placed in his studio, representing philosophers, priests and all the doctors of the Church, both Greek and Latin, accomplished with the most marvellous artistry."[6] This was how Vespasiano da Bisticci, in his *Lives of Illustrious Men of the 15th Century* (*c.* 1482), described Federico da Montefeltro's *studiolo* in the castle of Urbino, a building Baldassare Castiglione later described as "a city in the shape of a palace". We cannot fail to be captivated by the image of Federico, the "warlord" immersed in the political and military affairs of the Italy of his day, retiring to his *studiolo* amongst the exquisite paintings and inlaid woodwork to read and reflect on the writings of Plutarch or Livy, Seneca or Cicero, from his trilingual library with its volumes in Latin, Greek and Hebrew. From the *studiolo* of Isabella d'Este in the Palazzo Ducale in Mantua to Cardinal Alessandro Farnese's *studiolo* in Caprarola and the *camerino* of Alfonso d'Este in Ferrara, inventories and the testimony of eye-witnesses reveal a succession of valuable archaeological collections, now lost, together with works by great artists, including Mantegna, Giovanni Bellini, Perugino and Titian.

Worthy of special mention is the *studiolo* of Grand Duke Francesco I de' Medici, in the Palazzo Vecchio in Florence, because it is one of the very few to have survived in its original location and to have retained the painted cabinets in which the collections were kept (see ill. p. 13). "The little room that is being rebuilt is to be used as a cabinet for rare and precious objects in terms of both their value and artistry, such as jewels, medals and carved stones, as well as cut crystal and vases, instruments and other similar small items, placed in individual cupboards according to their kind,"[7] wrote Vincenzo Borghini in a letter to Giorgio Vasari in 1570, when the Grand Duke's *studiolo* was being built. The main theme of the *studiolo* as regards its iconography was the four natural elements (Air, Fire, Earth and Water) which, governed by human intellect, produced "artifice", the prodigious results brought about by scientists, craftsmen and artists. The series of bronze sculptures and paintings on display in the cabinets (by Allori, Santi di Tito, Stradanus and Zucchi, to name a few) serve as both illustration and commentary on the thematic narrative that unifies the whole room. Inside the painted cabinets, which were opened only on rare occasions for the amusement of the prince, his friends and guests, were the *rariora, naturalia* and *exotica* listed by Borghini: pearls, coral, shells, glasswork, rock crystal, precious stones and rare artefacts.

The assembling of collections during the Renaissance was marked by a desire to list objects by way of an encyclopaedic approach. This was the concept behind Paolo Giovio's museum, which was created to be a "temple to fame". In his villa-museum Giovio systematically gathered a large collection of portraits of illustrious men divided according to type: writers, artists, rulers and warriors.[8] History, considered as a succession of exceptional individuals on the model of Plutarch's *De viris illustribus*, was the principle behind Vasari's second edition of his *Lives*, which he also chose to illustrate with woodcut portraits of the artists just as his friend Giovio had done before him in his own biographies.

The desire to understand the shimmering spectacle of history and the world by means of the systematic ordering of objects, art and knowledge is at the root of the modern concept of the museum, and was equally the guiding principle behind the creation of the cabinet of curiosities[9] (see ills. pp. 33, 38, 45). The princely collection of Albert V of Bavaria in Munich, for example, employed a system of classification based on five classes: sacred history and family genealogy; works of art; items from the natural world; musical instruments and exotic objects; and paintings, prints and engravings. The purpose of relying on an entirely empirical system of classification was to achieve a global vision of history and the world, thereby transforming the museum into a universal theatre. This explains why the Belgian physician Samuel Quiccheberg (see ill. p. 22) in 1565 gave his account of the collections of Albert V of Bavaria the title *Inscriptiones vel tituli theatri amplissimi* (Inscriptions or Titles of the Most Ample Theatre).

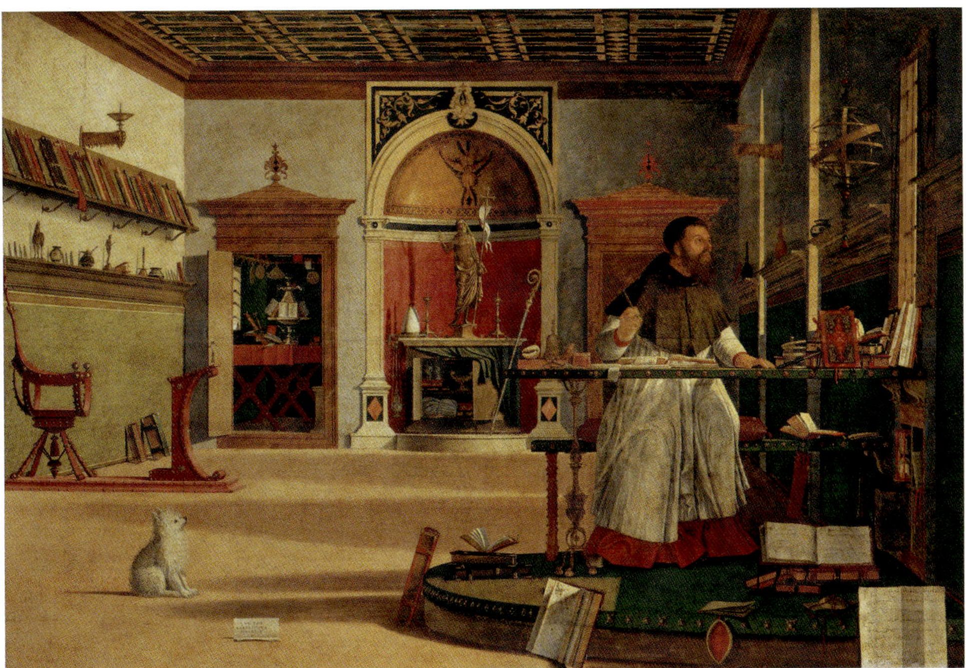

Vittore Carpaccio
*St. Augustine in his Study / Der heilige Augustinus in
seinem Studierzimmer / La Vision de saint Augustin,*
c. 1502–1508
Oil on canvas, 141 x 210 cm / 55½ x 82⅝ in.
Venice, Scuola di San Giorgio degli Schiavoni

Pages 16–17
Andrea Domenico Remps
*Cabinet of Curiosities / Kunstkammer /
Cabinet des merveilles,* 1690
Oil on canvas, 99 x 137 cm / 39 x 54 in.
Florence, Opificio delle Pietre Dure

From the outset then, first in Italy during the late Middle Ages and the early Renaissance
and subsequently throughout Europe under the authoritarian regimes of the Counter-
Reformation, the early museums were shaped by a compulsion for voracious and encyclopaedic knowledge. As shown above, the *studioli* of Italian princes, collectors and humanists
(in Florence as in Ferrara, or in Mantua, Venice or Rome) were already, in essence, universal
museums. Even if their interests and inclinations may have varied, the common objective
was to collect and classify everything: items representative of the arts, sciences and
natural curiosities, archaeological finds and selected paintings, sacred relics and ethno-
graphical documents (see ills. pp. 31, 34, 36, 37, 49, 51, 53, 54–55). This all-encompassing
and omnivorous model of the "universal museum" found its highest expression in the
cabinet of curiosities collections of the European royal families, including those in Prague,
Stuttgart or Ambras Castle in the Tyrol, which was established and furnished by Archduke
Ferdinand II beginning in 1573; also at Fontainebleau, the residence of the kings of France,
or Florence, as already noted, where at the end of the 16th century Buontalenti's Tribune at
the Uffizi was created and also the peculiar alchemical *studiolo* of Grand Duke Francesco I.

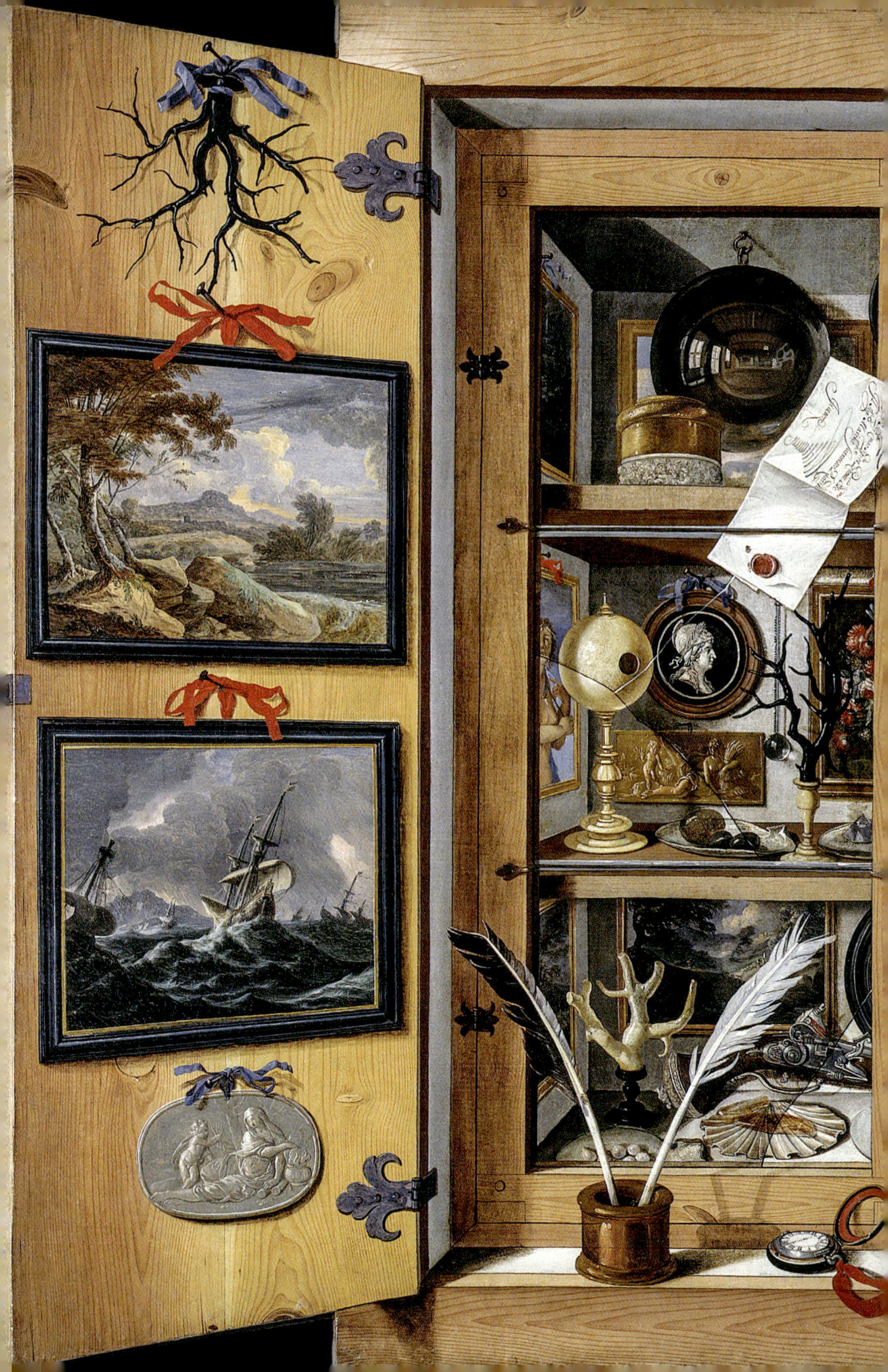

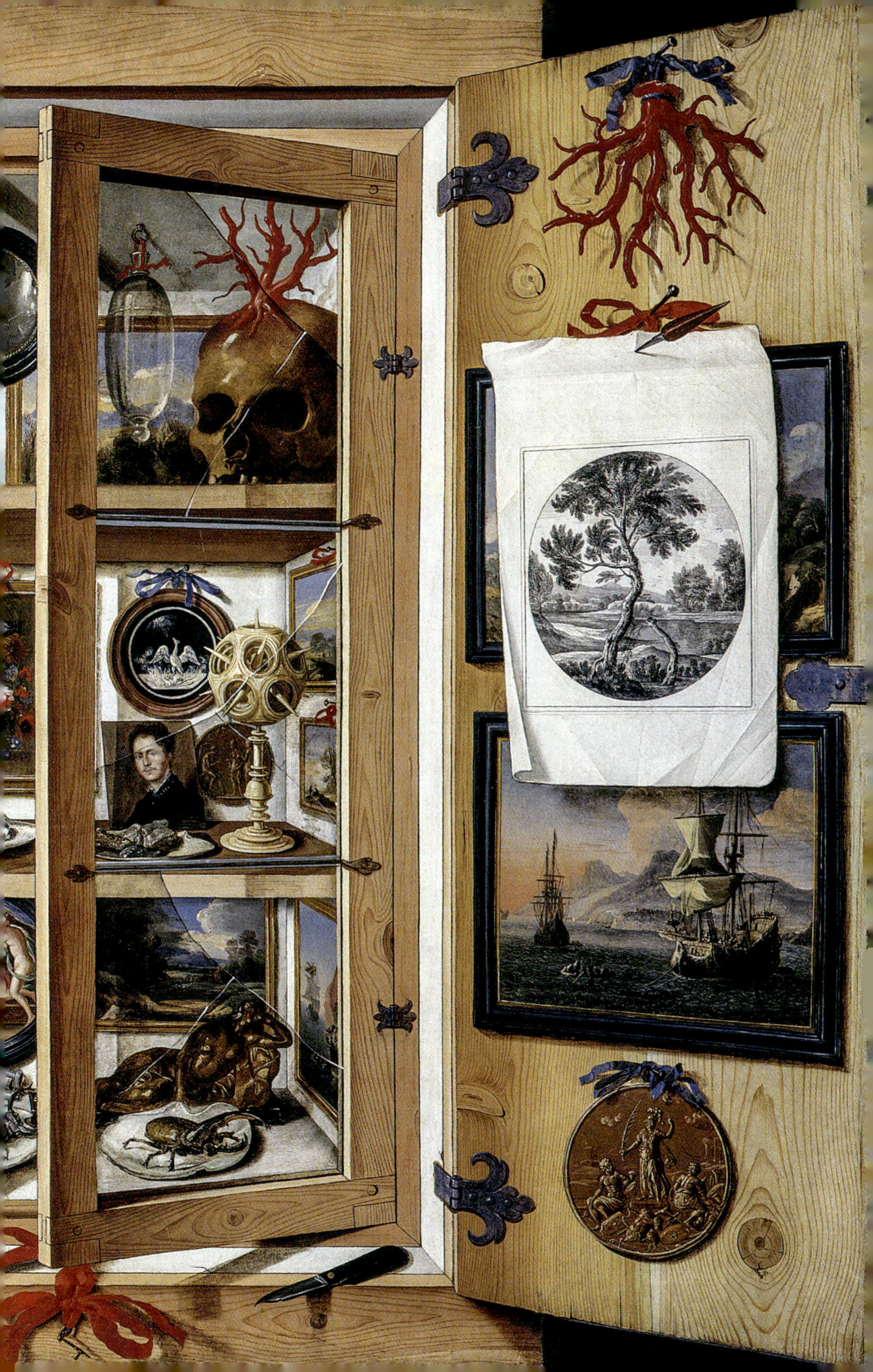

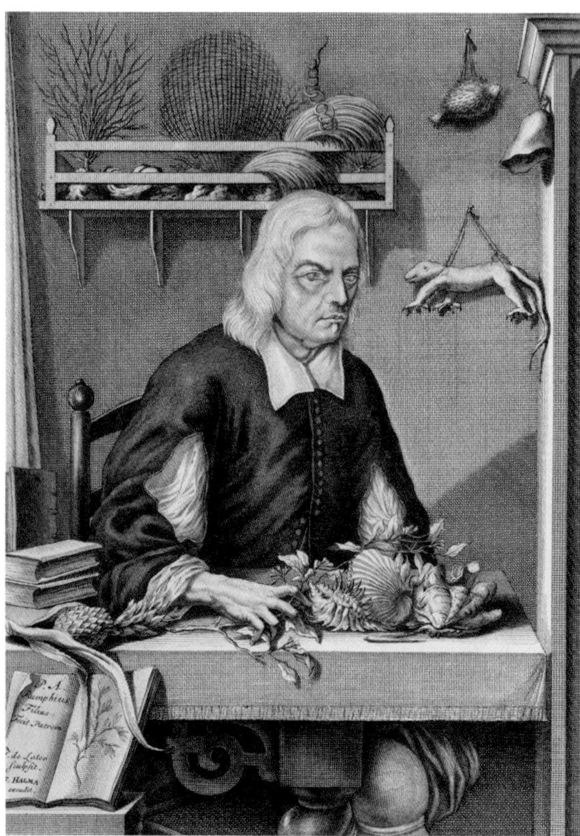

Portrait of Georg Eberhard Rumph, 1705
in Georg Eberhard Rumph, *D'Amboinsche Rariteitkamer*,
Amsterdam, 1705, p. 19

At times it could be said that a kind of madness or sense of anguish manifested itself in the obsessive collecting taken up by European rulers during this period. A case in point is the cabinet of curiosities of Ambras Castle near Innsbruck, a collection every bit as chilling as it is fascinating (see pp. 144–165). Visitors to this gloomy Tyrolean castle, chosen by Archduke Ferdinand II of Habsburg to be his residence and where he surrounded himself with a court of poets and artists, are greeted by Paul Reichel's masterpiece, *Death* (see ill. p. 157), lost in thought yet aware of the viewer's presence, as if to underline the vanity of all that we are about to see. Once inside the castle it becomes evident that the collection is organised into categories (*naturalia, artificialia* and *mirabilia*), because here amidst the nightmarish madness there is rationality, but present above all to awaken curiosity and the sense of wonder, to challenge preconceived notions and convictions. There are images of dwarfs, giants and natural monsters, human beings entirely covered in hair, but alongside these are also portraits of rulers, military captains and illustrious men. In the same way the pensive figure of *Death*, the guardian and also the emblem of Ambras Castle, teaches us that all is vanity, a fleeting apparition, whether the horrors and marvels of Nature or the glory of kings. Is there then one single image that could sum up all the splendours and horrors of Archduke Ferdinand's cabinet of curiosities? The answer is yes, and this is where the photographic eye of Massimo Listri comes into the equation, keeping the whole multiplicity of objects under close control with the unyielding fixity of his images. If Ambras is hyperbole, excess and exaggeration, let us pause a while and contemplate the portrait of Gregor Baci, whose eye was impaled by a lance (see ill. p. 149), the dancing skeleton (see ill. p. 156), the crocodile that seems to be climbing up the wall or the ivory artefact worked to the very limits of the carver's art. In this way we can halt for a moment the kaleidoscopic and iridescent spectacle of a universe which, like Jorge Luis Borges's *The Aleph*, might otherwise overwhelm us.

The most beautiful and most important cabinet of curiosities in Italy is in the Pitti Palace in Florence (see ill. p. 65). In the northern part of the palace, known as the "Summer Apartment", is the Tesoro dei Granduchi, the "Treasury of the Grand Dukes", an extraordinary assemblage of rare and precious objects (see pp. 268–305). In the great reception hall exquisite frescoes as luminous as silk tapestries, by Florentine painters of the Baroque period such as Giovanni da San Giovanni and Francesco Ferrini, illustrate the glories of the House of Medici and the destiny of Florence itself, which, following the Turkish occupation of Constantinople, became the new Athens, a beacon of civilisation and culture for the whole world. The frescoes immortalise Lorenzo the Magnificent, surrounded by the artists and intellectuals of his circle as embodied by Marsilio Ficino and the Platonic Academy.

The Great Hall by Giovanni da San Giovanni is the heart of the Tesoro dei Granduchi. Surrounding it on all sides, distributed among several rooms, are the treasures amassed by the Medici family over the centuries, which Anna Maria Luisa, the Electress of the Palatinate and last heir of the dynasty, bequeathed to the Grand Dukes of Lorraine, with a legal restriction forbidding the removal or dispersal of the treasures from the palace. Inside the Tesoro dei Granduchi are Byzantine and Sassanid vases collected by Lorenzo the Magnificent, items of furniture made of amber and some of the rarest and most exquisite pietra dura tables in the world. There are artefacts made of lapis lazuli designed by Bartolomeo Buontalenti and rock crystal objects carved by the great Milanese goldsmiths, cameos and jewels that once belonged to the Medici princesses and ethnographic finds from remote parts of the Americas. This marvellous, glittering "chamber of wonders" also features the group of artefacts known as the Coburg Ivories.[10] In March 1635, during the Thirty Years' War, Imperial troops attacked and captured the fortress of Coburg. Mattias de' Medici, fighting on the side of the Catholic army, seized the collection of ivories that belonged to the Lutheran prince and took it to Florence as spoils of war. These 27 translucent, extremely fragile ivories are masterpieces of art and science. The viewer is uncertain whether to be more astounded by the creative imagination of the craftsman who brought the manipulation of his material almost to the point of transfiguration, or by the technical quality of the precision lathe that has managed to deliver such extraordinary results with the finest accuracy.

As he captures his images of the Coburg Ivories, Listri's gaze succeeds in somehow merging with the subject at the same time as participating with it. He is fascinated by the way organic matter—an elephant's tusk—has been manipulated and transformed by artifice, and communicates his sense of wonder, which is immediately shared by the viewer, at the coiled twists and miraculous, threadlike work achieved with the lathe. At the same time he wants to convey—and does so magnificently—the translucent, diaphanous, luminous beauty of these objects which appear to have spilled out from the coffers of Paradise to cast their quiet radiance upon the amber, lapis lazuli and silver of the Medici treasure.

Perhaps only Angelo Maria Ripellino, in *Magic Prague* (1973), has been able to evoke the full hypnotic and sinister allure of Prague Castle, the residence of the Habsburg Emperor Rudolf II (see ill. p. 23). He died at the age of 60 in 1612, before his castle was destroyed and his collections dispersed during the Thirty Years' War. But in the course of his life, the emperor—an irascible visionary, misanthropic and given to hypochondria, who surrounded himself in his castle with a court of adventurers, engineers, alchemists, astrologers and magicians—was driven by a boundless compulsion to accumulate things, so much so that in all of Europe there was not a collection of wonders to rival his in terms of size or the astonishing items it contained. In the cabinets and glass cases of Prague Castle could be found everything: there were automata designed by the Imperial engineers and rock crystal carved by Saracchi and Miseroni from Milan, cups made from rhinoceros horn or ostrich eggs as well as masterpieces of art (paintings, sculptures, enamels, tapestries, gold artefacts, armour and weaponry) collected by generations of Habsburg rulers over the centuries. The objects from Rudolf's Prague collection which escaped destruction during the war, together with other Habsburg treasures from different locations, now make up the Kunstkammer of the Kunsthistorisches Museum in Vienna. In 1891, Franz Joseph I established the Imperial collection of 2,100 pieces (see pp. 166–181); this assemblage is so awe-inspiring, so overflowing with masterpieces—such as Benvenuto Cellini's gold *Salt Cellar* (see ill. p. 56) or the mechanical automata, those hybrid forms (hence fascinating for that reason) born of the cross-pollination of art and technology—that even Listri's photographic eye falters before it, as if momentarily intimidated.

Some cabinet of curiosities collections possess the beguiling charm of enchanted palaces, like magical visions suspended in time. One such example is the royal residence of Rosenborg Castle in Copenhagen (see pp. 196–235). Alongside precious objects associated with Nordic legends (the *Oldenburg Horn*, or the Throne Chair made from the long, spiralling tusks of narwhals) are displayed the porcelain collection and the thousand glass pieces from Murano, a gift from the Republic of Venice to King Frederick IV following his visit to the city, immortalised in a famous painting by Carlevarijs (see ill. p. 59). Listri's camera examines the glass cases teeming with objects, pauses before the portraits with their glowing, almost tactile other-worldly presence, and is captivated by the hoards of ivories, gold artefacts and masterpieces of glasswork. The impression gained is one of "orderly excess", a glittering, variegated abundance kept in check by a sense of deliberate and rigorous order.

Michelangelo Merisi da Caravaggio
Head of the Medusa / Medusenhaupt / Méduse,
c. 1597/98
Oil on canvas attached to wood, d. 58 cm / 22⅞ in.
Florence, Gallerie degli Uffizi

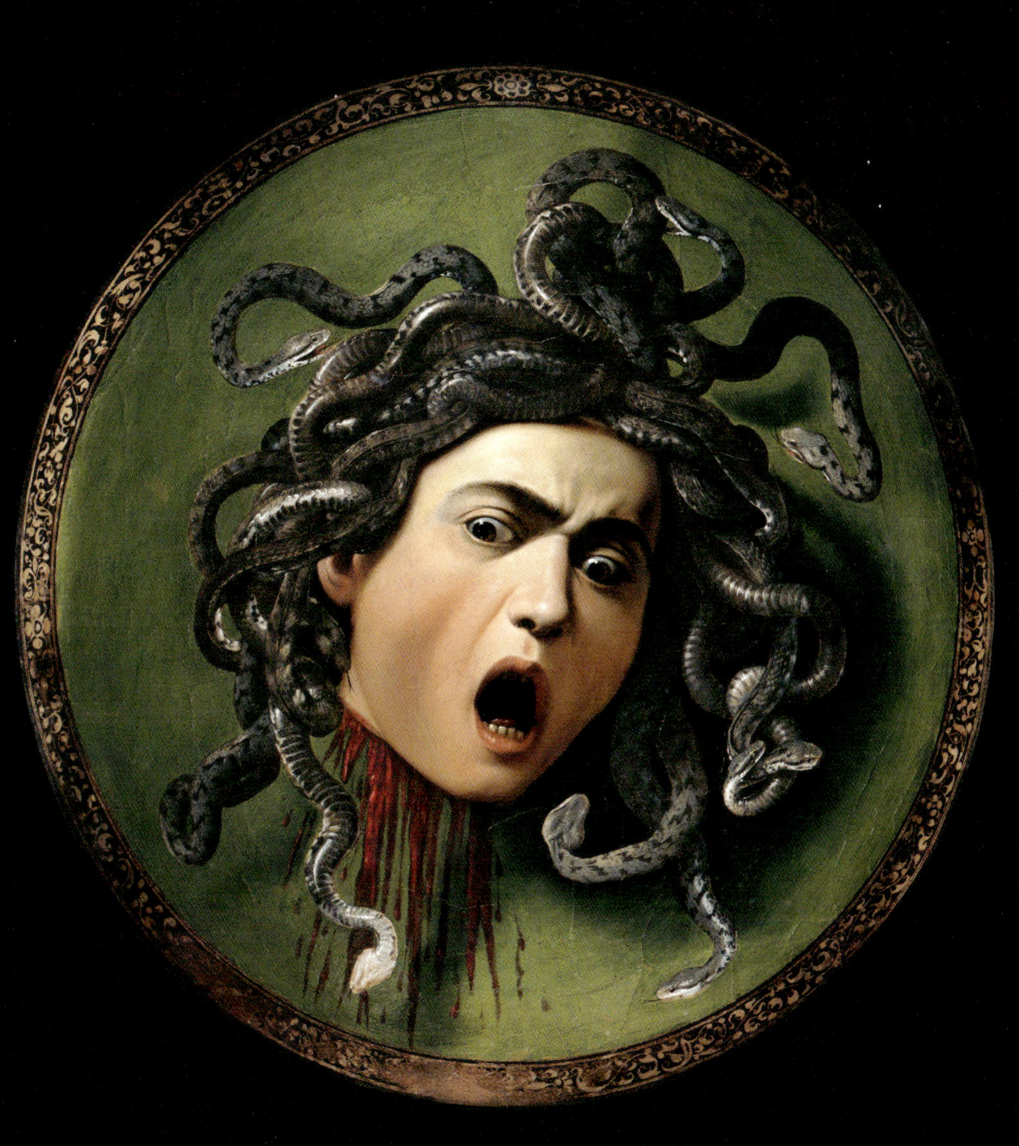

The 17th century was marked by Galileo's discovery that the sky extends to infinity, and Blaise Pascal's enquiries into the vertiginous abyss of the human soul; this resulted in a growing awareness of the immense vastness that surrounds us, but also of the infinitesimal presences that exist within the pulsating mechanism of the human body, and in every other creature in the world. Only during such a time as this could an object be conceived and constructed to be, in a manner of speaking, as big as the world itself, to be a metaphor and an image of the world. The object in question may be found today in the Gustavianum Museum in Sweden, in the art collections of Uppsala University, and is the cabinet King Gustav II Adolf of Sweden received from the German city of Augsburg, a masterpiece created by Philipp Hainhofer, the greatest cabinet-maker of his day (see pp. 236–267). It features hundreds of drawers, some visible but most of them hidden from sight, together with sliding panels and tilting mirrors, and contains over a thousand objects made of ivory, enamel or pietra dura, concealed in its numerous compartments. The whole world is here, expressed and enshrined in a piece of furniture. The Uppsala cabinet bewilders even Listri as he photographs it, yet he succeeds in conveying its particular, almost hypnotic sense of accumulation and multiplication. In his photographs this microcosm becomes the image of the cosmos, in precisely the same way that Hainhofer and the king wished to see and possess it. Perhaps only a country as philosophically inclined as Germany could sustain such a quasi-mystical notion of a "chamber of wonders" (see ill. p. 63).

In Dresden, the "Florence of the North" as it is called in eulogistic literature, the city museums are famous for Raphael's *Sistine Madonna*, a painting that enchanted Dostoyevsky, and for the masterpieces by Correggio and Parmigianino that were acquired by Augustus, Elector of Saxony, from the Este family in Modena. However, few people know that since 1560 the Residenzschloss of the great Prince-Elector, subsequently king of Saxony, has housed one of the most exquisite and fascinating cabinets of curiosities

Hans Mielich
Portrait of Samuel Quiccheberg
in Samuel Quiccheberg, *Declaratio psalmorum poenitentialium*, 1565, f. 131r
Munich, Bayerische Staatsbibliothek

Wenzel Maler
Portrait of Emperor Rudolph II, 1606
Wax in high relief, framed and glazed,
29.2 x 21.6 x 5.5 cm / 11½ x 8½ x 2⅛ in.
London, Victoria and Albert Museum

in Europe. The rooms were filled with seemingly endless series of *naturalia* and especially *artificialia* (clocks, automata and scientific instruments), and at the heart of it all was the Grünes Gewölbe (Green Vault). The castle was destroyed during the Second World War, in the appalling bombing of Dresden in February 1945. Its reconstruction and the replacement of the objects from the collection (including over 3,000 masterpieces of goldsmithing and jewellery), now displayed in a highly sophisticated exhibition, must be acknowledged as one of the most enlightened and important initiatives to have been achieved in the latter part of the 20th century (see pp. 66–111).

In following the sequence of the great cabinet of curiosities collections in the western world we return to the very roots of the history of thought and science. Massimo Listri has taken us on a journey through the collections which came into being in the first place to facilitate the pursuit of scientific aims and study. His images permit us to gain access to the Benedictine abbey of Seitenstetten, in Austria, where, in a calmly resplendent Rococo setting, may be found one of the most important collections of minerals in Europe (see pp. 42, 182–195). Similarly—although in this case the objects are organised according to the selective classification criteria of the Enlightenment—upon entering the marine paradise of the Cabinet of Clément Lafaille, in the Muséum d'Histoire Naturelle in La Rochelle, France, we cannot fail to be amazed by the limitless curiosity of the man who created this collection, who loved the sea and, ahead of his time in the 18th century, wanted to know all its secrets, and thus selected and amassed so many starfish, shells and madrepores (see pp. 354–373).

Back in Italy, in the civic museums of Reggio Emilia can be seen various documents and materials gathered by Lazzaro Spallanzani, one of the fathers of modern experimental science (see pp. 306–317), and in the Palazzo Patrizi in Bracciano, near Rome, those looking in are greeted by the *splendor marmorum* (splendour of marble). Ancient Rome, the city of Domitian and Martial, Hadrian and Aristides, Commodus and Apuleius, Constantine and Diocletian, was a colourful place, built not just of white marble but

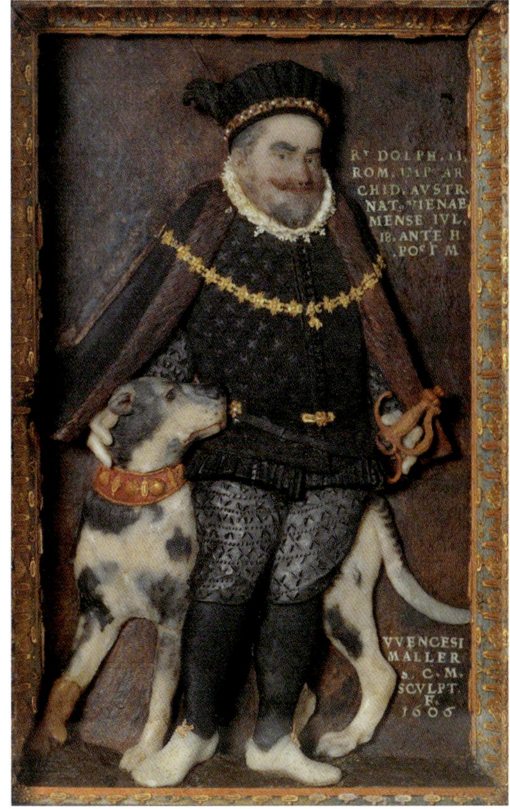

also porphyry and *rosso antico* (red porphyry), grey and green granite from Africa and Anatolia, black basalt, Spanish jasper, yellow breccia, alabaster and Portasanta. All of this is known from Raniero Gnoli, the author of a number of invaluable books on the subject of ancient Roman marbles, and who put together the huge and extraordinary collection in the Palazzo Patrizi of examples of the various different stones that made the splendour and glory of Rome (see pp. 334–343).

Even though its existence is known to only a few, and fewer still visit it, the ancient Ospedale di Santo Spirito in Sassia, on the Lungotevere in Rome and not far from the Vatican, is a true cabinet of curiosities of the history of health: therapeutic practices, surgical instruments, pharmacopoeia and care for the sick are all represented through five centuries' worth of material, documents and publications, preserved in the most important medical history library in Italy today (see pp. 318–333).

It is fair to ask, in closing, whether the notion of the cabinet of curiosities still exists in the imagination and aspirations of today's collectors, and whether the impulse behind such omnivorous, extravagant collecting has survived until the present, providing modern counterparts of Rudolf of Habsburg, Athanasius Kircher (see ill. p. 41) and Francesco de' Medici. The answer is yes (see ills. pp. 6–8, 26–28, 46). When we look at Alessandro Orsi's collection in Azzate in Varese (see pp. 344–353), or the collection of glyptic art in Guy Ladrière's gallery in Paris (see pp. 388–395), or the ancient ivories in the Kugel gallery (see pp. 396–407), also in Paris, there is no avoiding the conclusion that the impulse behind the historical creation of the great European collections of *mirabilia* has not been extinguished. At the same time it is true though that the collections I have described here, and which have been illustrated by Massimo Listri, belong in the majority of cases to art-dealers. Overwhelmed by the clamour of advertising and the fickle trends of the market, the private collector of today struggles to achieve the mindset required for the patient, meticulous pursuit of things, the things we fall in love with and which make us happy to own. And yet it is this attitude, and no other, that we must encourage and support.

Notes

1 Campanella 1602, pp. 35–38.
2 Bocchi 1591, pp. 106–110, 111–112.
3 Paolucci 2007, pp. 87–90.
4 Giambattista Marino 1620, p. 48.
5 De Benedictis 1991, pp. 32–37, 168–178.
6 Da Bisticci *c.* 1482, p. 209; Reynaud & Ressort 1991, pp. 82–114.
7 Frey 1930, p. 529; Berti 1967.
8 De Vecchi 1977, pp. 87–93.
9 De Benedictis 1991, pp. 116–125, 287–298.
10 Schmidt & Sframeli 2013.

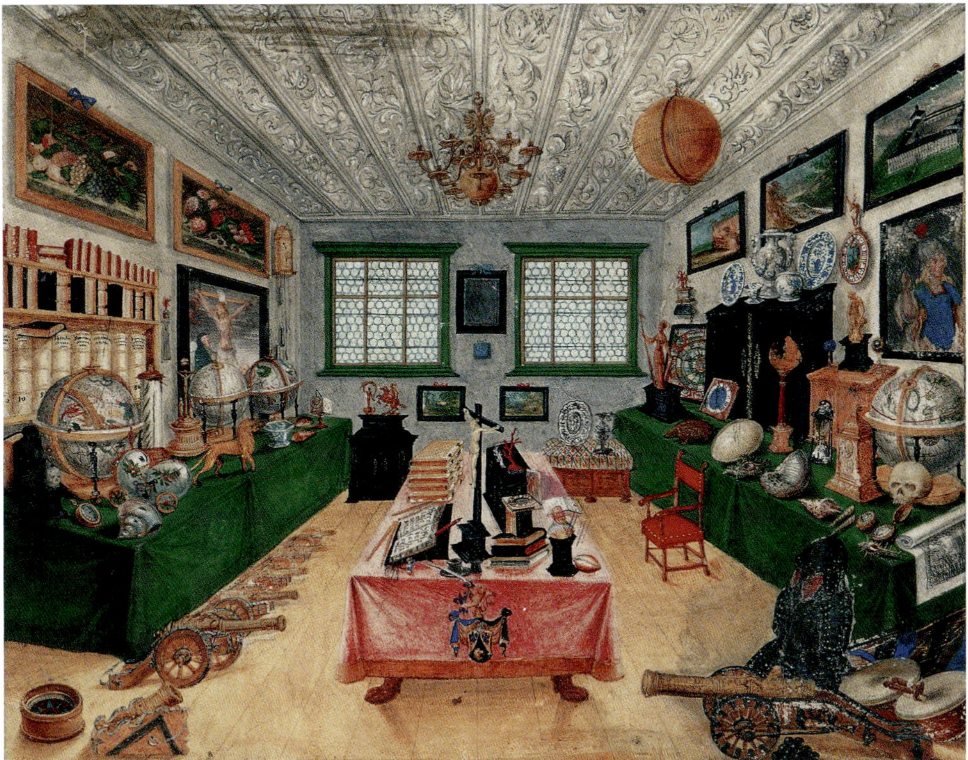

Joseph Arnold
*The Cabinet of Curiosities of the Dimpfel Family of
Regensburg, Iron Wholesale Merchants and Miners /
Die Kunstkammer der Regensburger Großeisen-
händler- und Gewerkenfamilie Dimpfel / Le Cabinet
des merveilles de la famille Dimpfel, commerçants de
fer en gros et membres d'une société minière, 1668 (?)*
Gouache, 14.9 x 19.1 cm / 5⅞ x 7½ in.
Ulm, Ulmer Museum

Pages 26–27
*Display cases with examples of semi-precious stones
from Egypt and India, and other ancient items / Schau-
kästen mit Objekten aus Halbedelsteinen aus Ägypten
und Indien sowie weitere antike Sammlungsstücke /
Vitrines d'exposition avec des exemples de pierres
semi-précieuses d'Égypte et d'Inde, et d'autres
pièces anciennes*
Rome, Dario del Bufalo Collection

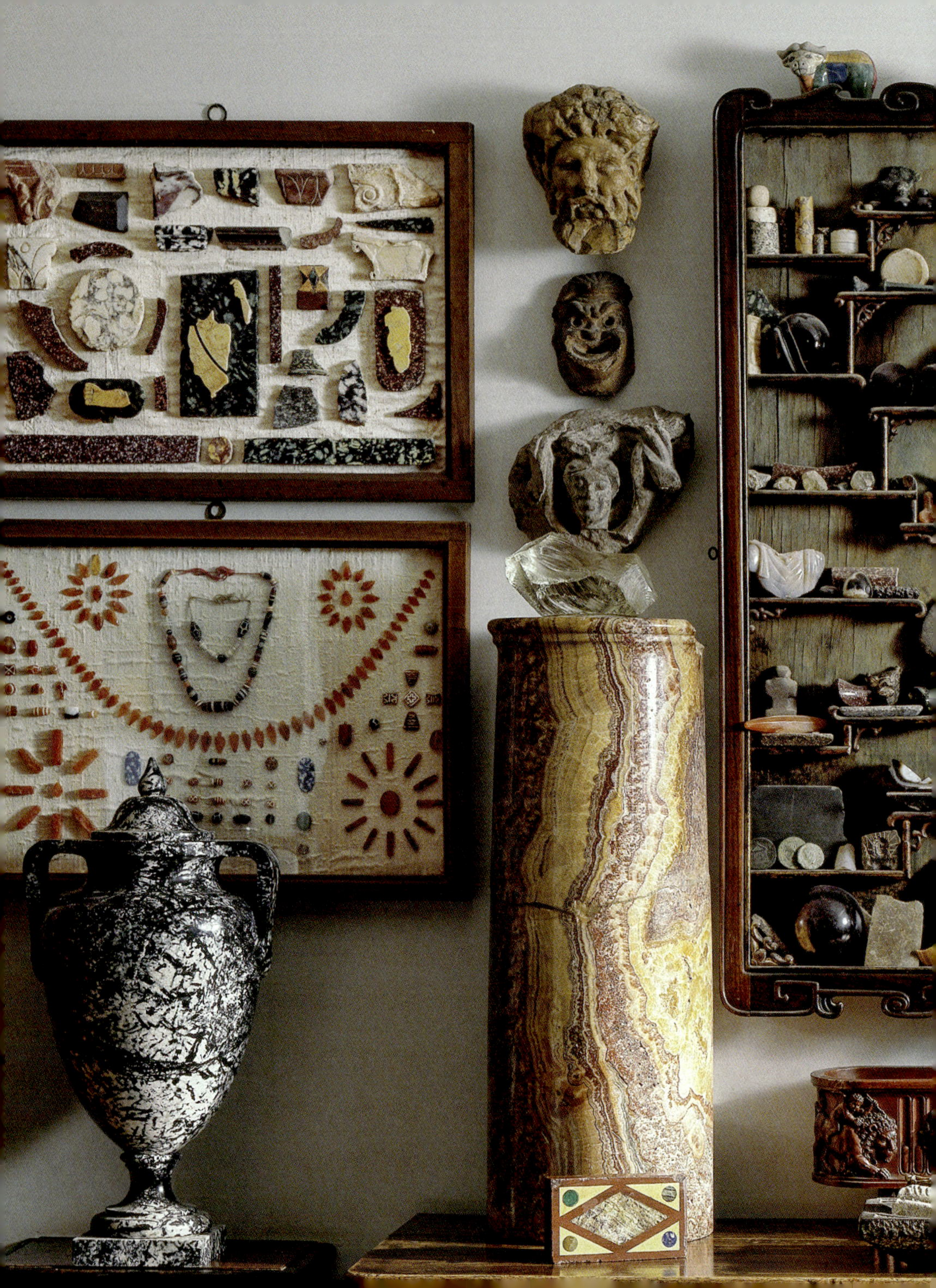

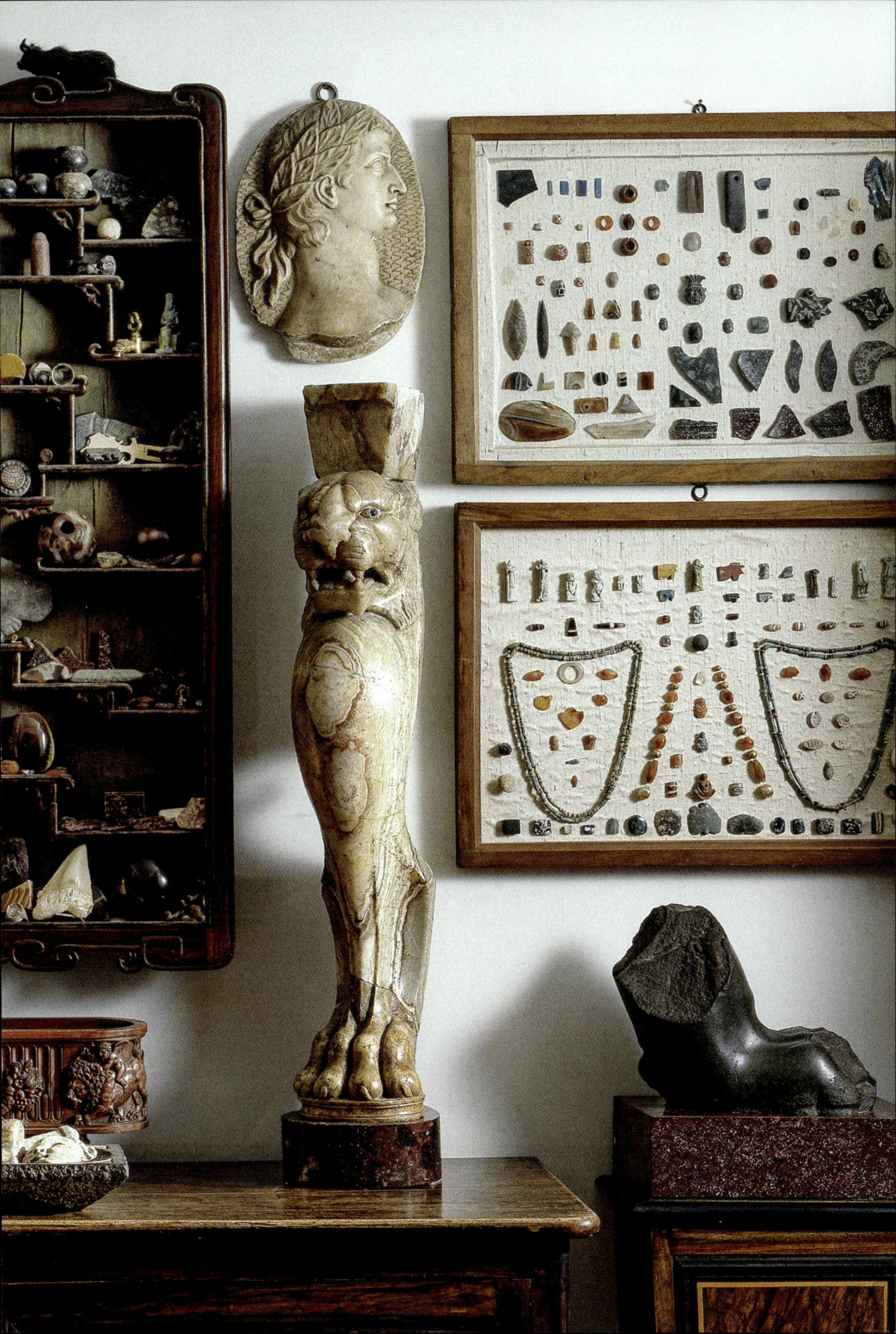

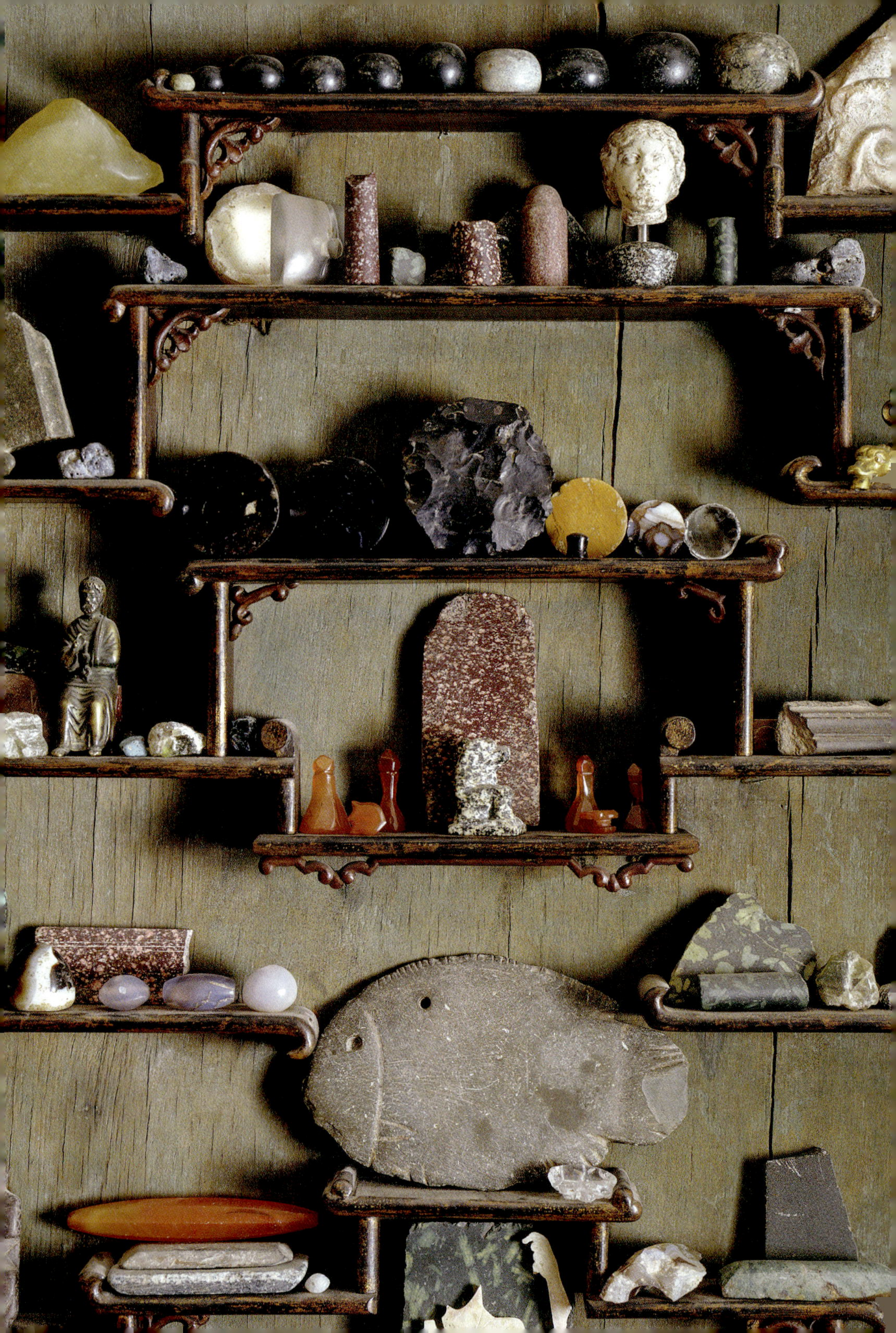

Artificialia und Naturalia: Die Welt als Sammlung

Antonio Paolucci

Die Wunderkammer galt einst als Stätte der Sensationen, Raritäten und Wunderwerke, ja sogar als Spiegel und Abbild des Weltuniversums (Abb. S. 16–17). In der Wunderkammer fand alles, aber wirklich alles, seinen Platz: bildende Kunst, wissenschaftliche Geräte, Astrologie und Medizin, Zoologie und Botanik, Gemmologie und Metallurgie, Esoterik und Alchemie (Abb. S. 25).

Der italienische Philosoph, Theologe und Utopist Tommaso Campanella (1568–1639) beschreibt in seiner Schrift *Civitas Solis* (*Der Sonnenstaat*) von 1602 (Abb. S. 10), in der er die Utopie eines Gemeinwesens entwirft, detailliert sein „imaginäres Museum", einen ringförmig gebauten Tempel, in dem alle Künste und Wissenschaften anschaulich dargestellt werden: „Auf der Innenseite der Mauer des ersten Ringes erblickt man alle mathematischen Figuren [...]. Auf der nach außen gewölbten Außenseite der Mauer steht zunächst die genaue und vollständige Beschreibung der ganzen Erde. Darauf folgen besondere Darstellungen jeder einzelnen Gegend. Dabei sind auch die Sitten und Gebräuche [...] und die Alphabete aller Völker über dem Alphabet des Sonnenstaates. Auf der Innenseite der Mauer des zweiten Ringes [...] erblickt man alle Arten von edlen und gewöhnlichen Steinen, Mineralien und Metallen, echte und gemalte, ebenso wirkliche Bruchstücke davon als Proben. [...] Auf der Außenseite sind [...] Weine und Öle und überhaupt alle Flüssigkeiten mit Angabe ihres Herkommens, ihrer Eigenschaften und Kräfte. Dabei stehen in Mauernischen Gefäße mit teilweise hundert bis dreihundert Jahre alten Flüssigkeiten zur Heilung der verschiedenen Krankheiten. [...] Auf der Innenseite des dritten Ringes sind alle Arten von Bäumen und Kräutern abgebildet, [...] ihre Kräfte und Eigenschaften sowie ihre Beziehungen zu den Himmelserscheinungen, den Metallen, den Teilen des menschlichen Körpers, [...] ferner ihr Gebrauch in der Heilkunde und so weiter. Auf der Außenseite finden sich alle Gattungen der Fische der Flüsse, Seen und Meere, ihre Lebensgewohnheiten und Eigenschaften [...]. Auf der Innenwand des vierten Ringes sieht man alle Arten von Vögeln dargestellt, ihre Eigenschaften, Größen, Farben, ihr Leben, ihre Gewohnheiten und so weiter. Auch der Phönix gilt ihnen für durchaus wirklich." So geht es weiter mit der Darstellung aller lebenden Arten bis zum sechsten und letzten Ring, wo „alle mechanischen Künste dargestellt sind, die dazu nötigen Werkzeuge und ihre Handhabung bei den verschiedenen Völkern. Auf der Außenseite sieht man die Bildnisse aller Entdecker und Erfinder wissenschaftlicher und technischer Dinge, ebenso die der Gesetzgeber, unter denen sah ich Moses, Osiris, Jupiter, Merkur [...];

sogar Mohammed ist abgebildet. [...] Am würdigsten Platze jedoch sah ich das Bildnis Jesu Christi und der zwölf Apostel, die sie für besonders ehrwürdig und gleichsam für Übermenschen halten. Ich sah ferner Cäsar, Alexander, Pyrrhus und vor allem Römer." Aber auch technische Errungenschaften aus dem Fernen Osten finden Erwähnung: „Steinschleudern und Schießgewehre wurden, ebenso wie die Druckerkunst, bei den Chinesen erfunden, und zwar früher als bei uns."[1]

Die überbordende Fantasie, die uns in Campanellas Werk begegnet, war typisch für den damaligen Zeitgeist und brachte eine regelrechte Blüte der Wunderkammern hervor, die in Europa wie Pilze aus dem Boden schossen.

Auch die Galleria degli Uffizi in Florenz war ursprünglich eine Kunstkammer: Im oberen Stockwerk des weitläufigen, von Giorgio Vasari erbauten Gebäudekomplexes, der „fast über dem Fluss zu schweben scheint", hatte sich Francesco I. de' Medici bereits 1581 eine private Schatzkammer eingerichtet (Abb. S. 13). Als Herzstück der Uffizien gilt seit jeher, geografisch wie symbolisch, die berühmte Tribuna von Bernardo Buontalenti (Abb. S. 60–61). Dort platzierte man die wertvollsten Stücke der Medici-Sammlung, um sie illustren Gästen vorzuführen. In einem zeitgenössischen Reiseführer, *Le bellezze della città di Firenze* von Francesco Bocchi aus dem Jahr 1591, heißt es dazu: „In der Mitte der Galerie ist eine Kuppel, von allen nur Tribuna genannt, darunter ein achteckiger Saal mit einem Durchmesser von zehn Ellen und sehr schönem Licht, entworfen von Bernardo Buontalenti."[2] Dabei sind es weniger die hier versammelten Kunstwerke, antiken Skulpturen (etwa die *Venus Medici* oder der *Schlafende Eros*), Gemälde berühmter Künstler wie Andrea del Sarto, Pontormo, Leonardo und Raffael (mit dem *Porträt Leos X.*) oder die Bronzen Giambolognas, die Bocchi am meisten beeindruckten, sondern die Kuriositäten. Voller Bewunderung äußerte er sich beispielsweise über einen Kopf von Julius Cäsar „aus einem wunderbaren Edelstein, tiefblau und hand-werklich unvergleichlich kunstvoll", ein „Arrangement aus Perlen und Edelsteinen", von Großherzog Francesco I. selbst angefertigt, oder eine Wunderkugel aus Elfenbein mit sechs Porträtgemmen darin – ebenfalls aus Elfenbein – des Herzogs von Bayern, seiner Frau und seiner Kinder. Derartige Wunderwerke erstaunten ihn ebenso wie das mit Perlmutt ausgeschlagene Gewölbe, die meteorologischen, astronomischen und astrologischen Darstellungen oder der mit einer Wetterfahne verbundene Zeiger oben in einer Laterne. Dieser ursprüngliche Charakter, wie ihn die Uffizien zu Zeiten der Medici hatten, ist später allmählich verloren gegangen, als man im Laufe des 18. und 19. Jahrhunderts zunehmend dazu überging, die Bestände chronologisch, nach Schulen oder Themen, Material oder Stilrichtung zu ordnen. Wie diese Kunstkammer einmal ausgesehen hat, weiß man daher nur aus alten Texten. Ein Beispiel: Zu Caravaggios Meisterwerken, die der Besucher heute in den Uffizien bewundern kann, zählt neben der *Opferung Isaaks* auch das als Rundschild gedachte *Medusenhaupt* (Abb. S. 21). Als Kardinal Francesco Maria Del Monte – nicht nur Botschafter der Medici beim Papst, sondern auch feinsinniger Kunstkenner sowie Freund und Förderer Caravaggios – das

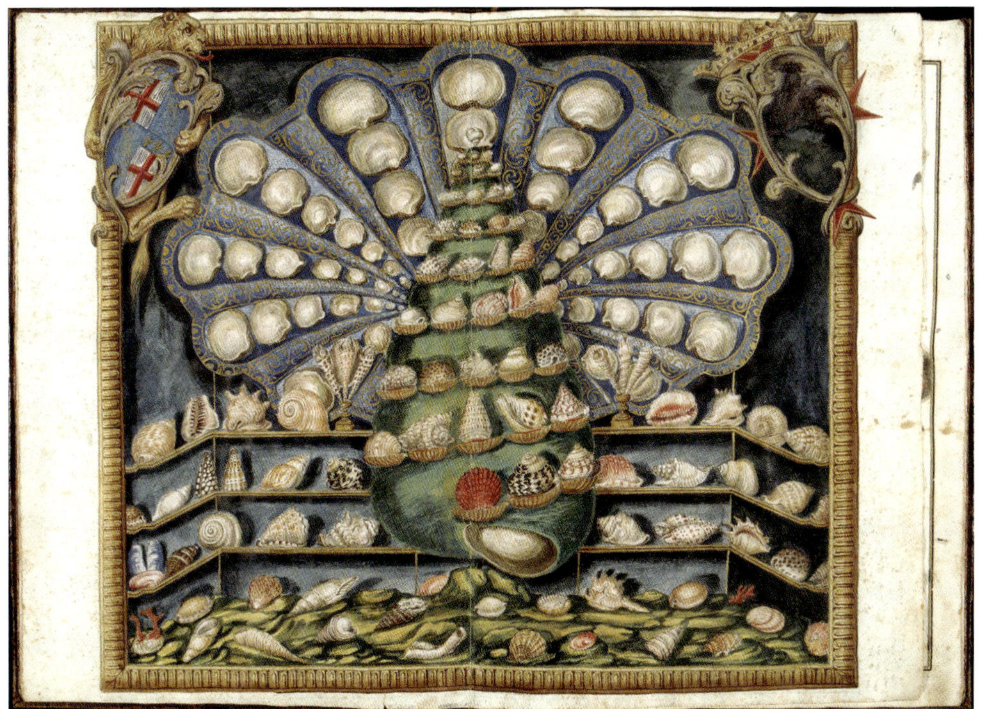

Page 28 *A shelving system displaying a wealth of ancient items in various materials, including Roman weights made from black nephrite and fragments of polychrome marble / Wandregal mit antiken Fragmenten, römischen Gewichten aus schwarzem Nephrit und Fragmenten aus mehrfarbigem Marmor / Étagère avec des fragments antiques, des poids romains en néphrite noire et des fragments de marbre polychrome* Rome, Dario del Bufalo Collection

Jacopo Tosi
Cabinet with shells / Kabinettschrank mit Muscheln / Cabinet avec coquillages, in *Testacei cioè nicchi chiocciole e conchiglie di più spezie con piante marine*, 1683, f. 3v–4r
Pen, tempera and watercolour,
43.5 x 30.5 cm / 17⅛ x 12 in.
Bologna, Biblioteca Universitaria,
Collezione Cospi, MS. 4312

Werk seinem Dienstherrn Ferdinando de' Medici zum Geschenk machte, gelangte das *Medusenhaupt* am 7. September 1598 in die Obhut des Waffenmeisters Antonio Maria Bianchi. Der wiederum ließ das Bild, das heute mit Werken der Naturalisten des 17. Jahrhunderts ausgestellt ist (mit Gherardo delle Notti, Manfredi, Stomer, Ribera und anderen), in die Waffenkammer bringen. Ende des 16. Jahrhunderts hatten die Uffizien drei Rüstkammern. Zeitgenössischen Inventaren nach wimmelte es dort nur so von Piken, Lanzen und Schwertern – darunter auch das berühmte Schwert Karls des Großen –, von Helmen, Schilden und Rossstirnen. Es gab Pfeile und Bögen, eisenbewehrte Schutzschilde, Geschütze, Armbrüste, Feldschlangen, Steinschleudern, türkische Scimitare, „indische" Dolche, deutsche Halsbergen, Mailänder Klingen, burgundische Beckenhauben und „ungarische" Helme. Und unter all dem Kriegsgerät befand sich in dieser ästhetisch wie technisch beeindruckenden Sammlung die *Medusa* Caravaggios. Man stelle sich diesen Prunkschild in der ursprünglichen Aufstellung vor – das war eine große Inszenierung. Mitten in einem blinkenden Wald aus tod- und verderbenbringenden Waffen stand ein Holzpferd mit blau-rotem Überwurf: „Den unteren Saum zierten feinziselierte, mit Tiefblau und Gold bemalte Eisenplättchen, die mit Messingspangen an dem rot-gelben, mit rotem Leinen gefütterten Saum befestigt waren", so die zeitgenössische Beschreibung. Darauf saß ein orientalischer Krieger in einer goldverzierten Rüstung, auf dem Kopf trug er einen Turban „aus golddurchwirktem Stoff mit Pfauenaugen"[3]. In der einen Hand hielt er eine Lanze und in der anderen – und das ist der Höhepunkte der theatralischen Inszenierung – „einen Schild, der mit einem furchterregenden Medusenhaupt bemalt war, von der Hand des Caravaggio". Man stelle sich Caravaggios *Medusa* zwischen all dem Rüstzeug vor – als Teil einer prachtvollen Kavallerierüstung, die der Schah von Persien, Abbas der Große, dem toskanischen Großherzog geschenkt hatte. Es fällt nicht leicht, diesen Anblick nachzuvollziehen. Die Zeilen des Dichters Giambattista Marino jedoch, die dieser nach einem Besuch in der Rüstkammer der Uffizien 1601 schrieb, lassen das Bild Gestalt annehmen:

> *Nun, was für Feinde wären das, die nicht sofort*
> *zu kaltem Stein würden,*
> *wenn sie, Herr, auf eurem Schild*
> *jene stolze und grausame Gorgo erblicken,*
> *der auf schreckliche Weise*
> *ein Gewirr von Vipern*
> *einen hässlichen und furchtbaren Haarschmuck bilden?*[4]

Die manieristische Emphase des Dichters entspricht der des Waffenmeisters, der Caravaggios *Medusa* effektvoll in Szene setzte und sie so zum symbolischen Herzstück der mediceischen Waffenkammer machte. Wegweisendes Vorbild für die Kunst- und Wunderkammer aus der Zeit des Manierismus und des Barocks war das *studiolo*, das Studierzimmer. In der italienischen Renaissance galt es als klassisches Requisit des humanistischen Intellektuellen, fand aber auch im Hochadel Verbreitung, quasi als Aushängeschild der geistigen Ambitionen des Landesfürsten, der sich dorthin zurückzog, um sich eingehend mit historischen, künstlerischen und philosophischen Fragen zu beschäftigen (Abb. S. 11, 15). Im Studierzimmer bewahrte man seine Kostbarkeiten und Raritäten auf, um sie ungestört zu bewundern und zu erforschen. Man sammelte archäologische Fundstücke, seltene Metalle, Edel- und Halbedelsteine, Goldschmiedearbeiten, Bücher,

Levinus Vincent
Cabinet of the Levin Museum / Wunderkammer von Levins Museum / Cabinet des merveilles du musée de Levin
in *Wondertooneel der Nature*, Amsterdam, 1706, plate III
Göttingen, Niedersächsische Staats- und Universitätsbibliothek

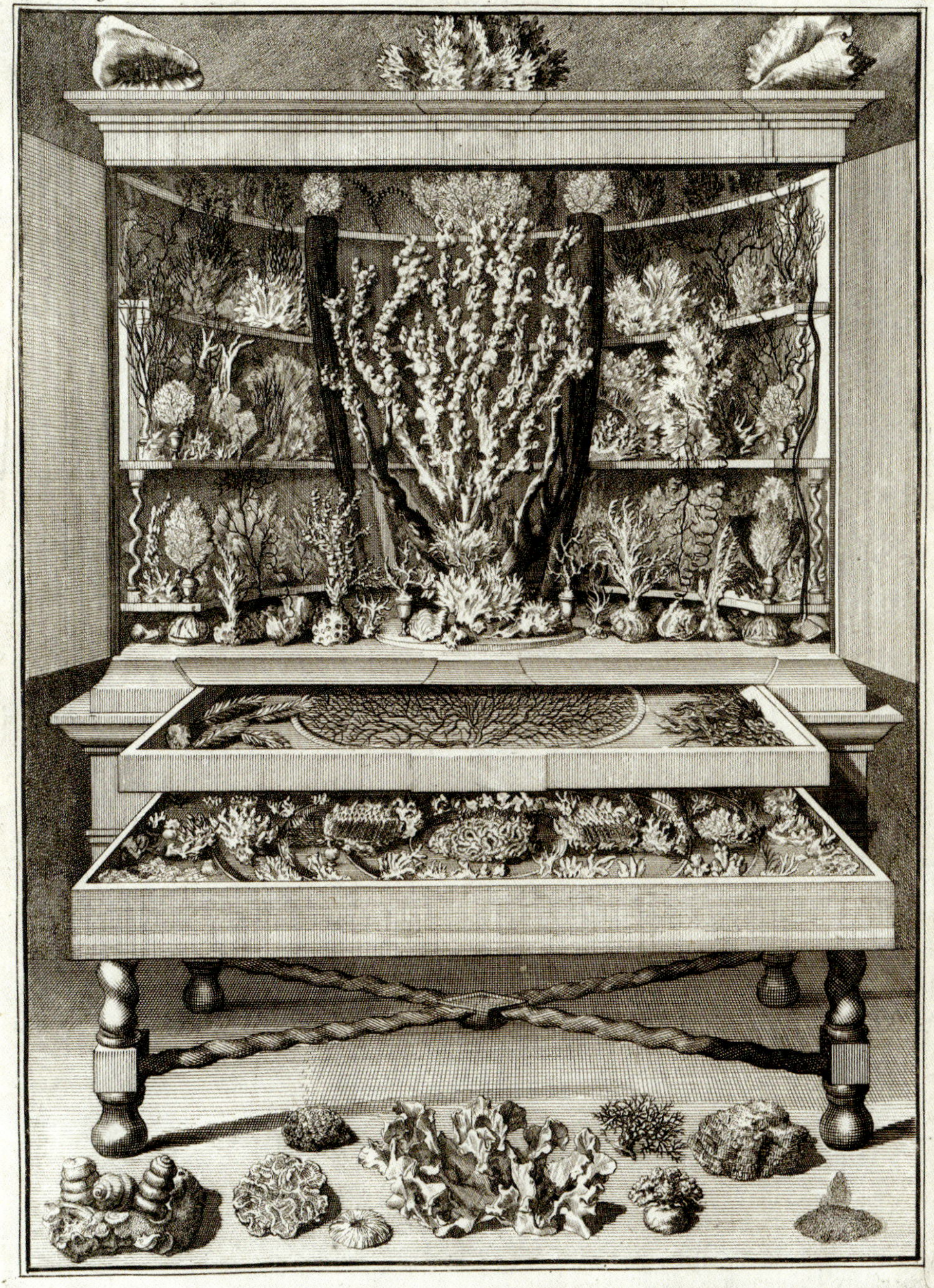
Pinac. 3.
TAB. III.

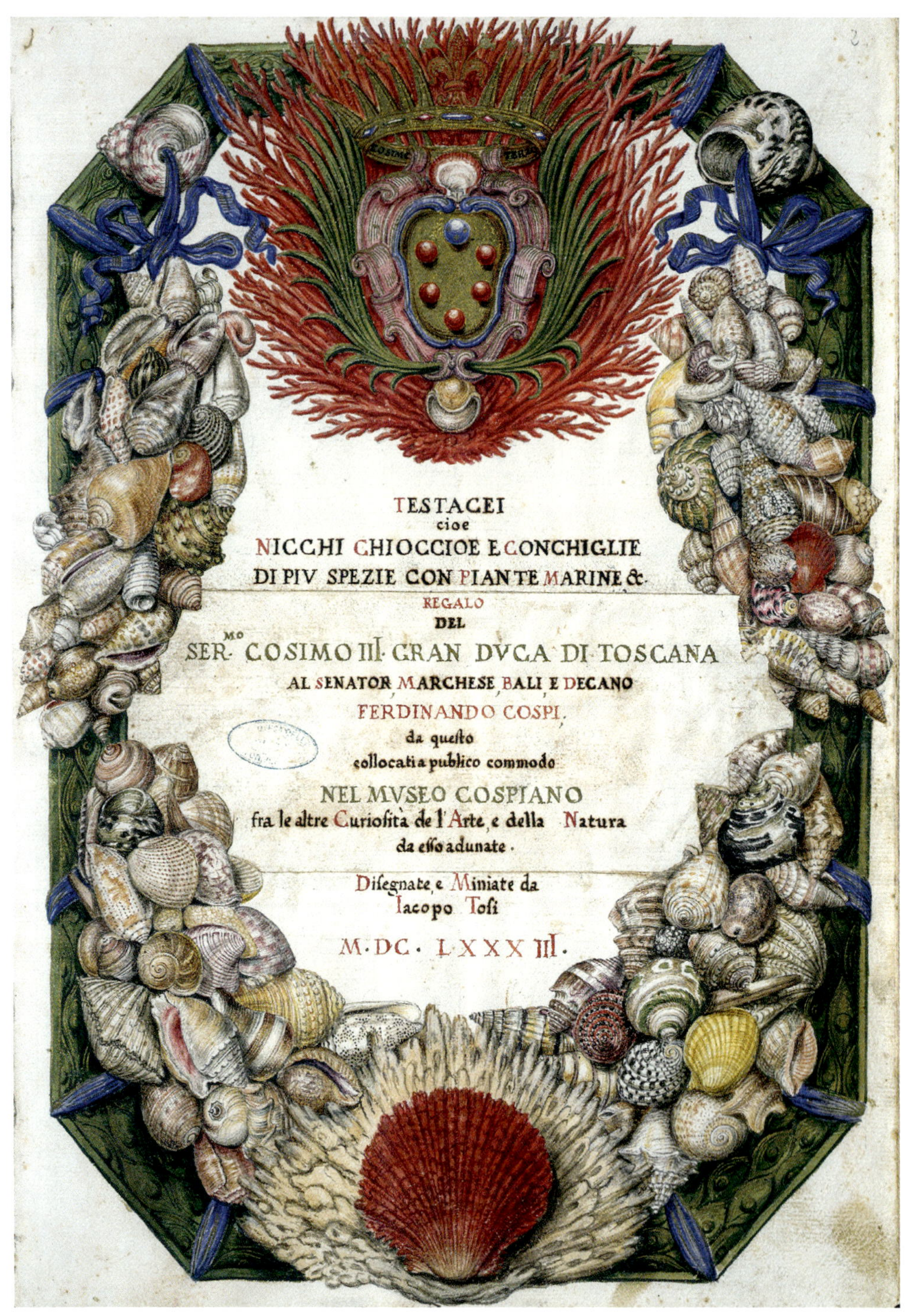
TESTACEI
cioe
NICCHI CHIOCCIOE E CONCHIGLIE
DI PIV SPEZIE CON PIANTE MARINE &.
REGALO
DEL
SER.mo COSIMO III. GRAN DVCA DI TOSCANA
AL SENATOR MARCHESE, BALI E DECANO
FERDINANDO COSPI,
da questo
collocati a publico commodo
NEL MVSEO COSPIANO
fra le altre Curiosità de l'Arte, e della Natura
da esso adunate.
Disegnate, e Miniate da
Iacopo Tosi
M.DC. LXXX III.

wissenschaftliche Geräte, Gemälde und Skulpturen, *Exotica* und *Naturalia* (Abb. S. 18).
Von zahlreichen berühmten Studierzimmern wissen wir allerdings nur aus der Literatur,
wie sie einmal ausgesehen haben, weil die kostbare Einrichtung[5] später oft durch
politische oder dynastische Wirren verloren ging. Das gilt für das Studierzimmer von
Leonello und Borso d'Este im Palazzo Belfiore in Ferrara sowie für das Studierzimmer des
Dogenpalasts in Urbino, das reich mit herrlichen Intarsien von Botticelli und Benedetto da
Mariano sowie mit Gemälden der Flamen Giusto di Gand und Pedro Berruguete ausgestat-
tet war (Abb. S. 11). „Außer Bücherregalen gibt es dort ein Studierzimmer [...] mit einem
Tisch in der Mitte und Sitzgelegenheiten mit Lehnen rundherum: alles reich mit Intarsien
und Schnitzarbeiten versehen. Die Holzverkleidung bedeckt den Boden und die Wände
bis zur Decke, den oberen Teil nehmen Porträts ein, die berühmte antike oder moderne
Schriftsteller zeigen und in die Wandverkleidung eingelassen sind." Die Schöpfer dieser
Porträts kamen von weither, denn da „sich Federico in der Malerei bestens auskannte und
in Italien keine geeigneten Maler fand, ließ er einen Meister aus dem fernen Flandern kom-
men, der ihm für sein Studierzimmer herrliche Porträts von Philosophen, Priestern und
griechischen wie römischen Kirchenvätern malte."[6] So beschreibt Vespasiano da Bisticci
in *Vite degli uomini illustri del XV secolo* um 1482 das Studierzimmer von Federico da
Montefeltro in dem Palast, den Baldassare Castiglione als „Stadt in Form eines Palastes"
bezeichnet hat. Eine faszinierende Vorstellung, dass sich ein machtbewusster, politisch
und militärisch engagierter „Kriegsherr" wie Federico in sein Studierzimmer zurückzieht,
um sich in die Schriften von Plutarch, Titus Livius, Seneca und Cicero zu vertiefen oder
andere Bücher aus der dreisprachigen Bibliothek (Latein, Griechisch und Hebräisch) zu
konsultieren. Wie wir aus Inventaren und zeitgenössischen Berichten wissen, gehörte
es im Hochadel – etwa bei Isabella d'Este aus Mantua, Kardinal Alessandro Farnese aus
Caprarola oder Alfonso d'Este aus Ferrara – zum guten Ton, sich ein Studierzimmer einzurichten, es von berühmten Künstlern, darunter Mantegna, Giovanni Bellini, Perugino und
Tizian, gestalten zu lassen und mit wertvollen Antiken zu bestücken.

Besondere Aufmerksamkeit verdient jedoch das Studierzimmer, das sich Francesco I.
de' Medici im Palazzo Vecchio in Florenz einrichten ließ, auch weil es zu den wenigen
gehört, deren Einrichtung mit bemalten Sammelschränken erhalten ist (Abb. S. 13). „In
der Kammer ist alles nagelneu, damit meine ich Schränke zur Aufbewahrung seltener
und kostbarer Dinge, von materiellem und künstlerischem Wert, als da wären Schmuck,
Medaillen, geschnittene Steine, Kristallgefäße, Apparate und Ähnliches, für jede Sorte
gibt es einen speziellen Schrank."[7] So schrieb Vincenzo Borghini 1570 in einem Brief an
Giorgio Vasari, als das Studierzimmer noch im Bau war. Bestimmend im Bildprogramm
waren die vier Elemente Feuer, Wasser, Luft, Erde, die, durch menschliches Genie

Jacopo Tosi
Title-page of / Titelblatt von / Page de titre de
Testacei cioè nicchi chiocciole e conchiglie di
più spezie con piante marine, 1683

Pen, tempera and watercolour,
43.5 x 30.5 cm / 17⅛ x 12 in.
Bologna, Biblioteca Universitaria,
Collezione Cospi, MS. 4312

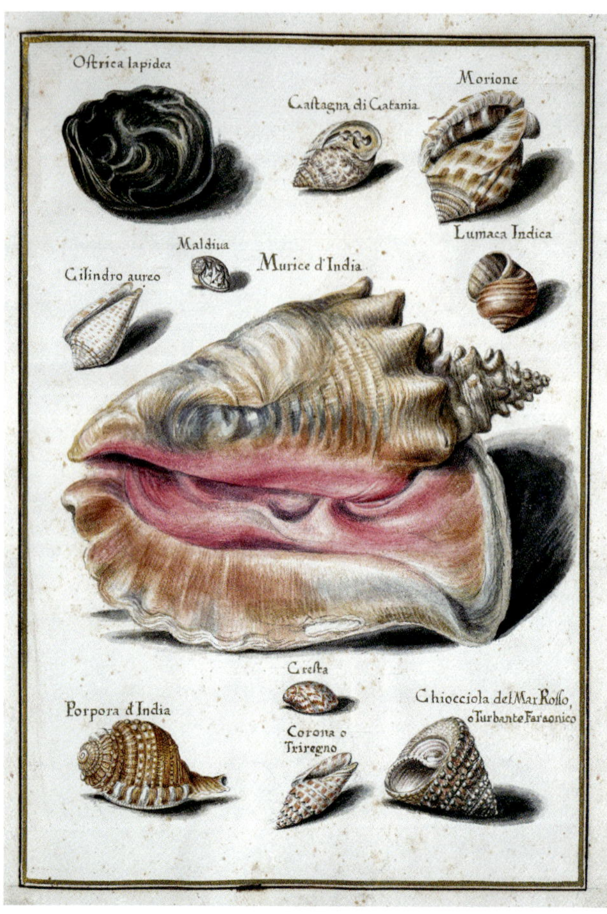

beherrscht, etwas „Künstliches" hervorbringen, mithin die Wunderwerke aus Kunst, Handwerk und Wissenschaft. Die Bronzefiguren und Malereien – von Allori, Santi di Tito, Stradano, Zucchi und vielen anderen –, mit denen die Schränke dekoriert sind, illustrieren und kommentieren das mythologische Gesamtprogramm. In den bemalten Schränken, die nur bei besonderen Gelegenheiten für den Fürsten, seine Freunde und Gäste geöffnet wurden, befanden sich *Rariora*, *Naturalia* und *Exotica*, die Borghini wie folgt aufzählt: Perlen, Korallen, Muscheln, Glas, Bergkristall, Edelsteine und besonders kunstvolle Handwerksprodukte.

Der umfassende enzyklopädische Anspruch ist charakteristisch für die Sammler der Renaissance. Ihm begegnen wir auch in dem als „Ruhmeshalle" gedachten Haus von Paolo Giovio. Seine Villa am Comer See beherbergte eine umfangreiche, systematisch angelegte Sammlung mit Porträts bedeutender Persönlichkeiten, unterteilt nach Literaten, Künstlern, Staatsmännern und Feldherren.[8] Seine am plutarchischen Model *De viris illustribus* geschulte Auffassung der Geschichte als Summe außergewöhnlicher Individuen blieb bis zur zweiten Auflage der *Vite* aktuell, die Giorgio Vasari nach dem Vorbild seines Freundes mit Porträtstichen der Künstler ausstatten ließ.

Die Einrichtung der ersten Kunst- und Wunderkammern[9] und damit die Geburt der modernen Museumsidee ging aus dem brennenden Wunsch hervor, über die Systematisierung empirischer Dinge zur Erkenntnis der Ordnungsprinzipien der Welt und der Geschichte vorzudringen (Abb. S. 33, 38, 45). Als Beispiel kann die Sammlung des bayrischen Großherzogs Albrecht V. gelten, die in fünf Klassen eingeteilt war: Sakralgeschichte und Familiengenealogie, Kunstprodukte, Naturprodukte, Musikinstrumente und exotische

Gegenstände, Gemälde und Druckerzeugnisse. Damit sollte alles Wissen gebündelt werden, um dadurch zu einer umfassenden Sicht der Welt und der Geschichte zu gelangen, einem universellen Theater. Daher gab der belgische Arzt Samuel Quiccheberg (Abb. S. 22) seinem 1565 verfassten Traktat über die Münchner Kunstkammer Albrechts V. auch den Titel *Inscriptiones vel tituli theatri amplissimi*.

Angetrieben von einem alles verschlingenden enzyklopädischen Wissenshunger, nahmen schon die ersten Museen, zunächst im Italien des Spätmittelalters und der Frührenaissance, dann im Europa des Absolutismus und der Gegenreformation, die Form einer Universalsammlung an. Wie schon erwähnt waren die Studierzimmer der italienischen Fürsten, Sammler und Humanisten bereits als Universalmuseen angelegt (wie in Florenz, Ferrara, Mantua, Venedig und Rom). Das heißt, im Grunde versuchte man, wenn auch mit unterschiedlichen Interessen und Vorlieben, alles Erdenkliche zu sammeln und zu klassifizieren: symbolträchtige Gegenstände aus Kunst und Wissenschaft ebenso wie Naturkuriositäten, archäologische Funde und Gemälde, Reliquien und ethnografische Stücke (Abb. 31, 34, 36, 37, 49, 51, 53, 54–55). Dieses allumfassende Konzept eines „Universalmuseums" fand seinen höchsten Ausdruck in den Kunst- und Wunderkammern der europäischen Fürsten: in Prag wie in Stuttgart, in Schloss Ambras in Tirol, das sich Großherzog Ferdinand II. ab 1573 herrichten ließ, in der Residenz der französischen Könige in Fontainebleau, wie in Florenz, wo man wie bereits erwähnt

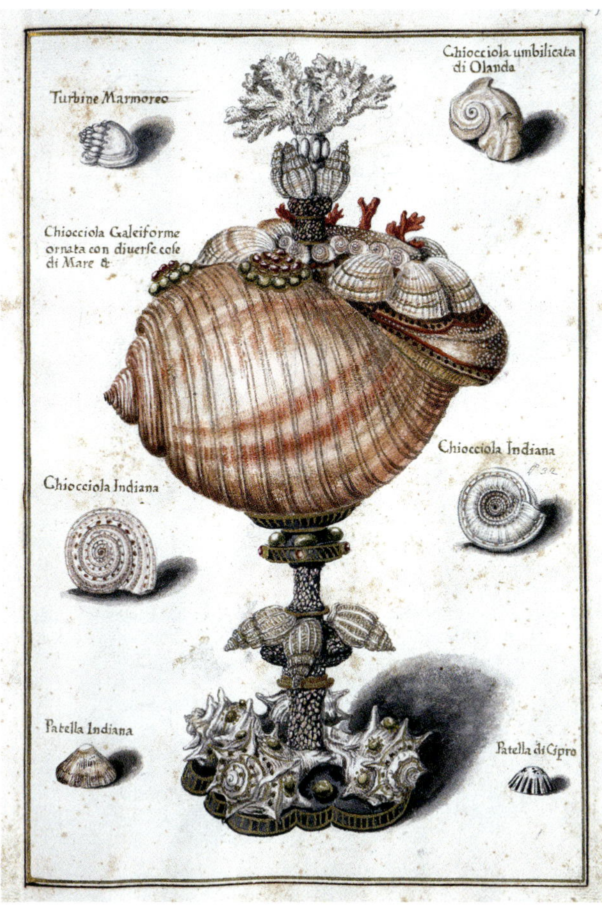

Shellfish and conches / Muscheln und Schnecken / Coquillages et escargots in *Testacei cioè nicchi chiocciole e conchiglie di più spezie con piante marine*, 1683
Pen, tempera and watercolour, 43.5 x 30.5 cm / 17⅛ x 12 in.
Bologna, Biblioteca Universitaria, Collezione Cospi, MS. 4312, f. 37, 29

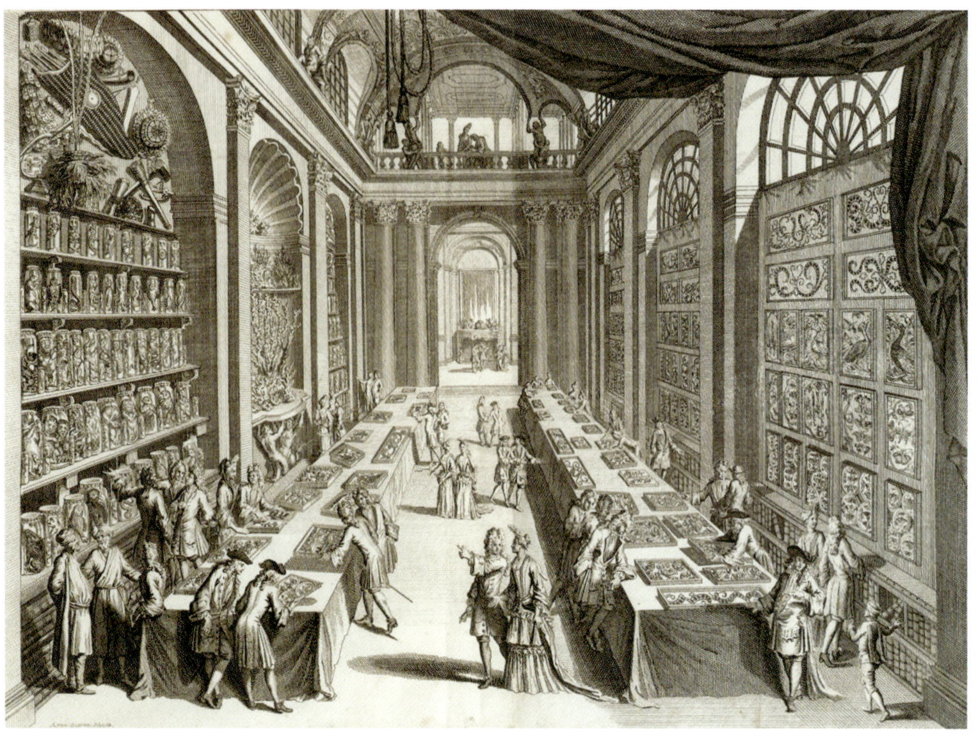

Levinus Vincent
The Cabinet of the Levin Museum in Haarlem /
Die Wunderkammer von Levins Museum in Haarlem /
Le cabinet du musée de Levin à Haarlem

in *Wondertooneel der Nature*, Amsterdam, 1706
Göttingen, Niedersächsische Staats- und
Universitätsbibliothek

Ende des 16. Jahrhunderts in den Uffizien die Tribuna des Buontalenti erbaute oder im
Palazzo Vecchio das alchemistische Studierzimmer Francescos I.

Mitunter, so könnte man meinen, nahm die Sammelwut der europäischen Autokraten
im Ancien Régime fast wahnhafte Züge an. Nehmen wir beispielsweise Schloss Ambras
bei Innsbruck, ein ebenso faszinierendes wie unheimliches Produkt unbändiger Sammelleidenschaft (S. 144–165). In dem finsteren Schloss, das sich Erzherzog Ferdinand II. von
Habsburg als Residenz erwählte und wo er sich mit einem Hof aus Dichtern und Künstlern
umgab, empfängt uns gleich am Eingang der *Tödlein-Schrein* (Abb. S. 157), ein Meisterwerk von Paul Reichel. Wie ein Sinnbild der Vergänglichkeit all dessen, was wir nun zu
sehen bekommen, blickt er gedankenverloren vor sich hin, ist sich der Anwesenheit des
Betrachters aber bewusst. Die Sammlung ist streng nach Kategorien geordnet (*Naturalia,
Artificialia und Mirabilia*), die Ordnung existiert selbst im Wahn und im Albtraum, sie
will aber vor allem Neugier wecken, Erstaunen auslösen und vorgefasste Ansichten und
Überzeugungen hinterfragen. Es gibt Bildnisse von Zwergen, Riesen und Haarmenschen,

aber auch Porträts von Herrschern, Feldherren und Gelehrten. Im Grunde, so scheint
der sinnierende Tod, Wächter und Sinnbild von Schloss Ambras in einer Gestalt, uns
zu bedeuten, ist alles eitel, vergänglicher Schein: Schrecken und Wunder der Natur
genauso wie der Ruhm der Herrscher. Glanz und Schrecken, die Ferdinands Kunst- und
Wunderkammer ausstrahlen, werden durch das unbestechliche Auge des Fotografen
Massimo Listri inszeniert, das die überbordende Vielfalt im Bild festhält und ordnet.
Wenn Ambras unmäßig, überzogen und exzessiv ist, müssen wir inne vor dem Porträt
Gregor Bacis, dessen Auge von einer Lanze durchbohrt wurde (Abb. S. 149), dem tanzen-
den Skelett (Abb. S. 156), dem Krokodil, das die Wand hinaufzuklettern scheint, und
dem unglaublich fein ziselierten Elfenbein inne halten. Das ist seine Methode, das schil-
lernde Kaleidoskop eines Universums anzuhalten, das uns sonst, wie Jorge Luis Borges'
Das Aleph, unweigerlich mit sich fortreißen würde.

Die schönste und bedeutendste Kunstkammer Italiens befindet sich in Florenz, im
Palazzo Pitti (Abb. S. 65). Gemeint ist das Museum des Tesoro dei Granduchi, die „groß-
herzogliche Schatzkammer", eine einzigartige Sammlung von Kostbarkeiten (S. 268–305).
Wir befinden uns im Nordteil des Palazzo Pitti, in der sogenannten Sommerwohnung. Mit
spielerischer Leichtigkeit entführen uns die farbenprächtigen, fein wie Seide glänzenden,
beschwingten Wandgemälde der beiden Florentiner Barockmaler Giovanni da San
Giovanni und Francesco Ferrini im großen Festsaal in die Glanzzeit der Medici und die
Blütezeit von Florenz, das nach der Besetzung Konstantinopels durch die Türken gern
als Neu-Athen bezeichnet wurde, ein Leuchtturm der Kultur für die ganze Welt. Dort
begegnen wir Lorenzo dem Prächtigen mit seinem Kreis aus Gelehrten und Künstlern und
Marsilio Ficino, Leiter der Platonischen Akademie. Rund um diesen Saal, der das Herz des
Museums bildet, erstrecken sich die Räume mit den Kunstschätzen der Medici, die von
der Kurfürstin Anna Maria Luisa, der letzten Vertreterin des Hauses, an die Großherzöge
Lothringens weitergegeben wurden, unter der strengen Auflage, die Sammlung zusam-
menzuhalten. Dazu gehören Gefäße byzantinischen und sassanidischen Ursprungs,
Möbel und Einrichtungsgegenstände aus Bernstein, Tische mit wertvollen Intarsien
aus seltenen Steinen, Lapislazuli-Objekte nach Entwürfen von Bartolomeo Buontalenti,
Werke der berühmten Mailänder Goldschmiede aus geschliffenem Bergkristall; ferner
Kameen und Schmuck sowie Volkskunst aus Amerika. Zu den heutigen Beständen der
Kunstkammer zählt auch das „Coburg-Elfenbein".10 Als Coburg im Dreißigjährigen Krieg
im März 1635 von den Kaiserlichen Truppen eingenommen wurde, erbeutete Mattias de'
Medici den Elfenbeinschatz und brachte ihn nach Florenz: Siebenundzwanzig Stücke aus
hauchdünnem Elfenbein – künstlerische und technische Meisterwerke. Tatsächlich weiß
man nicht, was man mehr bewundern soll, den Einfallsreichtum der Handwerker oder die
geradezu atemberaubende Technik der neuartigen Präzisionsdrehbank. Massimo Listris
Blick ist mimetisch und lässt den Betrachter zugleich teilnehmen. Ihn fasziniert das
organische Material, wie das der Stoßzähne eines Elefanten, das durch die Bearbeitung
verändert und verwandelt wird; er lässt uns teilhaben an seinem Staunen angesichts der

kunstvollen Spiralen, der vielgestaltigen Wunderwerke, die aussehen, als wären sie direkt aus dem Paradies gekommen, und überzieht Bernstein, Lapislazuli und Silber mit einem milden Glanz.

Das Prager Schloss und seine düstere, hypnotische Wirkung, Residenz des großen Sammlers Rudolfs II. von Habsburg (Abb. S. 23), beschreibt Angelo Maria Ripellino in seinem Buch *Magisches Prag* (1973) vermutlich am besten. Rudolf starb 1612 im Alter von sechzig Jahren, gerade noch rechtzeitig, um nicht mehr miterleben zu müssen, wie seine Sammlungen im Dreißigjährigen Krieg geplündert und zerstreut wurden. Solange er lebte, galt er als cholerischer, visionärer Hypochonder und Misanthrop, der an seinem Hof Abenteurer, Ingenieure, Alchemisten, Astrologen und Zauberer um sich scharte und alles Erdenkliche sammelte. In Europa gab es keine umfangreichere, erstaunlichere Kuriositätensammlung als die seine. Schränke und Vitrinen im Schloss waren mit allem Möglichen vollgestopft: Automaten, die seine Ingenieure für ihn bauten, Objekte aus Bergkristall aus den Mailänder Werkstätten Saracchi und Miseroni, Pokale aus Rhinozeroshorn oder Straußeneiern, Kunstschätze – Gemälde, Plastiken, Emailarbeiten und Wandbehänge, Goldschmiedearbeiten und Waffen –, die Generationen von Habsburgern in Jahrhunderten zusammengetragen hatten. Alles, was den Verwüstungen des Krieges entging, bildet heute zusammen mit den Habsburgerschätzen anderer Herkunft die Bestände der Kunstkammer des Kunsthistorischen Museums in Wien. 1891 wurde die aus 2100 Exponaten bestehende kaiserliche Sammlung von Kaiser Franz Joseph persönlich eröffnet (S. 166–181); die fulminante Sammlung umfasst eine derartige Menge von Meisterwerken – etwa das goldene Salzfass von Benvenuto Cellini (Abb. S. 56), die Tischautomaten, Hybride aus Kunst und Technik, und gerade deshalb faszinierend –, dass selbst das Fotografenauge eines Massimo Listri respektvoll davor innehält.

Verzaubert wie ein Märchenschloss, als wäre die Zeit stehen geblieben, so wirken manche Kunst- und Wunderkammern heute. So auch Schloss Rosenborg, die ehemalige Residenz der dänischen Könige in Kopenhagen (S. 196–235). Neben geheimnisumwitterten Objekten der nordischen Sagenwelt wie dem *Oldenburger Wunderhorn* oder dem ungewöhnlichen Narval-Thron finden sich hier umfangreiche Porzellan- und Glassammlungen, darunter auch die herrliche, aus tausend Einzelteilen bestehende Murano-Sammlung, ein Geschenk der Republik Venedig an den dänischen König Friedrich IV., dessen feierliche Übergabe Carlevarijs in einem Gemälde festhielt (Abb. S. 59). Listris Objektiv sucht sorgfältig die überbordenden Vitrinen ab, hält bei Bildnissen von Menschen inne, die aussehen wie Außerirdische, widmet sich der Faszination von Elfenbein, Gold und Glas. In seinen Fotos spiegelt sich die Idee einer „geordneten Überfülle", einer überwältigenden Vielfalt, die zugleich jedoch stets einer strengen, durchdachten Ordnung unterworfen ist.

Athanasius Kircher
The Museum of Athanasius Kircher / Das Museum von Athanasius Kircher / Le musée d'Athanase Kircher, in *Romani Collegii Societatis Jesu musaeum celeberrimum*, Amsterdam, 1678, frontispiece
Rome, Biblioteca Angelica

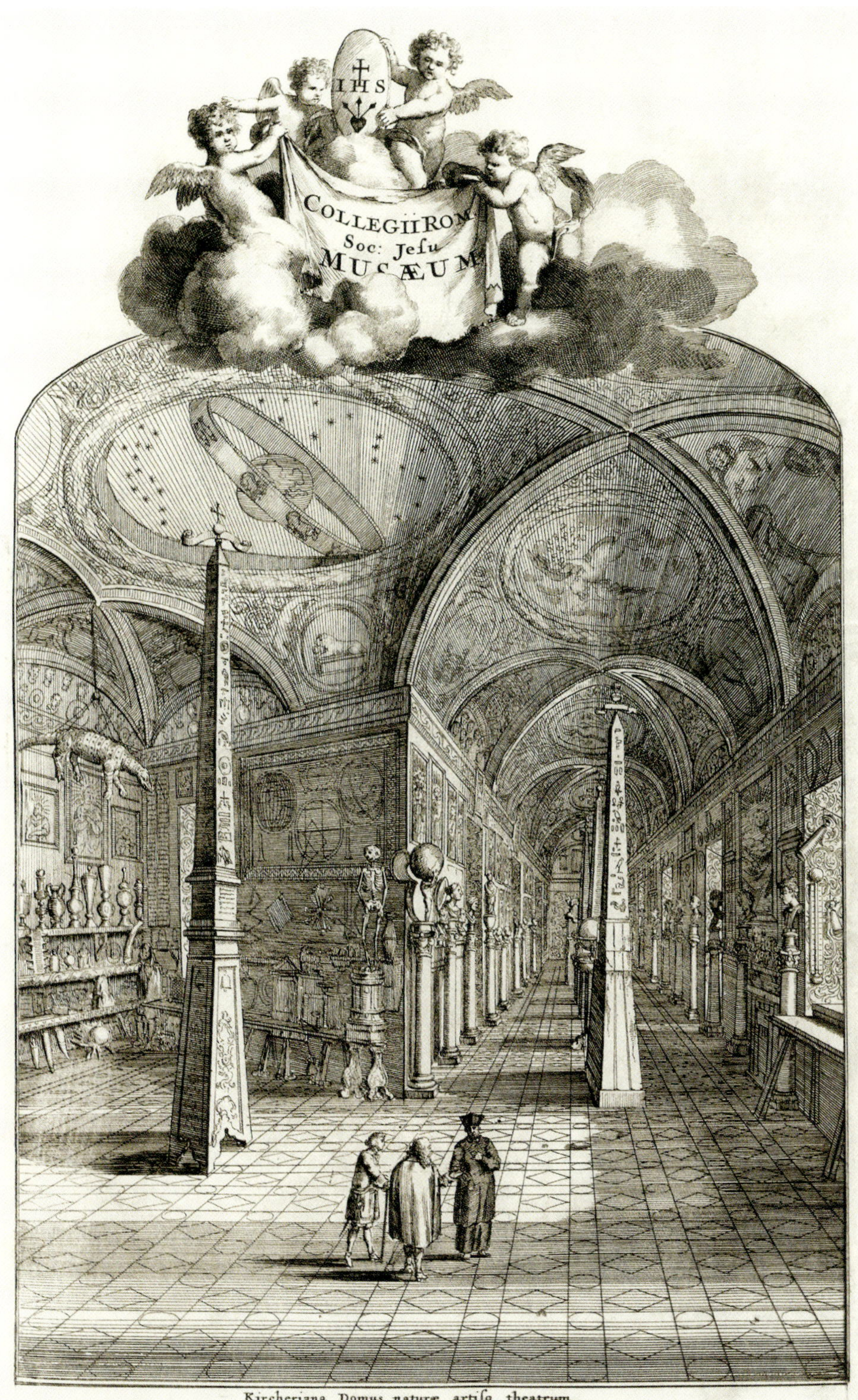

Kircheriana Domus naturæ artisq. theatrum.
Par cui vix alibi cernere posse datur.

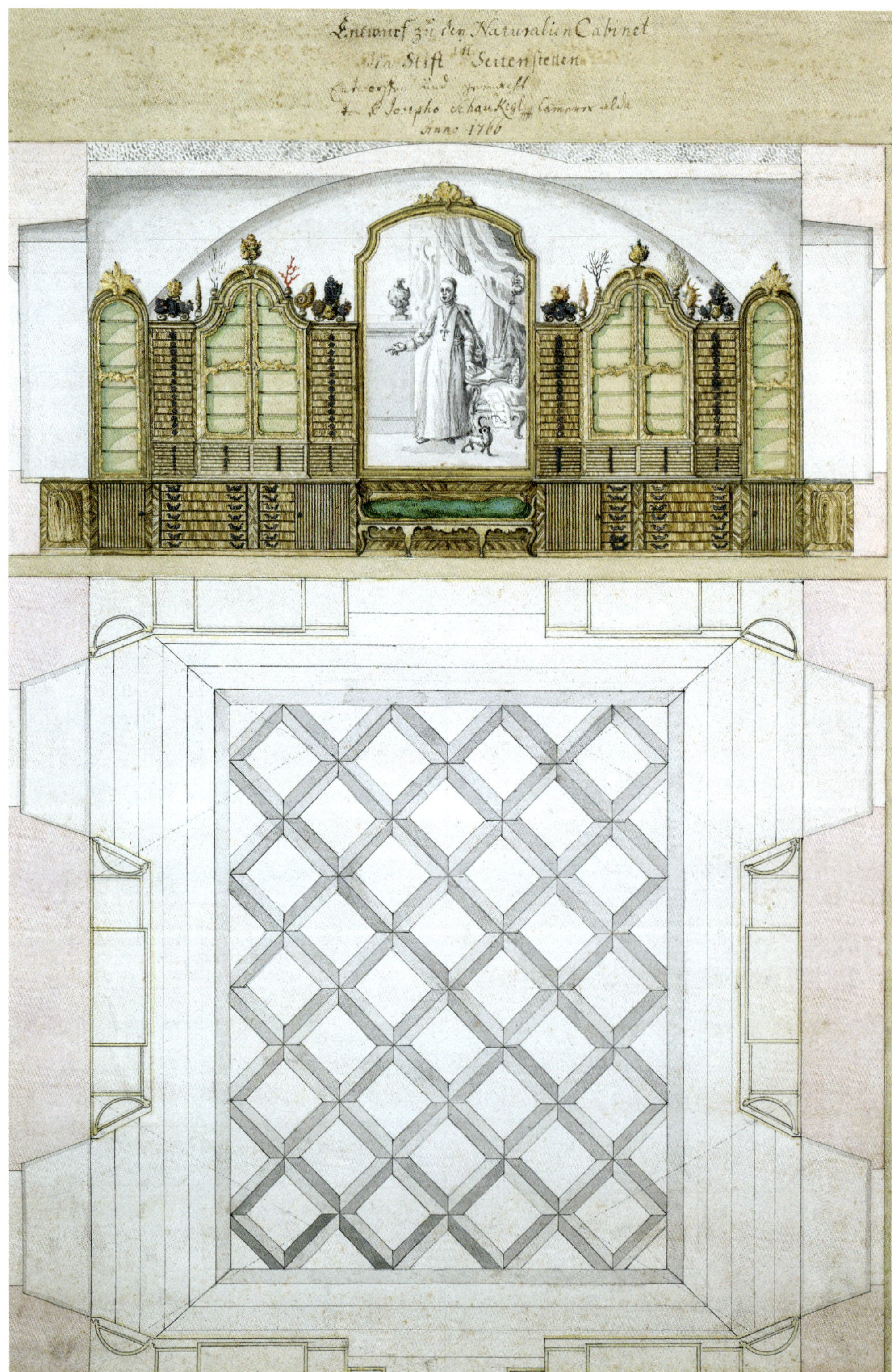
Entwurf zu dem Naturalien Cabinet
in Stift Seitenstetten
Entworfen und gemacht
von Josepho Schaukegl Cammerdiener alda
Anno 1766

Das 17. Jahrhundert war eine Zeit bahnbrechender Entdeckungen, mit Galileo Galilei richtete sich der Blick in die unendlichen Weiten des Alls und mit Blaise Pascal in die schwindelerregenden Abgründe der menschlichen Seele. Man war sich der Unendlichkeit des Universums genauso bewusst wie des Mikrokosmos, der sich im pulsierenden Organismus des Menschen und jeder noch so winzigen Kreatur spiegelt. Nur ein solches Jahrhundert konnte ein Möbelstück hervorbringen, das in gewisser Hinsicht ebenso groß ist wie Welt und zugleich ihre Metapher und ihr Abbild. Gemeint ist damit ein sogenannter Kunstschrank, wie er im Museum Gustavianum, der Kunstsammlung der Universität Uppsala in Schweden, besichtigt werden kann (S. 236–267). Dabei handelt es sich um eine Art Riesenschrankkoffer nach einem Entwurf des damals für seine Ebenholzmöbel berühmten Philipp Hainhofer, den der schwedische König Gustav II. Adolf von der Stadt Augsburg als Geschenk erhielt. Der Schrank enthält ein ausgeklügeltes System aus Schubladen, Geheimfächern, Schiebetüren, ausklappbaren Türchen und Klappspiegeln und beherbergt Tausende von Objekten aus Elfenbein, Email und Stein. Ein Abbild der gesamten Welt in einem einzigen Möbelstück. Trotz der verwirrenden Vielfalt gelingt es Massimo Listri, uns das fast Hypnotische dieser Anhäufung nahezubringen. Auf seinen Fotos wird der Mikrokosmos zum Abbild des Kosmos. Genau das entsprach Hainhofers Absicht und den Wünschen des schwedischen Königs. Vielleicht war man nur in Deutschland dazu in der Lage, eine fast mystische Vorstellung der Wunderkammer zu entwickeln (Abb. S. 63).

Die Museen in Dresden, dem Florenz des Nordens, verdanken ihre Berühmtheit Raffaels *Sixtinischer Madonna*, die schon Fjodor Dostojewski begeisterte, oder den Werken von Parmigianino und Correggio, die August von Sachsen in Modena von den Este erwarb. Vielleicht weniger bekannt ist hingegen die Tatsache, dass im Residenzschloss des großen Kurfürsten, des späteren Königs von Sachsen, schon seit 1560 eine der prächtigsten Kunstkammern Europas existierte. Endlose Reihen von *Naturalia* und vor allem *Artificialia*, wie Uhren, Automaten und wissenschaftliche Geräte, bevölkerten die Säle, deren Herz das Grüne Gewölbe bildete. Bei den grauenhaften Bombardierungen im Zweiten Weltkrieg wurde das Schloss im Februar 1945 fast vollständig zerstört. Zweifellos gehören der Wiederaufbau der Gebäude und die Neueinrichtung der Ausstellung – man denke nur an die über dreitausend Meisterwerke der Goldschmiede- und Juwelierkunst – zu den wichtigsten und intelligentesten Restaurierungen der zweiten Hälfte des 20. Jahrhunderts (S. 66–111).

Begibt man sich mit Massimo Listri auf Entdeckungsreise durch die großen Sammlungen der westlichen Welt, taucht man tief in die Geistes- und Wissenschaftsgeschichte ein und stößt dabei unweigerlich auf die ersten naturwissenschaftlich

Joseph Schaukegl
*Design for the Cabinet of Minerals at Seitenstetten /
Entwurf für das Mineralienkabinett Seitenstetten /
Projet pour le Cabinet des minéraux de Seitenstetten*

1766, Pen, ink and watercolour,
c. 37 x 28 cm / 14½ x 11 in.
Seitenstetten, Benediktinerstift, Mineralienkabinett

inspirierten Sammlungen. So etwa in der Benediktinerabtei Seitenstetten in Österreich, die in verspielter Rokokoausstattung eine der bedeutendsten Mineraliensammlungen Europas präsentiert (Abb. S. 42, 182–195). Oder, wenn auch mit den strengeren Auswahl- und Katalogisierungskriterien der Aufklärung, in dem Meeresparadies Clément Lafailles im Muséum d'Histoire Naturelle von La Rochelle, wo dank der unerschöpflichen Neugier des Forschers, der mitten im 18. Jahrhundert die Geheimnisse des Meeres erkundete, Seesterne, Muscheln und Steinkorallen zu bestaunen sind (S. 354–373).

Nächste Etappe ist die Sammlung von Lazzaro Spallanzani, Mitbegründer der experimentellen Biologie, im städtischen Museum von Reggio Emilia (S. 306–317); dann geht es weiter nach Bracciano, nicht weit von Rom, wo im Palazzo Patrizi der „Glanz des Marmors" auf uns wartet. Das antike Rom, die Stadt von Domitian und Martial, Hadrian und Aristeides, Commodus und Apuleius, Konstantin und Diokletian, war eine farben-prächtige Stadt, in der man neben weißem auch farbigen, teilweise von weither impor-tierten Marmor als Baustoff verwendete: *rosso antico*, roten Porphyr, grünen und grauen Granit aus Afrika und Anatolien, schwarzen Basalt, Jaspis aus Spanien, gelbe Brekzie, Alabaster und Portasanta. Die damit verbundenen Erkenntnisse sowie die eindrucksvolle Mustersammlung aus dem Palazzo Patrizi ist der bahnbrechenden Forschungsarbeit von Raniero Gnoli zu verdanken (S. 334–343).

Weniger bekannt und noch weniger besucht, handelt es sich bei dem uralten römi-schen Ospedale di Santo Spirito in Sassia am Tiberufer, nicht weit vom Vatikan, doch um eine echte Wunderkammer der Medizingeschichte: Behandlungsmethoden, chi-rurgische Instrumente, Arzneibücher, Krankenpflege, all dies kann man hier in seiner fünfhundertjährigen Entwicklung studieren – anhand von Hilfsmitteln, Unterlagen und Publikationen, die in der bedeutendsten Fachbibliothek zur Geschichte der Medizin bereitstehen (S. 318–333).

Bleibt schließlich die berechtigte Frage, ob das Prinzip der Kunst- und Wunder-kammer heute noch eine Rolle spielt. Gibt es derzeit überhaupt noch begeisterte Liebhaber, haben berühmte Sammler wie Rudolf von Habsburg, Athanasius Kircher (Abb. S. 41) oder Francesco de' Medici Nachfolger, die in ihre Fußstapfen treten? Die Antwort lautet Ja (Abb. S. 6–8, 26–28, 46). Die moderne Wunderkammer von Alessandro Orsi in Azzate di Varese (S. 344–353), die glyptische Sammlung von Guy Ladrière in Paris (S. 388–395) oder die Elfenbeinsammlung in der Galerie Kugel, ebenfalls in Paris (S. 396–407), zeigen, dass die Liebhaberei für *Mirabilia* keineswegs ausgestorben ist. Einschränkend muss jedoch gesagt werden, dass es sich hier, wie von Massimo Listri dokumentiert, zum größten Teil um Antiquare handelt. Angesichts der beständigen Verlockungen eines unübersichtlichen Marktes und aggressiver Werbung ist es für den privaten Sammler heutzutage fast unmöglich, mit Muße und Gelassenheit nach jenen Dingen zu suchen, die man ins Herz schließt und an deren Besitz man sich erfreuen kann. Dennoch sollten wir gerade diese Haltung unterstützen und kultivieren.

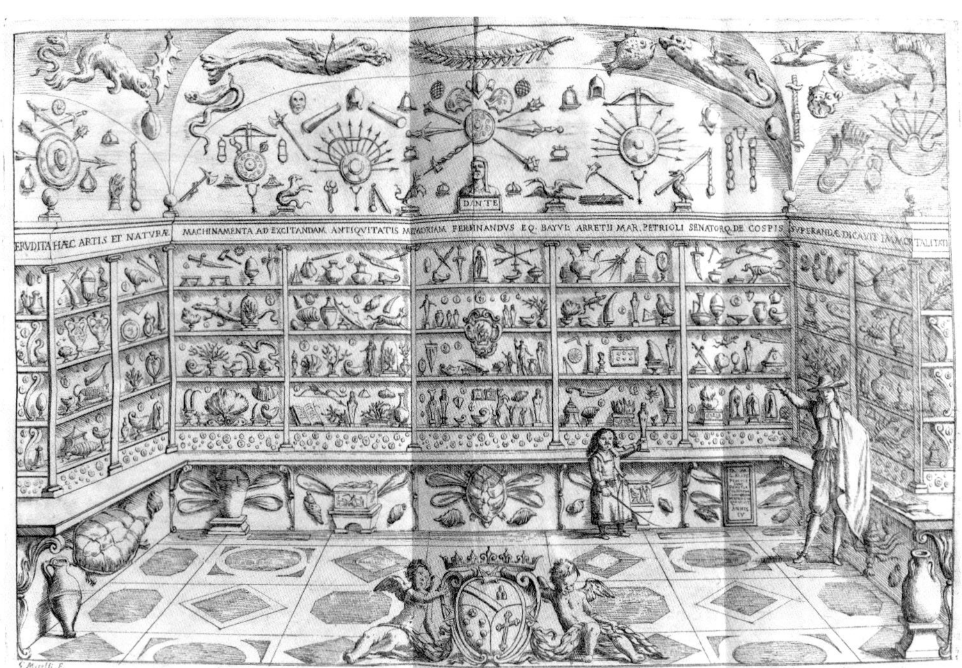

Ferrante Imperato
*Cabinet of Curiosities of Ferrante Imperato / Die Wunderkammer
von Ferrante Imperato / Le Cabinet des merveilles de Ferrante
Imperato,* in *Dell'historia naturale*, Naples, 1599
Rome, Biblioteca Angelica

Notes

1   Campanella 1602, S. 120 ff.
2   Bocchi 1591, S. 106–110, 111–112.
3   Paolucci 2007, S. 87–90.
4   Marino 2009, S. 51.
5   De Benedictis 1991, S. 32–37, 168–178.
6   Da Bisticci *c.* 1482, S. 209;
    Reynaud & Ressort 1991, S. 82–114.
7   Frey 1930, S. 529; Berti 1967.
8   De Vecchi 1977, S. 87–93.
9   De Benedictis 1991, S. 116–125, 287–298.
10 Schmidt/Sframeli 2013.

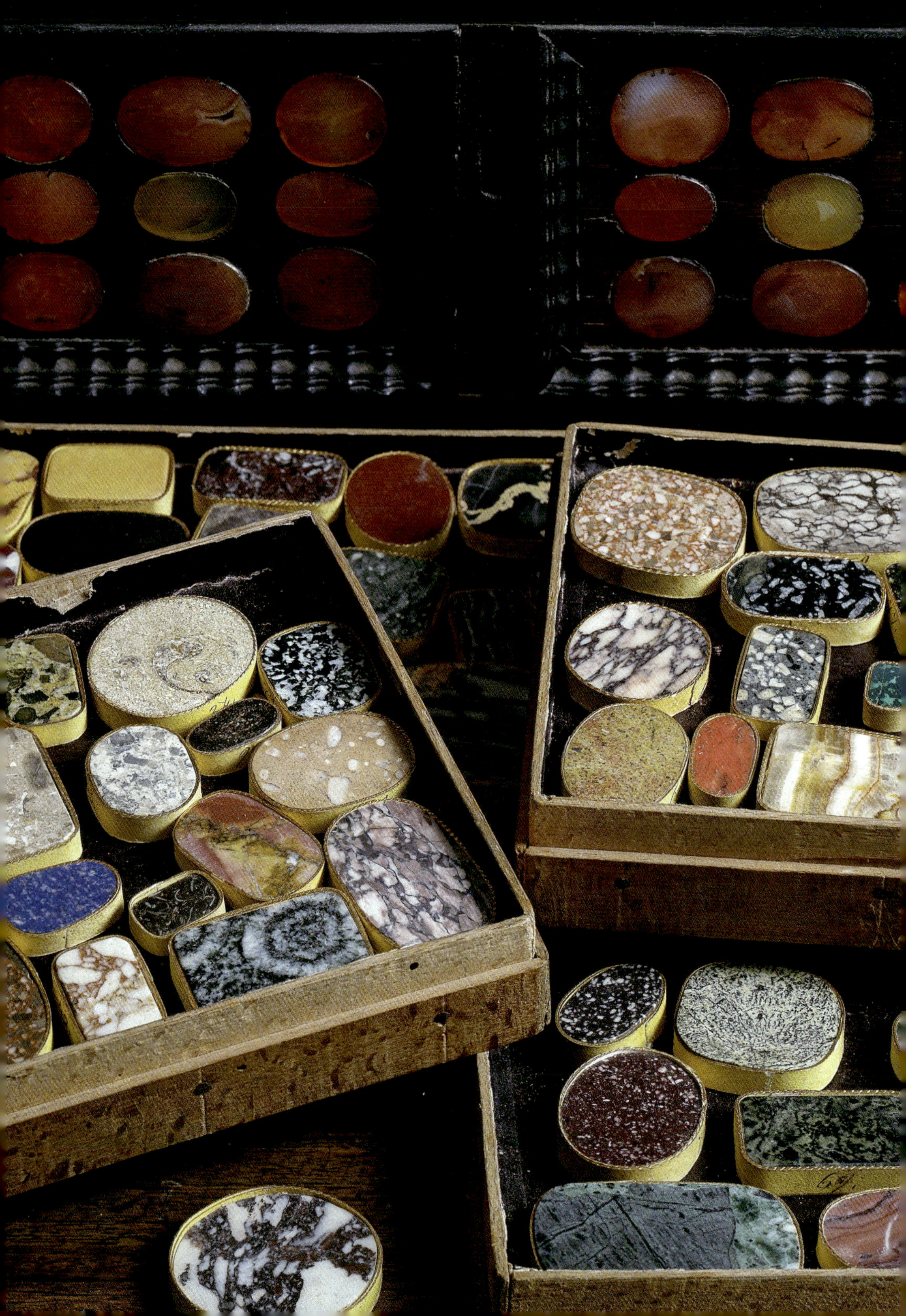

Artificialia et naturalia : Collections des splendeurs du monde

Antonio Paolucci

Le Cabinet des merveilles est émotion et stupeur, rareté et prodige, mais aussi miroir et figure de l'univers monde (ill. p. 16–17). Fondamentalement, tout, absolument tout, ainsi que l'imaginait Tommaso Campanella (1568–1639) dans son musée idéal, a sa place dans le Cabinet des merveilles : les arts figuratifs et les instruments scientifiques, l'astrologie et la médecine, la zoologie et la botanique, la gemmologie et la métallurgie, les sciences ésotériques et l'alchimie (ill. p. 25).

Dans *Civitas Solis (La Cité du Soleil* ; 1602) Tommaso Campanella, philosophe, théologien et utopiste, dépeint son « musée imaginaire » (ill. p. 10), édifice conçu et organisé tel un temple de tous les arts et de tous les savoirs. On y progresse par cercles successifs dont le philosophe donne la description suivante : « À l'intérieur du premier cercle sont dessinées, avec les propositions qui s'y rapportent, toutes les figures mathématiques [...]. À l'extérieur sont peintes la carte du monde, les planches de toutes les provinces avec leurs us et coutumes, leurs lois et leurs lettres confrontées avec l'alphabet de la ville. À l'intérieur du deuxième cercle, on trouve toutes les pierres précieuses et non précieuses, les minéraux, les métaux réels ou figurés [...]. À l'extérieur, ce sont toutes les sortes de lacs, de mers et de cours d'eau, de vins, d'huiles, et autres liqueurs accompagnées de leurs vertus, origines et qualités ; on trouve là des flacons remplis de diverses liqueurs comptant de cent à trois cents ans d'âge avec lesquelles ils guérissent presque toutes les maladies. L'intérieur du troisième cercle montre peintes toutes les sortes d'herbes et d'arbres du monde [...], quelles sont leurs vertus, leurs analogies avec les étoiles, les métaux, les membres du corps humain et leur usage spécifique en médecine. À l'extérieur du même cercle figurent tous les poissons des fleuves, des lacs et des mers, leurs caractères, leur genre de vie [...]. À l'intérieur du quatrième cercle, la peinture a représenté les oiseaux, avec leurs caractères distinctifs, leur grandeur, leurs mœurs ; on voit même le phénix qui n'est pas, pour les Solariens, un oiseau fabuleux. » Poursuivant son parcours, Campanella évoque toutes les espèces vivantes avant d'atteindre le sixième et dernier cercle où « apparaissent tous les métiers, leurs inventeurs respectifs et les techniques dont on en use à travers les diverses régions du monde ». En plus des illustrations techniques et scientifiques du génie de l'homme sont représentés les grands esprits de l'histoire : « Moïse, Osiris, Jupiter, Mercure, Mahomet et bien d'autres encore.

En un lieu prestigieux, car ils en font grand cas, se trouvaient Jésus-Christ avec les douze Apôtres, puis César, Alexandre, Pyrrhus et tous les Romains. » Dans le musée imaginaire de Tommaso Campanella, on trouve encore les connaissances technologiques de l'Extrême-Orient puisque « les Chinois avaient des bombardes et l'imprimerie avant nous[1] ». L'imagination débordante que nous découvrons dans l'œuvre de Campanella est un trait caractéristique de cette époque et provoqua l'apparition des Cabinets des merveilles, qui se multiplièrent alors en Italie et dans le reste de l'Europe.

C'est en qualité de Cabinet des merveilles, de lieu des merveilles, qu'à Florence voit le jour la galerie des Offices, le palais des magistratures que Giorgio Vasari a édifié « au-dessus du fleuve et presque dans les airs » et dont le grand-duc François Ier Médicis fait aménager le dernier étage en galerie des trésors de la couronne en 1581 (ill. p. 13). La fameuse Tribune de Bernardo Buontalenti a été de tout temps le cœur géographique et symbolique de la galerie des Offices (ill. p. 60–61). Les trésors les plus précieux de la dynastie y étaient conservés et offerts à la curiosité et à l'émerveillement des visiteurs illustres, des hôtes éminents. Voici la description qu'en fournit Francesco Bocchi en 1591 dans *Le bellezze della città di Firenze* : « Au milieu de la galerie se trouve une salle avec coupole que tout le monde appelle Tribune, de forme octogonale, d'un diamètre de dix brasses, dessinée par Bernardo Buontalenti et du meilleur effet[2]. » Elle abrite des chefs-d'œuvre de la statuaire gréco-romaine (la *Vénus* dite des Médicis, l'*Éros endormi*), ceux de la peinture (d'Andrea del Sarto, de Pontormo, Léonard de Vinci et Raphaël avec le *Portrait de Léon X*), et les petits bronzes de Giambologna. Toutefois, ce sont d'autres œuvres qui impressionnent Bocchi : une tête de Jules César « d'une pierre précieuse bleu foncé, d'une grande beauté, fruit d'une extrême habileté et d'une incomparable ingéniosité » ; « un monticule de perles et de gemmes » de la main du grand-duc François ; une boule d'ivoire contenant six boules ovales, en ivoire elles aussi, avec les portraits du duc de Bavière, de son épouse et de leurs enfants. Telles sont les merveilles qui fascinent Bocchi tout comme la voûte incrustée de nacre ou encore les informations météorologiques, astronomiques et astrologiques fournies par la lanterne et sa girouette.

Au temps des Médicis, la galerie des Offices constituait un parcours merveilleux, caractère qui s'est peu à peu estompé tandis qu'entre le 18e et le 19e siècle s'affirmaient des critères muséographiques modernes faisant appel à la répartition des œuvres d'art selon un ordre chronologique didactique et à leur regroupement par école, iconographie, matériau ou style.

Seule l'étude des documents anciens permet de reconstituer l'aménagement du Cabinet des merveilles des Offices. En voici un exemple : parmi les chefs-d'œuvre de Caravage que le visiteur découvre aujourd'hui dans le musée, au côté du *Sacrifice d'Isaac* se trouve la *Méduse* (ill. p. 21), une rondache ou rouelle, bouclier de parade peint, de forme circulaire, que le cardinal Francesco Maria Del Monte, ambassadeur du grand-duc auprès du Saint-Siège, intellectuel raffiné, ami et protecteur de Caravage, offrit à Ferdinand de Médicis et remit à l'armurier Antonio Maria Bianchi, le 7 septembre 1598. Aujourd'hui conservée aux

Offices avec les œuvres
des maîtres naturalistes
du 17e siècle (Gherardo
delle Notti, Manfredi,
Stomer et Ribera, entre
autres), la *Méduse* faisait
alors partie de l'armurerie
médicéenne. À la fin du
16e siècle, trois salles de
l'actuel musée des Offices
abritaient le Cabinet des
merveilles des armes. Si
l'on en croit les inventaires
de l'époque, tout n'est que
reflets de piques, lances,
épées (dont la mythique
épée dite de Charlemagne),
casques, boucliers et
têtières de cheval. Des arcs
et des flèches avoisinent
des plaques hérissées de
pointes d'acier, des lances
se muant en bouches à feu
jouxtent des arquebuses,
des couleuvrines et des
espringales. S'y ajoutent

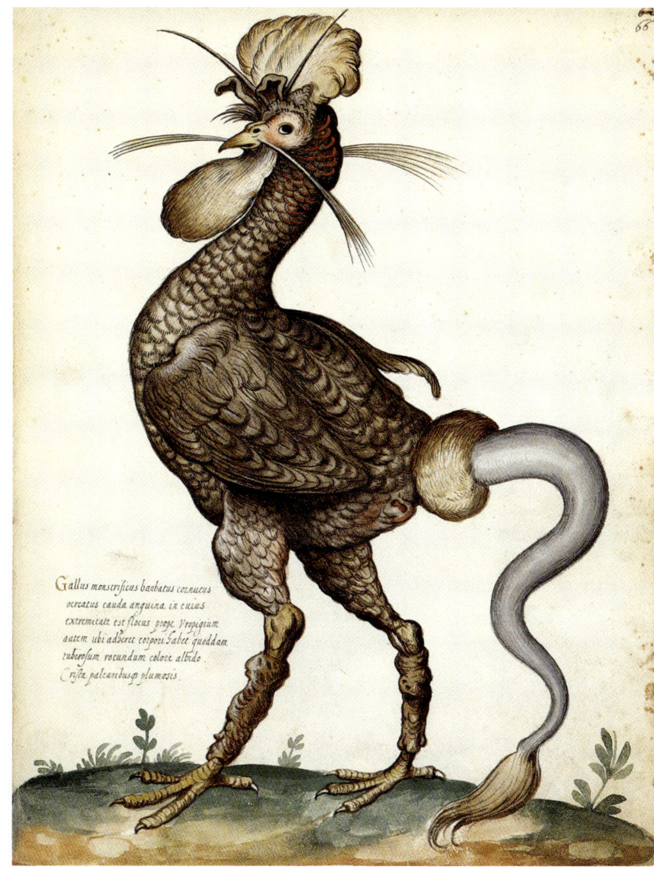

des armes et des équipements originaires du monde entier : des cimeterres turcs et des
poignards « à l'indienne », des gorgerins allemands et des lames milanaises, des bassinets
bourguignons et des casques « à la hongroise ». Dans ce prodigieux musée de la beauté
formelle et de l'excellence technique, parmi d'autres pièces d'équipement guerrier, se
trouve la *Méduse* de Caravage. Il faut imaginer la rondache dans sa disposition originelle
qui était du pur théâtre.

Page 46
*Cornelian-inlaid drawers of a 17th-century cabinet
in Rome, with ancient examples of marble in 18th-
century boxes / Schubläden eines römischen Schrankes
des 17. Jahrhunderts mit eingelassenen Karneolen
und antike Marmorstücke in Kassetten des 18. Jahrhunderts / Tiroirs incrustés de cornaline d'un cabinet
romain du 17e siècle et pièces de marbre antiques dans
des boîtes du 18e siècle*
Rome, Dario del Bufalo Collection

Ulisse Aldrovandi
Gallus monstrificus
Mythical creature resembling a rooster with a
lizard-like tail / Mythisches Wesen, das einem Hahn
ähnelt, der den Schwanz einer Schlange hat / Créature
mythique ressemblant à un coq avec une queue de
lézard, in *Corpus Aldrovandino di Storia Naturale*,
second half of 16th century, vol. I, f. 66
Watercolour, 42 x 27.5 cm / 16⅝ x 10⅞ in.
Bologna, Biblioteca Universitaria

Dans la mise en scène que décrit l'inventaire de l'armurerie, au cœur de la forêt de cruauté et de mort créée par cette accumulation d'armes de toutes les formes, destinées à tous les usages, se dressait un cheval de bois habillé de bleu et de rouge : « avec une bordure de plaque de fer ouvragée et dorée, de couleur bleu foncé, fixée avec des mailles et des épingles de laiton, avec une frise ourlant cette bordure rouge et jaune, doublée de toile rouge », précise le document. Ce cheval était monté par un guerrier oriental cuirassé d'or et d'acier, coiffé d'un turban « orné d'ocelles d'or[3] ». Dans une main, le cavalier tenait une lance, dans l'autre – coup de théâtre ! – « un bouclier où Caravage avait peint une tête de Méduse couronnée de serpents ». Il paraît difficile d'imaginer la *Méduse* de Caravage dans l'armurerie des Offices faisant partie intégrante d'une magnifique et terrifiante armure de cavalier, don du shah de Perse Abbas le Grand à la couronne grand-ducale. Cependant, les vers que le poète Giovanni Battista Marino a rédigés en 1601, après avoir visité l'armurerie, concrétisent parfaitement cette vision :

Aujourd'hui, quels ennemis
Ne seraient pas changés en marbres froids
En fixant, monseigneur, sur votre bouclier
Cette Gorgone fière et cruelle
Dont la chevelure, par un horrible nœud de vipères,
Est muée en effrayante et hirsute parure.[4]

L'hyperbole maniériste du poète se reflète donc dans l'hyperbole maniériste de l'armurier scénographe qui a fait de la *Méduse* de Caravage le cœur symbolique de la salle d'armes médicéenne.

À l'origine, le Cabinet des merveilles des époques maniériste, puis baroque, a pour modèle le *studiolo* de la Renaissance italienne, attribut de l'intellectuel humaniste et lieu de prestige d'une cour, reflet des intérêts artistiques, historiques et philosophiques du seigneur, quasi-incarnation de sa personnalité spirituelle (ill. p. 11, 15). Le *studiolo* est une pièce secrète dont la fonction est d'abriter les objets rares et précieux que le propriétaire aime étudier et collectionner en privé. Il peut s'agir de pièces archéologiques, de métaux rares, de pierres précieuses ou semi-précieuses, d'objets d'orfèvrerie, de livres, d'instruments scientifiques, de peintures ou de sculptures particulièrement appréciées, d'*exotica* et de *naturalia* (ill. p. 18). La littérature et les documents nous ont transmis le souvenir des *studioli* italiens les plus célèbres, dont la plupart virent bien souvent leurs trésors dispersés à la suite de successions dynastiques ou d'événements politiques[5]. Ainsi en advint-il des *studioli* de Lionello et Borso d'Este, aménagé dans le palais de Belfiore près de Ferrare, ainsi que du précieux cabinet du palais ducal d'Urbino, rehaussé de marqueteries dues à Botticelli et Benedetto da Mariano et de peintures flamandes signées par Juste de Gand et Pedro Berruguete (ill. p. 11).

« Au-delà de la bibliothèque se trouve une petite pièce destinée à l'étude [...] meublée de sièges en bois avec des appuis sur le pourtour, et d'une table au milieu : le tout est orné avec le plus grand soin de marqueteries et de sculptures. Le bois habille le sol comme les murs à hauteur d'homme, voire un peu plus, tandis que plus haut les parois accueillent des tableaux dont chacun propose le portrait d'un écrivain célèbre, ancien ou moderne. » Les auteurs de ces tableaux venaient de très loin car « Frédéric était un grand connaisseur de peinture et, comme il ne trouvait pas de maîtres à son goût en Italie, il chargea un envoyé de trouver dans les Flandres un maître talentueux qu'il fit venir à Urbino ; il le chargea de réaliser de nombreuses et excellentes peintures pour son cabinet, qui représentaient des philosophes, des prêtres et tous les Docteurs de l'Église, grecque comme latine, figurés de manière admirable[6] ». C'est en ces termes que, dans ses *Vite degli uomini illustri del XV secolo*, Vespasiano di Bisticci décrit vers 1482 le *studiolo* de Frédéric de Montefeltre aménagé dans le palais d'Urbino, dans lequel Baldassare Castiglione vit « une ville en forme de palais ». Comment ne pas être fasciné par l'idée de

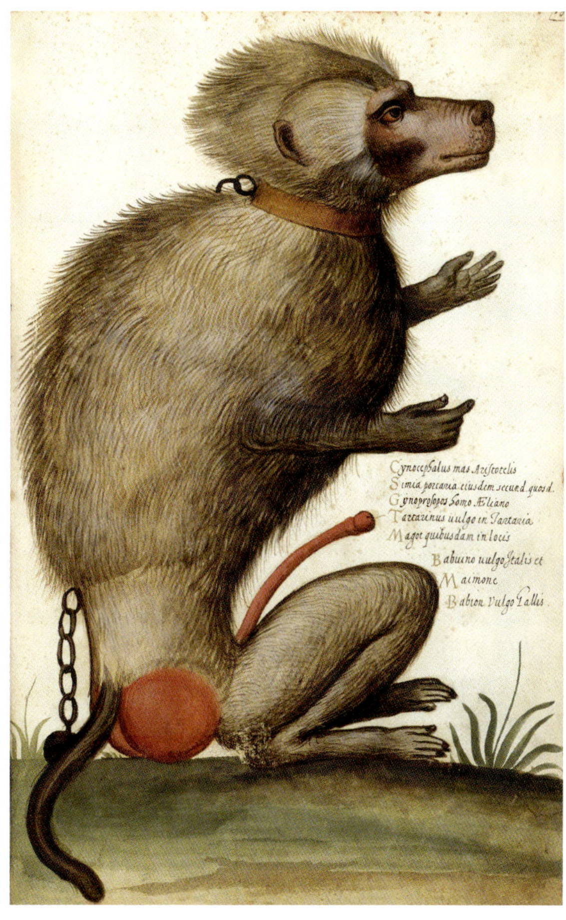

Ulisse Aldrovandi
Cynocephalus
Baboon / Pavian / Babouin
Ibid., vol. V, f. 22
Watercolour, 42 x 27.5 cm / 16⅝ x 10⅞ in.

Frédéric, « seigneur de guerre » prenant part aux événements politiques et militaires de l'Italie de son temps, qui se retire dans son *studiolo*, entouré de peintures et de sculptures de grande qualité, pour lire et méditer les écrits de Plutarque et de Tite-Live, de Sénèque et de Cicéron, ouvrages conservés dans sa bibliothèque trilingue, latine, grecque et hébraïque. Du *studiolo* d'Isabelle d'Este à Mantoue à celui du cardinal Alexandre Farnèse à Caprarola et au « camerino » d'Alphonse d'Este à Ferrare défilent, dans les inventaires et les témoignages contemporains, de précieuses collections archéologiques aujourd'hui dispersées et les noms de grands artistes, dont ceux de Mantegna et de Giovanni Bellini, du Pérugin et de Titien.

De tous les *studioli*, celui du grand-duc François Ier de Médicis, aménagé dans le palazzo Vecchio de Florence, mérite une attention particulière, car il est l'un des très rares à avoir conservé son agencement d'origine et notamment les armoires peintes où étaient conservées les collections (ill. p. 13). « La petite pièce que l'on aménage ex-novo devrait servir, si j'ai bien compris, de cabinet de choses rares et précieuses par leur valeur et leur art, autrement dit des bijoux, des médailles, des pierres gravées, des cristaux ouvragés, des vases et autres objets similaires, des choses de petites dimensions qui trouvent place, selon leur genre, dans l'une ou l'autre armoire[7]. » Voilà ce qu'écrivait Vincenzo Borghini en 1570 dans une lettre adressée à Giorgio Vasari alors que le *studiolo* était en cours de construction. Le thème iconographique principal est celui des quatre éléments naturels (air, feu, terre et eau) qui, maîtrisés par l'intelligence humaine, produisent l'« artifice », c'est-à-dire les prodiges sortis des mains de scientifiques, d'artisans et d'artistes. La série de sculptures en bronze et les peintures ornant les armoires (par Allori, Santi di Tito, Stradano, Zucchi, entre autres) illustrent et commentent l'ensemble des mythographies. Dans les armoires peintes, qui n'étaient ouvertes qu'en de rares occasions pour le plaisir du prince, de ses amis et de ses hôtes, sont conservées les *rariora*, les *naturalia* et les *exotica* que Vincenzo Borghini énumère : perles, coraux, coquillages, verrerie, cristaux de roche, pierres précieuses et produits artisanaux confectionnés avec soin.

L'ambition d'élaborer des encyclopédies exhaustives caractérise le collectionnisme de la Renaissance, comme en témoigne le musée de Paul Jove, conçu comme « Temple de la gloire ». En effet, sa villa-musée abritait une vaste collection systématique de portraits d'hommes illustres divisée par genre (lettrés, artistes, souverains, guerriers)[8]. Le concept d'histoire comme somme d'individualités d'exception sur le modèle plutarquien du *De Viris illustribus* se perpétua jusqu'à la deuxième édition des *Vies des meilleurs peintres, sculpteurs et architectes* que Giorgio Vasari choisit d'orner de gravures avec les portraits des artistes, à l'instar du répertoire iconographique de son ami Paul Jove.

Le désir de comprendre le chatoyant spectacle de l'histoire et du monde par la systématisation des objets, des créations de l'homme et des savoirs a inspiré le concept moderne de musée et conduit à la naissance du Cabinet des merveilles[9] (ill. p. 33, 38, 45). Ainsi, la collection princière d'Albert V de Bavière à Munich se répartissait en cinq classes : histoire sacrée et généalogie familiale, produits artistiques, produits naturels, instruments de musique et objets exotiques, peintures, sculptures et gravures. Cette classification totalement empirique était censée donner lieu à une vision globale du monde et de l'histoire, de manière à transformer le musée en théâtre universel. C'est ainsi qu'en 1565 le médecin belge Samuel Quiccheberg (ill. p. 22) intitule *Inscriptiones vel tituli theatri*

Monstro tribus capitis
Monstrous creature with three heads /
Monsterhaftes Wesen mit drei Köpfen /
Créature tricéphale monstrueuse
Ibid., vol. V, f. 84
Watercolour, 42 x 27.5 cm / 16⅝ x 10⅞ in.

Pages 54–55
Rhinoceros / Nashorn / Rhinocéros
Ibid., vol. I, f. 91
Watercolour, 27.5 x 42 cm / 10⅞ x 16⅝ in.

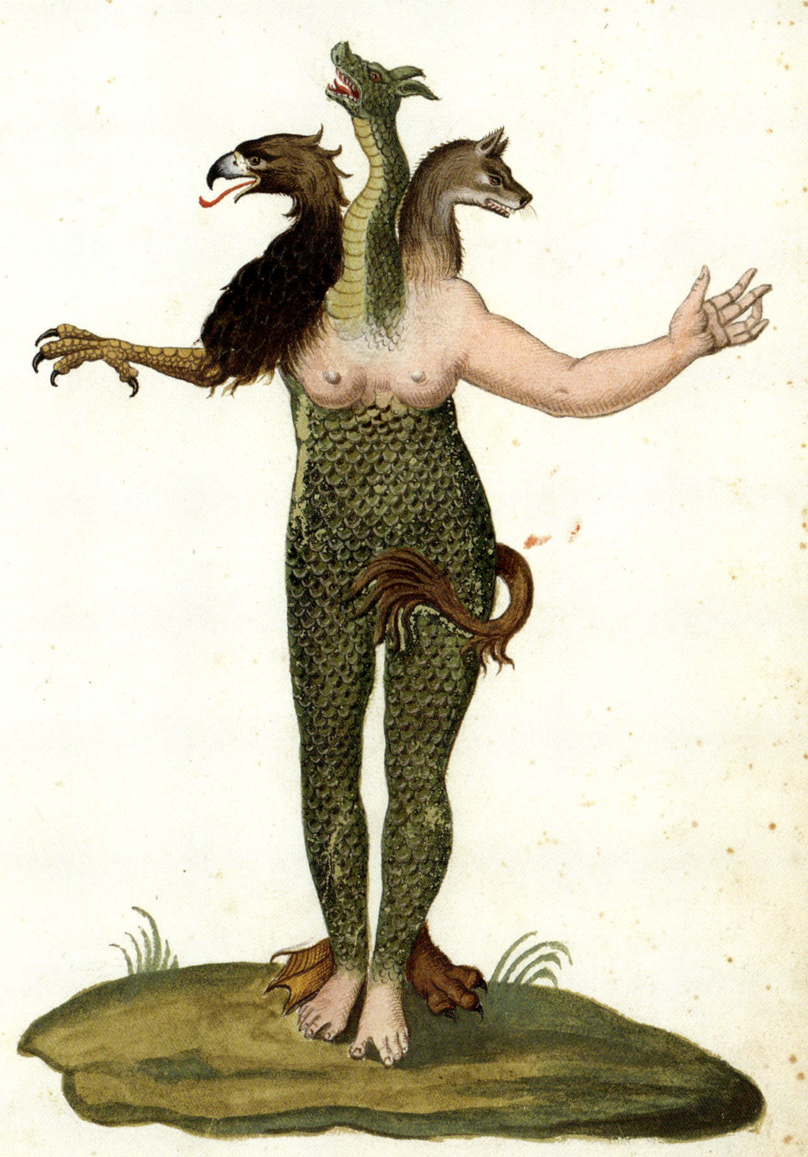

Monstro tribus capitis nempe Dracontino, Aquilino
et Volpino corpore squamoso instar draconis Ab uno
latere brachium humanum cum manu ab altero
aquilinum pedem habet mammas humanas caud-
am loninam, pedes quatuor omnino diuersos leoni-
num unum humanos duos reliquum anserinum,
tribus digitis preditum. Monstrum hoc Amphybiæ
naturæ versabatur in Ægypto iuxta Nili ripam
homines aliaq; ammantia deuorans.

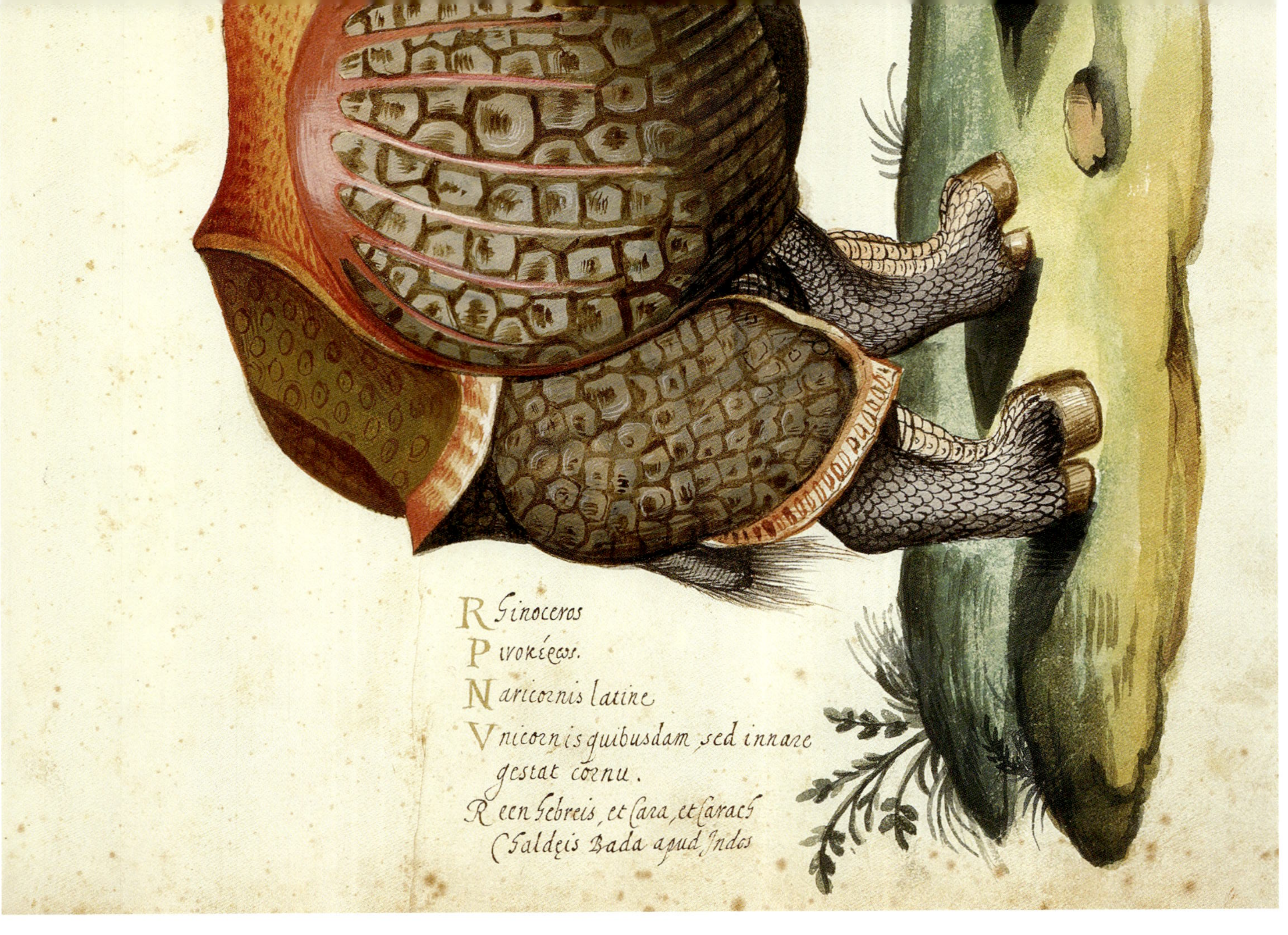

R Sinoceros
P ινοκέρως.
N aricornis latine
V nicornis quibusdam, sed innare
  gestat cornu.
R een Sebreis, et Cara, et Caracħ
Chaldęis Bada apud Indos

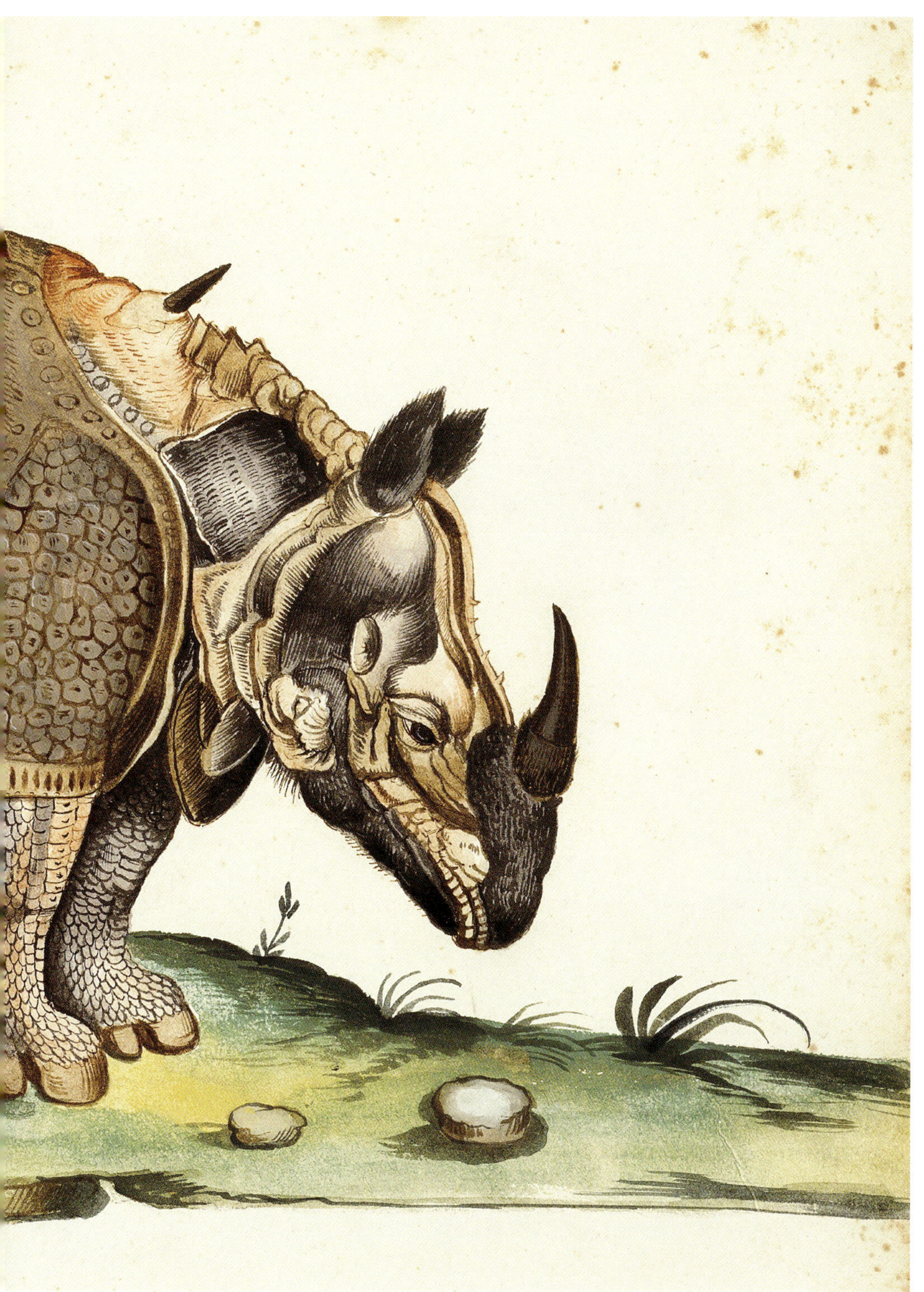

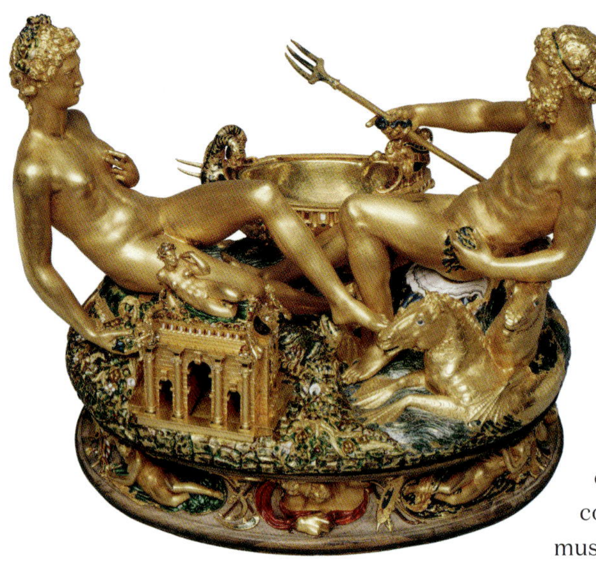

amplissimi sa description des collections d'Albert V de Bavière.

À ses débuts, dans l'Italie de la fin du Moyen Âge et du commencement de la Renaissance, puis dans l'Europe des absolutismes et de la Contre-Réforme, le musée est le fruit de pulsions encyclopédiques insatiables. Les *studioli* des princes, des collectionneurs et des humanistes italiens (à Florence comme à Ferrare, à Mantoue comme à Venise et à Rome) sont des musées universels en germe dans la mesure où, pour satisfaire les inclinations et les intérêts les plus divers, on cherche à tout réunir et à tout classifier : objets symboliques des arts et des sciences, et curiosités naturelles, vestiges archéologiques et peintures appréciées, reliques sacrées et documents ethnographiques (ill. p. 31, 34, 36, 37, 49, 51, 53, 54–55). Ce modèle globalisant et infiniment étendu de « musée universel » trouve sa plus haute expression dans les Kunst- und Wunderkammern du collectionnisme princier européen : à Prague comme à Stuttgart, dans le château d'Ambras au Tyrol, aménagé par l'archiduc Ferdinand II à partir de 1573, comme à Fontainebleau, résidence des rois de France, et à Florence, où à la fin du 16e siècle virent le jour la Tribune dessinée par Buontalenti aux Offices et, au palazzo Vecchio, le *studiolo* alchimique et des mystères du grand-duc François Ier.

Parfois, un vent de folie mêlée d'angoisse semble parcourir le collectionnisme des autocrates européens sous l'Ancien Régime. Songeons à la Kunst- und Wunderkammer du château d'Ambras près d'Innsbruck, collection éblouissante et terrifiante à la fois (voir p. 144–165). En effet, dans ce sombre château tyrolien que l'archiduc Ferdinand II de Habsbourg choisit pour résidence où il s'entoure d'une cour de poètes et d'artistes, le visiteur est d'emblée accueilli par la *Mort*, chef-d'œuvre de Paul Reichel, une Mort plongée dans une profonde méditation, comme pour signifier au visiteur la vanité de tout ce qu'il s'apprête à découvrir (ill. p. 157). Dans le château d'Ambras, ce qui est offert au regard est strictement présenté par catégories (*naturalia*, *artificialia* et *mirabilia*),

Benvenuto Cellini
Salt Cellar or Saliera / Sogenannte Saliera / Salière, c. 1540–1543

Gold, enamel, ebony, ivory,
28.5 x 21.5 x 26.3 cm / 11¼ x 8½ x 10⅜ in.
Vienna, Kunsthistorisches Museum

car la rationalité existe même dans la folie et dans le cauchemar, une rationalité surtout destinée à éveiller la curiosité, à étonner, à remettre idées et croyances en question. Ainsi trouve-t-on des représentations de nains, de géants, de monstres, d'hommes au corps entièrement recouvert de poils, mais également des portraits de souverains, de condottieres et d'hommes illustres. Au fond – nous dit la Mort pensive, à la fois gardienne et emblème du château d'Ambras –, tout est vanité, tout est apparition éphémère, les horreurs et les prodiges de la nature comme la gloire des souverains. En dominant et en maîtrisant la pluralité par l'implacable fixité de l'image, l'œil photographique de Massimo Listri donne une image des beautés et des horreurs qui peuplent le Cabinet des merveilles de l'archiduc Ferdinand. Puisque Ambras est hyperbole, excès, démesure, arrêtons-nous devant le portrait de Gregor Baci, dont l'œil a été percé par une lance (ill. p. 149), le squelette dansant (ill. p. 156), le crocodile qui semble ramper sur le mur, l'ivoire ouvragé jusqu'à l'exacerbation. Telle sera la manière d'arrêter le kaléidoscopique et le changeant spectacle d'un univers qui, autrement, à l'instar de l'*Aleph* de Jorge Luis Borges, nous emporterait inexorablement.

Le plus beau, le plus important des Cabinets des merveilles italiens se trouve à Florence, dans la partie septentrionale du palais Pitti, dans une zone dite « appartement d'été » (voir p. 268–305 et ill. p. 65). Il s'agit du cabinet du Tesoro dei Granduchi, le « Trésor des Grands-Ducs », extraordinaire réunion d'objets rares et précieux. Dans le grand salon de réception, de délicats peintres florentins de l'âge baroque comme Giovanni da San Giovanni et Francesco Ferrini ont retracé, dans des fresques aussi légères et lumineuses que des tapisseries de soie, les fastes de la Maison de Médicis et le destin de Florence appelée à être une nouvelle Athènes, un phare de civilisation et de culture pour le monde entier après la prise de Constantinople par les Turcs. Ces fresques évoquent la mémoire de Laurent le Magnifique entouré d'un cercle d'artistes et d'intellectuels, et celle de Marsile Ficin et de l'Académie platonicienne.

Le salon de Giovanni da San Giovanni est le cœur du Tesoro dei Granduchi. Tout autour sont répartis dans plusieurs salles les trésors accumulés au cours des siècles par la Maison de Médicis, que l'électrice palatine, Anne-Marie-Louise, dernière héritière de la dynastie, légua à ses successeurs, les grands-ducs de Lorraine, avec interdiction de les disperser ou de les aliéner. Au musée sont conservés, notamment, les vases d'origine byzantine et sassanide collectionnés par Laurent le Magnifique, des meubles et des décors en ambre, des tables en marqueterie de pierres dures parmi les plus rares du monde. Le musée abrite également des objets en lapis-lazuli dessinés par Bartolomeo Buontalenti, des cristaux de roche taillés par de grands orfèvres milanais, les camées et les bijoux ayant appartenu aux princesses de Médicis et des pièces ethnographiques originaires d'Amérique. Cette prestigieuse et scintillante « salle des merveilles » recèle encore les « ivoires de Cobourg[10] ». En mars 1635, pendant la guerre de Trente Ans, les Impériaux assiégèrent et conquirent Cobourg ; Matthias de Médicis, qui était au service de l'armée catholique, confisqua la collection d'ivoires du prince luthérien et l'emporta à

Florence comme butin de guerre. Il s'agit de vingt-sept ivoires diaphanes et très fragiles, véritables chefs-d'œuvre d'art et de technique. Et l'on ne sait ce qu'il faut le plus admirer : la fantaisie créatrice de l'artiste qui travaille la matière jusqu'à la transfigurer ou presque, ou bien l'époustouflante qualité technique des tours de précision capables de prodiges millimétriques.

En présence des ivoires Cobourg, le regard de Massimo Listri parvient à être mimétique tout en jouant une part active. Fasciné par la matière organique – la défense d'éléphant – travaillée et transformée par l'artifice, il réussit à nous communiquer sa stupeur, à la faire nôtre, devant les enroulements vrillés et les miracles filiformes. Dans le même temps, il se propose de nous faire saisir la beauté transparente, diaphane et lumineuse de ces objets qui semblent descendus des coffres-forts du Paradis pour illuminer d'une paisible lumière les ambres, les lapis-lazuli et l'argenterie du trésor des Médicis.

Personne n'a su évoquer mieux qu'Angelo Maria Ripellino dans *Praga Magica* (1973) la fascination hypnotique et sinistre du château de Prague, résidence de l'empereur Rodolphe II de Habsburg (ill. p. 23) qui mourut en 1612 à l'âge de 60 ans, à temps pour ne pas voir son château dévasté et ses collections dispersées lors de la guerre de Trente Ans. Mais tant que vécut cet homme colérique, visionnaire, hypocondriaque et misanthrope, qu'entourait une cour d'aventuriers, d'ingénieurs, d'alchimistes, d'astrologues et de mages, un homme en proie à une fièvre de collectionneur boulimique, il n'y eut point en Europe de collection plus vaste et plus étonnante que la sienne. Les armoires et les vitrines du château de Prague renfermaient les objets les plus variés : des automates conçus par les ingénieurs au service de Rodolphe, des cristaux de roche taillés par les Milanais Saracchi et Miseroni, des coupes réalisées à partir d'une corne de rhinocéros ou d'un œuf d'autruche, des trésors artistiques (peintures, sculptures, émaux, tapisseries, pièces d'orfèvrerie et armes) que des générations de souverains habsbourgeois avaient accumulés au long des siècles. La partie des collections pragoises de Rodolphe qui a échappé aux désastres de la guerre constitue aujourd'hui, avec les trésors habsbourgeois de diverses provenances, la Kunstkammer du Kunsthistorisches Museum de Vienne. En 1891, François-Joseph inaugura les collections impériales qui réunissent deux mille cent objets (voir p. 166–181) et forment un ensemble si admirable, si riche de chefs-d'œuvre – la *Salière* d'or de Benvenuto Cellini (ill. p. 56) et de précieux automates, fascinante alliance d'art et de technologie – que l'œil photographique de Massimo Listri en est comme effaré.

Certains Cabinets des merveilles possèdent un charme de château enchanté, ils s'apparentent à des visions magiques dans un temps suspendu. C'est le cas du château de Rosenborg à Copenhague, résidence royale (voir p. 196–235) où, aux côtés de divers objets mythiques inspirés par les sagas nordiques (la *Corne des Oldenbourg*, le trône ésotérique constitué de longues dents de narval torsadées), se déploient les collections de porcelaines et de verreries, dont celle de Murano offerte par la République de Venise au roi Frédéric IV lors de son voyage dans la lagune immortalisé par Carlevarijs dans une toile célèbre (ill. p. 59). L'objectif de Massimo Listri scrute les vitrines regorgeant d'objets,

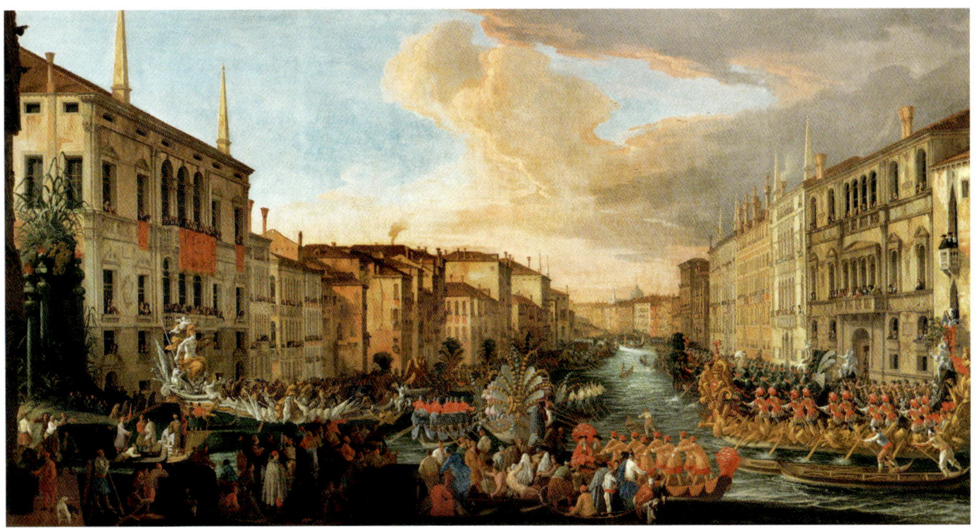

Luca Carlevarijs
*Regatta on the Grand Canal in Honour of King
Frederick IV of Denmark / Regatta auf dem Canal
Grande zu Ehren König Friedrichs IV. von Dänemark /
Régate sur le Grand Canal en l'honneur du roi
Frédéric IV de Danemark*, 1711
Oil on canvas, 135.3 x 259.7 cm / 53⅜ x 102¼ in.
Los Angeles, J. Paul Getty Museum

Pages 60–61
Johan Joseph Zoffany
*The Tribuna of the Uffizi / Die Tribuna der Uffizien /
La Tribune aux Offices*, c. 1772–1777
Oil on canvas, 123.5 x 155 cm / 48⅝ x 61 in.
Windsor, Royal Collection

s'arrête devant les portraits qui possèdent la lumineuse évidence tactile de créatures
extra-terrestres et se laisse séduire par une accumulation d'ivoires, d'objets d'orfèvrerie
et de verrerie. Il transmet une impression de « démesure ordonnée », de plénitude variée
et scintillante que régit néanmoins un ordre savant et rigoureux.

Le 17ᵉ siècle est celui qui découvre l'infinité des cieux avec Galilée et les vertigineux
abysses de l'âme humaine avec Pascal. Il reflète la prise de conscience de l'immensité qui
nous entoure, mais aussi de l'infiniment petit qui habite la machine palpitante du corps
humain et la moindre créature présente dans l'univers. Seul un siècle comme le 17ᵉ pouvait
imaginer et construire un meuble grand comme le monde en quelque sorte, un meuble
qui fût métaphore et représentation. Un tel objet appartient au Museum Gustavianum,
dans les collections d'art de l'université d'Uppsala en Suède ; il s'agit du cabinet que la
Ville d'Augsbourg offrit au roi Gustave II de Suède, véritable chef-d'œuvre de Philipp
Hainhofer, le plus grand ébéniste de son temps (voir p. 236–267). Il comporte des centaines
de petits tiroirs, visibles pour certains, secrets pour la plupart, des volets coulissants,
des miroirs rabattables et, partout, plus d'un millier d'objets en ivoire, en émail, en pierre
dure dissimulés dans d'innombrables compartiments. Le monde entier est symbolisé et
enfermé dans ce meuble. Le cabinet d'Uppsala peut déconcerter, y compris l'objectif de

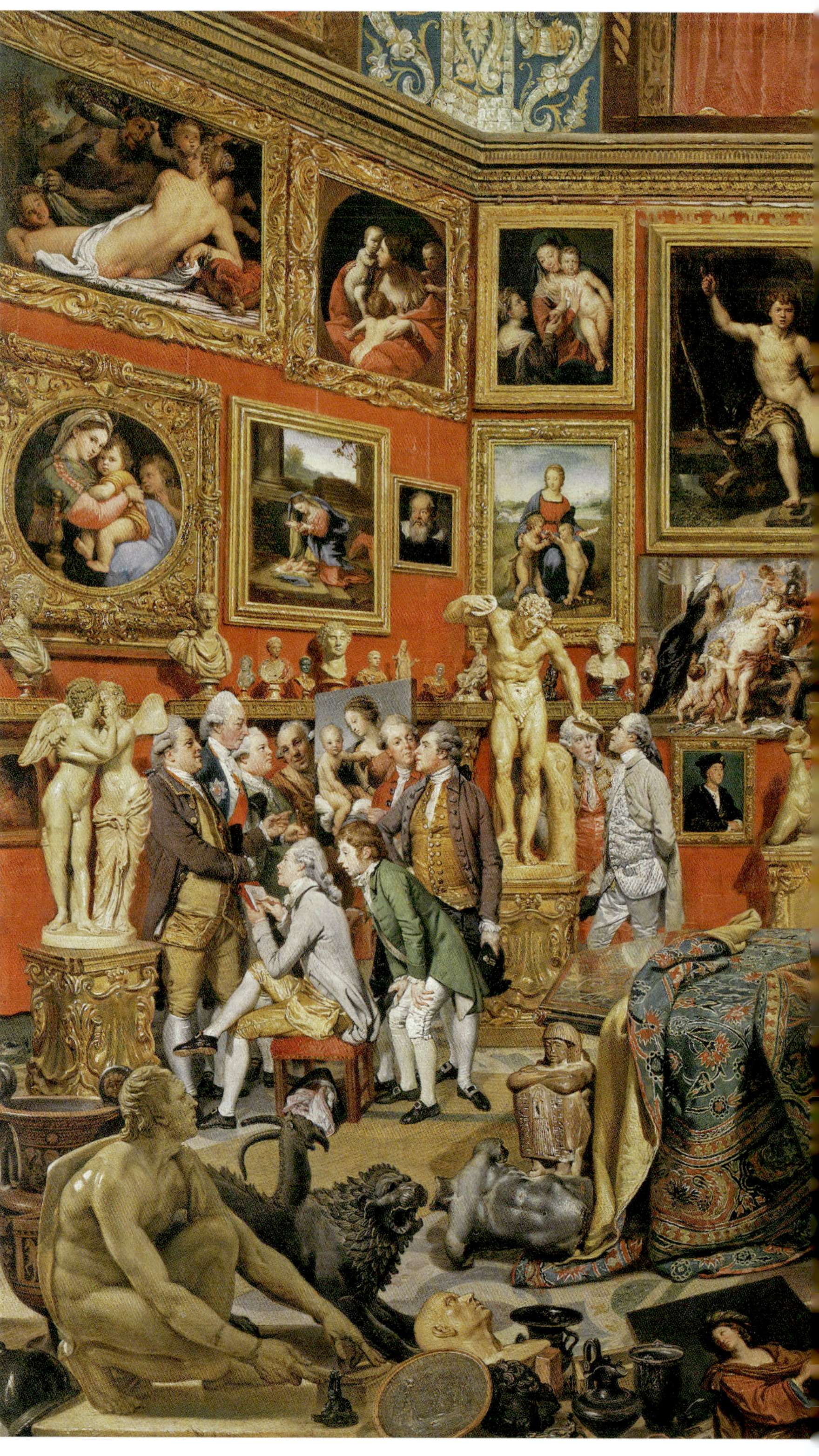

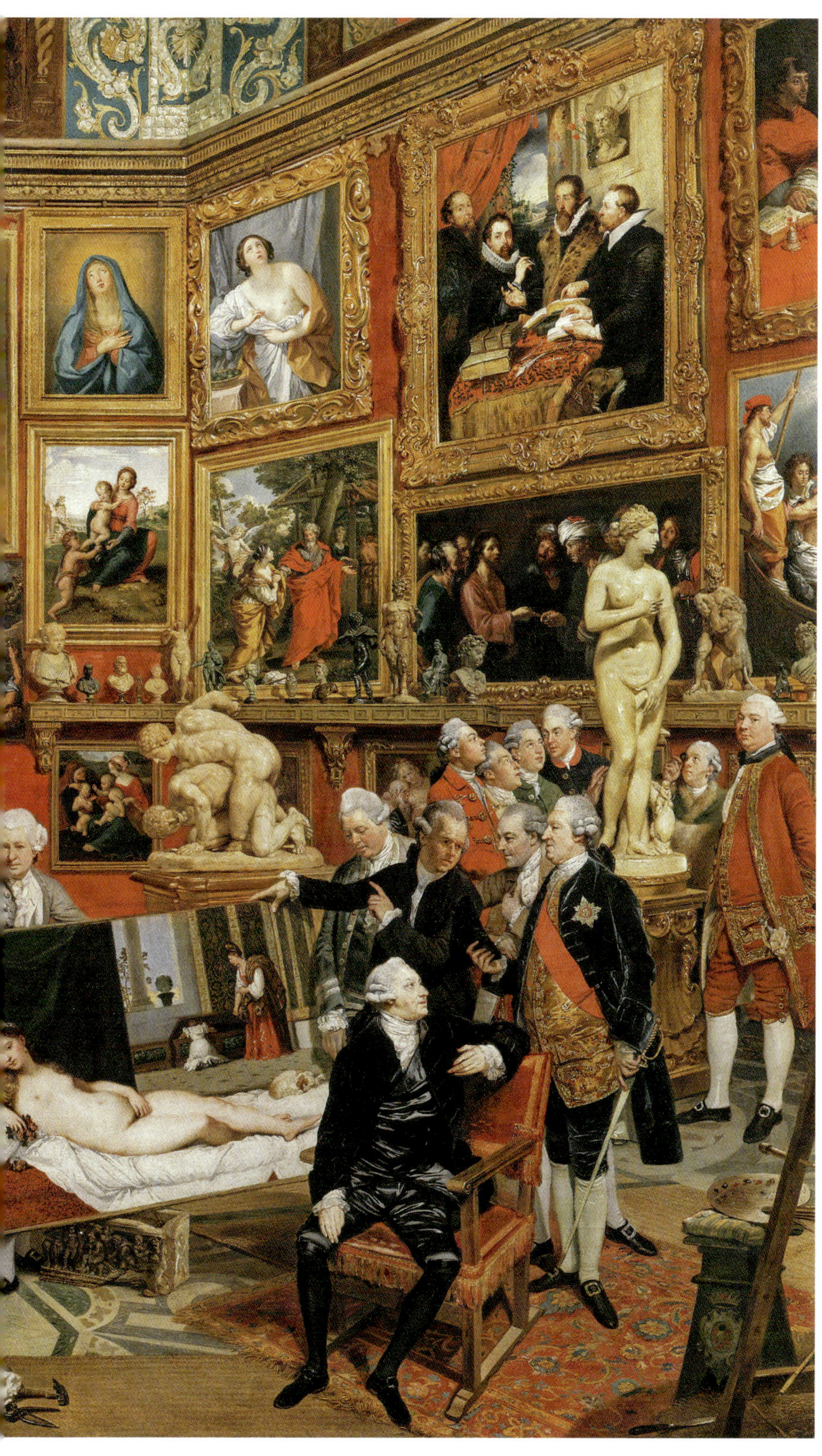

Massimo Listri qui parvient néanmoins à communiquer la dimension quasi hypnotique de l'accumulation et de la multiplication. Dans ses photographies, le microcosme devient image du cosmos. C'est exactement ce que Philipp Hainhofer et le roi Gustave de Suède désiraient voir et posséder. Seule l'Allemagne, parvint, semble-t-il, à élaborer une conception quasi mystique de la « chambre des merveilles » (ill. p. 63).

Les musées de Dresde, ville surnommée de manière élogieuse la Florence du Nord, doivent leur célébrité à la *Madone Sixtine* de Raphaël qui fascina Dostoïevski, aux tableaux du Corrège et à ceux du Parmesan qu'Auguste de Saxe acheta aux ducs d'Este de Modène ; mais rares sont les visiteurs qui savent que le château de la Résidence du grand prince électeur, futur roi de Saxe, a abrité dès 1560 l'une des plus envoûtantes et fastueuses Kunstkammern d'Europe. De richissimes collections de *naturalia* et d'*artificialia* surtout (horloges, automates, instruments scientifiques) occupaient des salles dont le cœur était la Grünes Gewölbe (la Voûte verte). Durant la Seconde Guerre mondiale, le terrible bombardement que subit Dresde en février 1945 a détruit le château. Sa reconstruction et le réaménagement de ses collections – que l'on songe aux quelque trois mille chefs-d'œuvre de joaillerie et d'orfèvrerie – selon de nouveaux critères de grande qualité constituent l'une des opérations les plus intelligentes et les plus judicieuses de la seconde moitié du 20ᵉ siècle (voir p. 66–111).

Parcourir les lieux qui abritent le grand collectionnisme d'Occident signifie remonter aux origines de l'histoire de la pensée et des sciences. Massimo Listri propose un voyage à travers des collections issues de préoccupations et d'ambitions scientifiques. Ainsi, lorsqu'il entre dans l'abbaye bénédictine de Seitenstetten en Autriche où triomphe un rococo aux couleurs tendres, le visiteur découvre l'une des collections minéralogiques les plus importantes d'Europe (voir p. 42, 182–195). De même, en pénétrant dans le paradis marin du cabinet Lafaille au Muséum d'Histoire Naturelle de La Rochelle, cabinet organisé selon les critères de sélection et de catalogage fixés au siècle des Lumières, comment ne s'étonnerait-il pas devant l'infinie curiosité d'un homme, Clément Lafaille, qui aimait la mer et qui en plein 18ᵉ siècle aspirait à en percer tous les secrets en sélectionnant et en accumulant des étoiles de mer, des coquillages et des madrépores (voir p. 354–373).

À Reggio Emilia, les Musei civici conservent les instruments et les documents réunis par Lazzaro Spallanzani, l'un des fondateurs de la science expérimentale moderne (voir p. 306–317), tandis que près de Rome le palazzo Patrizi de Bracciano accueille le visiteur avec un *splendor marmorum*. La Rome antique, celle de Domitien et de Martial, d'Hadrien et d'Aristide, de Commode et d'Apulée, de Constantin et de Dioclétien, était une ville colorée, une ville de marbres blancs mais aussi de porphyre et de rouge antique, de granits verts et gris importés d'Afrique et d'Anatolie, de basalte noir, de jaspes venus d'Espagne, de brèches jaunes, d'albâtres et de marbre *portasanta*. Voici ce que révèle Raniero Gnoli, auteur d'études fondamentales sur les marbres romains antiques, qui a réuni au palazzo Patrizi la plus vaste et la plus étonnante collection d'échantillons des pierres ayant contribué à la beauté et la gloire de Rome (voir p. 334–343).

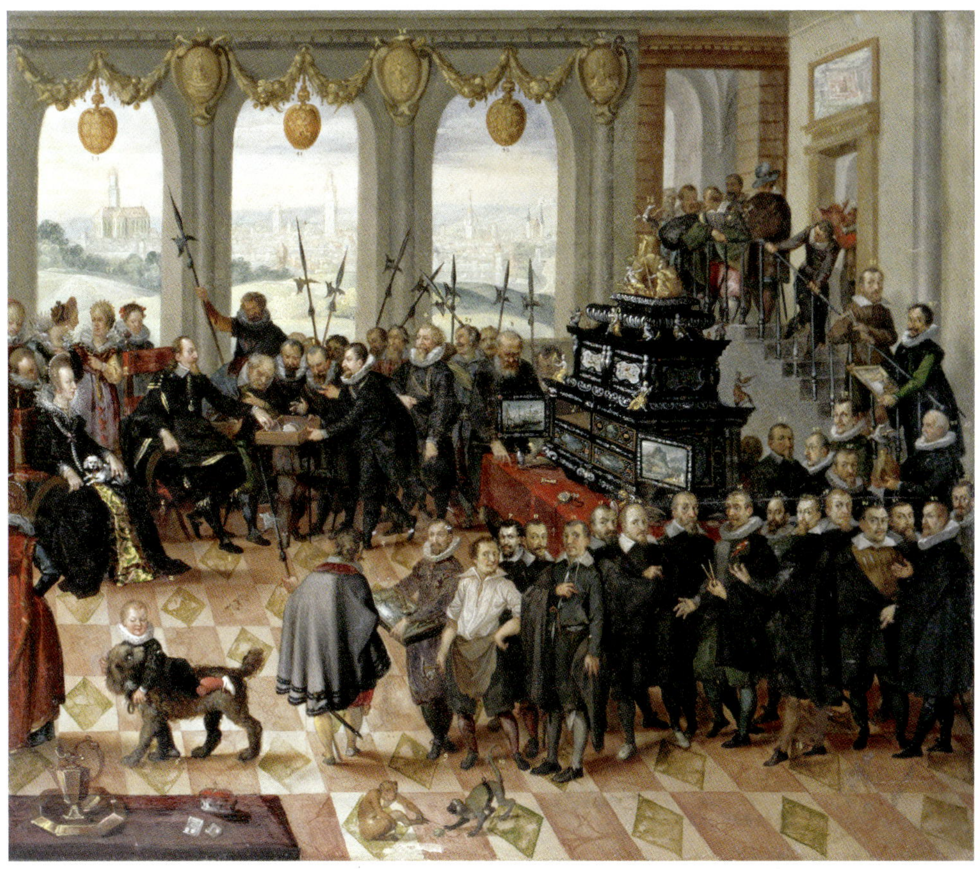

Anton Mozart
Presentation of the Pomeranian Art Cabinet /
Die Übergabe des Pommerschen Kunstschranks /
La Présentation du cabinet poméranien, c. 1614/15

Oil on wood, 39.5 x 45.4 cm / 15½ x 17⅞ in.
Berlin, Kunstgewerbemuseum

Rares sont ceux qui connaissent le très ancien Ospedale di Santo Spirito in Sassia
situé sur les rives du Tibre, non loin du Vatican, et plus rares encore ceux qui le visitent;
c'est un véritable Cabinet des merveilles sanitaire : pratiques thérapeutiques, instruments chirurgicaux, pharmacopée, assistance aux malades. Tout cela est documenté par
cinq siècles de matériaux, d'archives et de publications conservés dans la plus importante
bibliothèque d'histoire de la médecine existant aujourd'hui en Italie (voir p. 318–333).

À ce stade, il est légitime de se demander si le Cabinet des merveilles est encore
présent dans le désir et l'imaginaire des collectionneurs, si le goût de la collection démesu-
rée n'a pas disparu, si aujourd'hui les Rodolphe de Habsbourg, Athanase Kircher (ill. p. 41)
et François de Médicis ont des héritiers. La réponse est oui (ill. p. 6–8, 26–28, 46). Devant
la collection d'Alessandro Orsi à Azzate di Varese (voir p. 344–353) ou la collection de

glyptique que Guy Ladrière a réunie dans sa galerie parisienne (voir p. 388–395) ou encore devant les ivoires anciens de la galerie Kugel (voir p. 396–407), parisienne elle aussi, nous devons admettre que subsiste aujourd'hui encore la passion qui a conduit à l'avènement des *mirabilia* dans l'histoire du grand collectionnisme européen. Précisons toutefois que les exemples cités ici et que Massimo Listri a photographiés, sont ceux d'antiquaires pour la plupart. De nos jours, pour le collectionneur privé, désorienté par le brouhaha publicitaire et les sirènes du marché, il est presque impossible de se lancer à une recherche patiente et minutieuse d'objets susceptibles de lui plaire et de faire son bonheur. Telle est néanmoins l'attitude qu'il nous faut favoriser et encourager.

Notes

1 Campanella 2000, p. 14–15.
2 Bocchi 1591, p. 106–110, 111–112.
3 Paolucci 2007, p. 87–90.
4 Giambattista Marino 1620, p. 48.
5 De Benedictis 1991, p. 32–37, 168–178.
6 Da Bisticci *c.* 1482, p. 209;
   Reynaud & Ressort 1991, p. 82–114.
7 Frey 1930, p. 529; Berti 1967.
8 De Vecchi 1977, p. 87–93.
9 De Benedictis 1991, p. 116–125, 287–298.
10 Schmidt – Sframeli 2013.

Giovanni Battista Foggini
Elector Palatine's cabinet / Der Kabinettschrank des pfälzischen Kurfürsten / Le cabinet de l'Électeur palatin, 1709
Ebony, gilded bronze, semi-precious stones, mother-of-pearl, crystal,
280 x 162 x 54 cm / 110¼ x 63¾ x 21¼ in.
Florence, Palazzo Pitti, Tesoro dei Granduchi

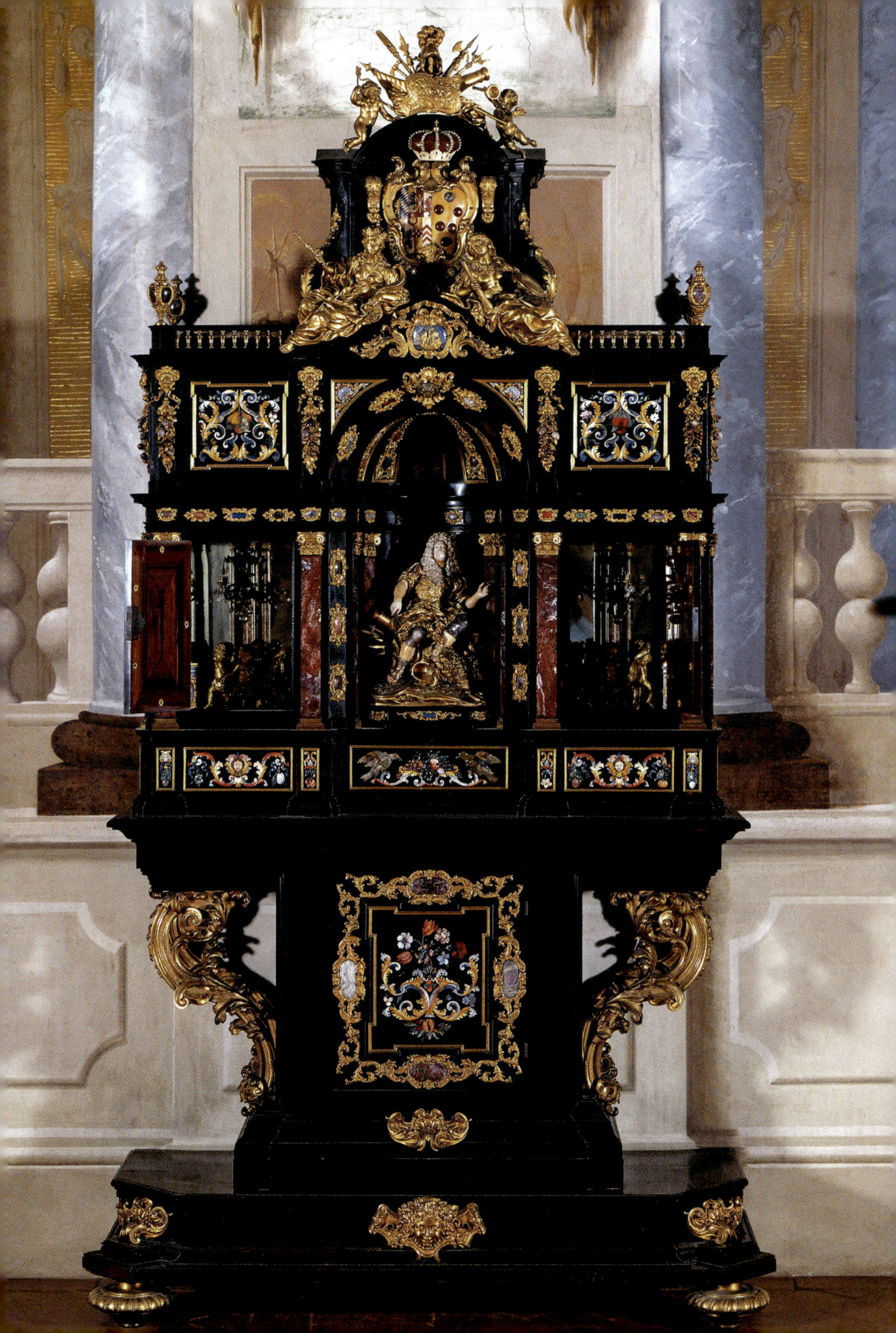

Grünes Gewölbe

Staatliche Kunstsammlungen, Dresden

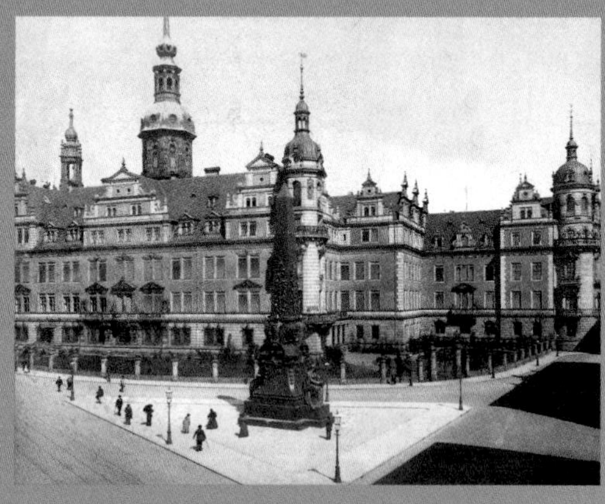

Founded 1560 (the museum was opened in 1723)

Key item A nautilus shell cup embellished with an elaborate black décor and engraved with grotesques. Mounted in gilt silver, the cup is supported by a cloven-hoofed grotesque figure wearing mask and armour who is sitting astride a saddle shaped like a turtle that is strapped to a dragon partially made out of a large piece of coral. In 1724 Johann Heinrich Köhler combined two older pieces from the collection to create this exceptional artwork.

Besonders sehenswert Nautiluspokal aus vergoldetem Silber, dessen Oberfläche mit einem feinen Gespinst aus Grotesken in Schwarzgravur und Flachrelief überzogen ist. Die Fußgruppe besteht aus einer bocksbeinigen, maskierten und gepanzerten Groteske, die auf einem schildkrötenförmigen Sattel sitzt und einen Drachen reitet, dessen Hinterleib aus einem großen Korallenzinken besteht. Johann Heinrich Köhler fügte die beiden älteren, ursprünglich separaten Teile 1724 zu einem neuen Kunstwerk zusammen.

À voir absolument Nautile monté en argent doré, orné de grotesques incisées et sculptées, soutenu par un personnage grotesque en armure assis sur une tortue en guise de selle et chevauchant un dragon constitué pour moitié d'une branche de corail. Johann Heinrich Köhler assembla en 1724 les deux parties plus anciennes, initialement séparées, créant ainsi une nouvelle œuvre d'art.

The Royal Palace and the wing with the Grünes Gewölbe (Green Vault). Photograph, 1905.

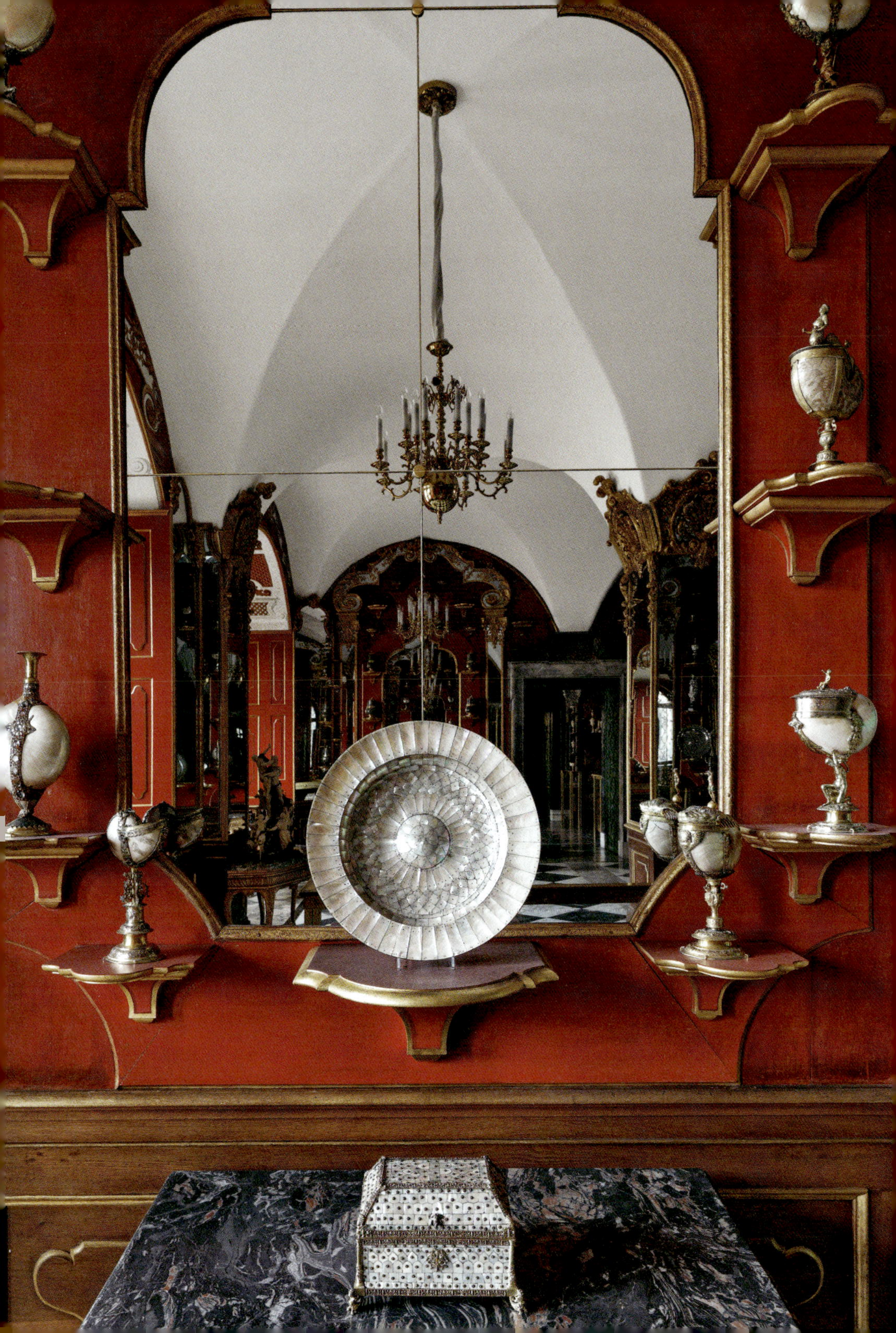

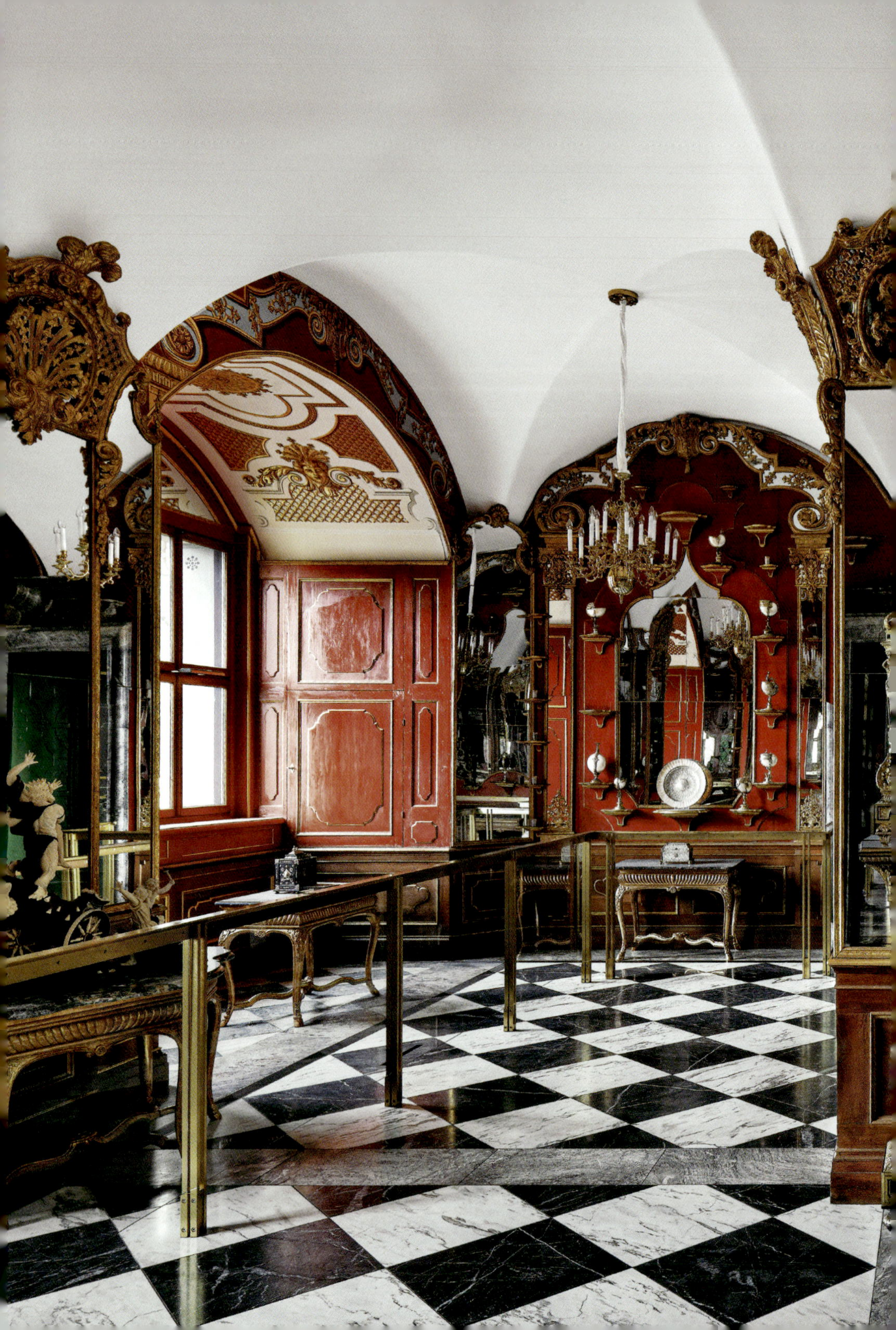

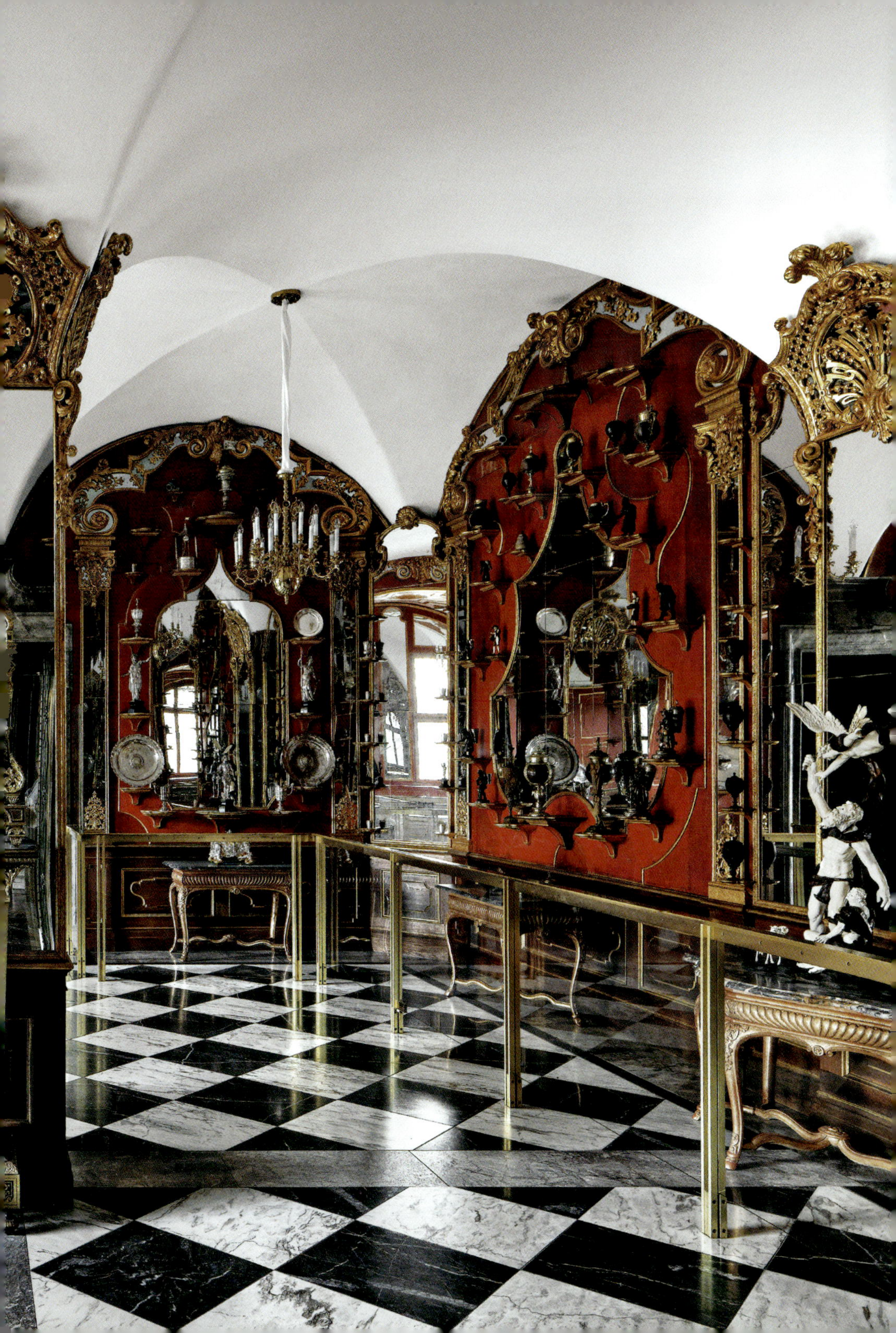

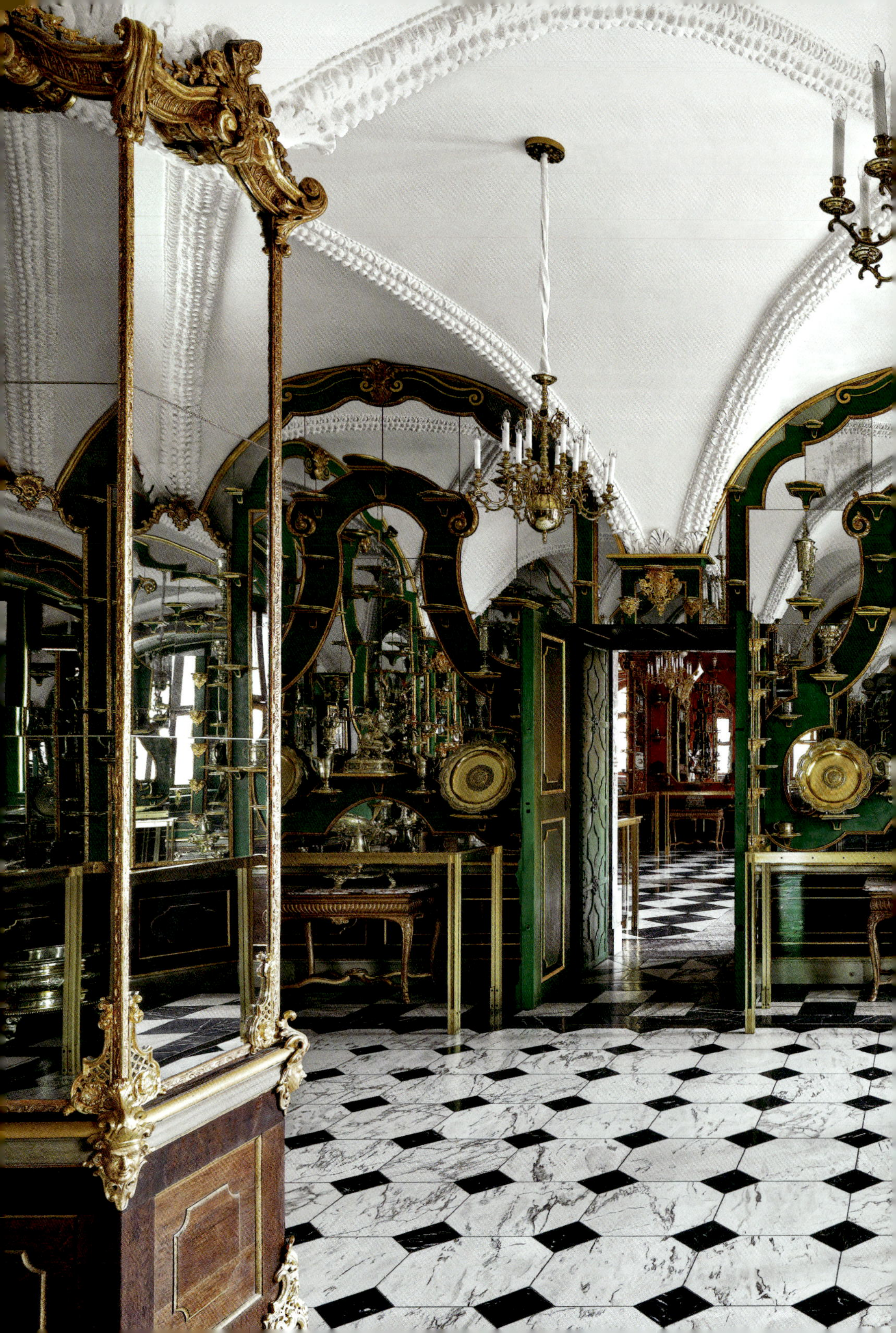

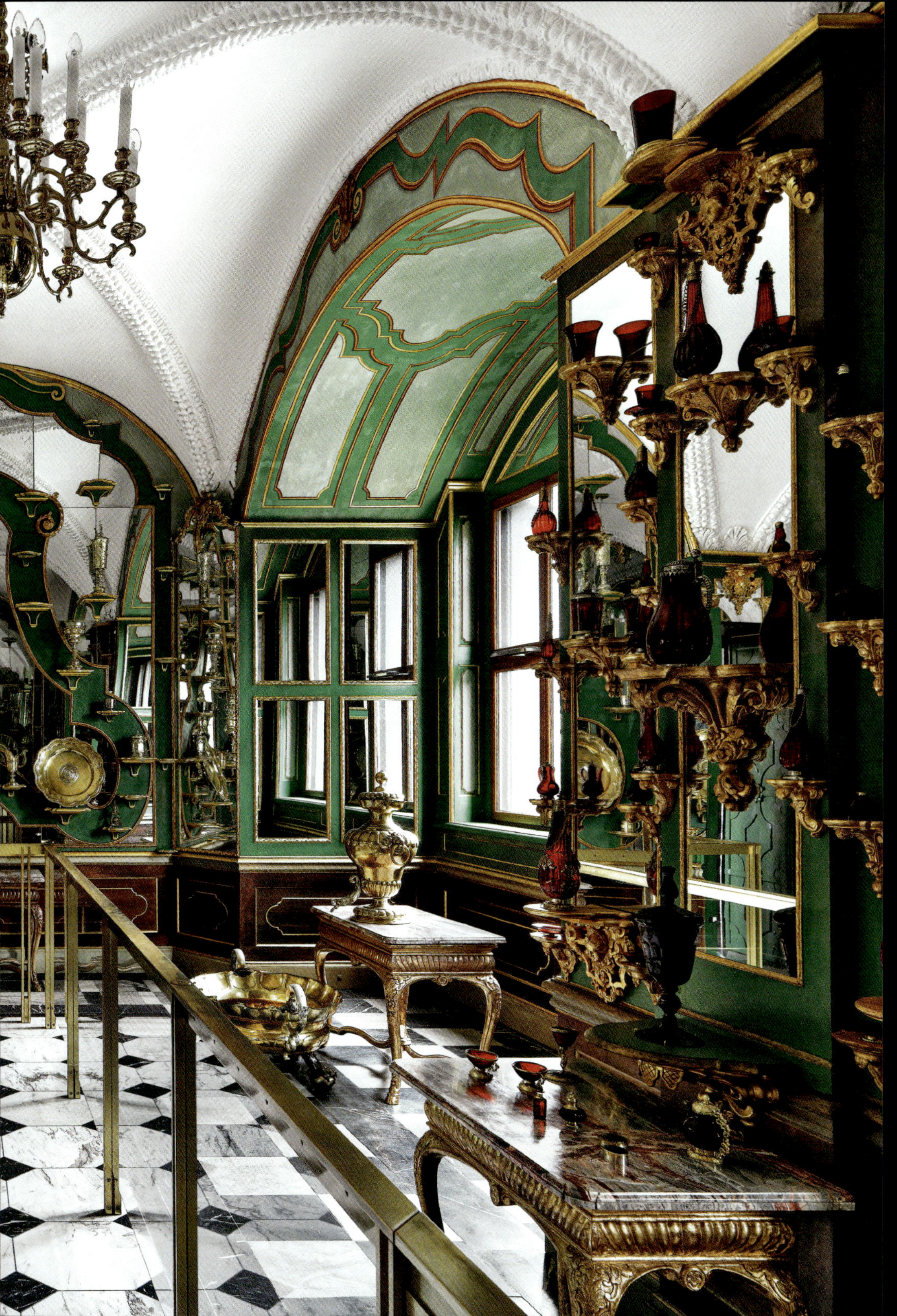

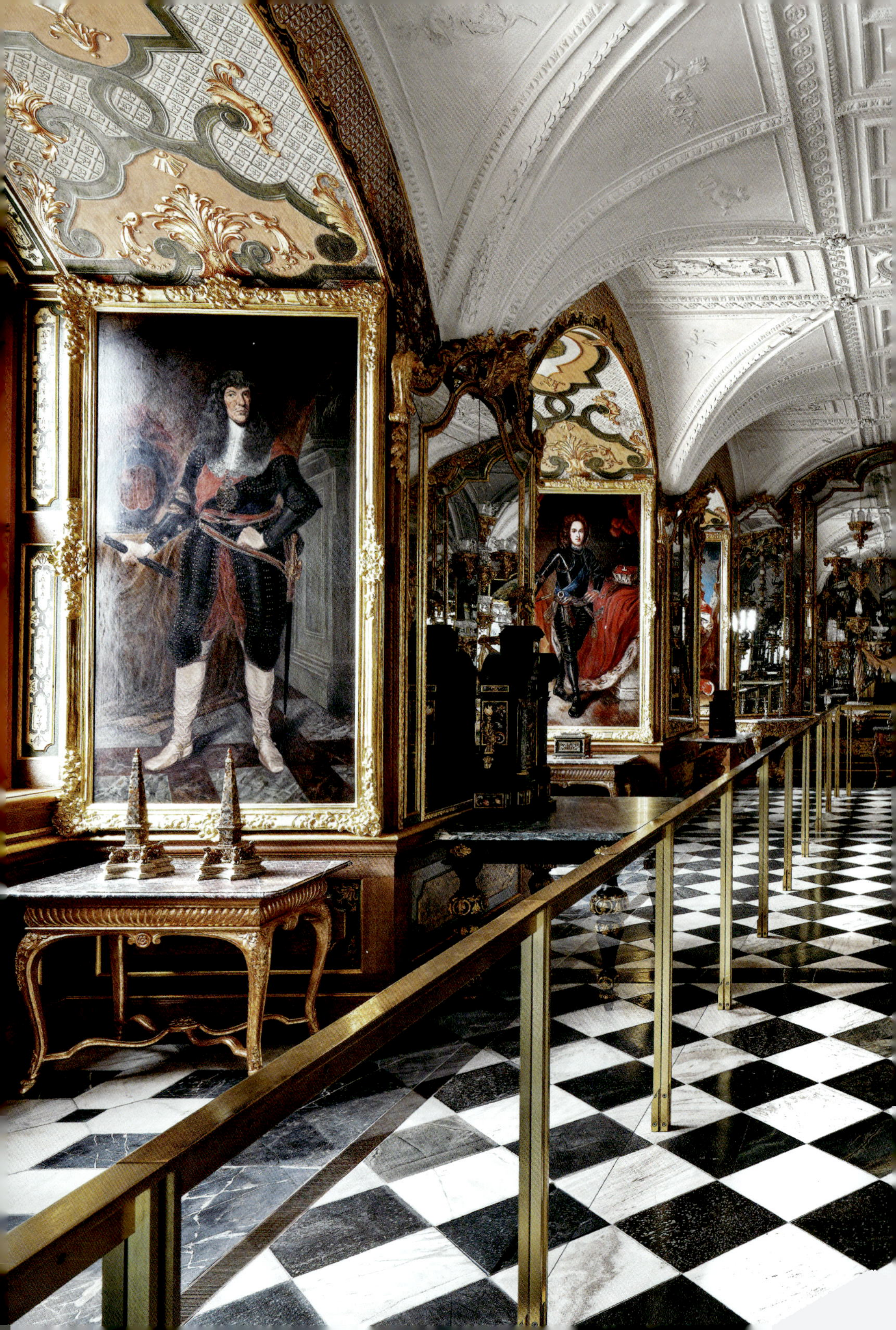

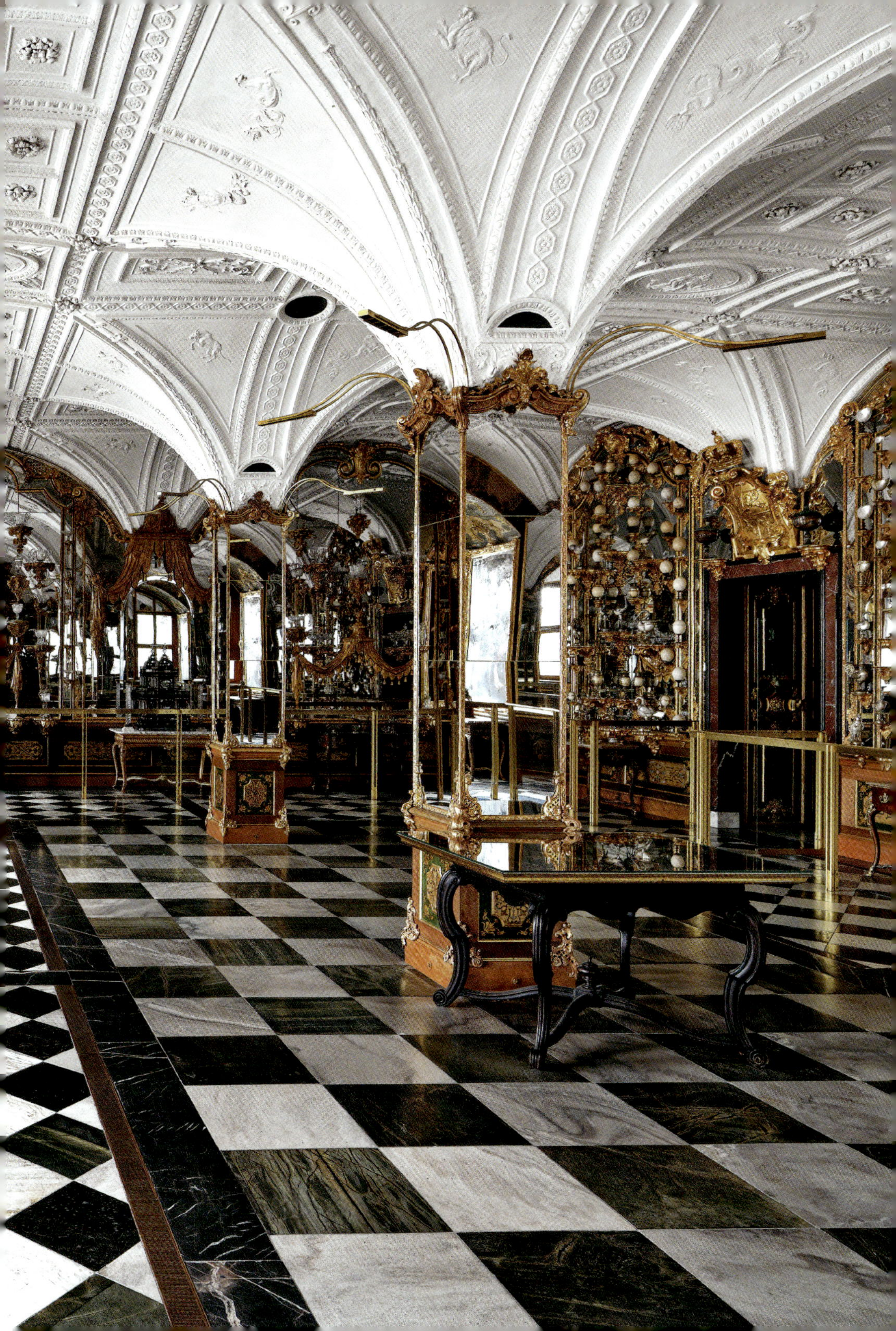

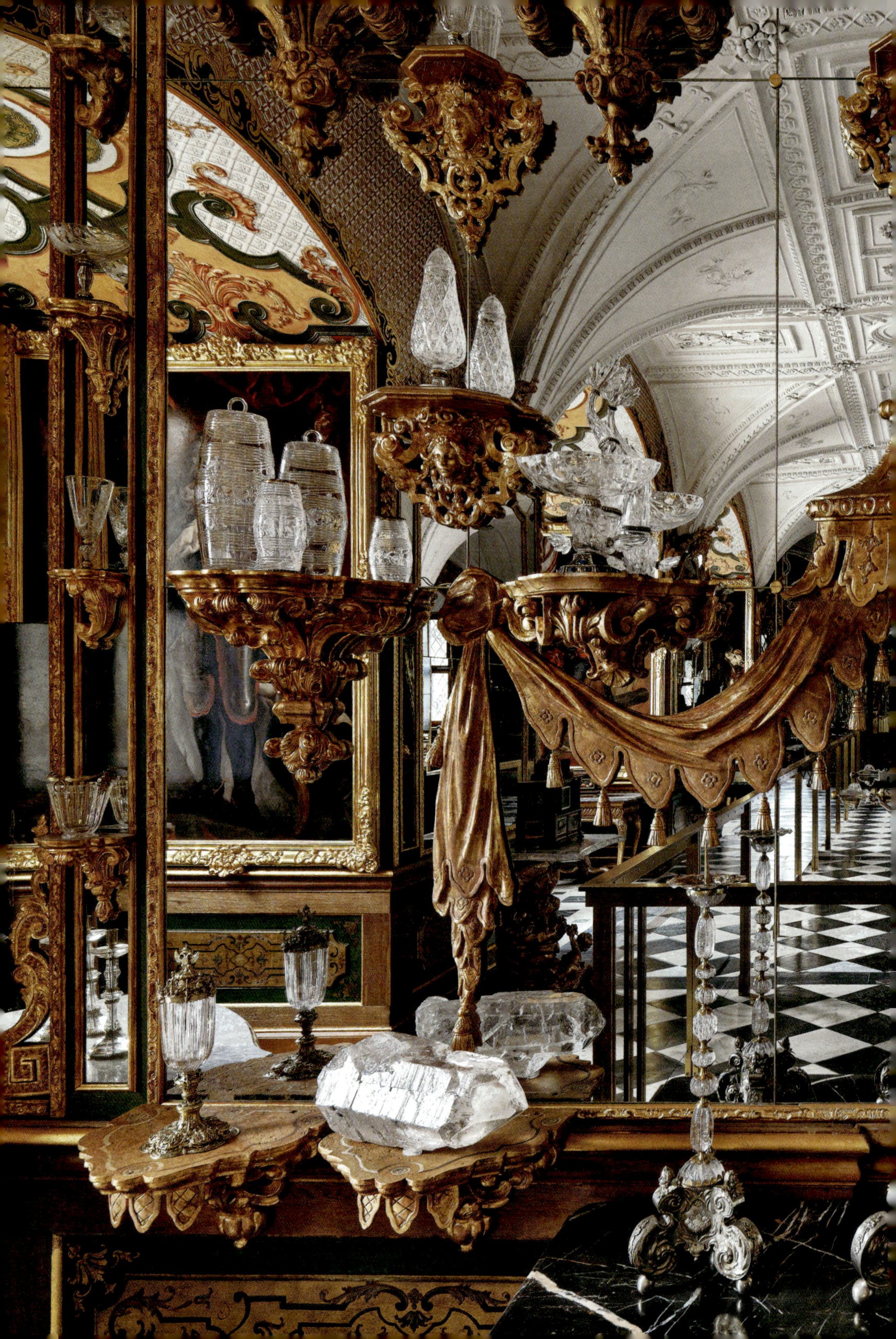

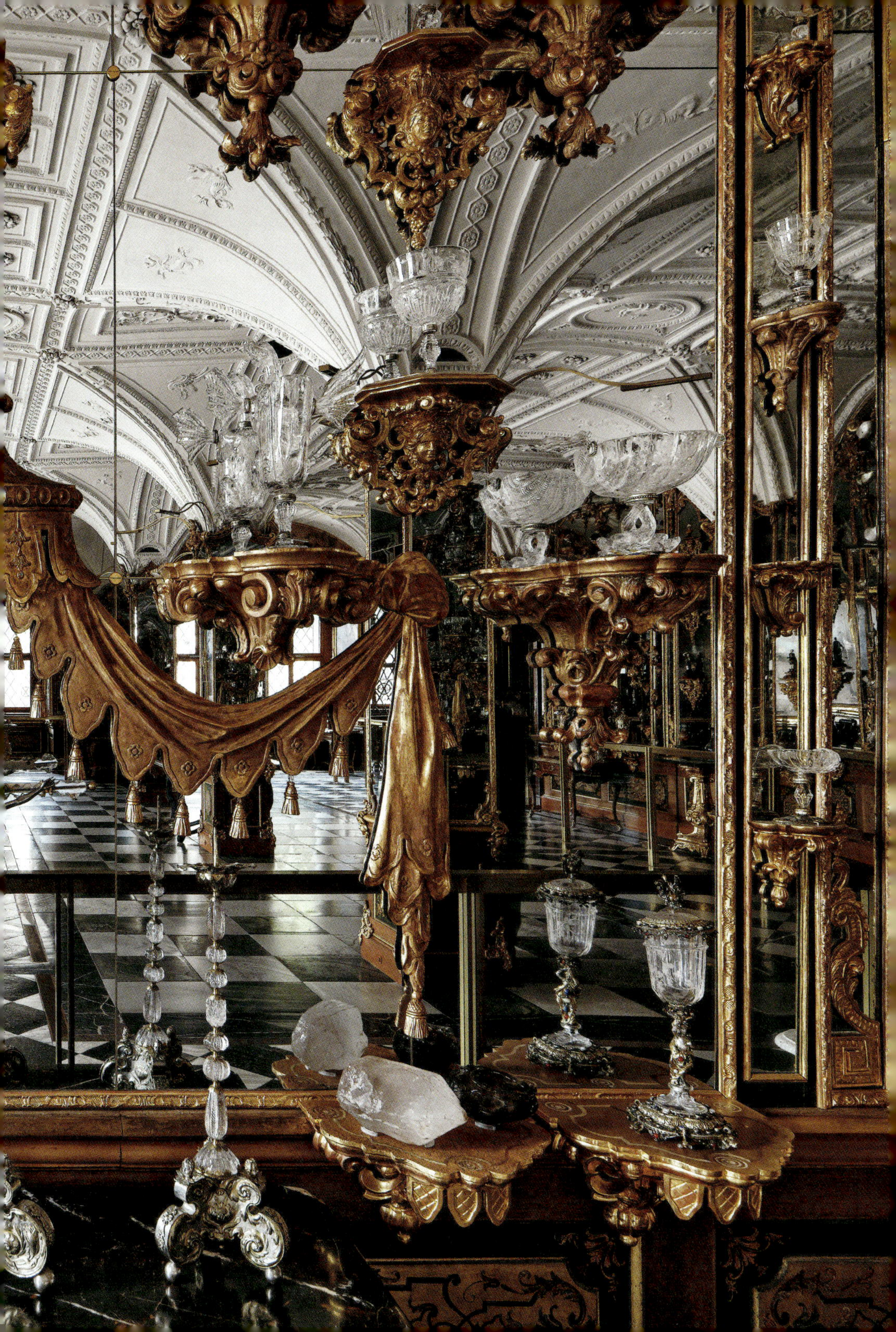

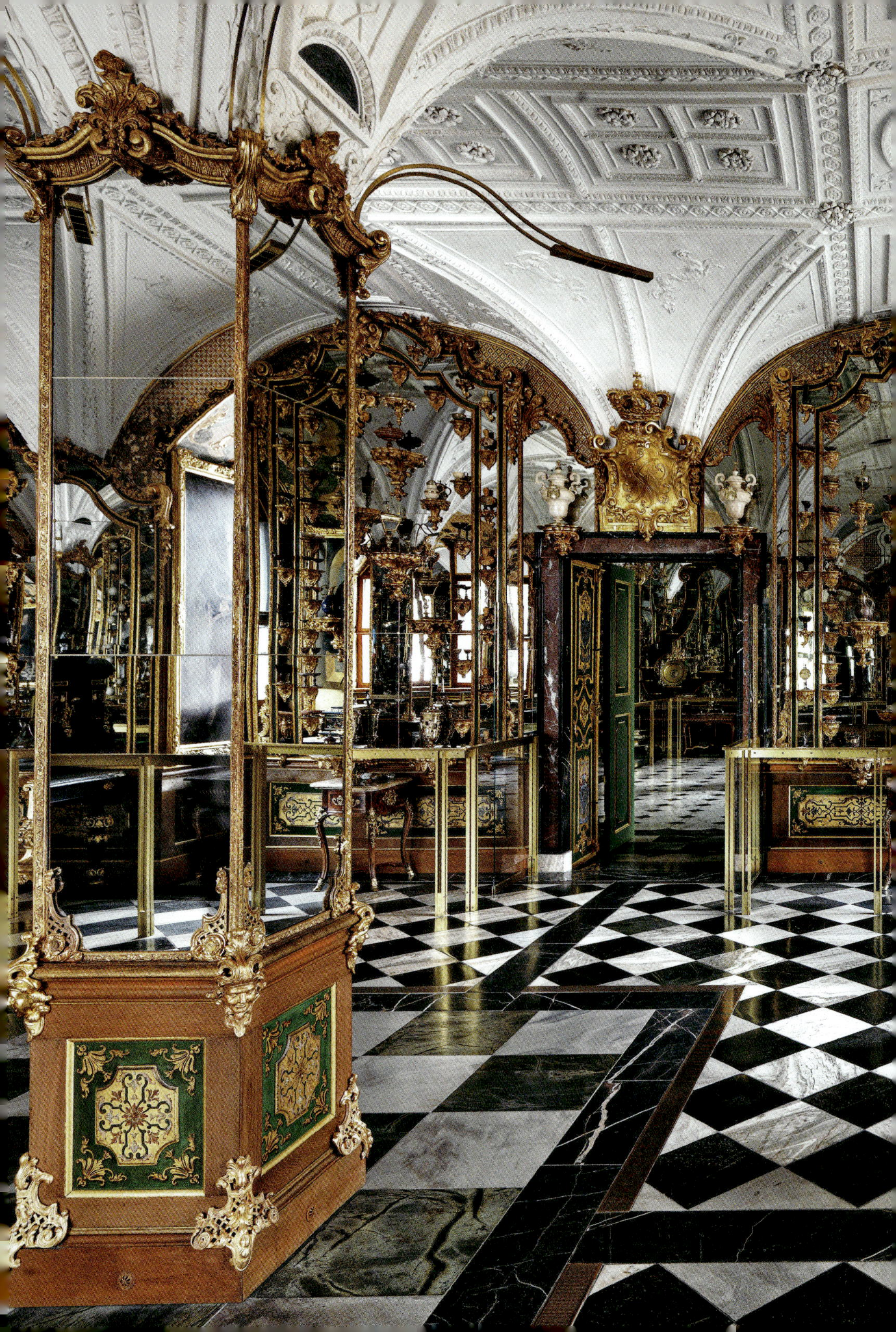

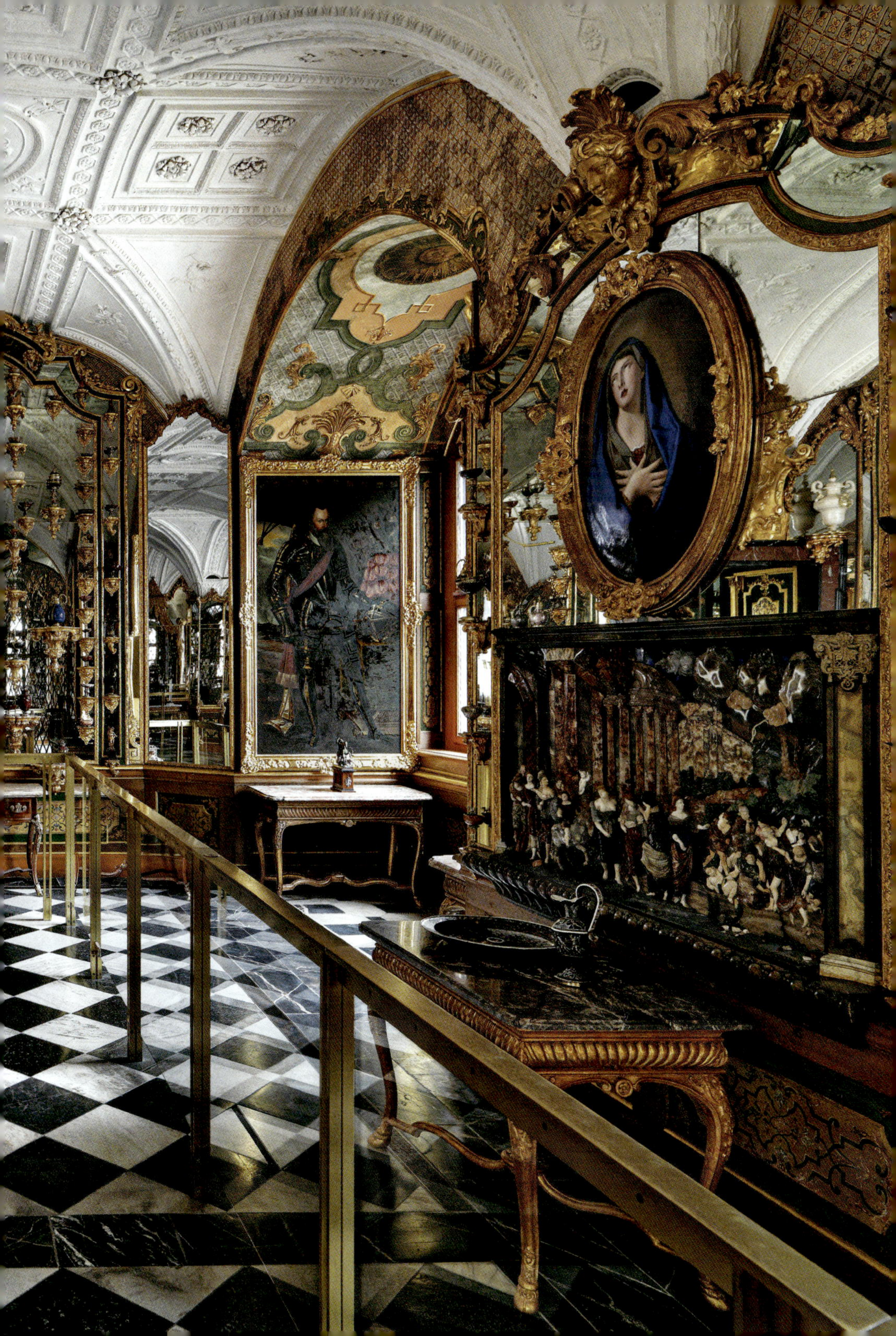

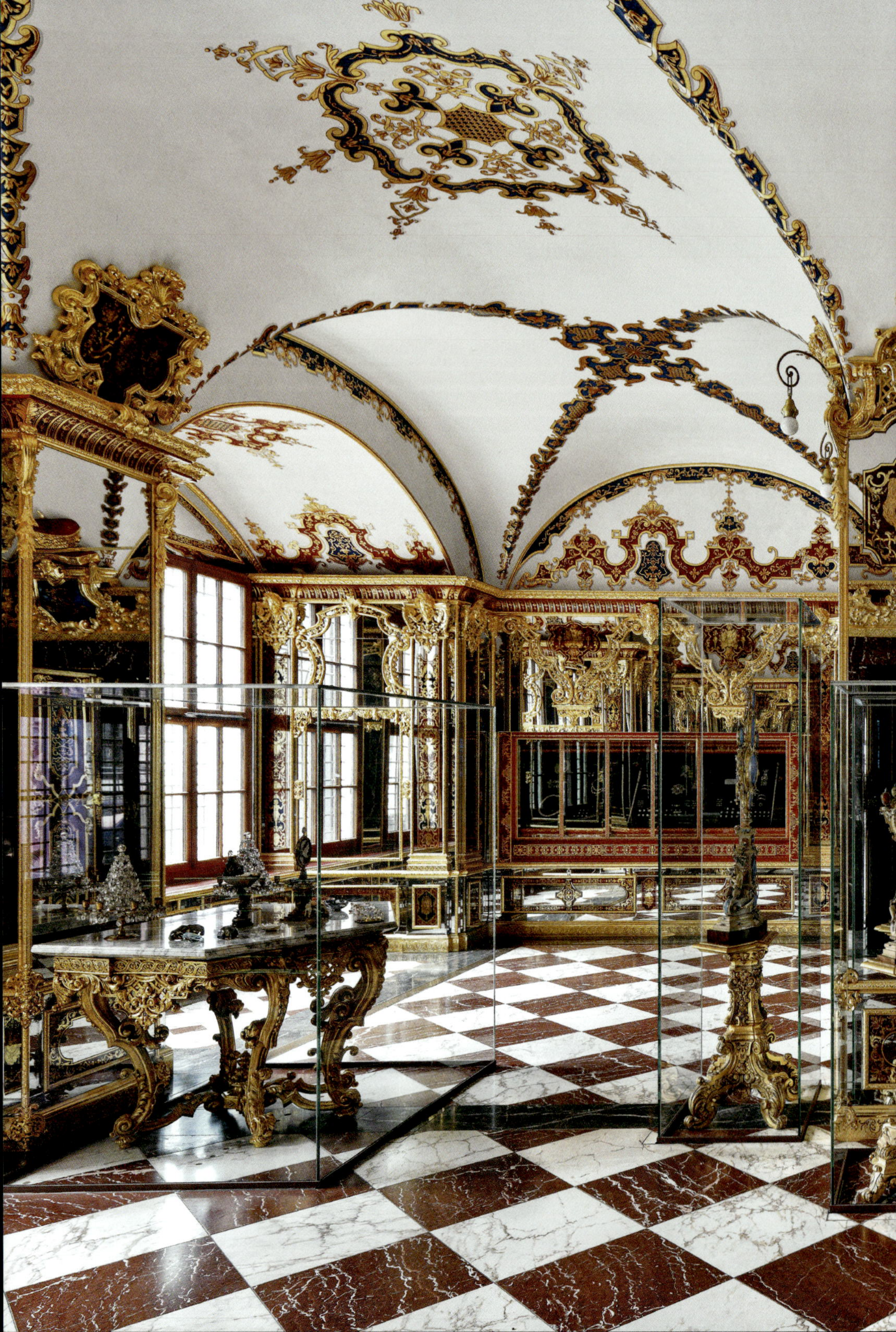

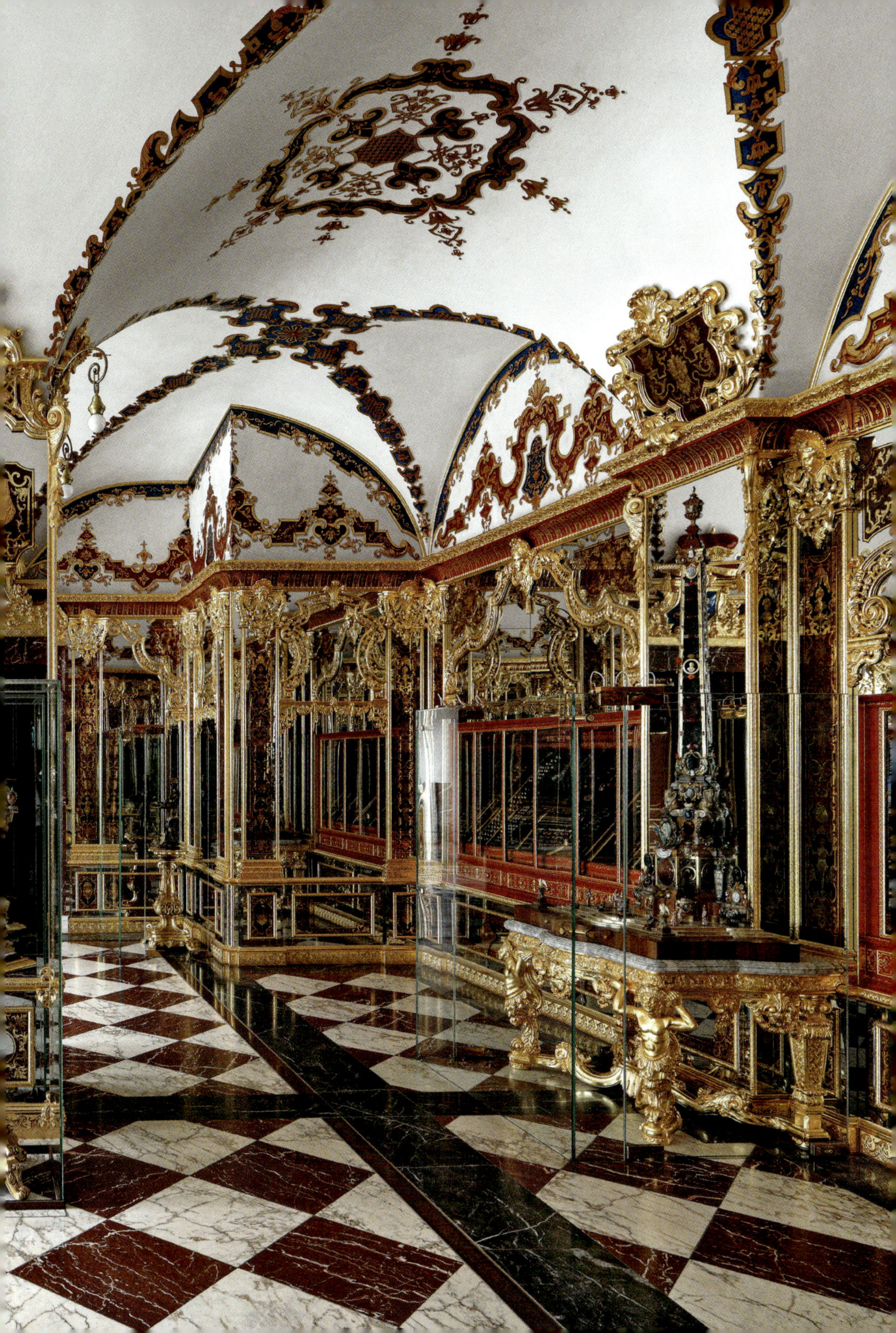

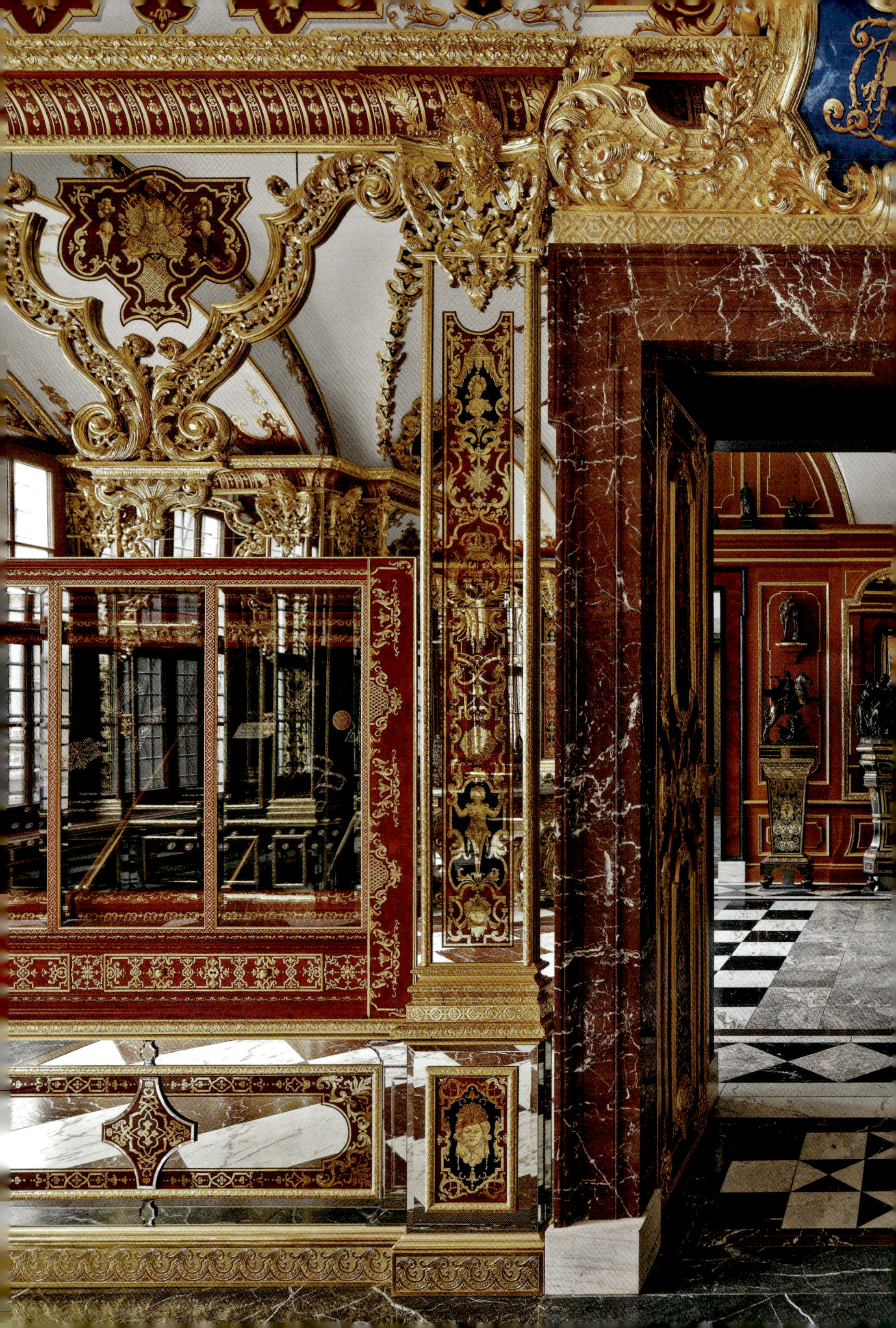

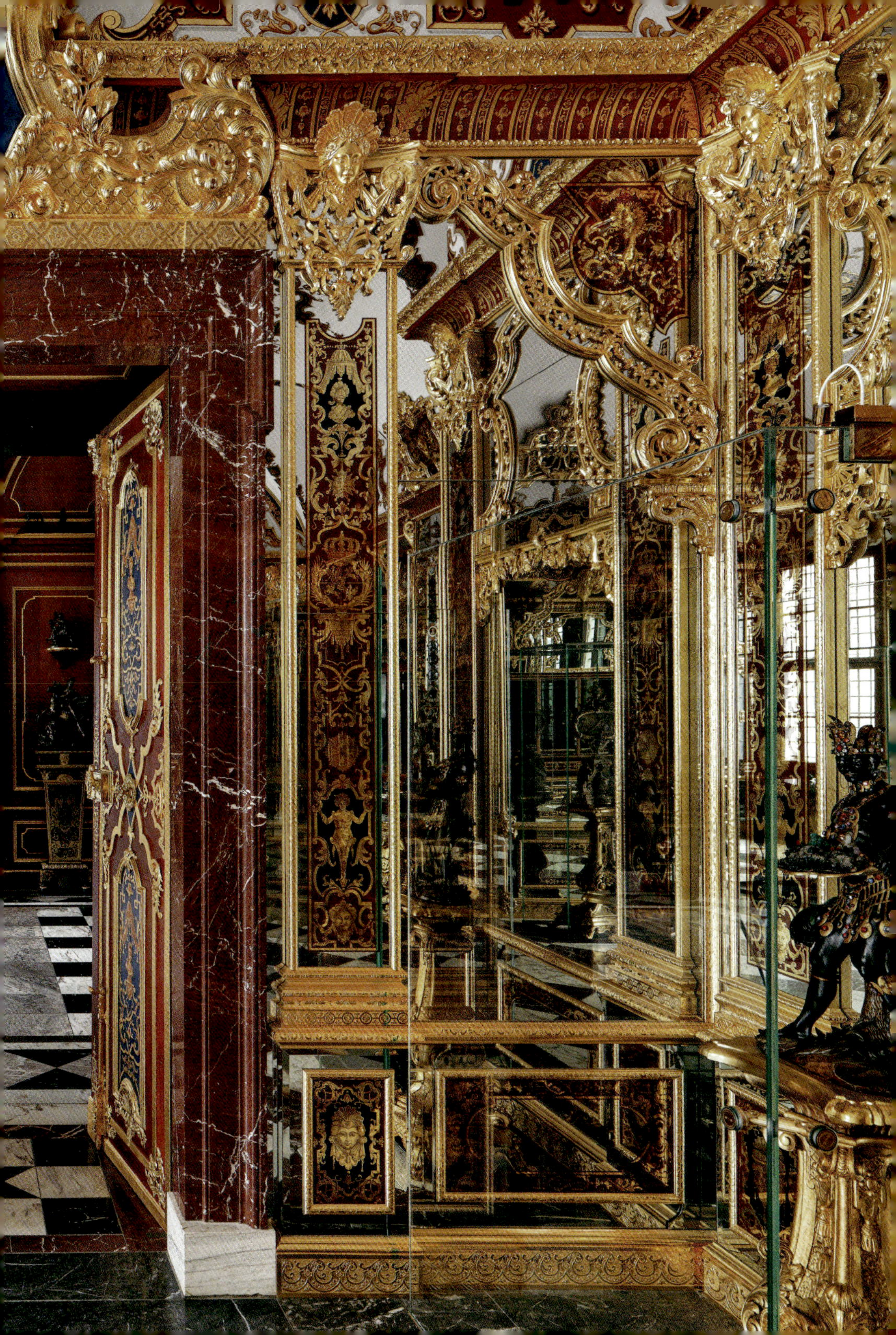

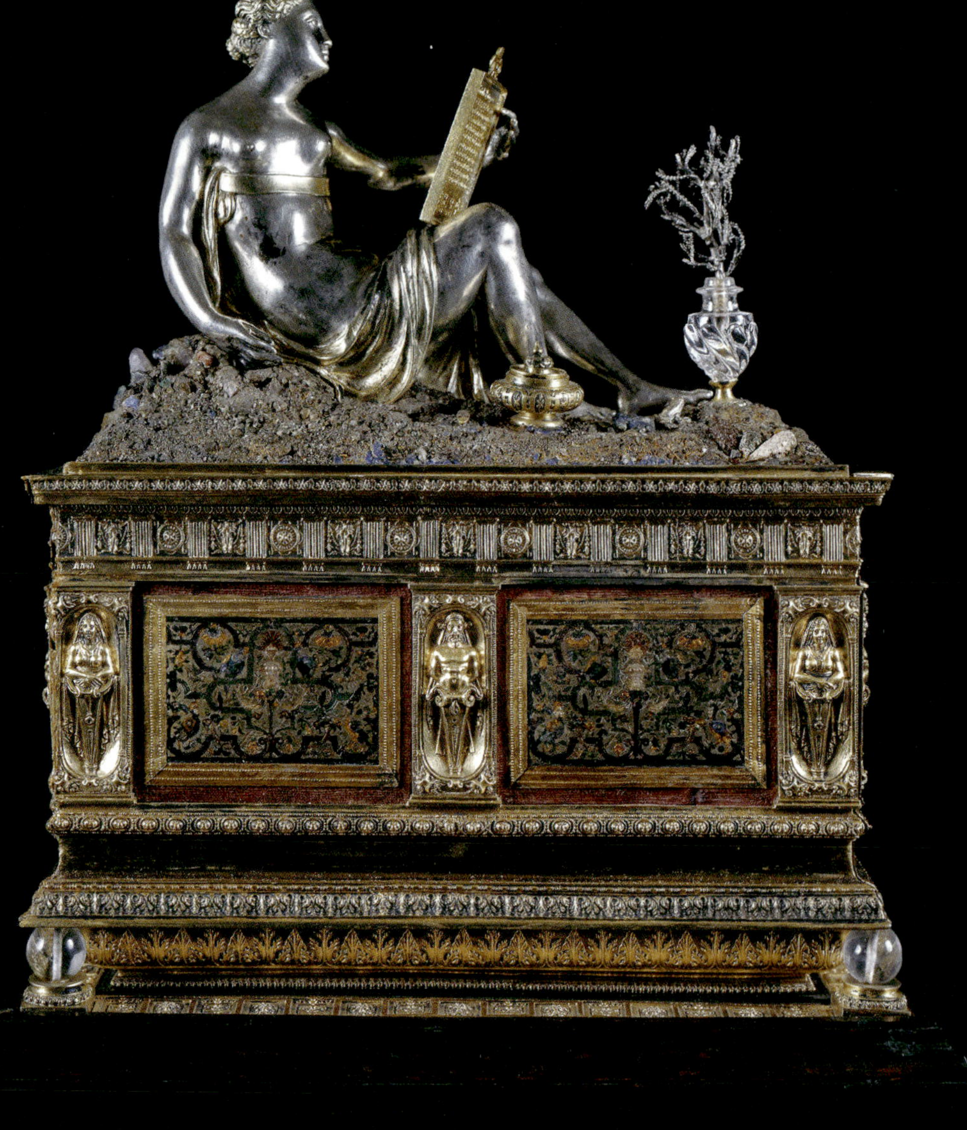

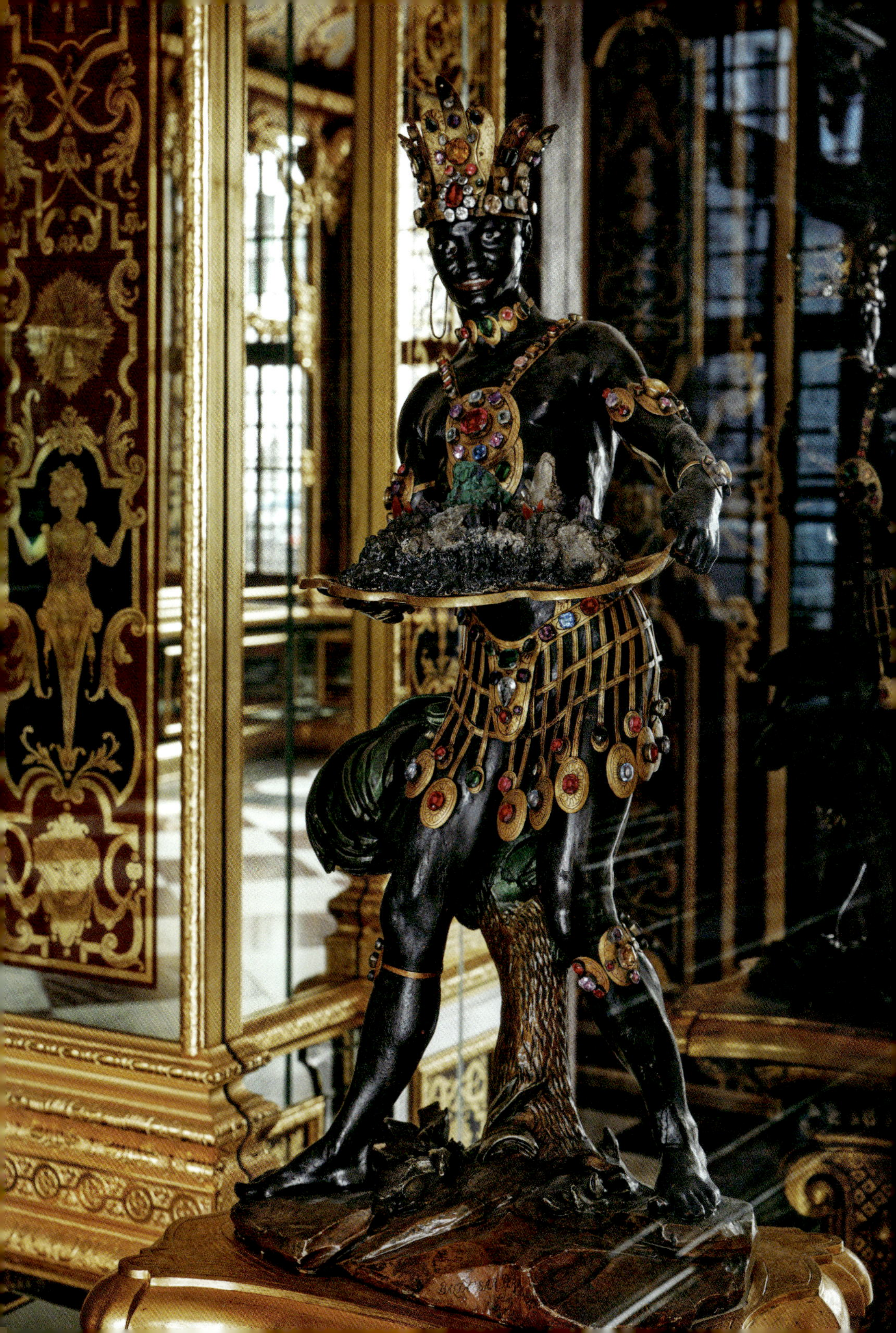

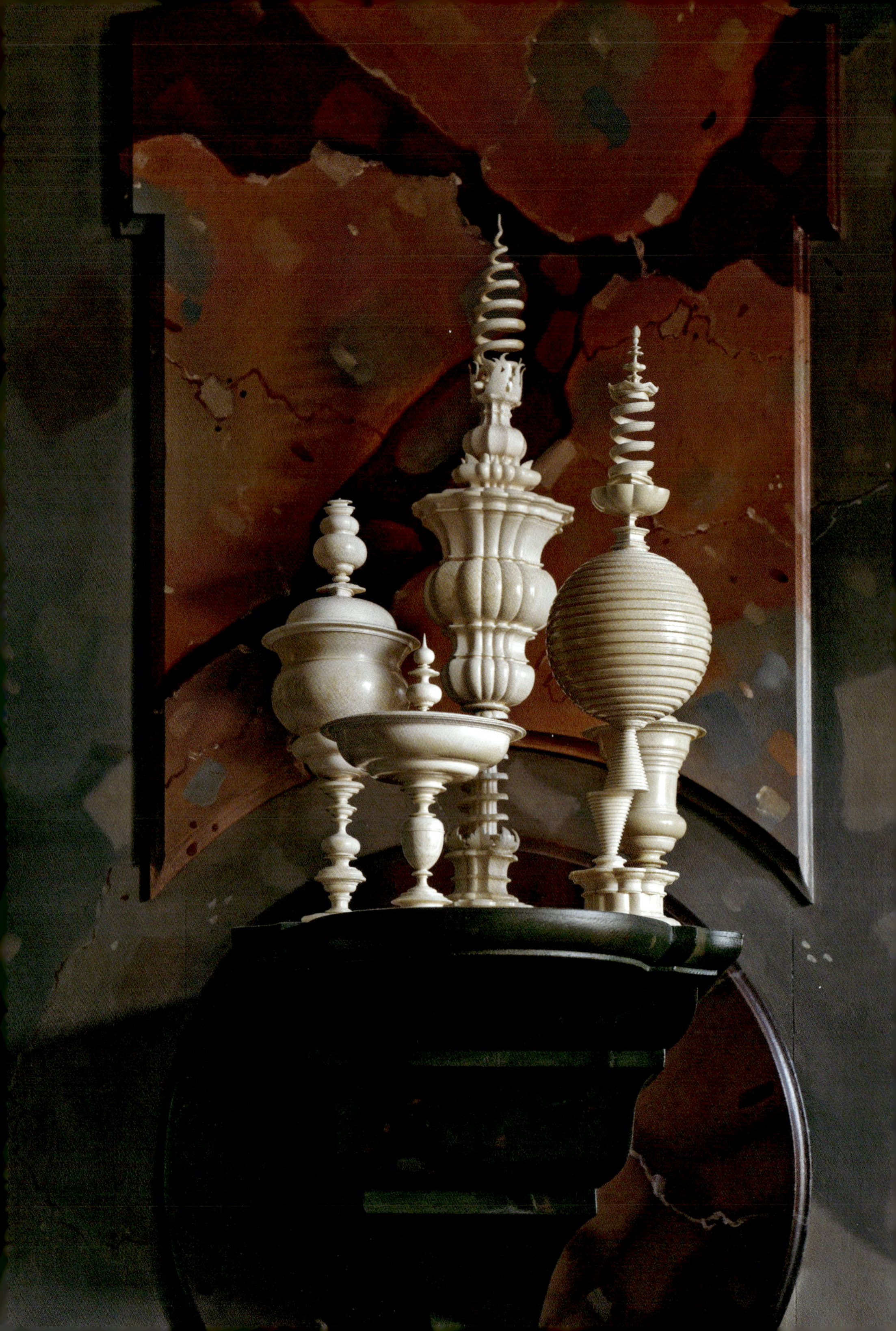

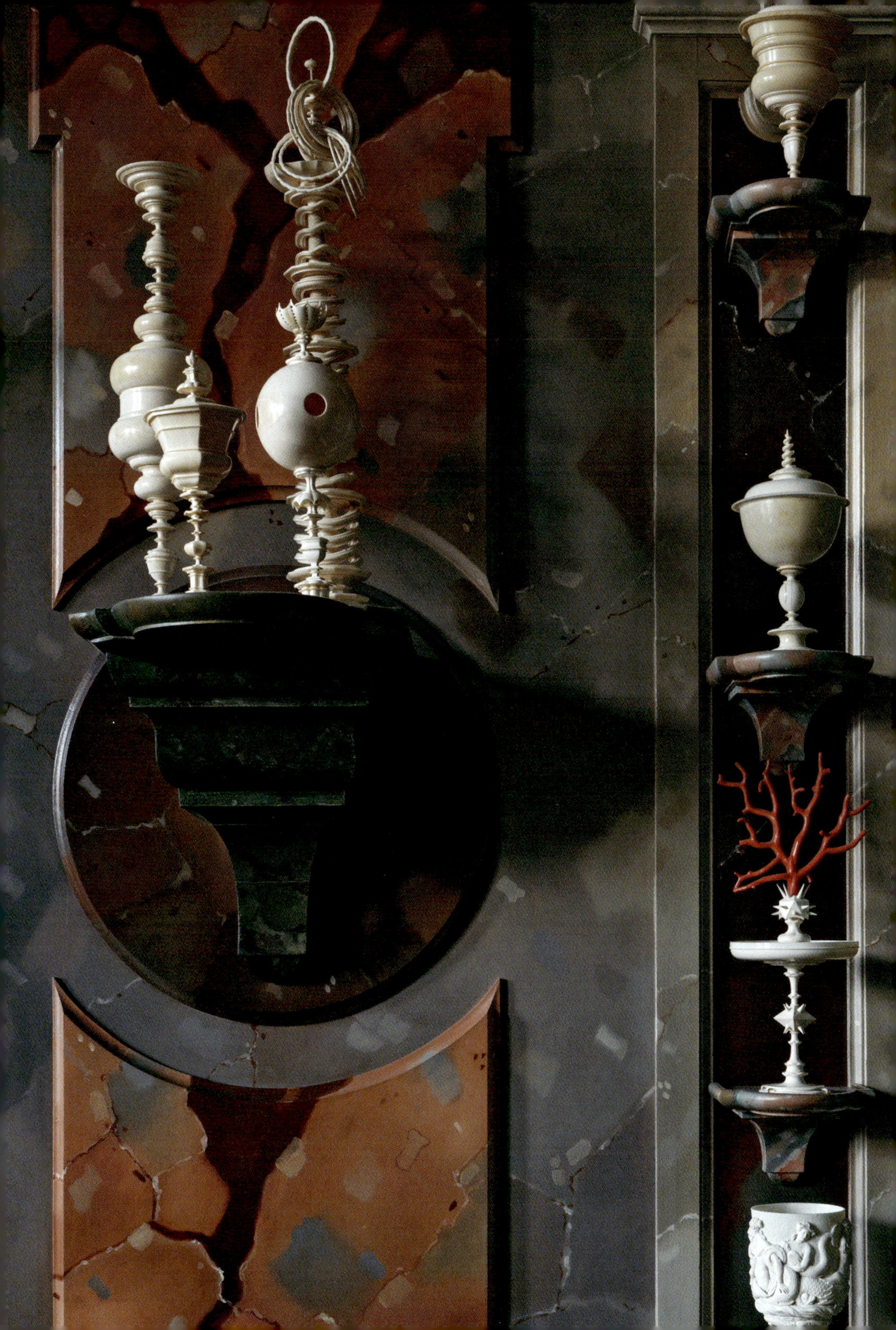

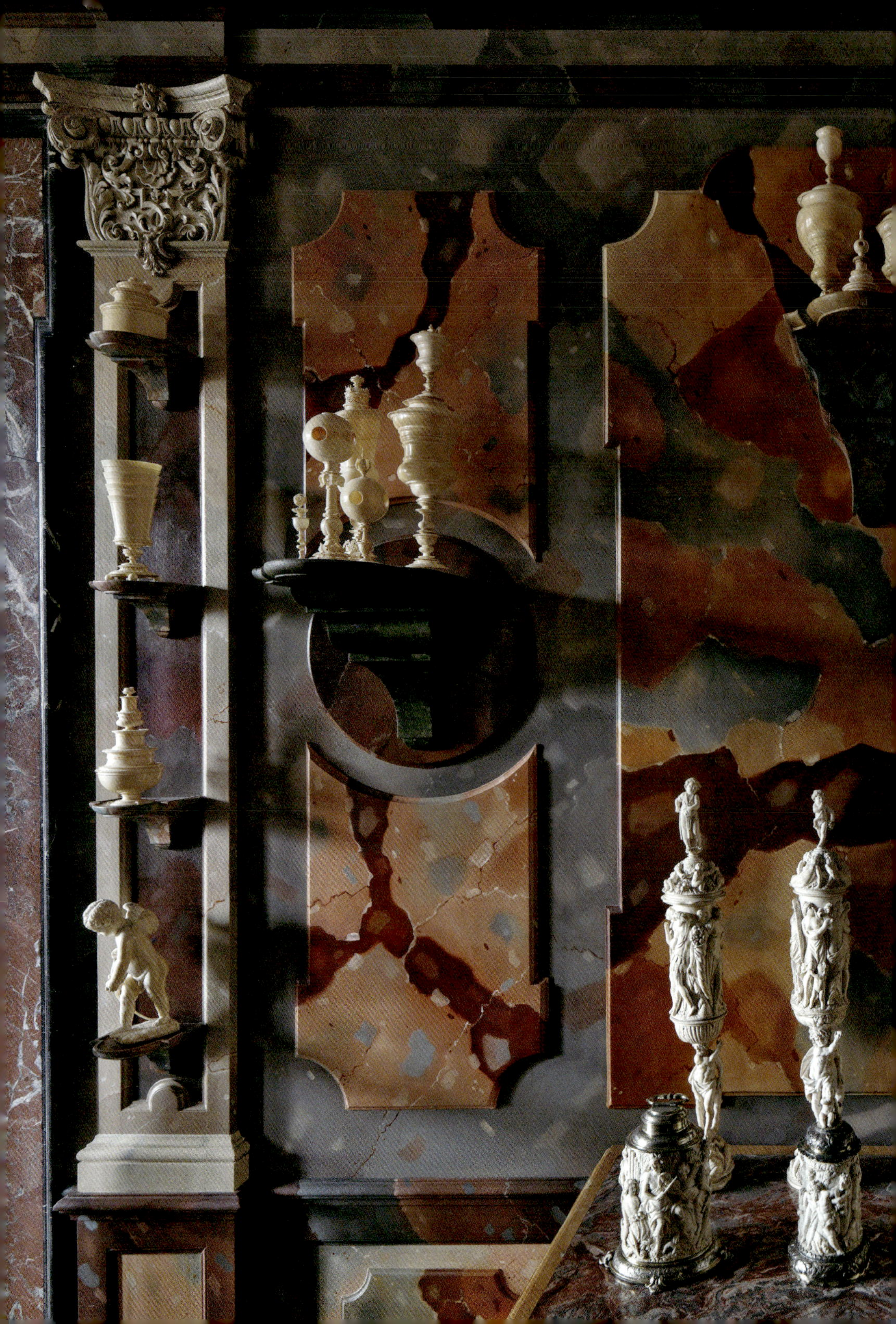

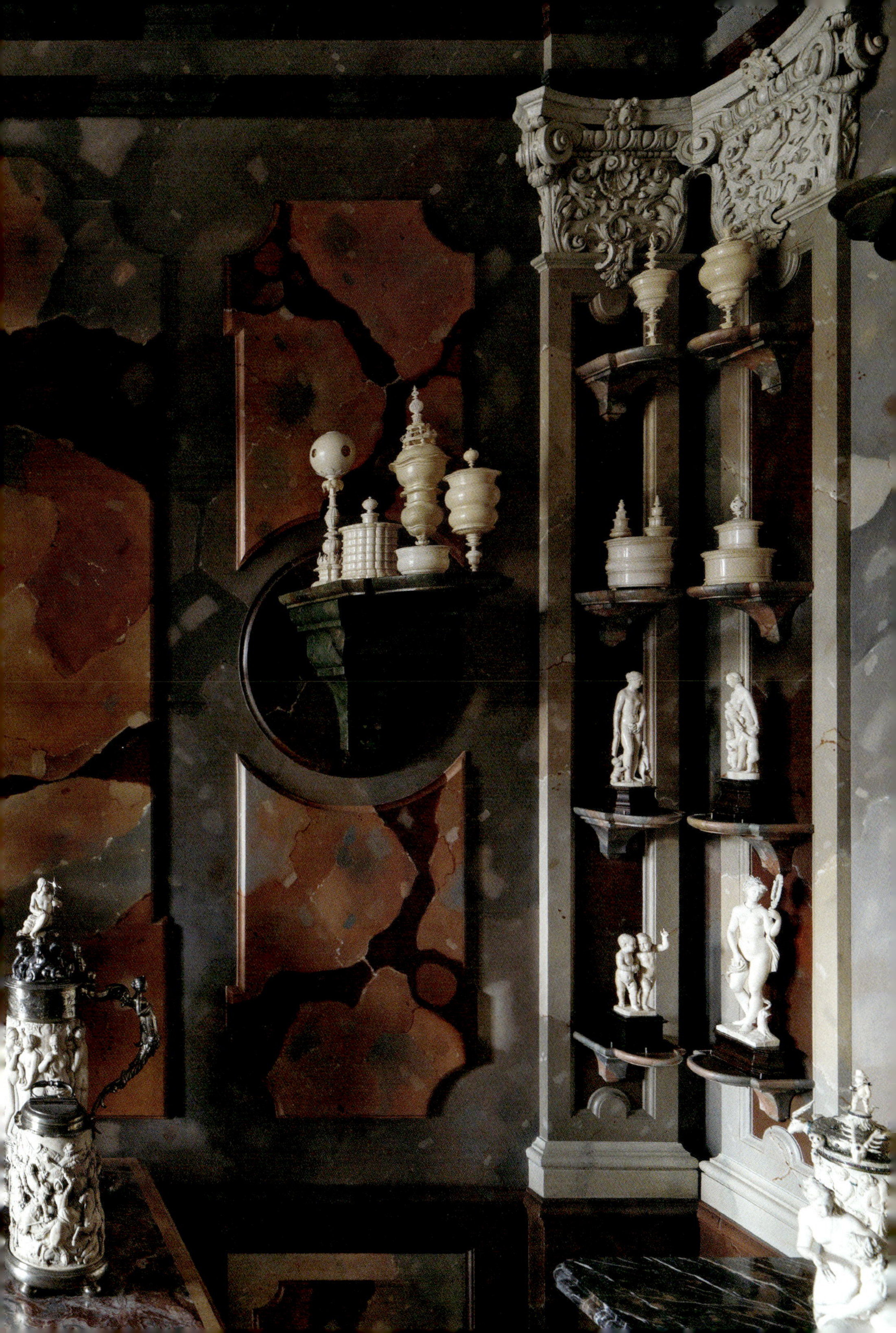

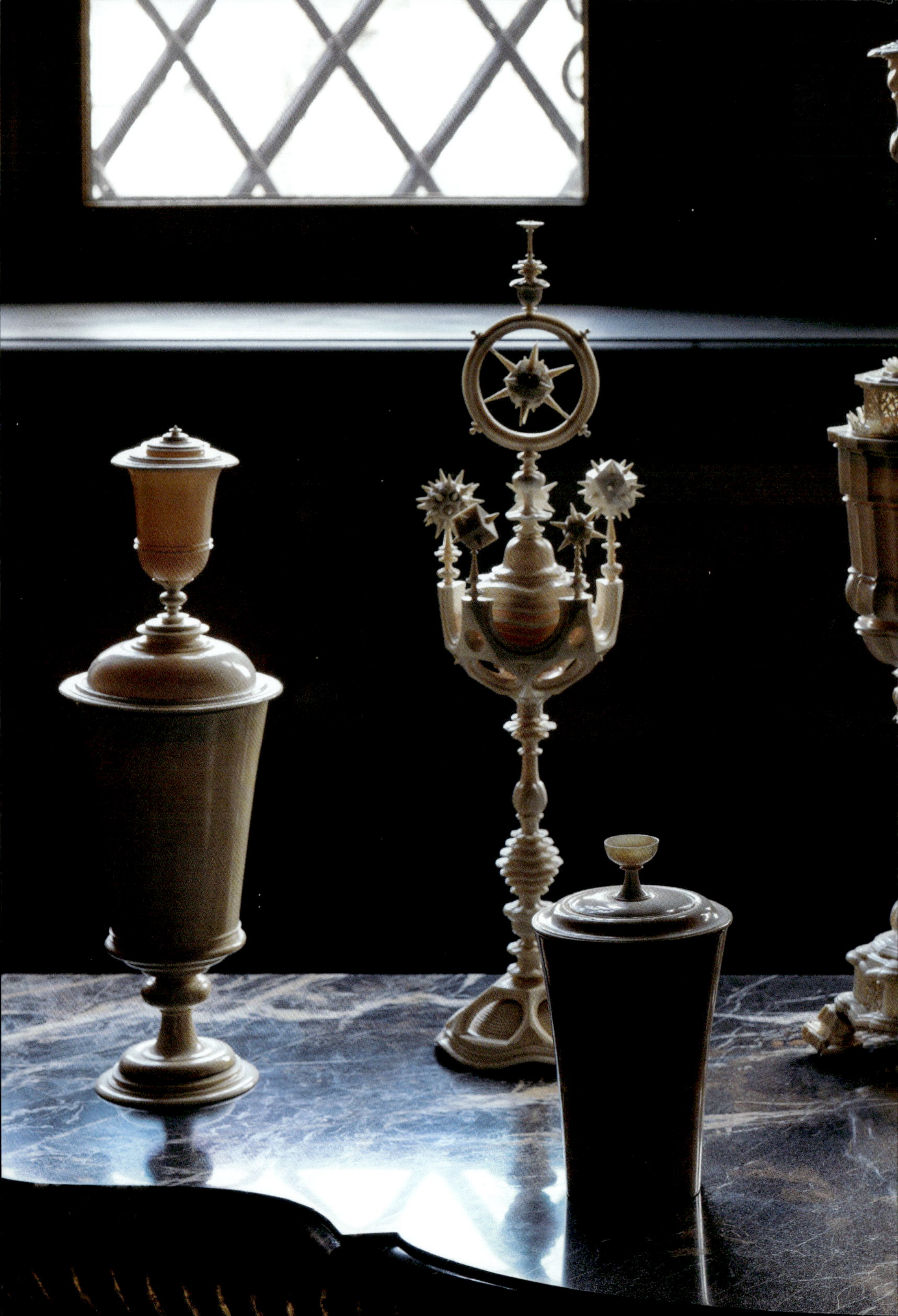

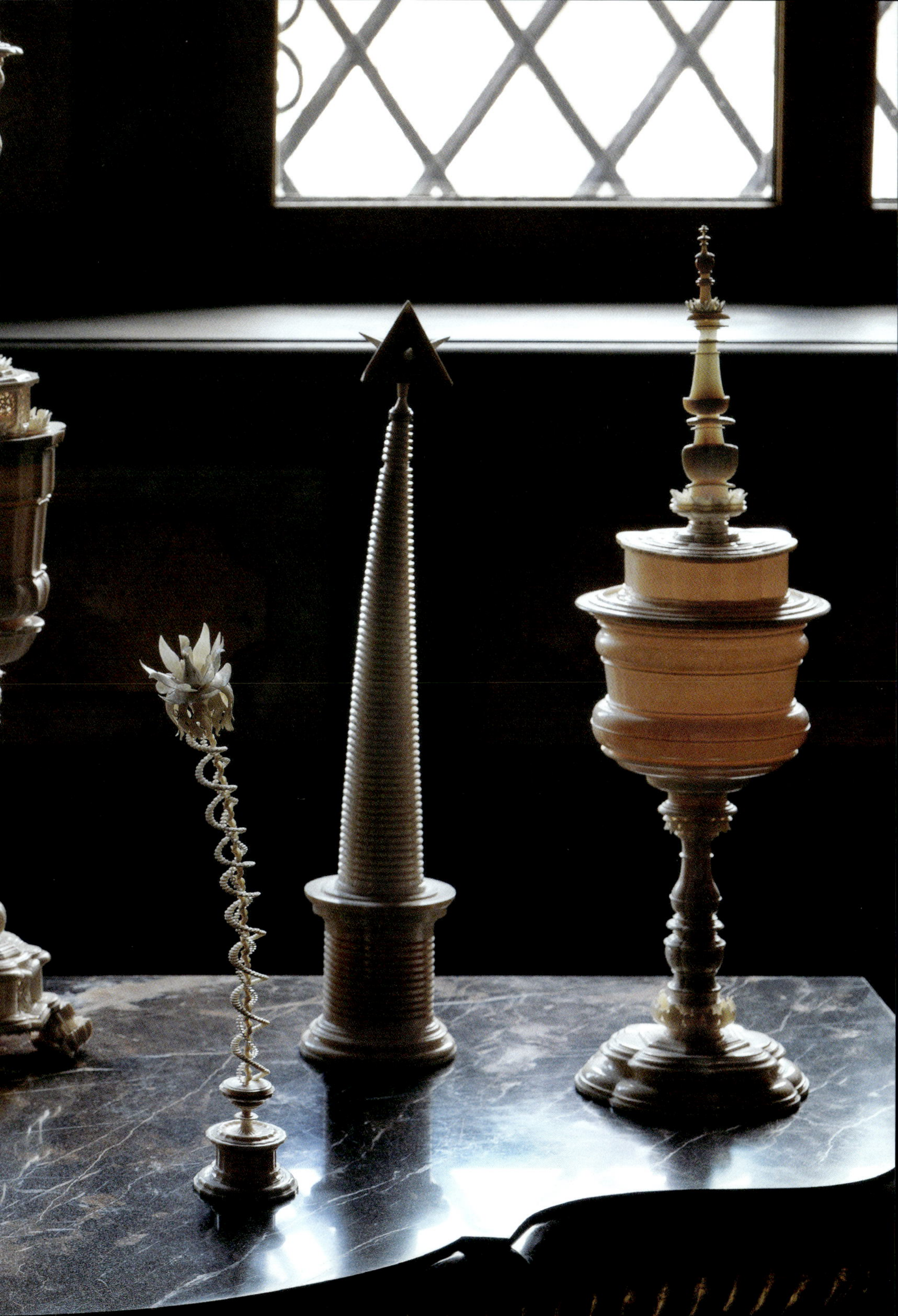

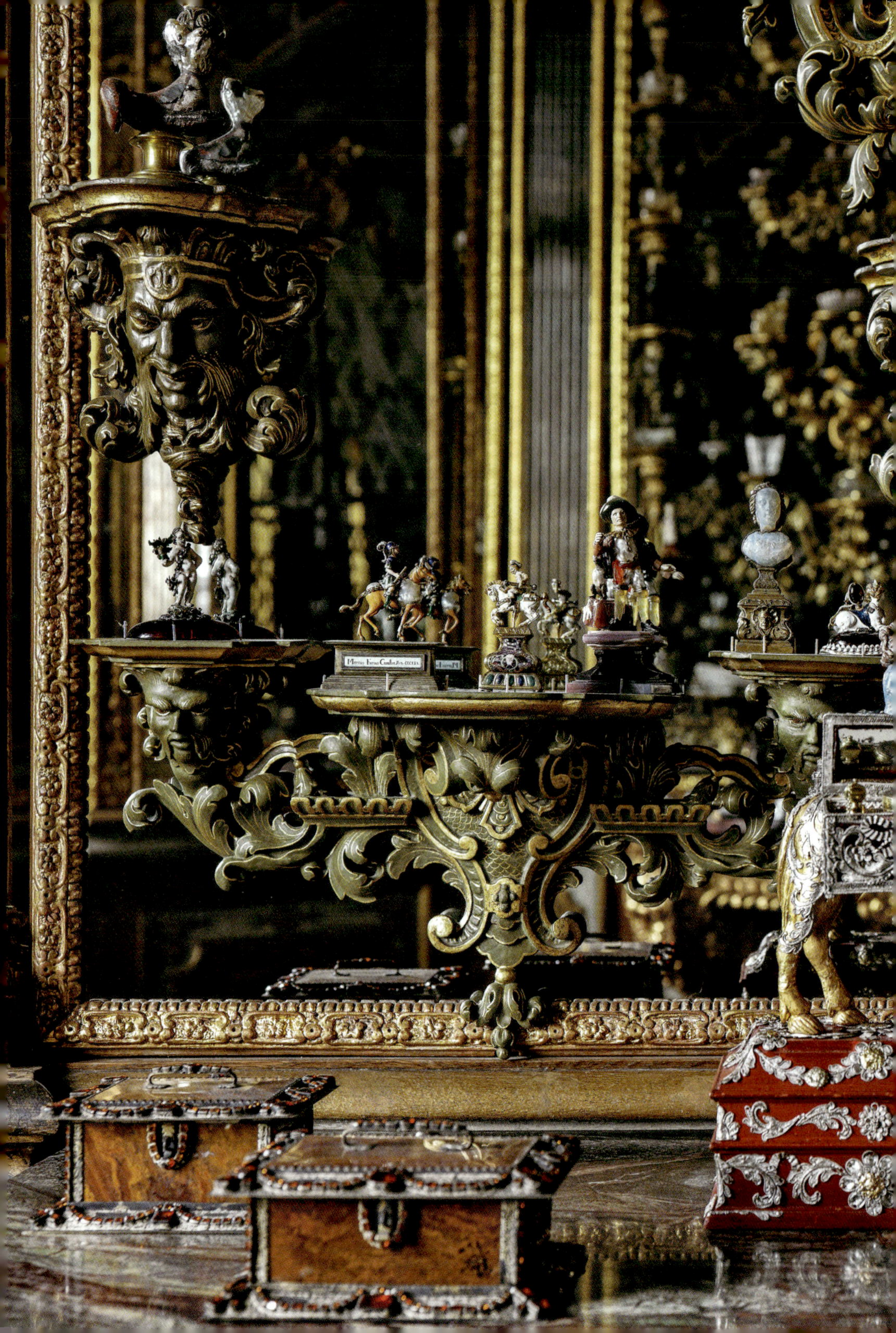

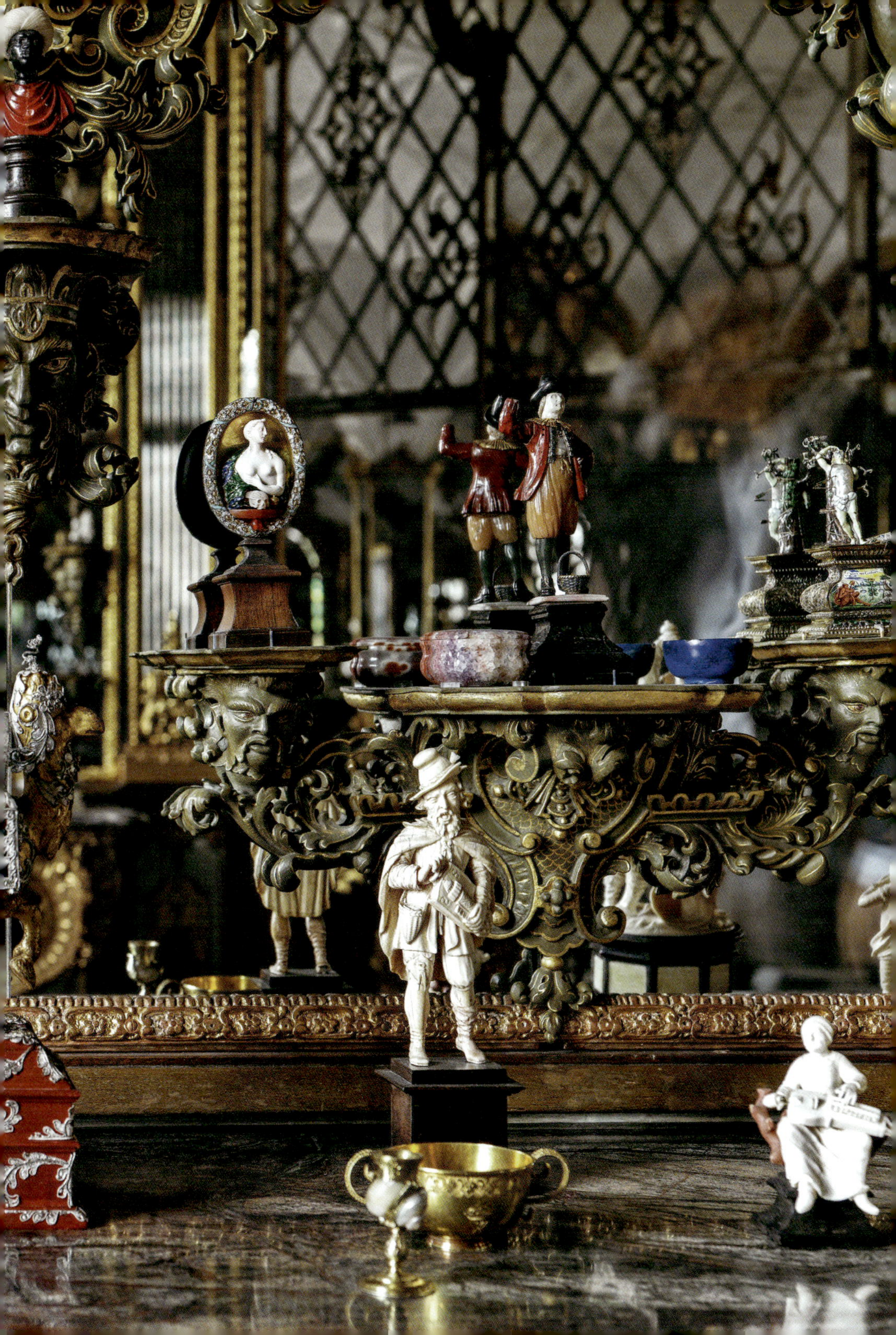

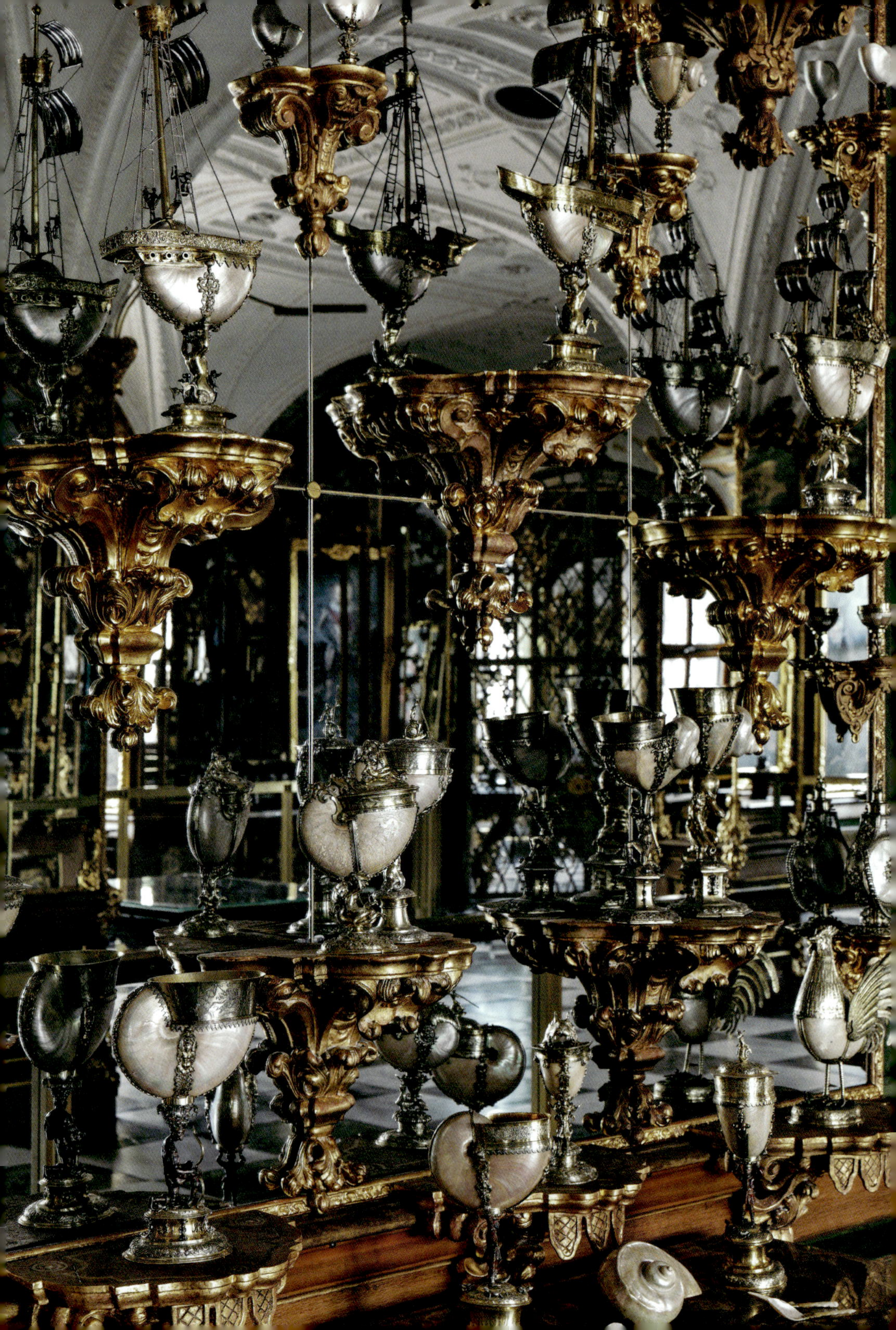

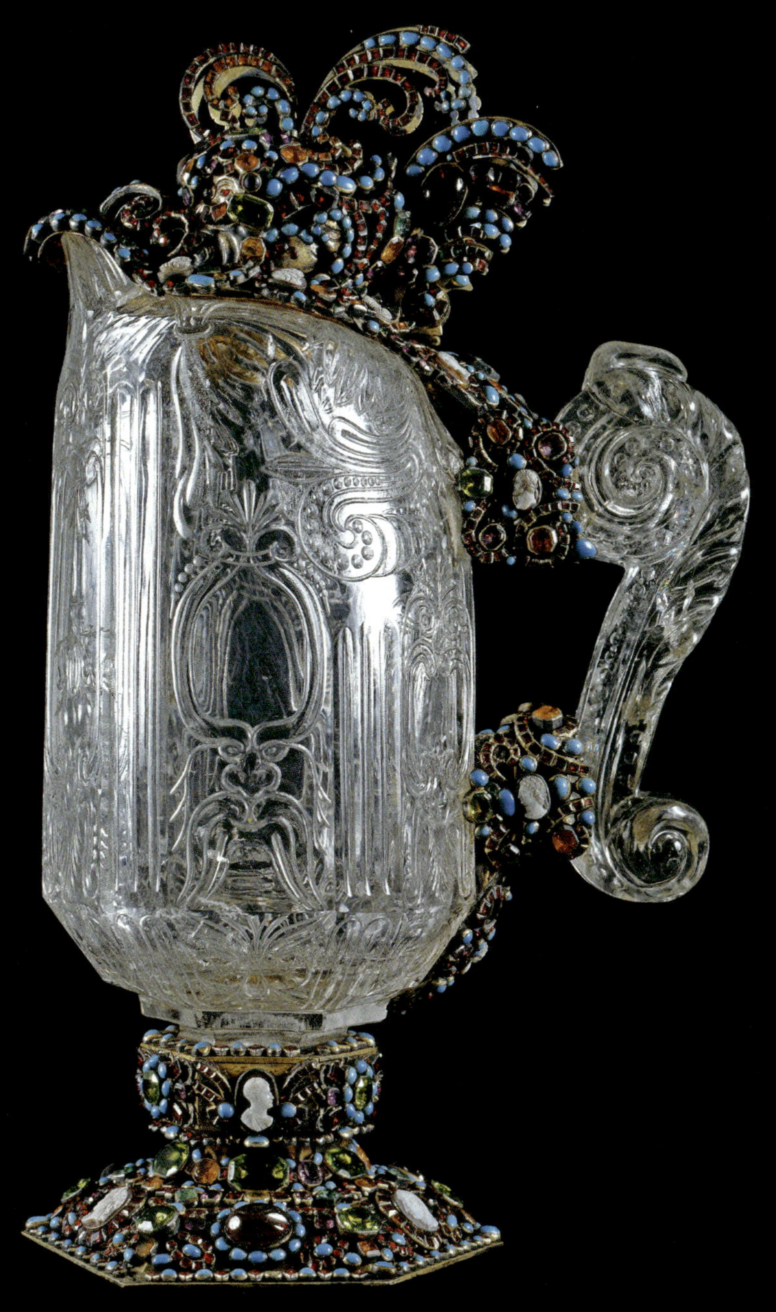

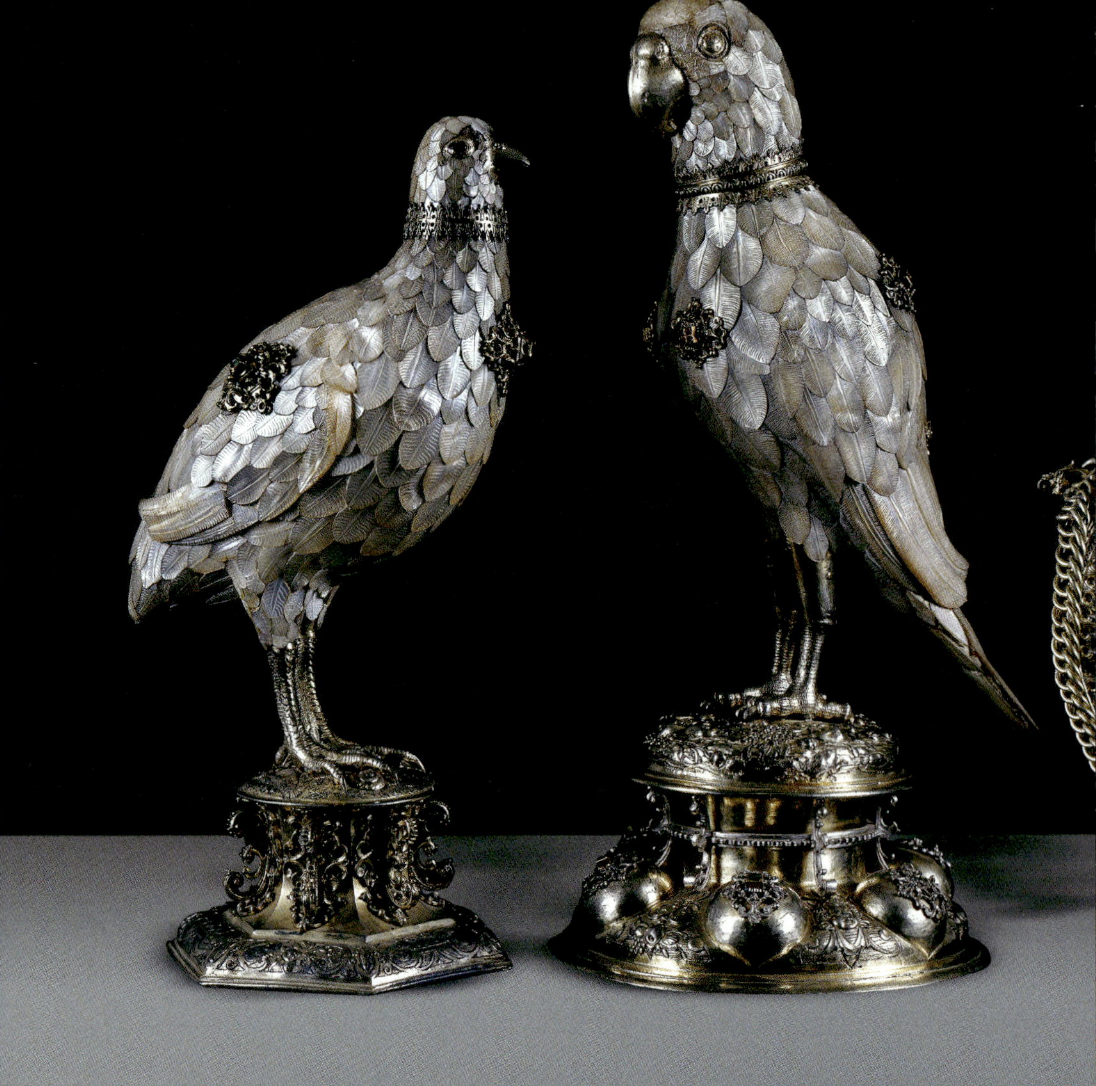

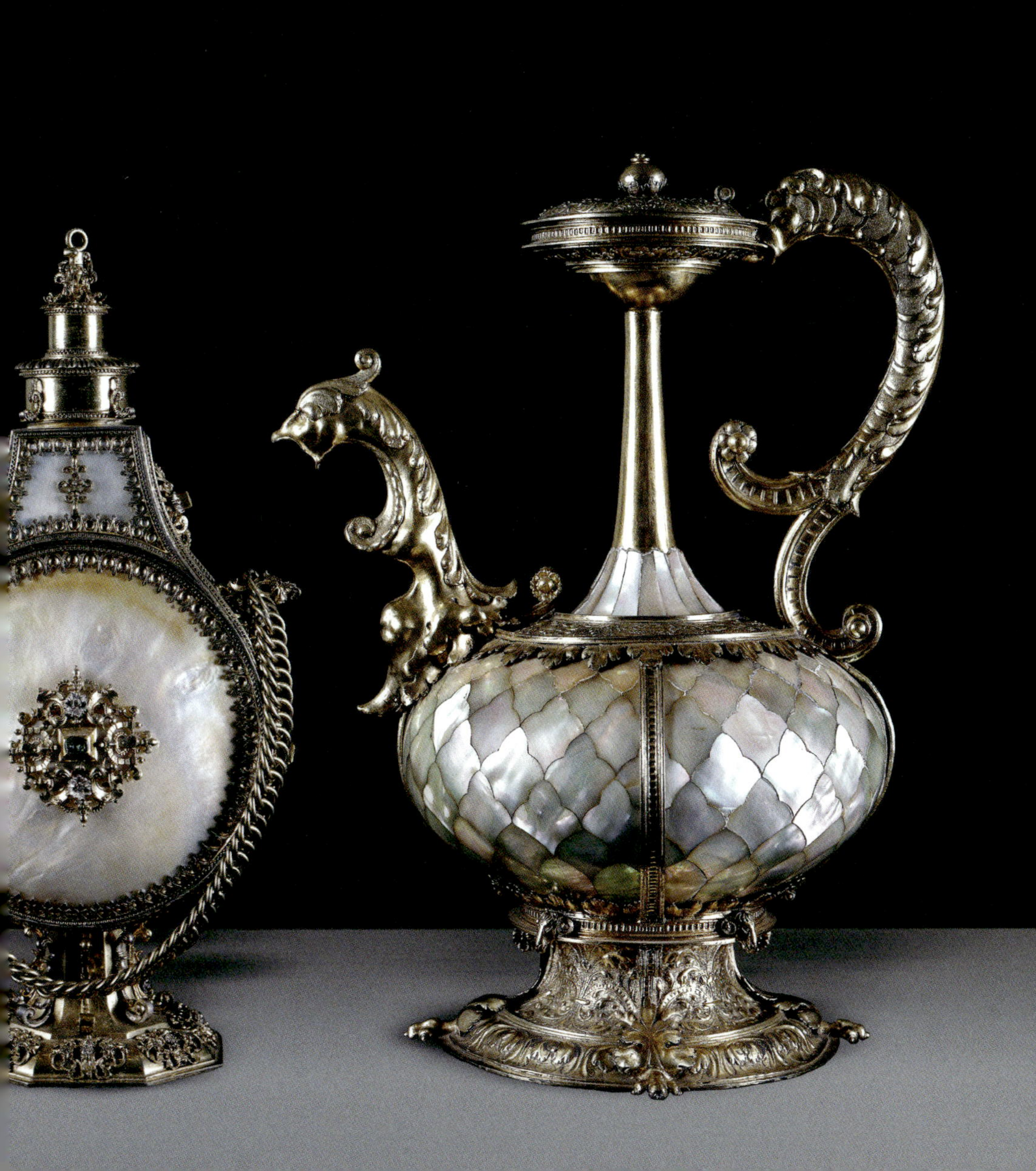

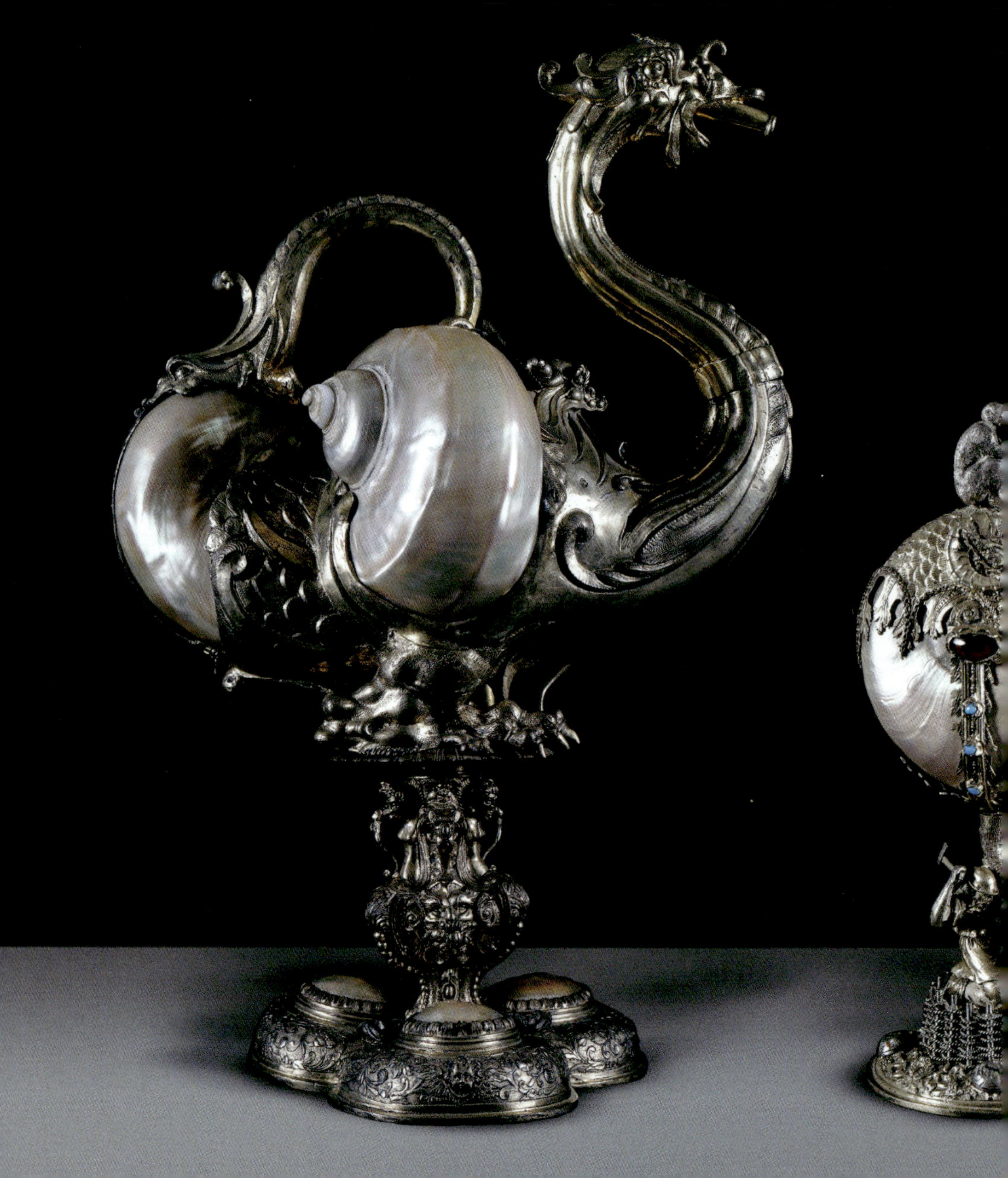

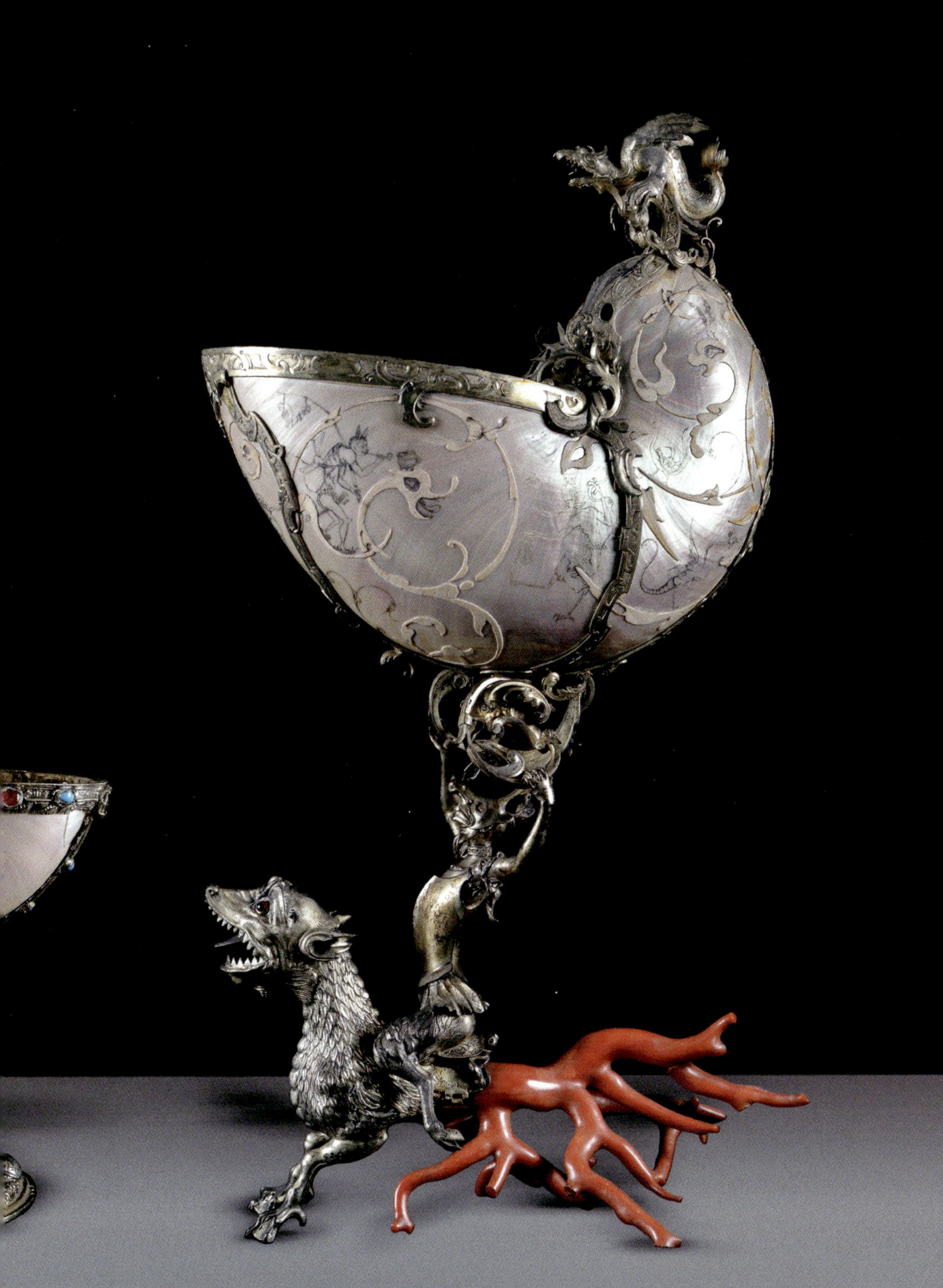

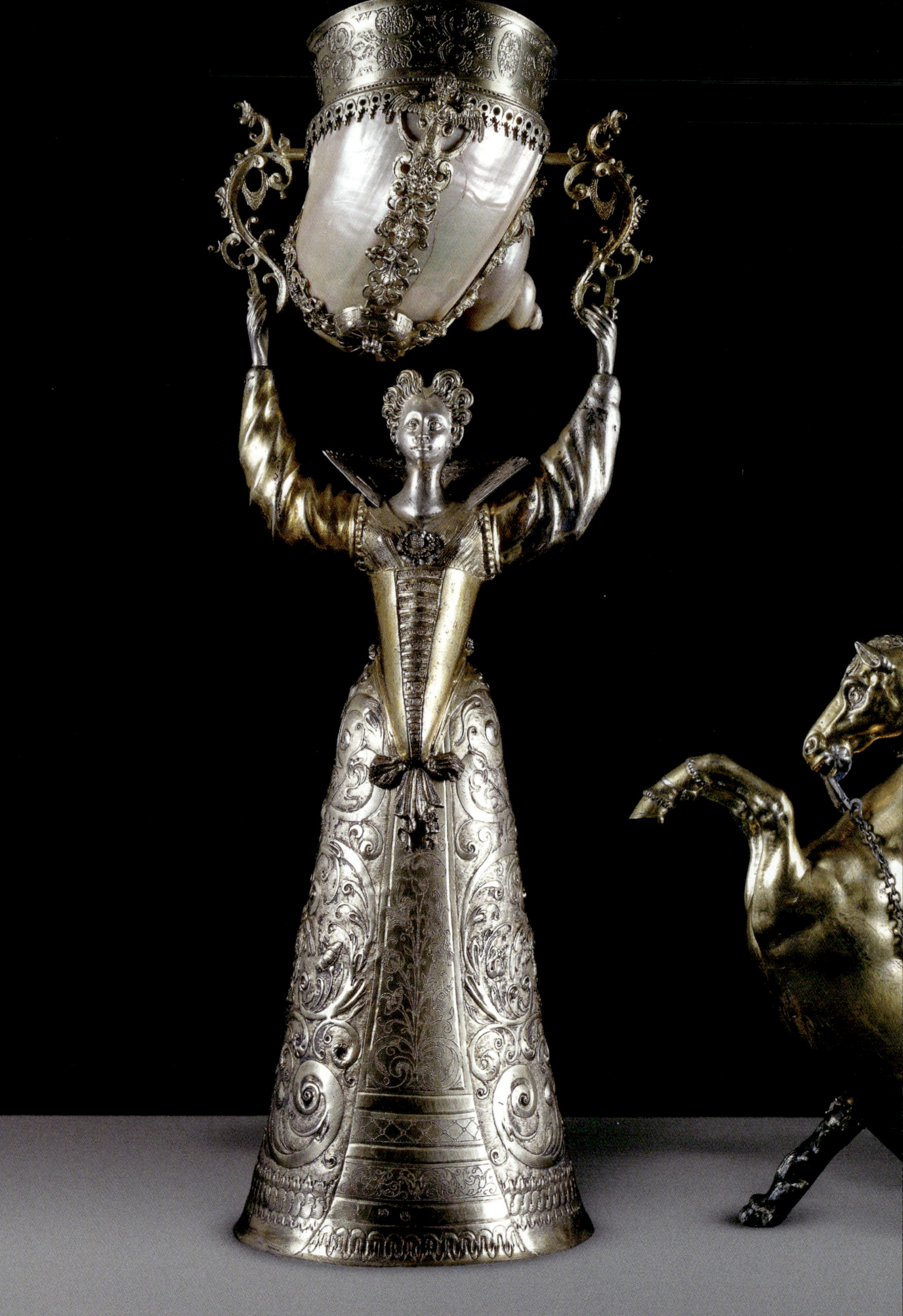

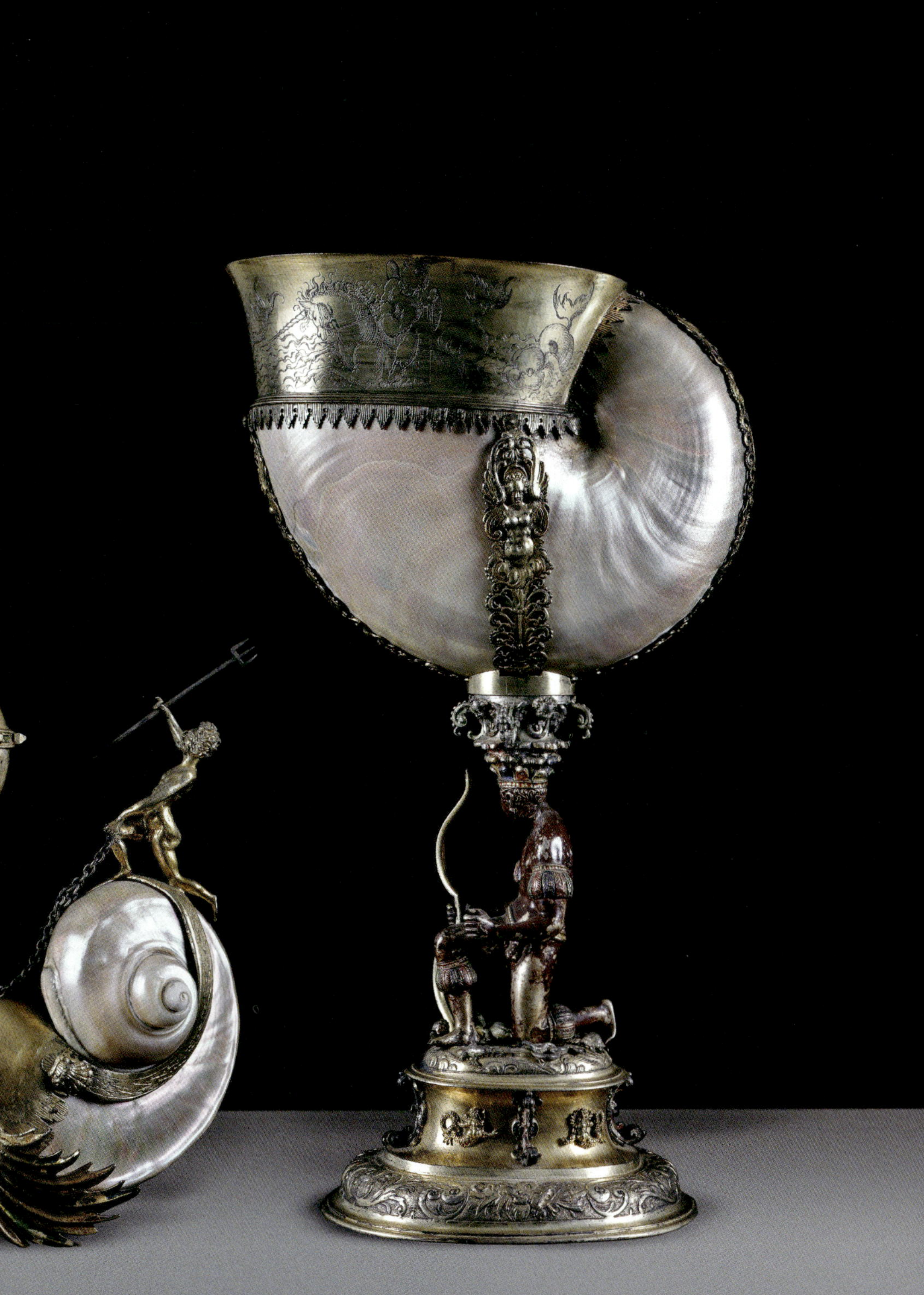

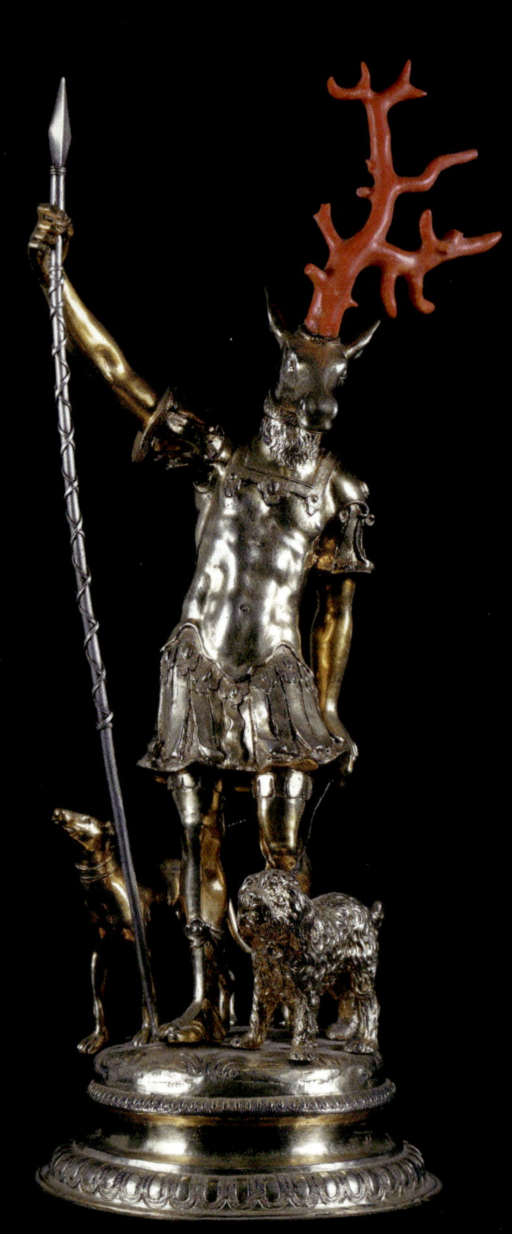

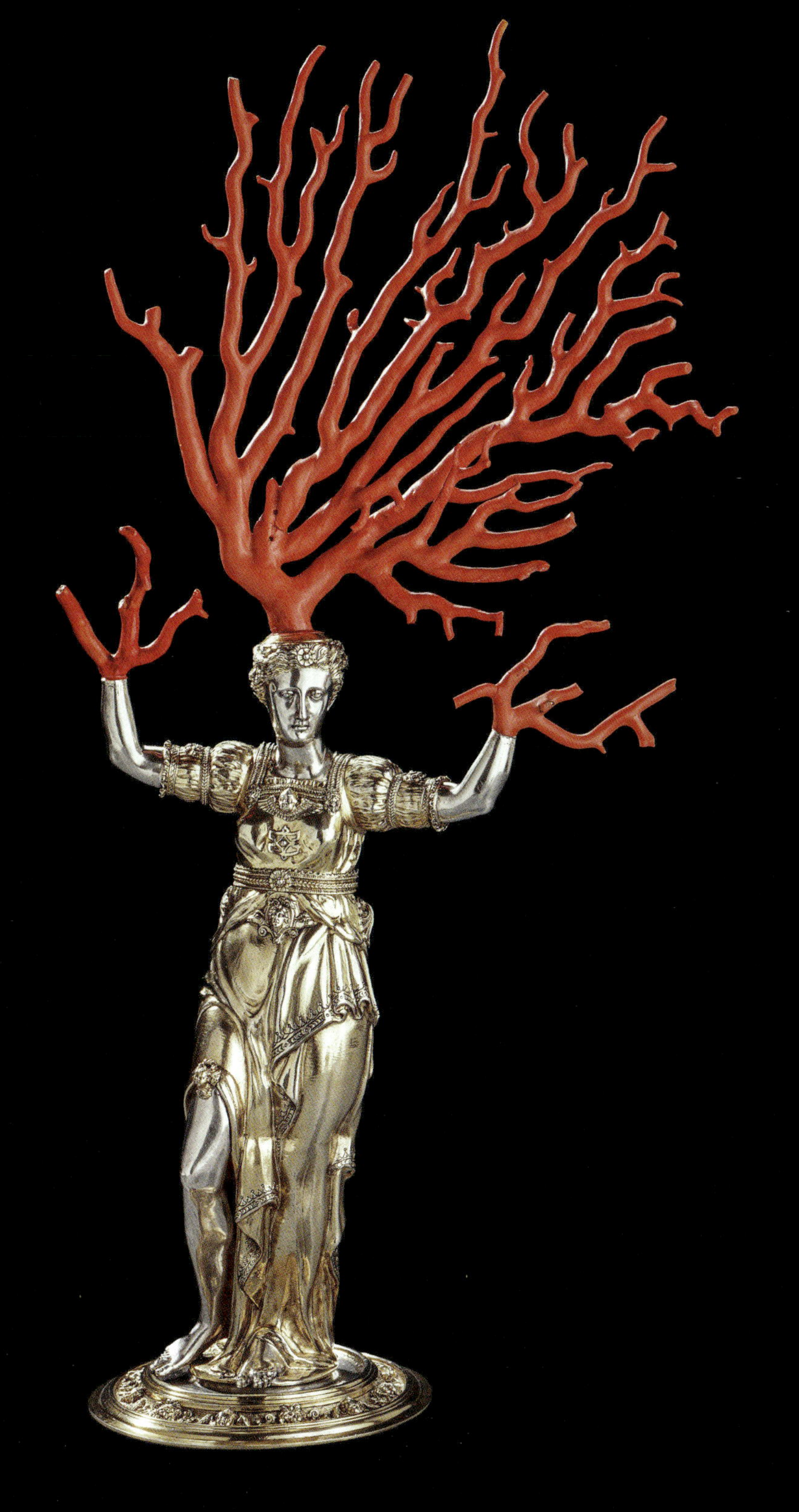

The Staatliche Kunstsammlungen (State Art Collections) in Dresden are some of the oldest and most important museum institutions in the world. In 1560, Augustus I, Elector of Saxony (1526–1586), established a cabinet of curiosities in the royal palace in Dresden which included various examples of *naturalia* although his main interest was *artificialia*: clocks, scientific instruments, automata, lathe-turned ivories, works of art, jewels and curiosities. In the late Renaissance, a cabinet of curiosities functioned as an encyclopaedic and universal collection, primarily focused on technological innovations and scientific instruments. However, what sets the collections in Dresden apart is the artistic sensibility of Augustus II the Strong (1670–1733), who was not only an avid collector of porcelain and jewellery but also wanted to create the perfect setting for his collection, and thus commissioned a series of lavishly appointed galleries that included the Grünes Gewölbe (Green Vault). Entering the Green Vault—so called because of the colouring, now no longer visible, that was originally used to highlight architectural details in the main hall—creates a literally dazzling effect, with reflected light dancing off the gold and the countless precious stones. Undoubtedly this was the effect Augustus the Strong set out to achieve when he commissioned his court architect Matthäus Daniel Pöppelmann (1662–1736) to create this luxurious Baroque *Gesamtkunstwerk* (total work of art), which was built between 1723 and 1729 and initially open only to select visitors, who would have instantly understood that something so spectacular could only belong to a ruler who was both powerful and unimaginably wealthy. Almost completely destroyed during the Second World War, the palace has been under reconstruction since the 1980s and its treasures have been put on show at two different locations: the Historical Green Vault and the New Green Vault. More than 3,000 masterpieces are displayed in the Historical Green Vault in 10 richly decorated rooms, some of which are devoted to a particular material, such as bronze, ivory, silver or amber. Among the most extraordinary items are those produced by the court jeweller Johann Melchior Dinglinger (1664–1731), such as the *Golden Coffee Service* and *The Birthday of the Grand Mogul Aurangzeb*, together with the *Dresden Green*, a huge diamond that was acquired in 1742.

◉ ◈ ◉

Die Staatlichen Kunstsammlungen Dresden gehören zu den ältesten und bedeutends-ten Museen der Welt. Bereits 1560 ließ der sächsische Kurfürst August (1526–1586) in seiner Dresdner Residenz eine Kunstkammer einrichten, die neben zahlreichen *Naturalia* vor allem *Artificialia* umfasste: Uhren, wissenschaftliche Instrumente, Automaten, Elfenbeindrechseleien, Kunstwerke, Schmuckstücke und Kuriositäten. In der Spätrenaissance fungierte die Kunstkammer als eine Art enzyklopädische Universalsammlung, die vor allem aus technischen Neuheiten und Instrumenten jeder Art bestand. Ihre herausragende Sammlung verdanken die Dresdener jedoch dem ausgeprägten Kunstsinn des sächsischen Kurfürsten August des Starken (1670–1733), der nicht nur ein großer Liebhaber von Porzellan und Pretiosen war, sondern seine

Sammlung auch entsprechend in Szene setzten wollte und eigens dafür besonders prachtvolle Ausstellungsräume errichten ließ, darunter das Grüne Gewölbe. Tatsächlich kann einem beim Betreten des Grünen Gewölbes, benannt nach dem heute nicht mehr sichtbaren Grün an Architekturteilen des Hauptsaals, im wahrsten Sinn des Wortes leicht schwindelig werden, denn Gold und Edelsteine glitzern und funkeln so stark, dass man bei ihrem Anblick ganz benommen ist. Genau darauf hatte es August der Starke vermutlich auch abgesehen, als er sich 1723 bis 1729 von seinem Hofbaumeister Matthäus Daniel Pöppelmann (1662–1736) dieses überaus prunkvolle barocke Gesamtkunstwerk errichten ließ, um einen kleinen, erlesenen Besucherkreis zu beeindrucken: Denn eine solche Pracht konnte sich nur ein mächtiger, ungewöhnlich reicher Herrscher erlauben. Seit den 1980er Jahren wird das im Zweiten Weltkrieg fast vollständig zerstörte Schloss wiederaufgebaut. Daher sind die Kunstschätze heute als Dauerausstellung in zwei verschiedenen Räumlichkeiten zu bewundern, dem Historischen Grünen Gewölbe und dem Neuen Grünen Gewölbe. In Ersterem sind mehr als 3000 Meisterwerke auf zehn prächtig ausgestattete Säle verteilt, von denen einige einem speziellen Material gewidmet sind: Bronze, Elfenbein, Silber, Bernstein, usw. Zu den herausragendsten Exponaten gehören die Arbeiten des Hofjuweliers Johann Melchior Dinglinger (1664–1731), darunter *Das Goldene Kaffeezeug* und der *Thron des Großmoguls Aureng-Zeb,* sowie der 1742 erworbene *Dresdener Grüne Diamant.*

◎ ❖ ◎

Au nombre des pôles muséaux les plus importants et les plus anciens du monde figurent les Staatliche Kunstsammlungen (collections d'art nationales) de Dresde. En 1560 le prince-électeur de Saxe, Auguste (1526–1586) de Saxe fonda la somptueuse *Kunstkammer* (cabinet d'art) aménagée dans le château résidentiel de Dresde, qui comptait quelques *naturalia* et une majorité d'*artificialia* – horloges, instruments scientifiques, automates, ivoires tournés, œuvres d'art, bijoux et curiosités. Reflet de l'esprit de la Renaissance tardive, le cabinet d'art était une collection universelle de nature encyclopédique qui rassemblait surtout des innovations technologiques et des instruments en tous genres. Les Collections de Dresde doivent leur particularité au sens artistique du prince Auguste II, dit le Fort (1670–1733), amateur passionné de porcelaines et de bijoux, qui fit aménager les premières collections spéciales dont font partie la Grünes Gewölbe (Voûte verte). La Voûte verte, qui tire son nom de la couleur vert émeraude – elle n'est plus visible aujourd'hui – de parties architecturales de la salle principale, fait littéralement tourner la tête : les reflets lumineux se multiplient parmi les ors et les pierres précieuses de l'une des collections les plus riches d'Europe. Sans doute faut-il y voir l'effet recherché par Auguste II quand, entre 1723 et 1729, il passa commande à l'architecte Matthäus Daniel Pöppelman (1662–1736) de son œuvre d'art totale, somptueuse et baroque, qui, pour la première fois, fut accessible à un public choisi : seul un souverain exceptionnellement riche et puissant pouvait se permettre une telle splendeur. Presque entièrement détruit durant la Seconde Guerre mondiale, le château est en reconstruction depuis les années 1980. Aujourd'hui, le visiteur peut admirer les œuvres d'art dans deux espaces d'exposition distincts offerts à son admiration dans leur présentation baroque d'origine aussi bien dans l'Historisches Grünes Gewölbe (Voûte verte historique) que dans la Neues Grünes Gewölbe (Nouvelle Voûte verte). Dans la première, plus de 3000 chefs-d'œuvre d'orfèvrerie et de joaillerie sont exposés dans dix cabinets luxueusement décorés dont certains sont consacrés à un matériau : bronze, ivoire, argent, ambre etc. Parmi les pièces les plus fabuleuses, on citera les créations de Johann Melchior Dinglinger (1664–1731), joaillier à la cour de Dresde, tels le *Service à café en or* et la *Cour du Grand Moghol Aurangzeb* ainsi que le *Diamant vert de Dresde* acquis en 1742.

1 *The Silver Room.* Displayed here are a selection of nautilus shell goblets together with a casket and a large basin made of mother-of-pearl, both of which were costly and highly sought materials that came from Gujarat in India. The Green Vault houses the largest collection of such exotic artefacts in the world.
Weißsilberzimmer. Dieses Wandfeld im Weißsilberzimmer präsentiert eine Auswahl an Nautiluspokalen sowie eine Prunkkassette und ein großes Becken aus Perlmutter; die genannten Materialien sind Kostbarkeiten aus dem indischen Gujarat. Das Grüne Gewölbe besitzt weltweit die größte Sammlung derartiger exotischer Werke.
Chambre d'argent blanc. Ce panneau mural de la Chambre d'argent blanc présente une sélection de nautiles montés en coupes ainsi qu'une cassette de cérémonie et un grand bassin décoré de nacre, deux joyaux du Gujarat indien. La Voûte verte possède la plus grande collection d'œuvres d'art exotiques de ce genre au monde.

2 *The Silver Room.* Vermilion is the predominant colour in the Silver Room, which originally housed 377 silver artefacts displayed on the various tables and shelves. In 1772, severe financial difficulties forced the Elector to have almost the entire collection melted down, only three silver statues (visible in the background on the right) having survived.
Weißsilberzimmer. Auf den Tischen und Konsolen des zinnoberrot gehaltenen Weißsilberzimmers standen ursprünglich 377 Gegenstände aus Weißsilber. Geldnot führte 1772 dazu, dass der Bestand eingeschmolzen wurde. Lediglich drei Silberstatuetten (hinten rechts im Bild) blieben damals verschont.
Chambre d'argent blanc. 377 objets en argent blanc étaient posés à l'origine sur les tables et les consoles de la Chambre d'argent blanc, peinte en vermillon. Ils ont tous été fondus en 1772 en raison de difficultés financières. L'intervention n'a épargné que trois statuettes en argent (à l'arrière-plan à droite sur la photo).

3 *The Silver Gilt Room.* The Silver Gilt Room, lined with mirrors and panelled in lime green, houses a collection of silver-gilt tableware, most of it made in Augsburg and Nuremberg. The shelves on the right were once used to display vessels made of solid gold but today their place has been taken by a number of objects made of ruby glass.
Silbervergoldetes Zimmer. Das grün vertäfelte und verspiegelte silbervergoldete Zimmer ist den silbervergoldeten Geschirren vorbehalten, von denen die meisten aus Augsburg und Nürnberg stammen. Auf dem Wandfeld rechts im Bild standen einst Gefäße aus purem Gold, heute werden dort Objekte aus Rubinglas gezeigt.
Chambre vermeille. La chambre revêtue de panneaux vert tilleul et de miroirs est réservée aux vaisselles en vermeil, la plupart des pièces provenant d'Augsbourg et de Nuremberg. Sur le mur, à droite de l'image, se trouvaient jadis des récipients en or pur, aujourd'hui des objets en verre rubis y sont exposés.

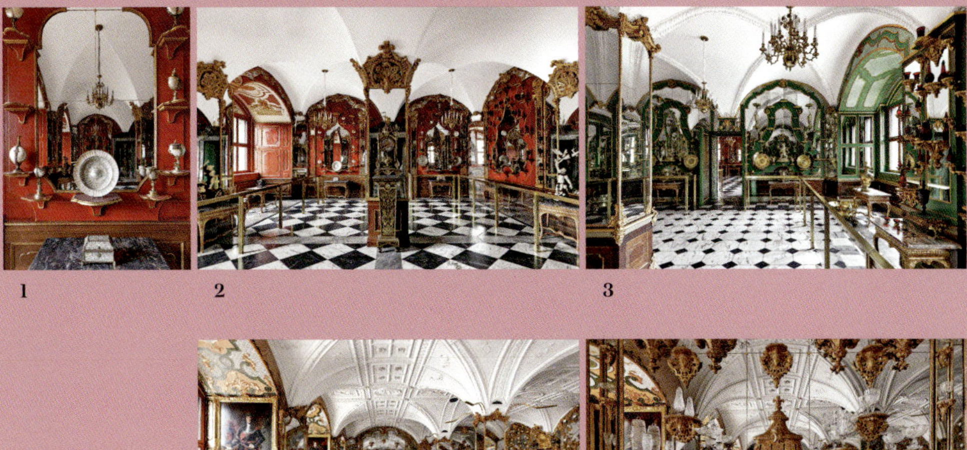

1   2   3

4   5

4 *The Hall of Treasures*. The mirrors in the Hall of Treasures and its sumptuous stucco ceiling date from the Renaissance, and these constitute the first of many highlights in the increasingly magnificent suite of rooms comprising the Green Vault. On show here are artefacts made of precious stones, sea snails, nautilus shells and ostrich eggs.
Pretiosensaal. Der verspiegelte und von einer prächtigen Stuckdecke aus der Renaissance überspannte Pretiosensaal bildet den ersten Höhepunkt im dramaturgisch sich steigernden Rundgang durch das Grüne Gewölbe. Neben Herrscherporträts sind hier Werke aus Edelsteinen, Seeschnecken, Nautilusgehäusen und Straußeneiern zu sehen.
Salle des objets précieux. La Salle des objets précieux, entièrement recouverte de miroirs et surplombée par un magnifique plafond en stuc de la Renaissance, constitue le premier point culminant de la visite de la Voûte verte au cours de laquelle les effets dramaturgiques

vont croissant. Des œuvres d'art en pierres précieuses, escargots de mer, coquilles de nautile et œufs d'autruche peuvent être admirés ici.

5 *The Hall of Treasures*. The artefacts made of rock crystal were first displayed on the tables and shelves of the Hall of Treasures during the reign of Augustus II the Strong. The gilt canopy marks the position where Johann Melchior Dinglinger's *Birthday of the Grand Mogul Aurangzeb* was originally intended to have been installed, while today it is housed in the New Green Vault.
Pretiosensaal. Auf Konsolen und Tischen der Ostwand des Pretiosensaals werden, wie bereits unter August dem Starken, Bergkristallobjekte präsentiert. Der vergoldete Baldachin markiert die Stelle, an der einst Johann Melchior Dinglingers *Thron des Großmoguls Aureng-Zeb* aufgestellt werden sollte. Dieser befindet sich heute im Neuen Grünen Gewölbe.

Salle des objets précieux. Sur les consoles et les tables du mur de la Salle des objets précieux, des objets en cristal de roche sont présentés aujourd'hui, comme au temps d'Auguste le Fort. Le baldaquin doré marque l'endroit où devait être placée à l'origine la *Cour du Grand Moghol Aurangzeb* de Johann Melchior Dinglinger. Il se trouve aujourd'hui dans la Nouvelle Voûte verte.

6 *The Hall of Treasures*. The window bays in the Hall of Treasures are lined on the sides with portraits of the Electors of Saxony, from Maurice (shown here) to Frederick Augustus II. The lost originals have been replaced by copies. Georg Friedrich Dinglinger's depiction of the Virgin Mary, painted on enamel (right), was once greatly admired for its unusually large format (90 x 68 cm / 35½ x 26¾ in.).
Pretiosensaal. In den Fensternischen des Pretiosensaals hängen Porträts der sächsischen Kurfürsten von Moritz (hier im Bild) bis Friedrich August II. Die verschollenen

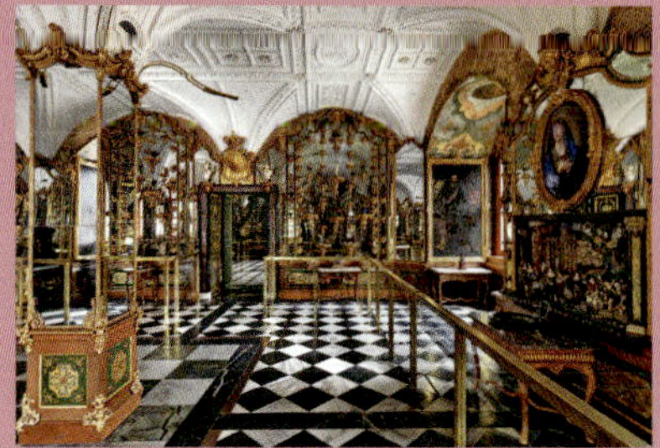

6

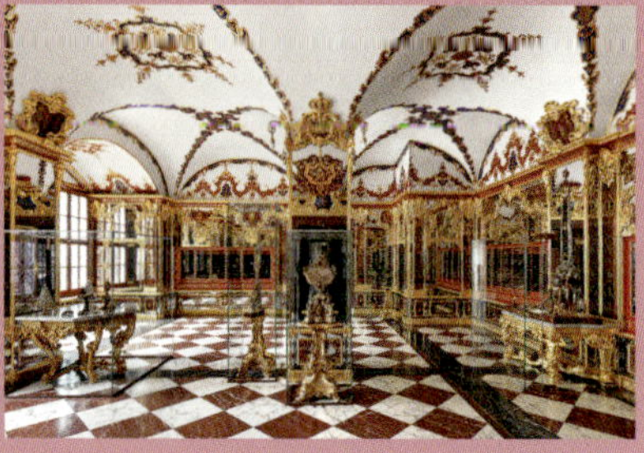

7

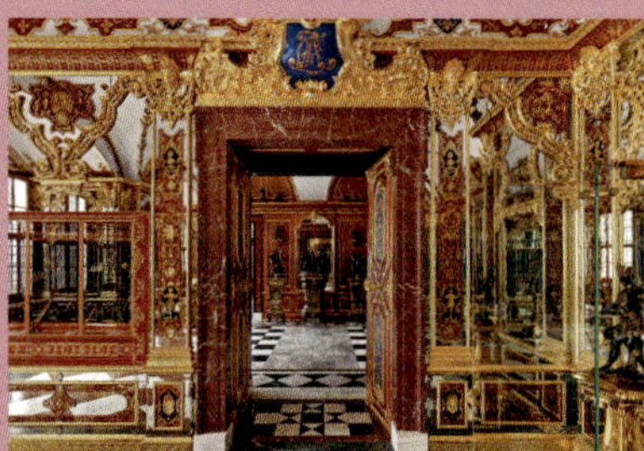

8

Originale wurden durch Kopien ersetzt. Das Marienbild Georg Friedrich Dinglingers in Emailmalerei (rechts) sorgte damals wegen seiner Größe (90 x 68 cm) für Aufsehen.

Salle des objets précieux. Dans les renfoncements de fenêtres de la Salle des objets précieux sont accrochés des portraits des électeurs saxons, de Maurice (ici sur la photo) à Frédéric-Auguste II. Les originaux perdus ont été remplacés par des copies. La Vierge Marie peinte sur émail par Georg Friedrich Dinglinger (à droite) a fait sensation à l'époque en raison de sa taille gigantesque (90 x 68 cm).

7 *The Jewel Chamber.* Completely destroyed in the bombing of 13 February 1945, the Jewel Chamber was carefully rebuilt between 2002 and 2006. Today, the wall-mounted vitrines once again house the former state treasure of the Saxon-Polish royal family—10 more or less complete sets of jewellery.

Juwelenzimmer. Das am 13. Februar 1945 zerstörte Juwelenzimmer wurde zwischen 2002 und 2006 sorgfältig rekonstruiert. In den Wandvitrinen wird heute wieder der Staatsschatz des sächsisch-polnischen Königshauses – zehn teils vollständig erhaltene Juwelengarnituren – präsentiert.

Salle des joyaux. Complètement détruite le 13 février 1945, la Salle des joyaux a été soigneusement reconstruite entre 2002 et 2006. Dans les vitrines murales, le trésor d'État unique en son genre de la royauté saxonne et polonaise – dix parures de bijoux plus ou moins entièrement conservées – est à nouveau présenté au public.

8 *The Jewel Chamber.* The sumptuous appointment of the Jewel Chamber gives it something of the appearance of a huge treasure chest. Above the entrance to the Heraldry Room is the monogram "CFA" (Churfürst Friedrich August/ Elector Frederick Augustus) set amongst scrolling acanthus leaves, while on the mirrors appear the Polish-Lithuanian arms and the emblems of the great chivalric orders.

Juwelenzimmer. Wegen seiner überaus reichen Ausstattung gleicht das Juwelenzimmer einem imposanten Schatzkästchen. Über dem Durchgang zum Wappenzimmer prangt zwischen üppigem Akanthuswerk das Monogramm CFA (für Churfürst Friedrich August), und auf den Spiegeln erkennt man das polnisch-litauische Wappen sowie Symbole großer Ritterorden.

Salle des joyaux. En raison de la richesse de son ameublement, la Salle des joyaux ressemble à un coffre au trésor. Le monogramme « CFA » (pour le prince-électeur Frédéric-Auguste) est gravé au-dessus du passage vers la Salle des armoiries entre les opulents décors de feuilles d'acanthe, les miroirs montrent les armoiries polono-lituaniennes ainsi que les symboles des grands ordres de chevalerie.

9 Wenzel Jamnitzer, *Writing Casket with an Allegory of Philosophy,* Nuremberg, 1562. Partially gilt silver, enamel, velvet, silk, rock

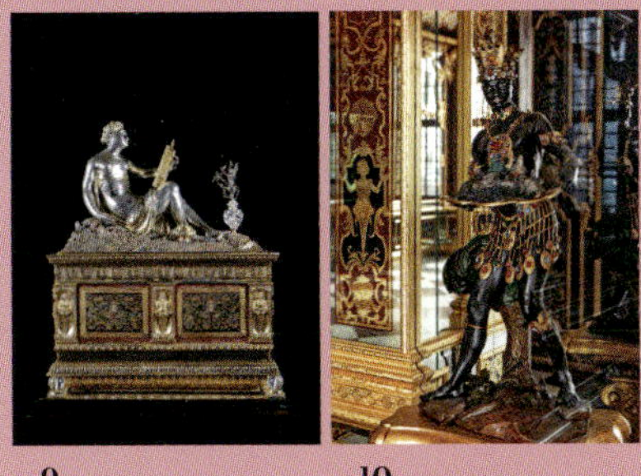

9   10

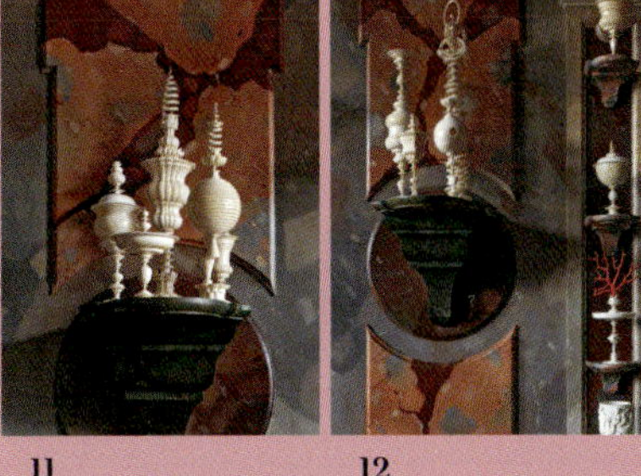

11   12

crystal, ebony and a large piece of silver ore, 31 x 24 x 11 cm / 12¼ x 9½ x 4⅜ in.
Wenzel Jamnitzer, *Schreibkassette mit Allegorie der Philosophie*, Nürnberg, 1562. Silber, teilvergoldet, Email, Samt, Seide, Bergkristall, Erzstufe, Ebenholz, 31 x 24 x 11 cm.
Wenzel Jamnitzer, *Nécessaire à écrire avec l'allégorie de la Philosophie*, Nuremberg, 1562. Argent en partie doré, émail, velours, soie, cristal de roche, spécimen de minerai, ébène, 31 x 24 x 11 cm.

10 Johann Heinrich Köhler (setting), *Moor with Tray of Minerals*, Dresden, 1724. Varnished wood, piece of silver ore with precious stones from a Saxon mine, gilt copper, brass, various semi-precious stones, 66.5 cm / 26⅛ in.
Johann Heinrich Köhler (Fassung), *Sogenannter Mohr mit Landsteinstufe*, Dresden, 1724. Holz, lackiert, Silbererzstufe mit sächsischen Edelsteinen, Kupfer, vergoldet, Messing, verschiedene Farbsteine, teils foliert, 66,5 cm.

Johann Heinrich Köhler (monture), *Le soi-disant Maure présentant un morceau de pierre du pays*, Dresde, 1724. Bois verni, spécimen de minerai d'argent avec pierres précieuses saxonnes, cuivre doré, laiton, pierres de différentes couleurs, 66,5 cm.

11–12 *The Ivory Room*. By the early 17th century, Dresden was the main centre for the art of lathe-turning ivory in Europe, and several court artists produced incredibly complex showpieces for its cabinet of curiosities. Once work on the Green Vault was completed, these artefacts were installed in the Ivory Room. Its panelled walls are painted to imitate Italian marble, creating a sophisticated setting for the ivory objects displayed here.
Elfenbeinzimmer. Im frühen 17. Jh. war Dresden das Zentrum europäischer Elfenbeindrechselkunst. Hofkünstler schufen faszinierend komplexe Werke für die Kunstkammer, die bei der Einrichtung des Grünen Gewölbes in das Elfenbeinzimmer überführt wurden.

Die holzverkleideten Wandflächen erinnern in ihrer Bemalung an italienischen Marmor und bilden eine ästhetisch anspruchsvolle Rahmung für die davor präsentierten Elfenbeinarbeiten.
Chambre d'ivoire. Au début du 17e siècle, Dresde était le centre du tournage européen de l'ivoire. Les artistes de la cour de Dresde ont créé des œuvres d'une complexité fascinante pour la Kunstkammer. Celles-ci ont été transférées dans la Chambre d'ivoire lors de l'installation de la Voûte verte. Les murs lambrissés de la Chambre d'ivoire sont peints en « style marbre italien », formant ainsi un cadre esthétiquement sophistiqué pour les travaux en ivoire présentés devant les murs.

13 *The Ivory Room*. The collection notably includes not only turned but also carved ivories, amongst which are statuettes, goblets, boxes, writing utensils and polyhedra, variously displayed on shelves and marble tables.

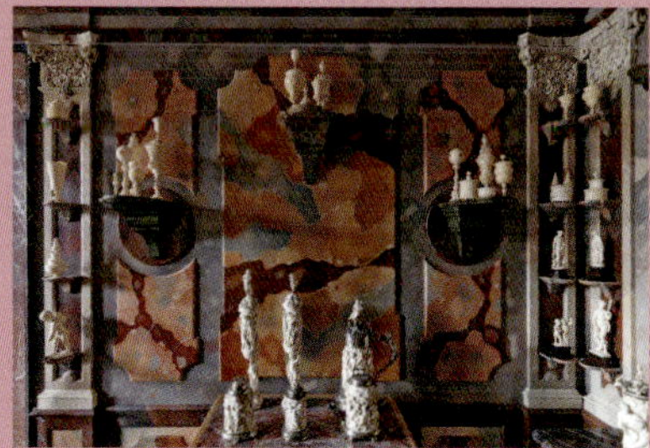

13

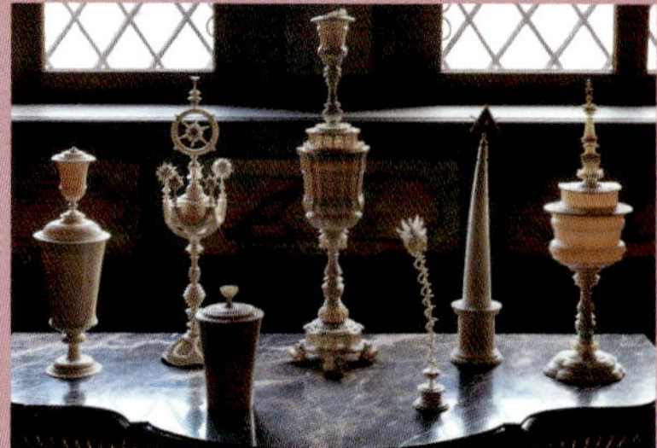

14

Elfenbeinzimmer. Neben der Drechselkunst gehören auch geschnitzte Elfenbeinarbeiten zum Sammlungskanon. Statuetten, Trinkgefäße, Dosen, Schreibzeuge oder geometrische Körper werden nicht nur auf den Wandkonsolen, sondern auch auf Marmortischen präsentiert.
Chambre d'ivoire. À côté de l'ivoire tourné, l'ivoire sculpté fait également partie du canon de la collection. Statuettes, récipients à boire, boîtes, ustensiles d'écriture ou corps géométriques sont présentés non seulement sur les consoles murales, mais aussi sur des tables en marbre.

14 *The Ivory Room.* The 16th- and 17th-century turned ivories displayed on a table in the Ivory Room are large-scale virtuoso works celebrated for their intricate geometric forms, complex construction and precise execution.
Elfenbeinzimmer. Bei diesen Drechseleien handelt es sich um großformatige, künstlerisch höchst anspruchsvolle Werke des 16. und

17. Jhs., deren Erscheinungsbild von komplexen geometrischen Formen und einer überaus präzisen Ausführung geprägt ist.
Chambre d'ivoire. Les objets en ivoire tournés sur la table de la Chambre d'ivoire sont des œuvres de grandes dimensions et d'une très grande exigence artistique créées aux 16e et 17e siècles. Leur aspect est caractérisé par des formes géométriques complexes et une exécution extrêmement précise.
Objects on the table (left to right):
Objekte auf dem Tisch (von links):
Objets sur la table (de gauche) :

14a Georg Wecker, *Lidded Goblet*, 1586, ivory, 45 cm / 17¾ in.
Georg Wecker, *Deckelbecher*, 1586, Elfenbein, 45 cm.
Georg Wecker, *Gobelet à couvercle*, 1586, ivoire, 45 cm.

14b *Centrepiece*, presumably Dresden, *c.* 1600, ivory, 58 cm / 22⅛ in.
Kunststück, wohl Dresden, um 1600, Elfenbein, 58 cm.

Objet d'art, probablement Dresde, vers 1600, ivoire, 58 cm.

14c *Lidded Goblet*, ivory, 21.8 cm / 8⅝ in.
Deckelbecher, Elfenbein, 21,8 cm.
Gobelet à couvercle, ivoire, 21,8 cm.

14d Jacob Zeller, *Lidded Goblet*, ivory, 74 cm / 29⅛ in.
Jacob Zeller, *Deckelpokal*, Elfenbein, 74 cm.
Jacob Zeller, *Coupe à couvercle*, ivoire, 74 cm.

14e *Centrepiece with Tulip*, ivory, 37 cm / 14⅝ in.
Kunststück mit Tulpe, Elfenbein, 37 cm.
Objet d'art avec tulipe, ivoire, 37 cm.

14f Egidius Lobenigk, *Ivory Column with Tetrahedron*, Dresden, 1588, ivory, 52.5 cm / 20⅝ in.
Egidius Lobenigk, *Elfenbeinsäule mit Tetraeder*, Dresden, 1588, Elfenbein, 52,5 cm.
Egidius Lobenigk, *Colonne en ivoire avec tétraèdre*, Dresde, 1588, ivoire, 52,5 cm.

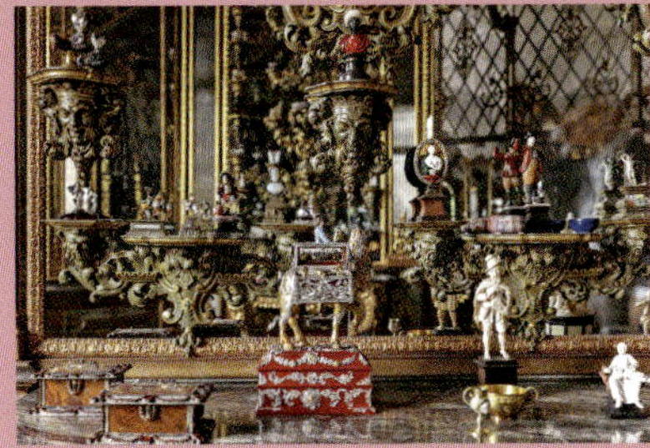

15

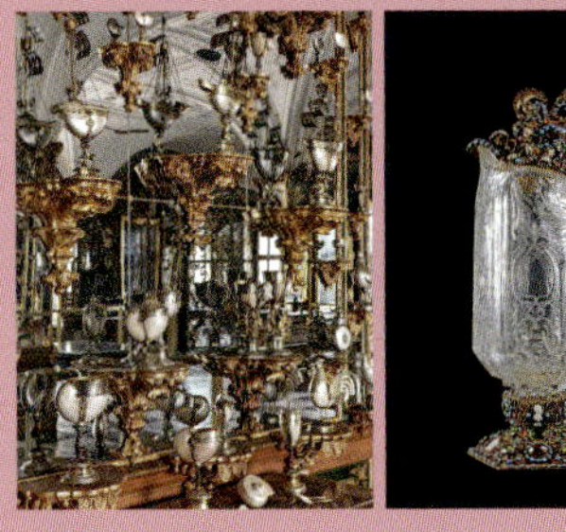

16   17

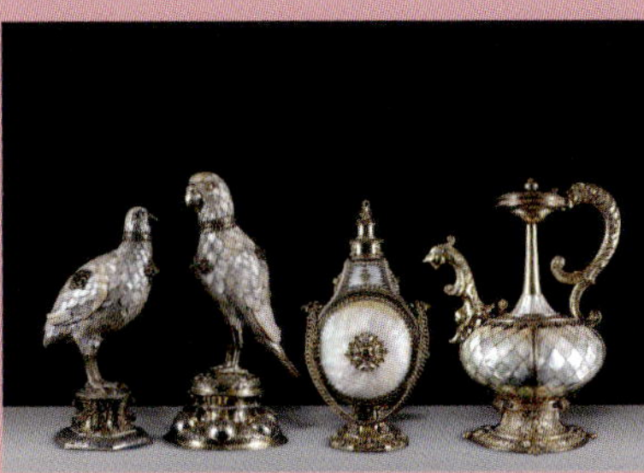

18

14g Jacob Zeller, *Lidded Goblet*, Dresden, *c.* 1620, ivory, 60 cm / 23⅝ in.
Jacob Zeller, *Deckelpokal*, Dresden, um 1620, Elfenbein, 60 cm.
Jacob Zeller, *Coupe à couvercle*, Dresde, vers 1620, ivoire, 60 cm.

15 *The Corner Cabinet.* The Corner Cabinet is a closed and almost completely mirrored small room located next to the Hall of Treasures. With its embellished shelves, detailed paintwork and small-scale artefacts, it functions as the intimate treasury within the main treasury.
Eckkabinett. Das Eckkabinett ist ein kleiner, in sich geschlossener und nahezu vollständig verspiegelter Raum, welcher an den Pretiosensaal grenzt. Mit den reich verzierten Wandkonsolen, der detaillierten Ausmalung und den kleinformatigen Werken fungiert das Eckkabinett als intimes Kleinod innerhalb der Schatzkammer.
Cabinet d'angle. Le Cabinet d'angle est une petite pièce indépendante et presque entièrement recouverte de miroirs, qui borde la Salle des objets précieux. Avec ses consoles murales richement ornées, son décor peint de manière détaillée et ses œuvres d'art de petites dimensions, le Cabinet d'angle opère comme une chambre au trésor intime au sein du Trésor.

16 *The Hall of Treasures.* The walls of the Hall of Treasures are lined with gilt shelves showcasing works from the goldsmith's art of the Renaissance and the Baroque, amongst which are the fascinating goblets made using nautilus shells and those of sea snails.
Pretiosensaal. Die Wände des Pretiosensaals sind bis zur Decke mit vergoldeten Konsolen bestückt. Auf ihnen werden Goldschmiedearbeiten der Renaissance und des Barock präsentiert, die unter Einbeziehung von Nautilusgehäusen und Seeschnecken zu fantasievollen Trinkgefäßen geformt wurden.
Salle des objets précieux. Les murs de la Salle des objets précieux sont équipés jusqu'au plafond de consoles dorées sur lesquelles sont présentés des travaux d'orfèvrerie de la Renaissance et du Baroque, transformés en récipients à boire très originaux à l'aide de coquilles de nautile et d'escargots de mer.

17 Dionysio Miseroni (hard-stone carver), *So-called Dragon Ewer*, Prague, after 1651, setting *c.* 1660. Rock crystal, partially gilt silver, various semi-precious stones and cameos, 42.2 x 25.4 cm / 16⅝ x 10 in.
Dionysio Miseroni (Steinschneider), *Sogenannte Drachenkanne*, Prag, nach 1651, Fassung um 1660. Bergkristall, Silber, teilvergoldet, Farbsteine und Kameen, 42,2 x 25,4 cm.
Dionysio Miseroni (tailleur de pierre), *Dite aiguière-dragon*, Prague, après 1651, monture vers 1660. Cristal de roche, argent, partiellement plaqué or, pierres et camées de différentes couleurs, 42,2 x 25,4 cm.

18a Friedrich Hillebrandt, *Drinking Game in the Shape of a Partridge*, Nuremberg, between

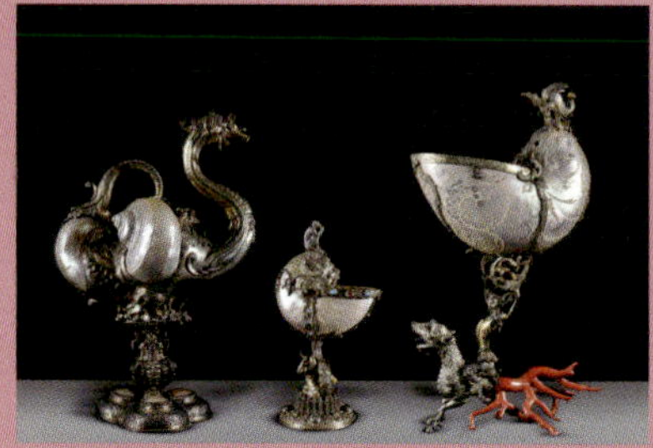
19

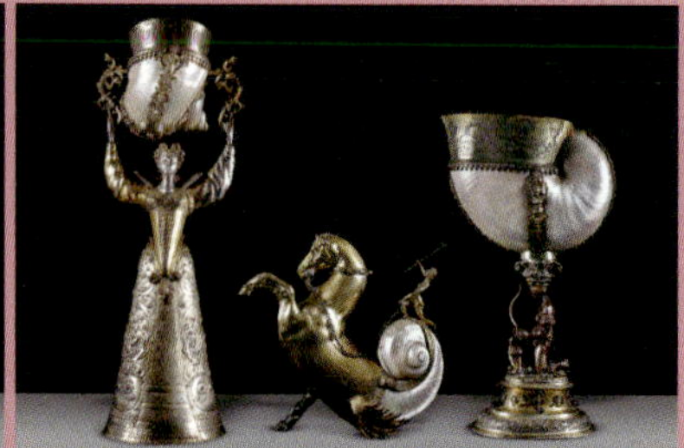
20

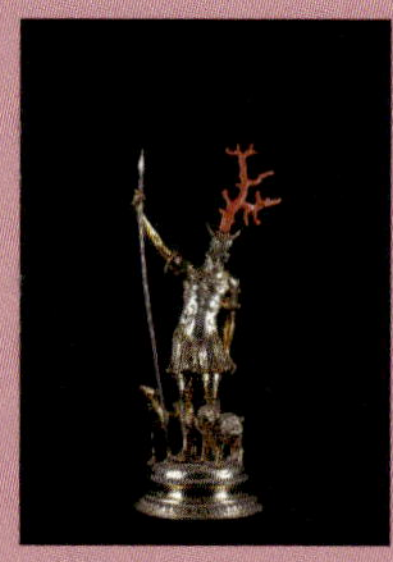
21

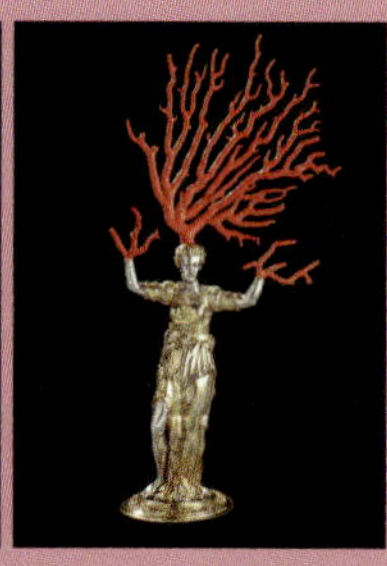
22

1593 and 1602. Gilt silver, emeralds, garnets, 27.2 x 12.3 x 14.4 cm / 10¾ x 4⅞ x 5⅝ in.
Friedrich Hillebrandt, *Trinkspiel in Gestalt eines Rebhuhns*, Nürnberg, zwischen 1593 und 1602. Silber, vergoldet, Perlmutterplättchen, Smaragde, Granate, 27,2 x 12,3 x 14,4 cm.
Friedrich Hillebrandt, *Jeu à boire en forme de perdrix*, Nuremberg, entre 1593 et 1602. Argent doré, plaquettes de nacre, émeraudes, grenats, 27,2 x 12,3 x 14,4 cm.

18b Hans I. Rappolt, *Drinking Game in the Shape of a Parrot*, Nuremberg, between 1593 and 1602. Embossed, cast, tooled, punched and gilt silver, cut and carved mother-of-pearl, rubies, emeralds, enamel, 32.5 x 19 cm / 12¾ x 7½ in.
Hans I. Rappolt, *Trinkspiel in Gestalt eines Papageis*, Nürnberg, zwischen 1593 und 1602. Silber, getrieben, gegossen, ziseliert, punziert, vergoldet, Perlmutter, geschnitten, graviert, Rubine, Smaragde, Email, 32,5 x 19 cm.

Hans I. Rappolt, *Jeu à boire en forme de perroquet*, Nuremberg, entre 1593 et 1602. Argent repoussé et coulé, ciselé, poinçonné, doré, nacre taillée, gravée, rubis, émeraudes, émail, 32,5 x 19 cm.

18c *Flask with Chain*, Nuremberg, c. 1598–1602. Embossed, cast, engraved, gilt silver, emeralds, small mother-of-pearl plates from Pinctada, a genus of pearl oyster, 27.4 x 9 x 8 cm / 10¾ x 3½ x 3⅛ in.
Kettenflasche, Nürnberg, um 1598–1602. Silber, getrieben, gegossen, graviert, vergoldet, Smaragde, Perlmutterplättchen von Perlmuscheln, 27,4 x 9 x 8 cm.
Flacon à chaîne, Nuremberg, vers 1598–1602. Argent repoussé et coulé, gravé, doré, émeraudes, plaques de nacre provenant d'une huître perlière du genre Pinctada, 27,4 x 9 x 8 cm.

18d *Mother-of-pearl Ewer*, Gujarat (India, mother-of-pearl), Antwerp or Nuremberg (setting), c. 1540. Embossed, cast, tooled, punched and gilt silver, copper, cut mother-of-pearl, 29 x 23.3 cm / 11⅜ x 9⅛ in.
Perlmutterkanne, Gujarat (Indien, Perlmutterarbeit), Antwerpen oder Nürnberg (Fassung), um 1540. Silber, getrieben, gegossen, ziseliert, punziert, vergoldet, Kupfer, Perlmutter, geschnitten, 29 x 23,3 cm.
Aiguière en nacre, Gujarat (Inde, travail en nacre), Anvers ou Nuremberg (monture), vers 1540. Argent repoussé et coulé, ciselé, poinçonné, doré, cuivre, nacre taillée, 29 x 23,3 cm.

19a Nicolaus Schmidt, *Ewer Made from Two Shells*, Nuremberg, c. 1600. Heavy turban shell, with gilt silver, 40 x 26.8 x 17 cm / 15¾ x 10½ x 6¾ in.
Nicolaus Schmidt, *Kanne aus Seeschneckengehäusen*, Nürnberg, um 1600. Turbanschneckengehäuse, Silber, vergoldet, 40 x 26,8 x 17 cm.
Nicolaus Schmidt, *Aiguière en coquilles d'escargot de mer*, Nuremberg, vers 1600. Coquille d'escargot (Turbinidae), argent doré, 40 x 26,8 x 17 cm.

19b *Small Nautilus Goblet with Man Cutting Tree and Monkey*, probably southern German, *c.* 1570. Nautilus shell, gilt silver, turquoises, garnets, rubies, enamel, polychrome work, 17.8 x 10.1 x 5.7 cm / 7 x 4 x 2¼ in.
Kleiner Nautiluspokal mit Baumfäller und Affe, wahrscheinlich Süddeutschland, um 1570. Nautilusgehäuse, Silber, vergoldet, Türkise, Granate, Rubine, Email, Farbfassung, 17,8 x 10,1 x 5,7 cm.
Petit nautile monté en coupe avec bûcheron et singe, probablement du sud de l'Allemagne, vers 1570. Coquille de nautile, argent doré, turquoise, grenats, rubis, émail, couleur, 17,8 x 10,1 x 5,7 cm.

19c Johann Heinrich Köhler (goldsmith), Cornelis van Bellekin (circle; mother-of-pearl carver), *Nautilus Goblet with Coral Branches*, base with dragon, probably Nuremberg, third quarter of the 16th century. Nautilus shell, gilt silver, coral, garnets, 42.3 x 26 x 13 cm / 16⅝ x 10¼ x 5⅛ in.
Johann Heinrich Köhler (Goldschmied), Cornelis van Bellekin (Umkreis; Perlmutterschnitzer), *Nautiluspokal mit Korallenzinken*, Fußgruppe mit Drachen, wahrscheinlich Nürnberg, 3. Viertel 16. Jh. Nautilusgehäuse, Silber, vergoldet, Koralle, Granat, 42,3 x 26 x 13 cm.
Johann Heinrich Köhler (orfèvre), Cornelis van Bellekin (entourage ; graveur de nacre), *Nautile monté en coupe à dents de corail*, pied formant un dragon, probablement Nuremberg, 3ᵉ quart du 16ᵉ siècle. Coquille de nautile, argent doré, corail, grenat, 42,3 x 26 x 13 cm.

20a Friedrich Hillebrandt, *Virgin's Goblet*, mainly gilt silver, with mother-of-pearl, 43 cm / 16⅞ in.
Friedrich Hillebrandt, *Jungfrauenbecher*, Nürnberg, um 1600. Silber, größtenteils Silber, größtenteils vergoldet, Perlmutterschnecke, 43 cm.
Friedrich Hillebrandt, *Coupe de mariage*, Nuremberg, vers 1600. Argent, en grande partie argent doré, escargot en nacre, 43 cm.

20b Elias Geyer, *Goblet in the Shape of a Hippocampus*, Leipzig, 1591–1593 or around 1600. Embossed, cast, tooled, engraved and gilt silver, shell of a pyramid snail, layered mother-of-pearl, polychrome work, 18.9 x 21 x 10.5 cm / 7½ x 8¼ x 4⅛ in.
Elias Geyer, *Hippocampus als Trinkgefäß*, Leipzig, 1591–1593 oder um 1600. Silber, getrieben, gegossen, ziseliert, graviert, vergoldet, Turboschneckengehäuse, Perlmutterschicht, Farbfassung, 18,9 x 21 x 10,5 cm.
Elias Geyer, *Hippocampe monté en récipient à boire*, Leipzig, 1591–1593 ou vers 1600. Argent, repoussé et coulé, ciselé, gravé, doré, coquille d'escargots de mer (Tectus fenestratus), revêtement nacre, couleur, 18,9 x 21 x 10,5 cm.

20c Hans Utten, *Nautilus Goblet Borne by a Kneeling Native American*, Nuremberg, 1609–1612. Partially gilt silver, nautilus shell, polychrome work, 33.5 cm / 13¼ in.
Hans Utten, *Nautiluspokal von kniendem Indianer getragen*, Nürnberg, 1609–1612. Silber, teilvergoldet, Nautilusgehäuse, Farbfassung, 33,5 cm.
Hans Utten, *Coupe-nautile portée par un Indien agenouillé*, Nuremberg, 1609–1612. Argent en partie doré, coquille de nautile, couleur, 33,5 cm.

21 Jeremias Ritter, *Goblet in the Shape of Actaeon*, Nuremberg, between 1609 and 1629. Partially gilt silver, coral, 50 cm / 19¾ in.
Jeremias Ritter, *Aktaeon als Trinkgefäß*, Nürnberg, zwischen 1609 und 1629. Silber, teils vergoldet, Koralle, 50 cm.
Jeremias Ritter, *Actéon en forme de récipient à boire*, Nuremberg, entre 1609 und 1629. Argent en partie doré, corail, 50 cm.

22 Abraham and Wenzel Jamnitzer, *Goblet in the Shape of Daphne, with Coral Branches*, Nuremberg, *c.* 1580–1586. Silver, partially gilt, coral, 64.6 cm / 25⅜ in.

Abraham und Wenzel Jamnitzer, *Pokal als Daphne mit Korallenzinken*, Nürnberg, um 1580–1586. Silber, zum großen Teil vergoldet, Koralle, 64,6 cm.
Abraham et Wenzel Jamnitzer, *Coupe en forme de Daphné avec branches de corail*, Nuremberg, vers 1580–1586. Argent, pour la plus grande partie doré, corail, 64,6 cm.

Schloss Friedenstein

Gotha

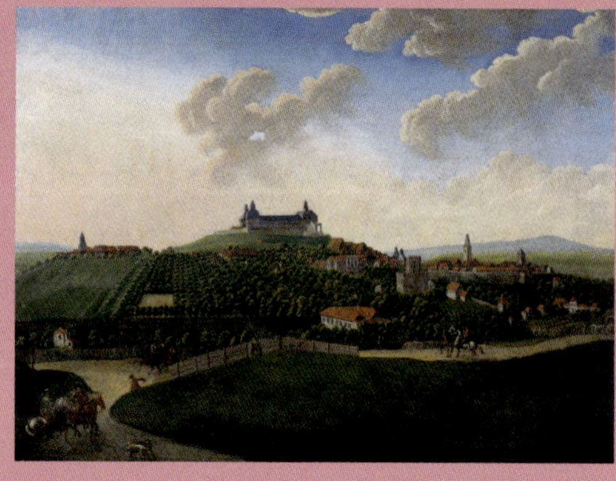

Founded 1643 (construction of the palace)

Key item The coin collection and the wax portraits of Duke Frederick and Duchess Magdalena Sibylle of Saxe-Gotha-Altenburg by Anna Maria Braun, *née* Pfründt (1642–1713).

Besonders sehenswert Das Münzkabinett und die Wachsbildnisse des Herzogs Friedrich I. von Sachsen-Gotha-Altenburg und seiner Gemahlin Magdalena Sibylle, geschaffen von Anna Maria Braun, geborene Pfründt (1642–1713).

À voir absolument La collection numismatique et les portraits en cire du duc Frédéric Ier de Saxe-Gotha-Altenbourg et de son épouse Madeleine Sibylle par Anna Maria Braun, née Pfründt (1642–1713).

Anonymous, *View of Gotha with the Friedenstein Palace, from the south-east, c.* 1730

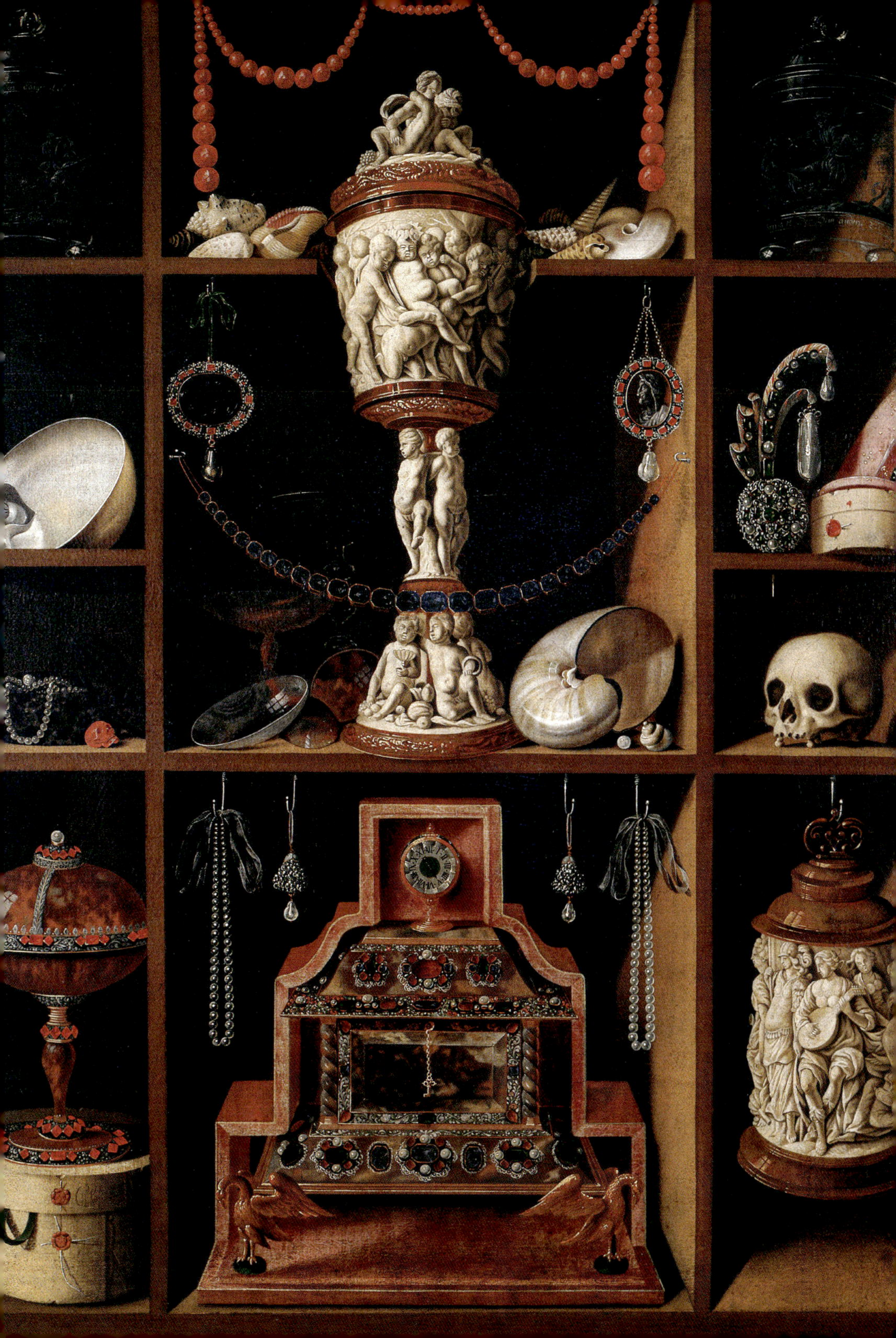

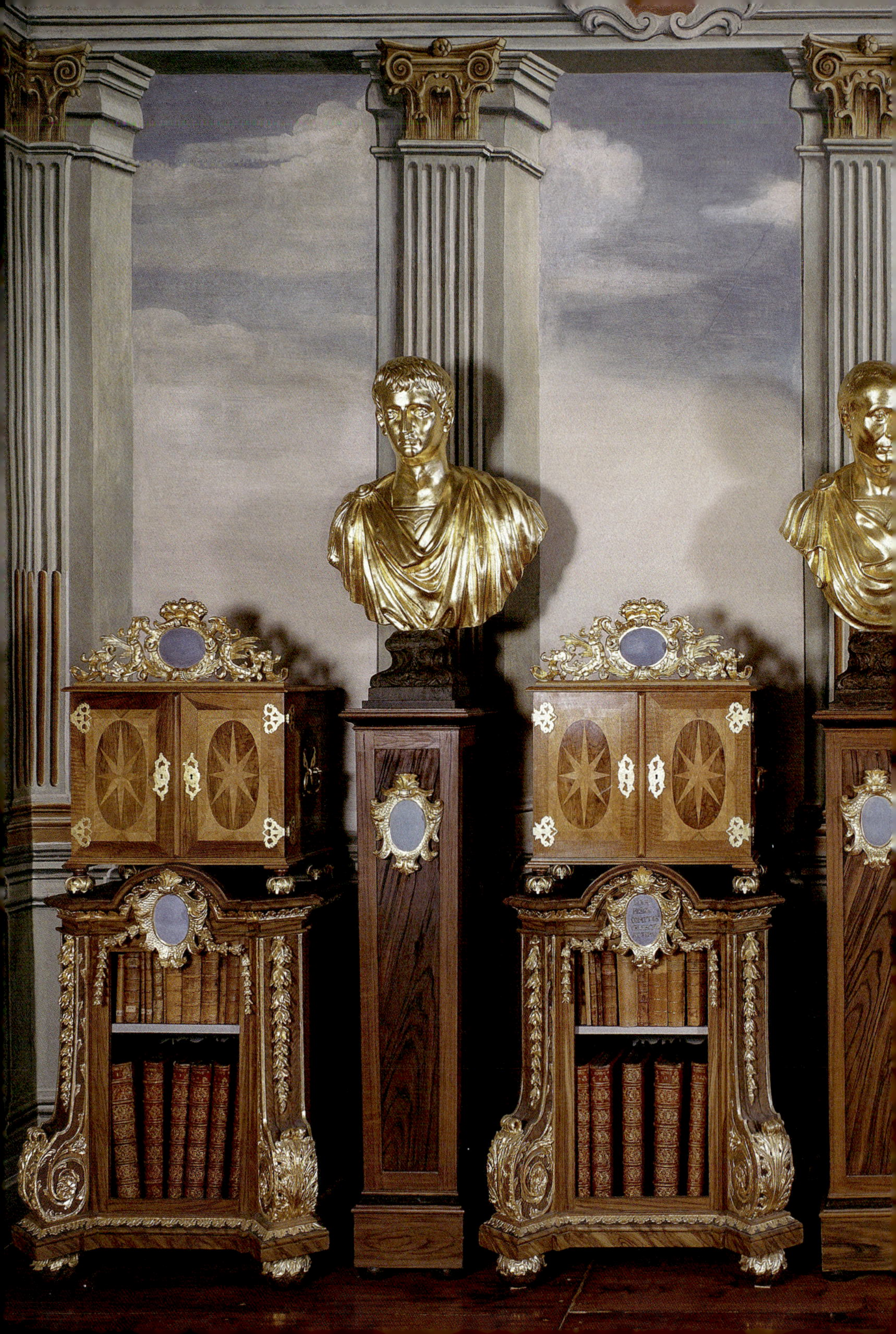

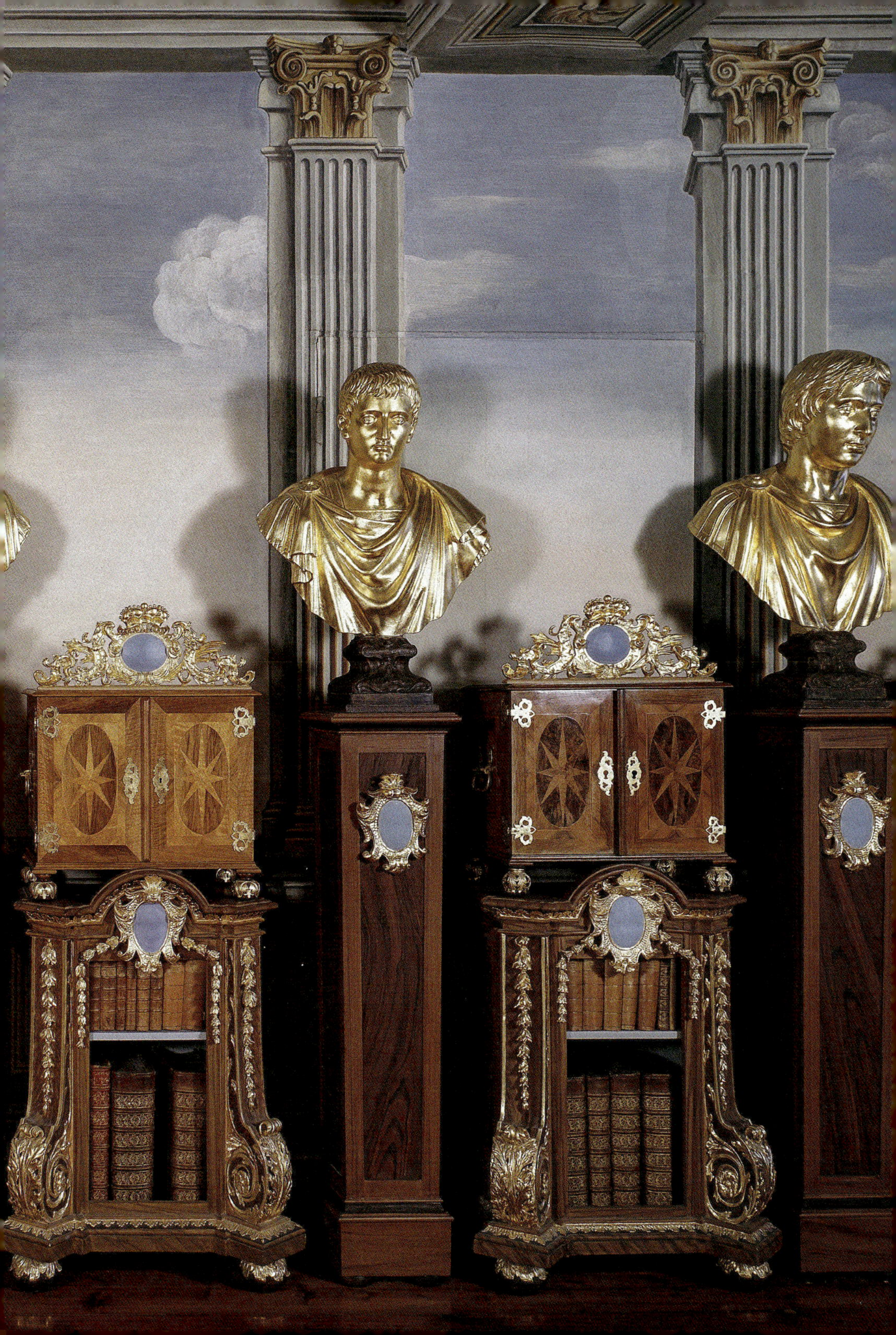

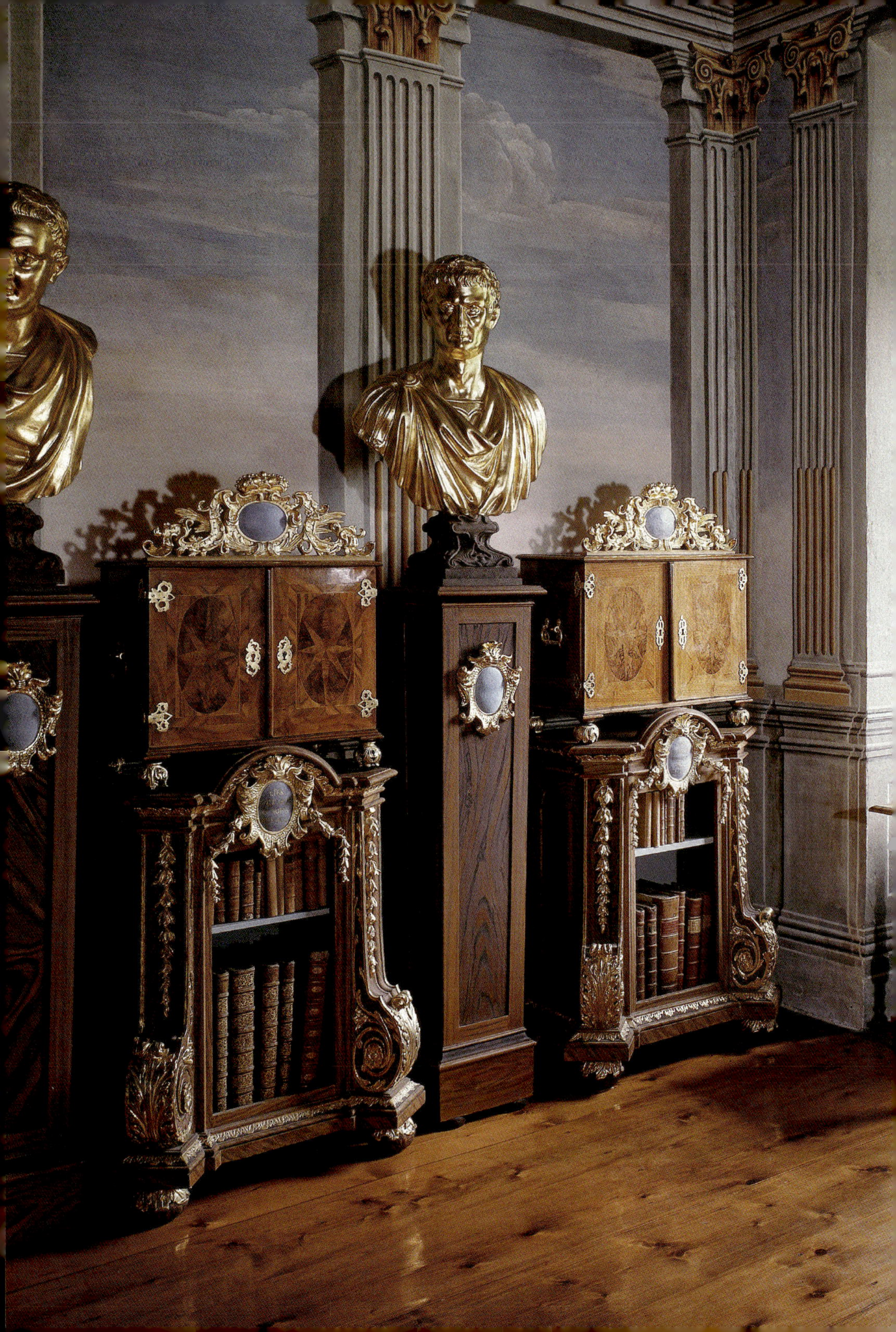

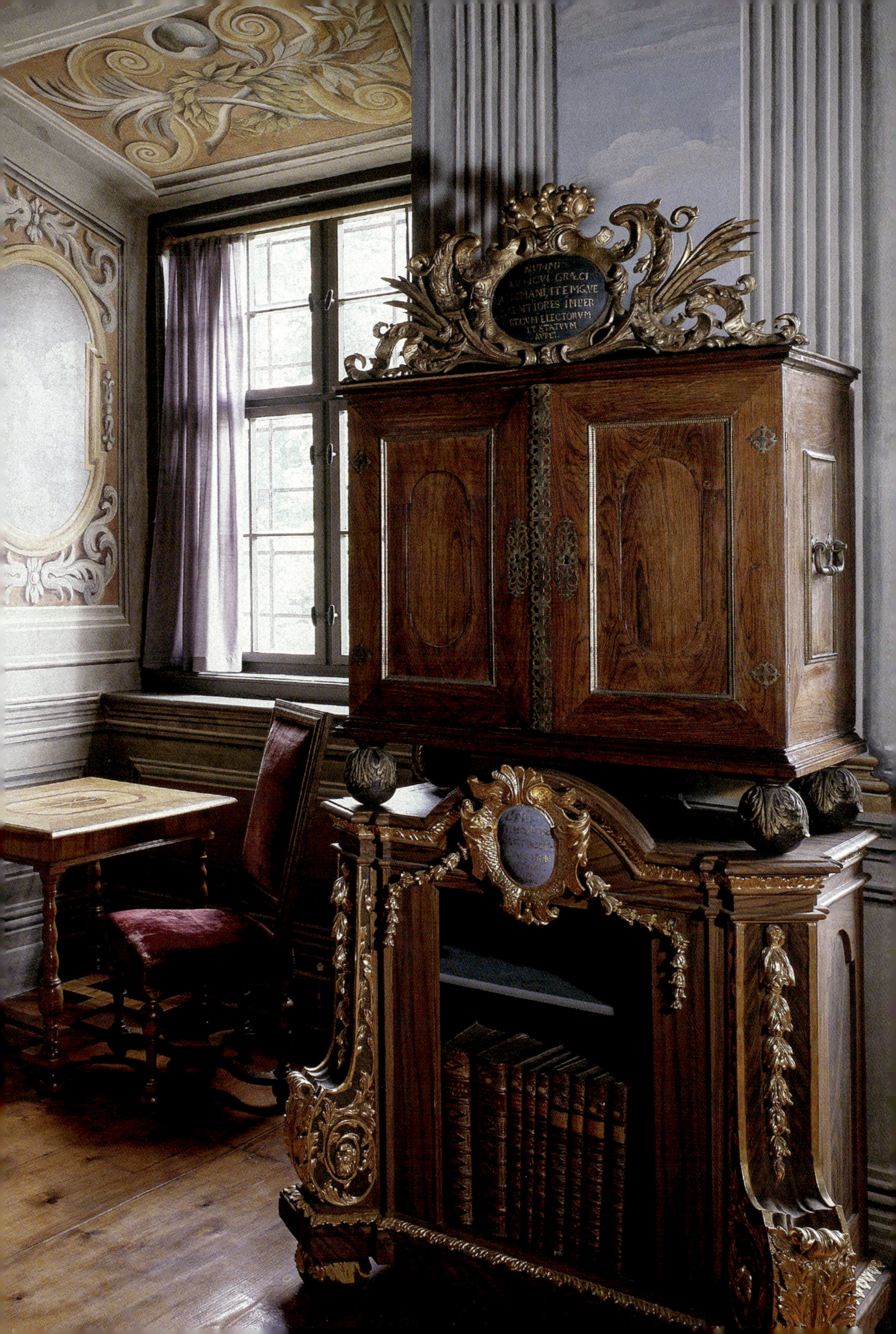

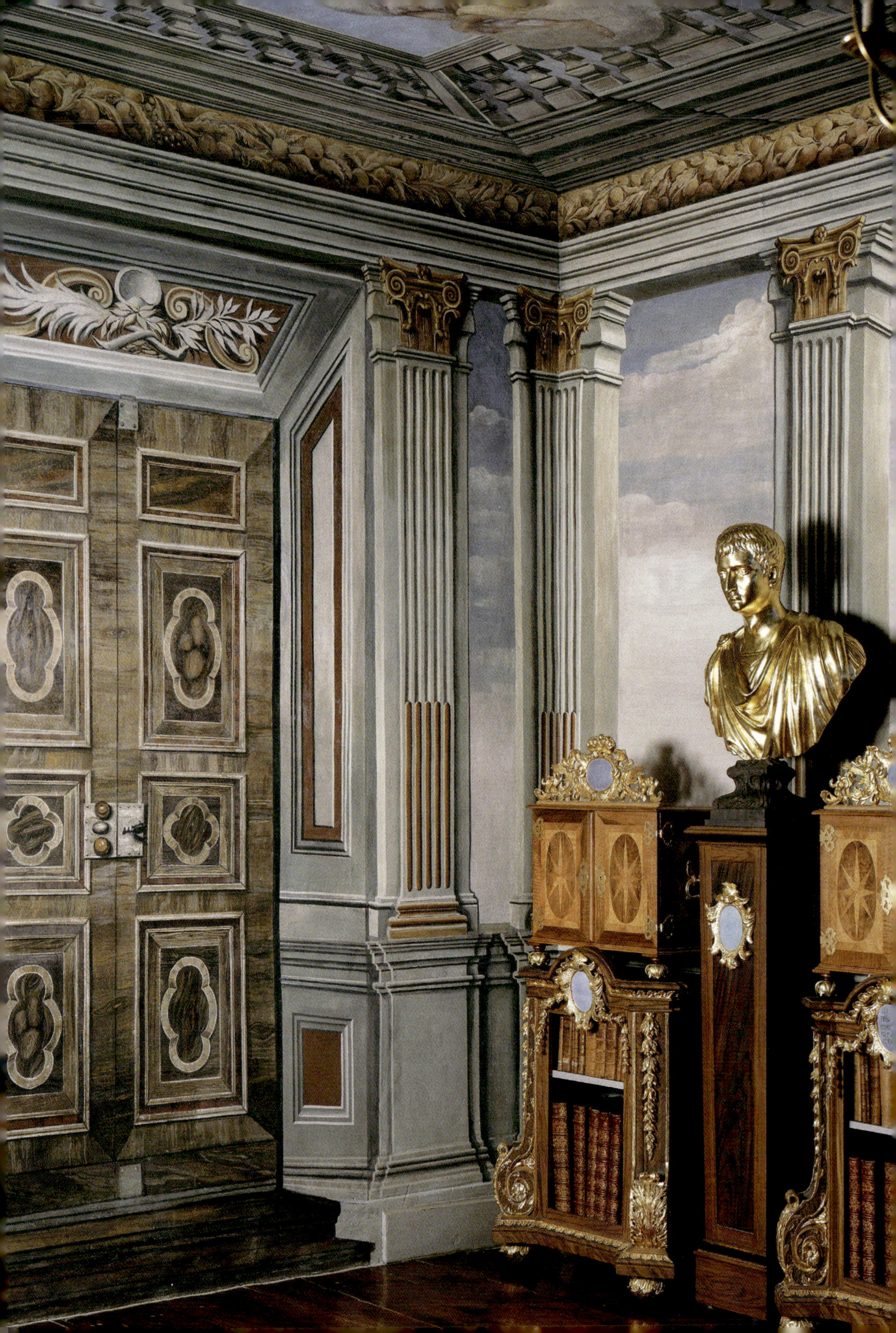

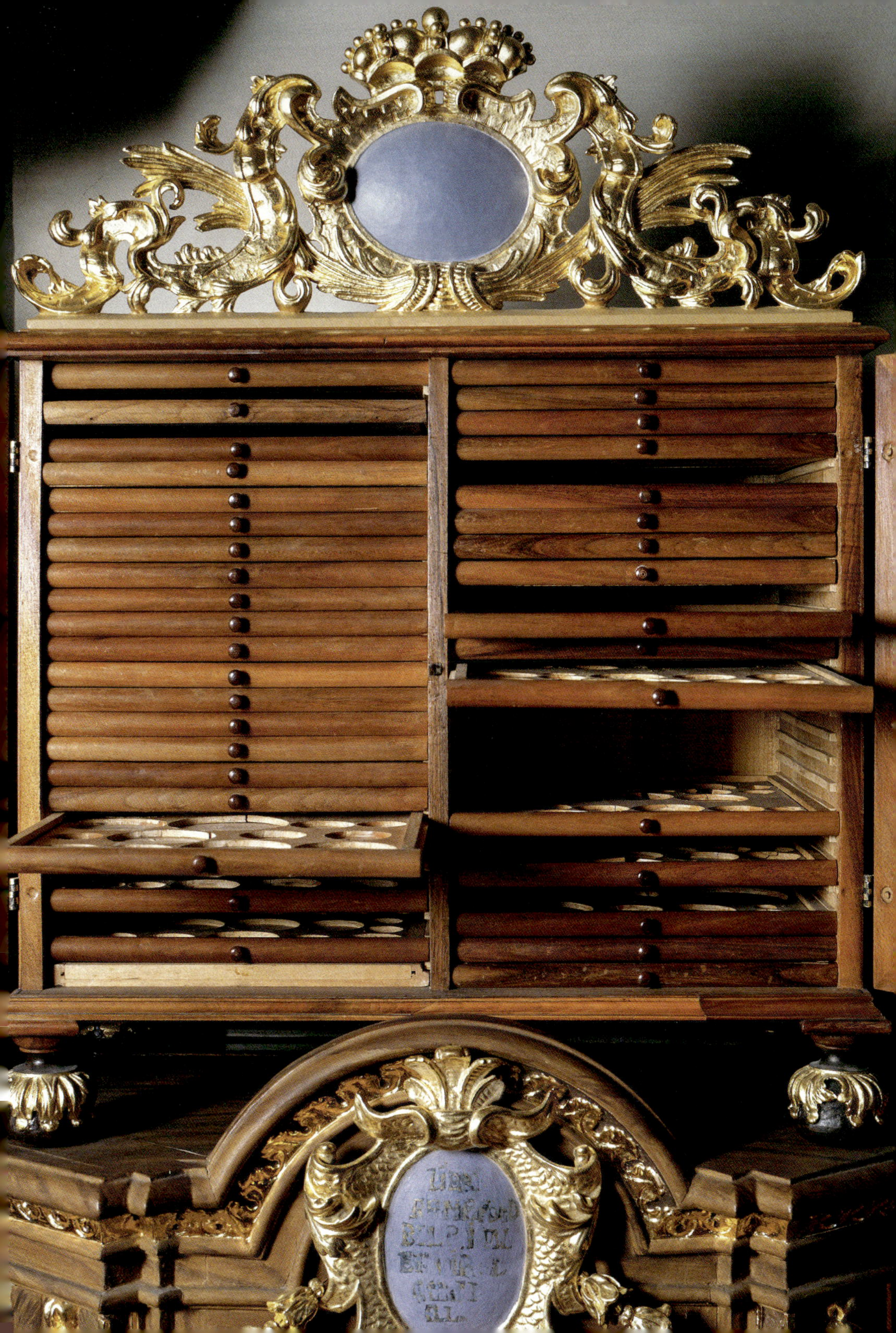

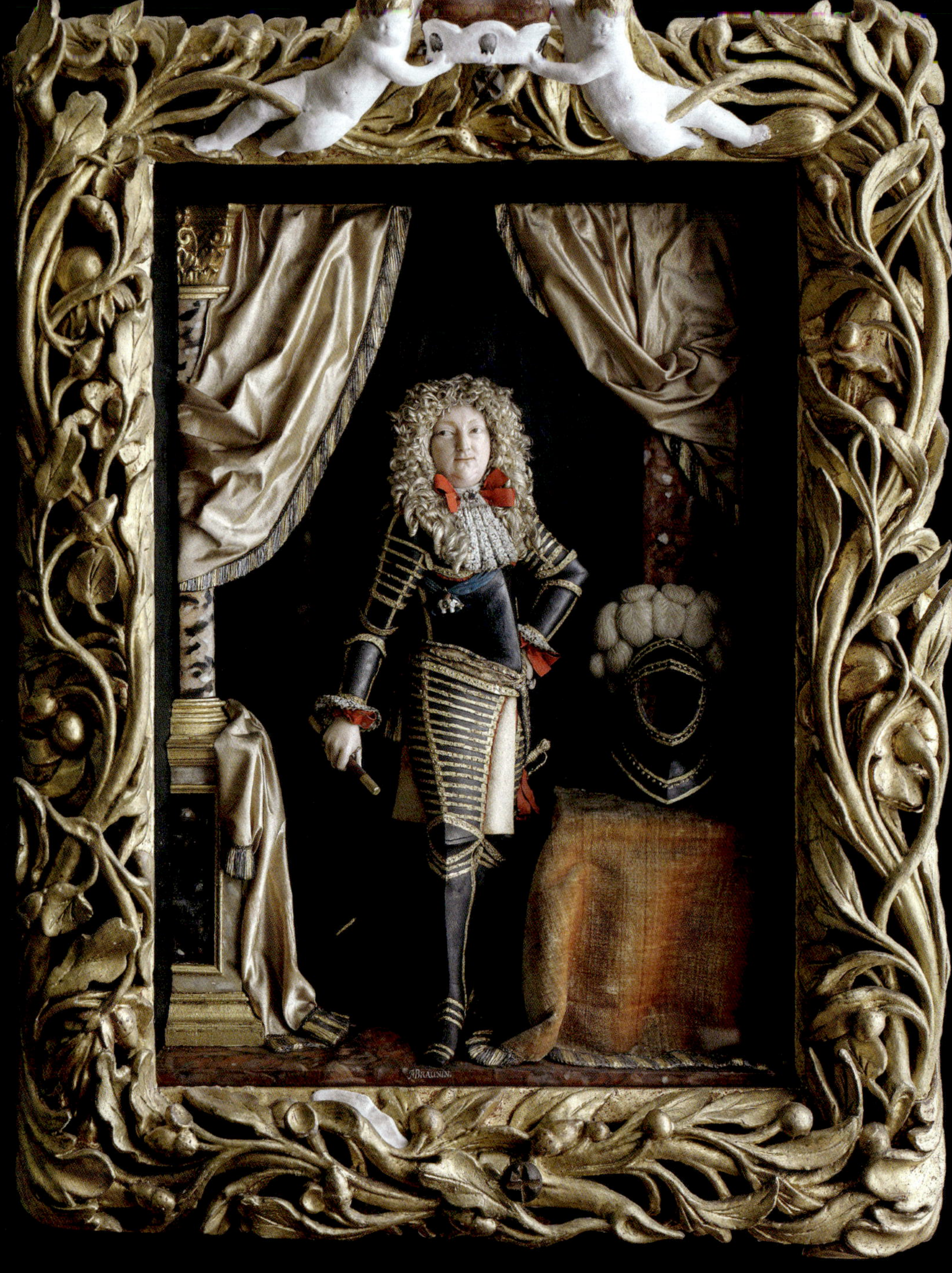
A.BRAUNIN.

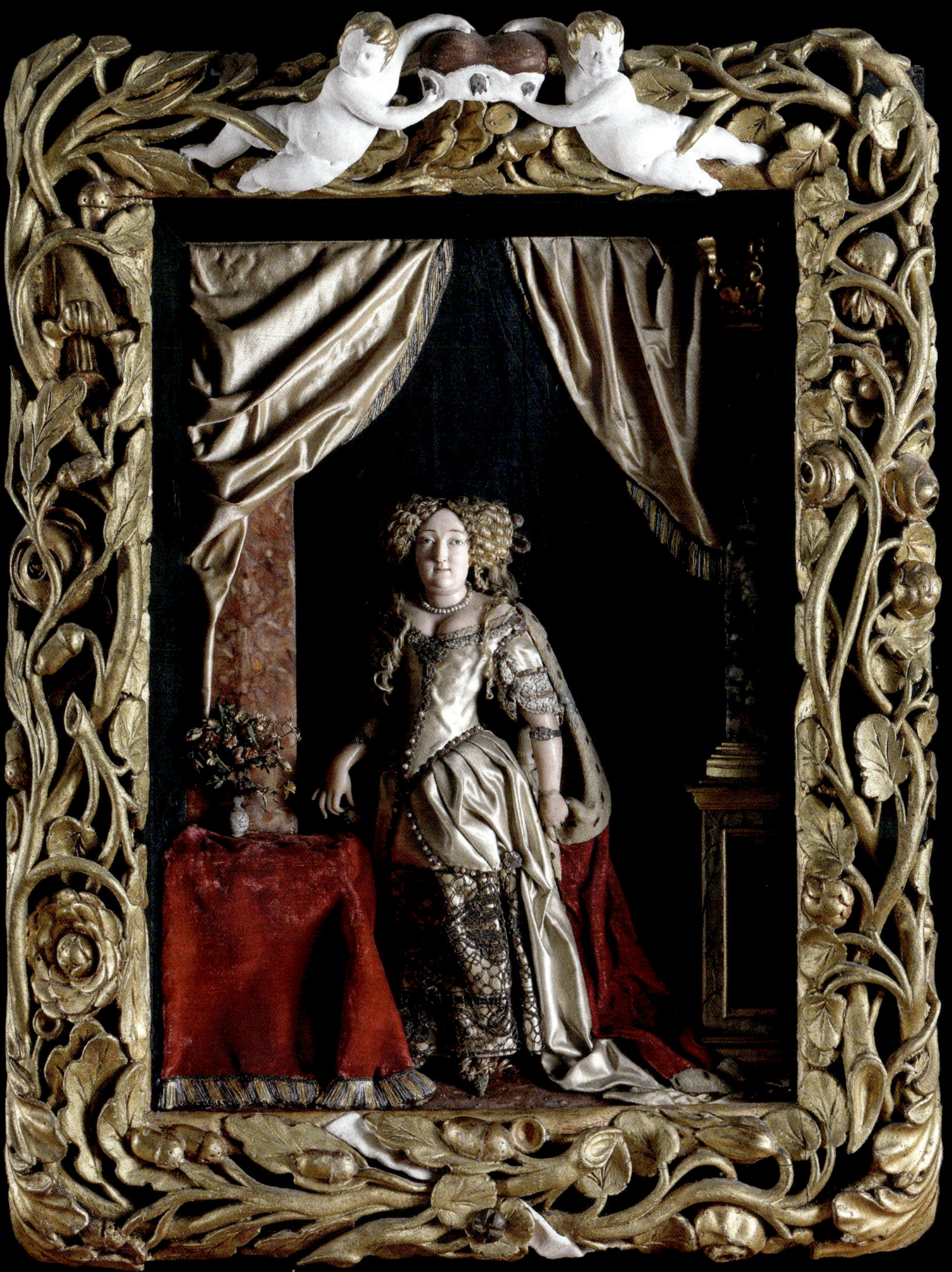

After the Duchy of Saxe-Gotha was founded in 1640 (becoming Saxe-Gotha-Altenburg from 1672), following the division of the paternal states, the new Duke Ernest I, the Pious (1601–1675) chose Gotha as his residential seat. Here, during the turmoil of the Thirty Years' War, he built an imposing castle complex and symbolically named it Friedenstein (Rock of Peace). From 1646 to 1918 the palace was the residence of the dukes of Saxe-Gotha-Altenburg and Saxe-Coburg and Gotha. Over the years new treasures were continually added so that it soon became the most magnificent palace in Thuringia. The Ballroom, Mirror Hall, Lilac Room and Pergola Room are just some of the sumptuously appointed attractions.

The castle contains a number of remarkable and important artefacts, the result of more than 350 years of ducal patronage: paintings, drawings, sculptures and *objets d'art*, coins, medals, rare books and scientific prints, antiques from the Far East, items relating to ancient Egyptian art and culture and various ethnological finds. The numismatic collection was begun by Ernest I, and much enlarged by his grandson Frederick II (1676–1732). The acquisition of the collection of Count Anton Günther II of Schwarzburg-Sondershausen-Arnstadt (1653–1716) in 1712 added over 18,000 pieces (dating from Antiquity to the 18th century), which made the Friedenstein coin collection one of the finest of its kind in Europe. The *trompe-l'œil* frescoes on the ceiling and walls are by Giovanni Francesco Marchini (*c.* 1672–1745), while the larger-than-life gilt-plaster busts of Caesar and the first 11 Roman emperors (from Augustus to Domitian) give the room a sense of gravitas intended to suggest a historical continuity between Imperial Rome and the dukes of Gotha. The busts alternate with purpose-built cabinets, seven on either side of the gallery, which house this priceless collection, while the related numismatic library is kept in the lower open sections underneath.

The Gotha coin collection suffered severe losses after the end of the Second World War, but today, with its 145,000 coins, medals and other numismatic objects, it ranks just behind the important collections in Berlin, Munich and Dresden.

◎ ◈ ◎

Nachdem 1640 aufgrund von Erbteilung das Herzogtum Sachsen-Gotha (ab 1672 mit Altenburg) entstanden war, erwählte sich der neue Herzog Ernst I., der Fromme (1601–1675), Gotha als Residenzstadt. Hier errichtete er noch während des Dreißigjährigen Krieges eine imposante Schlossanlage und gab ihr den symbolträchtigen Namen Friedenstein. Von 1646 bis 1918 war das Schloss die Residenz der Herzöge von Sachsen-Gotha-Altenburg und Sachsen-Coburg und Gotha. Im Laufe der Jahrhunderte kam es zu Modernisierungen, und als besonders eindrückliche Räumlichkeiten sind unter anderem der Festsaal, das Spiegelkabinett, das Flieder- und das Pergolazimmer zu nennen.

Das Schloss beherbergt bedeutende Sammlungen, die in mehr als 350-jähriger Sammeltätigkeit zusammengetragen wurden. Dazu gehören Gemälde, Grafiken, Skulpturen und Kunsthandwerk, Münzen, Medaillen, bibliophile Raritäten und wissenschaftliche

Druckwerke, ostasiatische und altägyptische Kunst neben ethnologischen Exponaten.
Die numismatische Sammlung wurde von Ernst I. begründet und konnte bereits von
seinem Enkel Friedrich II. (1676–1732) erheblich erweitert werden. Allein durch den
Erwerb der Sammlung des Grafen Anton Günther II. von Schwarzburg-Sondershausen
zu Arnstadt (1653–1716) kamen 1712 mehr als 18 000 Sammlungsobjekte von der Antike
bis zum 18. Jahrhundert hinzu, sodass die friedensteinische Münzsammlung mit einem
Schlag zu europäischem Rang aufstieg. Die illusionistische Wand- und Deckenbemalung
im Münzkabinett stammen von Giovanni Francesco Marchini (um 1672–1745), während
die überlebensgroßen vergoldeten Gipsbüsten von Cäsar und der ersten elf römischen
Kaiser, von Augustus bis Domitian, dem Raum einen besonderen feierlichen Ausdruck
verleihen und auf eine direkte Kontinuität bis zu den Gothaer Herzögen anspielen.
Zwischen den Büsten stehen kleine, eigens zu diesem Zweck angefertigte Schränke,
sieben auf jeder Seite, die die Münzen beherbergten und in deren offenem Unterteil
sich die entsprechende numismatische Literatur zu den Objekten befand.

 Herbe Verluste erlitt das Gothaer Münzkabinett infolge der Nachkriegsereignisse
des Zweiten Weltkriegs. Heute reiht es sich bedeutungsmäßig mit seinen ca. 145 000
Münzen, Medaillen und numismatischen Zeugnisse unmittelbar hinter die großen
Kabinette von Berlin, München und Dresden ein.

❂ ❖ ❂

Après la création due à un partage successoral du duché de Saxe-Gotha en 1640 (auquel
se rattacha Altenbourg à partir de 1672), le nouveau duc Ernest Ier dit le Pieux (1601–1675)
choisit Gotha comme ville de résidence. Pendant la guerre de Trente Ans, il y fit aménager
un majestueux château auquel, il donna le nom symbolique de Friedenstein. De 1646 à
1918, le château fut la résidence des ducs de Saxe-Gotha-Altenbourg, de Saxe-Cobourg
et de Gotha. Pendant des siècles des modernisations furent réalisées, et la salle des Fêtes,
le cabinet des Miroirs, la salle des Lilas et celle de la Pergola ne sont que quelques-unes
des magnifiques pièces.

 Le château abrite des collections remarquables par leur intérêt et leur importance,
fruit de 350 ans de collectionnisme de la cour de Gotha : peintures, dessins, sculptures
et œuvres d'art appliqué, monnaies, médailles, trésors de bibliophilie et gravures
scientifiques rares, objets d'Extrême-Orient, documents liés à la culture et à l'art
anciens égyptiens, vestiges archéologiques. La collection numismatique a été fondée
par Ernest Ier et put déjà être considérablement étendue par son petit-fils Frédéric II
(1676–1732). En 1712, avec l'acquisition de la collection du comte Anton Günther II de
Schwarzbourg-Sondershausen-Arnstadt (1653–1716), le Cabinet numismatique s'enrichit
de 18 000 nouvelles monnaies, de l'Antiquité au 18e siècle, de sorte que la collection
de Friedenstein se hissa soudain au rang européen. Les fresques en trompe-l'œil du
plafond et des murs sont l'œuvre de Giovanni Francesco Marchini (vers 1672–1745),
tandis que les bustes en plâtre doré de César et des onze premiers empereurs romains

(de Auguste à Domitien), plus grands que nature, confèrent à la salle un caractère particulier en suggérant une sorte de continuité entre les ducs de Gotha et l'ancienne dignité impériale romaine. Alternant avec les bustes, des cabinets adéquats (sept de chaque côté) abritaient les pièces de monnaie, et leur partie inférieure ouverte contenait la littérature numismatique correspondante sur les objets.

Cependant, la collection numismatique Gotha a subi de lourdes pertes à la suite des événements consécutifs à la Seconde Guerre mondiale. Aujourd'hui, avec ses quelque 145 000 pièces de monnaie, médailles et témoignages numismatiques, elle occupe une place importante juste derrière les grands cabinets de Berlin, Munich et Dresde.

1 Georg Heinz, *Cabinet of Curiosities* (detail), 1666. Oil on canvas, 114.5 x 93.3 cm / 45⅛ x 36¾ in. Georg Heinz, *Kunstkammerschrank* (Detail), 1666. Öl auf Leinwand, 114,5 x 93,3 cm. Georg Heinz, *Le Cabinet des merveilles* (détail), 1666. Huile sur toile, 114,5 x 93,3 cm.

2–5 *Views of the Numismatic Cabinet.* Duke Frederick II commissioned a custom-made cabinet in the eastern wing of the castle to house his coin collection. *Trompe l'œil* paintings decorate the ceiling and walls of the room, while the gilt-plaster busts of Roman emperors, presented larger than life, give the room a particular flavour that suggests a sort of continuity between the dukes of Gotha and the Imperial gravitas of ancient Rome. Between the busts, special cabinets housed the precious collection in drawers at the top, with the numismatic library shelved in the open sections underneath.
Das Münzkabinett. Herzog Friedrich II. beauftragte ein maßgeschneidertes Kabinett für seine Münzsammlung im Ostflügel des Schlosses. Die Trompe-l'Œil-Fresken der Decke und Wände geben dem Raum eine besondere Atmosphäre: Sie suggerieren, dass die altrömische Kaiserwürde in den Herzögen Gothas einen würdigen Nachfolger findet. Büsten wechseln sich mit Spezialschränken für die kostbare Sammlung ab; im darunterliegenden offenen Schrankteil ist die numismatische Bibliothek untergebracht.
Partie du Cabinet numismatique. Le duc Frédéric II a fait réaliser dans l'aile est du château un cabinet sur mesure pour sa collection de pièces de monnaie. Les peintures en trompe-l'œil décorent le plafond et les murs de la salle, tandis que les bustes en plâtre doré des empereurs d'autrefois, plus grands que nature, donnent aux lieux une atmosphère particulière, suggérant une sorte de continuité entre les ducs de Gotha et la gravité impériale de la Rome antique. Entre les bustes, des cabinets adéquats abritaient la précieuse collection ; la partie inférieure ouverte contient la bibliothèque numismatique.

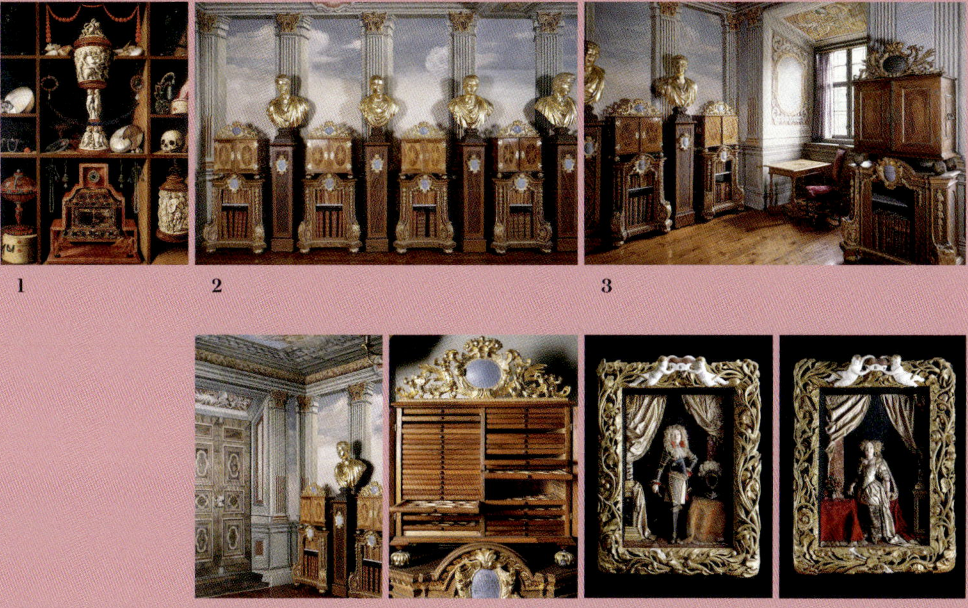

6–7 Anna Maria Braun, *Wax Portraits of Duke Frederick and Duchess Magdalena Sibylle of Saxe-Gotha-Altenburg*. Braun was a renowned wax modeller whose various assignments took her to several courts in different parts of Europe, including London, Vienna and Stockholm, as well as a number of small German capital cities, such as Gotha in around 1700. These figures are partially clothed in fabric and are part of the original core of the cabinet of curiosities collection.
Anna Maria Braun, *Wachsporträts von Herzog Friedrich I. und Herzogin Magdalena Sibylle von Sachsen-Gotha-Altenburg*. Braun war eine namhafte Wachsmodelliererin, die für verschiedene europäische Höfe arbeitete, darunter London, Wien und Stockholm, sowie für kleinere deutsche Residenzstädte wie für Gotha um 1700. Diese Figuren tragen teilweise Originalkleidung und gehören zum ursprünglichen Kernbestand der Kunstkammer-sammlung.
Anna Maria Braun, *Portraits en cire du duc Frédéric Ier de Saxe-Gotha-Altenbourg et de son épouse Madeleine Sibylle*. Anna Maria Braun était une modeleuse de cire réputée. Ses missions l'amenèrent dans de nombreuses cours européennes telles que Londres, Vienne, Stockholm, et dans plusieurs petites villes allemandes comme Gotha, vers 1700. Ces figurines sont en partie revêtues de tissu et font partie du noyau original de la collection de la Kunstkammer.

Kunst- und Naturalienkammer

Franckesche Stiftungen, Halle

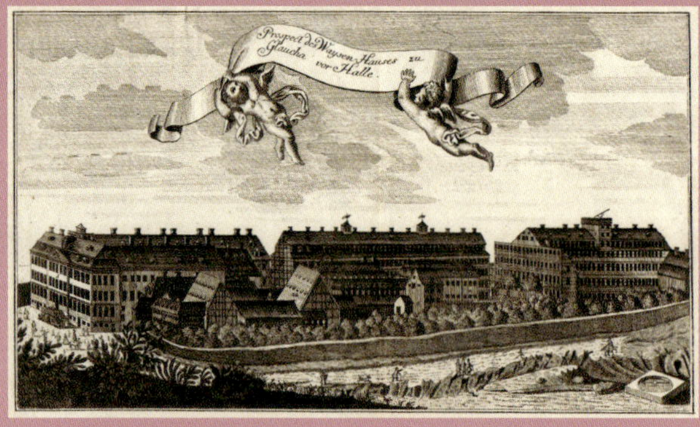

Founded 1698 (foundation of the schools)

Key item The huge planetary system with the Earth positioned at the centre of the universe, illustrating the theory of the Danish astronomer Tycho Brahe (1546–1601).

Besonders sehenswert Ein riesiges Modell des Planetensystems nach der Theorie des dänischen Astronomen Tycho Brahe (1546–1601) mit der Erde im Mittelpunkt des Universums.

À voir absolument Le gigantesque système planétaire avec la Terre au centre de l'univers réalisé pour illustrer la théorie de de l'astronome danois Tycho Brahe (1546–1601).

Gottfried August Gründler, *The Francke Foundations in Halle*, 1749

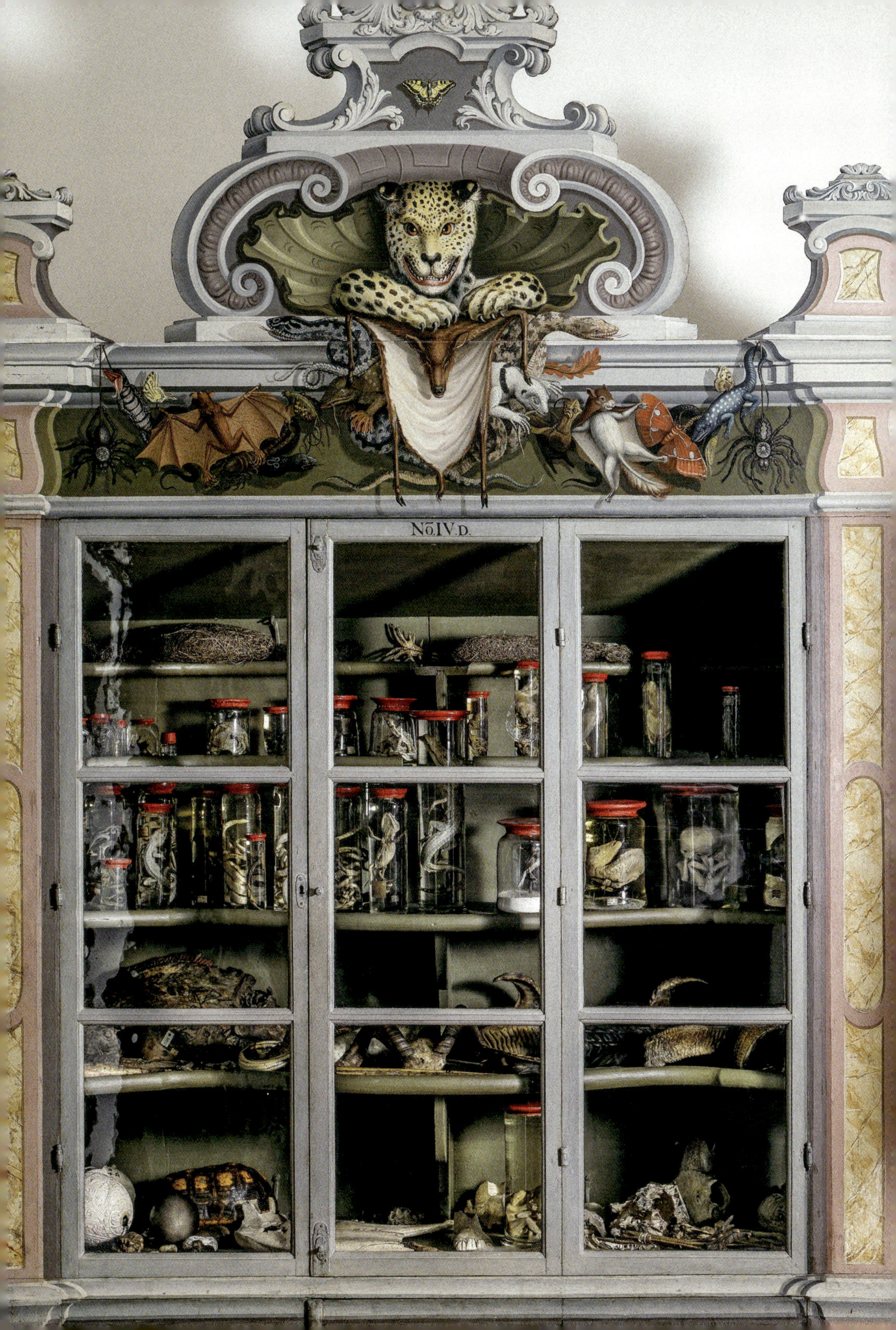

No. IV. D.

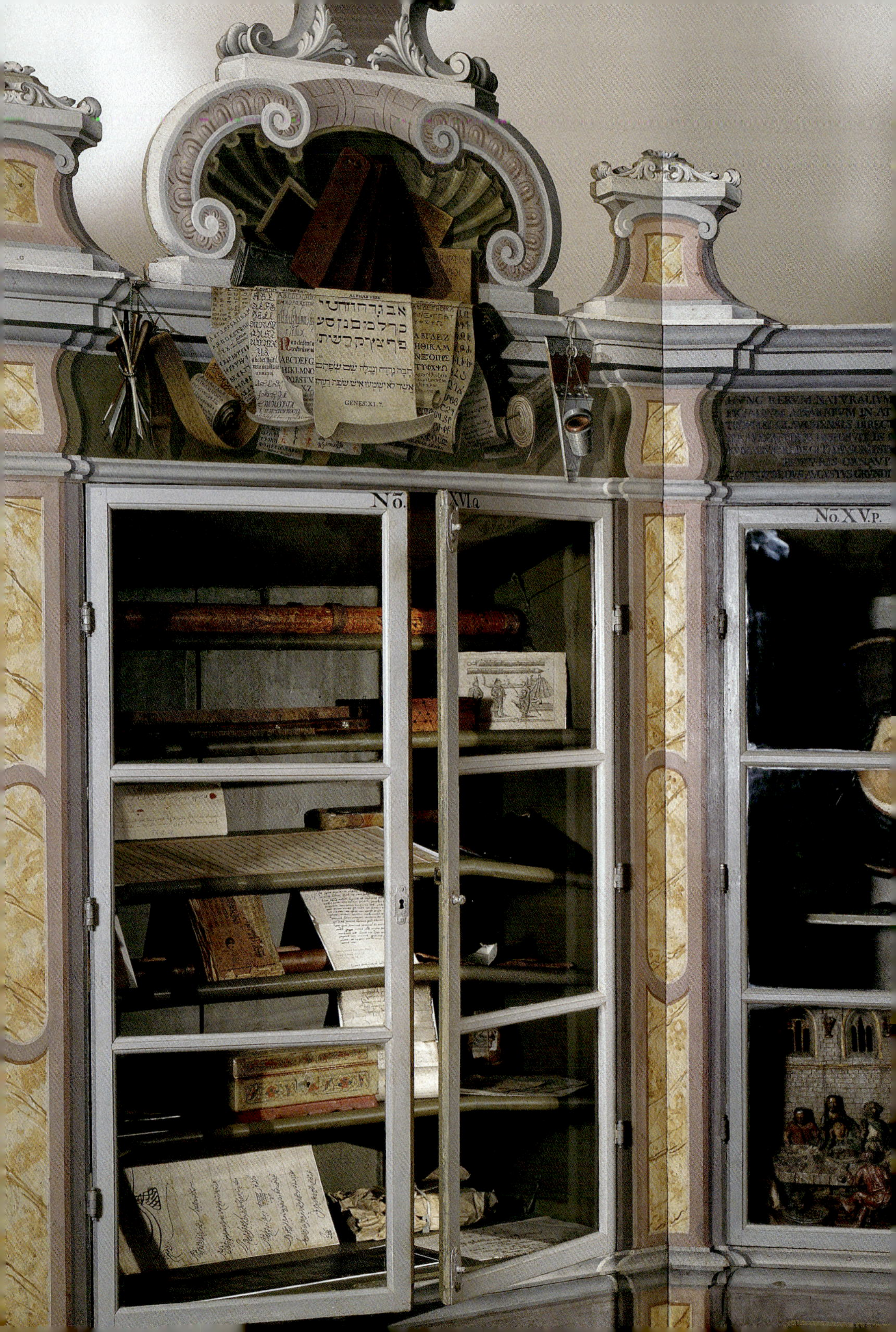

No. XVIa
No. XVp
GENES XI. 7

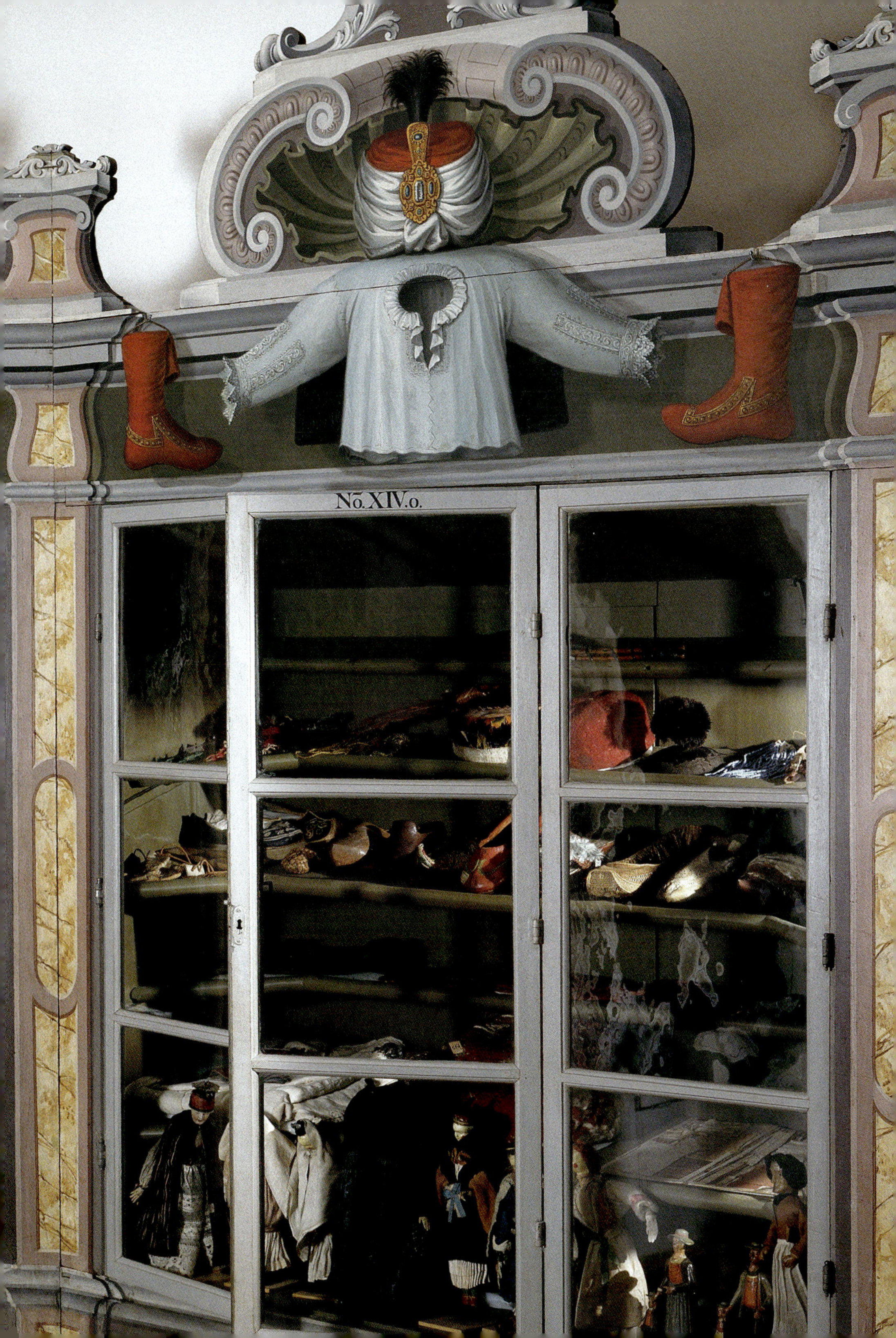
No. XIV.o

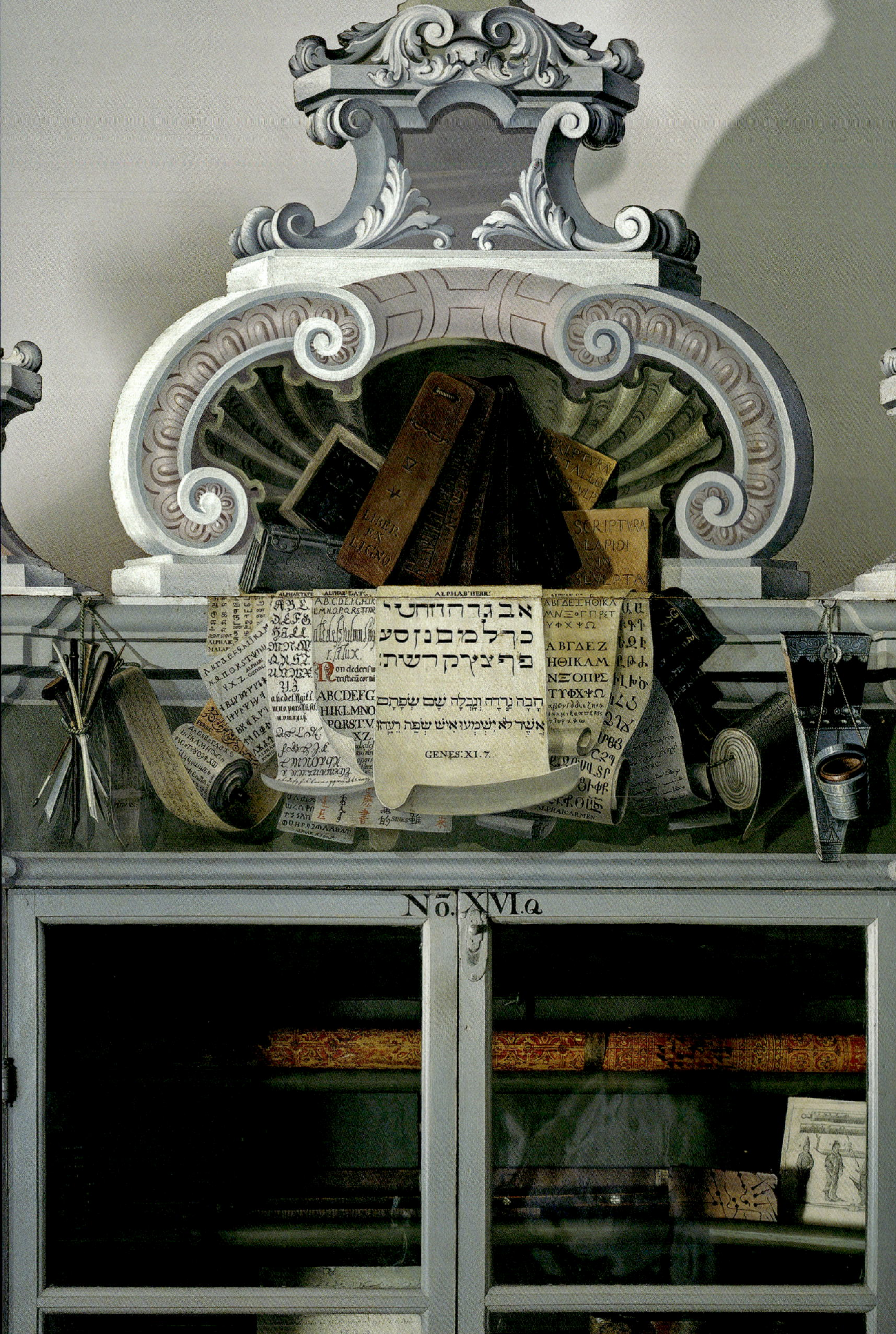
LIBER EX LIGNO
SCRIPTURA IN METALLO
SCRIPTURA LAPIDI INSCULPTA
ALPHAB. HEBR.
GENES: XI. 7.
Nō. XVI.a

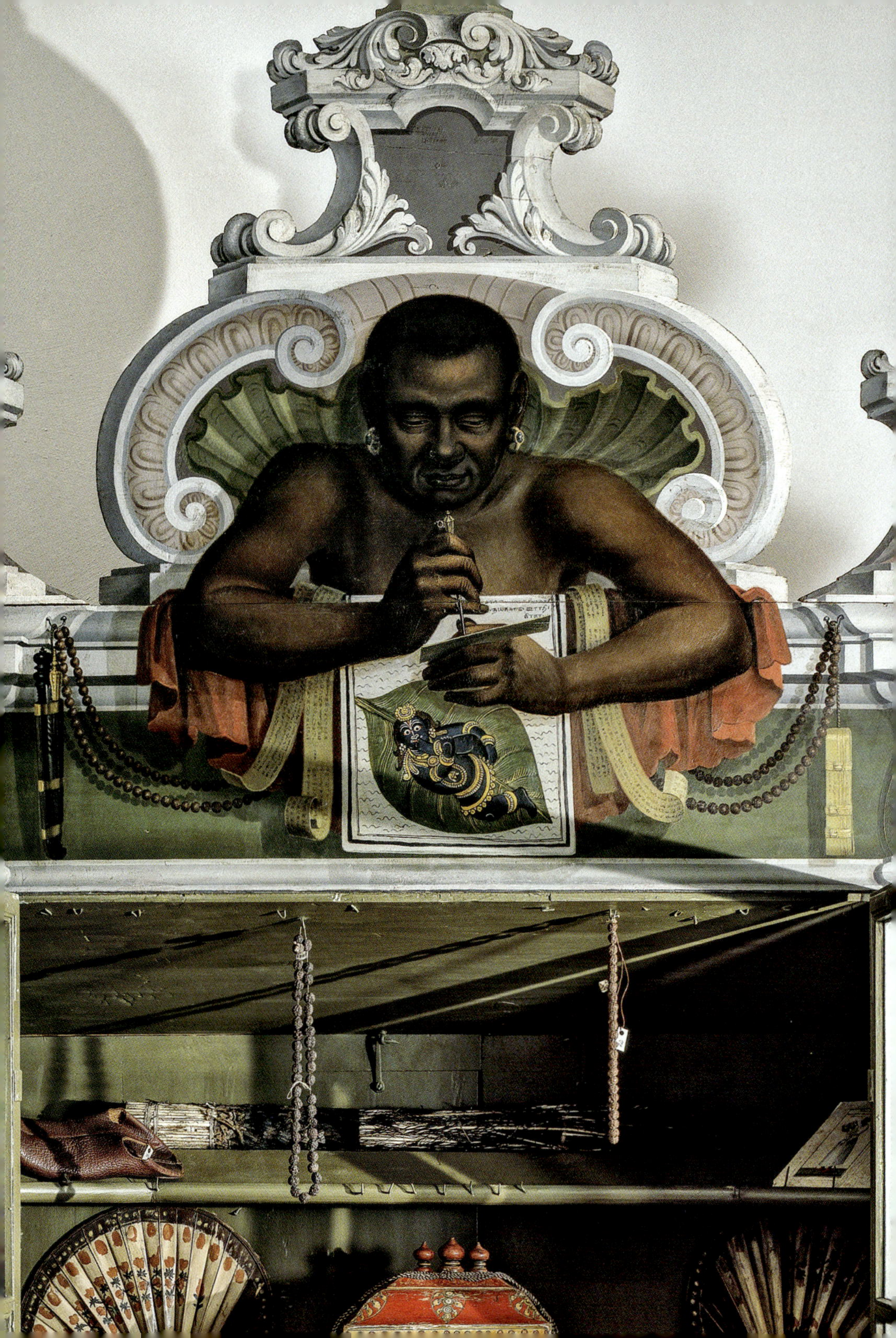

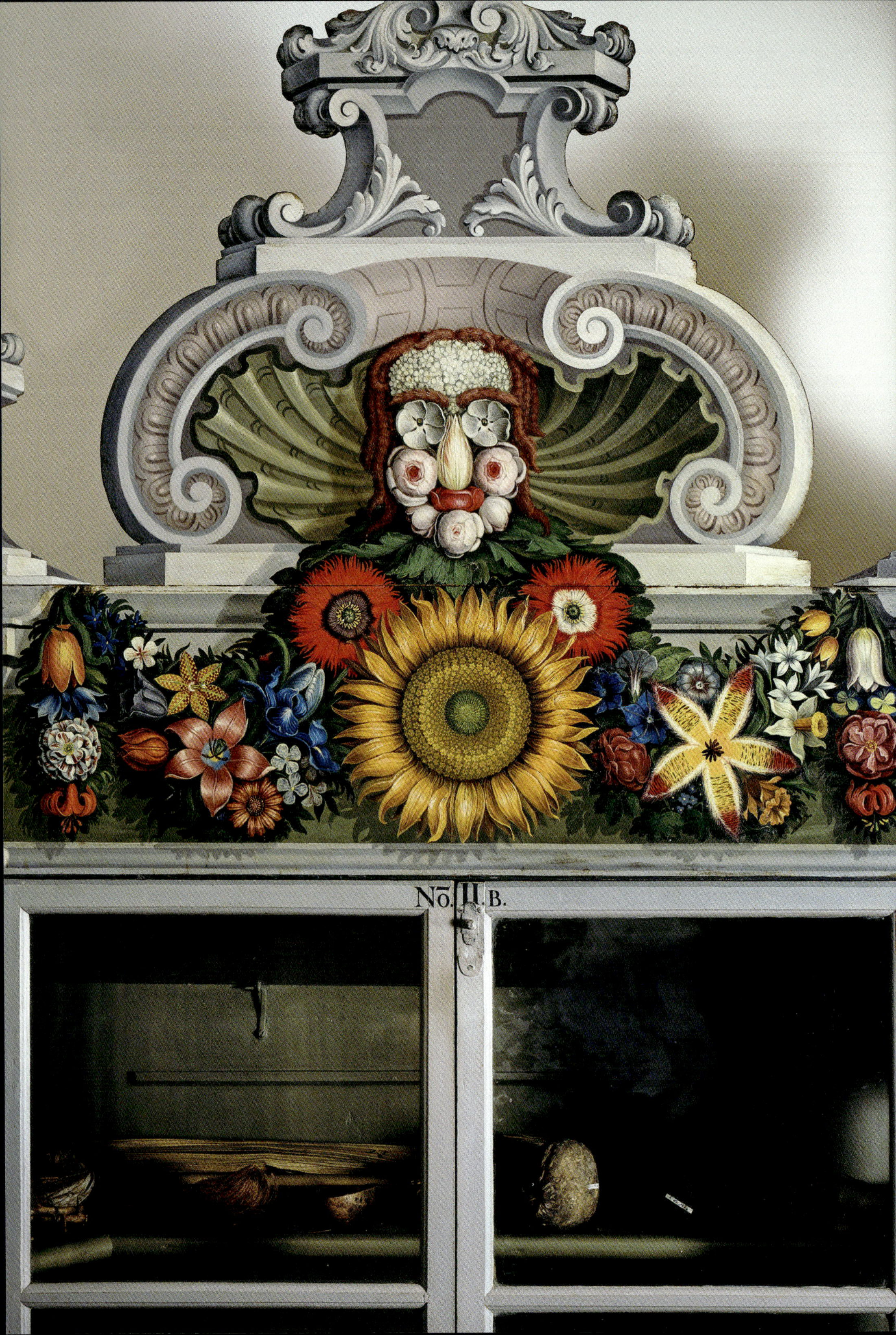
Nō. II.B.

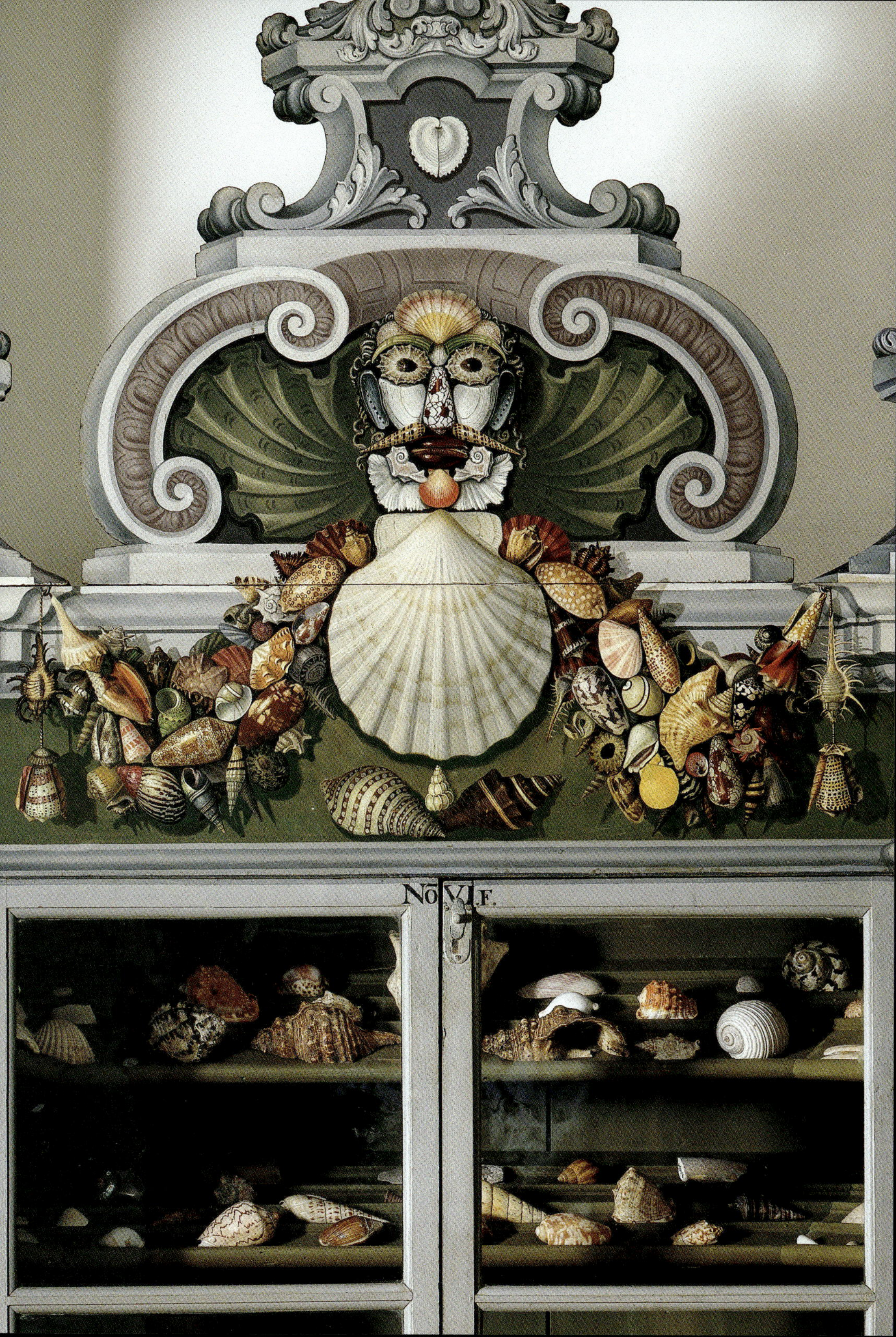
Nº VI.F.

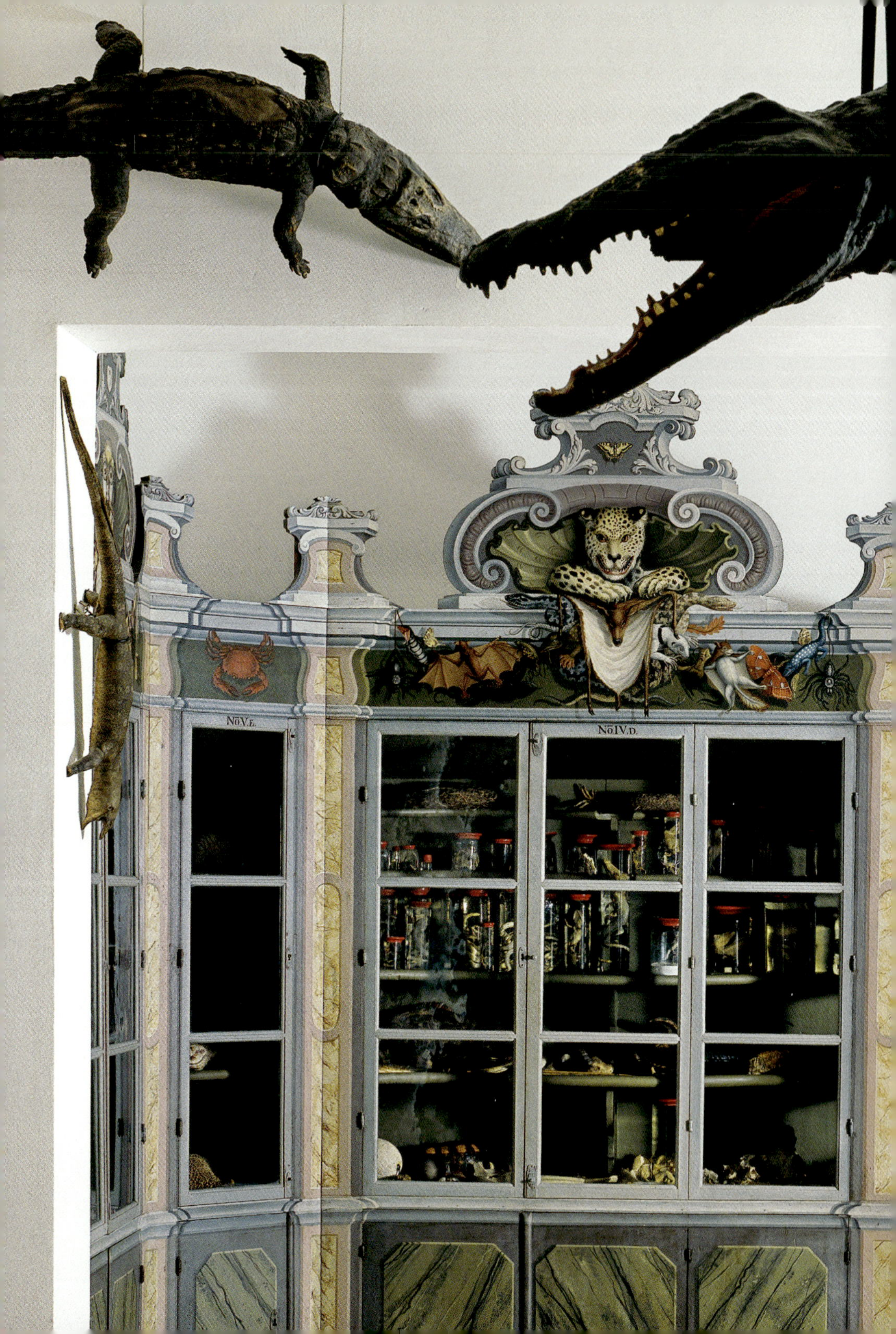

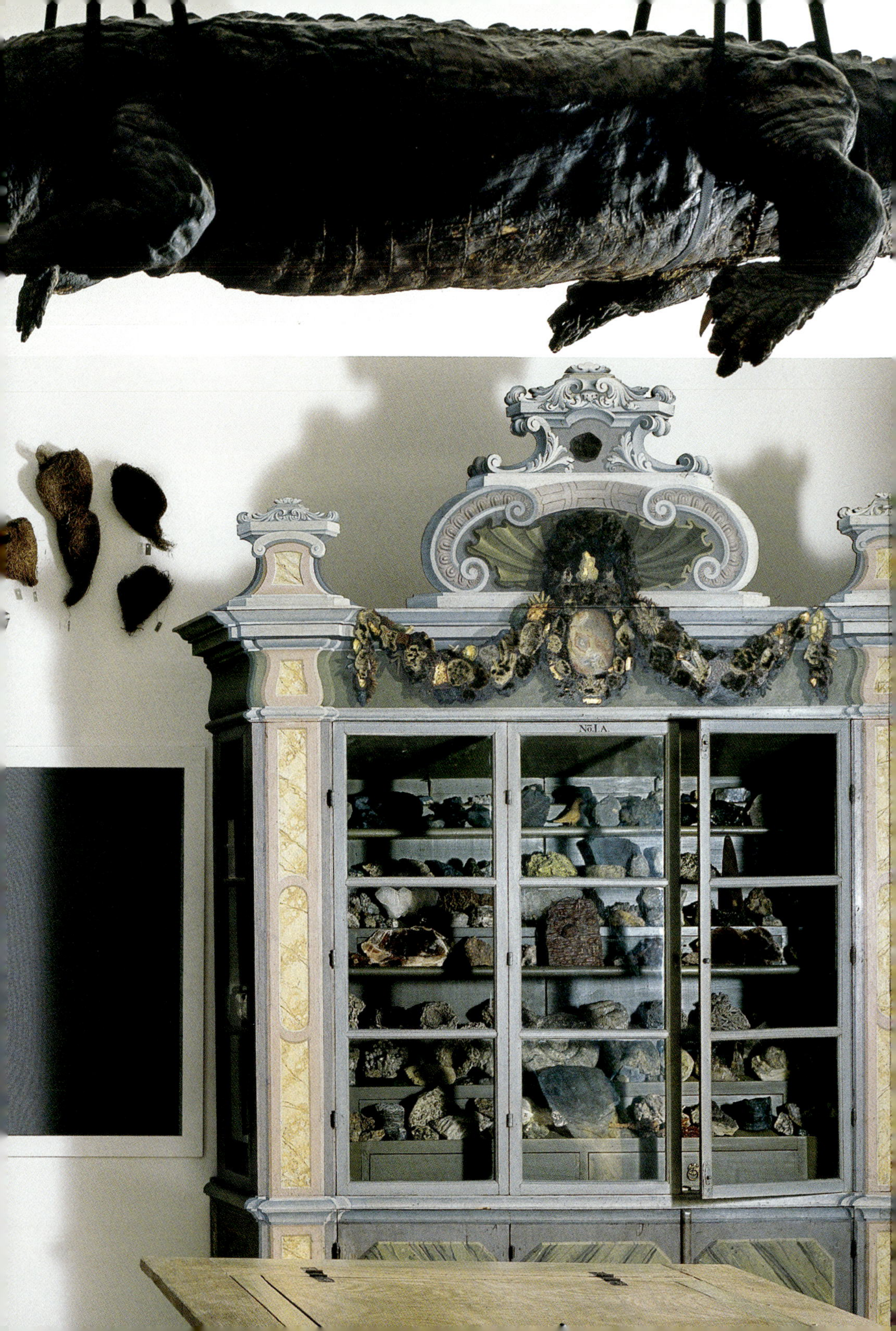

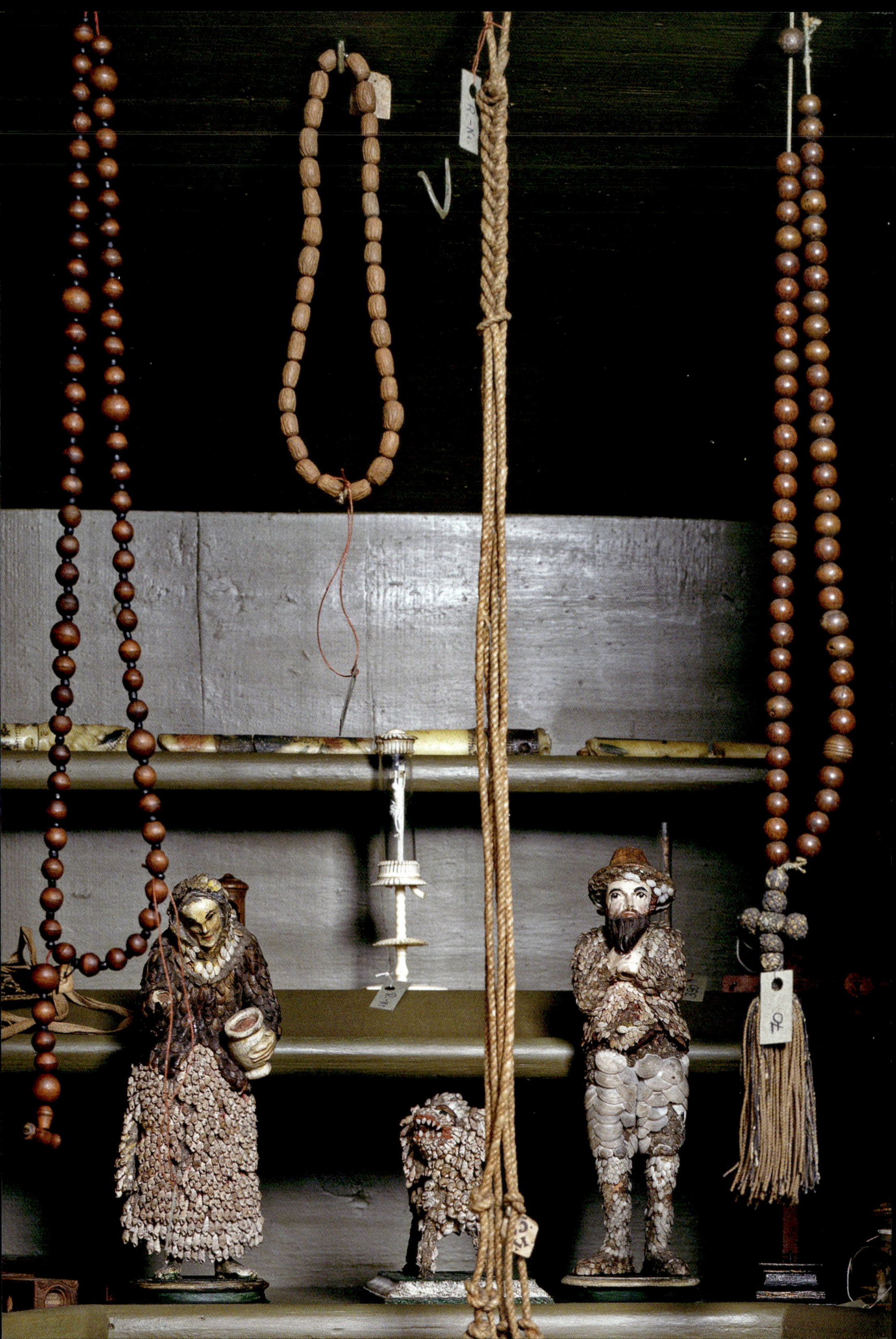

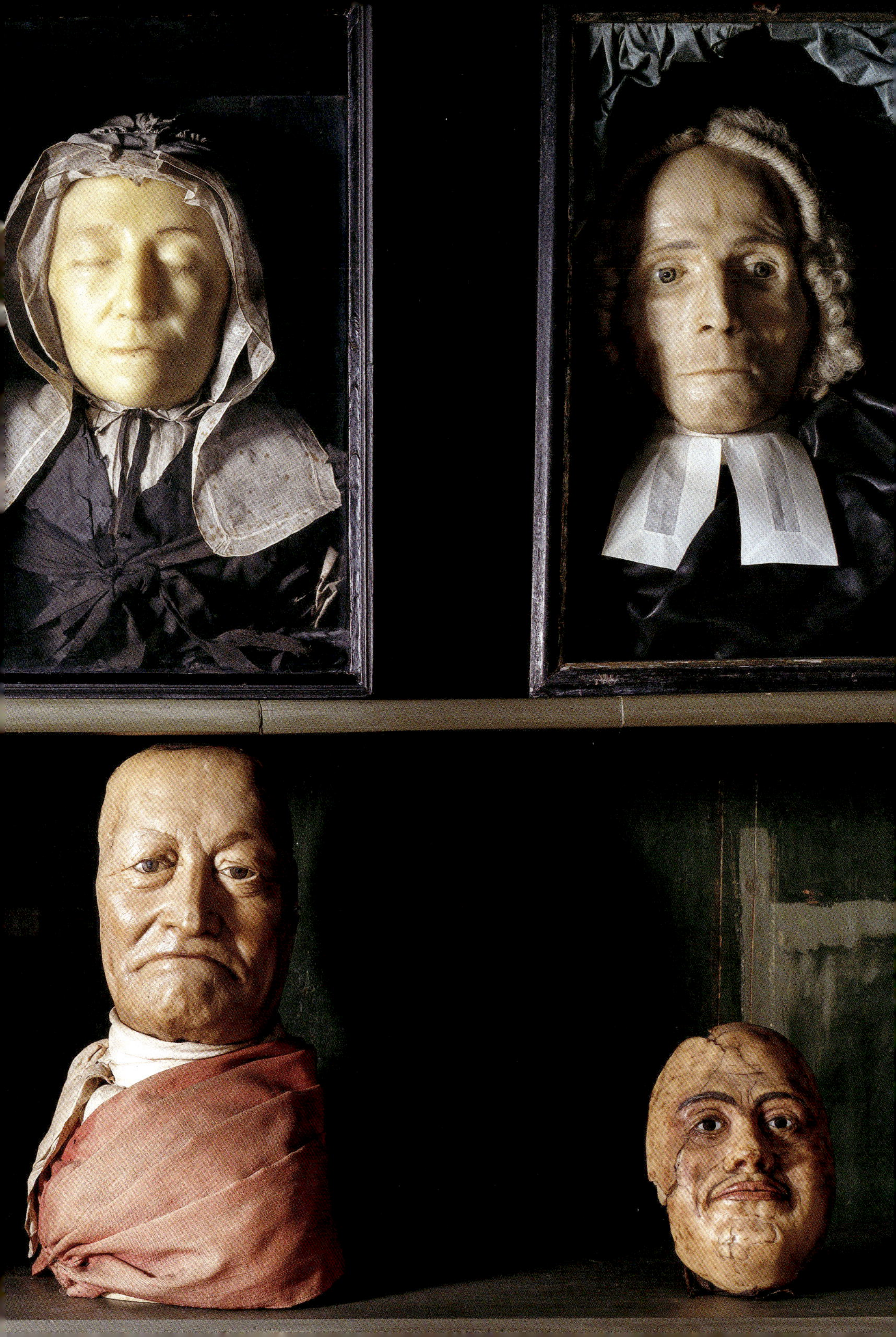

When the Lutheran theologian and educator August Hermann Francke (1663–1727) first arrived at Halle University as a professor and pastor in 1691, he was struck by the social neglect in the community and by the large number of children who were illiterate, rejected by society and reduced to a life in poverty. In 1698 he thus proceeded to found a series of schools which are still known today as the Franckesche Stiftungen (Francke Foundations).

With the support of the elector Frederick III of Brandenburg (1657–1713), Francke began his mission by building an orphanage, where he installed his collection of artworks and curiosities with a clear educational intent, in keeping with the pietistic spirit that characterised the rest of his work. Over time new pieces were added to the collection, whether simply for display or to be used during lessons, until in 1734 it was decided to catalogue them and arrange them in cabinets especially designed by the painter, engraver and naturalist Gottfried August Gründler (1710–1775). Gründler had been one of the sponsors of the first German edition of the *Systema naturae* by Carl Linnaeus (1707–1778), and in 1741 he reorganised the 4,696 objects in Francke's collection according to an encyclopaedic system, whereby the *naturalia* were distinguished from the *artificialia*. This symmetrical arrangement of the collection was believed to be inherent in nature, reflecting the harmonious unity of the world, a microcosm whose purpose was to reflect the miraculous macrocosm of God's creation. Different categories were represented in individual cabinets, each of which was carefully designed and decorated on the top with friezes illustrating its contents. The *naturalia* included rocks, minerals and fossils, plants, shells and specimens from the animal kingdom; the *artificialia* consisted of mathematical instruments, coins and wax masks, oil paintings, mechanical models, sacred objects from religions outside Christianity, clothes, manuscripts and a number of objects related to the art of writing. The collection was expanded in the 18th century, in part through gifts presented by pietist followers, many of whom had travelled around the world working as missionaries. From America came articles of clothing from some of the indigenous peoples and seeds of local plants, from Russia came a large number of curiosities and ethnographic items, while an entire cabinet was devoted to pieces from the flourishing mission to southern India.

During the 19th century the collection fell into neglect, but in 1909 it was rediscovered. Following an impressive campaign of restoration the collection has now been returned to its original splendour.

◎ ◈ ◎

Als der protestantische Theologe und Pädagoge August Hermann Francke (1663–1727) 1691 als Universitätsprofessor und Pfarrer nach Halle kam, war er entsetzt über die soziale Verwahrlosung in seiner Gemeinde, vor allem der vielen Kinder, die keinerlei Bildung genossen, weder lesen noch schreiben konnten und deren einziges Los es zu sein schien, ihr Leben in Armut zu fristen. Deshalb gründete er 1698 die Bildungseinrichtungen, die noch heute unter dem Namen Franckesche Stiftungen bekannt sind.

Mit Unterstützung des brandenburgischen Kurfürsten Friedrich III. (1657–1713) errichtete er zunächst ein Waisenhaus, in dem auch seine Kunst- und Kuriositätensammlung Platz fand, die er ganz im Geiste seiner pietistischen Gesinnung zu didaktischen Zwecken einsetzte. In der Folge wurde die Sammlung laufend ergänzt und im Unterricht genutzt. 1734 entschloss man sich dann, die Bestände zu katalogisieren und in eigens dafür hergestellten Schauschränken auszustellen, die von dem Altenburger Maler, Kupferstecher und Naturkundler Gottfried August Gründler (1710–1775) angefertigt wurden. 1741 katalogisierte Gründler, der auch die erste deutsche Ausgabe von Carl von Linnés (1707–1778) *Systema naturae* mitfinanziert hatte, die aus 4696 Stücken bestehenden Bestände und unterteilte sie enzyklopädisch in *Naturalia* und *Artificialia*. Dabei galt die symmetrische Anordnung als Abbild der Natur: Sie spiegelte die harmonische Einheit der Welt als Mikrokosmos, der den Makrokosmos als wunderbare Schöpfung Gottes fassbar machen sollte. Jeder Schrank stand für eine Kategorie, wurde sorgfältig bestückt und oben mit einem bemalten Fries versehen, der den Inhalt beschrieb. Zu den *Naturalia* gehörten Steine, Mineralien, Fossilien, Pflanzen, Muscheln und Objekte aus dem Tierreich, während die *Artificialia* mathematische Instrumente, Münzen, Wachsmasken, Ölgemälde, mechanische Modelle, Kultobjekte fremder Religionen, Kleidungsstücke, Manuskripte und Schreibutensilien umfassten. Im 18. Jahrhundert wurde die Sammlung durch Spenden aus aller Welt bereichert, oft von pietistischen Gefolgsleuten, die als Missionare weit gereist waren. Dazu gehörten indianische Objekte und Samen aus Amerika, Kuriositäten und volkskundliche Stücke aus Russland und ein ganzer Schrank mit Stücken aus der florierenden Mission Südindien.

Im 19. Jahrhundert geriet die Sammlung in Vergessenheit und wurde erst 1909 wiederentdeckt. Dank einer umfassenden Restaurierung erstrahlt sie heute in ihrem alten Glanz.

❀ ❖ ❀

En 1691, lors de son arrivée à l'université de Halle en qualité de professeur d'université et pasteur, le pédagogue et théologien luthérien August Hermann Francke (1663–1727) fut profondément affecté par l'état de déliquescence sociale qui régnait dans sa paroisse et par le nombre élevé d'enfants analphabètes dont le seul sort semblait être de devoir vivre dans la misère. Aussi décida-t-il en 1698 de fonder les écoles qui, aujourd'hui encore, sont connues comme Franckesche Stiftungen (Fondations Francke).

Grâce au soutien de l'électeur Frédéric III de Brandebourg (1657–1713), Francke lança la construction d'un orphelinat qui accueillit sa collection personnelle d'objets d'art et de curiosités dont le but ouvertement pédagogique était en accord avec le piétisme qui caractérisait son action. Pendant longtemps, les pièces qui rejoignaient la collection étaient simplement exposées ou utilisées durant les cours ; puis, en 1734, il fut décidé de les répertorier et de les présenter dans des vitrines dessinées par Gottfried August Gründler (1710–1775), peintre, graveur et naturaliste. Ce dernier, qui avait contribué à

financer la première édition allemande du *Systema naturae* de Carl von Linné (1707–1778),
réorganisa en 1741 les 4696 objets de la collection selon un principe encyclopédique
établissant une distinction entre *naturalia* et *artificialia*. La symétrie qui présidait à
l'organisation de la collection était considérée comme inhérente à la nature : elle reflétait
l'harmonieuse unité du monde, microcosme qui avait pour but de rendre tangible le
macrocosme comme miraculeuse création de Dieu. À chacune des armoires, exécutées
avec soin et ornées dans leur partie supérieure de frises peintes indiquant leur contenu,
correspond une catégorie d'objets. Parmi les *naturalia* se trouvent des pierres, des
minéraux et des fossiles, des plantes, des coquillages et des objets appartenant au règne
animal, tandis que parmi les *artificialia* figurent des instruments mathématiques, des
monnaies et des masques en cire, des peintures à l'huile, des maquettes mécaniques,
des objets de cultes non chrétiens, des vêtements, des manuscrits et des instruments
d'écriture. La collection s'enrichit au 18ᵉ siècle en partie grâce à des donations d'adeptes
piétistes, dont beaucoup avaient voyagé à travers le monde comme missionnaires.
D'Amérique vinrent des graines et des objets confectionnés par les natifs, de Russie des
curiosités et des objets ethnographiques, d'Inde du Sud toute une armoire de pièces
envoyées par les florissantes missions de cette région du monde.

Négligée au 19ᵉ siècle, la collection ne fut redécouverte qu'en 1909. Aujourd'hui, d'importants travaux de restauration lui ont restitué sa splendeur d'origine.

1 *Animal Kingdom.* The three-door cabinet IV.D., seemingly the main focus of the collection, contains items from the animal kingdom. A number of specimen jars can be seen with their contents, including human foetuses, in preserving fluid. One of the strangest items in the collection is a tattooed fish. A decorated ostrich egg, on the lower left side, is worthy of particular attention, and the dark-coloured egg of a cassowary beside it is one of the gifts that August Hermann Francke received from the electoral collection in 1698.
Tierreich. Der dreiflügelige Schrank IV.D. für das Tierreich ist das auffälligste Möbel im Saal und das Herzstück des Kabinetts. In ihm sind etliche Flüssigpräparate zu sehen , darunter auch menschliche Föten. Zu den merkwürdigsten Sammlungsstücken gehört ein tätowierter Fisch.

Besondere Aufmerksamkeit verdient das verzierte Straußenei unten links. Das dunklere Kasuarenei daneben ist eines der Geschenke, die August Hermann Francke 1698 aus der kurfürstlichen Kammer erhielt.
Le Règne animal. Le cabinet à trois vantaux IV.D. dédié au règne animal est certainement le meuble le plus remarquable de la salle et semble être le cœur de l'ensemble du Cabinet. On y voit plusieurs verres contenant des spécimens conservés en milieu liquide, notamment des fœtus humains. Parmi les pièces les plus extravagantes, on trouve un poisson tatoué. L'œuf d'autruche décoré, en bas à gauche, mérite une attention particulière. L'œuf de casoar voisin à la coquille foncée est l'un des cadeaux qu'August Hermann Francke reçut des collections du prince-électeur en 1698.

2 *Manuscripts and Writing Instruments, The Fine Arts* and *Clothing.* On the left, the two-door cabinet XVI.Q. is devoted to the art of writing, while all the collection's pictures are housed in the single-door cabinet XV.P. seen here in the centre, with the relief portrait of Martin Luther and the wooden relief depicting the Last Supper. The cabinet XIV.O. on the right contains only the collection's articles of clothing, while the painting on its pediment, topped by the magnificent turban, denotes the rare garments and fabrics which arrived here from all parts of the world.
Schriften und Schreibwerkzeuge und *Bildende Künste* und *Kleidung.* Der linke, zweiflügelige Schrank XVI.Q. widmet sich der Schreibkunst. In dem einflügeligen Schrank XV.P. sind bildliche Darstellungen eingeordnet. Besonders ins Auge fallen das Reliefporträt Martin

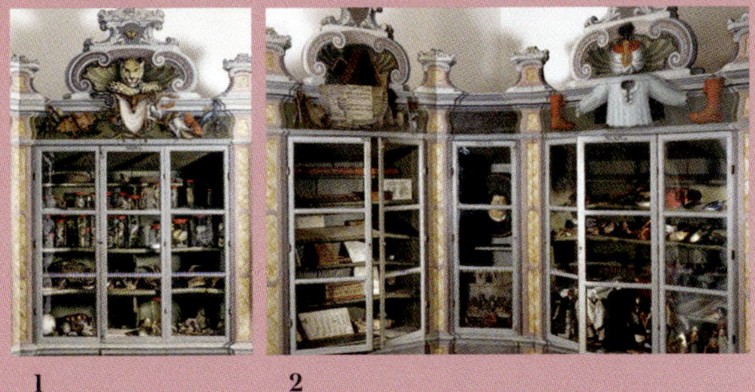

1   2

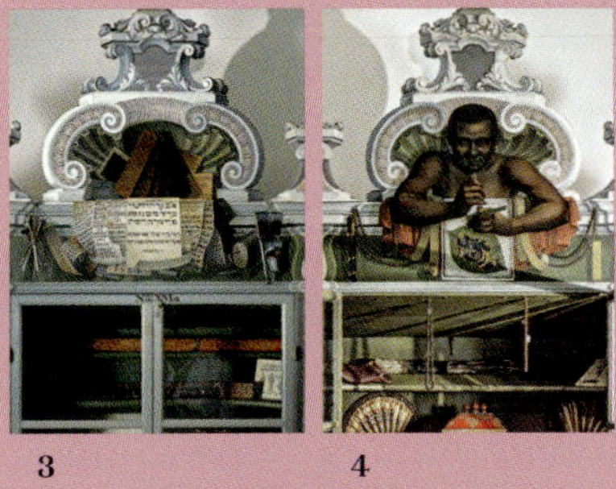

3   4

Luthers und das Holzrelief mit der Darstellung des Heiligen Abendmahls. Im Schrank XIV.O. sind Kleidungsstücke untergebracht. Die Bekrönungsmalerei mit dem prunkvollen Turban weist auf seltene Stoffe und Gewänder hin, die im Waisenhaus aus aller Welt eintrafen.
Manuscrits et instruments d'écriture et *Les beaux-arts* et *l'habillement*. À gauche, le cabinet à deux vantaux XVI.Q. est consacré à l'art de l'écriture. Toutes les images du Cabinet ont été placées dans le cabinet à un vantail XV.P. : le portrait en relief de Martin Luther et le relief en bois représentant la Cène attirent particulièrement l'attention. Seuls les vêtements sont conservés dans le cabinet XIV.O. La peinture du fronton, avec le magnifique turban au centre, montre les matériaux et vêtements rares qui sont arrivés de toutes les régions de la Terre.

3 *Manuscripts and Writing Instruments.* A closer view of the painting on the pediment reveals a whole kaleidoscope of images. At the top is a calendar with writing in runes on wooden leaves, supported on either side by other examples of materials used for writing. Beneath these are several pages showing specimens of 25 different scripts, as if they are hanging over the edge of the balustrade, while the different writing instruments on either side are shown hanging from their painted strings.
Schriften und Schreibwerkzeuge. Die Bekrönungsbemalung bietet bei genauem Hinsehen ein regelrechtes Bildprogramm: zentral sind ein Runenkalender und verschiedene Schreibmaterialien abgebildet. Darunter sieht man etwa 25 Schriftstücke, die scheinbar lose über die Brüstung hängen. Jeweils seitlich sind unterschiedliche Schreibgeräte dargestellt,

die gebündelt an einer Schnur zu baumeln scheinen.
Manuscrits et instruments d'écriture. Si on y regarde de plus près, le décor peint du fronton offre un véritable kaléidoscope d'images. Un calendrier runique et divers instruments d'écriture sont représentés au centre. En dessous, on voit environ 25 échantillons d'écriture différents, qui semblent pendre au-dessus de la balustrade. Enfin, différents instruments d'écriture sont visibles, pendant aux extrémités d'un cordon imaginaire.

4 *Danish-Halle Mission in India.* The two-door cabinet XI.L. is reserved for the collection's pieces that have come from India. The painting on this pediment shows a Tamil man concentrating while he paints the design on a palm leaf.
Dänisch-Hallesche Mission in Indien. Dieser zweiflügelige Schrank XI.L. ist Sammlungsgegenständen aus

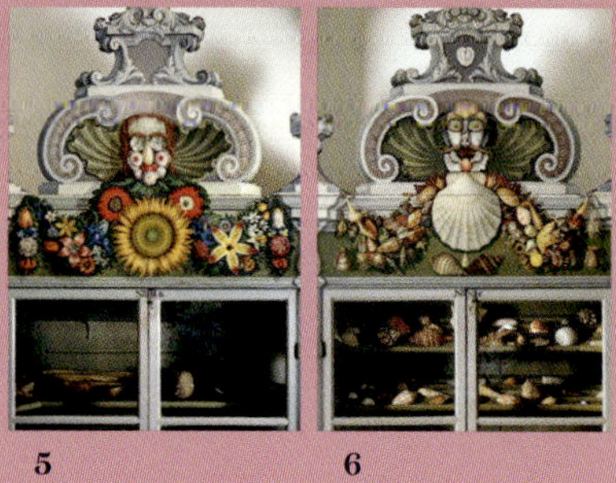

5   6

Indien vorbehalten. In seiner Bekrönung ist ein Tamile abgebildet, der konzentriert Palmblätter beschriftet.
Mission du Danemark-Halle en Inde. Le cabinet à deux vantaux XI.L. est réservé aux objets de collection provenant de l'Inde. Le fronton du cabinet représente un Tamoul, écrivant l'air concentré sur des feuilles de palmier.

5 *Land and Marine Plants.* The two-door cabinet II.B. is devoted to land and marine plants. A garland of flowers surmounted by a face formed entirely out of different parts of plants, in the style of Giuseppe Arcimboldo, embellishes the pediment.
Land- und Meerespflanzen. Der zweiflügelige Schrank II.B. ist Land- und Meerespflanzen gewidmet. Die Bekrönung ziert eine Blumengirlande mit einem Gesicht darüber, das nach der Manier Giuseppe Arcimboldos aus verschiedenen Pflanzenteilen zusammengesetzt ist.
Plantes terrestres et marines. Le cabinet à deux vantaux II.B. est

dédié aux plantes terrestres et marines. Le fronton est orné d'une guirlande de fleurs surmonté d'un visage composé de parties de plantes à la manière de Giuseppe Arcimboldo.

6 *Conchylia.* Cabinets V.E. and VI.F. contain what is left of the old collection of shells and molluscs. This includes starfish, sea urchins, various shellfish and also snails. In the centre of this cabinet is the shell of a giant clam which was brought to Halle from India in the second half of the 18th century.
Conchylien. In den Schränken V.E. und VI.F. sind die Reste der alten Conchyliensammlung untergebracht. Neben Seesternen und -igeln sind vor allem Schnecken und Muscheln vertreten. Im Zentrum des Schrankes befindet sich eine Riesenmuschel, die in der zweiten Hälfte des 18. Jhs. aus Indien nach Halle kam.
Conchylia. Les cabinets V.E. et VI.F. abritent les vestiges de l'ancienne collection de coquillages et mollusques. Outre les étoiles de

mer, les oursins, les escargots et les coquillages étaient surtout représentés. Au centre du cabinet on voit un coquillage géant originaire de l'Inde et arrivé à Halle dans la seconde moitié du 18e siècle.

7 *Natural History Collection.* In the southern part of the room the collection of natural history is completed by those exhibits kept outside of the cabinets, as a result of which not all of these items have survived. The crocodile, suspended from the ceiling right at the entrance to the collection, is known to have been on display in Gottfried August Gründler's time (1710–1775). The cabinets in the background are for the animal, mineral and fossil collections.
Naturaliensammlung. Die Naturaliensammlung im Süden des Saals wird durch Exponate außerhalb der Schränke ergänzt. Nicht alle haben überlebt. Das Entrée bildet ein Krokodil, das an der Decke hängt und bereits bei Gottfried August Gründler (1710–1775) nachweisbar ist. Im Hintergrund

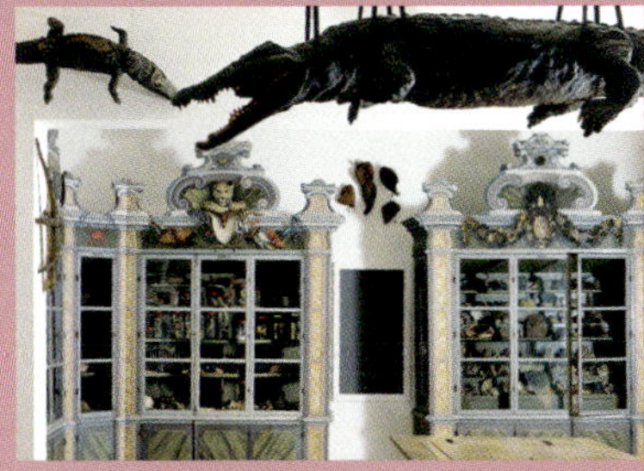

7

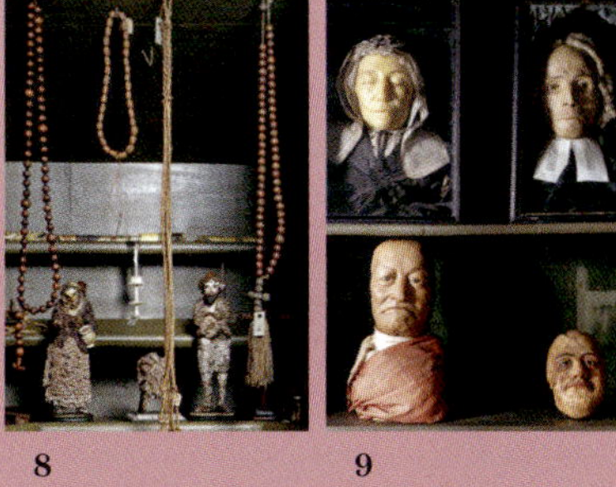

8   9

stehen Animalien-, Mineralien- und Fossilienschränke.
Collection d'Histoire naturelle. La collection d'histoire naturelle dans le sud de la salle est complétée par les expositions à l'extérieur des cabinets. Tous n'ont pas survécu. Le crocodile suspendu au plafond à l'entrée de la Collection se trouvait déjà dans la collection de Gottfried August Gründler (1710–1775). À l'arrière-plan se trouvent les cabinets consacrés aux animaux, aux minéraux et aux fossiles.

8 *Religions.* Cabinet XII.M. contains items from religions other than Christianity. At the same time, items used in Catholic rites but which would not be considered rare in any way, such as consecrated candles and rosaries, still found their way into this pietistic cabinet and thus acquired some sort of curiosity value. Even so, they are certainly less striking than the flagellum of a Capuchin monk, or the small bottle from the Roman catacombs containing the blood of the first Christians. The small

figure of a Chinese dragon and the Indian domestic idol are relics from civilisations further afield.
Religionen. Der Schrank XII.M. enthält religiöse Objekte. Gegenstände, die im katholischen Ritus keinen Seltenheitswert besaßen, wie geweihte Kerzen oder Rosenkränze, wurden in der pietistischen Kammer zur Kuriosität. Aufregender war etwa die Geißel eines Kapuzinermönchs oder ein Fläschchen mit Blut der ersten Christen aus den römischen Katakomben. Der chinesische Drache und der indianische Hausgötze sind Zeugen ferner Zivilisationen.
Religions. Le cabinet XII.M. contient des objets religieux. Des objets communs dans le rite catholique (bougies consacrées, chapelets) sont devenus une curiosité dans la chambre piétiste. Le fouet d'un moine capucin, ou un flacon contenant le sang des premiers chrétiens des catacombes romaines, était plus excitant. Le dragon chinois et l'idole domestique indienne sont les témoins de civilisations lointaines.

9 *Masks and Coins.* Constructed as an independent piece, this cabinet contains some 30 flat drawers where coins, medallions and small plaques are kept. This separate collection includes around 600 pieces in all, with a number of wax masks housed in the centre of the cabinet.
Masken und Münzen. Dieser Schrank wurde als Solitär konstruiert. Er enthält rund 30 flache Schubladen zur Aufbewahrung von Münzen, Medaillen und Plaketten. Allein diese Sammlung zählt rund 600 Stücke. Das Zentrum im Schrank nehmen die Wachsmasken ein.
Masques et pièces de monnaie. Ce cabinet est construit comme un solitaire. Il contient une trentaine de tiroirs plats pour pièces de monnaie, médailles et plaques. Cette collection compte à elle seule un total d'environ 600 pièces. Toutefois, les masques de cire occupent le centre du cabinet.

Die Kunst- und Wunderkammer

Schloss Ambras, Innsbruck

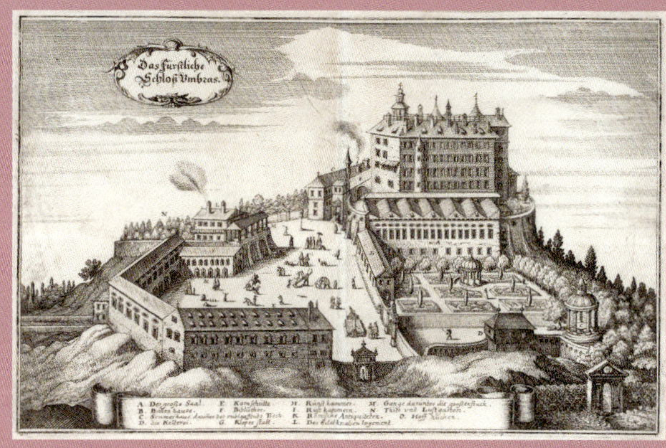

Founded 1565

Key item *Death,* c. 1583, by Paul Reichel. Inside an ebony shrine, within an arched niche carved from Kelheim limestone, stands a human skeleton, also made of limestone, representing Death absorbed in contemplation.

Besonders sehenswert Der *Tödlein-Schrein* von Paul Reichel, um 1583. In einem Schrein aus Ebenholz steht in einer rundbogigen Nische ein menschliches Skelett; ebenso wie die Nische ist es aus Kelheimer Stein geschnitten und stellt den Tod in einer nachdenklichen Pose dar.

À voir absolument *Écrin de la mort*, par Paul Reichel, vers 1583. Dans un écrin d'ébène, une niche cintrée en pierre de Kelheim abrite un squelette humain du même grès, qui semble plongé dans une profonde réflexion.

Matthäus Merian, *View of Ambras Castle*, in *Topographia provinciarum austriacarum*, Frankfurt am Main, 1649

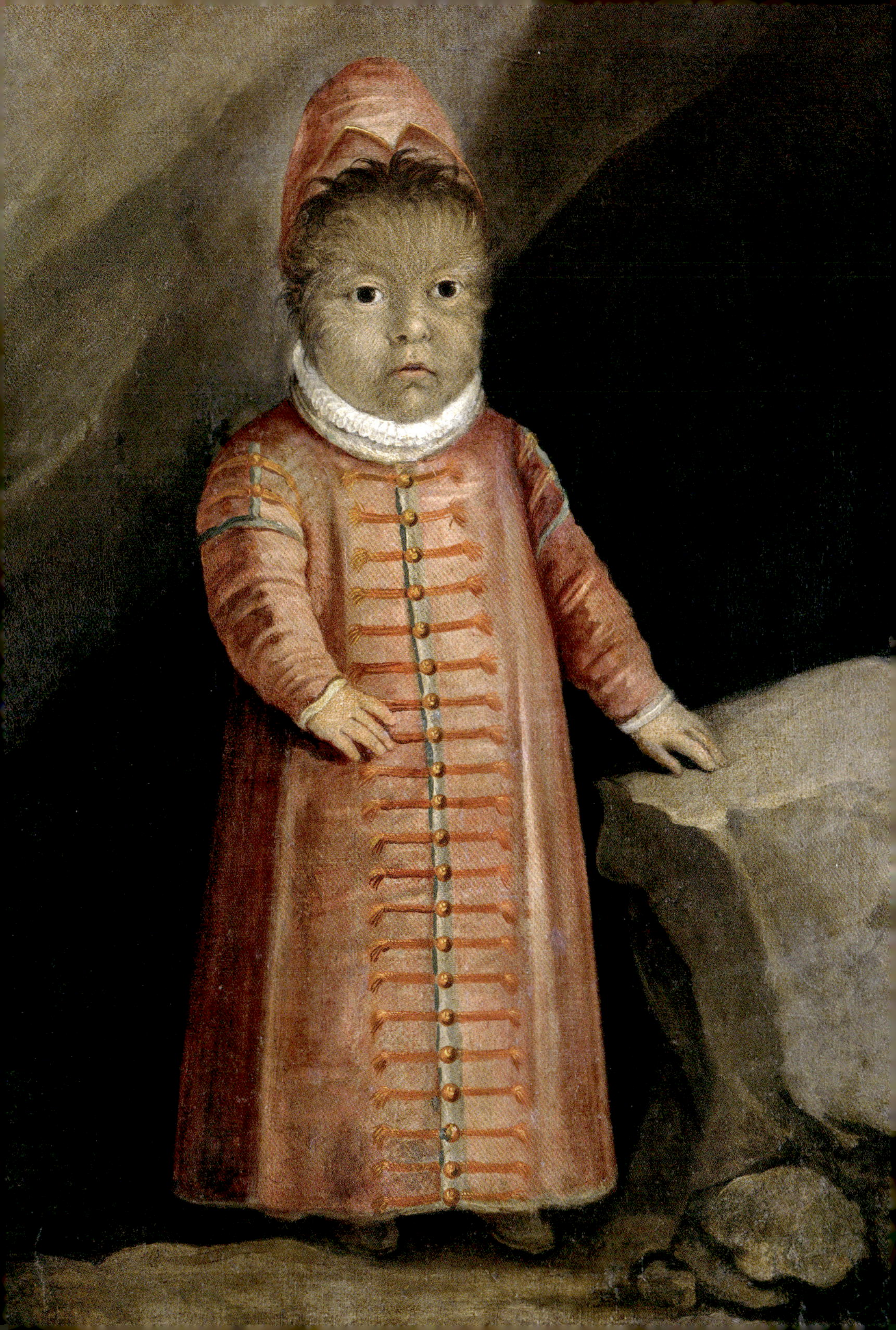

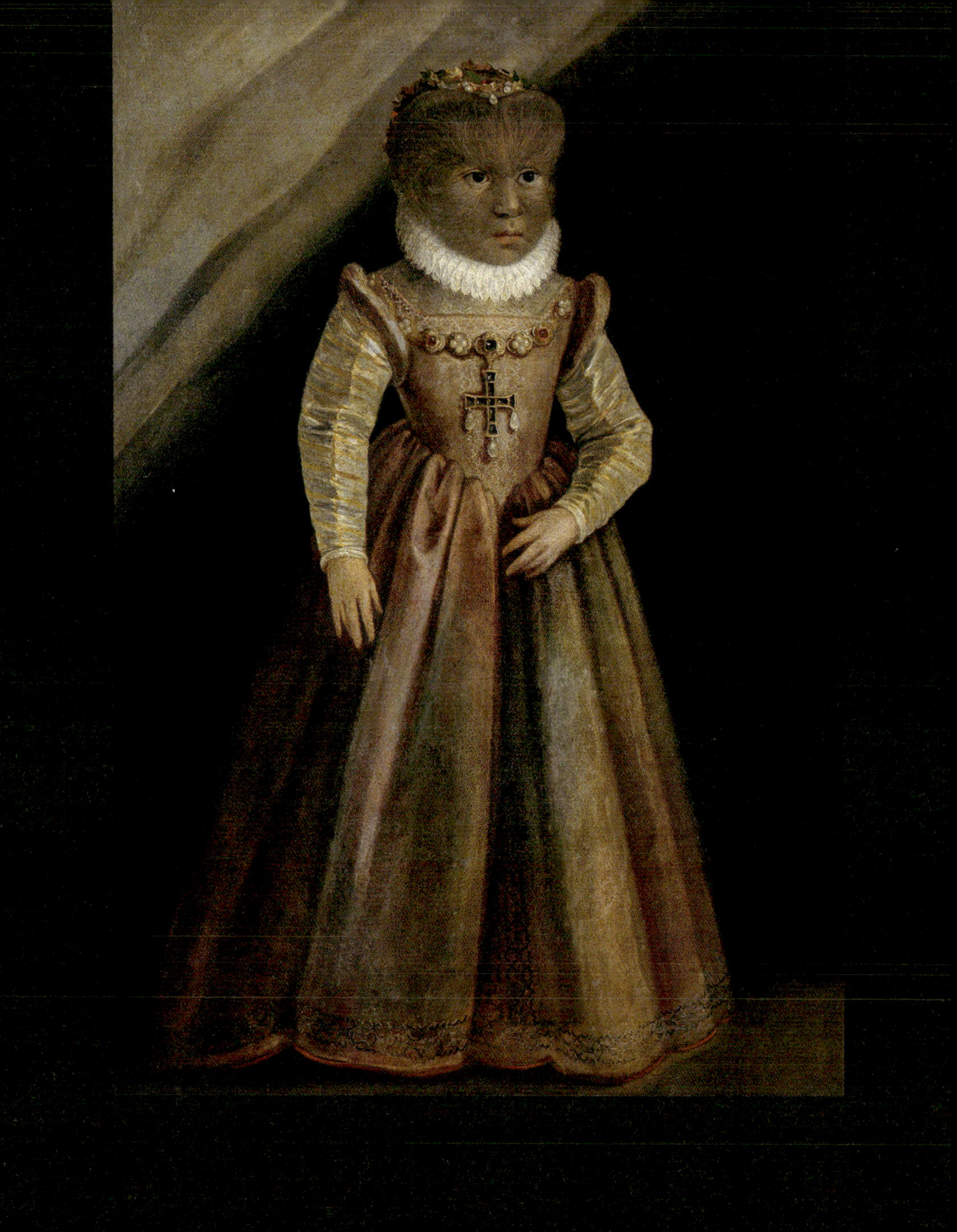

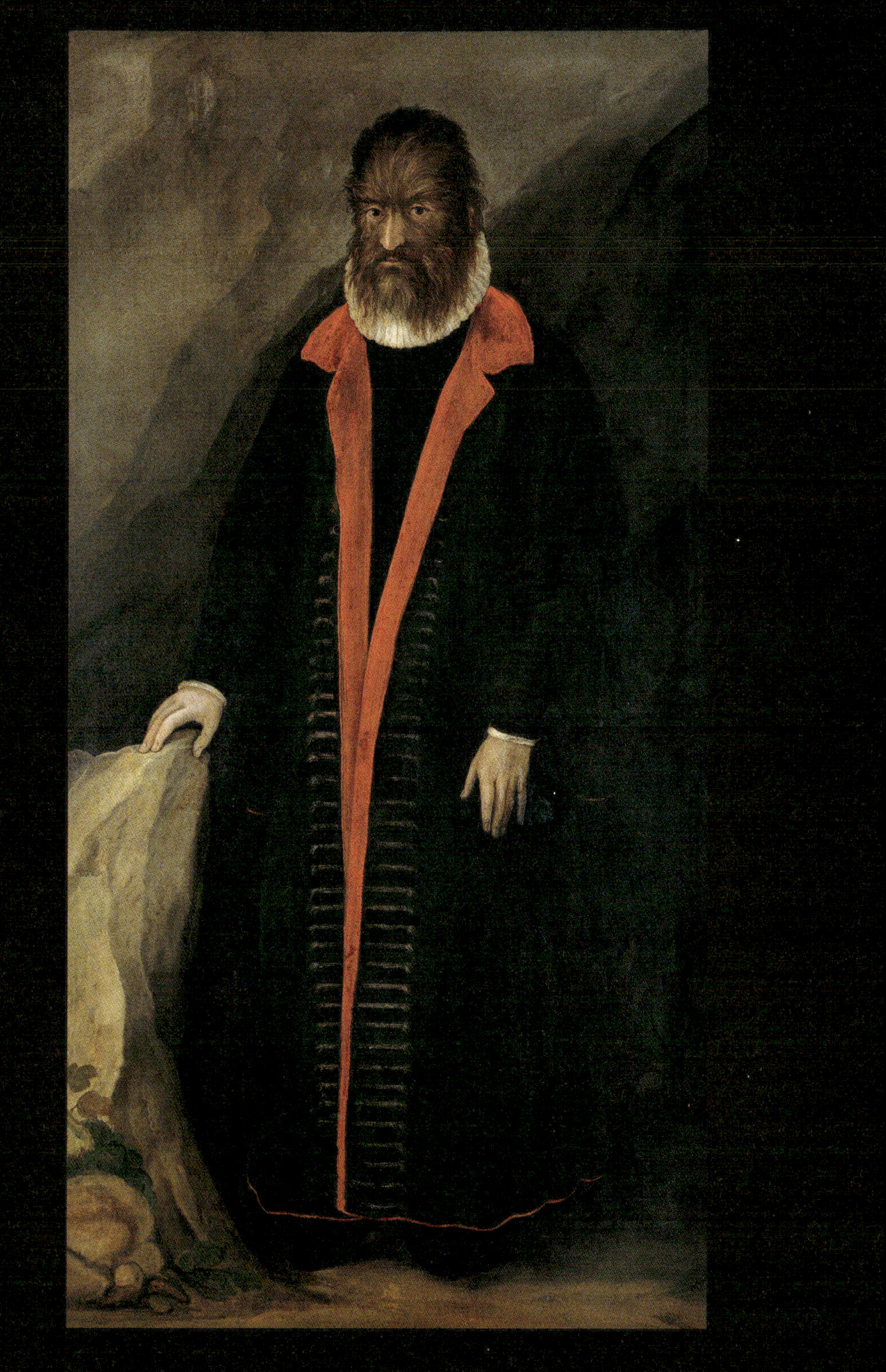

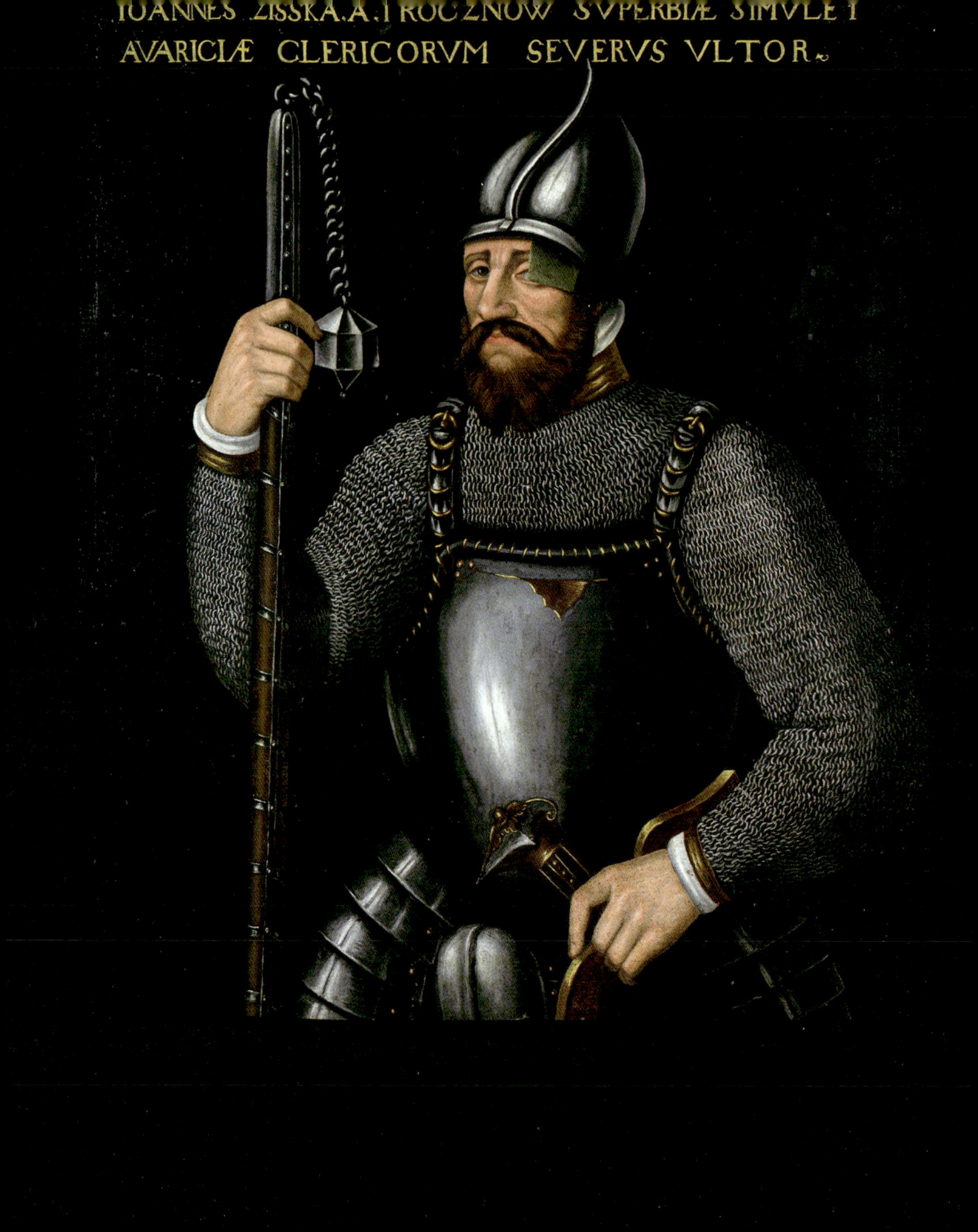

IOANNES ZISSKA A TROCZNOW SVPERBIÆ SIMVL ET
AVARICIÆ CLERICORVM SEVERVS VLTOR.

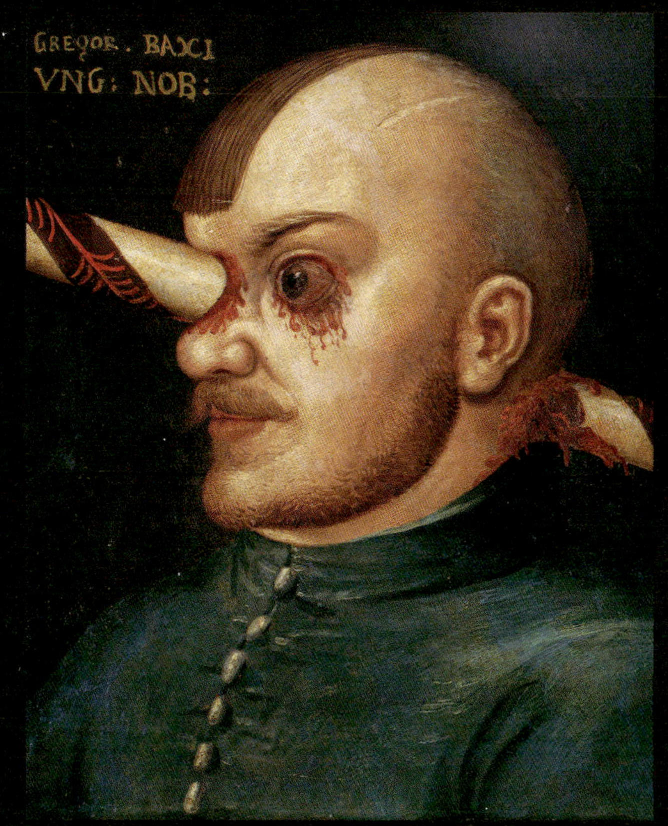
GREGOR . BAXI
VNG: NOB:

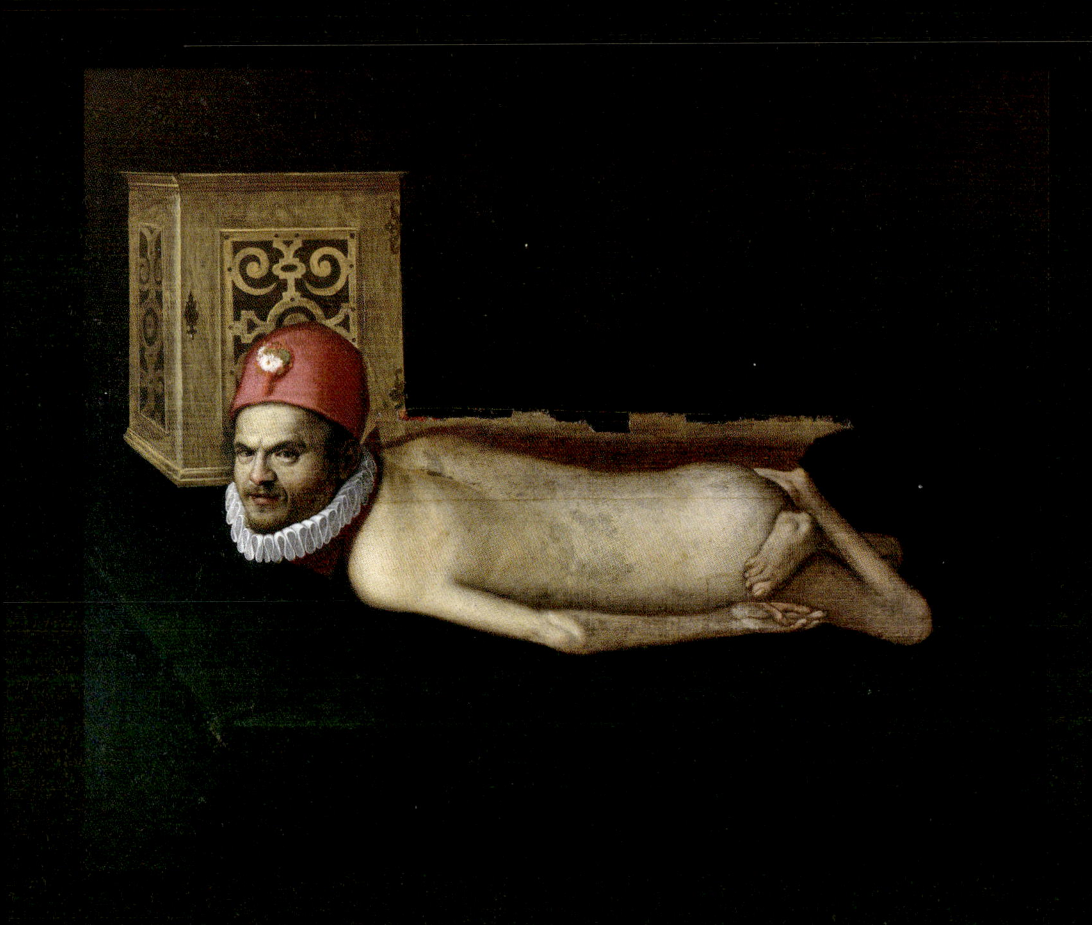

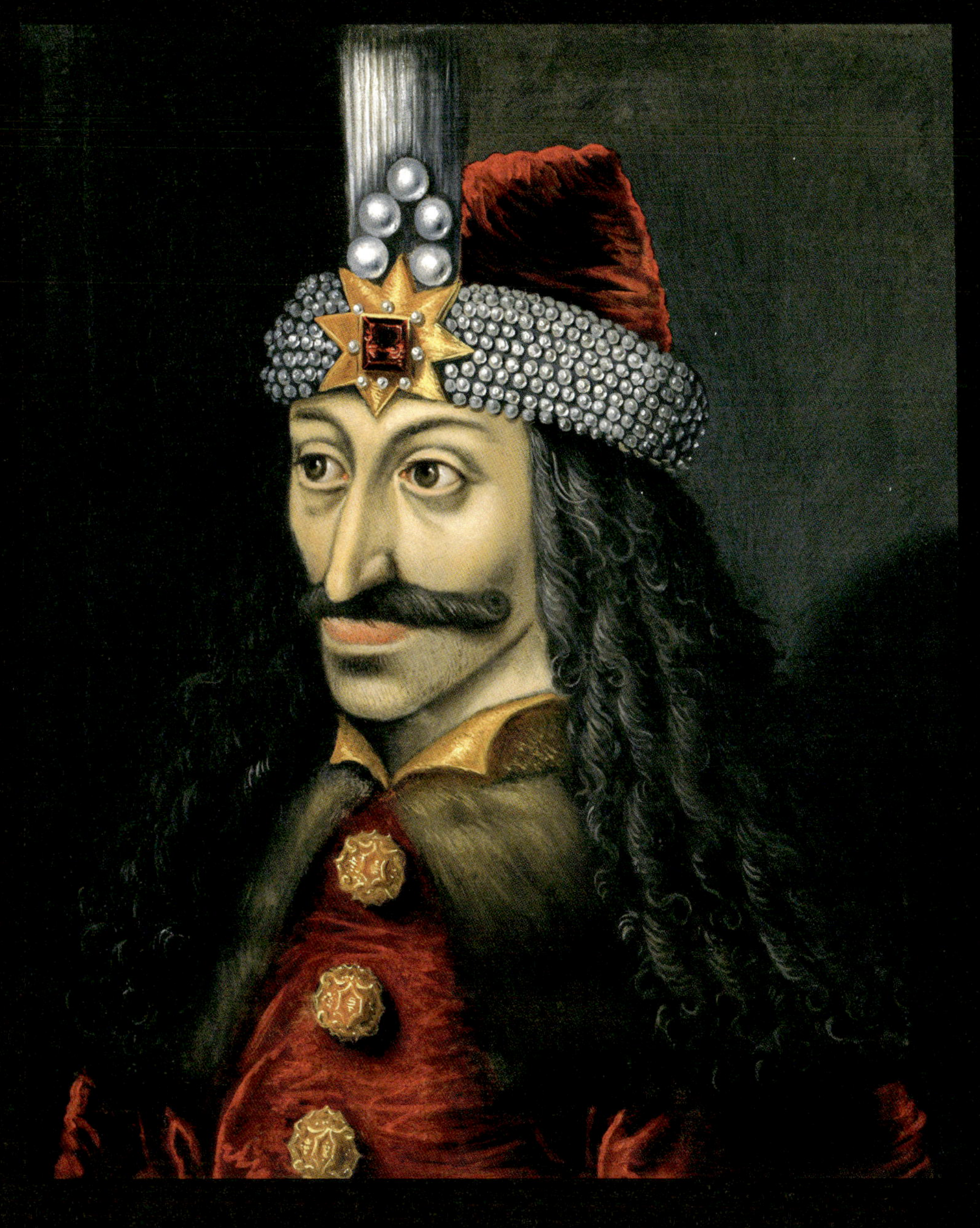

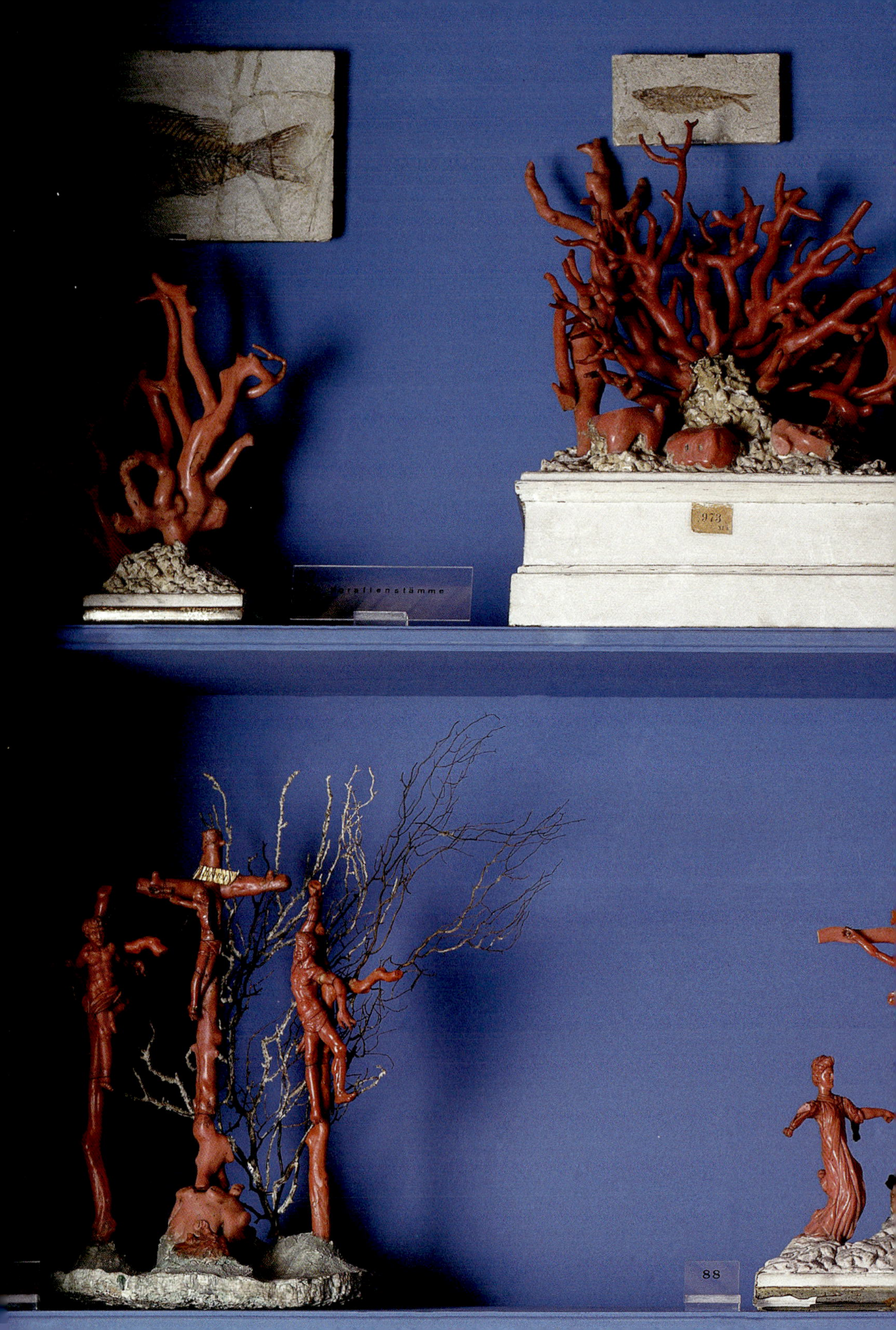
Korallenstämme
973
88

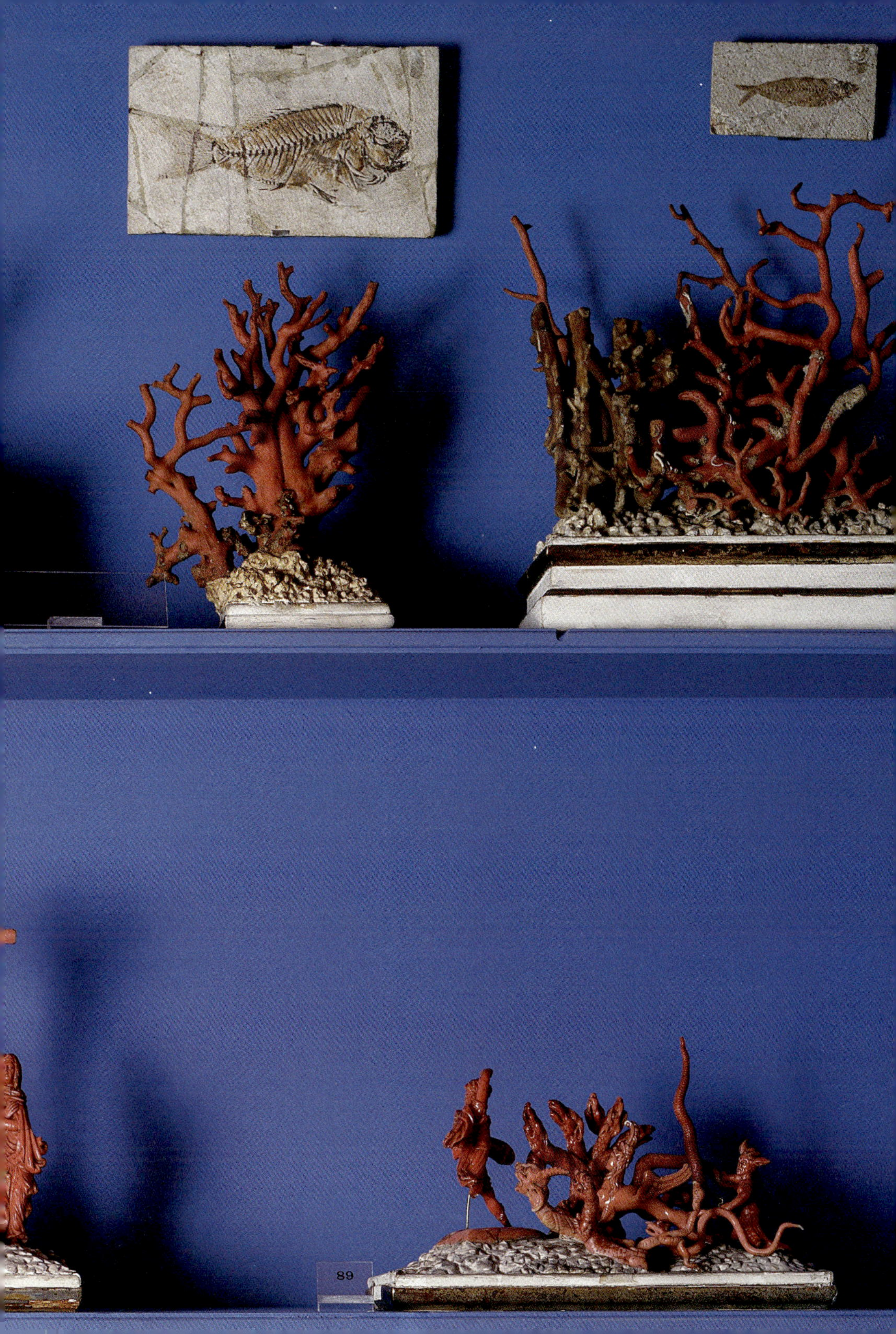
89

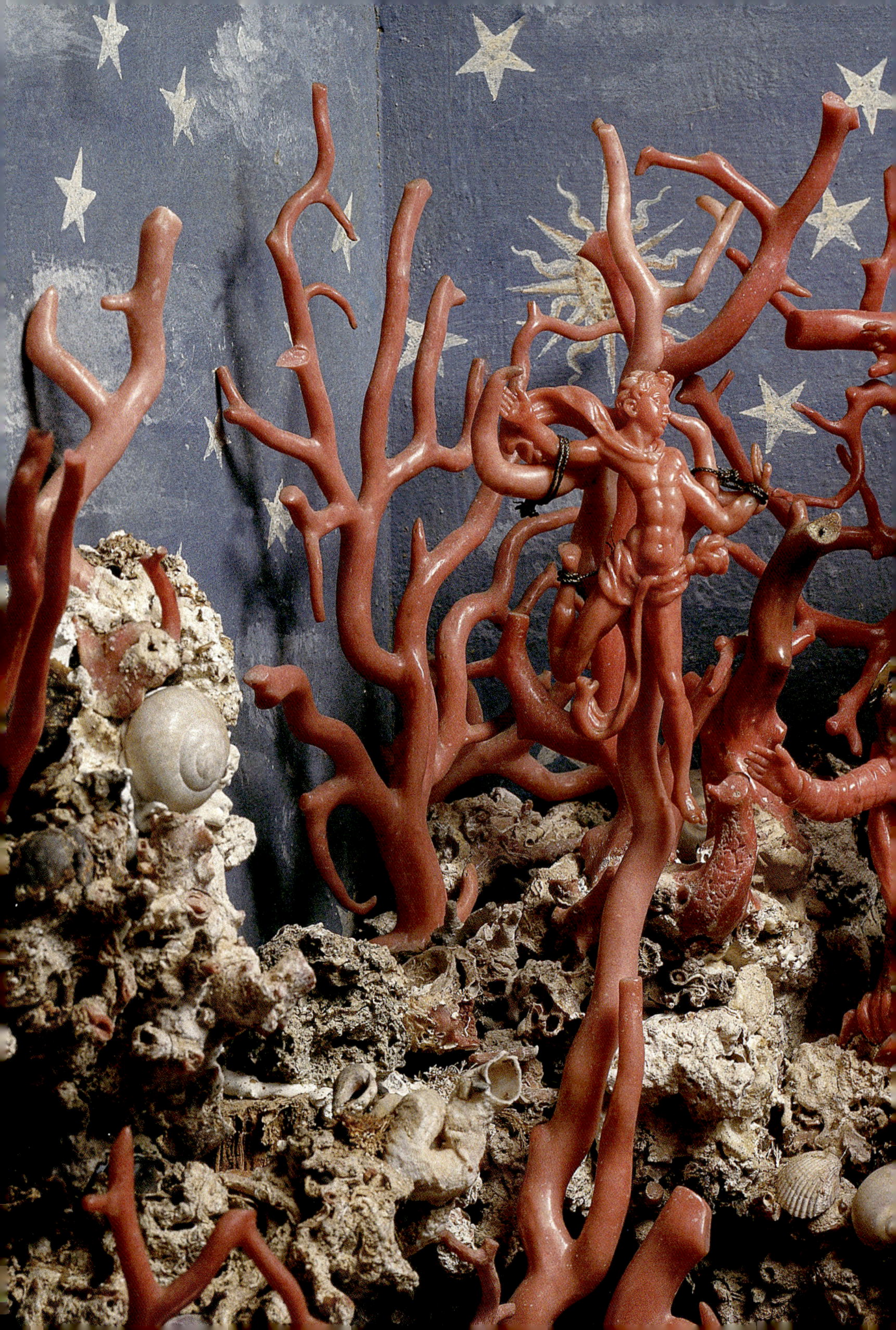

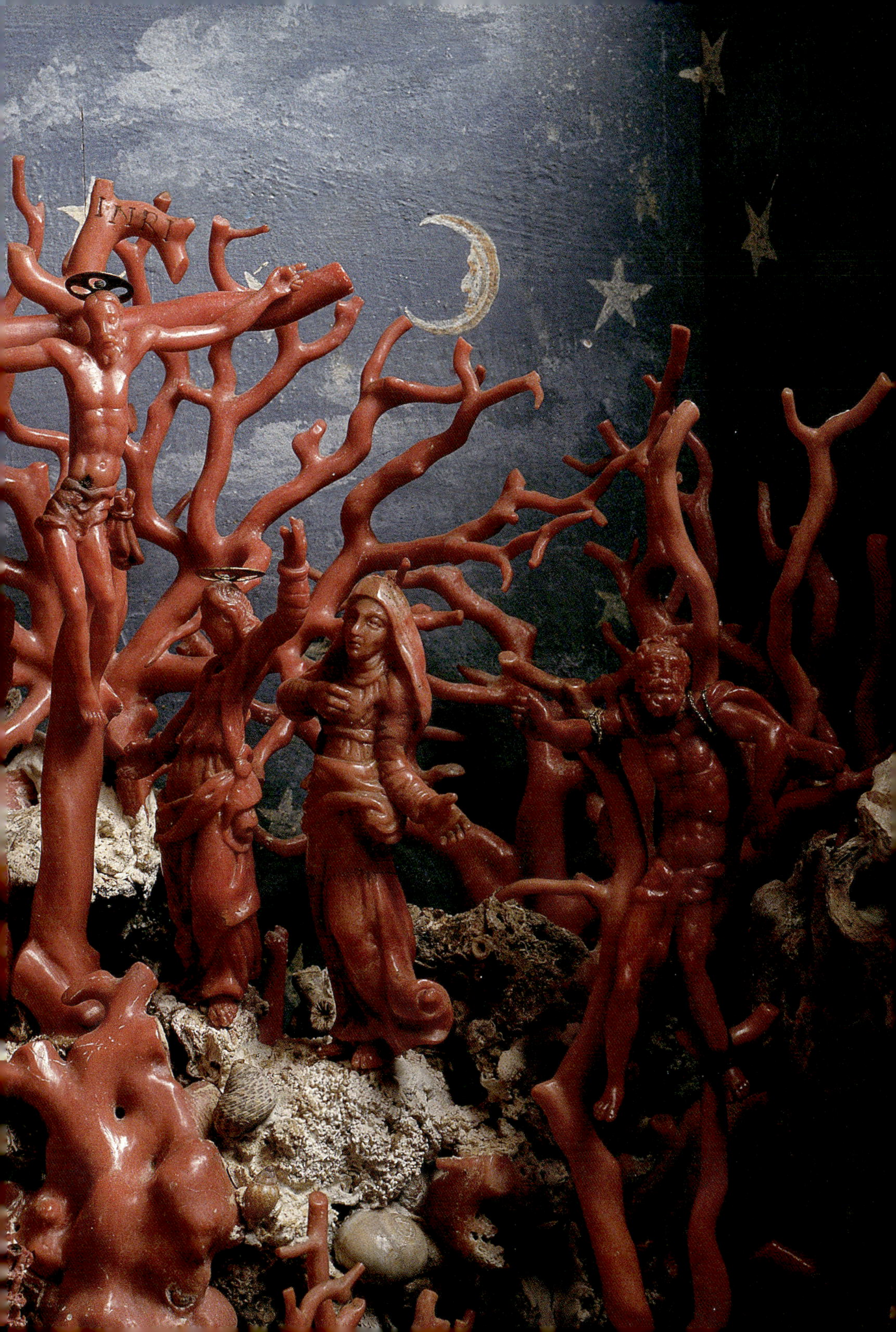

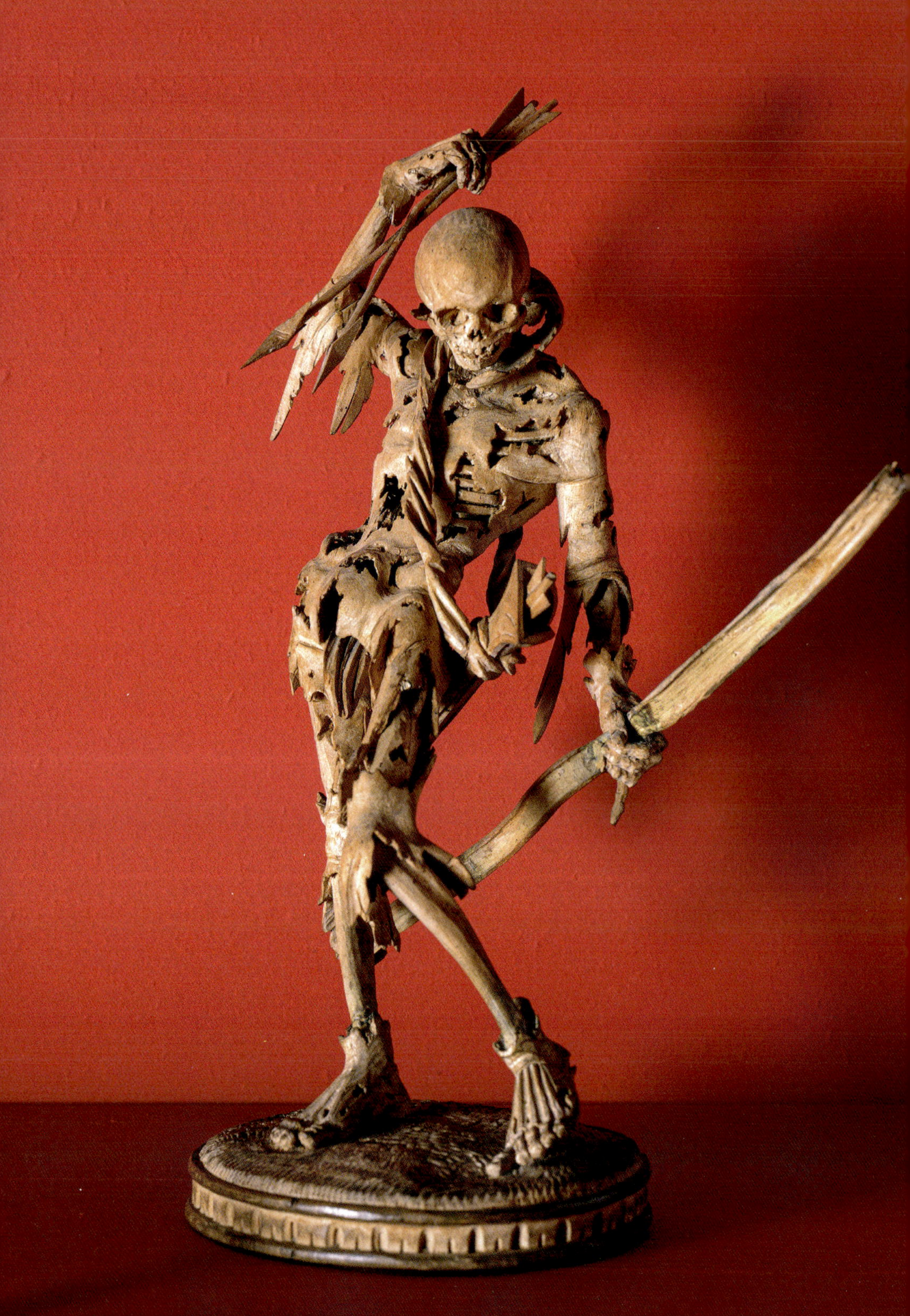

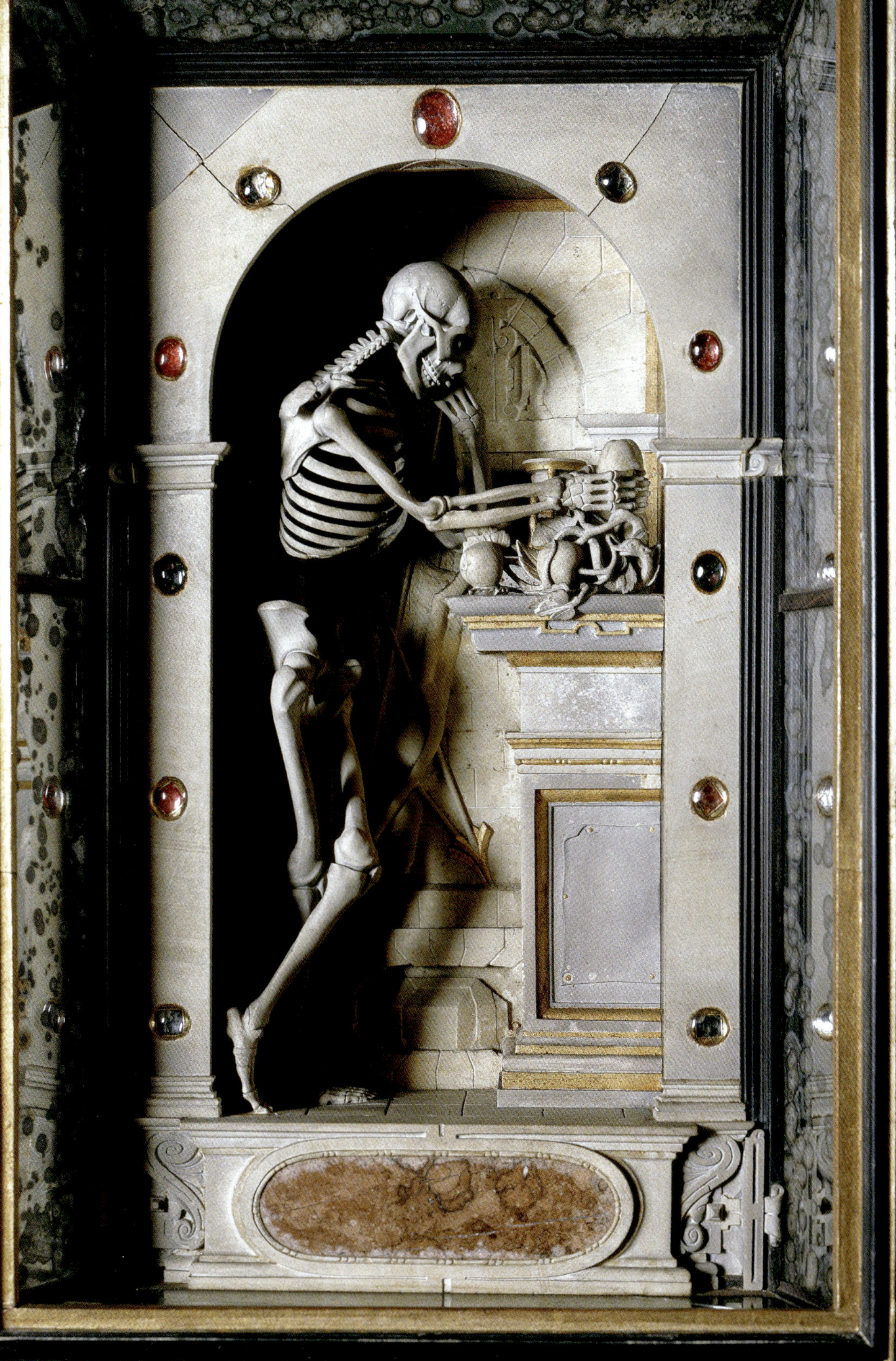

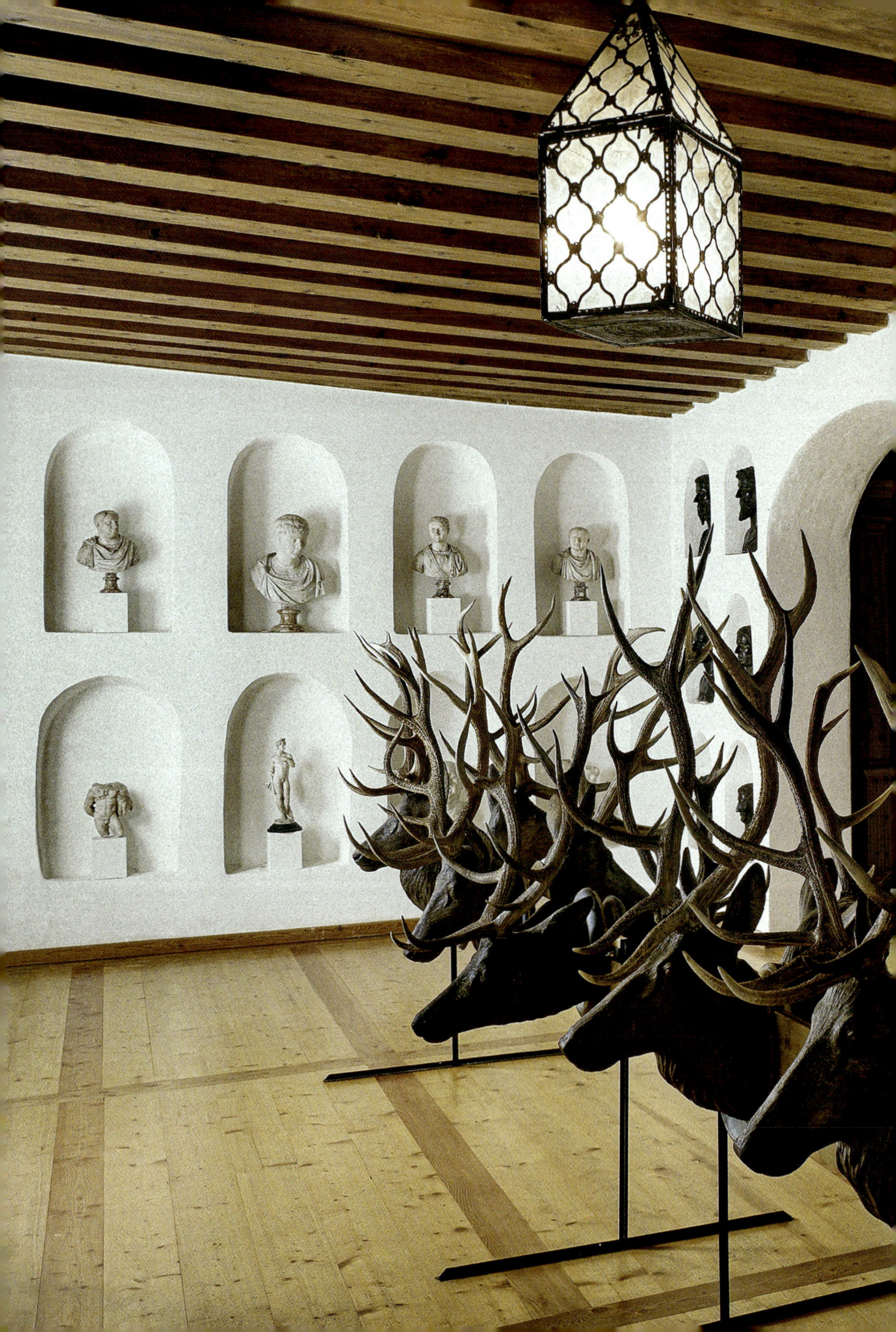

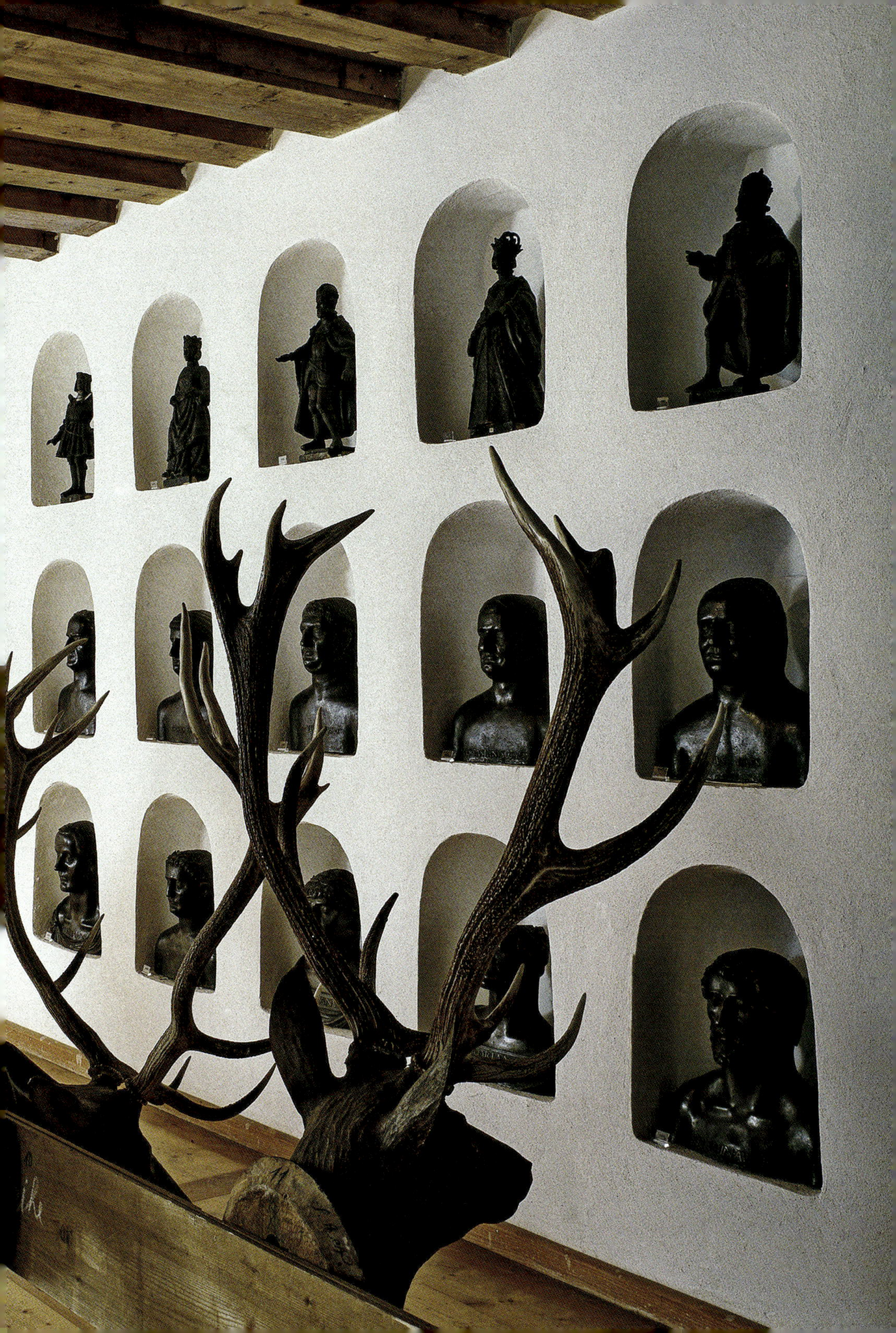

The history of Ambras Castle is closely bound up with that of Archduke Ferdinand II
of Habsburg (1529–1595), the second son of Emperor Ferdinand I and Anna of Bohemia.
Ferdinand was only 18 when his father appointed him governor of Bohemia, and upon the
Emperor's death in 1564 he became ruler of the Tyrol and moved to Ambras Castle with
his retinue of advisors, friends, poets and artists. He then had the sombre medieval castle,
formerly owned by the Andechs family, rebuilt as a Renaissance palace, and a number
of lower buildings constructed around the pentagonal court for his extensive collection;
when completed, the Hochschloss (upper castle) housed his private apartments while the
Unterschloss (lower castle) became his museum. Following the death of his morganatic
wife, Philippine Welser (1527–1580), Ferdinand devoted himself almost entirely to building
up his collection.

The Ambras collection was created at the dawn of modern museum history in Europe,
but its roots can be traced back to medieval encyclopaedias and the *ars memoriae*, a philosophical system of learning and memorising subjects by subdividing them into categories.
A portrait gallery of Habsburg rulers and generals takes pride of place, and the same
figures are also celebrated in Ferdinand's *Armamentarium heroicum*. Located next to the
armouries are the Library (containing some 3,500 books) and the Archduke's cabinet of
curiosities, the only one in the world to have survived *in situ*. For his collection, Ferdinand
devised a special form of presentation, so that objects made of the same material—ivory,
wood, coral, rock crystal—were displayed together in one of the 18 vitrines. Prints and
smaller pictures were kept in chests and cupboards, the walls were closely hung with
paintings, and crocodiles, fish and bones were suspended from the ceiling. The collection
was divided into three groups: *naturalia*, everything found in nature; *artificialia*, natural
objects worked and altered by man; and *mirabilia*. This third and most unusual category
included anything out of the ordinary, whether made of rare materials or objects that
were especially fragile or strange, and often conceived without any practical function:
impossible locks, a chair that traps the person sitting on it, writing utensils made of wood
shavings, portraits of dwarfs, giants and people whose bodies were entirely covered with
hair, and so on. Initially only selected guests were invited to visit the Archduke's cabinet,
but in the early 17th century the collection was opened up to the public, making it a kind
of museum before the concept properly existed. Today, the palace and collection are
administered by the Kunsthistorisches Museum in Vienna with their own director.

❂ ❧ ❂

Die Geschichte von Schloss Ambras ist eng mit dem Habsburger Ferdinand II. verbunden (1529–1595). Er war der zweitgeborene Sohn von Kaiser Ferdinand I. und Anna
von Böhmen. Schon im Alter von achtzehn Jahren wurde er von seinem Vater mit der
Verwaltung des Königreichs Böhmen betraut. Als ihm nach dessen Tod im Jahre 1564
die Herrschaft über Tirol zufiel, zog er mit seinem gesamten Hofstaat aus Beratern,
Freunden, Dichtern und Künstlern nach Ambras. Die finstere mittelalterliche Burg,

einstmals im Besitz der Familie Andechs, wurde zu einem Renaissanceschloss umgebaut. Um einen fünfeckigen Hof ließ Ferdinand II. mehrere flache Gebäude errichten, um darin seine Sammlungen unterzubringen: So wurde das Hochschloss zum Wohnbereich, das Unterschloss zum Museum. Nach dem Tod seiner bürgerlichen Ehefrau Philippine Welser (1527–1580), widmete er sich fast ausschließlich dem Aufbau des Museums.

Trotz ihrer Entstehung zu Beginn der modernen europäischen Museumsgeschichte reichen die Wurzeln der Sammlung Ambras weit zurück, bis zu den mittelalterlichen Enzyklopädien und der *Ars memoriae,* einer philosophischen Methode zur Speicherung und Abrufbarkeit nach Kategorien. Einen Ehrenplatz nimmt die Porträtgalerie der Herrscher und Feldherren aus dem Hause Habsburg ein, an die auch in der sogenannten „Heldenrüstkammer" erinnert wird. Neben den Rüstkammern befanden sich die Bibliothek – bestehend aus etwa 3500 Bänden – und die Kunst- und Wunderkammer, die als einzige historische Renaissance-Sammlung der Welt an Ort und Stelle erhalten geblieben ist. Für seine Sammlung entwickelte Ferdinand II. eine besondere Art der Präsentation, bei der die Objekte nach Materialien – wie Elfenbein, Holz, Koralle und Kristall – sortiert und in 18 Vitrinen ausgestellt wurden. Drucke und kleinformatige Gemälde lagerten in Truhen und Schränken, die Wände waren mit Bildern vollgehängt, und von der Decke baumelten Krokodile, Fische und Knochen. Die Bestände wurden in drei Klassen eingeteilt: *Naturalia*, also alles, was direkt aus der Natur kam, *Artificialia*, durch Menschenhand bearbeitete und veränderte Natur, und *Mirabilia*. Zu letzterer Kategorie gehörte alles, was nicht der Norm entsprach oder aus seltenem Material bestand, Absonderlichkeiten jeder Art und erlesene, äußerst zerbrechliche Dinge, die zumeist nicht in Gebrauch waren: unbrauchbare Truhenschlösser, Fangstühle, Schreibzeug aus feinsten Holzspänen, Bildnisse von Zwergen, Riesen und Haarmenschen und Ähnliches. Der Zugang zu den Sammlungen war ausgewählten Gästen Erzherzog Ferdinands vorbehalten. Im frühen 17. Jahrhundert war das Museum schließlich für das gebildete Publikum zugänglich. Es handelt sich also um eine Art Museum *ante litteram*. Heute werden das Schloss und seine Sammlungen als Außenstelle des Kunsthistorischen Museums Wien mit eigener Direktion geführt.

◦ ◈ ◦

L'histoire du château d'Ambras est étroitement liée à celle de l'archiduc Ferdinand II (1529–1595) de Habsbourg, deuxième fils de l'empereur Ferdinand Ier et d'Anne Jagellon. Nommé gouverneur de Bohême à 18 ans, Ferdinand devenu archiduc du Tyrol à la mort de son père (1564) s'établit au château d'Ambras avec sa cour de conseillers, d'amis, de poètes et d'artistes. La sombre forteresse médiévale, qui avait jadis appartenu aux Andechs, fut transformée en château de la Renaissance. Dans la cour pentagonale, l'archiduc fit élever des corps de bâtiment plus bas destinés à abriter ses collections : de fait, le *Hochschloss* (partie haute du château) devint résidence et l'*Unterschloss* (partie basse) musée. À partir de 1580, date du décès de Philippine Welser (1527–1580), son épouse morganatique, l'archiduc se consacra entièrement à l'aménagement du musée.

Si la collection d'Ambras voit le jour à l'aube de l'histoire muséale des temps modernes en Europe, ses origines remontent aux encyclopédies médiévales et à l'*ars memoriae* comme méthode philosophique de conservation et d'évocation des contenus par catégorie. Les hôtes d'honneur en sont les portraits de souverains et de condottieres, également rappelés à la mémoire par l'*Armamentarium heroicum*. Jouxtant l'armurerie, se trouvent la Bibliothèque qui comptait près de 3500 volumes et la *Kunst- und Wunderkammer* (cabinet d'art et des merveilles), la seule au monde à subsister dans son intégralité. Ferdinand disposa sa collection à l'intérieur de 18 vitrines où les objets furent classés en fonction du matériau dont ils étaient constitués (ivoire, bois, corail, cristal, etc.). Des coffres et des cabinets abritaient des gravures et des portraits de dimensions réduites, tandis que les murs disparaissaient sous les tableaux et que des crocodiles, des poissons et des ossements étaient suspendus au plafond. Le fonds est rationnellement divisé en trois catégories : les *naturalia*, c'est-à-dire ce qui est présent dans la nature, les *artificialia*, ou ce qui provient de la nature et est ensuite transformé par la main et l'ingéniosité de l'homme, et les *mirabilia*. Cette dernière catégorie, la plus étonnante, réunit tout ce qui est hors norme, rare par sa matière, tout ce qui est bizarre, d'une extrême fragilité, et souvent inapproprié: serrures inutilisables, sièges qui piègent leur hôte, coffret de bureau constitué de minces copeaux de bois, portraits de nains, de géants, de personnes au corps entièrement recouvert de poils, etc. L'accès aux collections était réservé à des invités distingués de l'archiduc Ferdinand. Au début du 17e siècle, le musée devint finalement accessible à un public cultivé. Il s'agit donc d'un musée *ante litteram*. Aujourd'hui, le château est une annexe du Kunsthistorisches Museum de Vienne avec sa direction propre.

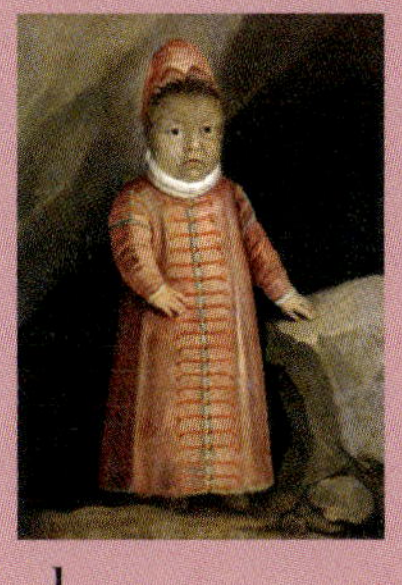

1

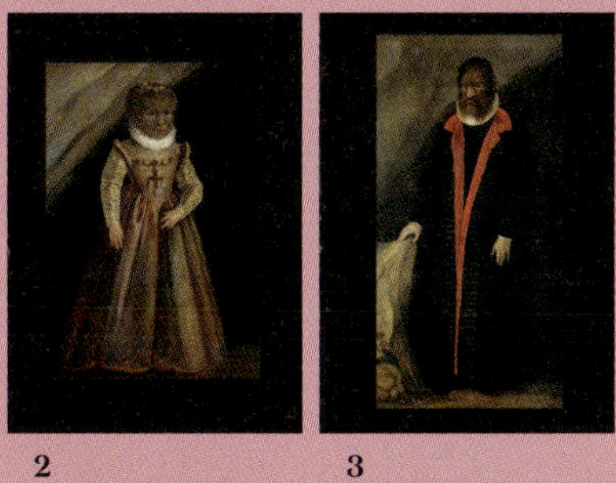

2   3

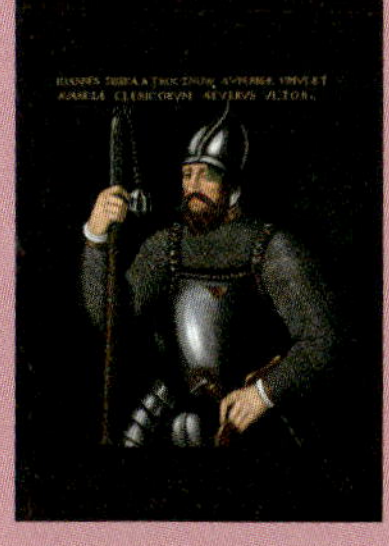

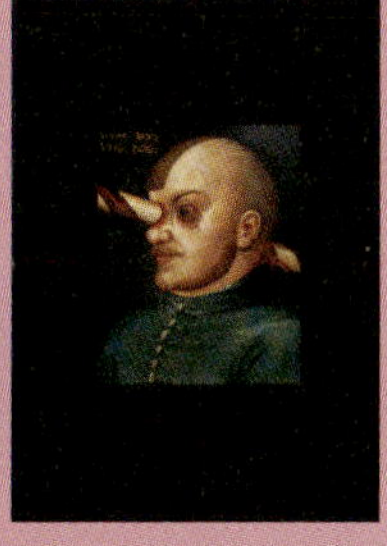

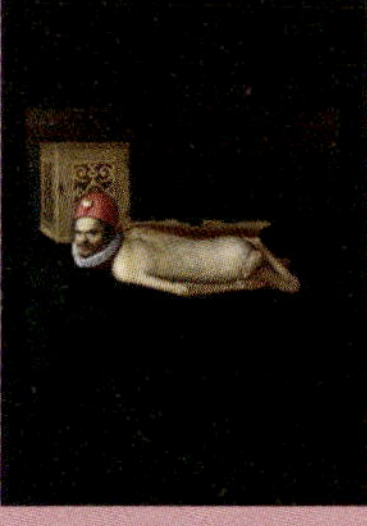

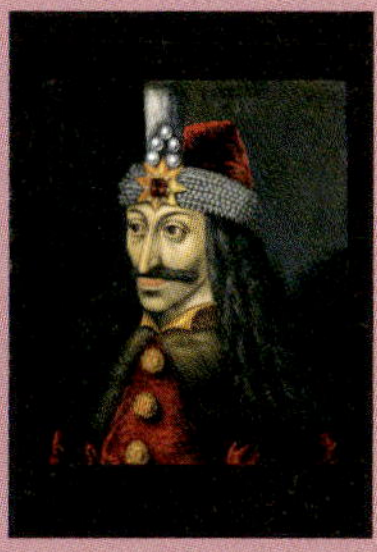

4   5   6   7

1 Anonymous, *Enrico Gonzalez, Son of Pedro Gonzalez, The Hairy Man*, c. 1580. Oil on canvas, 100 x 86.5 cm / 39½ x 34 in.
Anonym, *Enrico Gonzalez, Sohn des Haarmenschen Pedro Gonzalez*, um 1580. Öl auf Leinwand, 100 x 86,5 cm.
Anonyme, *Enrico Gonzalez, fils de Pedro Gonzalez, le Poilu*, vers 1580. Huile sur toile, 100 x 86,5 cm.

2 Anonymous, *Madeleine Gonzalez, Daughter of Pedro Gonzalez, The Hairy Man*, c. 1580. Oil on canvas, 123 x 86 cm / 48½ x 34 in.
Anonym, *Madeleine Gonzalez, Tochter des Haarmenschen Pedro Gonzalez*, um 1580. Öl auf Leinwand, 123 x 86 cm.
Anonyme, *Madeleine Gonzalez, fille de Pedro Gonzalez, le Poilu*, vers 1580. Huile sur toile, 123 x 86 cm.

3 Anonymous, *Pedro Gonzalez, The Hairy Man (born 1556)*, c. 1580.
Oil on canvas, 190 x 80 cm / 75 x 31½ in.
Anonym, *Pedro Gonzalez, der Haarmensch (geboren 1556)*, um 1580. Öl auf Leinwand, 190 x 80 cm.
Anonyme, *Pedro Gonzalez, le Poilu (né en 1556)*, vers 1580. Huile sur toile, 190 x 80 cm.

4 Anonymous, *Johann Ziska von Trocnov*, late 16th century. Oil on canvas, 100 x 83 cm / 39½ x 32½ in.
Anonym, *Johann Ziska von Trocnov*, Ende 16. Jh. Öl auf Leinwand, 100 x 83 cm.
Anonyme, *Johann Ziska von Trocnov*, fin du 16e siècle. Huile sur toile, 100 x 83 cm.

5 Anonymous, *Portrait of Gregor Baci*, 16th century. Oil on canvas, 39 x 31 cm / 15½ x 12 in.
Anonym, *Porträt von Gregor Baci*, 16. Jh. Öl auf Leinwand, 39 x 31 cm.
Anonyme, *Portrait de Gregor Baci*, 16e siècle. Huile sur toile, 39 x 31 cm.

6 Anonymous, *Portrait of a Disabled Man*, 16th century. Oil on canvas, 110 x 135 cm / 43½ x 53 in.
Anonym, *Bildnis eines behinderten Mannes*, 16. Jh. Öl auf Leinwand, 110 x 135 cm.
Anonyme, *Portrait d'un homme handicapé*, 16e siècle. Huile sur toile, 110 x 135 cm.

7 Anonymous, *Vlad III Dracula, Called the Impaler, Voivode of Wallachia*, second half of the 16th century. Oil on canvas, 60 x 50 cm / 23½ x 20 in.
Anonym, *Vlad III. Dracula, genannt Tzepesch, der Pfähler, Woiwode der Walachei*, 2. Hälfte 16. Jh. Öl auf Leinwand, 60 x 50 cm.
Anonyme, *Vlad III Dracula, dit Tepes, l'Empaleur, voïvode de la Valachie*. 2e moitié du 16e siècle. Huile sur toile, 60 x 50 cm.

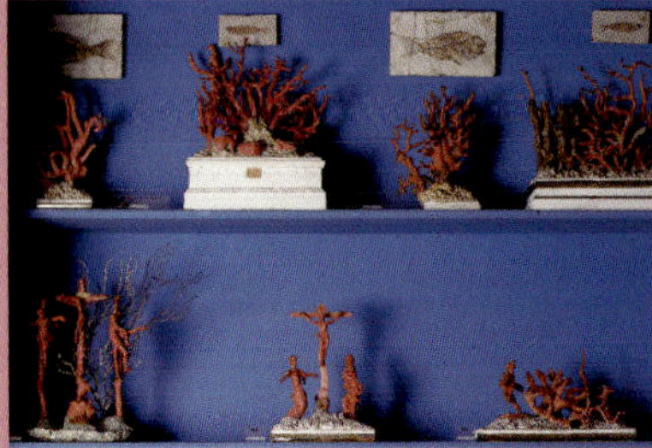

8

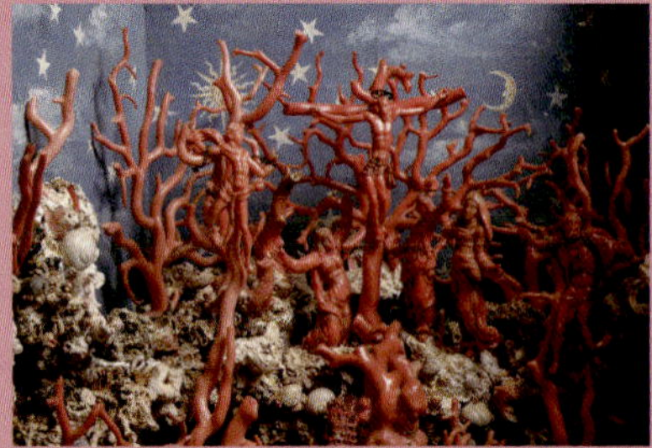

9

8 Objects made from coral are especially well represented in cabinets of curiosities throughout Europe from the Renaissance and Baroque period. The oldest and also the largest such collection is found in the cabinet assembled by Archduke Ferdinand II.

In den europäischen Kunstkammern der Renaissance und des Barock waren Objekte aus Korallen besonders zahlreich vertreten. Der älteste und zugleich größte Bestand hat sich in der Kunst- und Wunderkammer Erzherzog Ferdinands II. erhalten.

Les cabinets d'art européens de la Renaissance et du Baroque abritaient de nombreux objets de corail. La plus ancienne et la plus grande collection de coraux a été conservée dans la Chambre d'art et des merveilles de l'archiduc Ferdinand II.

8a–d Anonymous, *Selection of coral trunks*, Italy (Genoa?), second half of the 16th century. Coral, wood, plaster (from left to right), 23 cm; 25 cm; 24.5 cm; 26 cm / 9 in.; 9⅞ in.; 9⅝ in.; 10¼ in. Anonym, *Verschiedene Korallenstämme*, Italien (Genua?), 2. Hälfte 16. Jh. Koralle, Holz, Gips, 23 cm; 25 cm; 24,5 cm; 26 cm (von links). Anonyme, *Sélection de troncs de corail*, Italie (Gênes ?), 2ᵉ moitié du 16ᵉ siècle. Corail, bois, plâtre, 23 cm ; 25 cm ; 24,5 cm ; 26 cm (de gauche).

8e–f Anonymous, *Two calvaries*, Italy (Genoa?), second half of the 16th century. Coral, wood, plaster (from left to right), 28.3 cm; 20 cm / 11⅛ in.; 7⅞ in. Anonym, *Zwei Darstellungen mit dem Kalvarienberg*, Italien (Genua?), 2. Hälfte 16. Jh. Koralle, Holz, Gips, 28,3 cm; 20 cm (von links). Anonyme, *Deux calvaires*, Italie (Gênes ?), 2ᵉ moitié du 16ᵉ siècle. Corail, bois, plâtre, 28,3 cm ; 20 cm (de gauche).

8g Anonymous, *Hercules fighting the Hydra*, Italy (Genoa?), second half of the 16th century. Coral, wood, plaster, 18.5 cm / 7¼ in. Anonym, *Herkules im Kampf mit der Hydra*, Italien (Genua?), 2. Hälfte 16. Jh. Koralle, Holz, Gips, 18,5 cm. Anonyme, *Hercule se battant contre l'Hydre*, Italie (Gênes ?), 2ᵉ moitié du 16ᵉ siècle. Corail, bois, plâtre, 18,5 cm.

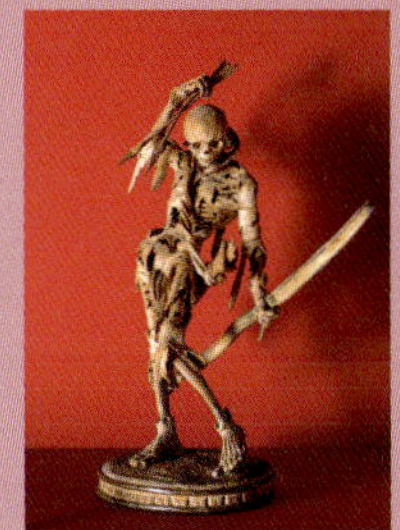

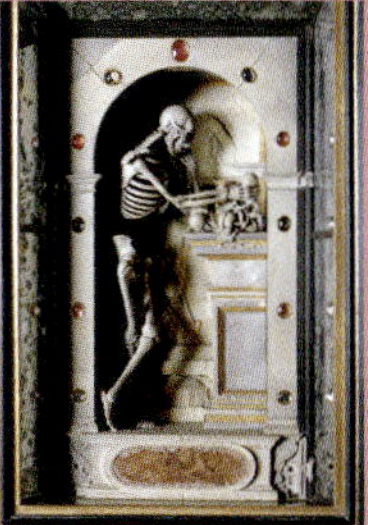

10

11

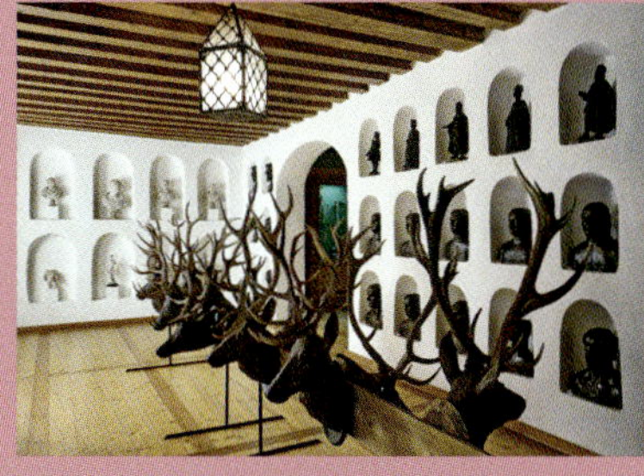

12

9 Anonymous, *Coral cabinet with scene of the Crucifixion*, southern Germany (cabinet, carving), Genoa (coral, carving), second half of the 16th century. Wood, pearls, mother-of-pearl, coral, plaster, mirrored glass, velvet, gold braid, bronze, lapis lazuli, gilding, 66 x 55 x 56.2 cm / 26 x 21⅝ x 22⅛ in.
Anonym, *Korallenkabinett mit der Darstellung der Kreuzigung Christi*, Süddeutschland (Kabinett, Schnitzarbeiten) und Genua (Korallen, Schnitzarbeiten), 2. Hälfte 16. Jh. Holz, Perlen, Perlmutter, Korallen, Gips, Spiegelglas, Samt, Goldborten, Bronze, Lapislazuli, Vergoldung, 66 x 55 x 56,2 cm.
Anonyme, *Cabinet de corail avec la représentation de la Crucifixion*. Allemagne du Sud (cabinet, sculpture) et Gênes (corail et sculpture), 2ᵉ moitié du 16ᵉ siècle. Bois, perles, nacre, corail, plâtre, miroir, velours, galons dorés, bronze, lapis-lazuli, dorure, 66 x 55 x 56,2 cm.

10 Hans Leinberger, *Depiction of Death*, before 1519. Pearwood, 22.5 cm / 8⅞ in.
Hans Leinberger, *Tödlein*, vor 1519. Birnbaumholz, 22,5 cm.
Hans Leinberger, *La « Petite Mort »*, avant 1519. Bois de poirier, 22,5 cm.

11 Paul Reichel, *Shrine with depiction of death*, around 1583. Kelheim limestone, gilded ebony, coloured glass stones, 82.3 x 32 cm / 32⅜ x 12⅝ in.
Paul Reichel, *Tödlein-Schrein*, um 1583. Kelheimer Kalkstein, vergoldetes Ebenholz, bunte Glassteine, 82,3 x 32 cm.
Paul Reichel, *Écrin de la mort*, vers 1583. Pierre de Kelheim, ébène doré, pierres de verre coloré, 82,3 x 32 cm.

12 *Room view of the Antiquarium* (*Hall of Antiquities*; the deer antlers are no longer on display in this room)
Blick in das Antiquarium (die Hirschgeweihe befinden sich dort heute nicht mehr)
Vue de l'Antiquarium (la salle des Antiquités ; les ramures de cerf ne sont plus exposées dans cette salle)

Kunstkammer

Kunsthistorisches Museum Wien

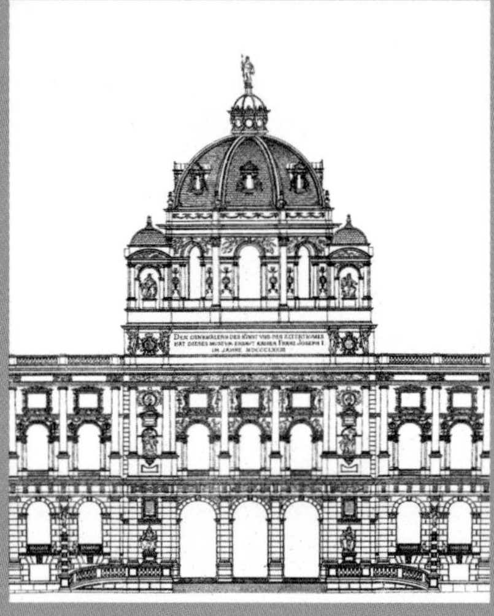

Founded 16th century
(the museum was opened in 1891)

Key item The rock crystal centre-piece in the form of a bird embellished with a real heron's feather on its head, produced in 1590 by the Saracchi workshop. This workshop in Milan was second only to that of the Miseroni family in terms of prestige.

Besonders sehenswert Ein Tafelaufsatz aus Bergkristall in Gestalt eines Vogels mit Reiherfeder auf dem Kopf, um 1590, Saracchi-Werkstatt. Saracchi war nach Miseroni die zweitwichtigste Werkstatt in Mailand.

À voir absolument Centre de table en cristal de roche en forme d'oiseau à la tête ornée d'une plume de héron, sorti de l'atelier des Saracchi et daté 1590. Par ordre d'importance, cet atelier milanais était le deuxième après celui des Miseroni.

Gottfried Semper and Carl von Hasenauer, *Drawing of the Façade of the K.K. Hofmuseum in Vienna* (detail), 1871, in *Allgemeine Bauzeitung*, 1894

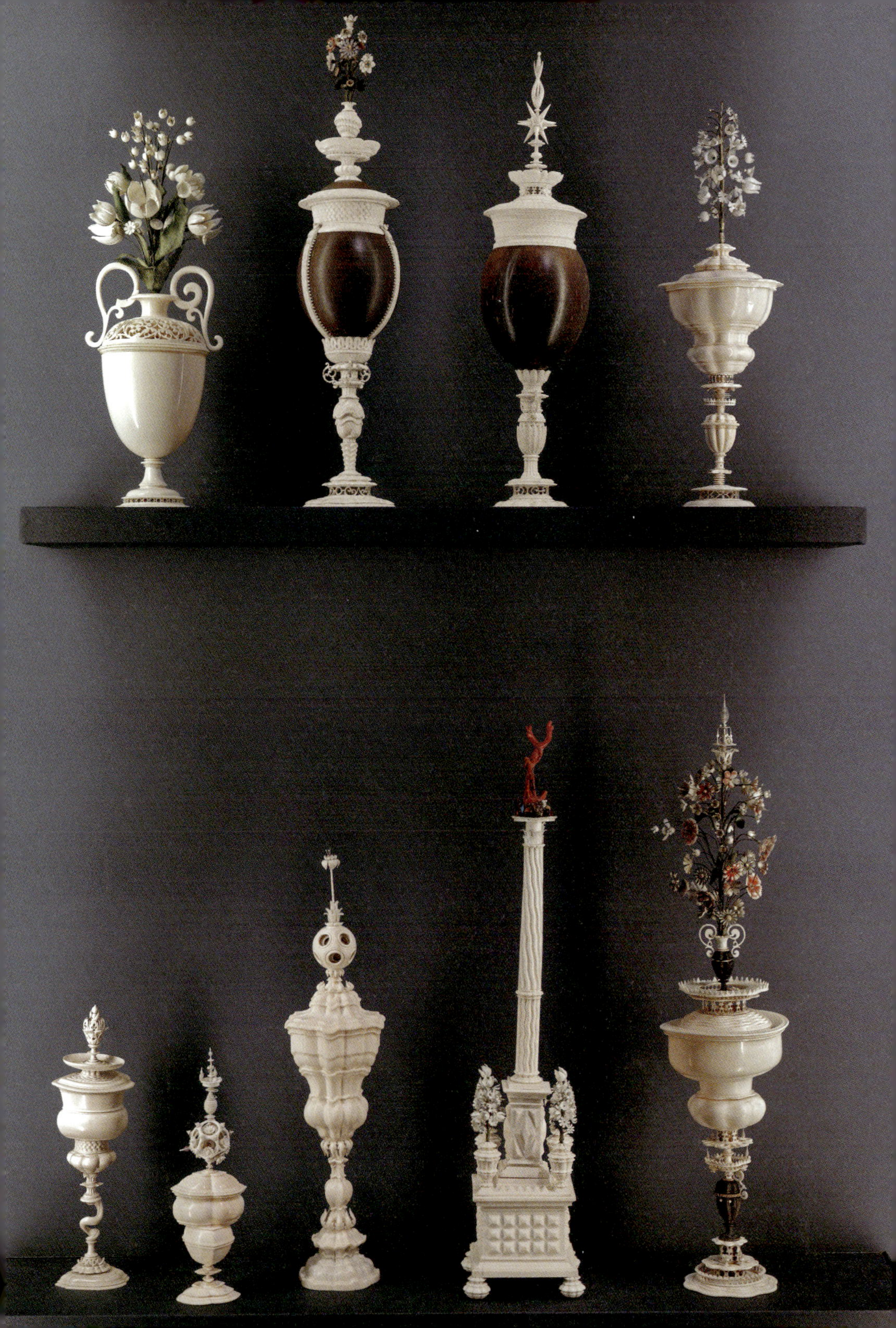

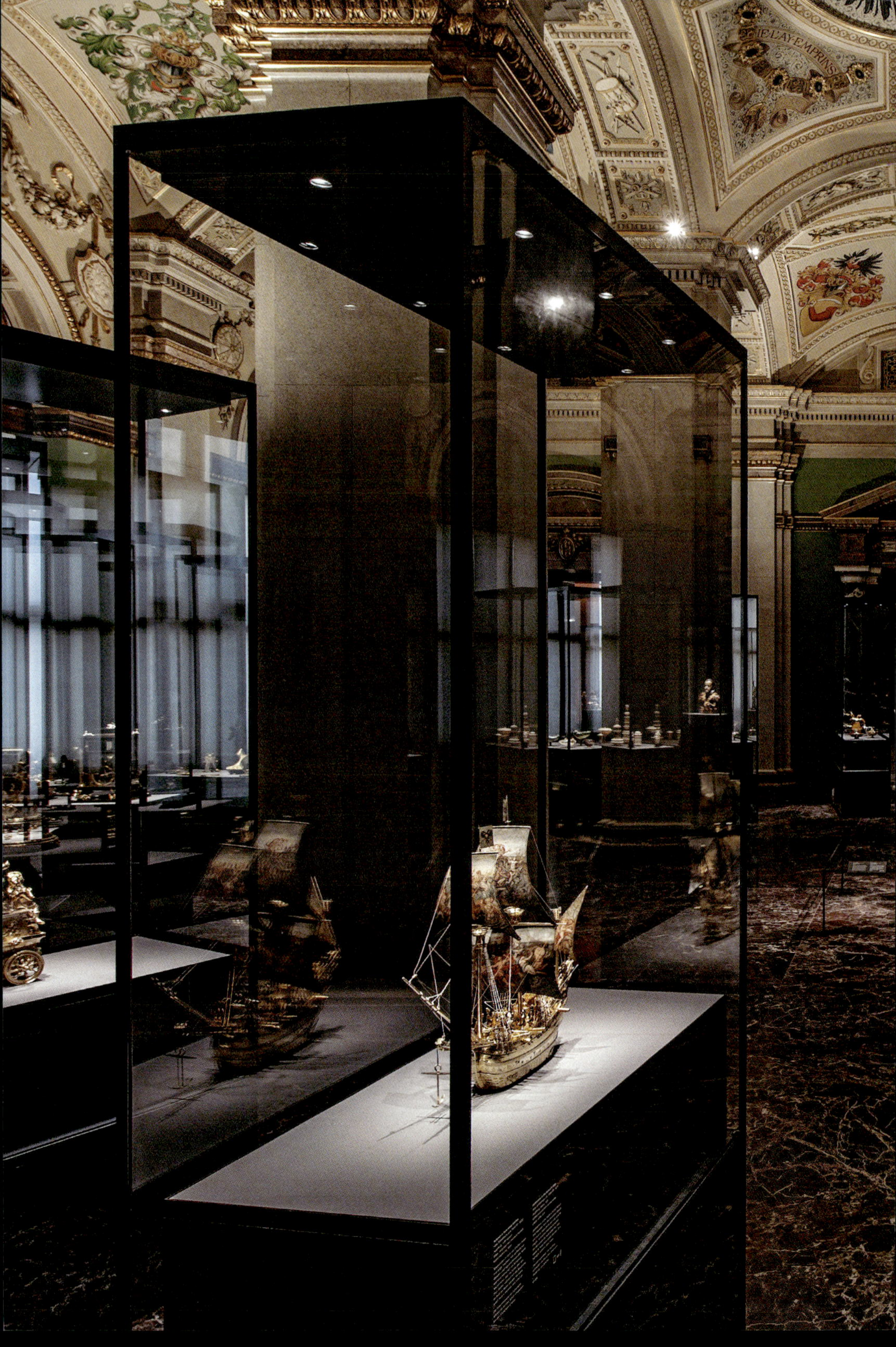

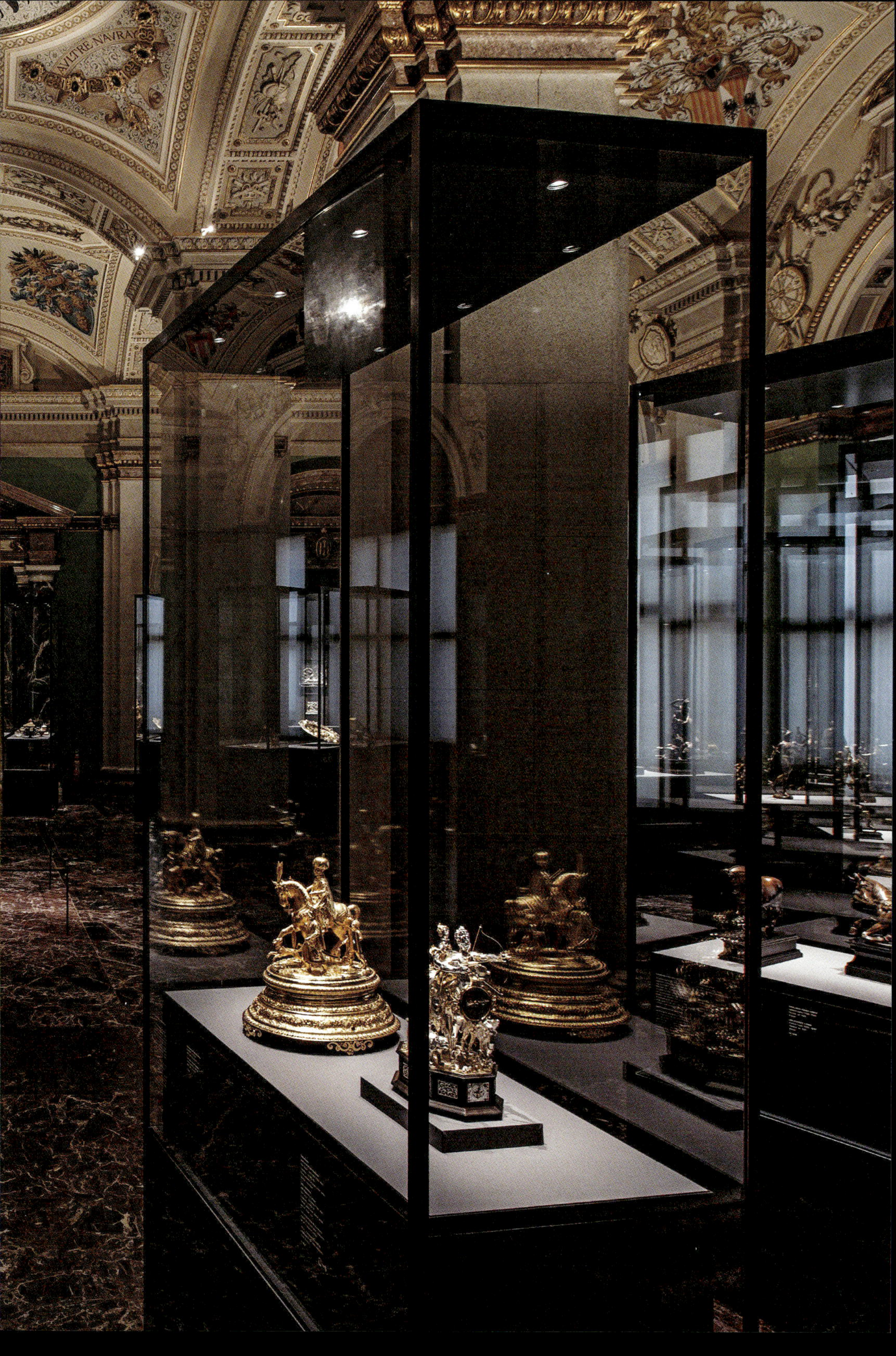

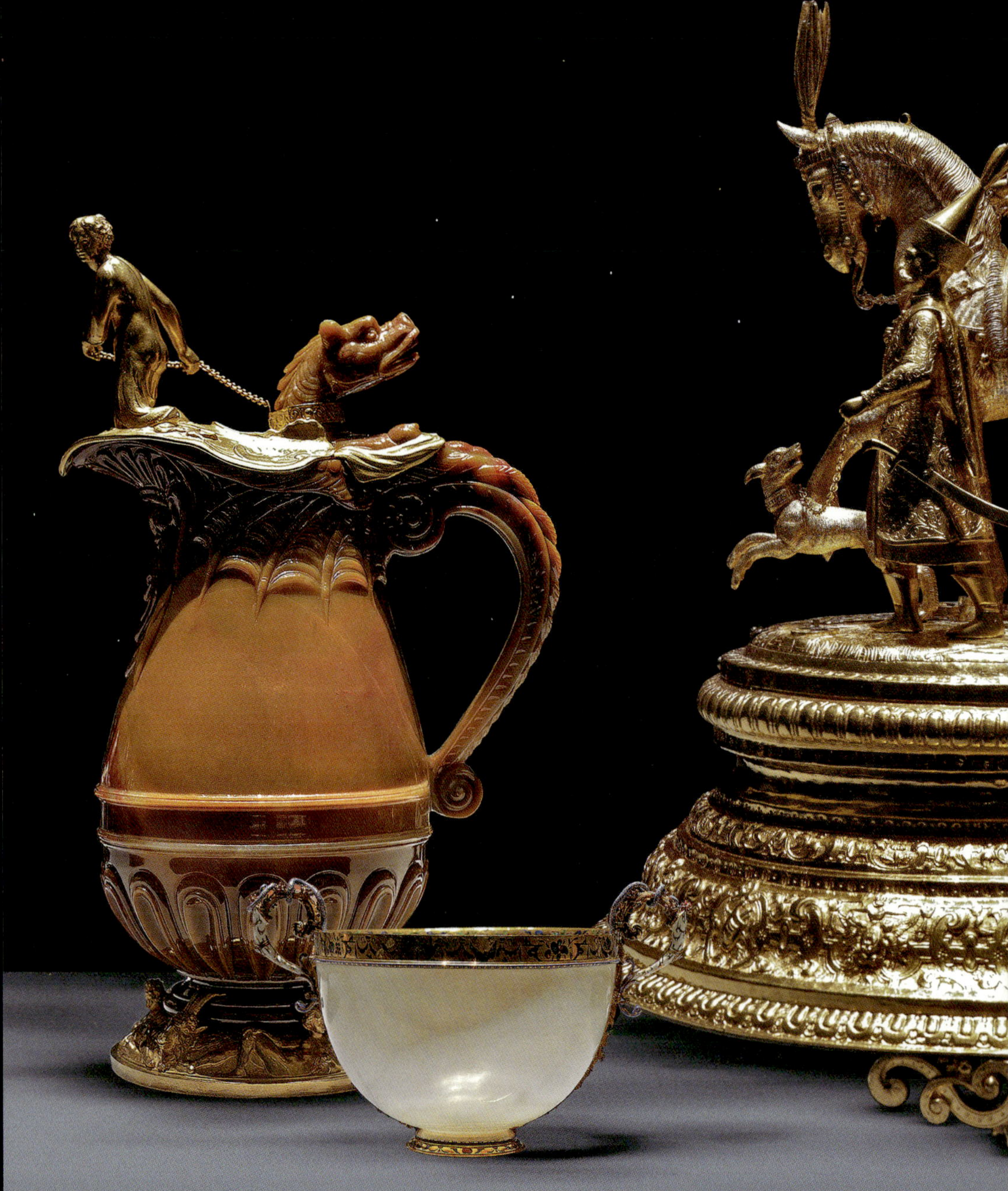

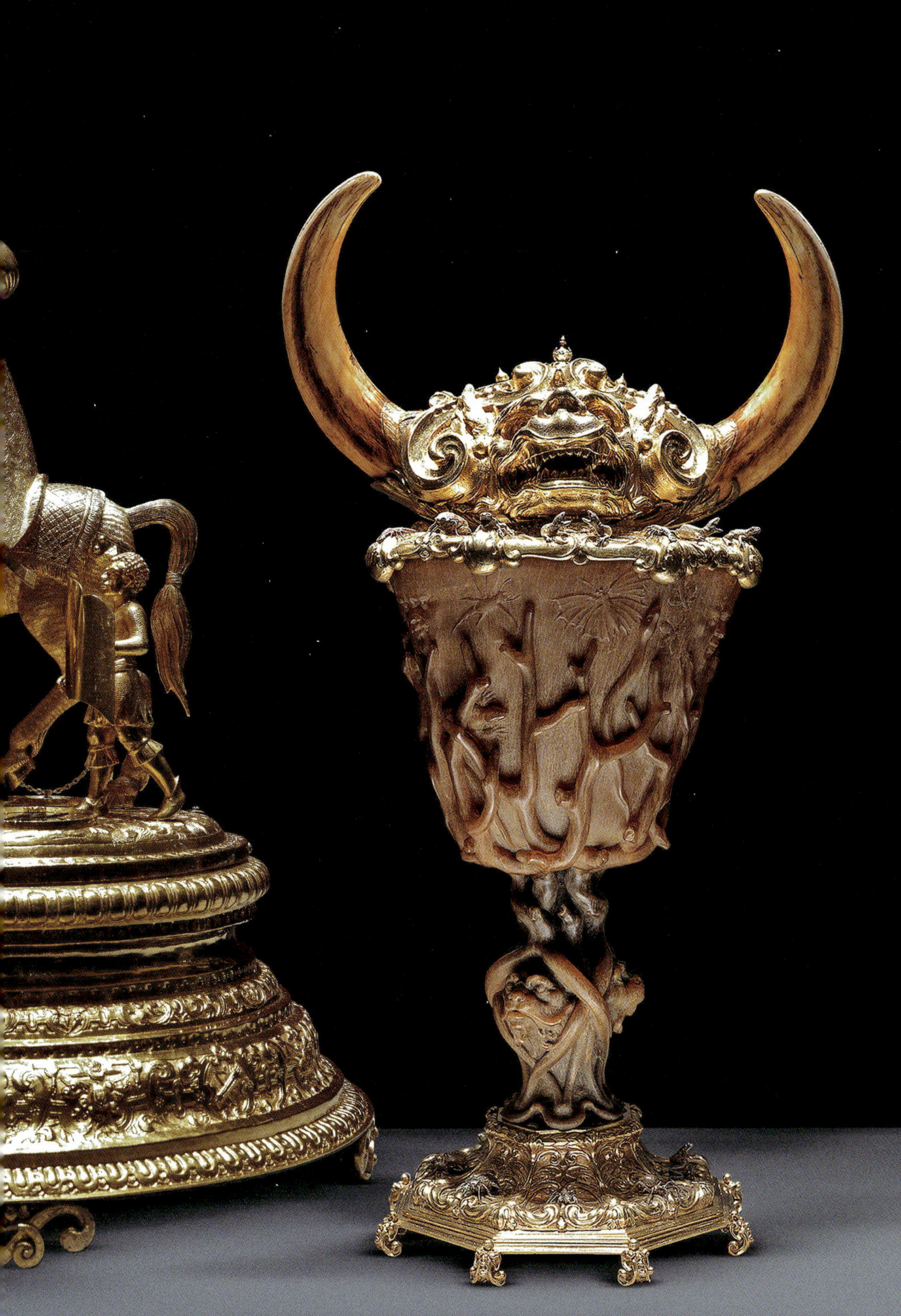

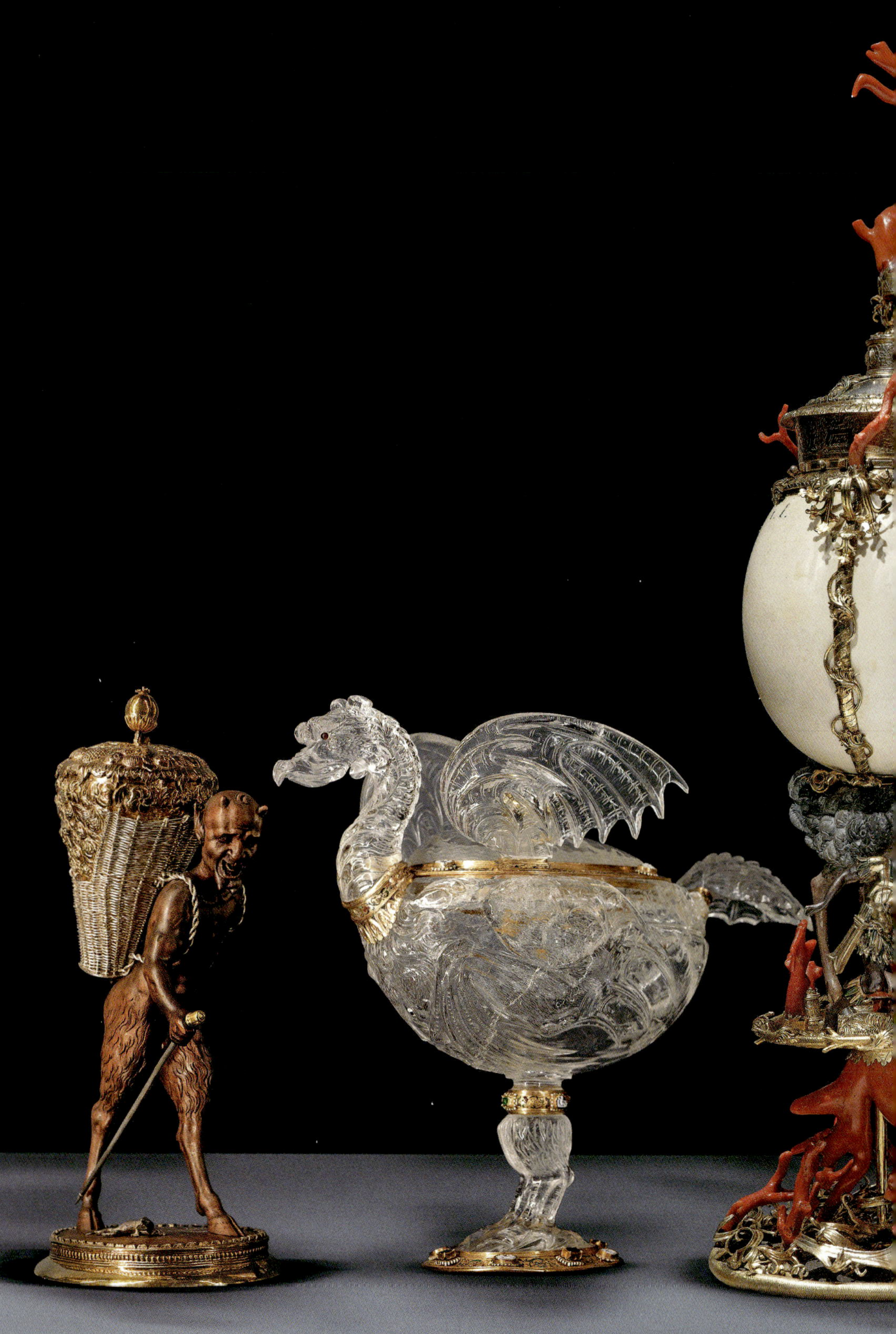

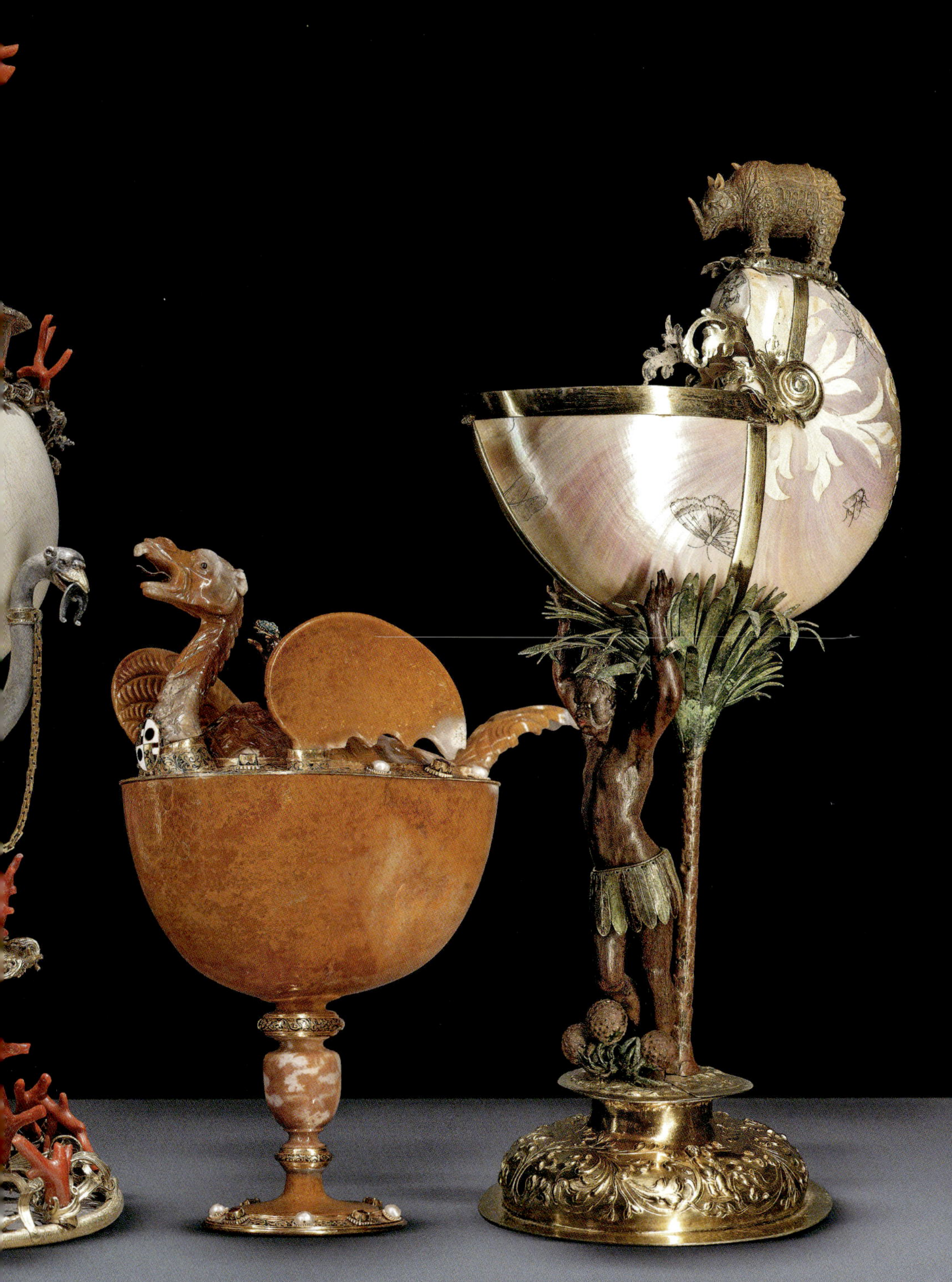

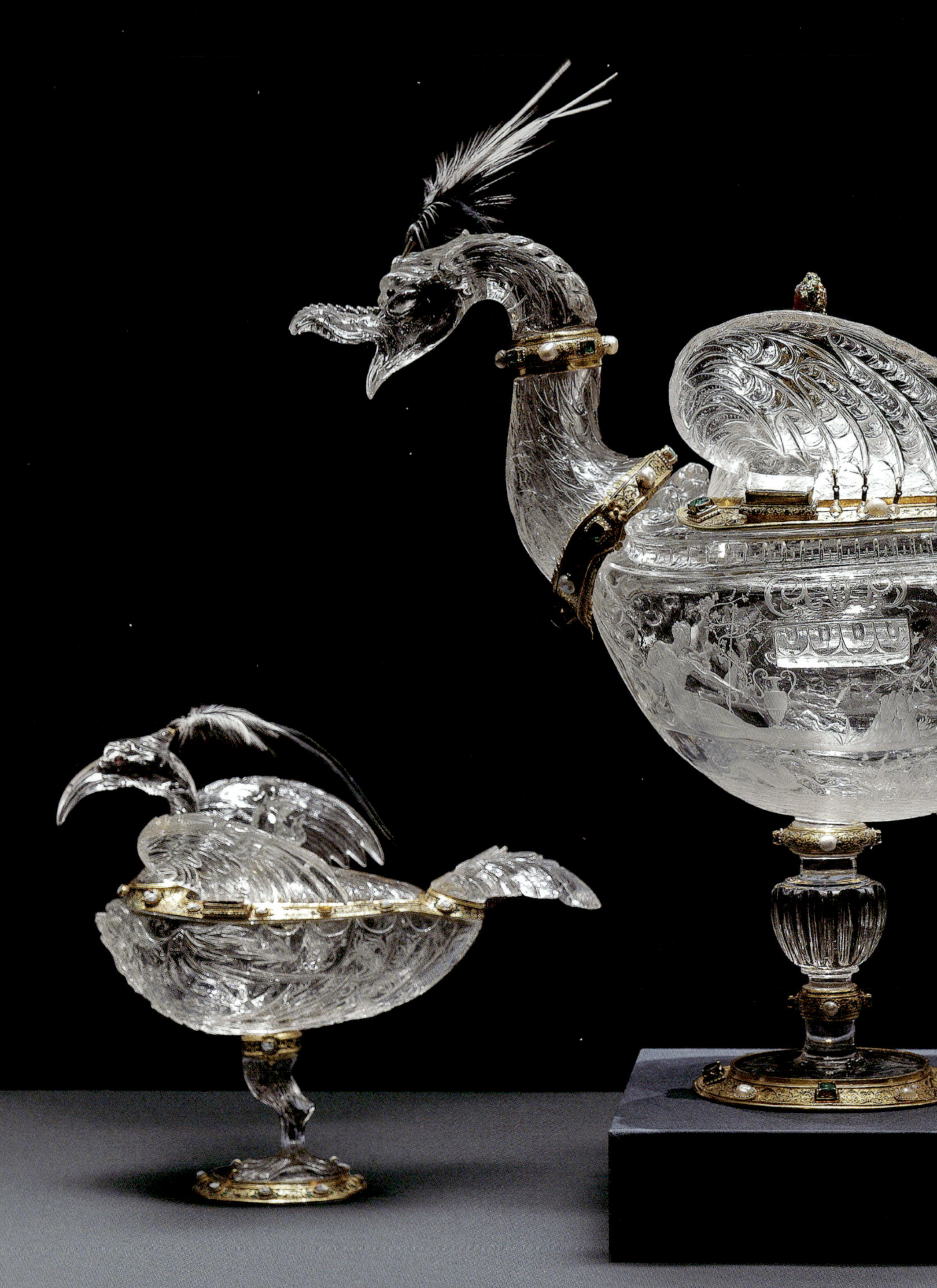

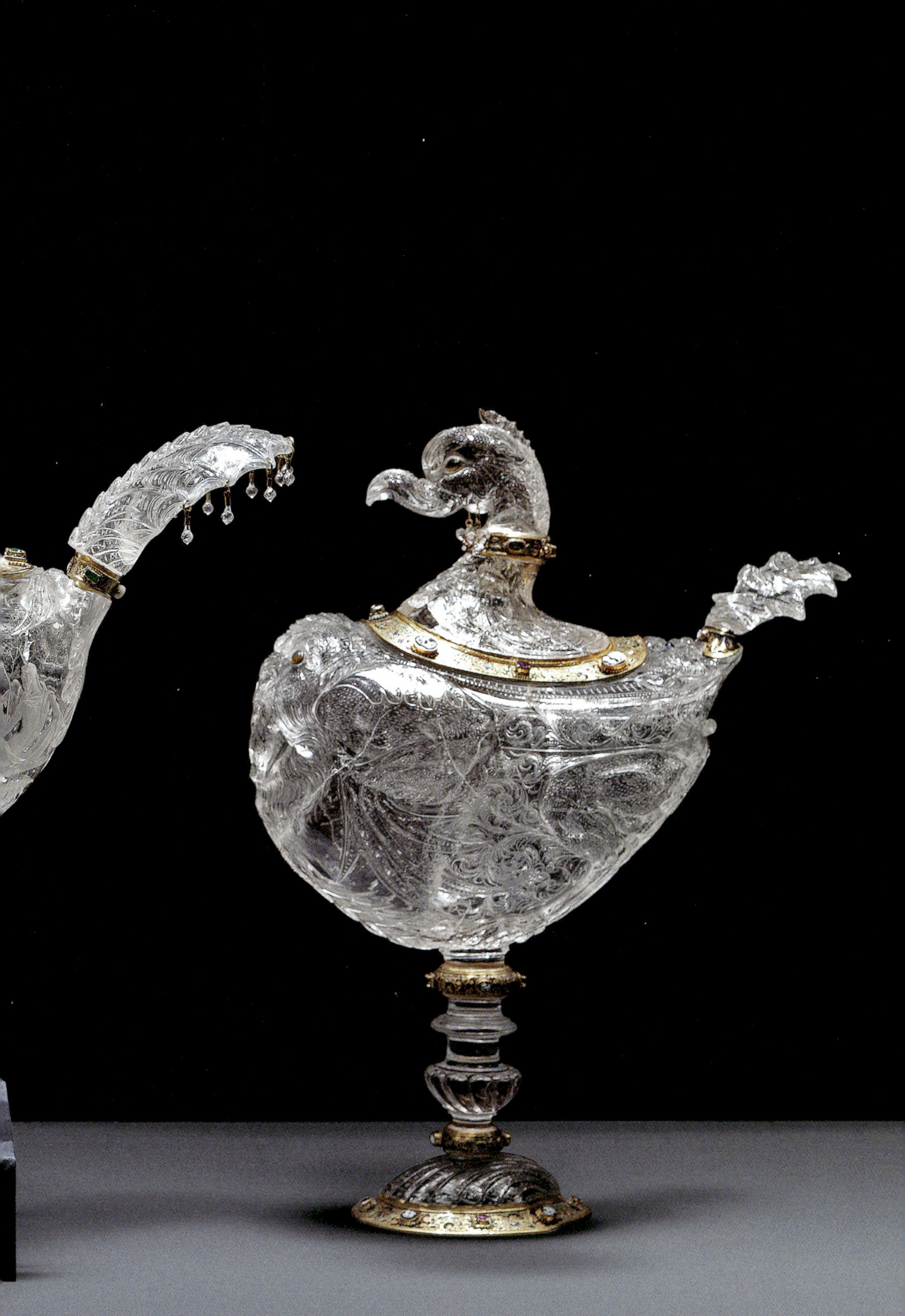

Emperor Rudolf II (1552–1612) was the greatest patron and collector of the House of Habsburg. He moved the Imperial capital to Prague and resided in its castle, where much of the empire's courtly ceremonial and cultural life now took place. A special gallery was built for his celebrated collection of paintings, and his cabinet of curiosities, already legendary during his lifetime, contained a wealth of *naturalia, scientifica* and *artificialia*. Many of these precious items were looted during the Thirty Years' War and are now dispersed among various collections. Following Rudolf's death, the Imperial capital was moved back to Vienna together with a large part of his collection, which is now in the Kunsthistorisches Museum. First opened in 1891 by Emperor Franz Joseph (1830–1916), the museum was designed to accommodate the enormous Habsburg art collection, which included items from the early cabinet of curiosities assembled by Archduke Ferdinand II (1529–1595) at Ambras Castle.

Today, the Kunstkammer forms one of the collections held in the Kunsthistorisches Museum and numbers over 2,100 artefacts, among them such outstanding masterpieces as the *Saliera* (salt cellar) by Benvenuto Cellini (1500–1571), the so-called *Krumau Madonna* from Český Krumlov, Diana Riding a Centaur—a remarkable automaton featuring a centaur that rolls its eyes and fires arrows—and the Automaton in the Form of a Ship, one of many inanimate objects that miraculously seem to come to life. There are also fantastic pieces such as the Goblet with a Lid made from rhinoceros horn, with warthog tusks, by Nikolaus Pfaff (1556?–1612), the Ostrich Egg Goblet by Clement Kicklinger (1561–1617) and numerous exotic curiosities from distant lands that were only just being discovered. Last but not least are the richly engraved rock crystal vessels made by the Miseroni in Milan. Already regarded as the leading producers of exquisite treasures in the 16th and 17th centuries, they created precious artworks using shells, gold and gems, enamel and rock crystal.

Following a comprehensive refurbishment, the Kunstkammer was reopened in 2013 and the treasures amassed by the Habsburgs are now installed in 20 galleries covering an area of more than 2,700 m² (over 29,000 square feet), including sculptures, exquisite goldsmith work, ivories, bronzes and amber artefacts, hardstone vessels, automata, clocks, scientific instruments and technical toys.

◉ ❖ ◉

Kaiser Rudolf II. (1552–1612) war der bedeutendste Kunstmäzen und Sammler des Hauses Habsburg. Die Prager Burg wurde unter ihm zur kaiserlichen Residenz. Große Teile des höfisch-zeremoniellen und des kulturellen Lebens fanden dort statt, und für seine bedeutende Gemäldesammlung ließ er eine eigene Galerie errichten. Seine Kunstkammer mit *Naturalia, Scientifica* und *Artificialia* war schon zu seinen Lebzeiten legendär. Während des Dreißigjährigen Kriegs kamen viele der wertvollen Objekte abhanden und befinden sich heute verstreut in anderen Sammlungen. Ein Großteil der Sammlung gelangte jedoch nach dem Tod Rudolfs II. durch die Rückverlegung der

Residenz von Prag nach Wien, wo sie heute im Kunsthistorischen Museum aufbewahrt wird. Gegründet wurde das 1891 von Kaiser Franz Joseph (1830–1916) eröffnete Museum, um die immense Kunstsammlung der Habsburger aufzunehmen, darunter auch die Bestände der historischen, von Erzherzog Ferdinand II. (1529–1595) gegründeten Kunstkammer in Schloss Ambras.

Zu den mehr als 2100 ausgestellten Objekten der heutigen Kunstkammer, die einen Sammlungsbereich innerhalb des Kunsthistorischen Museums darstellt, gehören unter anderem solche Meisterwerke wie die *Saliera* von Benvenuto Cellini (1500–1571), die sogenannte *Krumauer Madonna*, ein außergewöhnlicher Tischautomat mit Diana auf dem Kentauren, dessen Kentaur mit den Augen rollt und einen Pfeil abschießt, und der Automat in Form eines Schiffs, eines der vielen künstlich bewegten Objekte. Oder so fantastische Stücke wie der Deckelpokal aus Rhinozeroshorn mit Warzenschweinhauern von Nikolaus Pfaff (vermutlich 1556–1612), der Straußenei-Pokal von Clement Kicklinger (1561–1617) sowie weitere Kuriositäten aus fernen Ländern, die man damals gerade erst entdeckte. Und schließlich die reichverzierten Gefäße aus Bergkristall der Werkstatt Miseroni in Mailand. Dort war man bereits im 16. und 17. Jahrhundert auf exquisite Schatzkunst spezialisiert und fertigte aus Muscheln, Gold und Gemmen, Email und Kristall zahlreiche Meisterwerke.

Nach einer grundlegenden Sanierung wurde 2013 diese großartige Kunstkammer wieder eröffnet, und in 20 Räumen werden heute auf insgesamt 2700 m² die Kunstschätze der Habsburger präsentiert: Skulpturen, ausgefallenes Kunsthandwerk aus Gold, Elfenbein, Bronze und Bernstein, Steingefäße, Uhren, Automaten, wissenschaftliche Instrumente, technische Spielereien und vieles mehr.

◉ ❖ ◉

L'empereur Rodolphe II (1552–1612) fut le plus grand grand mécène et collectionneur de la maison Habsbourg. Sous son règne, le château de Prague devint la résidence impériale, et une grande partie de la vie cérémonielle et culturelle de la cour s'y déroulait. Il fit construire une galerie pour son importante collection de peintures, et sa *Kunstkammer* qui rassemblait *naturalia, scientifica* et *artificialia* devint légendaire de son vivant. Un grand nombre de pièces de valeur, perdues durant la guerre de Trente Ans, sont maintenant dispersées dans d'autres collections. Toutefois, après la mort de Rodolphe II, une grande partie de la collection a été transférée à Vienne lors du changement de résidence et est conservée aujourd'hui au Kunsthistorisches Museum. Inauguré en 1891 en présence de l'empereur François-Joseph (1830–1916), le musée était destiné à recevoir la très riche collection d'art des Habsbourg qui englobait les œuvres de l'ancienne *Kunstkammer* créée par Ferdinand II (1529–1595) au château d'Ambras.

Parmi les 2100 objets exposés de l'actuelle *Kunstkammer,* qui représente un domaine de collection au sein du Kunsthistorisches Museum, figurent plusieurs chefs-d'œuvre dont la *Salière* de Benvenuto Cellini (1500–1571), la *Vierge de Krumlov* provenant de Český

Krumlov, Diane chevauchant un centaure – automate d'une facture extraordinaire,
dont le centaure roule les yeux et tire une flèche –, et l'Automate en forme de nef, l'un
des nombreux objets pouvant être mis en mouvement. Ou des pièces aussi étonnantes
que la Coupe à couvercle en corne de rhinocéros avec des défenses de phacochère due
à Nikolaus Pfaff (1556 ?–1612) ou bien celle élaborée par Clement Kicklinger (1561–1617)
à partir d'un œuf d'autruche, entre autres curiosités provenant des mondes lointains
que l'on découvrait alors. Sans oublier les vases d'apparat en cristal de roche richement
décorés, créés par l'atelier des Miseroni à Milan. Spécialistes dès les 16ᵉ et 17ᵉ siècles de
pièces exquises destinées aux cabinets au trésor, ils fabriquaient de nombreux chefs-
d'œuvre en coquillages, or et pierres précieuses, émaux et cristaux.

Après avoir été rénovée en profondeur, cette magnifique *Kunstkammer* a été rou-
verte en 2013 et présente dans 20 salles sur un total de 2700 m² les trésors artistiques
des Habsbourg: sculptures, objets d'art insolites en or, ivoire, bronze et ambre, récipients en pierre, horloges, automates, instruments scientifiques, gadgets techniques
et bien plus encore.

1 View of a display case, con-
taining ivory objects made in
Germany from the 17th century.
Blick in eine Vitrine mit deutschen
Elfenbeinarbeiten des 17. Jhs.
Une étagère vitrée avec des
œuvres allemandes en ivoire du
17ᵉ siècle.
From top left to bottom right:
Von oben links nach unten rechts:
De gauche à droite et de haut
en bas :

1a *Vase of Flowers*, Germany, first
half of the 17th century. Ivory, gilded silver, fabric, 30.7 cm / 12⅛ in.
Blumenvase, Deutschland, 1. Hälfte
17. Jh. Elfenbein, Silber, vergoldet,
Textil, 30,7 cm.
Vase à fleurs, Allemagne, 1ᵉ moitié
du 17ᵉ siècle. Ivoire, argent doré,
tissu, 30,7 cm.

1b *Lidded Cup with Bouquet
of Flowers*, southern Germany,
first half of the 17th century.
Coconut, ivory, 38.2 cm / 15 in.
Deckelpokal mit Blumenbukett,
Süddeutschland, 1. Hälfte 17. Jh.
Kokosnuss, Elfenbein, 38,2 cm.
*Coupe à couvercle avec bouquet
de fleurs*, Allemagne du Sud,
1ᵉ moitié du 17ᵉ siècle. Noix de
coco, ivoire, 38,2 cm.

1c *Lidded Cup*, southern
Germany, first half of the
17th century. Coconut, ivory,
35.8 cm / 14⅛ in.
Deckelpokal, Süddeutschland,
1. Hälfte 17. Jh. Kokosnuss, Elfenbein, 35,8 cm.
Coupe à couvercle, sud de l'Allemagne, 1ᵉ moitié du 17ᵉ siècle.
Noix de coco, ivoire, 35,8 cm.

1d *Lidded Cup with Bouquet of
Flowers*, Germany, first half of the
17th century. Ivory, 32 cm / 12⅝ in.
Deckelpokal mit Blumenbukett,
Deutschland, 1. Hälfte 17. Jh.
Elfenbein, 32 cm.
*Coupe à couvercle avec bouquet
de fleurs*, Allemagne, 1ᵉ moitié du
17ᵉ siècle. Ivoire, 32 cm.

1e *Lidded Cup*, Germany, first
half of the 17th century. Ivory,
21.9 cm / 8⅝ in.
Deckelpokal, Deutschland,
1. Hälfte 17. Jh. Elfenbein, 21,9 cm.
Coupe à couvercle, Allemagne,
1ᵉ moitié du 17ᵉ siècle. Ivoire, 21,9 cm.

1f *Lidded Beaker with Spiny
Ball*, Germany, first half of the
17th century. Ivory, 18.8 cm / 7⅜ in.
Deckelbecher mit Stachelkugel,

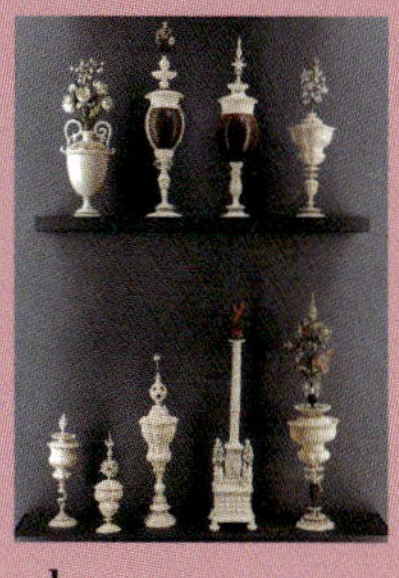

1

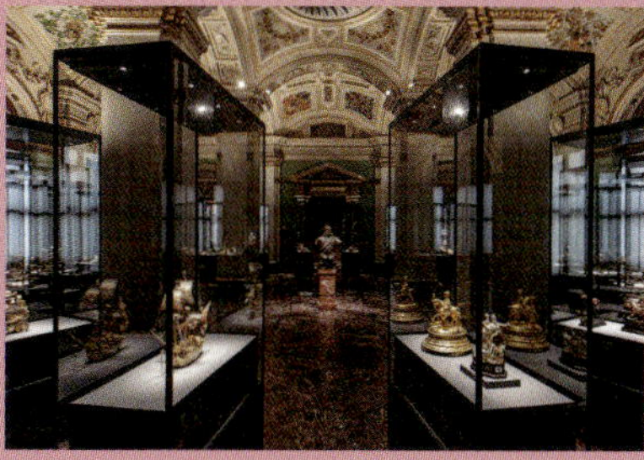

2

Deutschland, 1. Hälfte 17. Jh.
Elfenbein, 18,8 cm.
*Coupe à couvercle avec boule à
pointes*, Allemagne, 1ᵉ moitié du
17ᵉ siècle. Ivoire, 18,8 cm.

1g Johann Eisenberg, *Lidded
Cup with Contrefait (Portrait) Ball*,
Coburg, 1637. Ivory, 34.2 cm / 13½ in.
Johann Eisenberg, *Deckelpokal
mit Konterfettenkugel*, Coburg,
1637. Elfenbein, 34,2 cm.
Johann Eisenberg, *Coupe à
couvercle avec boule à portrait*,
Cobourg 1637. Ivoire, 34,2 cm.

1h Achilles Ag., *Columnar Centrepiece with St. Sebastian*, middle of
the 17th century. Ivory, coral,
44.1 x 9.8 x 10 cm / 17⅜ x 3⅞ x 4 in.
Achilles Ag., *Aufsatz in Säulenform
mit heiligem Sebastian*, Mitte 17. Jh.

Elfenbein, Koralle, 44,1 x 9,8 x 10 cm.
Achilles Ag., *Pièce centrale en forme
de colonne avec saint Sébastien*,
milieu du 17ᵉ siècle. Ivoire, corail,
44,1 x 9,8 x 10 cm.

1i *Lidded Cup with Bouquet of
Flowers*, Germany, second quarter
of the 17th century. Partially painted
ivory, wood, fabric, 46 cm / 18⅛ in.
Deckelpokal mit Blumenbukett,
Deutschland, 2. Viertel 17. Jh.
Elfenbein, teils bemalt, Holz,
Textil, 46 cm.
*Coupe à couvercle avec bouquet
de fleurs*, Allemagne, 2ᵉ quart
du 17ᵉ siècle. Ivoire en partie peint,
bois, tissu, 46 cm.

2 View of Room 27. In the centre
of this room, which is devoted to
Emperor Rudolf II and the cabinet

of curiosities he created in Prague,
is a bronze bust of Rudolf by Adriaen
de Vries, dated 1603. This sculpture, together with all the other
objects in this room, were originally
part of Rudolf's collection.
Blick in Saal 27. Das Zentrum dieses
Saals, der sich mit Kaiser Rudolf II.
und seiner Kunstkammer in Prag
auseinandersetzt, zeigt ihn in einer
Bronzebüste von Adriaen de Vries,
datiert 1603. Sie stammt ebenso
wie die sie umgebenden Objekte
aus der Kunstkammer des Kaisers.
Vue sur la salle 27. Au centre de
cette salle, consacrée à Rodolphe
II et à son Cabinet d'art à Prague,
l'Empereur est représenté dans un
buste en bronze d'Adriaen de Vries,
daté 1603. Celui-ci, ainsi que les
objets qui l'entourent, provient du
Cabinet d'art de l'Empereur.

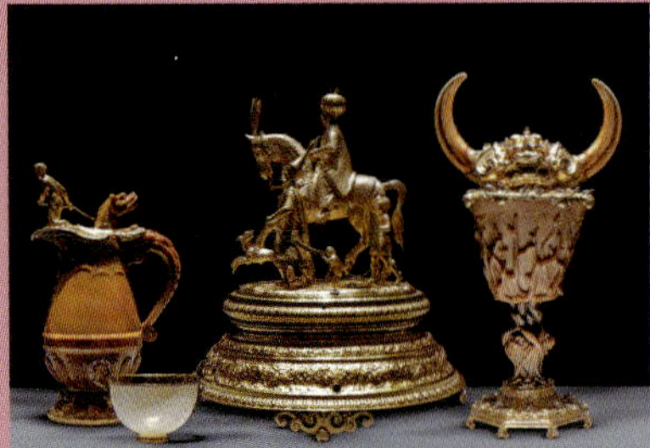

3

3a Ottavio Miseroni, Paulus van Vianen (mounting), *Jug*, Prague, *c.* 1588–1600; mounting dated 1608. Chalcedony, gold, 35.5 x 22 x 14.5 cm / 14 x 8⅝ x 5¾ in.
Ottavio Miseroni, Paulus van Vianen (Fassung), *Krug*, Prag, um 1588–1600; Fassung datiert 1608. Chalcedon, Gold, 35,5 x 22 x 14,5 cm.
Ottavio Miseroni, Paulus van Vianen (assemblage), *Pichet*, Prague, vers 1588–1600 ; assemblage daté de 1608. Calcédoine, or, 35,5 x 22 x 14,5 cm.

3b Attributed to Ottavio Miseroni, Jan Vermeyen (mounting), *Bowl with Handles*, Prague, *c.* 1600–1605. Chalcedony, gold, enamel, 10.2 x 17.2 cm / 4 x 6¾ in.
Ottavio Miseroni (zugeschrieben), Jan Vermeyen (Fassung), *Henkelschale*, Prag, um 1600–1605. Chalcedon, Gold, Email, 10,2 x 17,2 cm.
Ottavio Miseroni (attr.), Jan Vermeyen (assemblage), *Bol à poignées*, Prague, vers 1600–1605. Calcédoine, or, émail, 10,2 x 17,2 cm.

3c *Automaton of a Pasha on Horseback*, southern Germany,
c. 1580–1590. Gilded copper alloy, iron, 47.5 x 42 x 34 cm / 18¾ x 16½ x 13⅜ in.
Automatenuhr mit reitendem Pascha, Süddeutschland, um 1580–1590. Eisen, Kupferlegierung, vergoldet, 47,5 x 42 x 34 cm.
Horloge automatique avec un Pacha à cheval, Allemagne du Sud, vers 1580–1590. Alliage de cuivre doré, fer, 47,5 x 42 x 34 cm.

3d Nikolaus Pfaff, *Lidded Cup*, Prague, 1611. Rhinoceros horn, warthog tusks, gilded and partially painted silver, 49.7 x 27.5 x 17.7 cm / 19⅝ x 10⅞ x 7 in.
Nikolaus Pfaff, *Deckelpokal*, Prag, 1611. Rhinozeroshorn, Warzenschweinhauer, Silber, vergoldet, teilweise bemalt, 49,7 x 27,5 x 17,7 cm.
Nikolaus Pfaff, *Coupe à couvercle*, Prague, 1611. Corne de rhinocéros, défense de phacochère, argent doré, en partie peint, 49,7 x 27,5 x 17,7 cm.

4a Hans Heinrich II Rollenbutz, *Satyr with a Hod*, Zurich, first half of the 17th century. Boxwood, partially gilded silver, 24.8 cm / 9¾ in.
Hans Heinrich II. Rollenbutz, *Satyr als Buttenmännchen*, Zürich,
1. Hälfte 17. Jh. Buchsbaumholz, Silber, teilweise vergoldet, 24,8 cm.
Hans Heinrich II Rollenbutz, *Satyre portant une hotte en osier*, Zurich, 1ère moitié du 17e siècle. Buis, argent en partie doré, 24,8 cm.

4b Saracchi workshop, *Ornamental Vessel, so-called Dragon-bird*, Milan, *c.* 1575–1580. Rock crystal, gold, enamel, emeralds, garnets, cameos, 24.8 x 30 x 13.9 cm / 9¾ x 11¾ x 5½ in.
Werkstatt der Saracchi, *Prunkgefäß, sogenannter Vogeldrache*, Mailand, um 1575–1580. Bergkristall, Gold, Email, Smaragde, Granate, Kameen, 24,8 x 30 x 13,9 cm.
Atelier des Saracchi, *Récipient d'apparat, dit dragon oiseau*, Milan, vers 1575–1580. Cristal de roche, or, émail, émeraudes, grenats, camées, 24,8 x 30 x 13,9 cm.

4c Clement Kicklinger, *Lidded Cup with Ostrich Egg*, Augsburg, *c.* 1570–1575. Ostrich egg, coral, partially gilded and painted silver, 56.8 cm / 22⅜ in.
Clement Kicklinger, *Deckelpokal mit Straußenei*, Augsburg, um 1570–1575. Straußenei, Koralle, Silber, teilvergoldet und bemalt, 56,8 cm.

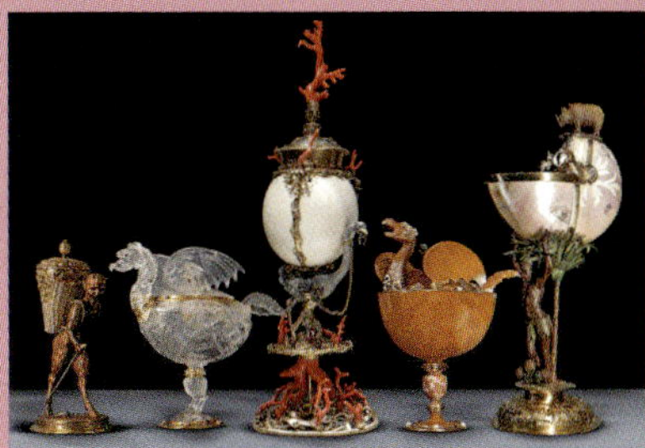

4

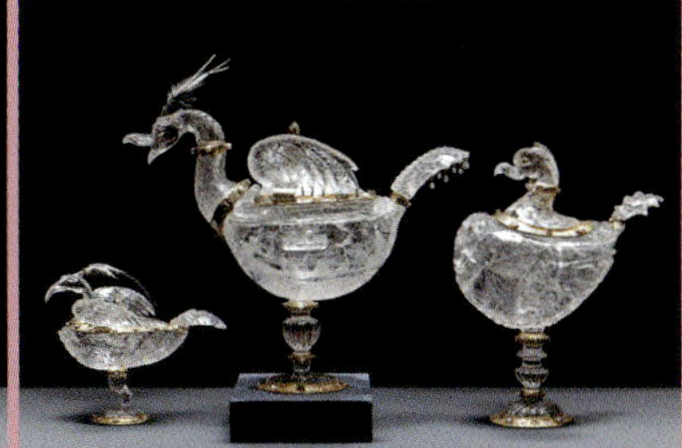

5

Clement Kicklinger, *Coupe à couvercle avec œuf d'autruche*, Augsbourg, vers 1570–1575. Œuf d'autruche, corail, argent en partie doré et peint, 56,8 cm.

4d Saracchi workshop, *Ornamental Vessel in the Form of a Dragon*, Milan, *c.* 1590. Chalcedony, gold, enamel, pearls, rubies, 28.5 x 26.4 x 13.3 cm / 11¼ x 10⅜ x 5¼ in.
Werkstatt der Saracchi, *Prunkgefäß in Gestalt eines Drachens,* Mailand, um 1590. Chalcedon, Gold, Email, Perlen, Rubine, 28,5 x 26,4 x 13,3 cm.
Atelier des Saracchi, *Récipient d'apparat en forme de dragon*, Milan, vers 1590. Calcédoine, or, émail, perles, rubis, 28,5 x 26,4 x 13,3 cm.

4e Johann Elias Geibinger, *Nautilus Cup*, Vienna, 1691. Nautilus shell, rhinoceros horn, wood, gilded and partially painted silver, 45 cm / 17¾ in.
Johann Elias Geibinger, *Nautiluspokal*, Wien, 1691. Nautilusgehäuse, Rhinozeroshorn, Holz, Silber, vergoldet, teils bemalt, 45 cm.
Johann Elias Geibinger, *Nautile monté en coupe*, Vienne, 1691.

Nautile, corne de rhinocéros, bois, argent doré et en partie peint, 45 cm.

5a Saracchi workshop, *Centrepiece, so-called Heron*, Milan, *c.* 1580. Rock crystal, garnets, cameos, gold, enamel, heron feathers, 23.7 x 29.3 x 16.4 cm / 9⅜ x 11½ x 6½ in.
Werkstatt der Saracchi, *Tafelaufsatz, sogenannter Raiger*, Mailand, um 1580. Bergkristall, Granate, Kameen, Gold, Email, Reiherfedern, 23,7 x 29,3 x 16,4 cm.
Atelier des Saracchi, *Centre de table, dit Héron*, Milan, vers 1580. Cristal de roche, grenats, camées, or, émail, plumes de héron, 23,7 x 29,3 x 16,4 cm.

5b Saracchi workshop, *Large Centrepiece in the Form of a Dragon-bird*, Milan, *c.* 1590. Rock crystal, emeralds, jacinth, rubies, pearls, glass, gold, enamel, heron feathers, 39.4 x 50 x 23.3 cm / 15½ x 19¾ x 9⅛ in.
Werkstatt der Saracchi, *Großer Tafelaufsatz in Gestalt eines Vogeldrachens*, Mailand, um 1590. Bergkristall, Smaragde, Hyazinth, Rubine, Perlen, Glasstein, Gold, Email, Reiherfedern, 39,4 x 50 x 23,3 cm.

Atelier des Saracchi, *Grand centre de table en forme de dragon oiseau*, Milan, vers 1590. Cristal de roche, émeraudes, hyacinthe, rubis, perles, pierre de verre, or, émail, plumes de héron, 39,4 x 50 x 23,3 cm.

5c Saracchi workshop, *Centrepiece in the Form of a Dragonbird*, Milan, *c.* 1580. Rock crystal, rubies, topaz, cameos, gold, enamel, 43.8 x 34 x 15.9 cm / 17¼ x 13⅜ x 6¼ in.
Werkstatt der Saracchi, *Tafelaufsatz in Gestalt eines Vogeldrachens*, Mailand, um 1580. Bergkristall, Rubine, Topas, Kameen, Gold, Email, 43,8 x 34 x 15,9 cm.
Atelier des Saracchi, *Centre de table en forme de dragon oiseau*, Milan, vers 1580. Cristal de roche, rubis, topaze, camées, or, émail, 43,8 x 34 x 15,9 cm.

Das Mineralienkabinett

Stift Seitenstetten

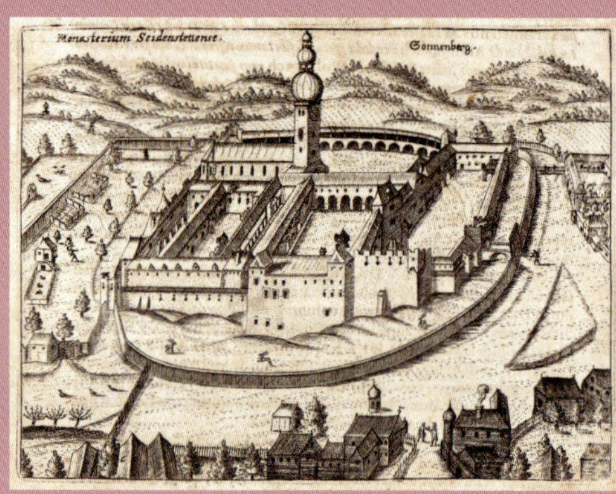

Founded 1766

Key item Among the rarest and most precious objects in the collection is a piece of limestone from the Dolomites measuring 14 x 12 cm (5½ x 4¾ in.) with a large silver vein (predominantly acanthite), which was found in a silver mine near Annaberg, Lower Austria.

Besonders sehenswert Ein 14 x 12 cm großer Kalkstein aus den Dolomiten mit einer dicken Silberader (zum größten Teil aus Akanthit), der in einem Silberbergwerk im niederösterreichischen Annaberg gefunden wurde.

À voir absolument Parmi les pièces les plus rares et les plus précieuses se trouve une pierre calcaire provenant des Dolomites, mesurant 14 x 12 cm et présentant une grande veine d'argent (d'acanthite surtout) découverte dans une mine d'argent d'Annaberg en Basse-Autriche.

Carolus Stengel, *Seitenstetten Abbey*, in *Monasteriologia*, Augsburg, 1638, p. 21

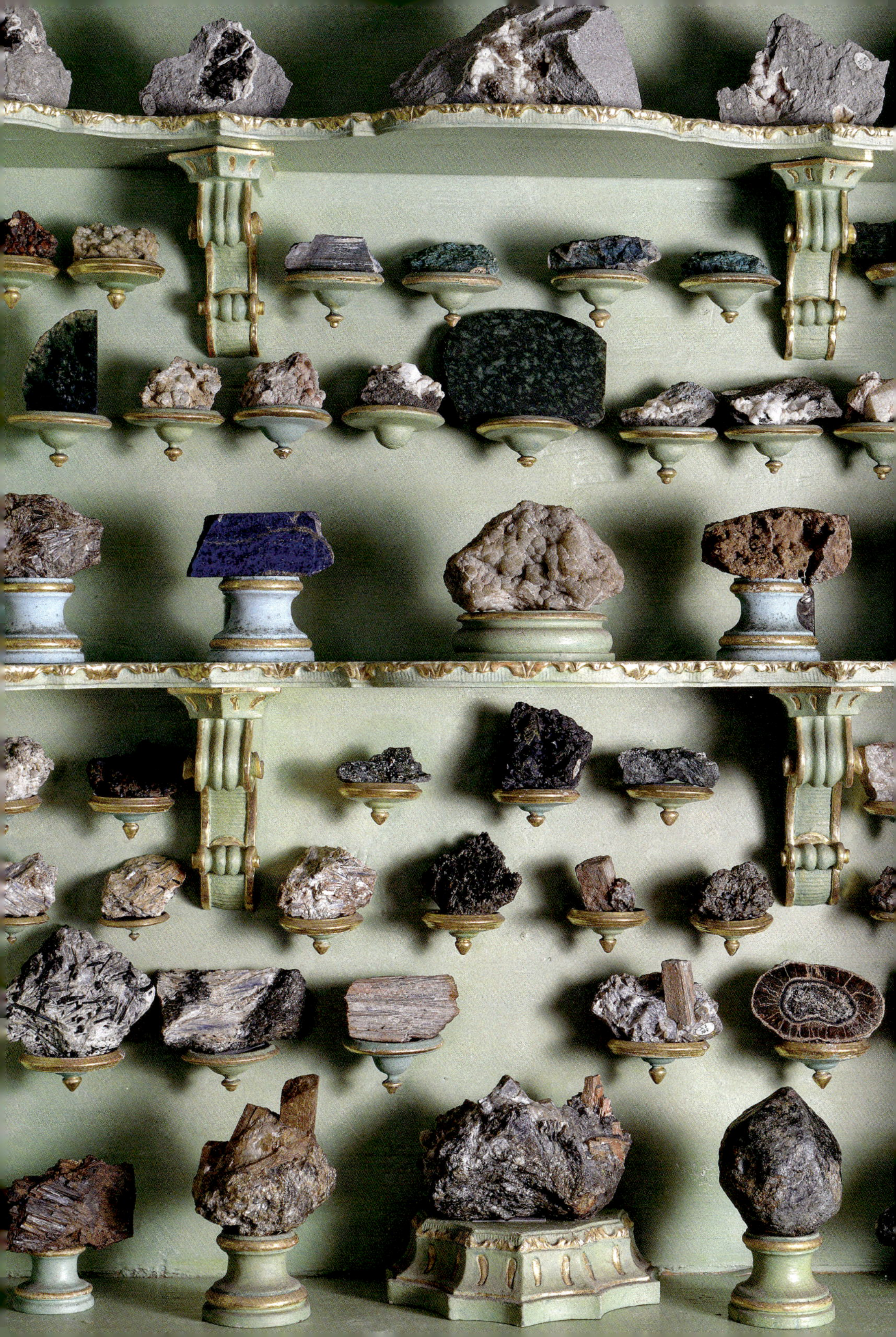

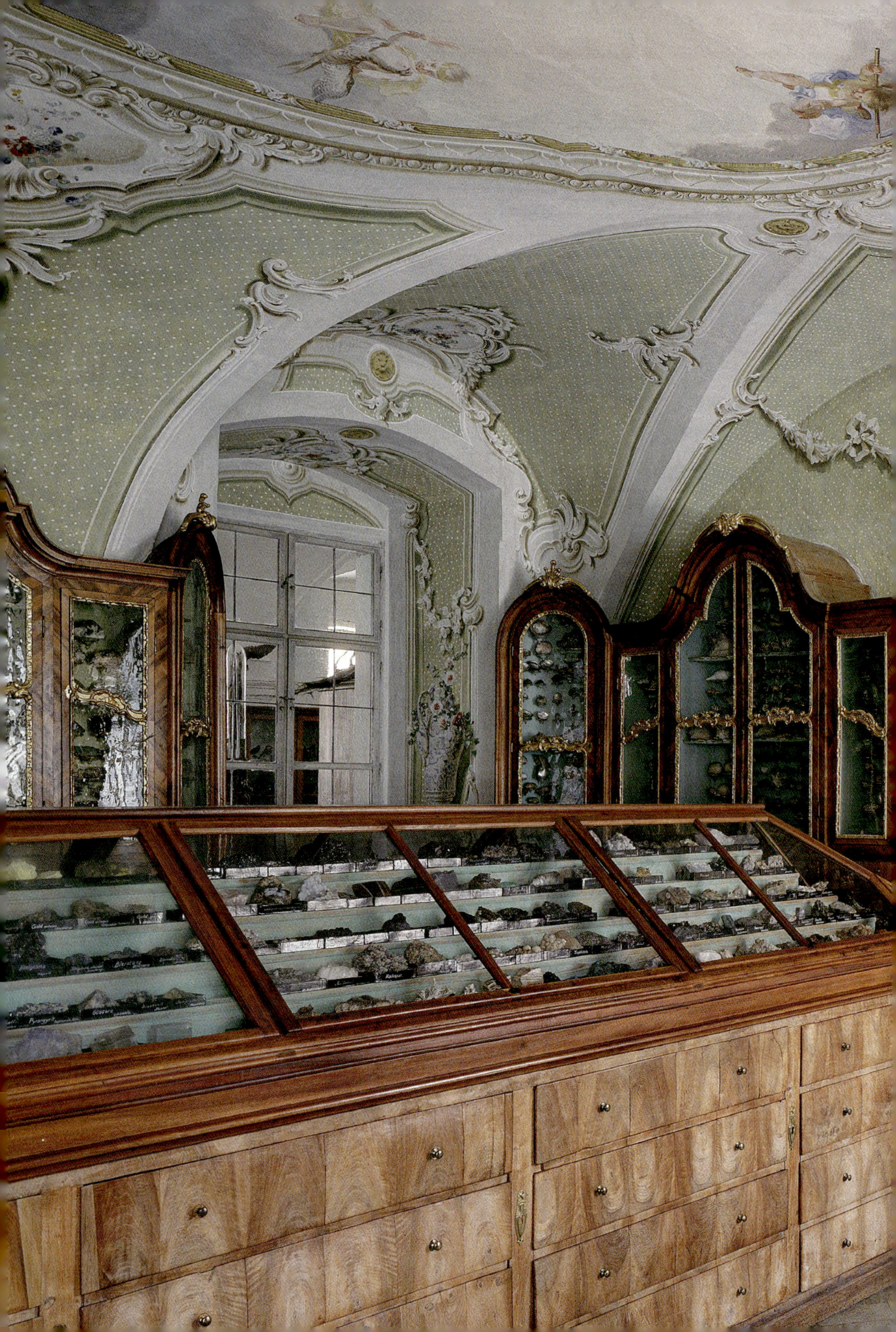

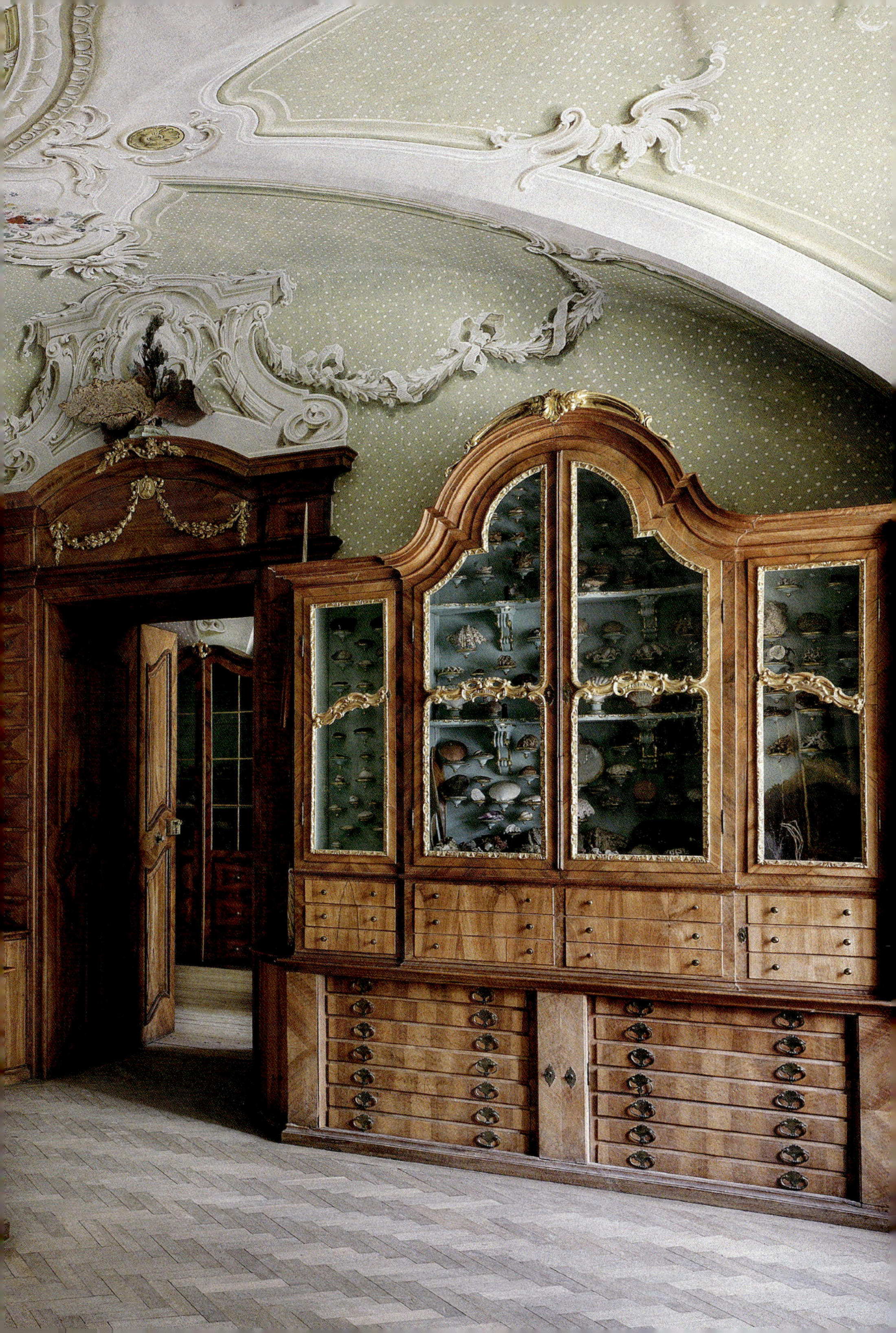

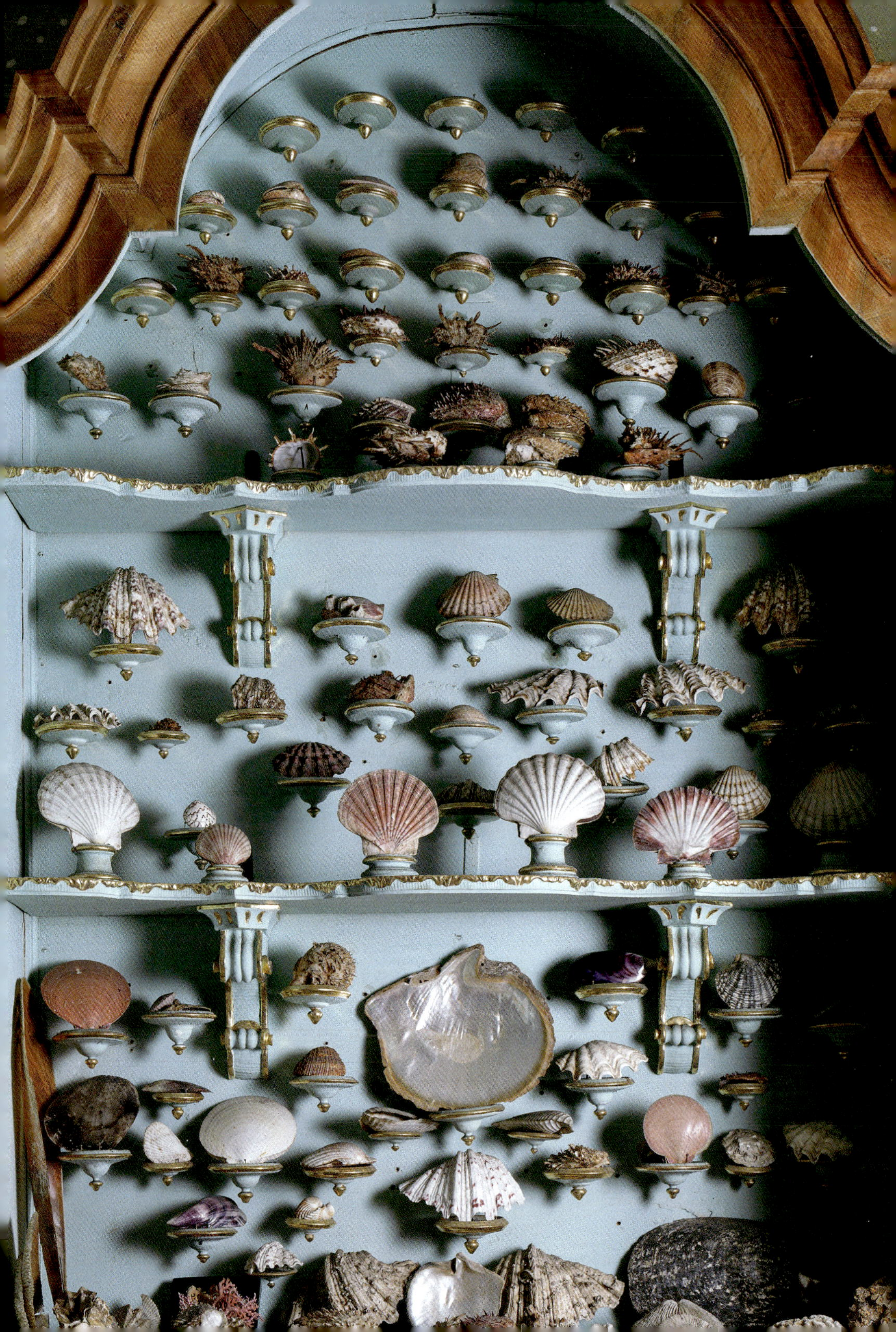

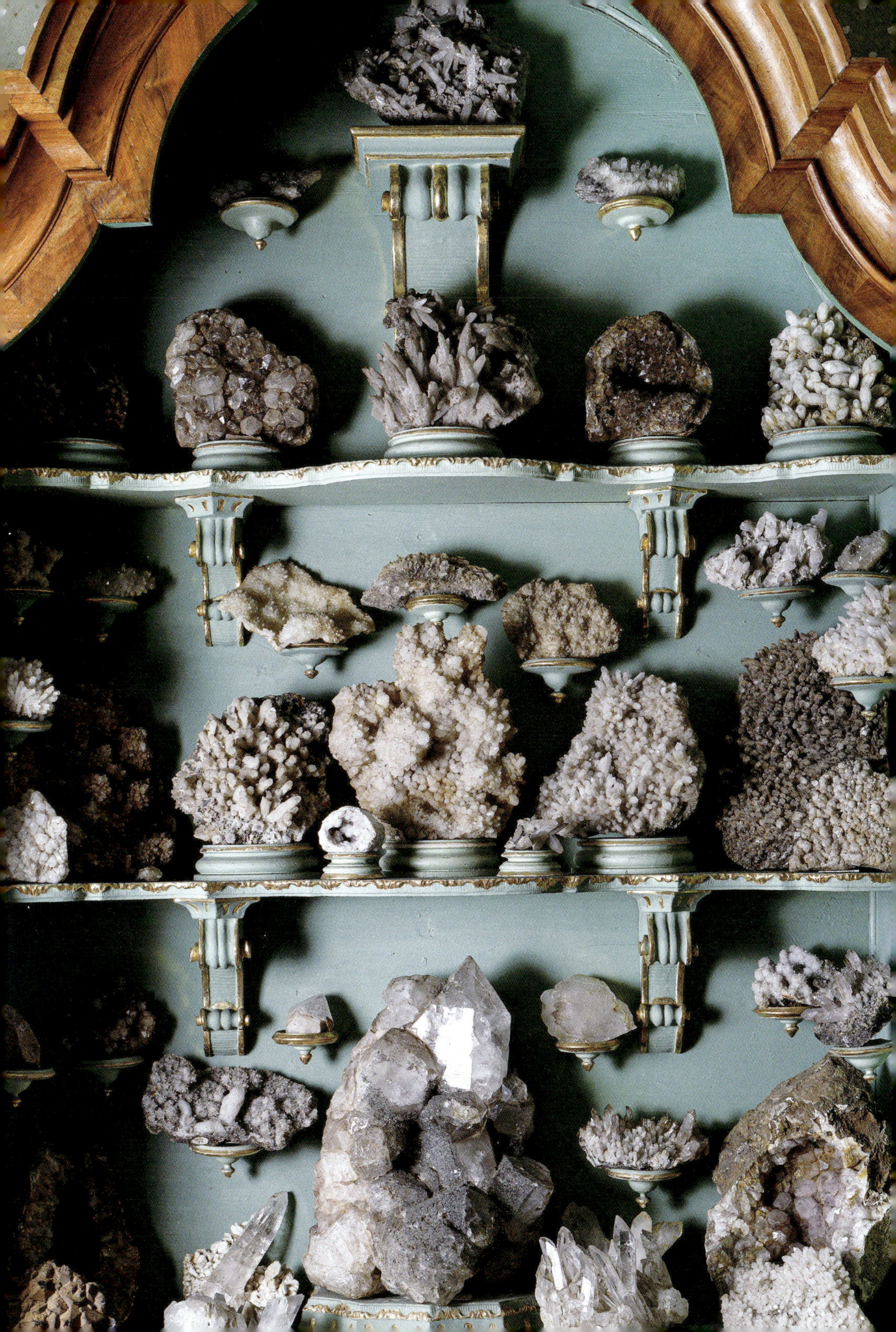

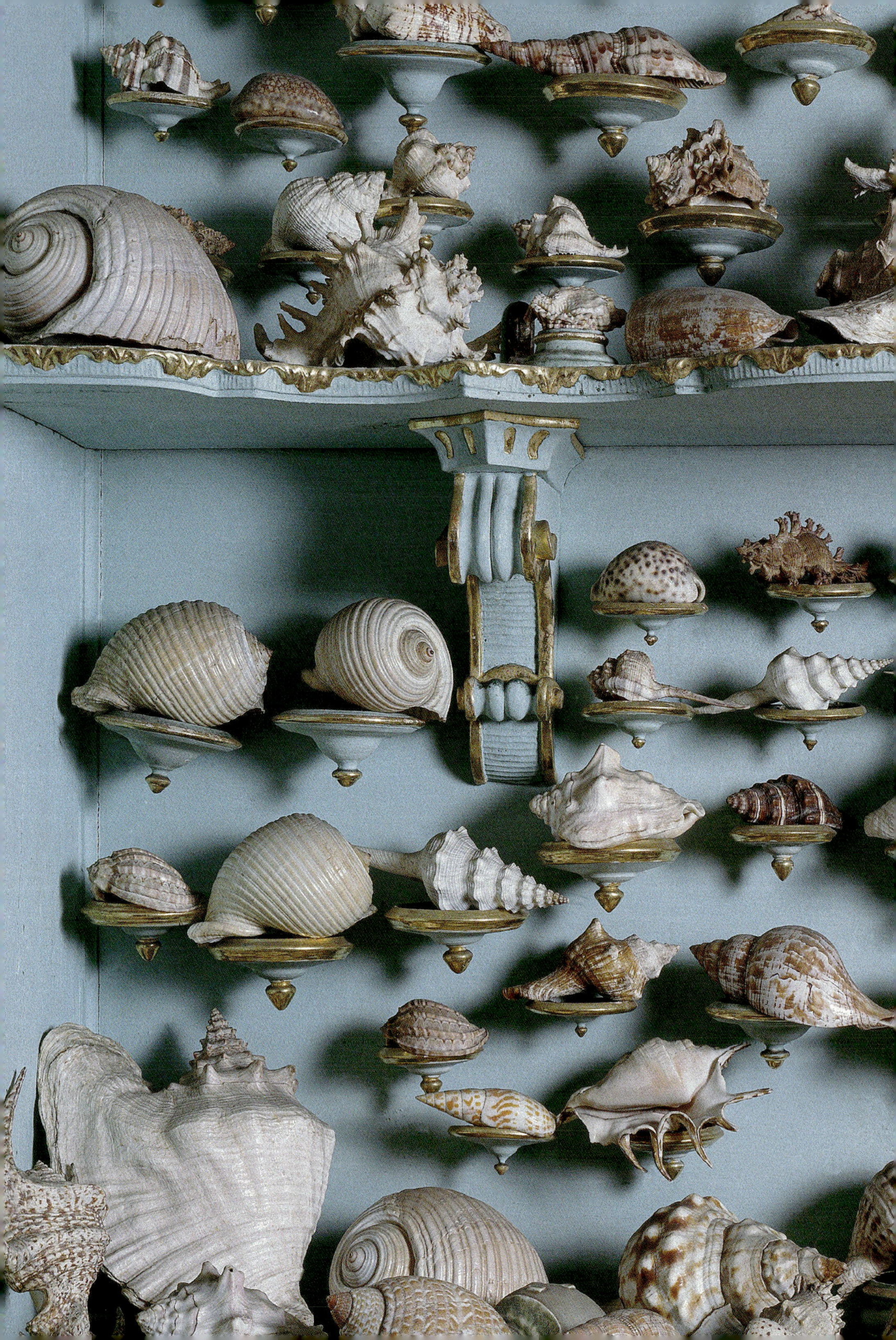

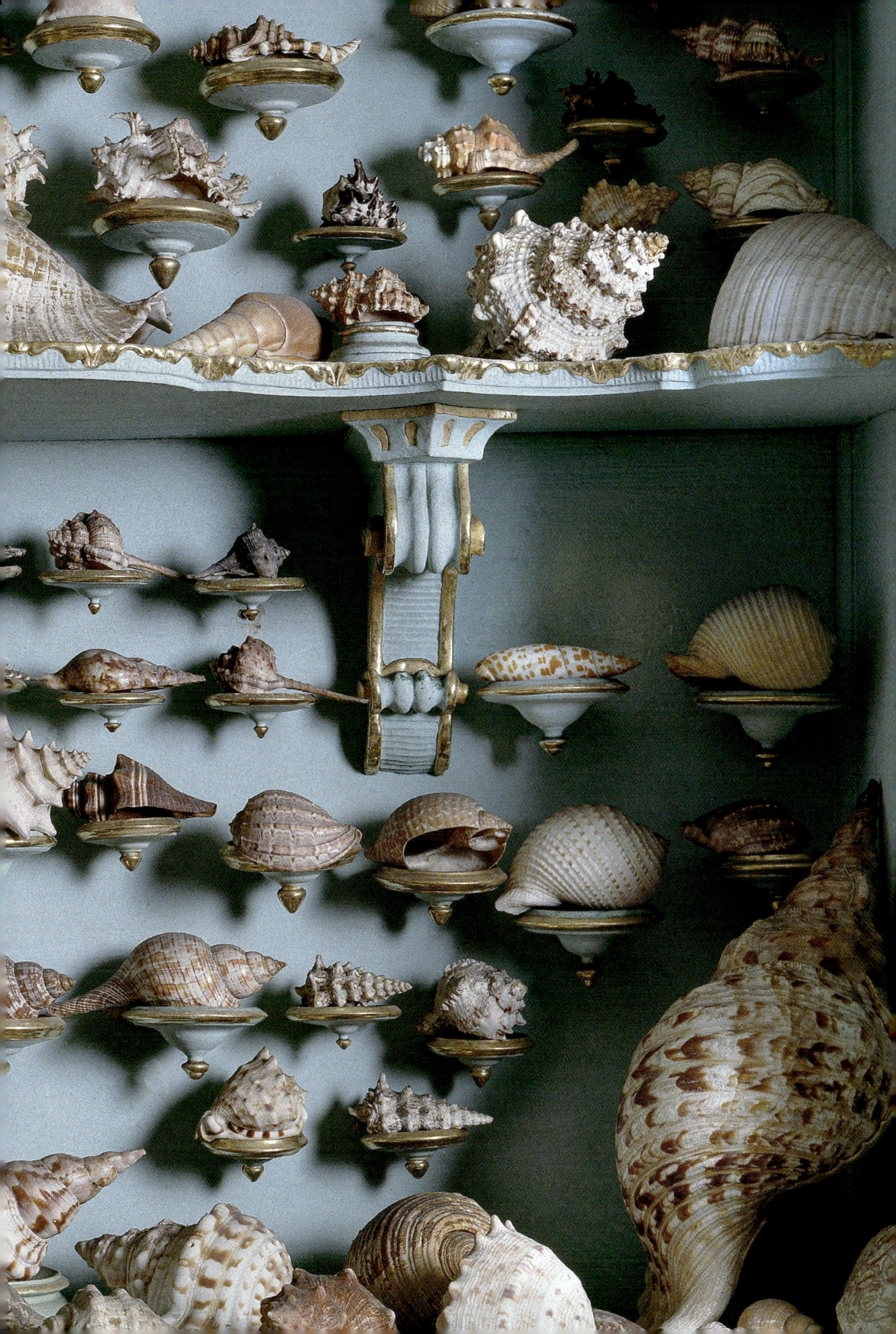

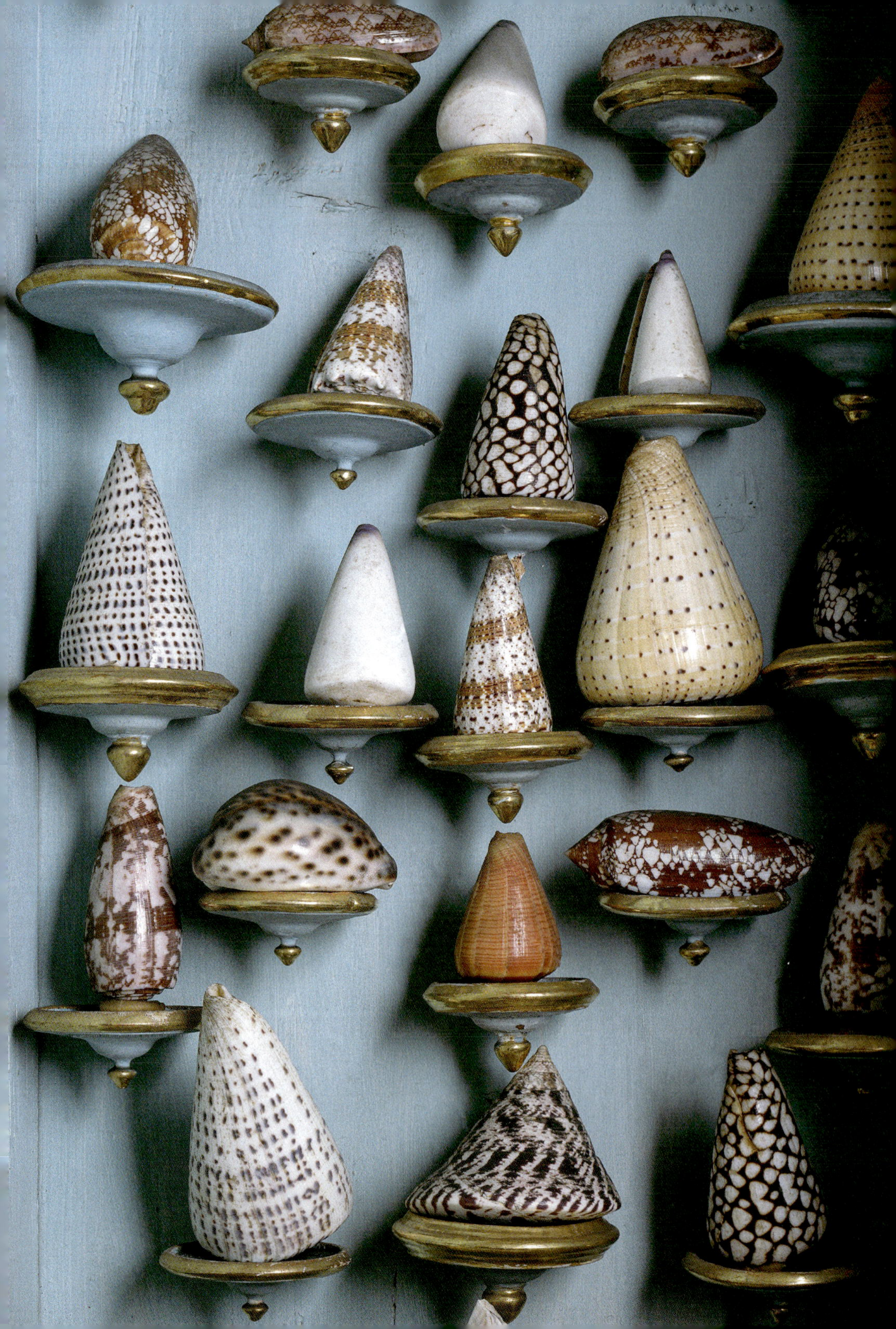

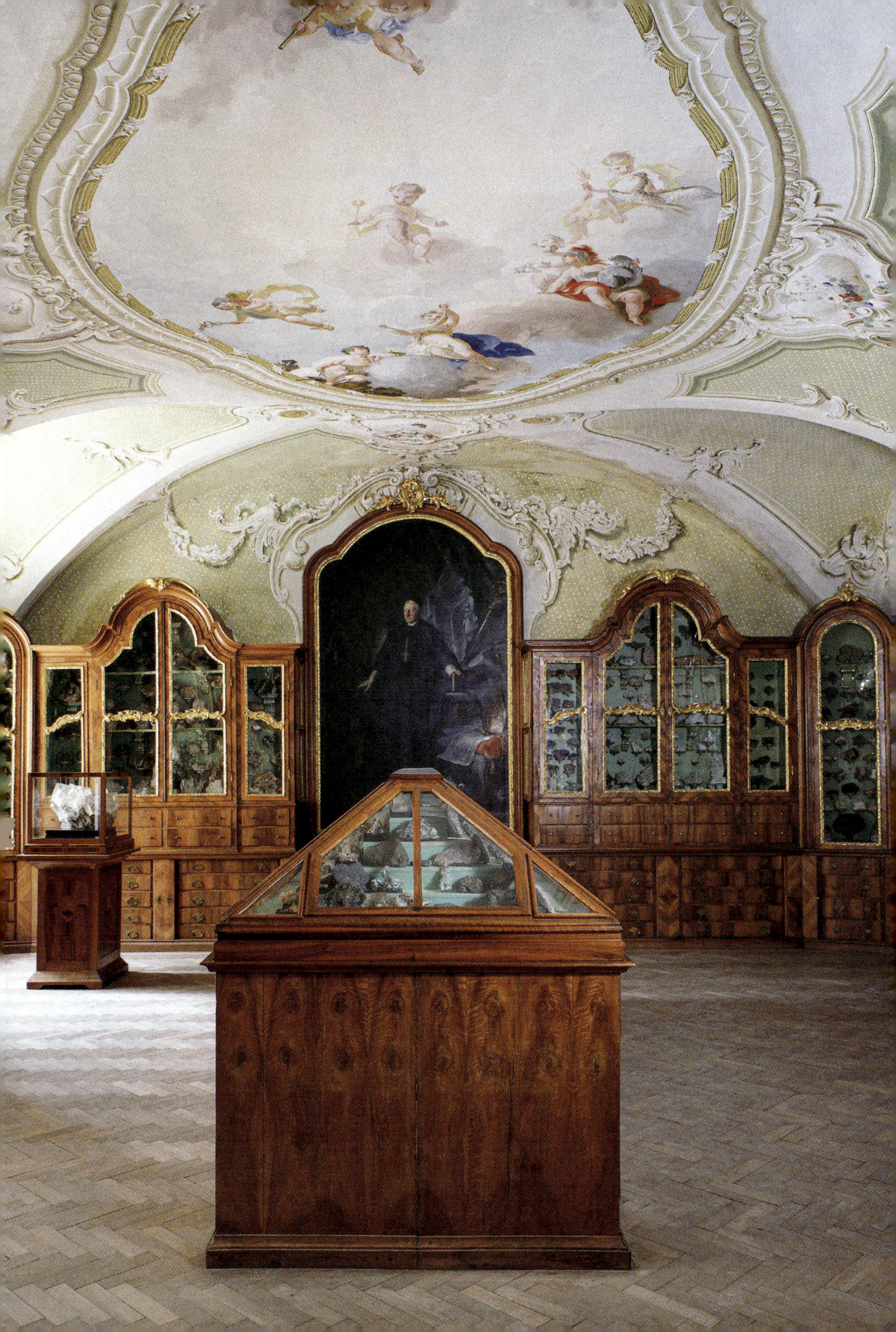

During the 18th century, several monasteries in Austria were rebuilt and enlarged by the addition of both monumental rooms and places of contemplation, such as libraries and scientific cabinets. In the Benedictine abbey of Seitenstetten (founded in 1112) the collection of natural curiosities stands adjacent to one of the most beautiful libraries in the world, which was built between 1741 and 1743, at the height of the Rococo. Some 20 years later, in 1766, the abbot Dominik Gußmann (active 1747–1777) entrusted father Joseph Schaukegl (1721–1798), who was also an architect, artist and keen naturalist, with the task of creating cabinets of *naturalia* and *mineralia*, which were intended to serve an educational purpose. Schaukegl's working drawings (still extant and which form part of the collection; see p. 42) make it clear that originally on top of each cabinet were arranged some of the rarer items, for decorative purposes, interspersed with vases or sculpted putti heads. This decorative scheme is not in place today, but the interiors of the glass cases and their Rococo ornamentations have remained intact, as have the ceiling frescoes showing the *Allegory of the Sun with the Seven Planets*.

The emergence of encyclopaedic approaches to thinking during the 18th century brought a revival of interest in shells and natural marvels, although this time the intention was to expand scientific knowledge, with *naturalia* being considered an entirely separate category from *mirabilia* as well as manufactured objects. The abbey's cabinet of *naturalia* was created for this exact reason, and was broadly divided into two sections, one containing minerals, the other shells. Coral, sponges and petrified plants were placed between the two. The mineral section was noted for its especially strong holding of oversized specimens; the collection numbered 3,814 mineral specimens, 1,240 rocks and 700 fragments, including a large selection of graphite, copper, gold and silver, but also malachite, amethyst, opal, quartz, aragonite and lazulite.

Viewed nowadays with a combination of detached amusement, wonder and a sense of nostalgia, the early obsession with the marvellous has faded and gradually given way to the spirit of scientific enquiry, and yet a taste for the decorative has endured. In fact, in this instance the cabinet was not organised according to any strict and methodical order, but as dictated by the size of the exhibits and the space available the objects were instead laid out so as to obtain a pleasant visual effect. This can be seen, for example, in some of the prints by Levinus Vincent (1658–1727), published in Amsterdam in 1706 (*Wondertooneel der Nature*), which show objects grouped symmetrically according to shape, size or colour, resulting in more animated, harmonious compositions.

❁ ❖ ❁

Im 18. Jahrhundert wurden in Österreich zahlreiche Klöster renoviert und um Räume für Sammlungen wie Bibliotheken und Wissenschaftskabinette erweitert. In der Benediktiner-Abtei Seitenstetten, deren Gründung auf das Jahr 1112 zurückgeht, befindet sich das Naturalienkabinett direkt neben der Bibliothek, die zwischen 1741 und 1743 in der Hochzeit des Rocaille-Stils erbaut wurde und zu den faszinierendsten der Welt zählt. Zwanzig Jahre später, 1766, betraute der Abt Dominik Gußmann (Amtszeit 1747–1777) den Architekten, Künstler und passionierten Naturforscher Pater Joseph Schaukegl (1721–1798) mit der Aufgabe, ein Naturalien- und Mineralienkabinett zu Lehrzwecken einzurichten. Aus Schaukegls Entwürfen, die ebenfalls dort ausgestellt sind (siehe S. 42), geht hervor, dass die Giebel der Schauschränke ursprünglich von seltenen Stücken bekrönt wurden, die sich mit Gefäßen und Putten abwechselten. Heute ist diese Giebelverzierung verschwunden, erhalten blieben aber der Inhalt der Vitrinen, das Rocaille-Dekor sowie das Deckenfresko mit einer *Allegorie der Sonne und der sieben Planeten*.

Mit dem Siegeszug des enzyklopädischen Denkens im 18. Jahrhundert erlebte das Interesse an Muscheln und anderen Schätzen der Natur eine neue Blüte. Allerdings ging man nun wissenschaftlich vor und führte eine strenge Unterscheidung zwischen *Naturalia* einerseits und *Mirabilia* und *Artificialia* andererseits ein. Diese neue Aufteilung spiegelt sich auch in dem Naturalienkabinett des Klosters wider, das in zwei Abteilungen untergliedert wurde: Mineralien und Muscheln. Dazwischen gruppierte man Korallen, Schwämme und versteinerte Pflanzen. Die Mineraliensammlung war bekannt für ihre Vielfalt an besonders großen Exemplaren: 3814 Mineralien, 1240 Steine und 700 Fragmente, darunter eine Fülle an Grafit, Kupfer, Gold und Silber, aber auch Malachit, Amethyst, Opal, Quarz, Aragonit und Lazulith.

Inzwischen sah man mit ungläubigem Staunen und fast schon nostalgisch auf den früheren Wunderkult zurück, der langsam immer mehr verblasste und von wissenschaftlichen Methoden abgelöst wurde, ohne jedoch den Sinn fürs Dekorative vollständig zu verlieren. Einer gefälligen Präsentation zuliebe war man daher durchaus bereit, in methodischer Hinsicht Konzessionen zu machen. Dies belegen zum Beispiel die Abbildungen von Levinus Vincent (1658–1727), die 1706 in Amsterdam veröffentlicht wurden (*Wondertooneel der Nature*): Die symmetrische Anordnung der Exponate nach Form, Größe und Farbe lässt das Bemühen um einen harmonischen Gesamteindruck erkennen.

◉ ❖ ◉

Au cours du 18ᵉ siècle, de nombreux monastères d'Autriche furent reconstruits et agrandis grâce à l'adjonction d'espaces de collection tels que bibliothèques ou cabinets scientifiques. Dans l'abbaye bénédictine de Seitenstetten dont la fondation remonte à 1112, la collection de curiosités naturelles jouxte la bibliothèque, l'une des plus fascinantes du monde, créée entre 1741 et 1743, à l'époque de la diffusion du style rocaille. Une vingtaine d'années plus tard, en 1766, l'abbé Dominik Gussmann (abbé de 1747 à 1777) confia au père Joseph Schaukegl (1721–1798) – architecte, artiste et naturaliste passionné – le soin de créer des cabinets de *naturalia* et de *mineralia* à but didactique. Les dessins réalisés par Schaukegl lui-même (et exposés ici, voir p. 42) montrent qu'à l'origine les vitrines aux lignes découpées étaient surmontées d'objets rares, à des fins ornementales, qui alternaient avec des vases, des sculptures ou des têtes de *putti*. Aujourd'hui, cette décoration a disparu, mais le contenu des vitrines et les ornements rocaille, tout comme les fresques du plafond représentant l'*Allégorie du soleil avec les sept planètes*, subsistent dans leur intégralité.

Au 18e siècle, la naissance de la pensée encyclopédique renouvela l'intérêt pour les coquillages et les prodiges de la nature : ici néanmoins, le projet est scientifique, les *naturalia* s'opposent aux *mirabilia* et aux créations artistiques. C'est dans cette optique que le cabinet naturaliste de l'abbaye vit le jour, qui présentait deux sections principales : l'une réunissait des minéraux, l'autre était consacrée aux coquillages. Entre les deux trouvaient place les coraux, les éponges et les végétaux pétrifiés. La section des minéraux était réputée pour la richesse de ses exemplaires aux dimensions exceptionnelles : 3814 minéraux, 1240 pierres et 700 fragments parmi lesquels une profusion de graphite, de cuivre, d'or et d'argent, sans oublier les malachites, les améthystes, les opales, les quartz, les aragonites et lazulites.

Considéré aujourd'hui avec un détachement amusé, une légère nostalgie et un certain étonnement, le culte des merveilles a peu à peu disparu pour faire place à l'esprit scientifique sans que l'on renonce pour autant au goût pour l'ornementation ; et de fait, pour des raisons liées aux dimensions des objets et au caractère des lieux, le cabinet pouvait se dispenser de suivre rigoureusement l'ordre méthodique et associer les objets dans une présentation agréable à l'œil. C'est ce qu'attestent les planches de Levinus Vincent (1658–1727) publiées à Amsterdam en 1706 (*Wondertooneel der Nature*), qui montrent les objets regroupés de manière symétrique, en fonction de leur forme, de leurs dimensions et de leur couleur afin de donner vie à des compositions harmonieuses.

1 According to the classic division of cabinets of curiosities of the time the Seitenstetten collection also featured *naturalia*, with a section devoted to various different categories of minerals.
Wie damals in Naturalienkabinetten üblich, gab es auch in der Seitenstettener Sammlung eine Mineralienabteilung mit verschiedenen Kategorien.
Conformément à la division classique des cabinets naturalistes de l'époque, le Cabinet Seitenstetten comportait lui aussi une section consacrée aux différentes catégories de minéraux.

2 The entrance to the Seitenstetten collection. The cabinets are adorned with gold friezes and rocaille decorations whose form echoes the decor of the vaulted ceiling.
Der Eingang zum Mineralienkabinett. Die Schränke sind mit Goldfriesen und Rocaillemotiven verziert, die das Gewölbedekor aufgreifen.
L'entrée du Cabinet Seitenstetten. Les armoires sont ornées de frises dorées et décorations rocaille qui font écho aux ornements du plafond voûté.

3 The shelves of the glass display cases are painted and decorated with gold, and present shells arranged symmetrically in harmonious compositions according to their shape, size and colour.
Die Glasvitrine ist durch bemalte, mit Gold verzierte Konsolen in Fächer geteilt, in denen nach Form, Größe und Farbe symmetrisch Gruppen von Muscheln arrangiert sind.
Les étagères des vitrines en verre sont peintes et décorées à l'or fin. Elles présentent des coquillages regroupés symétriquement selon

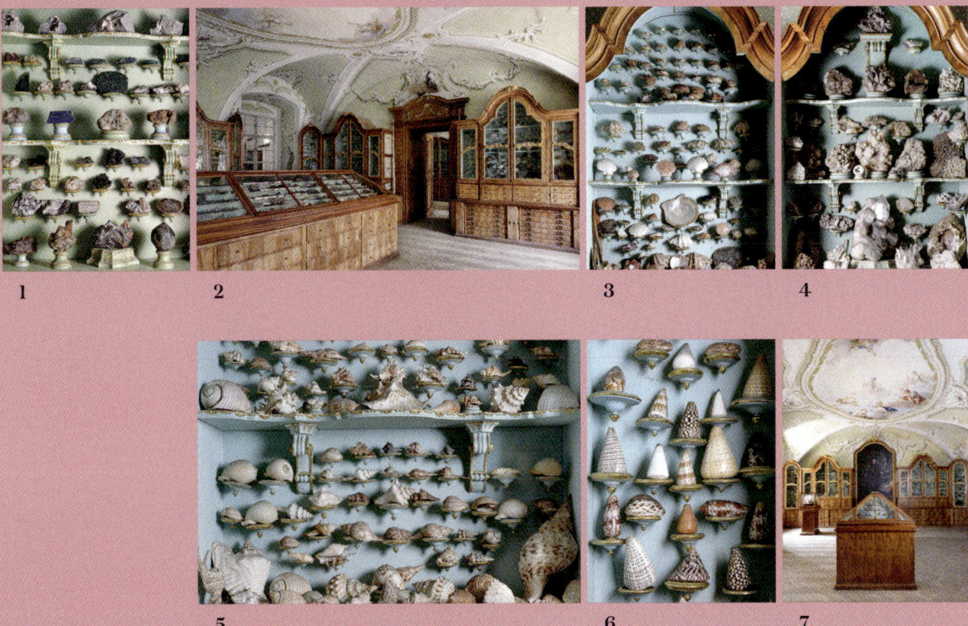

1

2

3

4

5

6

7

leur forme, leur taille et leur couleur, ce qui crée des compositions harmonieuses.

4 This display case contains crystals and quartzes of various sizes.
Diese Vitrine enthält Kristalle und Quarze unterschiedlicher Größe.
Cette vitrine contient des cristaux et du quartz de toutes tailles.

5 One of the cases with shells of various sizes; these are monovalve molluscs (Pectinidae).
In diesem Regal werden Kammmuscheln (Pectinidae) unterschiedlicher Größe präsentiert.
Une des étagères contenant des coquillages de différentes tailles ; ici nous voyons des mollusques univalves (Pectinidae).

6 This display case features some exceptional cowrie shells (Cypraea).
In dieser Vitrine sind außergewöhnliche Kaurischnecken (Cypraea) ausgestellt.
Cette vitrine abrite quelques coquillages extraordinaires du genre Cypraea.

7 The portrait of Dominik Gußmann on the back wall dominates the cabinet. It was painted in 1760 by Martin Johann Schmidt, and the ceiling fresco is by Johann Bergle.
Dominiert wird dieses Kabinett vom Porträt Dominik Gußmanns, das Martin Johann Schmidt 1760 schuf. Das Deckenfresko stammt von Johann Bergle.
Le portrait de Dominik Gussmann, à l'arrière-plan, domine le cabinet. Il a été peint en 1760 par Martin Johann Schmidt. La fresque du plafond est de Johann Bergle.

Rosenborg Slot

Copenhagen

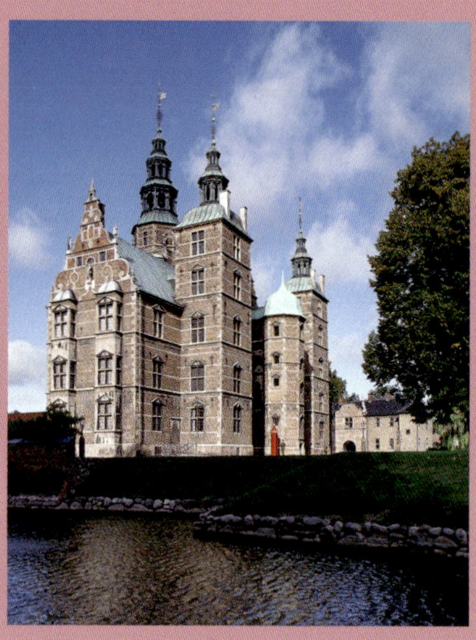

Founded 1658

Key item The famous *Oldenburg Horn*. According to legend, Count Otto, the founder of the Oldenburg dynasty, was given this mythical horn in the year 989 by a mysterious maiden while he was out on a hunting expedition. In fact, the horn was fashioned around 1465 and was probably donated by the Danish king Christian I to the cathedral of Cologne, from where, after the Reformation, it was returned to the Oldenburg family.

Besonders sehenswert Das berühmte *Oldenburger Wunderhorn*. Der Legende nach soll Graf Otto, Ahnherr der Oldenburger Grafen, das Trinkhorn im Jahre 989 auf der Jagd von einer Fee bekommen haben. Tatsächlich jedoch wurde es um 1465 angefertigt, dann vermutlich vom dänischen König Christian I. dem Kölner Dom geschenkt, von wo es nach der Reformation wieder in den Besitz der Grafen von Oldenburg zurückkehrte.

À voir absolument La célèbre *Corne des Oldenbourg*. Selon la légende, le comte Otto, fondateur de la dynastie, l'aurait reçu d'une mystérieuse et belle jeune fille au cours d'une partie de chasse, en l'an 989. En réalité, le cor mythique fut réalisé vers 1465 et, au lendemain de la Réforme, le roi danois Christian Ier l'a probablement offert à la cathédrale de Cologne avant qu'il ne soit à nouveau en possession des Oldenbourg.

Massimo Listri,
View of Rosenborg Castle

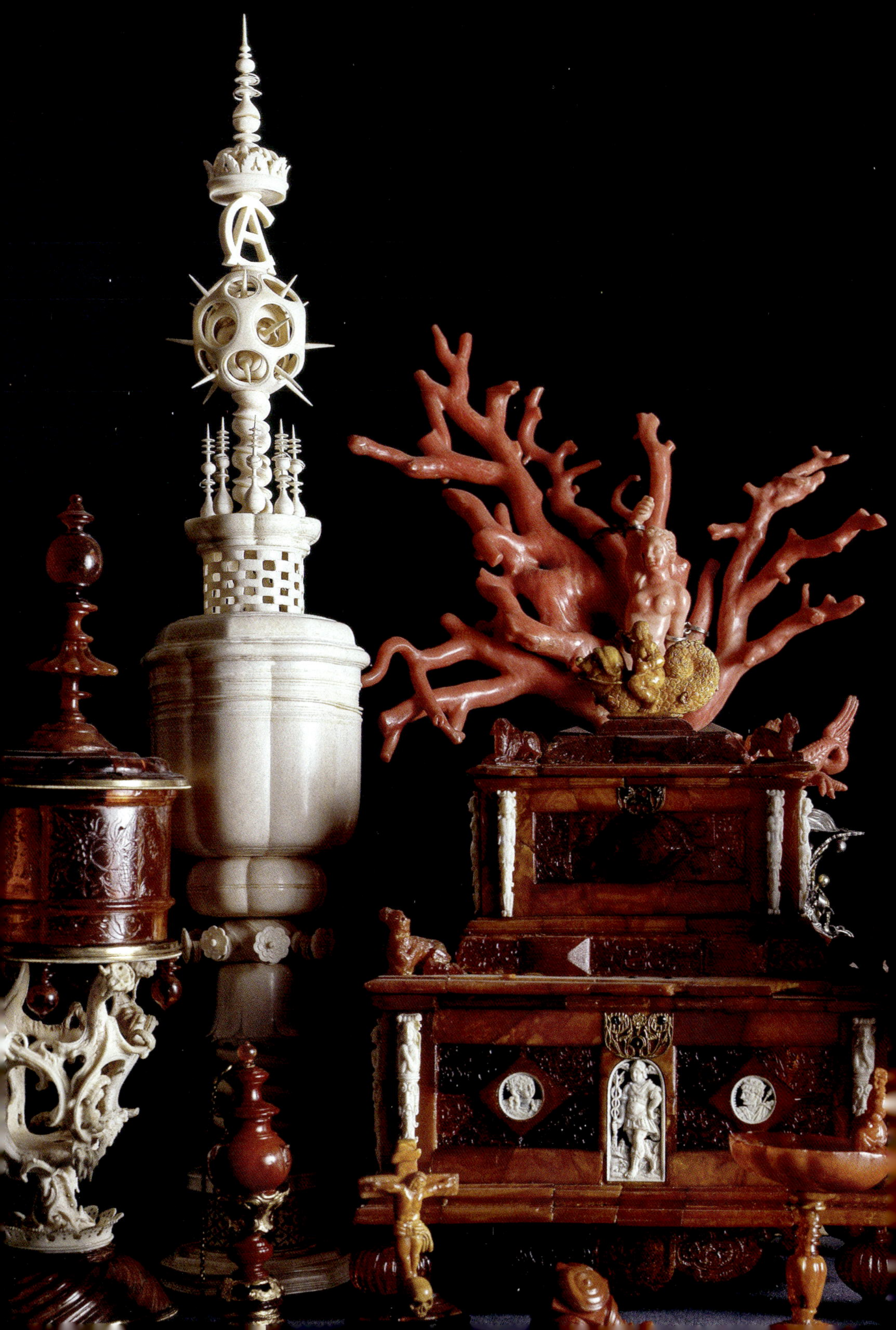

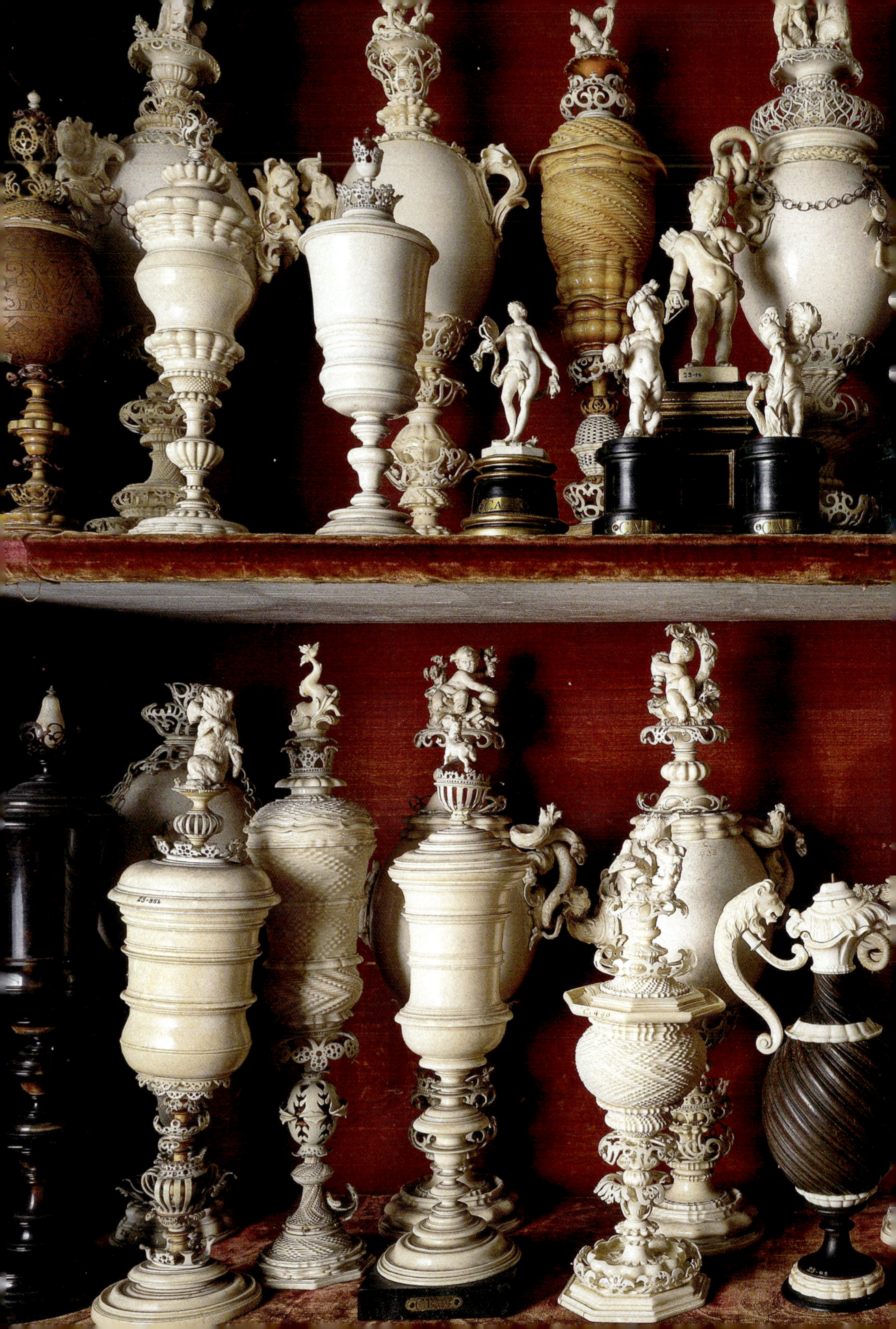

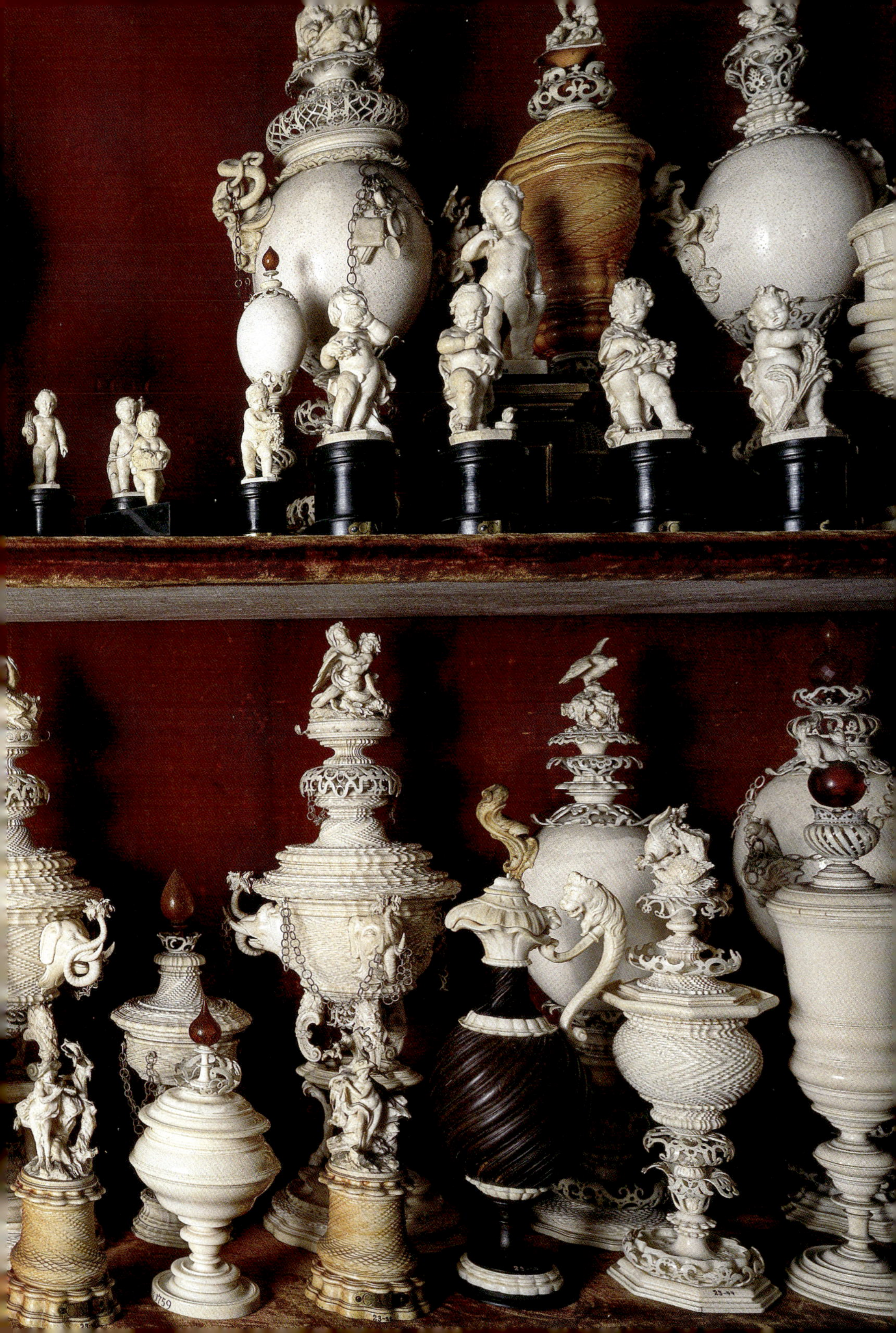

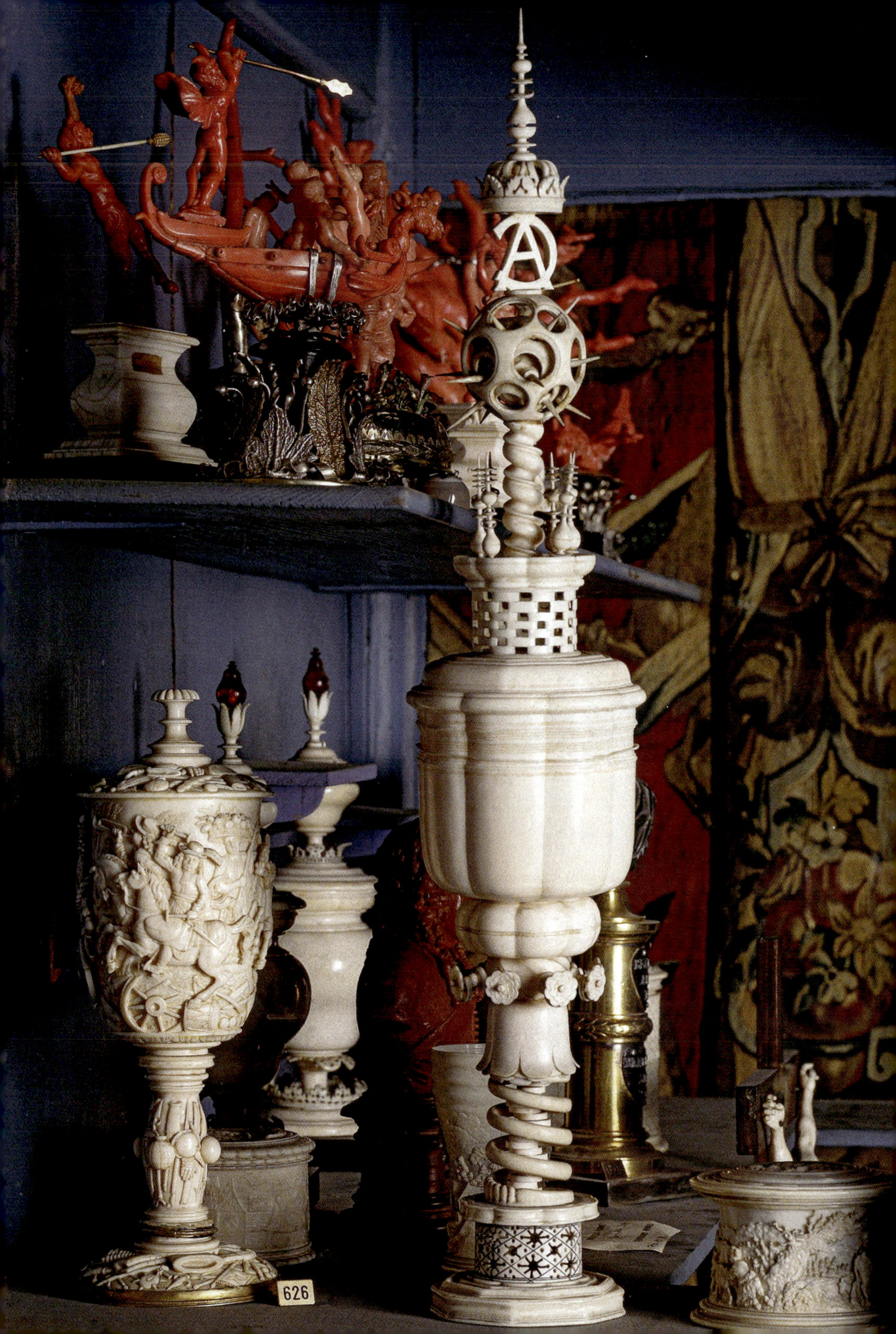

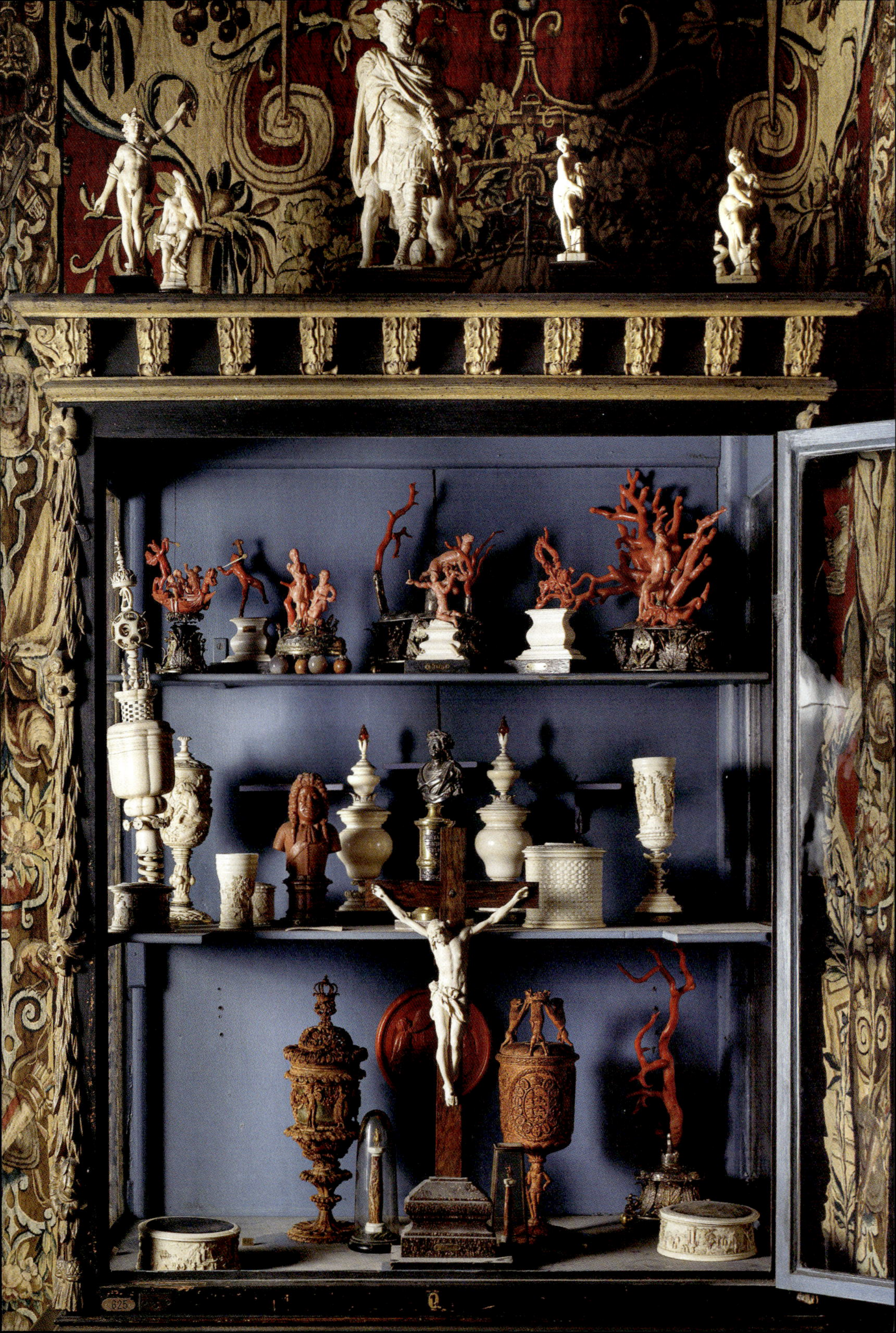

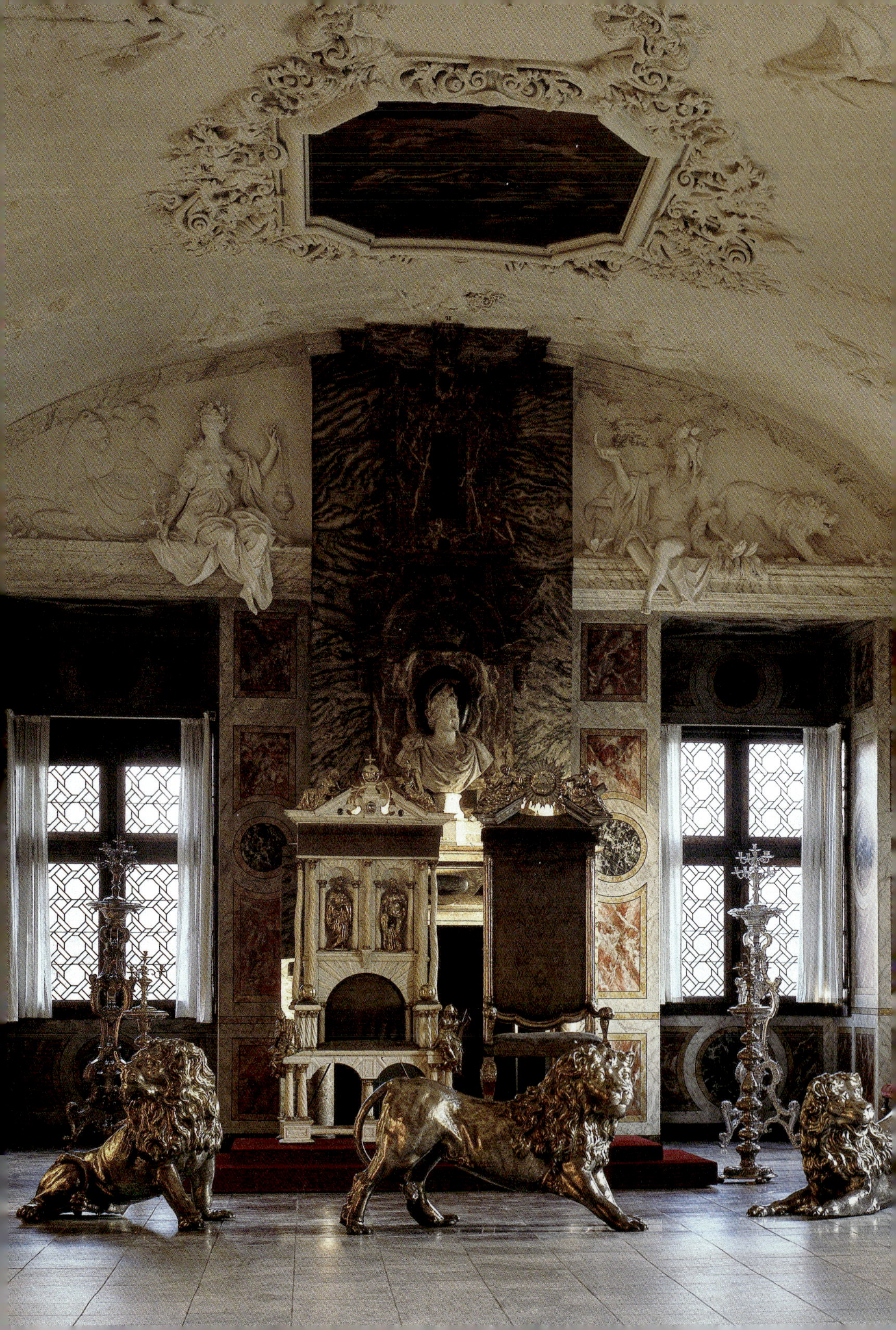

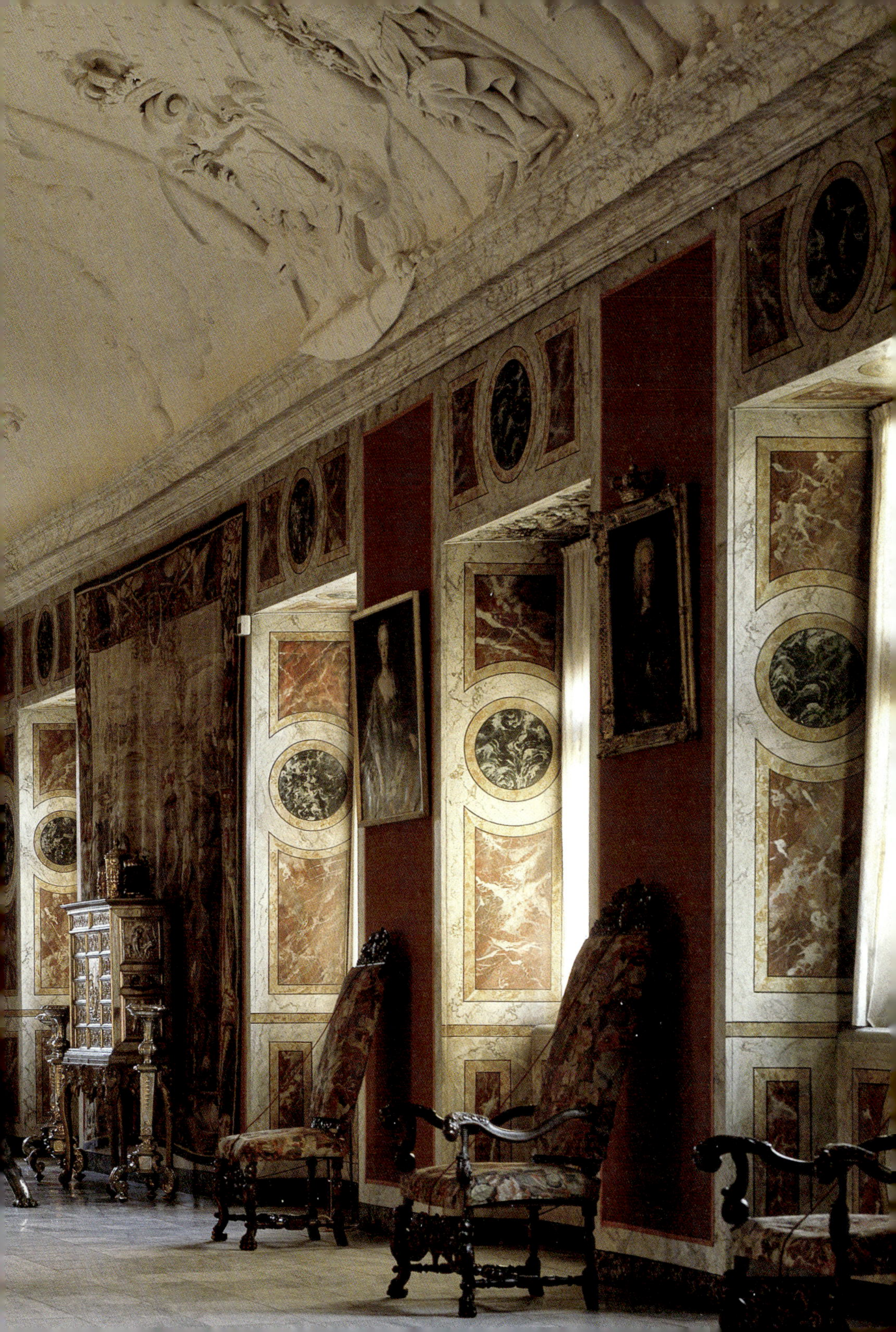

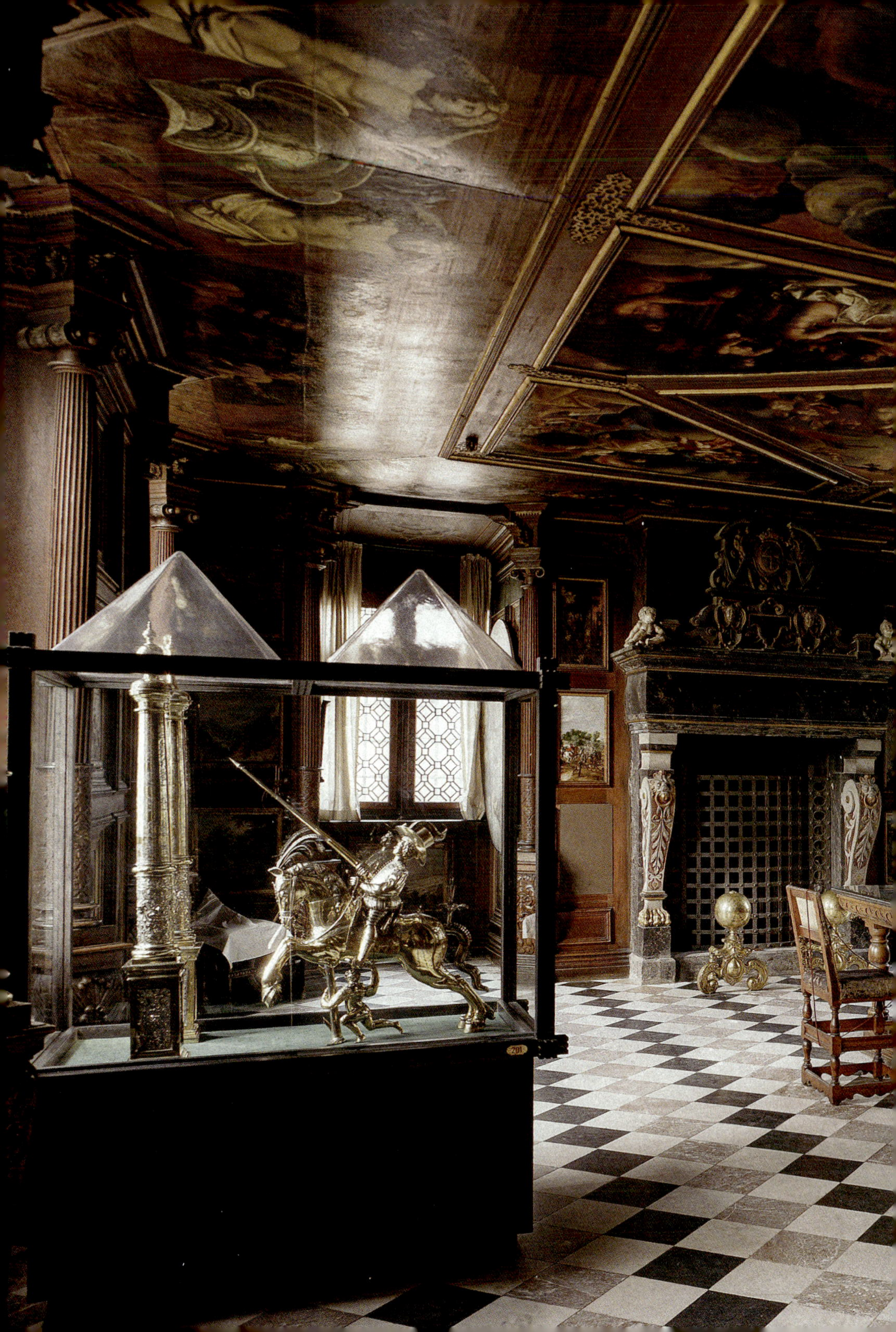

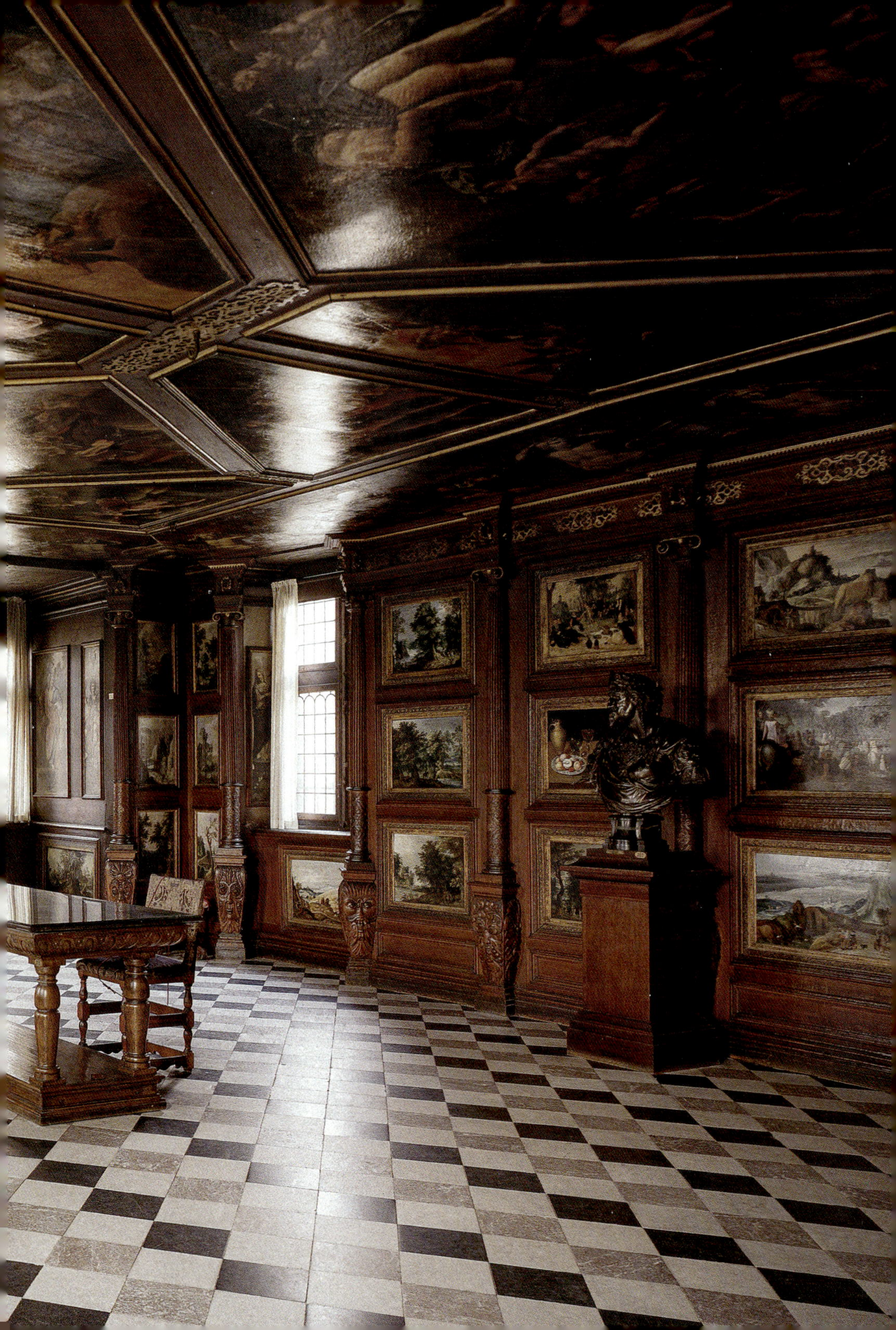

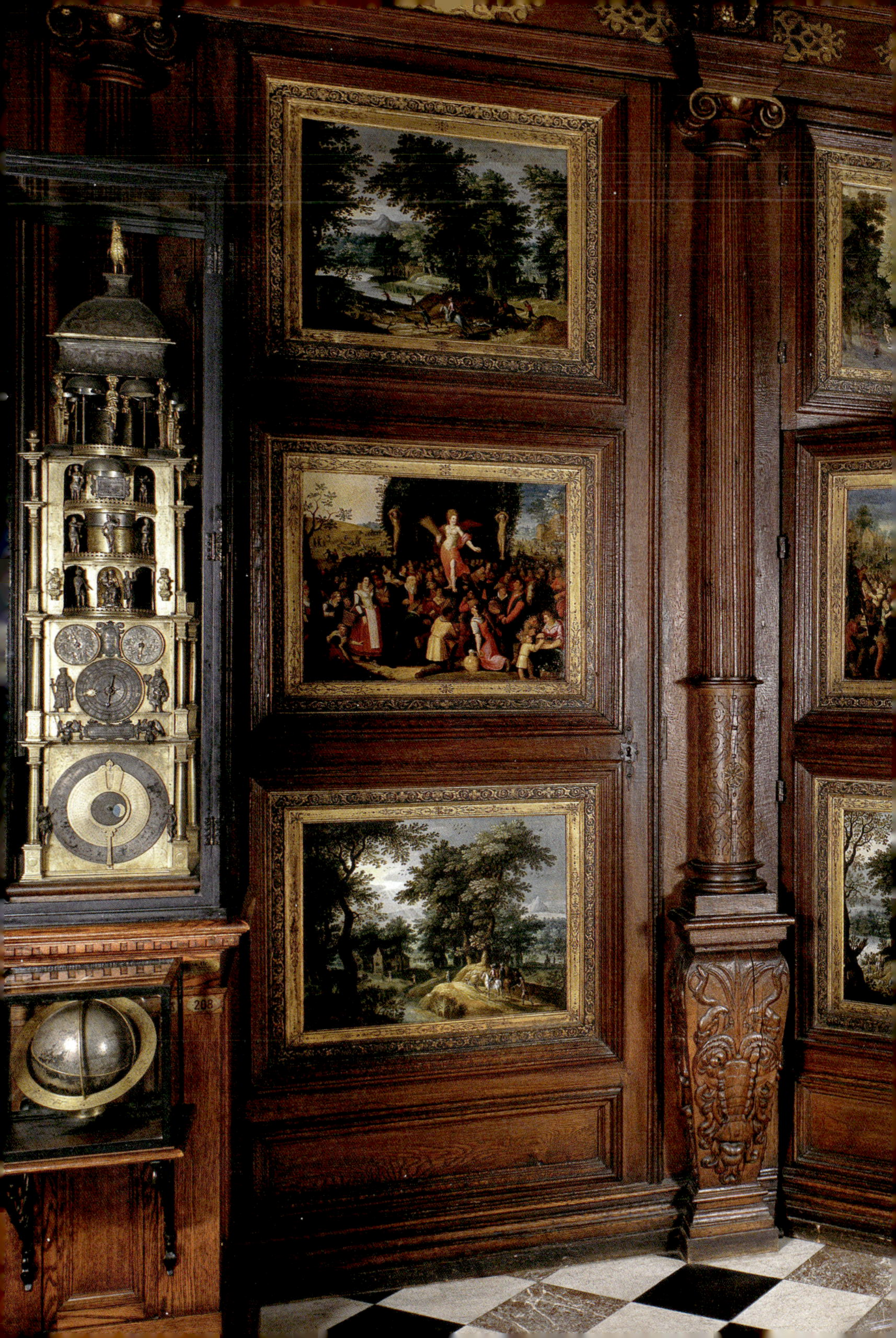

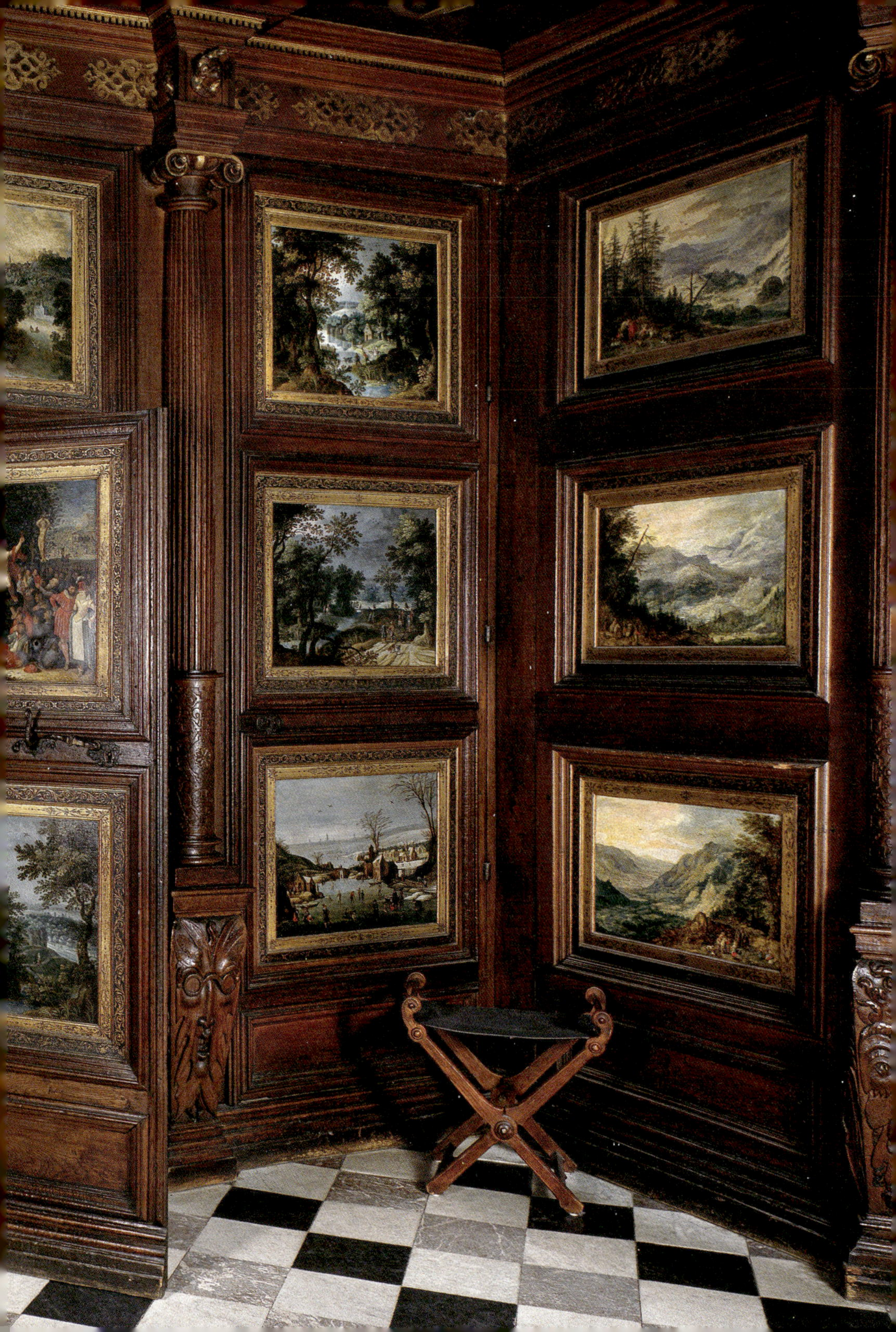

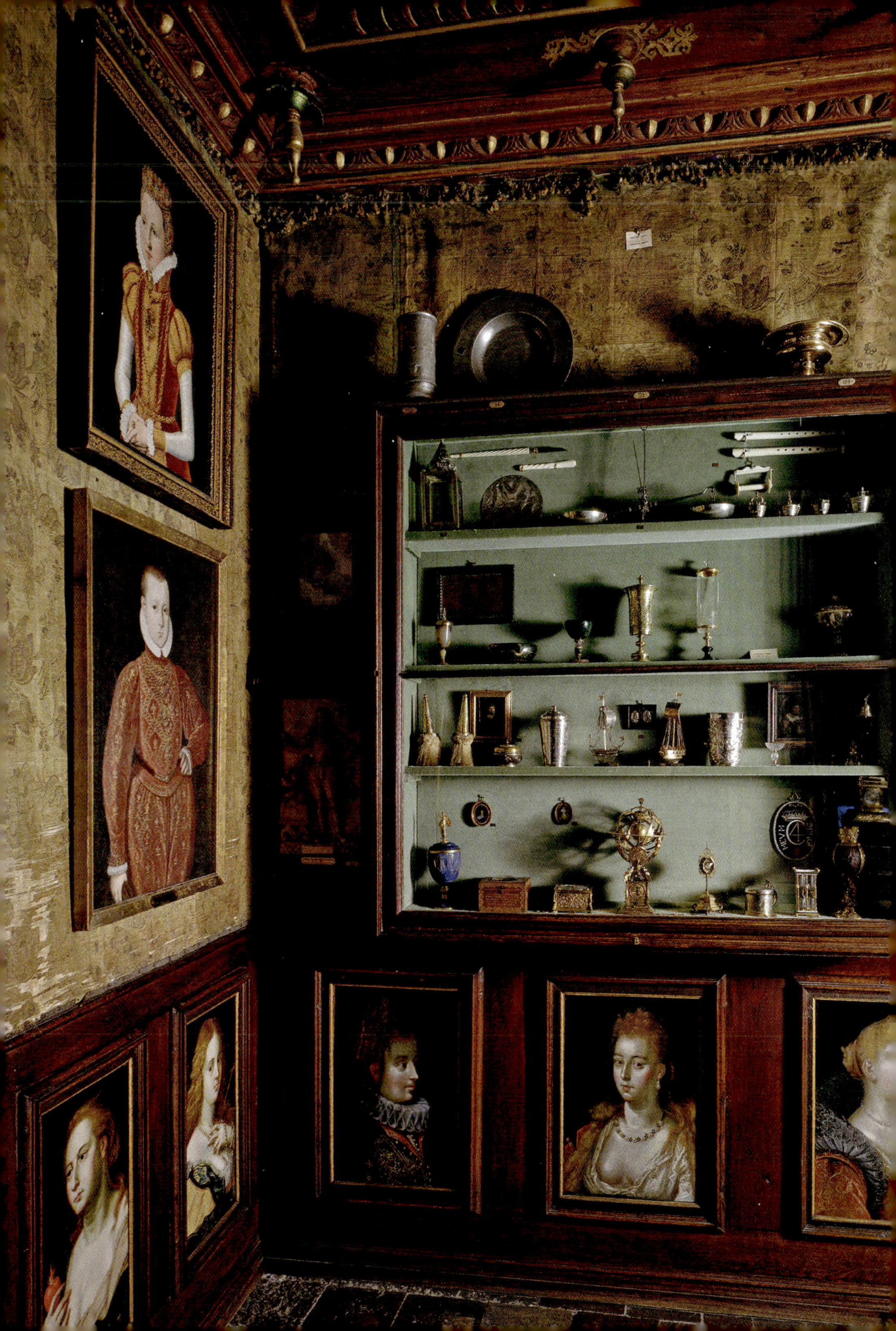

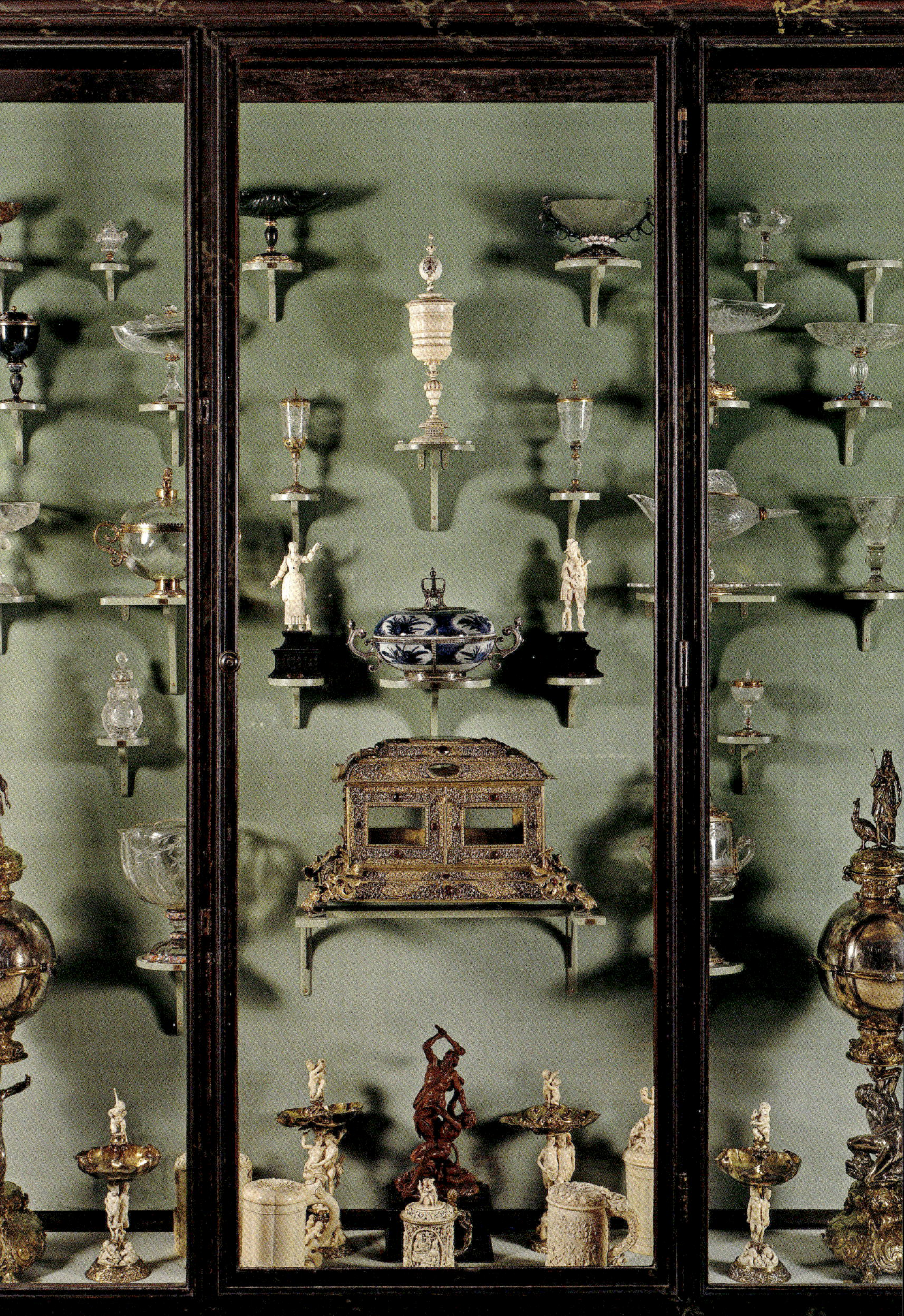

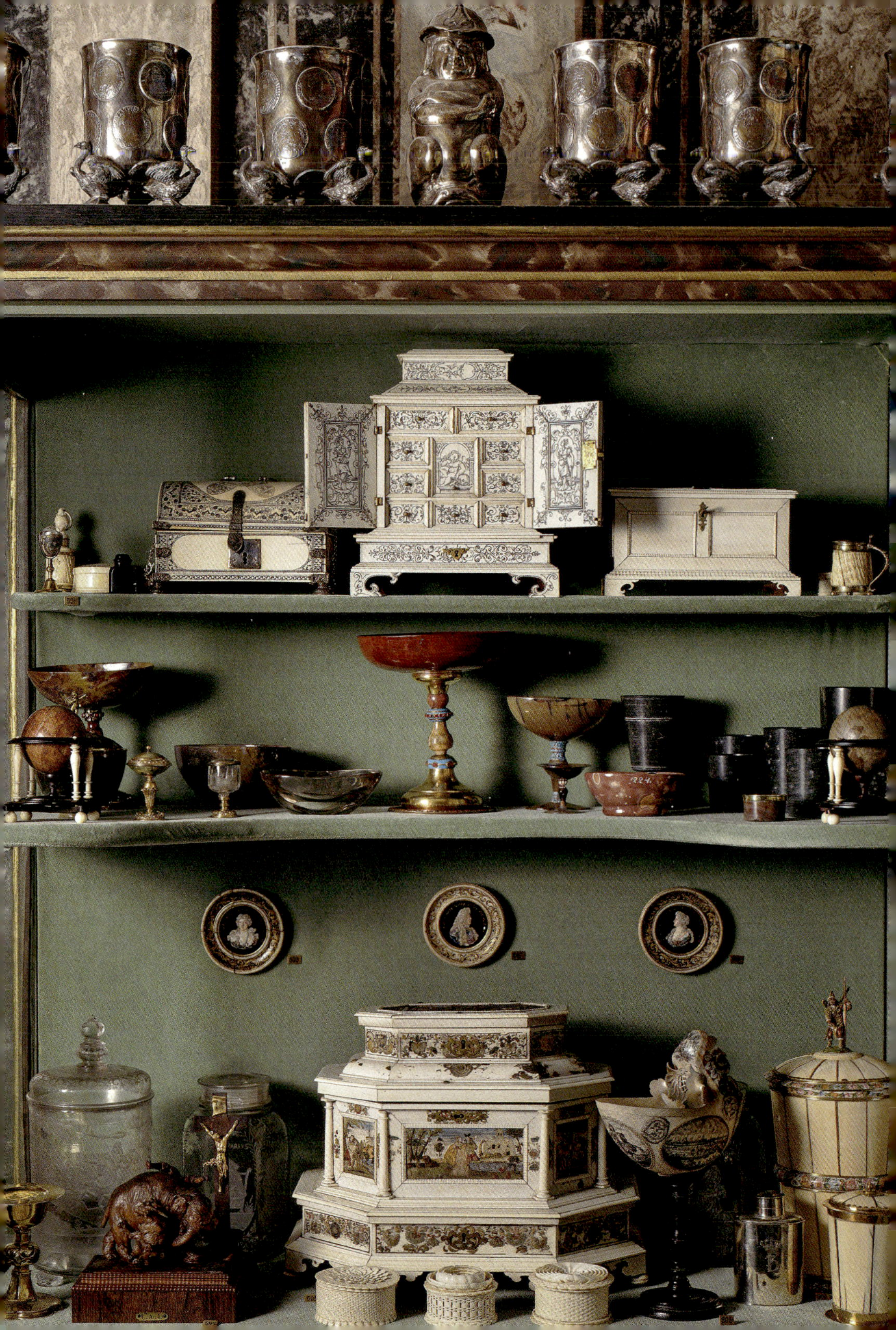

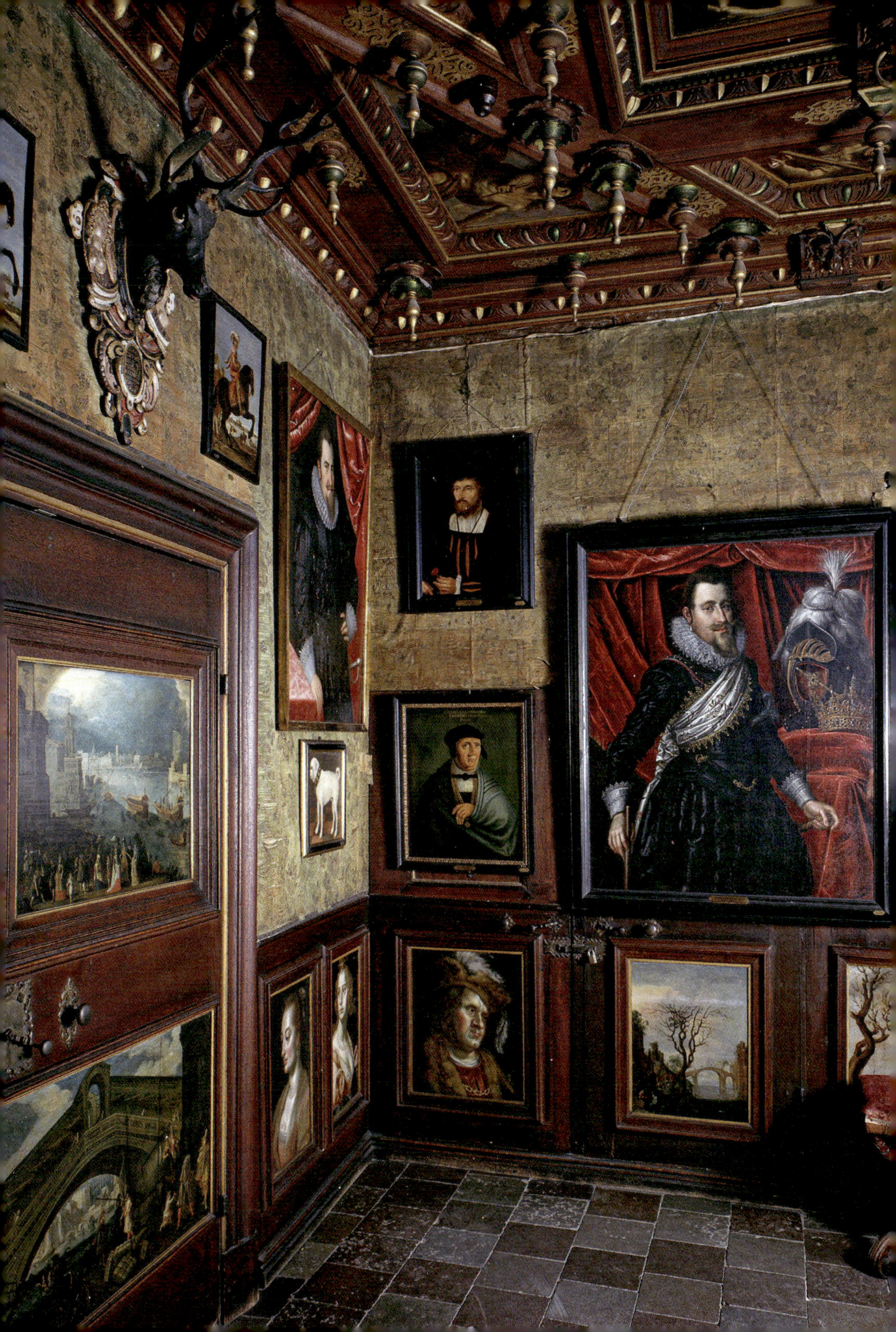

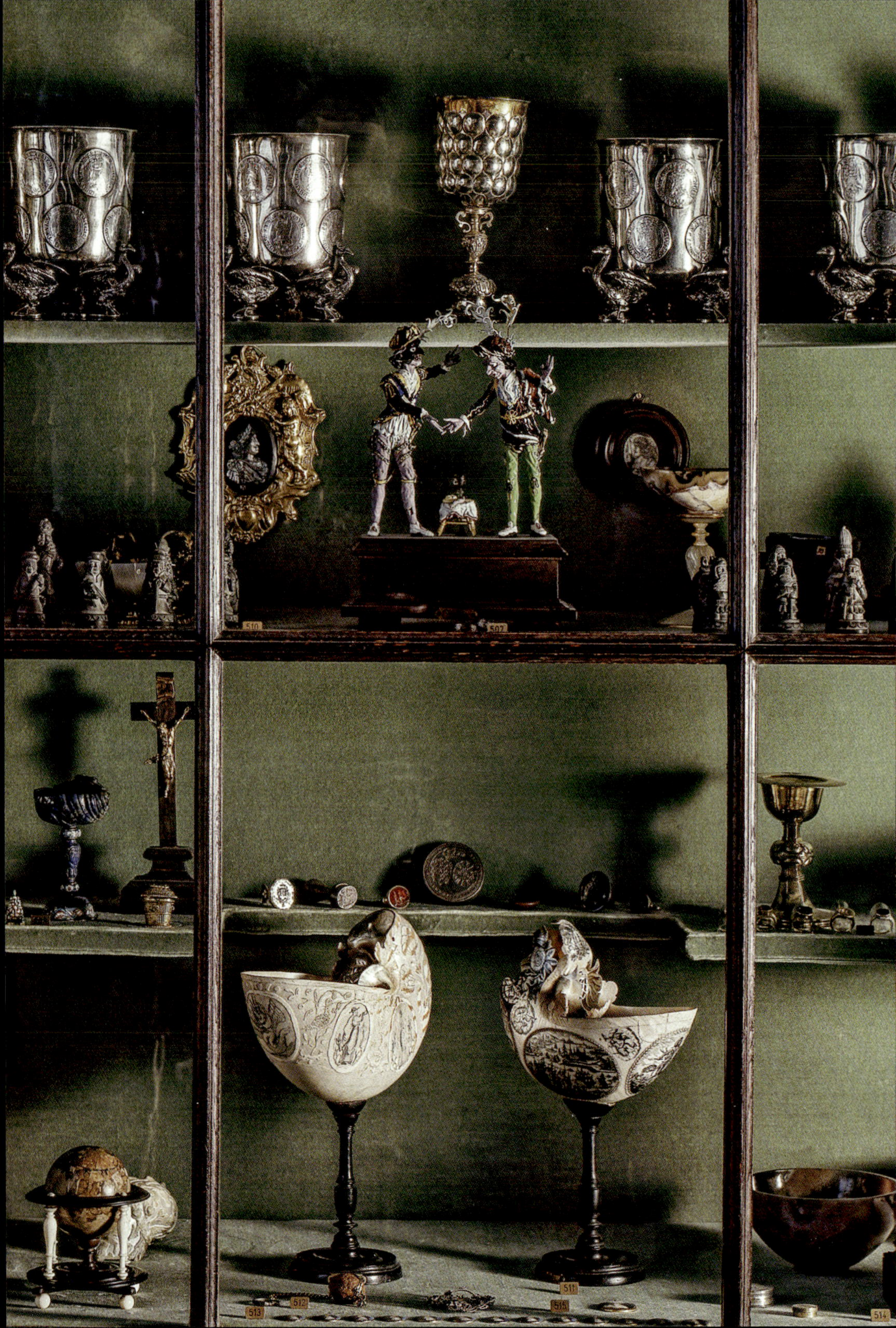
510
507
513
512
511
515
514

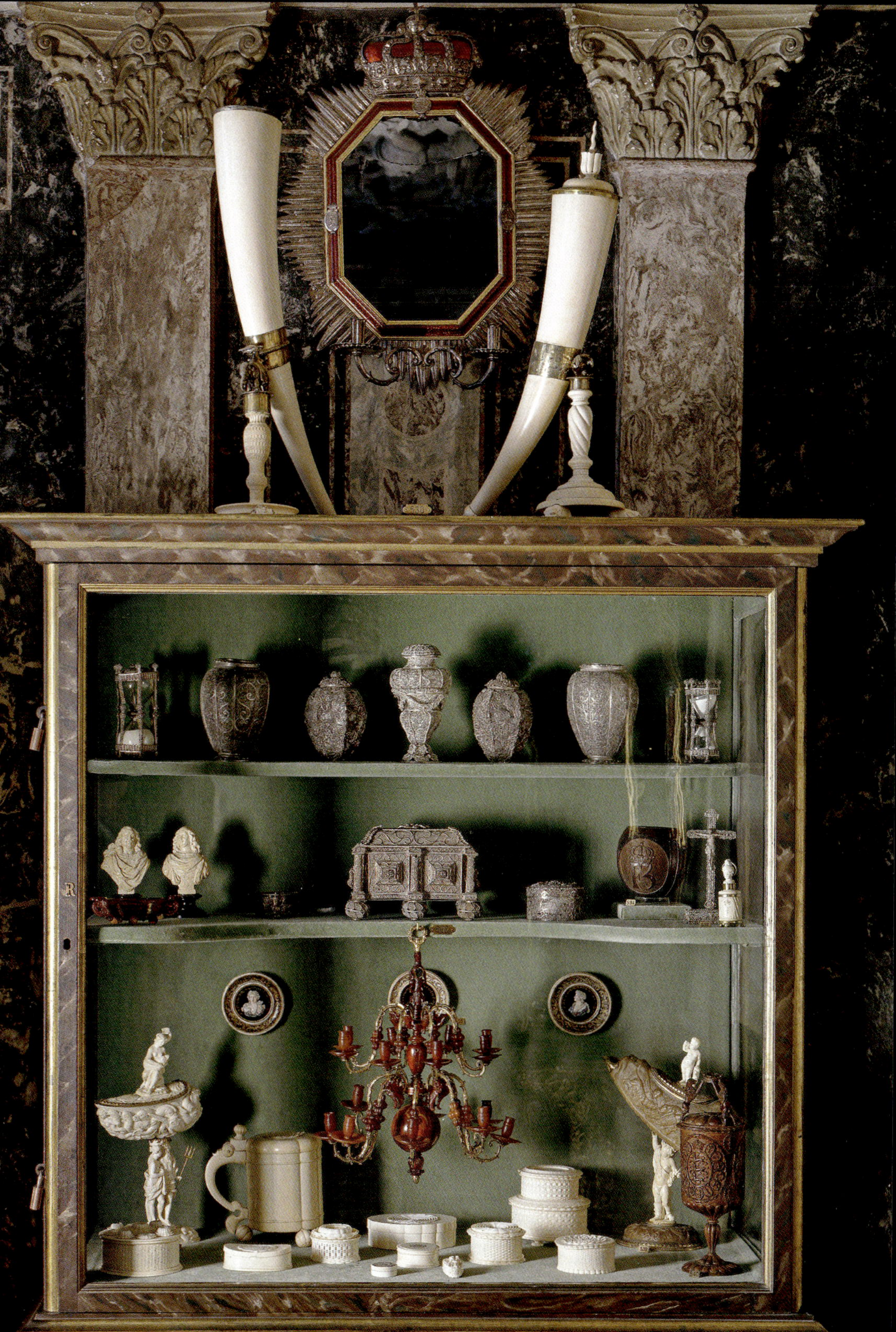

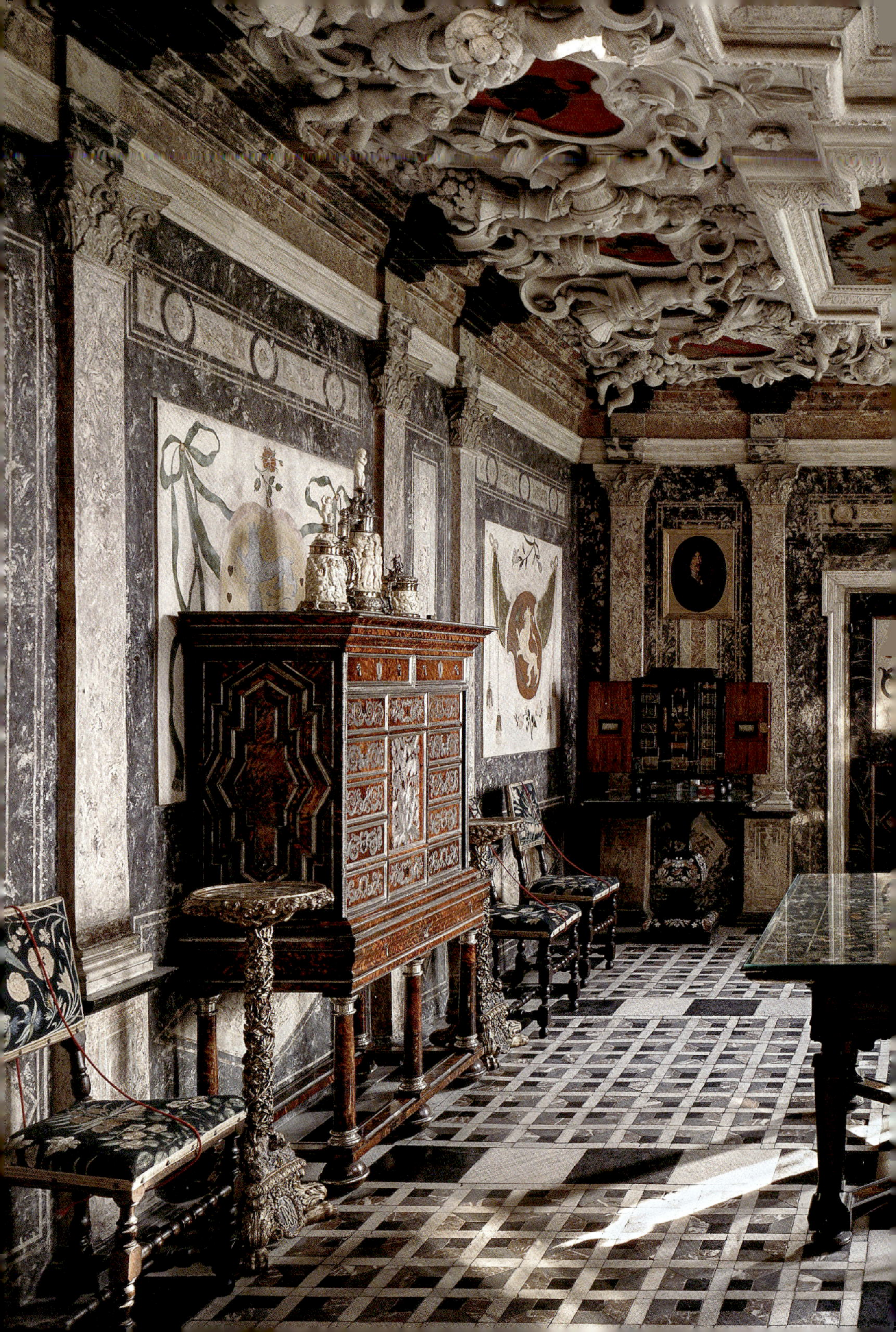

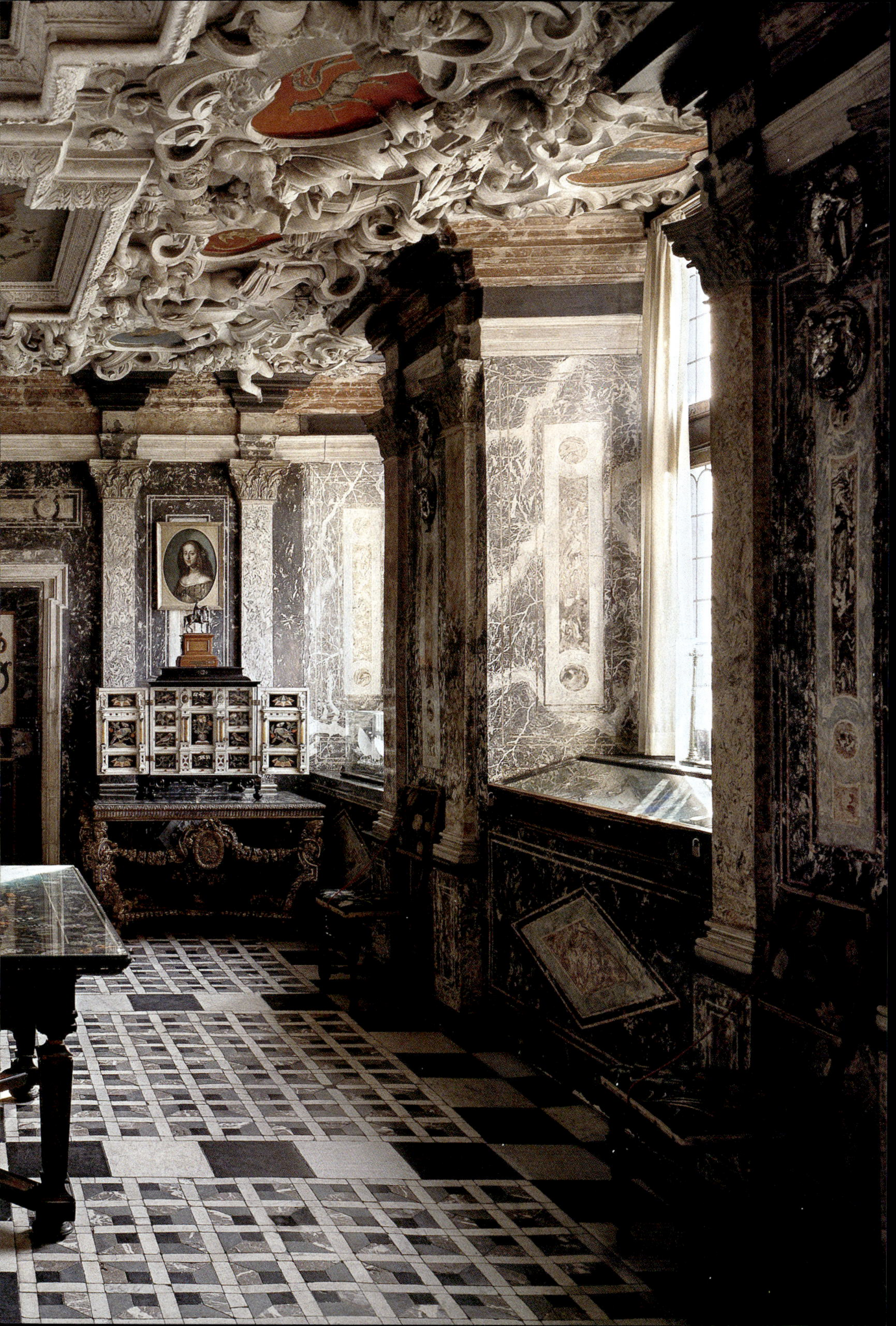

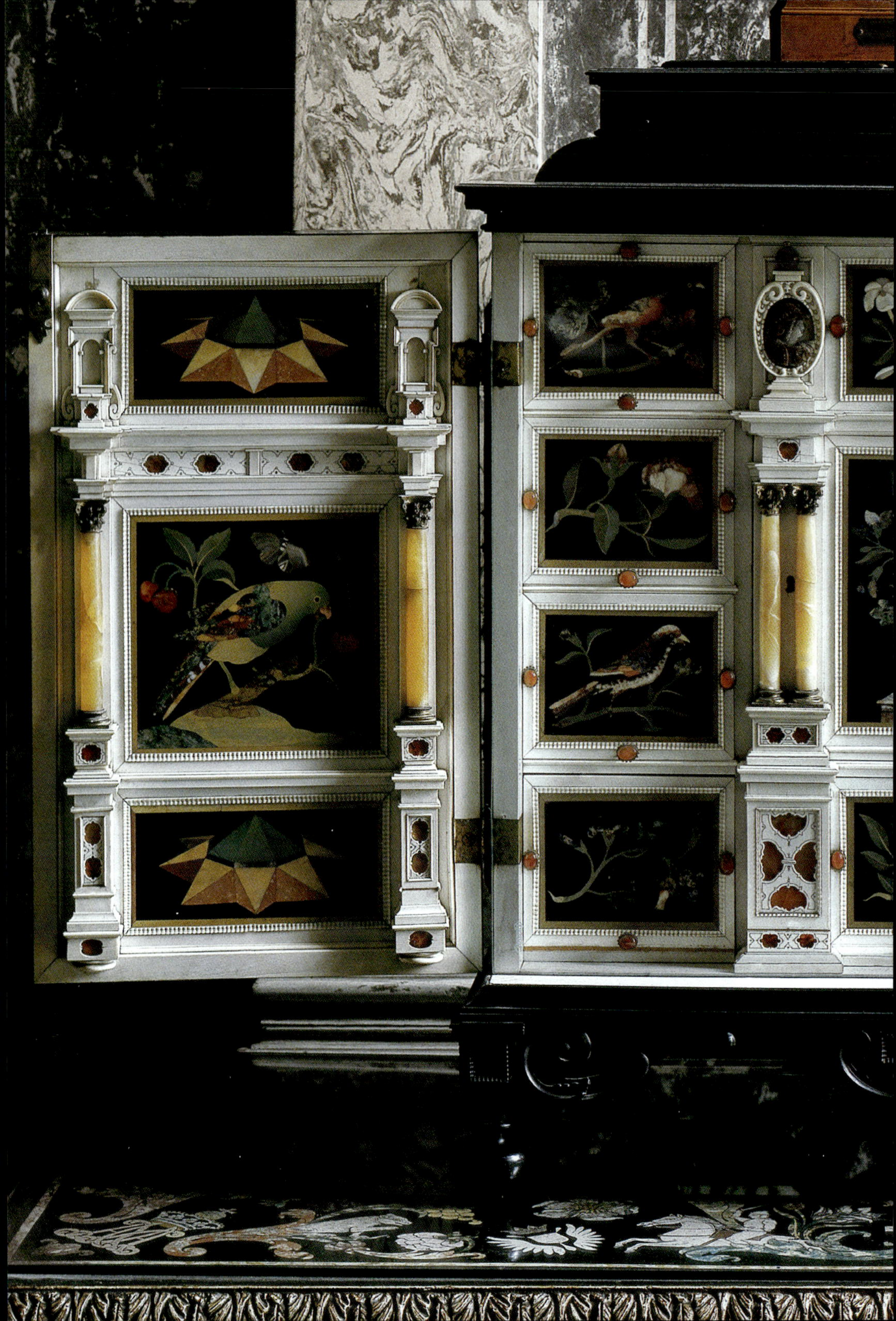

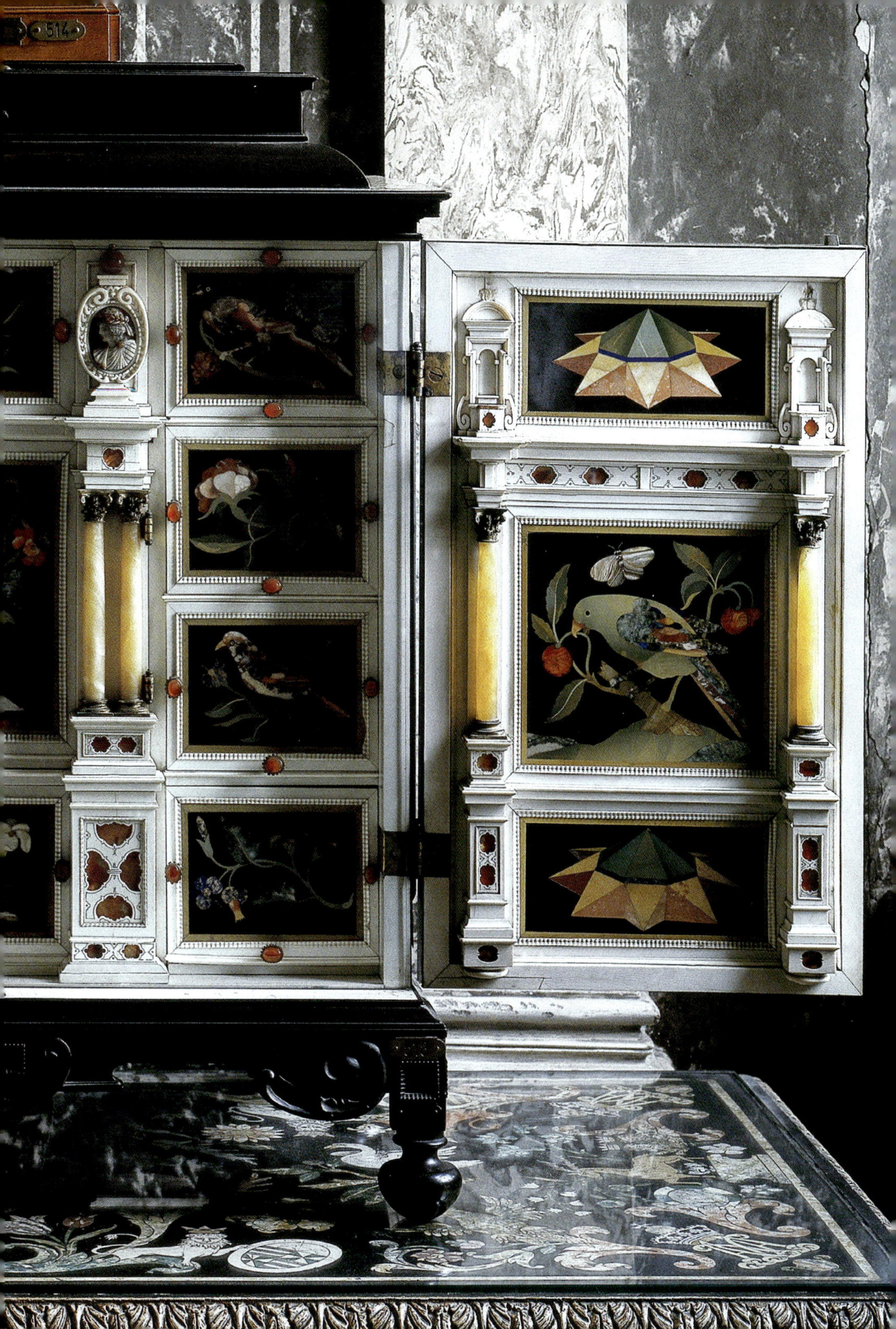

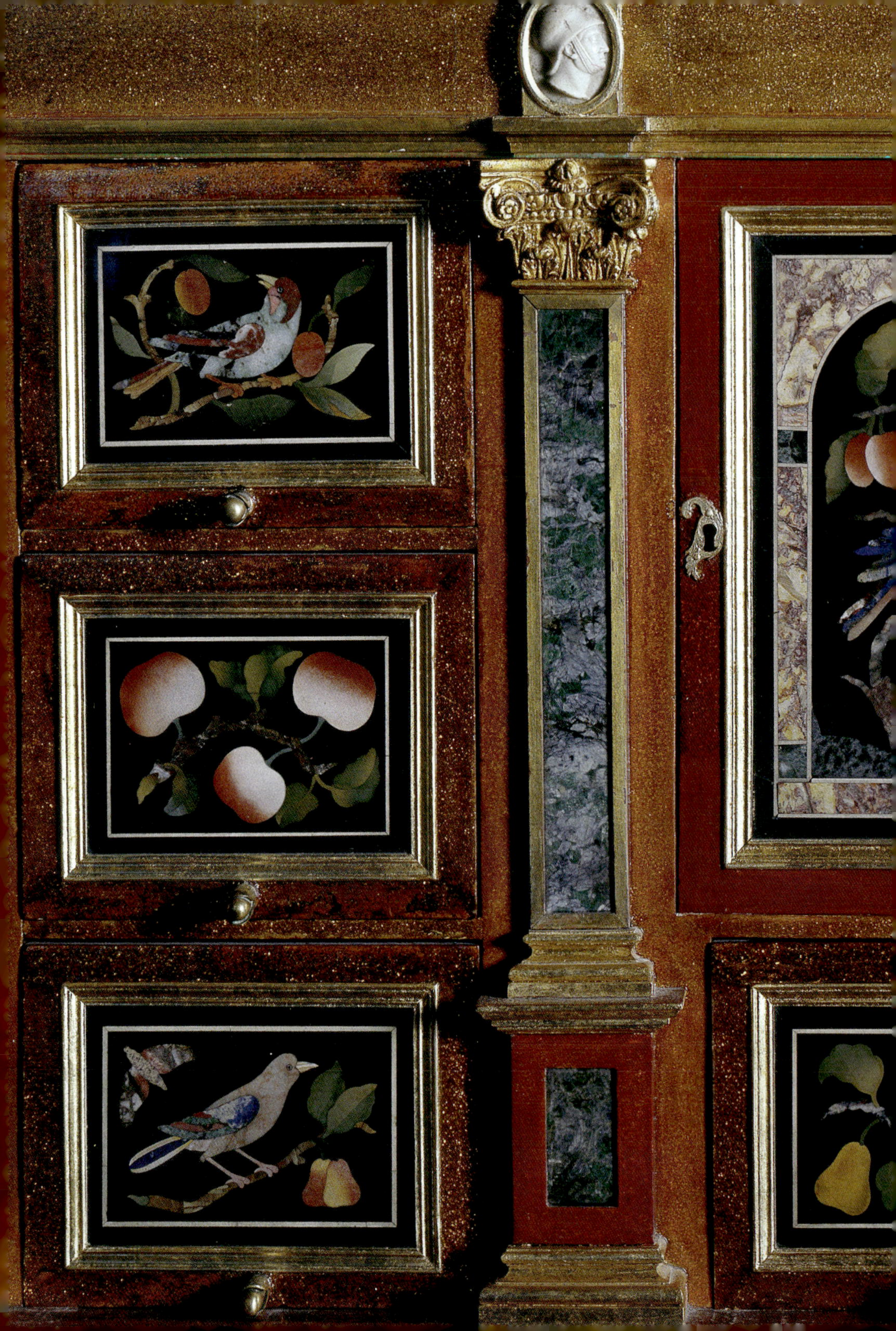

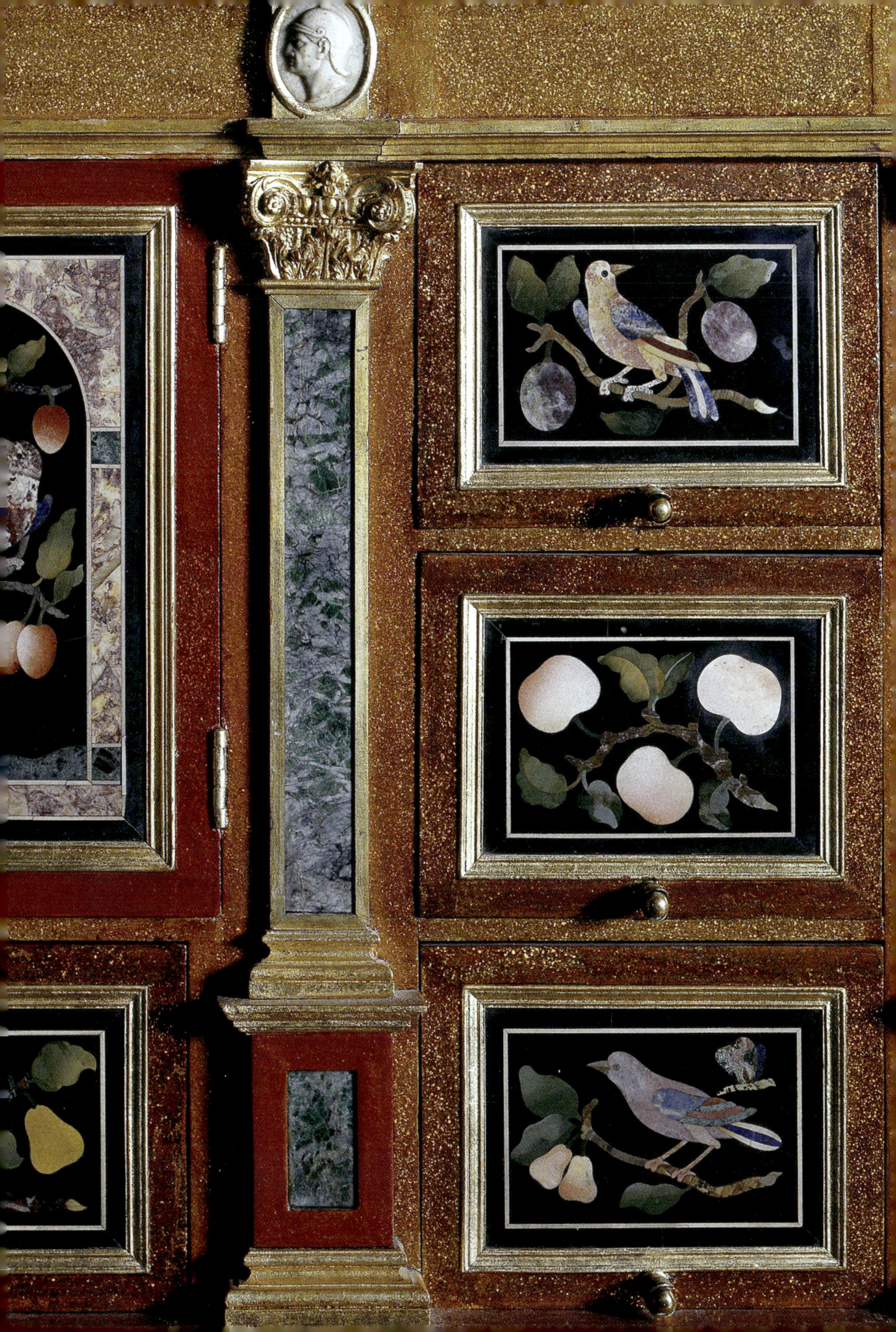

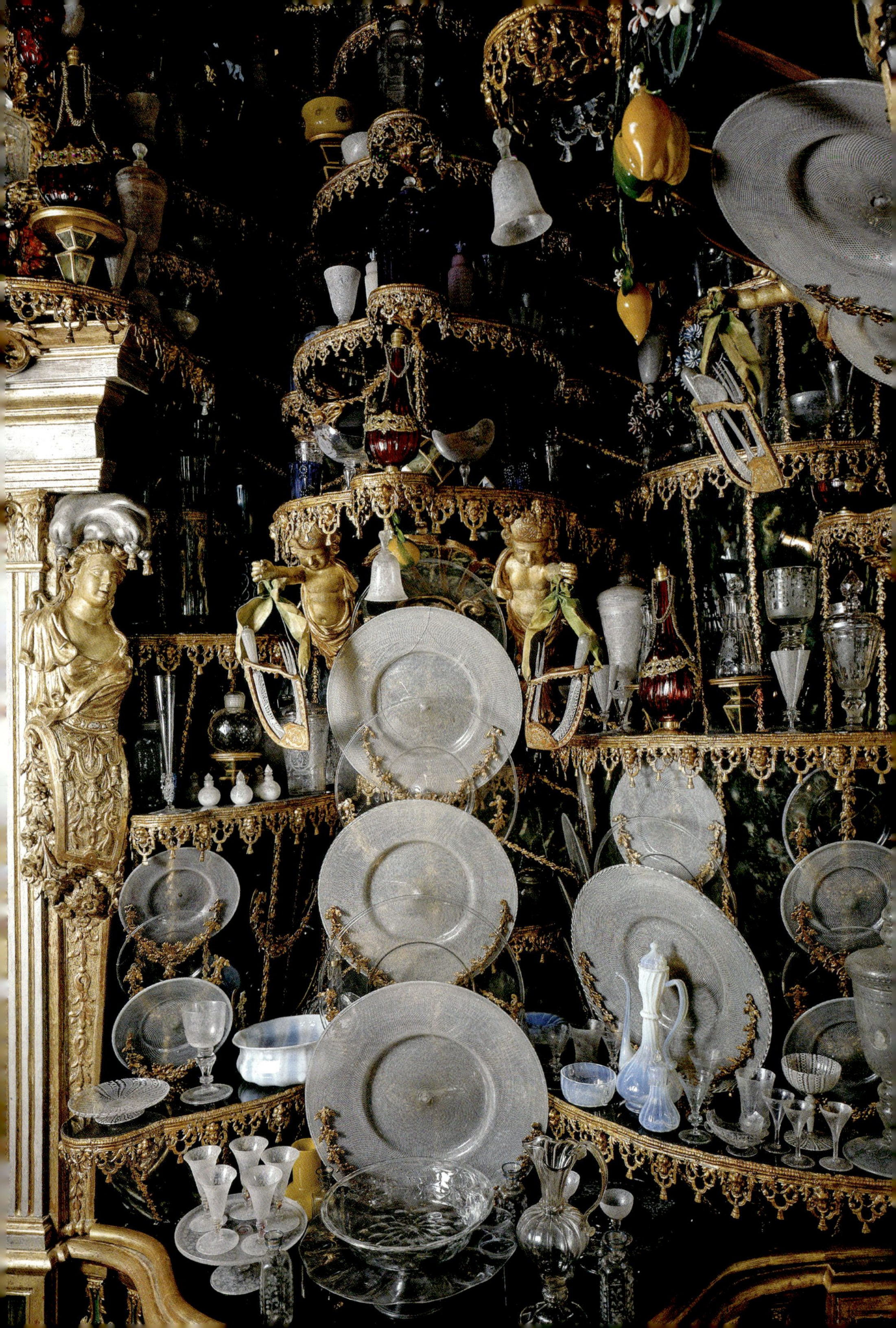

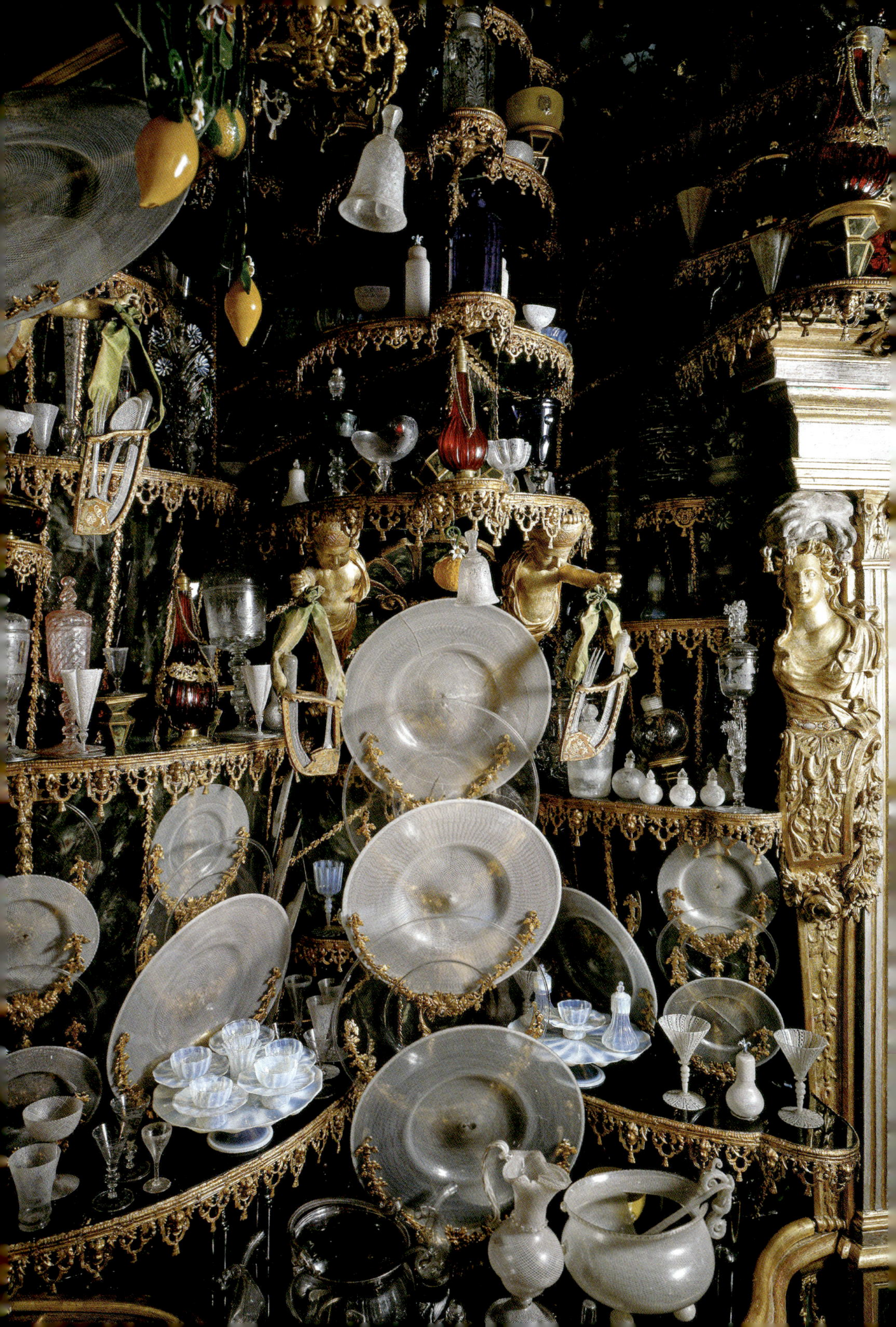

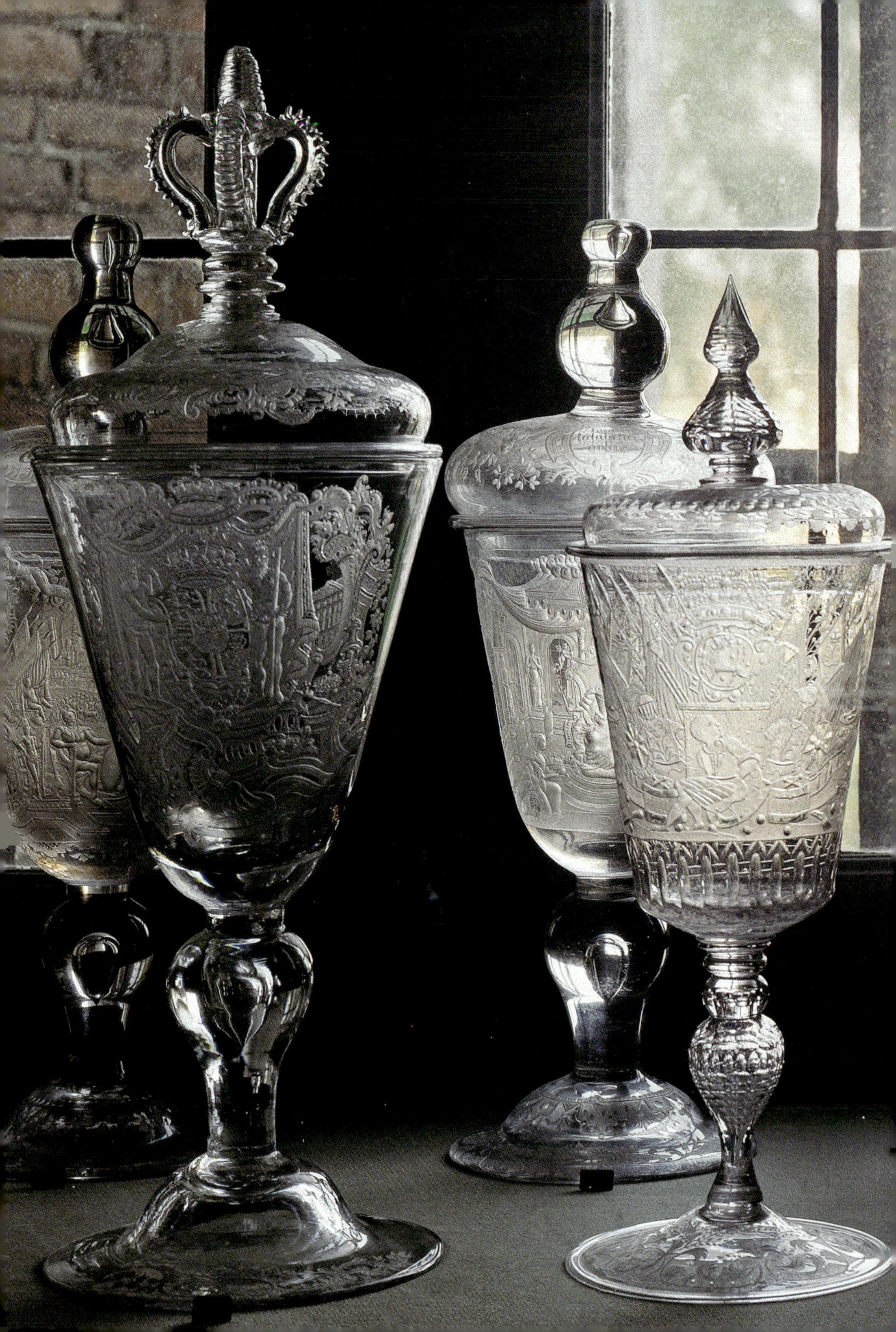

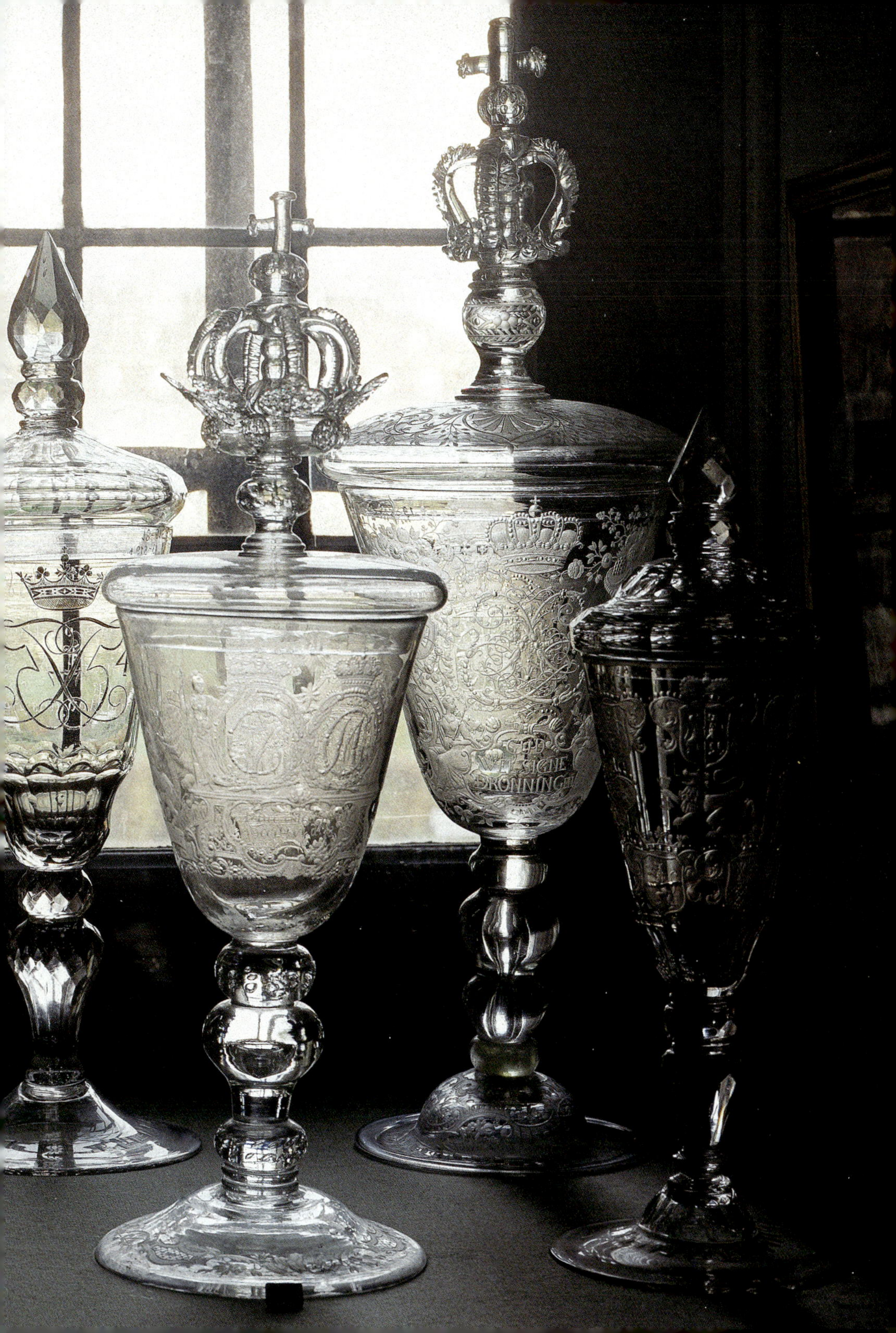
GVD
WELSIGNE
DRONNINGEN

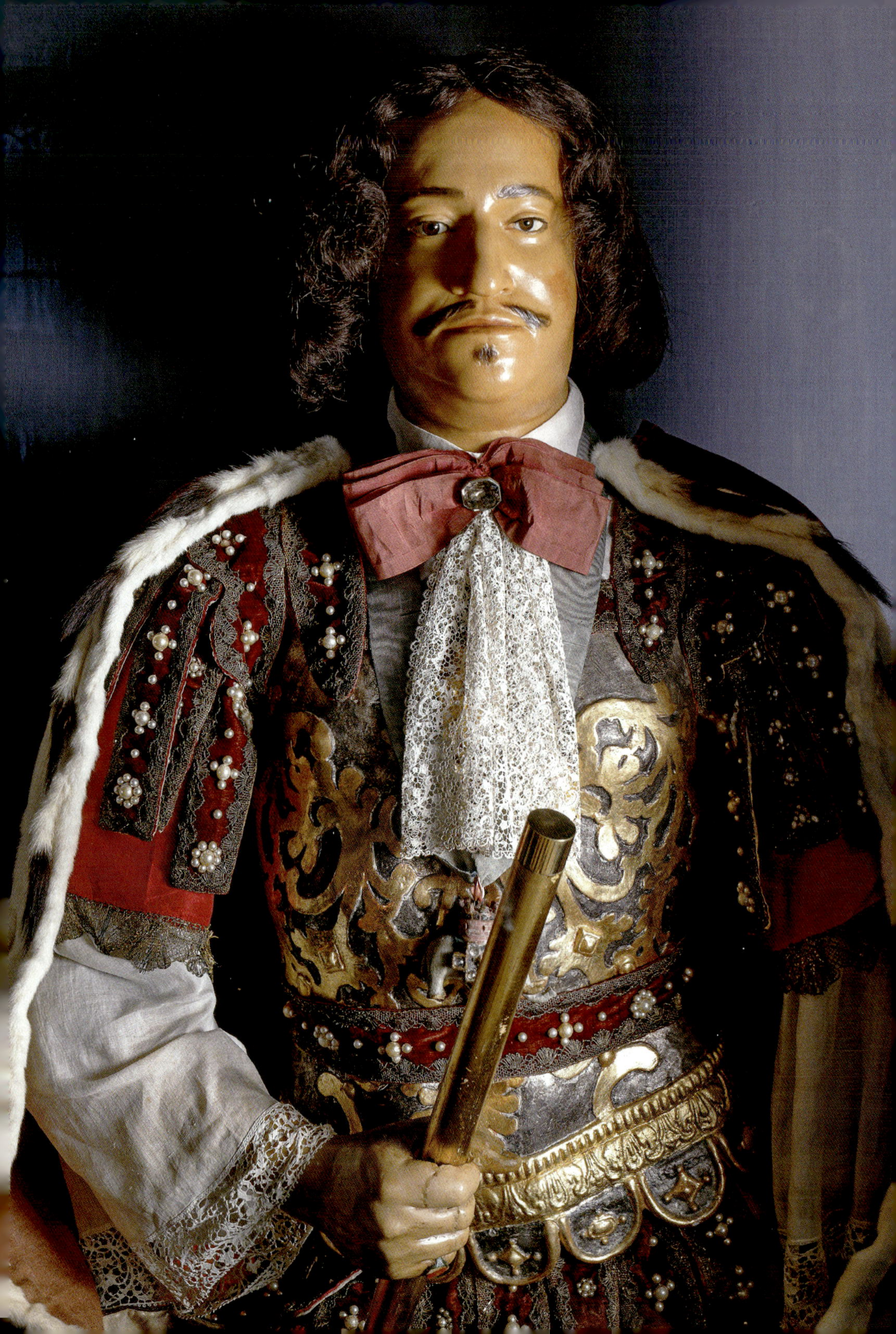

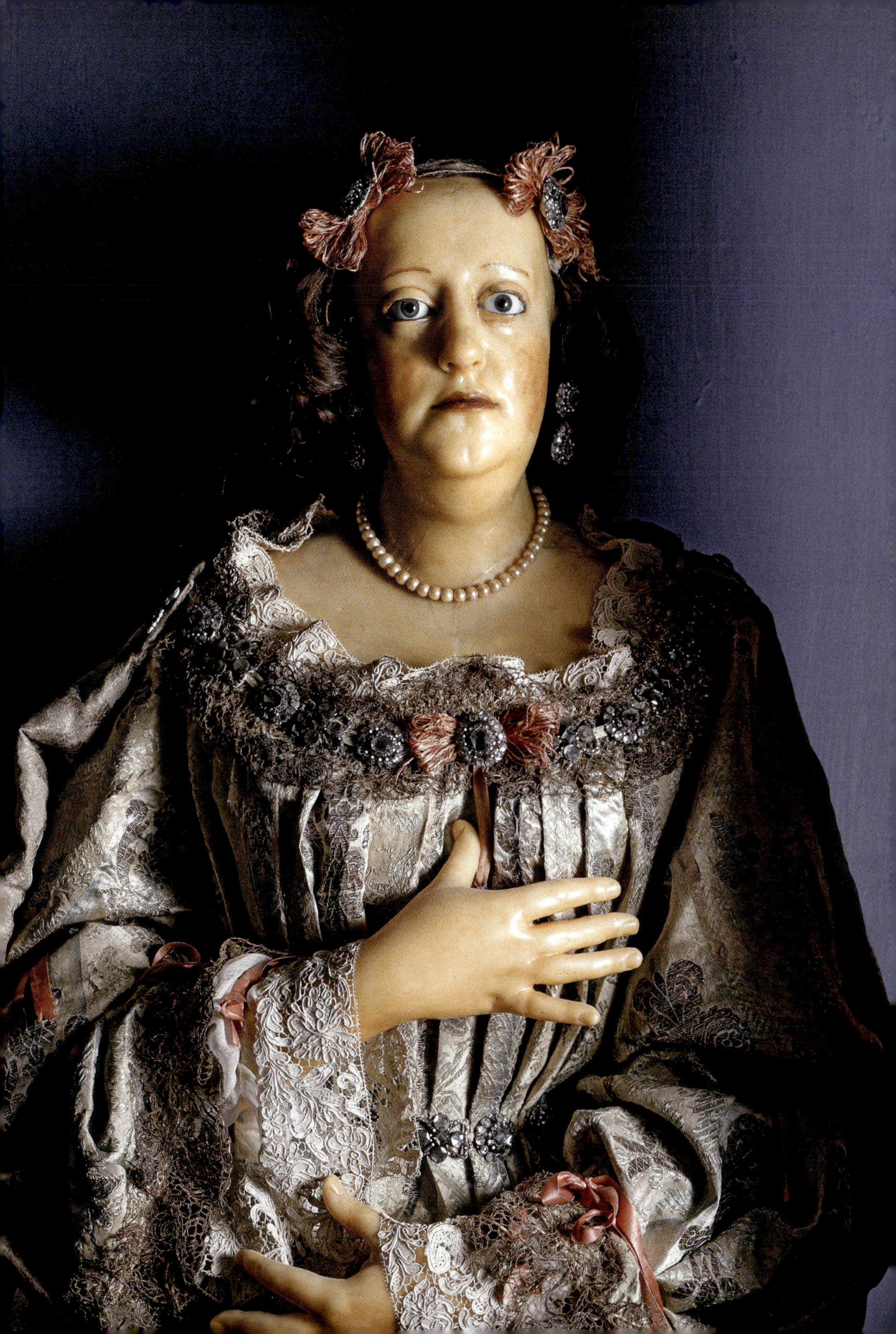

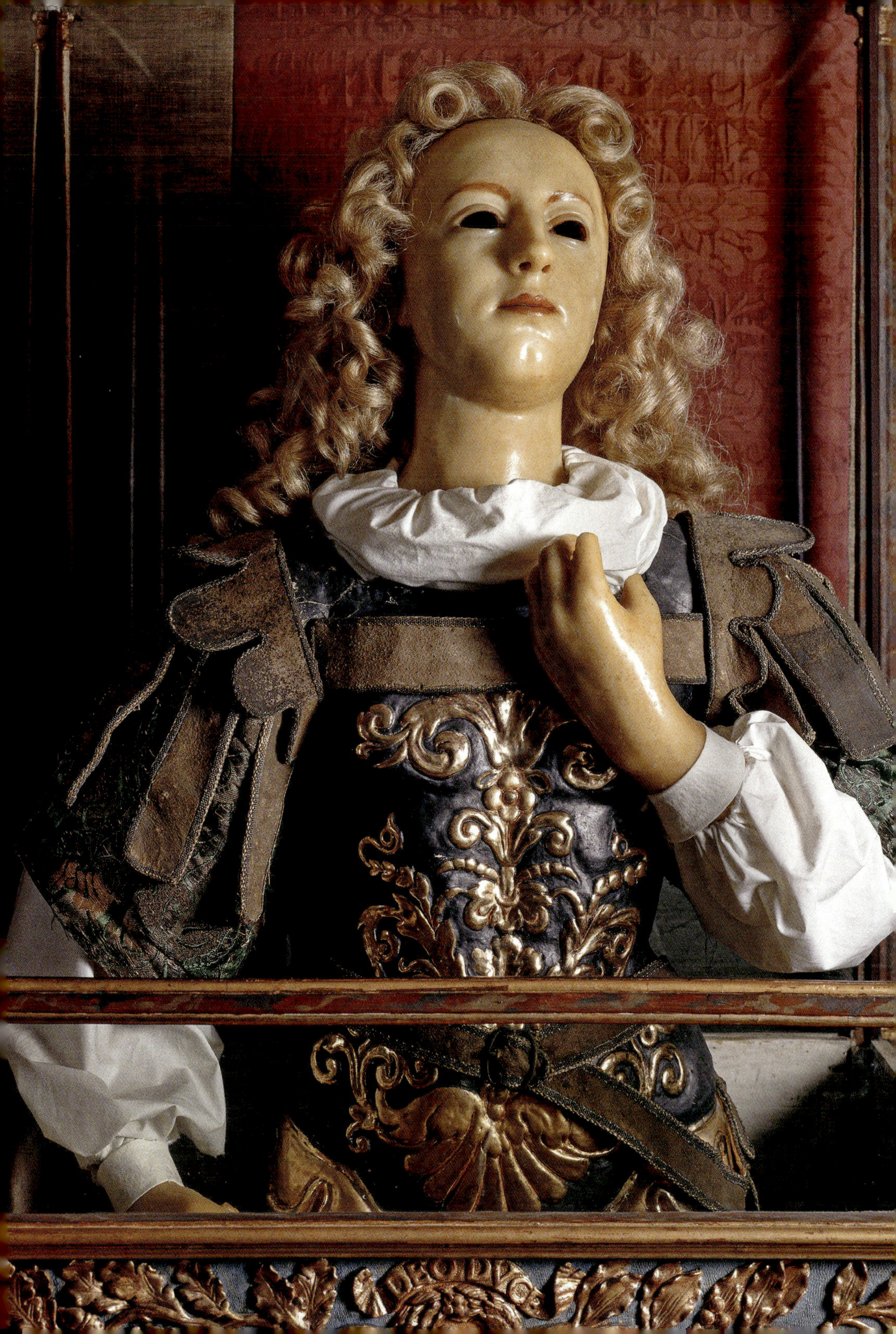

In a garden in the heart of Copenhagen is a little castle built of brown bricks and decorated with sandstone ornamentation, surrounded by the remains of an ancient moat. Rosenborg Castle was constructed in various stages on top of the ornamental pavilion which originally stood on the site, and was designed in the Renaissance style by King Christian IV (1577–1648) for his morganatic wife Kirsten Munk (1598–1658). The king gave her the title of Countess of Schleswig-Holstein, and her coat of arms featured three roses, which was perhaps the inspiration for the castle's name. The unimposing, but still exceptional building is enchanting and unique, not only because it houses the Danish crown jewels, but also because it is filled with a number of strange objects which could only be found in Nordic culture.

Rosenborg Castle was opened to the public in 1838, but the collection itself was originally established under Frederick II (1534–1588), at Frederiksborg Castle, before being transferred to Rosenborg in 1658. The royal family actually resided in the castle for only a century, from 1610 to 1710, and then maintained it as somewhere safe to keep the crown jewels and guard them from the fires that periodically affected the city; in consequence, the royal collection has remained intact and every object is well documented. The castle is like a treasure chest with its precious artefacts on display just as they were at the time when they were first used, whether the private chambers of Christian IV, the Marble Room of Frederick III, the King's Chamber of Christian V (1646–1699) or several of the other rooms. In the so-called Knights' Hall stands the Throne Chair built in 1671 for the coronation of Christian V. This magnificent throne is not of course made from unicorn horns (a powerful antidote against poison, according to legend) but from the long, spiralling tusks of narwhals, a type of whale that could only be hunted and caught by ships owned by the Danish kings since it was they who maintained absolute control of the sea routes to Greenland and back. The Glass Cabinet, one of the most magical rooms in the castle, came into being following a visit to Italy by Frederick IV (1671–1730), the last king to live in the castle. During one of his trips to Venice in 1706–1709, the Danish king was honoured by the city with a gift of 1,000 pieces of Murano glass. Whilst visiting Charlottenburg Palace Frederick IV saw the Porcelain Room and on his return to Copenhagen he decided to have a similar space designed for his Venetian glass. The room was completed in 1714, and subsequently the collection of Bohemian glass joined the original nucleus of artefacts. Cups, plates, jugs, vases, bottles and numerous other objects are displayed around the walls on shelves made to look like miniature castles, from which hang bunches of citrus fruit that are also made of glass. The beguiling effect of this room is further enhanced by the gallery of small paintings by Wolfgang Heimbach (1615–1678), which are quite extraordinary for the sense of light they manage to evoke and for the pictorial illusion they present of showing figures as if they were under glass.

◎ ❖ ◎

In einem Park im Herzen von Kopenhagen steht ein zierliches Schloss aus braunem, mit grauem Sandstein verziertem Backstein, umgeben von den Überresten eines alten Wassergrabens. Die heutige Gestalt von Schloss Rosenborg resultiert aus diversen Anbauten an einen ursprünglich vor der Stadt gelegenen Sommersitz, den der dänische König Christian IV. (1577–1648) ganz im Renaissancegeschmack für seine morganatische Gemahlin Kirsten Munk (1598–1658) errichten ließ. Als sie später zur Gräfin von Schleswig-Holstein wurde, gehörten drei Rosen zu ihrem Wappen: Daher stammt wahrscheinlich der Name Rosenborg. Obwohl äußerlich eher unscheinbar, hat der Ort doch etwas Magisches, nicht nur, weil hier die dänischen Kronjuwelen aufbewahrt werden, sondern auch zahlreiche andere Zeugnisse einer an Legenden reichen Kultur, wie man sie nur in einem Land des hohen Nordens findet.

Schloss Rosenborg wurde 1838 zur Besichtigung freigegeben, doch gegründet wurde die königliche Kunstsammlung bereits unter Friedrich II. (1534–1588). Aber erst 1658 wurde sie von Schloss Frederiksborg nach Rosenborg überführt. Nur hundert Jahre, von 1610 bis 1710, wurde das Schloss als Residenz genutzt und anschließend zur Aufbewahrung des Kronschatzes, um ihn vor den zahlreichen Bränden zu schützen, von denen die Stadt damals heimgesucht wurde. So ging nichts verloren und alles ist gut dokumentiert. Das Schloss ist daher ein wahres Schatzkästchen, in dem alles noch so aussieht wie zu Zeiten seiner Gründer: zum Beispiel die Wohnräume Christians IV., das Marmorzimmer Friedrichs III. und das Schlafzimmer Christians V. (1646–1699). Im sogenannten „Rittersaal" steht noch heute der Thron, der 1671 anlässlich der Krönung Christians V. angefertigt wurde. Als Material für diesen magischen Thron dienten die langen Stoßzähne des Narwals, auf die dänische Könige ein Monopol hatten, weil sie sämtliche Seewege nach Grönland kontrollierten und nicht etwa, wie damals angenommen, das Horn des Einhorns, das man der Legende nach für ein wirksames Mittel gegen Vergiftungen hielt. Friedrich IV. (1671–1730), der als letzter König in dem Schloss residierte, und seiner Italienreise verdankt das Schloss einen seiner schönsten Räume: das Glaskabinett. Anlässlich eines Aufenthalts in Venedig (1706–1709) schenkte ihm die Stadt tausend Stücke aus Muranoglas. Nachdem er in Charlottenburg die Porzellansammlung gesehen hatte, war Friedrich IV. davon so beeindruckt, dass er sich in Kopenhagen etwas Ähnliches für seine Glassammlung einrichten ließ. Das Glaskabinett wurde 1714 fertiggestellt und später um böhmisches Kristall ergänzt. Pokale, Teller, Kannen, Gefäße, Flaschen und andere Objekte reihen sich auf Wandregalen, die mit Girlanden aus gläsernen Zitrusfrüchten behängt sind. Noch attraktiver wird der Raum durch eine Galerie kleinformatiger Gemälde von Wolfgang Heimbach (1615–1678), die sich durch sein besonderes Gespür für Licht auszeichnen und die dargestellten Figuren wie „hinter Glas" aussehen lassen.

◎ ◈ ◎

Dans un jardin au cœur de Copenhague s'élève un petit château de briques brunies, rehaussé d'ornements en grès et entouré des vestiges de douves. Château de Rosenborg est une construction issue d'adjonctions successives à ce qui était originellement un pavillon d'agrément conçu dans le goût Renaissance par le roi Christian IV (1577–1648) pour son épouse morganatique Kirsten Munk (1598–1658). Le souverain accorda à cette dernière le titre de comtesse de Schleswig-Holstein dont les armoiries s'ornaient de trois roses, d'où le nom du château, semble-t-il. Le lieu, qui n'est nullement imposant ni même exceptionnel, est magique et précieux parce qu'il abrite le Trésor de la couronne danoise et des objets mystérieux ne pouvant appartenir qu'à la culture nordique.

Si le château de Rosenborg n'ouvre ses portes au public qu'en 1838, la famille royale a déjà commencé ses collections sous le règne de Frédéric II (1534–1588). Mais c'est seulement en 1658, que celles-ci seront transférées du château de Frederiksborg à Rosenborg. N'occupant cette demeure qu'un siècle durant, de 1610 à 1710, elle la conserva pour que le Trésor de la couronne s'y trouve en sécurité et à l'abri des incendies qui ravageaient la ville de temps à autre. Cela explique que rien n'a été dispersé et que tout est soigneusement documenté. Le château s'apparente à un écrin dont les trésors sont présentés comme au temps de ses fondateurs : les appartements privés de Christian IV, la salle des Marbres de Frédéric III, la chambre du roi Christian V (1646–1699), etc. Dans la salle dite des Chevaliers se trouve le trône réalisé en 1671 pour la cérémonie de l'onction de Christian V. Ce trône magique n'est pas fait d'une corne de licorne (puissant antidote contre les poisons, à en croire la légende), mais constitué de longues dents torsadées de narval, cétacé dont les rois du Danemark avaient le monopole de la chasse puisqu'ils contrôlaient toutes les routes maritimes du Groenland. C'est à Frédéric IV (1671–1730), dernier roi à utiliser la résidence, et à son voyage en Italie que le château doit l'une de ses salles les plus fascinantes : le Cabinet de verreries. À l'occasion d'un séjour du souverain danois à Venise (1706–1709), la Ville lui offrit mille pièces de verre de Murano. De retour à Copenhague, Frédéric IV qui avait admiré la salle des Porcelaines à Charlottenburg, décida de faire aménager un espace comparable pour ses verres vénitiens. Achevée en 1714, le Cabinet de verreries abrite également des cristaux de Bohême. Les coupes, plats, brocs, vases et flacons entre autres objets s'alignent le long des murs sur une superposition d'étagères festonnées d'agrumes en verre. La fascination exercée par les lieux est accrue par la galerie de petits tableaux de Wolfgang Heimbach (1615–1678) qui étonnent par leur traitement de la lumière et par leurs personnages qui semblent être « sous-verre ».

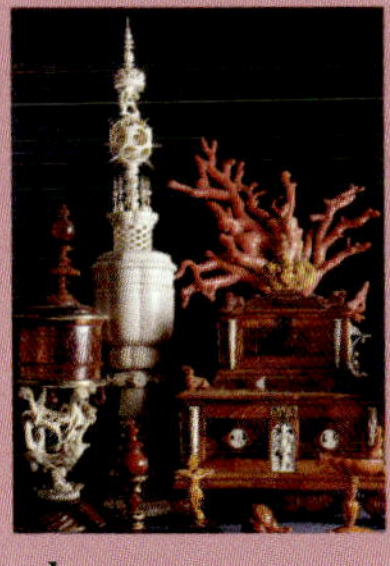

1

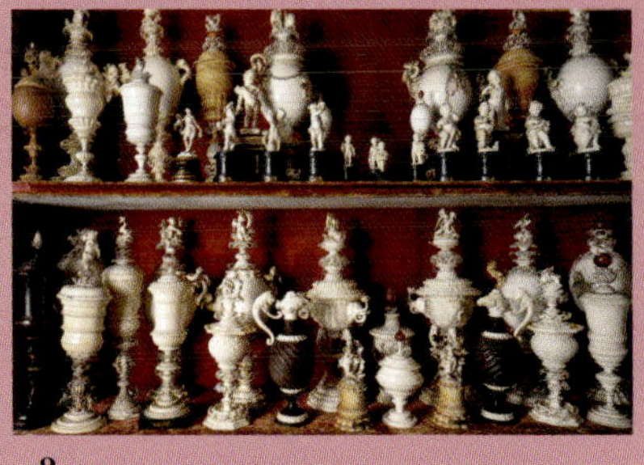

2

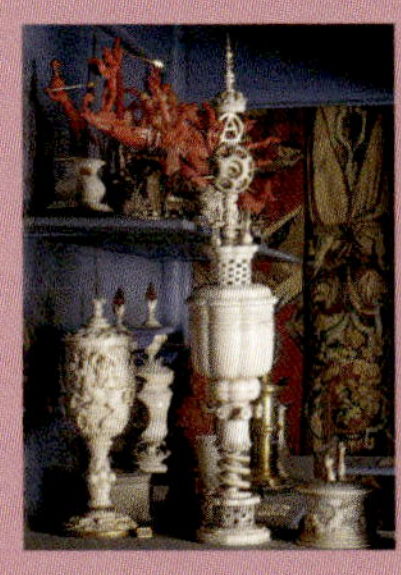

3

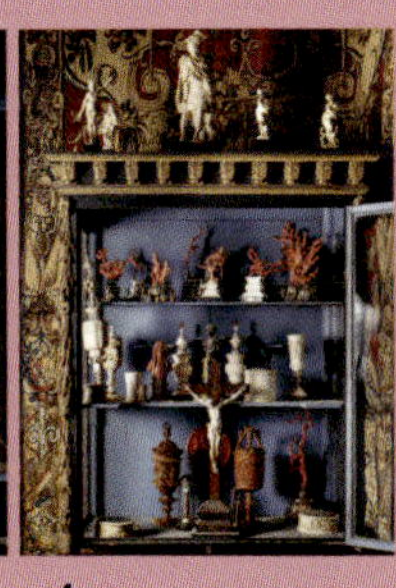

4

1–4 *Cellar Room.* Some of these splendid ivories and corals—carved in the shape of goblets, vessels and small mythological sculptures—date from the reign of Frederick IV. In the early 17th century, turning wood or ivory on a lathe was a popular hobby for young princes, and Frederick II as well as some of his successors were trained in this art. The most magnificent of the carved ivory goblets are the work of Lorenz Spengler, the court sculptor and a native of Germany.
Kellerraum. Einige der Schnitzereien – Meisterwerke aus Elfenbein –, Korallen in Pokalform, Gefäße und mythologische Kleinskulpturen stammen aus der Zeit Friedrichs IV. Das Drechseln mit Holz und Elfenbein war um 1600 eine angesehene Tätigkeit am Hofe. Friedrich II. und mehrere seiner Nachfolger ließen sich darin unterweisen. Besonders prächtige Elfenbeinschnitzereien in Pokalform fertigte der Hofbildhauer Lorenz Spengler.
La Salle de la cave. Certaines sculptures, chefs-d'œuvre en ivoire et coraux sous forme de coupes, de récipients et de figurines mythologiques, datent de l'époque de Frédéric IV. Le tournage du bois ou de l'ivoire était un passe-temps princier apprécié vers 1600. Frédéric II et plusieurs de ses successeurs se firent enseigner ce métier. Le sculpteur de la cour Lorenz Spengler, originaire d'Allemagne, a réalisé de magnifiques sculptures en ivoire en forme de coupes.

5 *The Knights' Hall.* The hall was completed in 1624 and houses the collection of solid-silver furniture, the two thrones and the three silver lions made by Ferdinand Küblich in Copenhagen in 1665–1670. The lions are used on solemn occasions when they act as guards surrounding the throne or the royal catafalque. The narwhal throne on the left has been much admired over the centuries, and the tusk of this creature was long taken to be the horn of the mythical unicorn.
Der Rittersaal. Der 1624 vollendete Saal beherbergt eine Sammlung von Silbermöbeln, darunter zwei Thronsessel und drei von Ferdinand Küblich in Kopenhagen zwischen 1665 und 1670 geschaffene, annähernd lebensgroße silberne Löwen. Bei besonderen Anlässen bewachen sie den Thron bzw. den königlichen Katafalk. Der Sage nach wurde der Ainkhürn (wörtlich Horn des Einhorns)-Thron aus dem Horn des namensgebenden Fabelwesens gefertigt, tatsächlich handelt es sich um Narwalstoßzähne.
La Salle des Chevaliers. Achevée en 1624, la salle abrite la collection de meubles en argent massif, les deux trônes et les trois lions en argent, fabriqués à Copenhague en 1665–1670 par Ferdinand Küblich. Ils étaient utilisés lors d'occasions solennelles, en tant que gardiens du trône et du catafalque royal. Le trône en dents de narval, à gauche, était une pièce convoitée ; avant que les scientifiques n'élucident le mystère de sa nature, on croyait à l'existence de la licorne mythique.

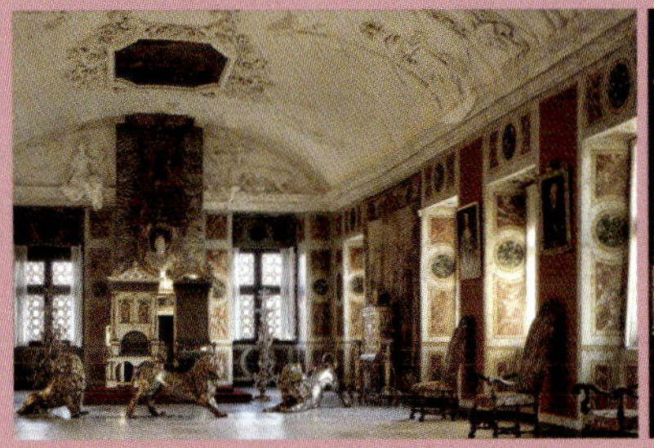

5

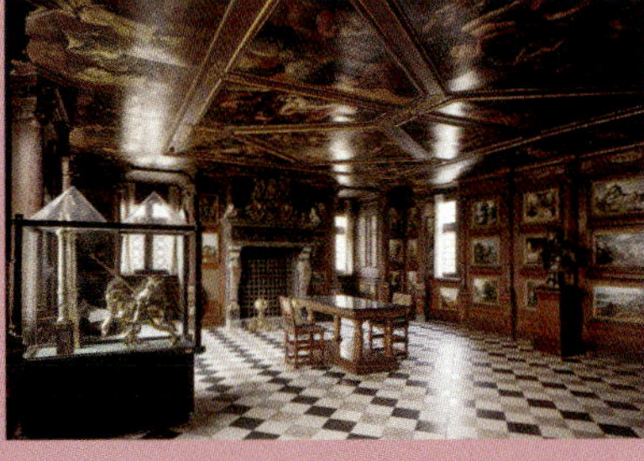

6

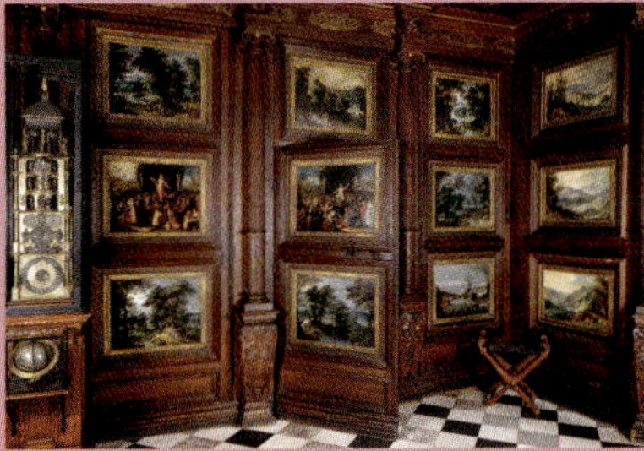

7

6 *Christian IV's Winter Room* is the best-preserved room in the old castle. In about 1770 the original stucco ceiling was replaced with mythological paintings by Pieter Isaacsz, among them *The Feast of the Gods* and *The Fall of the Giants*. On the left can be seen the gilt-silver statuette of Christian IV, made by the goldsmith Heinrich von Beust in Brunswick in 1598, while in the cupboards Frederick IV kept his private cabinet of curiosities, which included various spoils of war removed from Gottorf Palace.
Das Winterzimmer Christians IV. Dies ist das am besten erhaltene Zimmer des alten Schlosses. Um 1770 wurde die ursprüngliche Stuckdecke durch mythologische Gemälde von Pieter Isaacszs, darunter das *Festmahl der Götter* und der *Sturz der Giganten*, ersetzt. Die vergoldete Silberstatuette Christians IV. (links) schuf der Goldschmied Heinrich von Beust 1598 in Braunschweig. In Schränken verwahrte Friedrich IV. hier seine private Kunst- und Wunderkammer, zu der auch Kriegsbeute aus Schloss Gottorf zählte.
Le Salon d'hiver de Christian IV. La pièce la mieux conservée du château d'origine. Le plafond d'origine en stuc a été remplacé vers 1770 par les peintures mythologiques de Pieter Isaacsz, dont *La fête des dieux* et *La chute des géants*. À gauche : une figure en argent doré représentant Christian IV, réalisée par l'orfèvre Heinrich von Beust à Brunswick en 1598. Des placards abritaient le cabinet des merveilles privé de Frédéric IV, lequel incluait le butin de guerre du palais de Gottorp.

7 *Christian IV's Winter Room.* Work on the rich panelling was begun by the court cabinet-maker Gregor Greuss and completed around 1620. The inlaid paintings were purchased in Antwerp and constitute a unique collection of art from the Netherlands. On the left is a magnificent astronomical clock, complete with carillon and moving figures, made by the Swiss watchmaker Isaac Habrecht in 1594.
Das Winterzimmer Christians IV. Die prachtvolle Holzvertäfelung wurde vom Hoftischler Gregor Greuss um 1620 vollendet. Die um 1620 in Antwerpen erworbenen eingefügten Gemälde bilden eine einzigartige Sammlung niederländischer Kunst. Links: eine eindrucksvolle astronomische Uhr mit Glockenspiel und beweglichen Figuren, ein Werk des Schweizer Uhrmachers Isaac Habrecht von 1594.
Le Salon d'hiver de Christian IV. Commencé par l'ébéniste de la cour Gregor Greuss, le riche lambris a été achevé vers 1620. Les peintures intégrées ont été achetées à Anvers et constituent une collection unique de l'art des Pays-Bas. À gauche : le magnifique exemple d'une horloge astronomique, avec carillon et figures mobiles, réalisée par l'horloger suisse Isaac Habrecht en 1594.

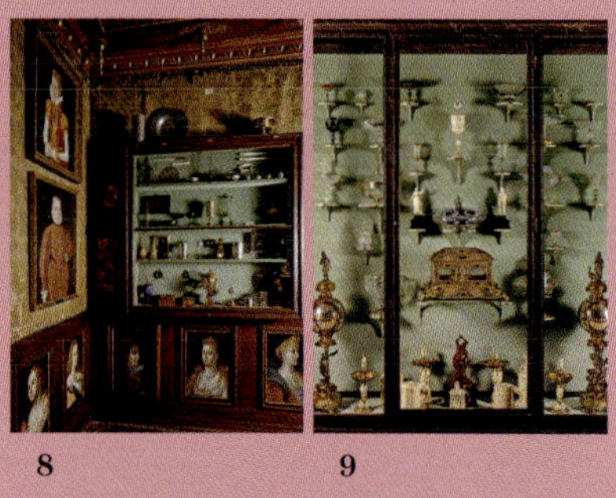

8   9

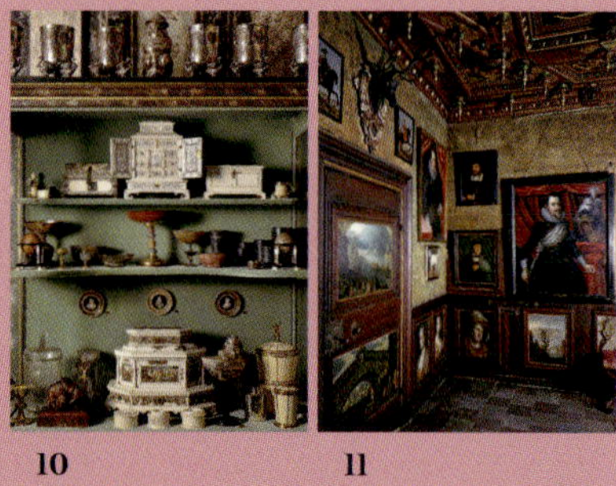

10   11

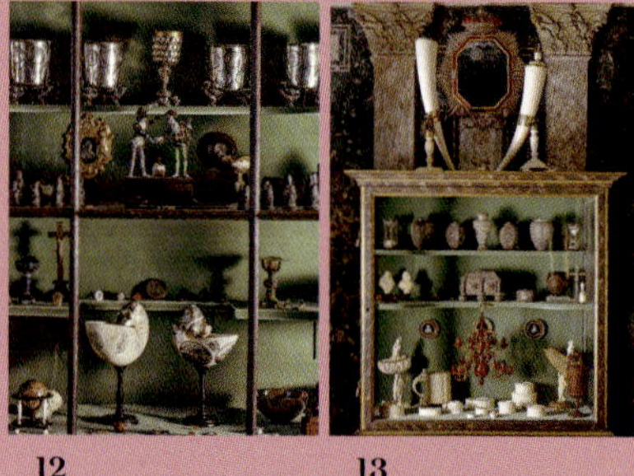

12   13

8-11 *Christian IV's Writing Room.* In this tower room, which is easy to keep warm, Christian IV wrote much of his vast correspondence. The room has been preserved more or less intact since his reign in the first half of the 17th century, although the wall coverings of green silk printed with gold ornaments date from around 1700. Most of the items displayed in this room are mementos of Christian IV, his immediate family or his ancestors. The two large portraits on the left (ill. 8) are by Hans Knieper and depict Queen Sophie, the wife of Frederick II, painted around 1572, and underneath her Christian IV at the age of seven (*c.* 1585).

Das Schreibzimmer Christians IV. In seinem leicht zu beheizenden Turmzimmer widmete sich Christian IV. seiner beeindruckend umfangreichen Korrespondenz. Der Raum blieb praktisch unverändert, die Einrichtung aus der ersten Hälfte des 17. Jhs., seiner Regierungszeit, ist nahezu komplett erhalten. Die Tapeten aus grüner, mit goldenen Ornamenten bedruckter Seide stammen aus der Zeit um 1700. Heute sind Erinnerungsstücke an Christian IV., seine engsten Familienmitglieder und Vorfahren ausgestellt. Die beiden großen Gemälde Hans Kniepers (Abb. 8, links) entstanden um 1585 und zeigen Christian IV. siebenjährig sowie Königin Sophie, die Gattin Friedrichs II., um 1572.

Le Salon d'écriture de Christian IV. C'est dans cette pièce de la tour, facilement chauffée, que Christian IV réalisait sa vaste correspondance. La pièce a été conservée, plus ou moins intacte, depuis l'époque de Christian IV dans la première moitié du 17e siècle. Les tentures murales en soie verte imprimée d'ornements dorés datent toutefois d'environ 1700. Les objets exposés dans le Salon d'écriture sont principalement des souvenirs de Christian IV, de sa famille proche et de ses ancêtres. Les deux grands tableaux à gauche (ill. 8) montrent Christian IV à l'âge de 7 ans, peint vers 1585 par Hans Knieper, et au-dessus la reine Sophie, épouse de Frédéric II, peinte par Hans Knieper, vers 1572.

12 *The Marble Room.* In the display case can be seen limestone chess pieces divided into 'Danes' and 'Swedes', following Charles X Gustav's victory over Frederick III in 1658, and two comedic masque figures playing a game of morra, made of coloured glass over a metal wire core in Venice in about 1600. The nautilus shells are decorated with angels, floral ornaments, the coat of arms of Copenhagen and depictions of Frederick III during the Siege of Copenhagen, 1658-1660.

Das Marmorzimmer. In der Vitrine Schachfiguren aus Kalkstein, die Dänen und Schweden nach Karl X. Gustavs Sieg über Friedrich III. im Jahr 1658 darstellen; zwei Maskenfiguren (morraspielende Komödianten) aus farbigem Glas über Metalldraht, entstanden um 1600 in Venedig; verzierte Nautiluspokale mit Engeln, Blumen-

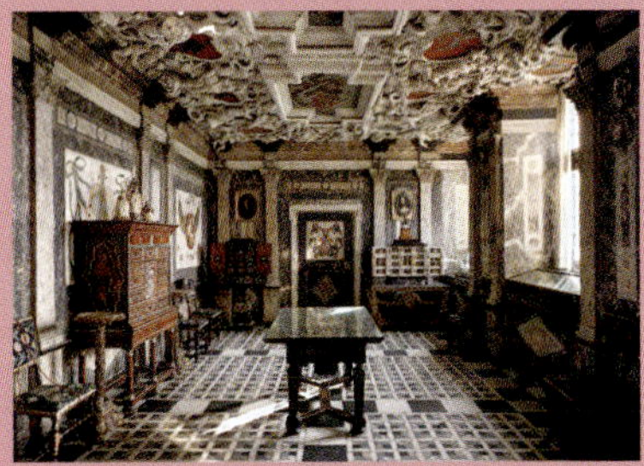

14

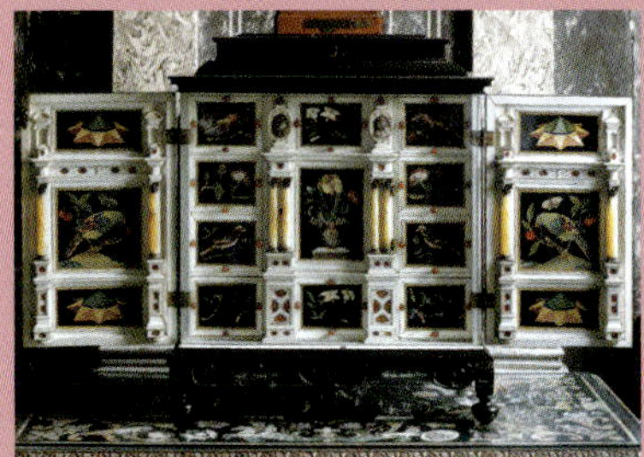

15

ornamenten, dem Kopenhagener Wappen und Darstellungen Friedrichs III. bei der Belagerung Kopenhagens 1658–1660.
La Salle des marbres. Dans la vitrine un jeu d'échecs avec des pièces « Danois » et « Suédois » taillées dans du calcaire, après la défaite de Frédéric III face à Charles X Gustave en 1658 ; deux masques (figures comiques, joueurs de morra) en verre coloré sur une armature en fil métallique, fabriqués à Venise vers 1600. Des coquilles de nautiles décorées d'anges, d'ornements fleuris, des armoiries de Copenhague et de représentations de Frédéric III pendant le siège de Copenhague, 1658–1660.

13 *The Marble Room*. On the top of the display case are two ivory drinking horns, and inside the case is a jewel box made of gilt silver and decorated with some 2,000 small diamonds. The box was made in Augsburg in around 1680 and is said to have been a present from the future Queen Anne of England to her mother-in-law, Queen Sophie Amalie of Brunswick-Lüneburg.
Das Marmorzimmer. Zwei Trinkhörner aus Elfenbein. In der Vitrine eine Schmuckschatulle aus vergoldetem Silber mit ungefähr zweitausend kleinen Diamanten besetzt. Sie entstand in Augsburg um 1680 und war angeblich ein Geschenk der späteren Königin Anne Stuart von Großbritannien an ihre Schwiegermutter, die dänische Königin Sophie Amalie von Braunschweig-Calenberg.
La Salle des marbres. Corne à boire en ivoire. Dans la vitrine une boîte à bijoux en argent doré, ornée d'environ deux mille petits diamants. La boîte, fabriquée à Augsbourg vers 1680, serait un cadeau de la future reine Anne d'Angleterre à sa belle-mère, la reine Sophie-Amélie de Brunswick-Lunebourg.

14 *The Marble Room*. The cabinet on the left is lined with pieces of tortoiseshell and silver decora-tions, Antwerp, *c.* 1680. It features a central section surrounded by 14 drawers, and the decoration consists of stylised plant, bird and animal motifs.
Das Marmorzimmer. Links: Kunst-schrank mit Schildpatt furniert und Silberornamenten eingelegt, Antwerpen, um 1680. Den Mittel-teil des Schrankes umrahmen 14 Schubladen. Die Dekoration zeigt stilisierte Pflanzen-, Vogel- und Tiermotive.
La Salle des marbres. À gauche: Cabinet plaqué d'écailles de tortue et incrusté d'ornements en argent, Anvers, vers 1680. Le cabinet com-porte une partie centrale entourée de 14 tiroirs, l'ensemble est décoré de motifs stylisés de plantes, d'oi-seaux et d'animaux.

15 Melchior Baumgartner (attrib.), *Jewel cabinet*, Augsburg, *c.* 1650. Ebony, ivory, pietra dura.
Melchior Baumgartner (zuge-schrieben), *Schmuckschrank*, Augsburg, um 1650. Ebenholz, Elfenbein, Pietra dura.

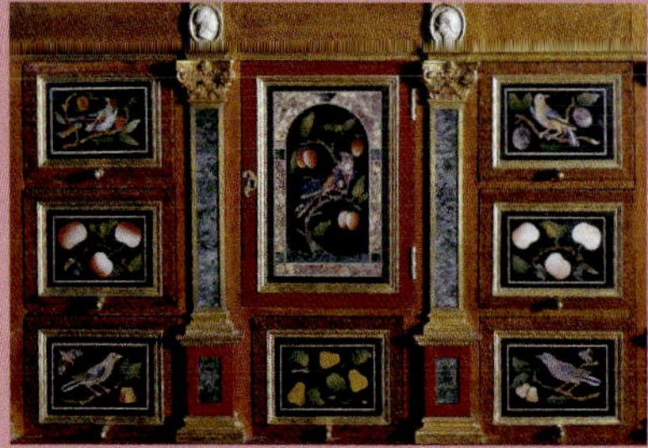

16

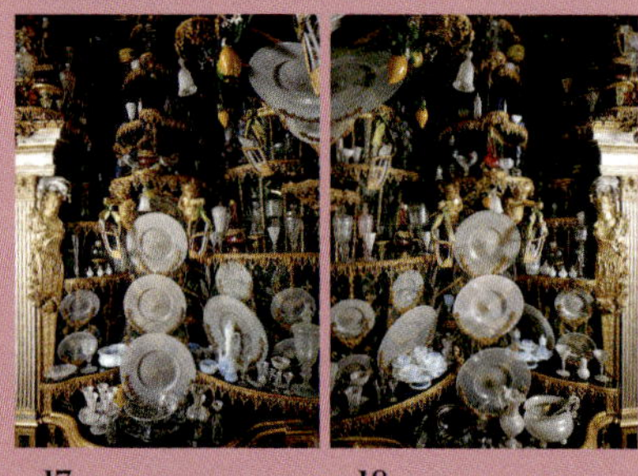

17   18

Melchior Baumgartner (attr.), *Cabinet à bijoux*, Augsbourg, vers 1650. Ébène, ivoire, incrusté de pietra dura.

16 *The Hall of Frederick IV*. This cabinet features lacquer work by Christian van Bracht and pietra dura pictures brought back from Florence in 1709 by Frederick IV. It was formerly owned by the king's sister, Princess Sophie Hedwig. *Der Saal Friedrichs IV.* Schrank mit Lackarbeiten von Christian van Bracht und Pietra-dura-Arbeiten, die Friedrich IV. 1709 aus Florenz mitbrachte. Aus dem Besitz Prinzessin Sophia Hedwigs, der Schwester des Königs. *La Salle de Frédéric IV*. Cabinet, décoré de laque de Christian van Bracht, et des images en pietra dura rapportées de Florence par Frédéric IV en 1709. Appartenait à la sœur du roi, la princesse Sophie-Hedwige.

17–18 *The Glass Cabinet*, dated 1713/14, was commissioned by Frederick IV. In the late 17th century porcelain cabinets were popular throughout Europe, but this is the only known glass cabinet. It was designed to house the exquisite glass collection presented to Frederick by the city of Venice during his visit there in 1706–1709. To display the precious glass artefacts, a number of pyramidal consoles were installed, covered with marbled paper and edged with festoons made of lead gilt. *Glaskabinett*, 1713/14. Friedrich IV. ließ den Raum als Glaskabinett einrichten. Porzellankabinette waren im späten 17. Jh. sehr beliebt, dies ist jedoch das einzige bekannte Glaskabinett. Es war für die erlesene Glassammlung bestimmt, die die Stadt Venedig Friedrich anlässlich seines Besuchs 1706–1709 zum Geschenk gemacht hatte. Präsentiert werden die kostbaren Gläser auf pyramidalen Konsolen, die mit marmoriertem Papier überzogen und mit Girlanden aus vergoldetem Blei gesäumt sind. *Le Cabinet des verreries*, 1713/14. Frédéric IV a fait concevoir la pièce comme un Cabinet des verreries. Les cabinets de porcelaines de ce type étaient assez courants en Europe à la fin du 17e siècle, mais c'est le seul cabinet des verres connu. Le Cabinet abrite l'exquise collection de verreries que Frédéric avait reçue en cadeau de la Ville de Venise, visitée en 1706–1709. Pour exposer les verres, des consoles pyramidales, recouvertes de papier marbré et bordées de festons de plomb doré, ont été fabriquées.

19 Cups made of Norwegian glass, engraved on the occasion of the coronation of Frederick V, in 1747. Pokale aus norwegischem Glas mit Gravuren zu Ehren der Krönung Friedrichs V., 1747.

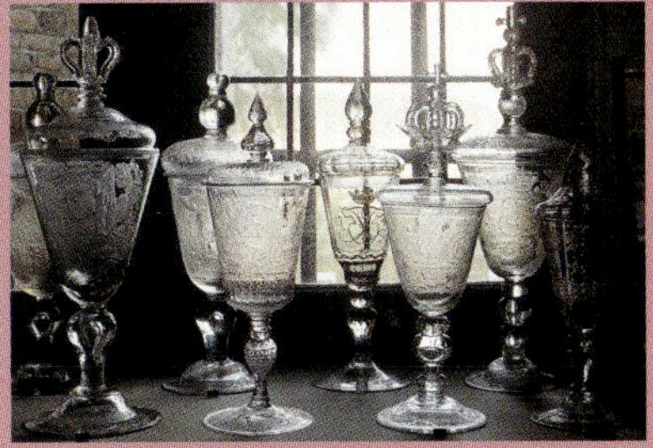

19

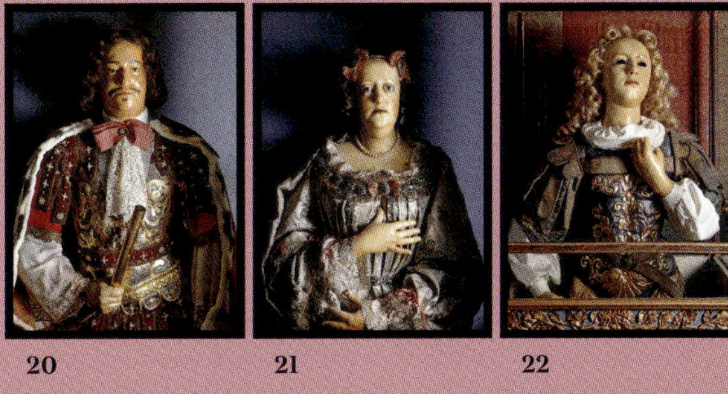

20   21   22

Tasses en verre norvégien, gravées à l'occasion du couronnement de Frédéric V, 1747.

20-22 *The Dark Room*. Wax busts of Frederick III, Sophie Amalie and prince George. The cabinet of curiosities contained wax portraits of several members of the royal family, and such images were also popular at other royal courts. Most of them were made using masks, whether taken from life or death. The king's bust was modelled by Louis-Augustin le Clerc in Copenhagen in 1751, almost a century after the king's death, but the queen's image was made during her lifetime. The figure of the prince, the younger brother of Christian V, was modelled in 1669 by Antoine Benoist.
Der dunkle Zimmer. Wachsbüsten Friedrichs III., Sophie Amalies und Prinz Georgs. In der Kunst- und Wunderkammer wurden auch Wachsporträts weiterer Mitglieder der königlichen Familie aufbewahrt. Ähnliches findet sich auch an anderen europäischen Königshöfen. Meist wurden solche Porträts nach einer Lebend- oder Totenmaske angefertigt. Louis-Augustin le Clerc schuf die Büste des Königs 1751 in Kopenhagen, fast ein Jahrhundert nach dem Tod des Herrschers. Die Büste der Königin entstand hingegen zu ihren Lebzeiten. Antoine Benoist modellierte Prinz Georg, den jüngeren Bruder von Christian V., im Jahr 1669.
Le Salon sombre. Bustes de cire de Frédéric III, Sophie-Amélie et prince George. Le Cabinet des merveilles contenait des représentations en cire de plusieurs membres de la famille royale. On retrouve cette coutume dans d'autres cours royales. Les bustes étaient généralement fabriqués d'après un masque moulé sur le visage d'une personne vivante ou morte. Le buste du roi a été modelé par Louis-Augustin le Clerc à Copenhague en 1751, presque un siècle après la mort du roi. Le buste de la reine a été fait de son vivant. Le buste de prince George, le frère cadet de Christian V a été modelé en 1669 par Antoine Benoist.

Det Augsburgska konstskåpet

Uppsala Universitet

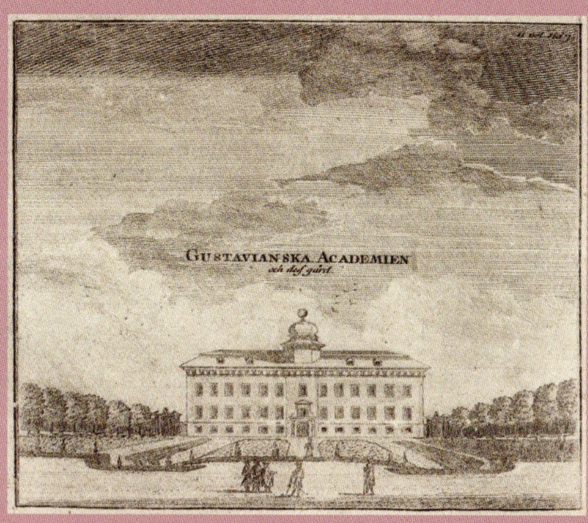

Founded 1625–1631

Key item The Cabinet designed by Philipp Hainhofer for King Gustav II Adolf of Sweden. On top of the cabinet the so-called "mountain" where the most precious objects, believed to have magical powers, were kept.

Besonders sehenswert Kunstschrank, entworfen von Philipp Hainhofer für König Gustav II. Adolf von Schweden. Der sogenannte „Gipfel" mit den kostbarsten Stücken, denen magische Wirkung zugesprochen wurde.

À voir absolument Cabinet de Philipp Hainhofer pour le roi Gustave II Adolphe de Suède. Le « mont » du cabinet qui rassemble les objets les plus précieux et auquel sont attribués des pouvoirs magiques.

Fredrik Akrel, *Gustavianum*, Uppsala, 1773

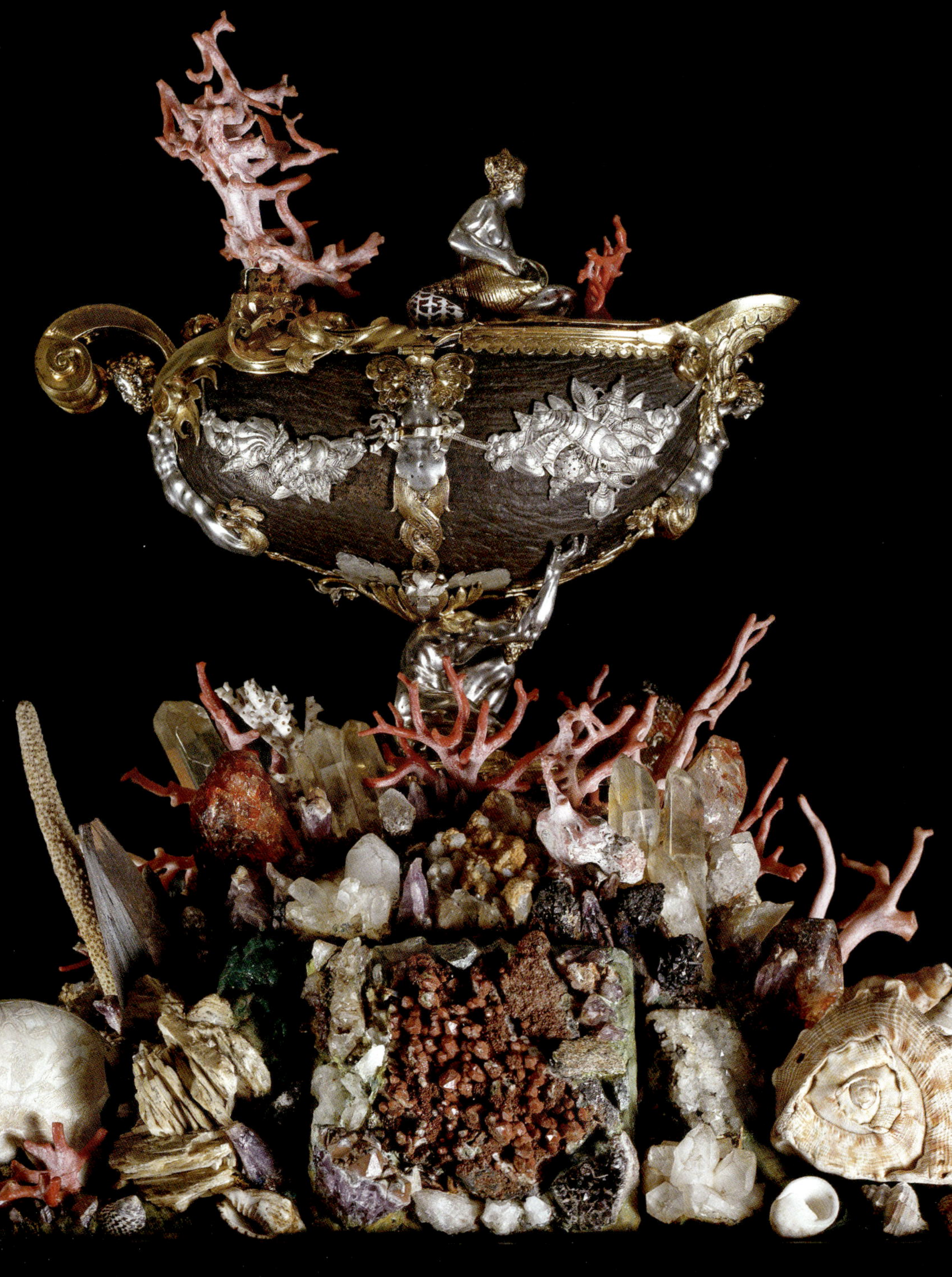

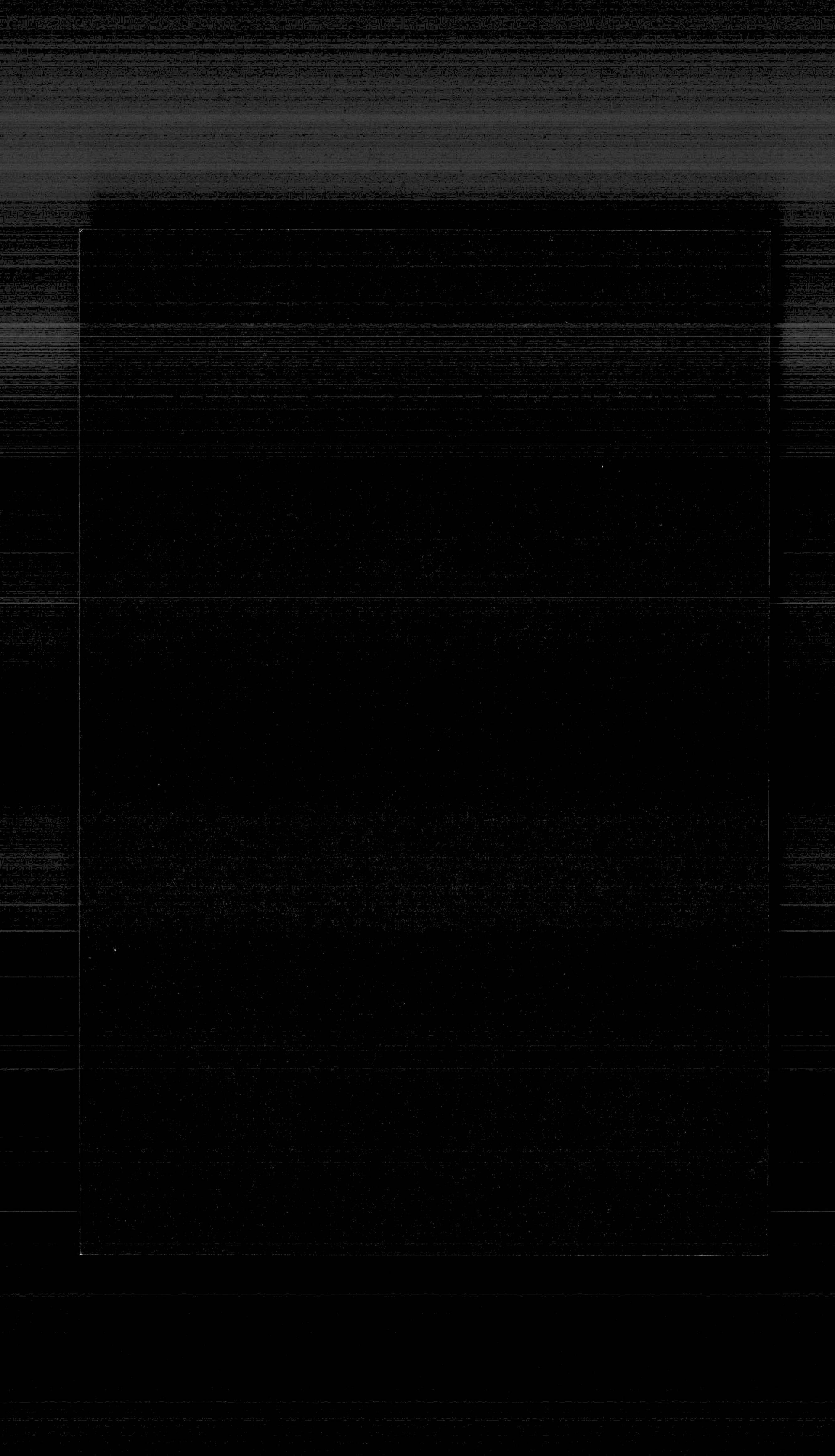

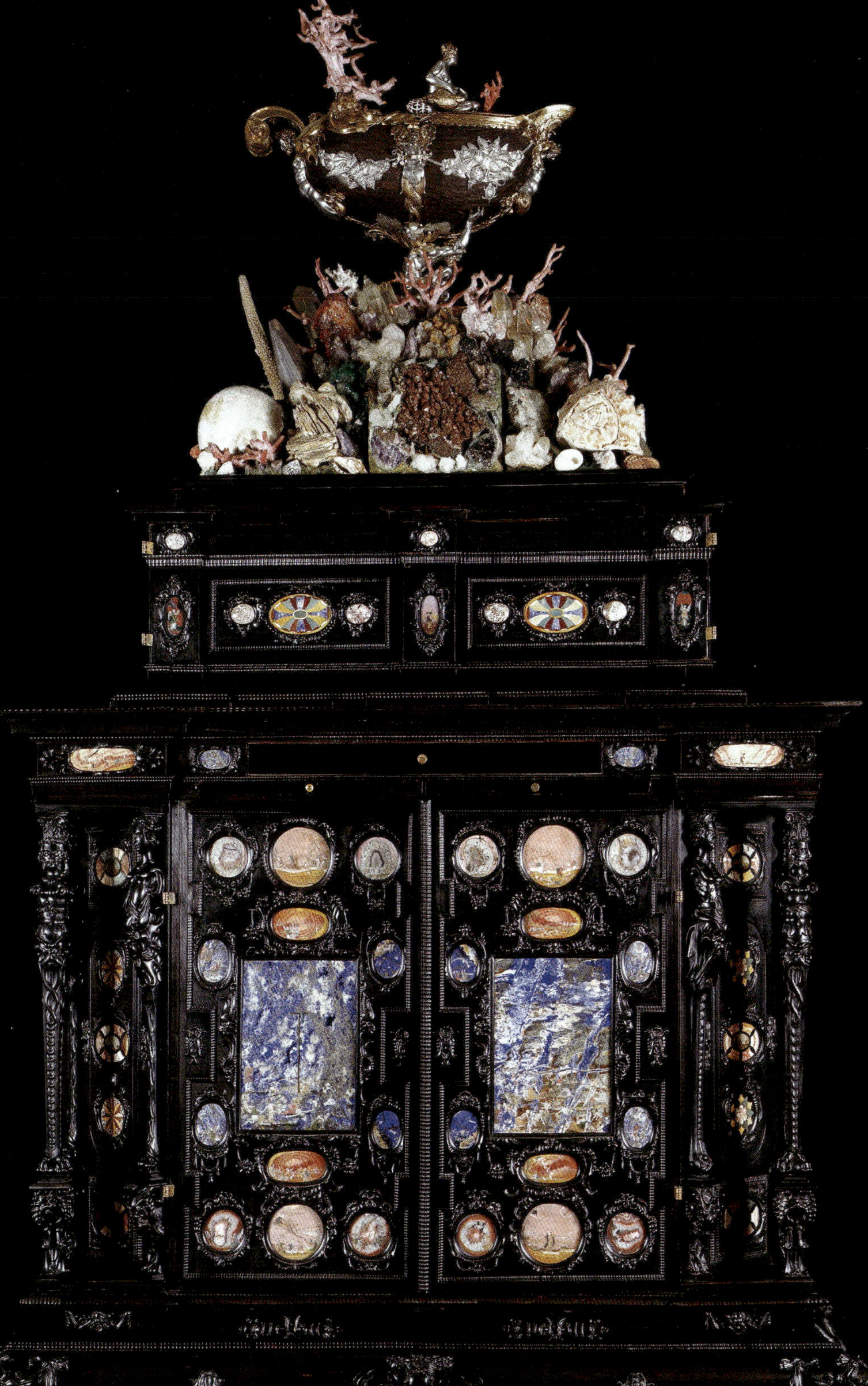

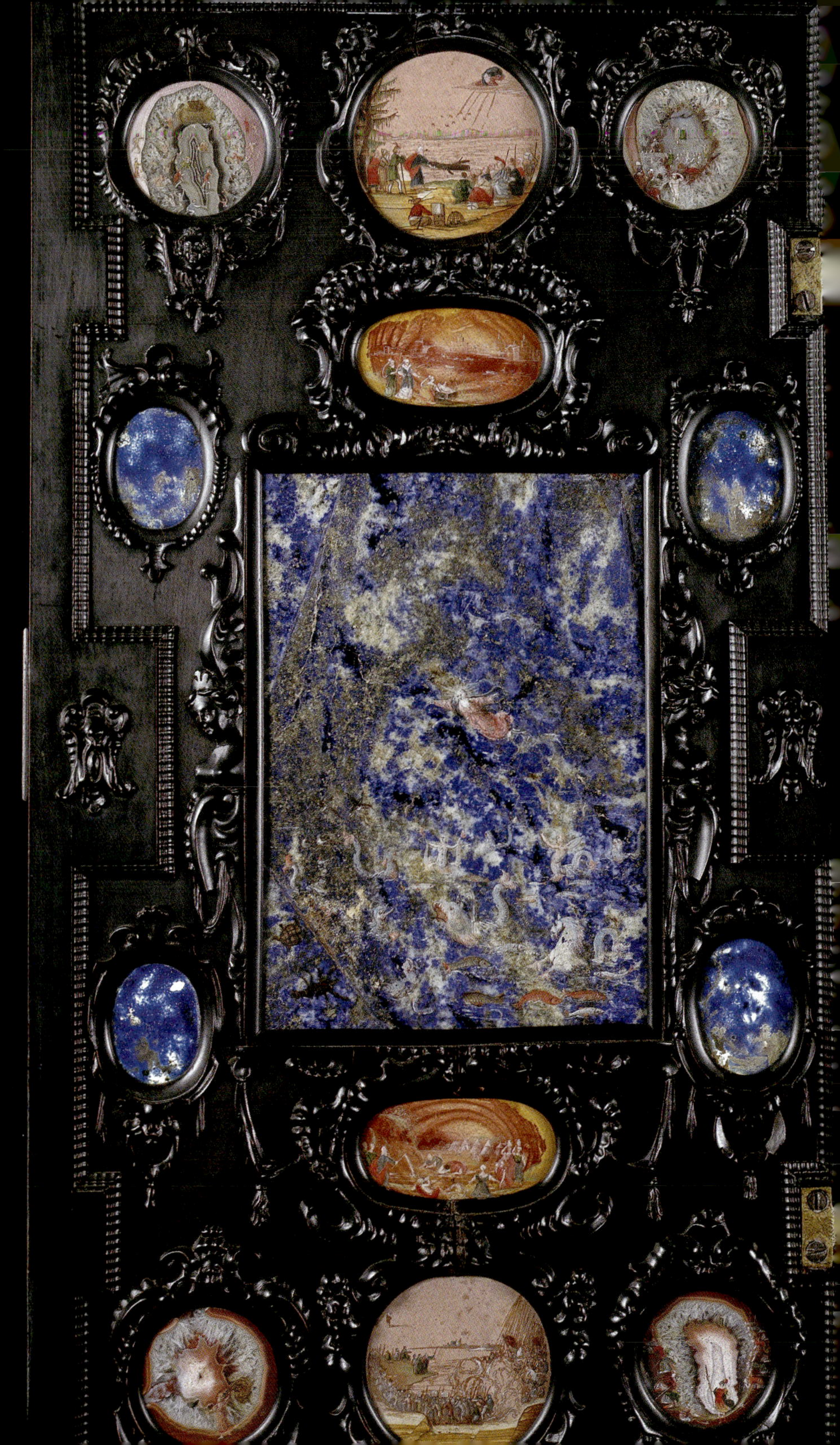

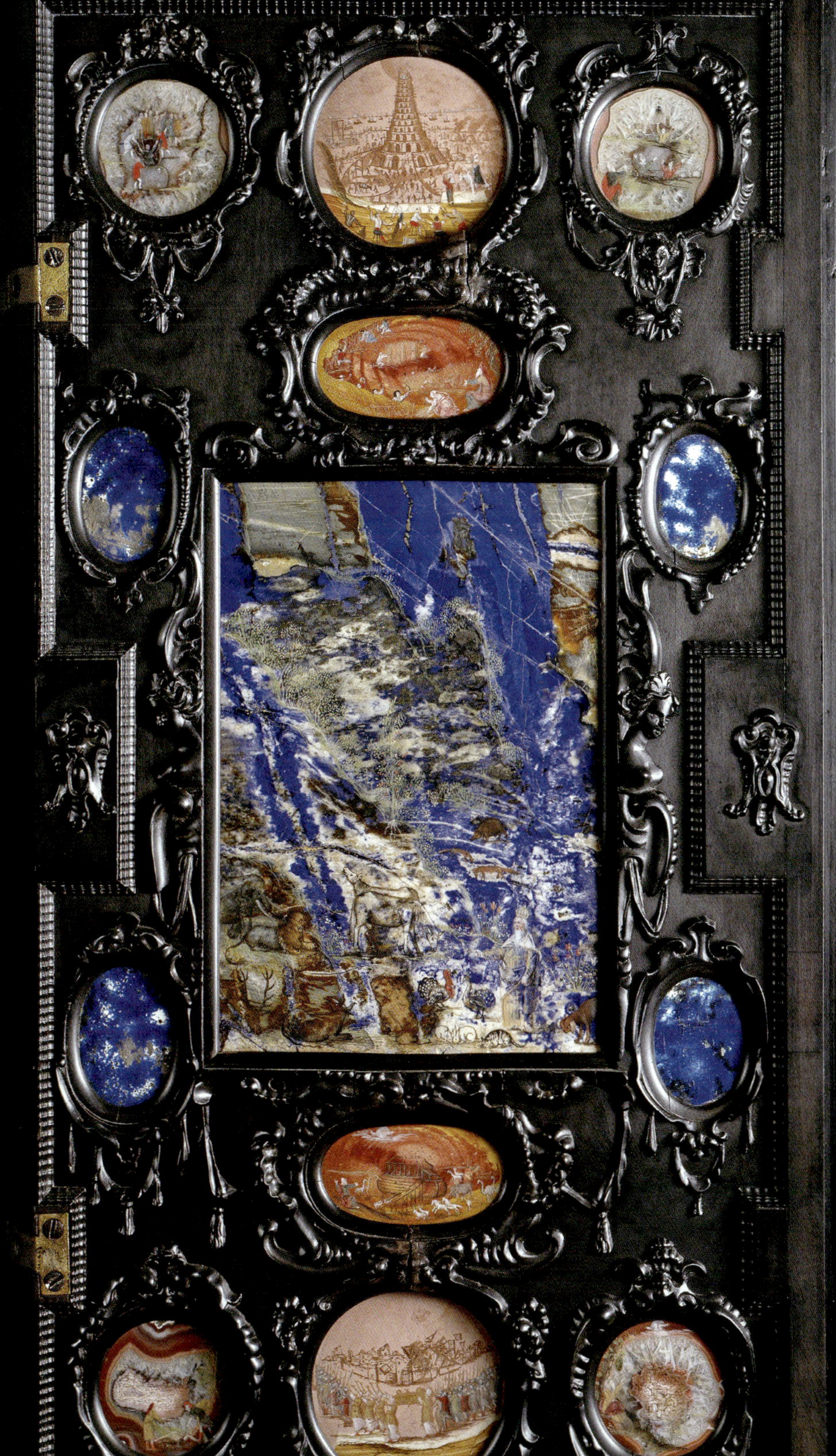

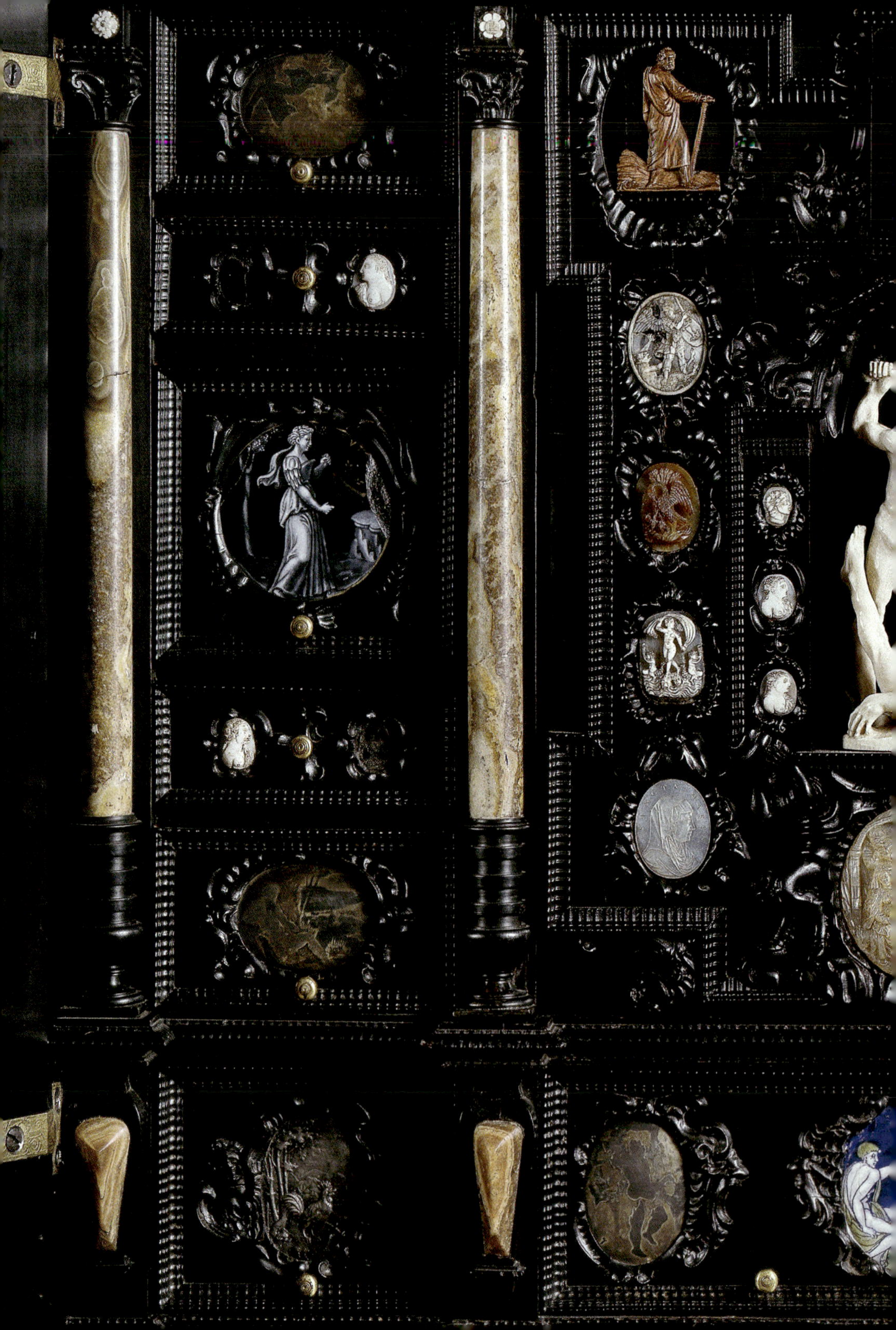

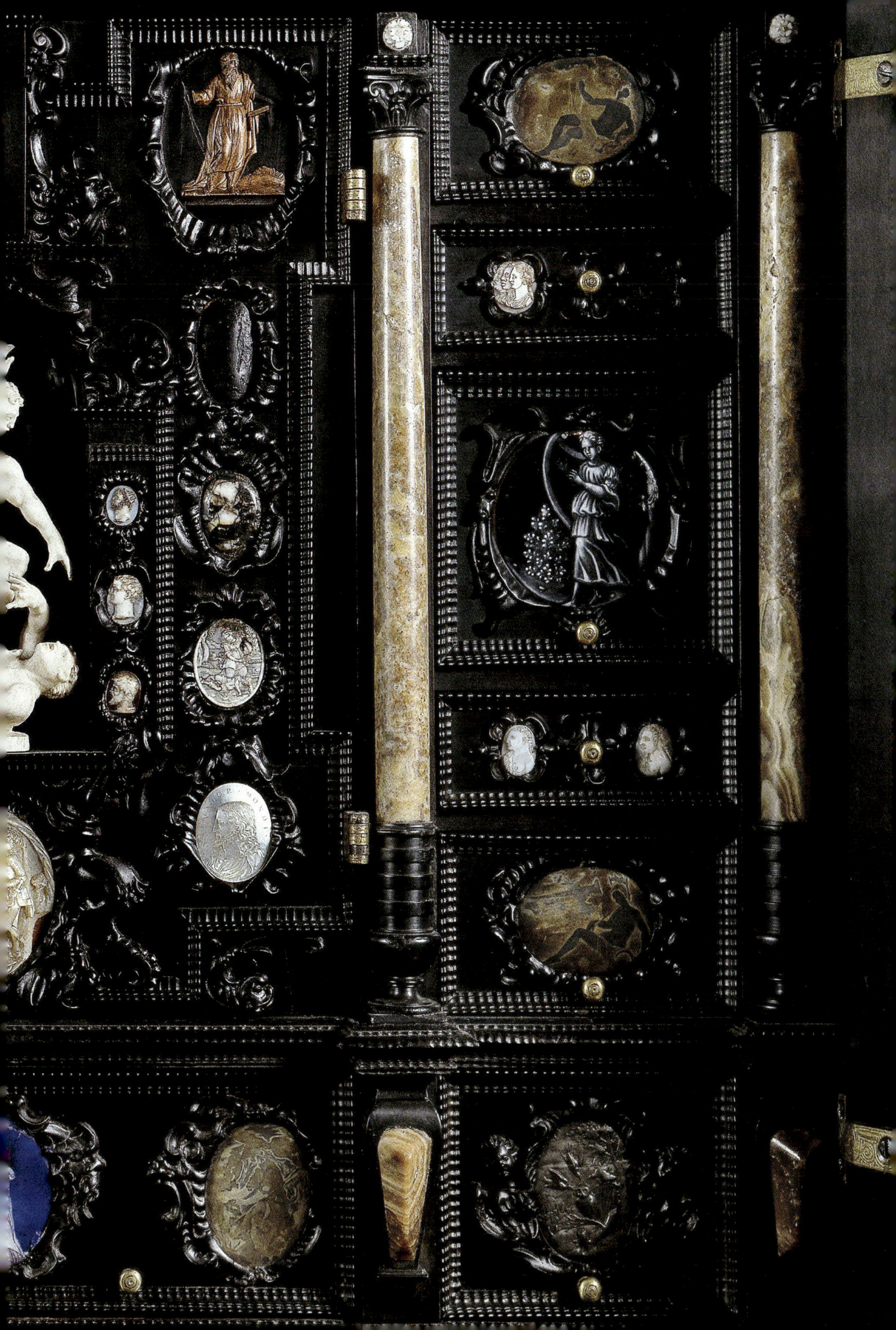

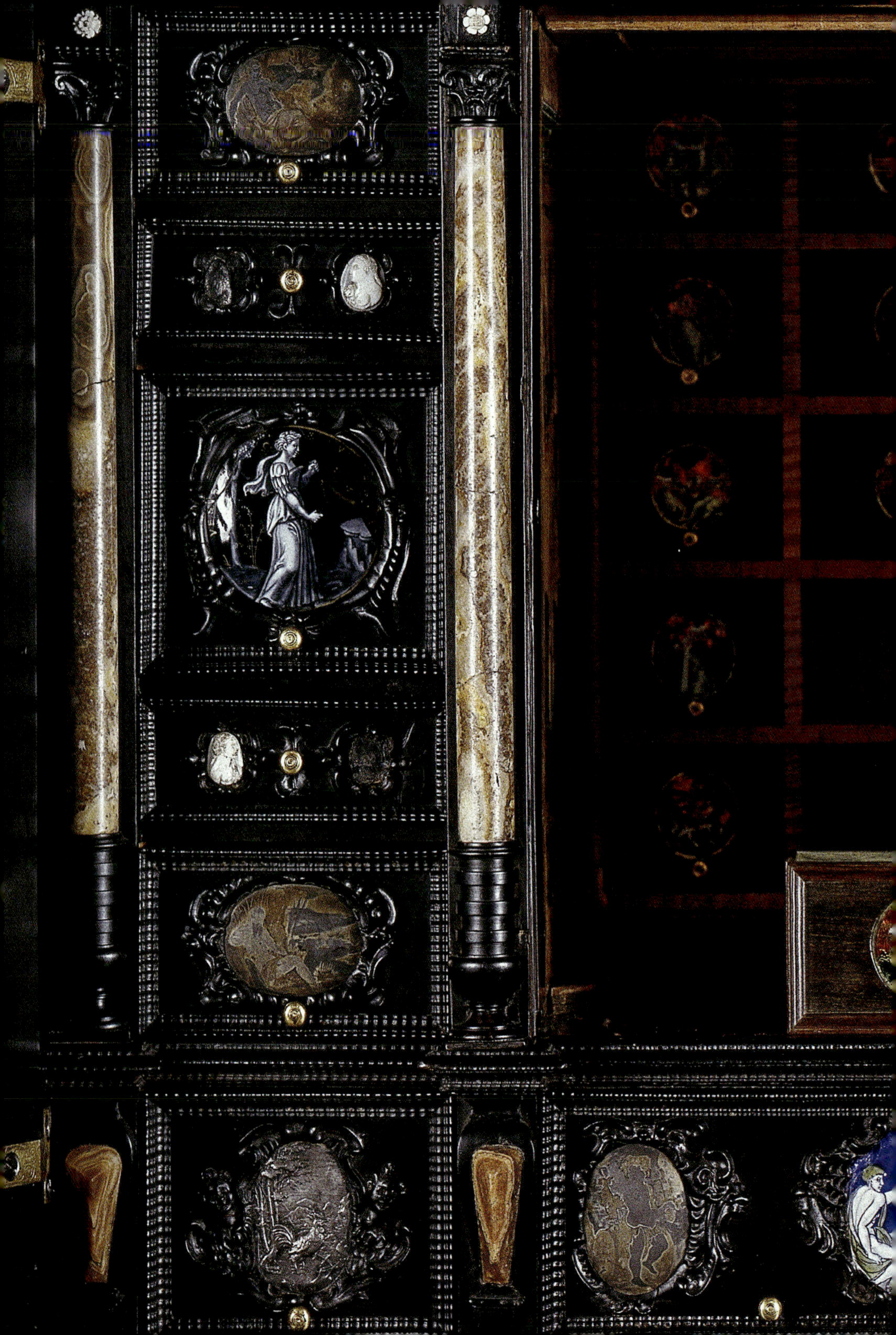

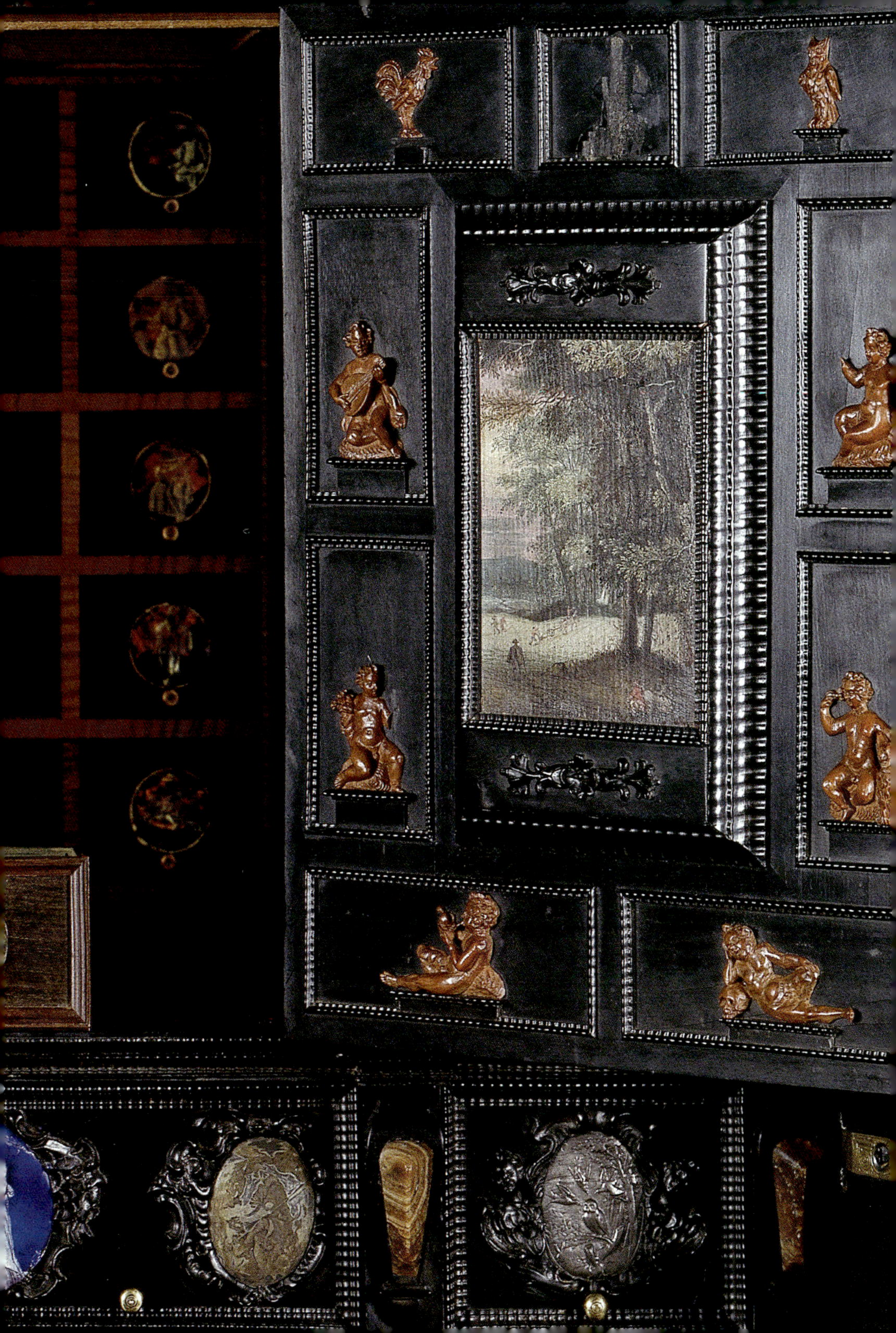

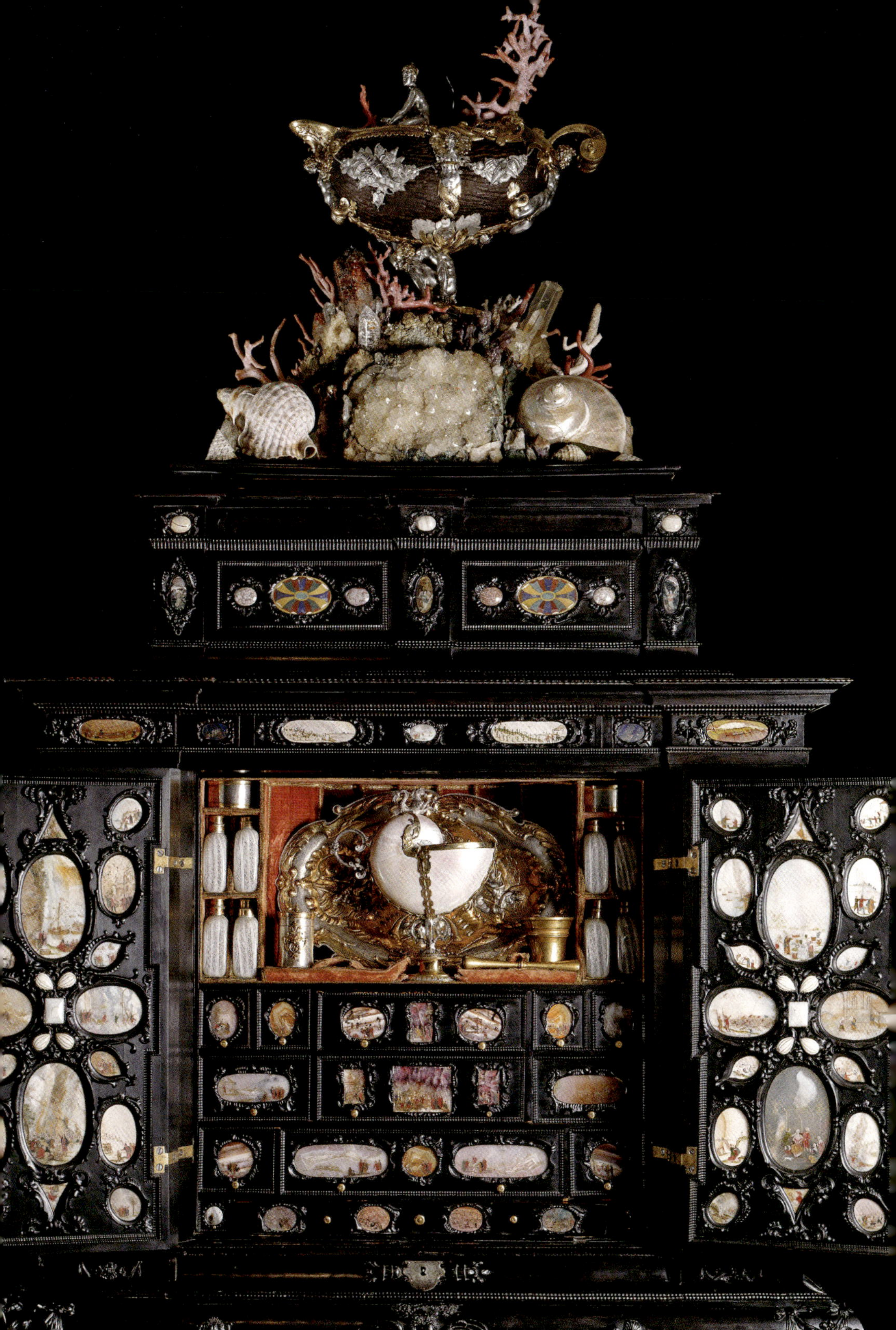

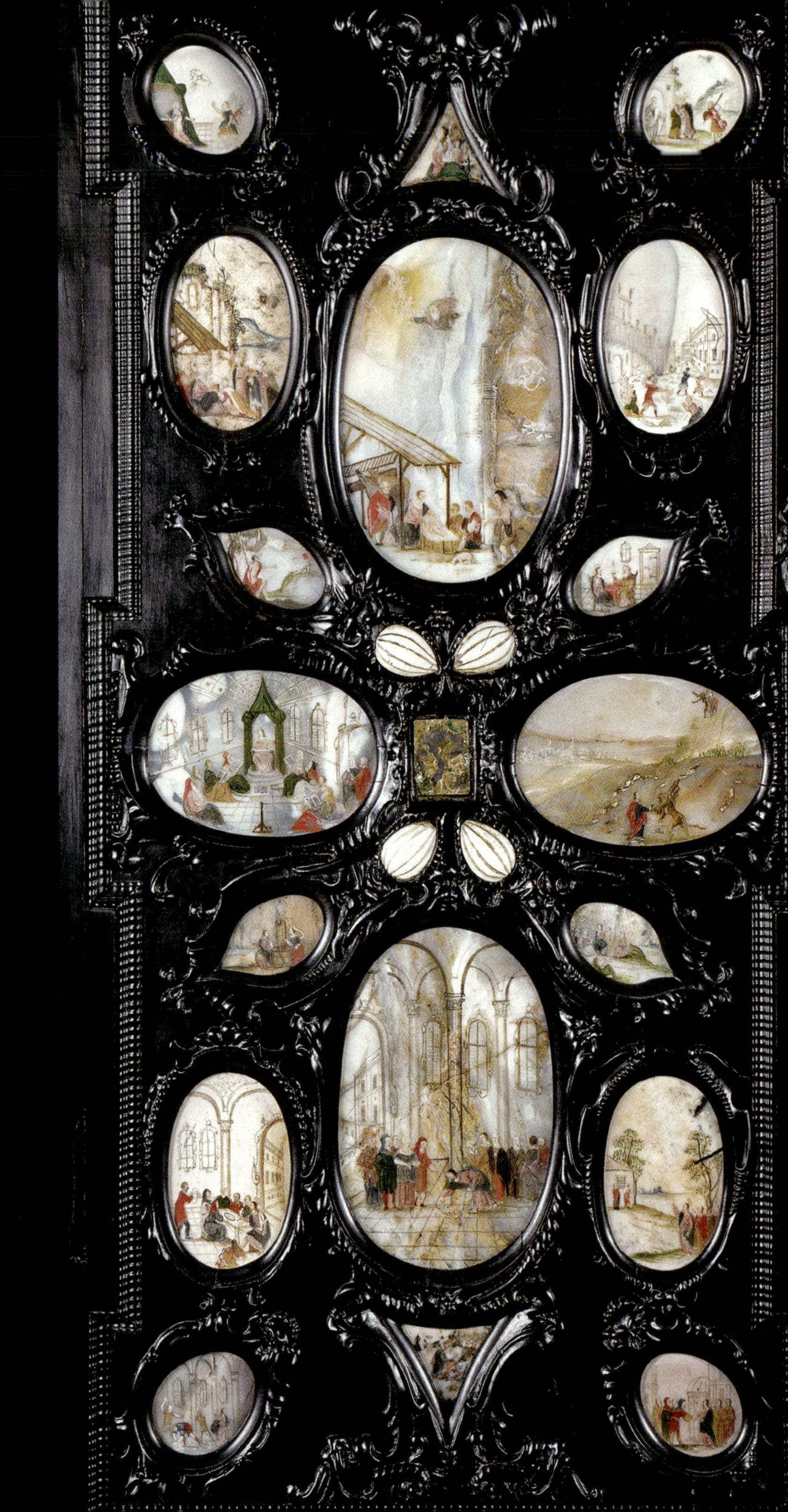

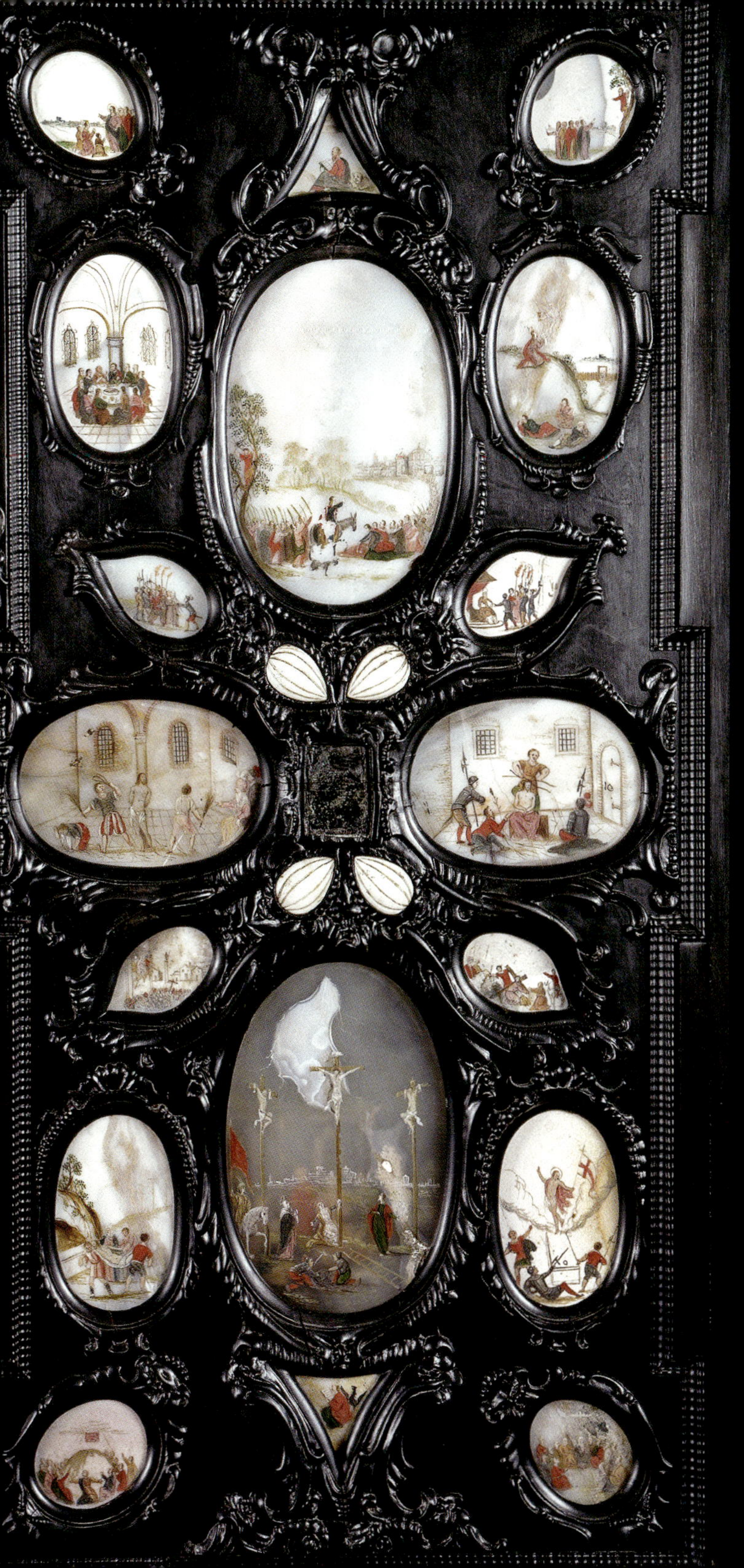

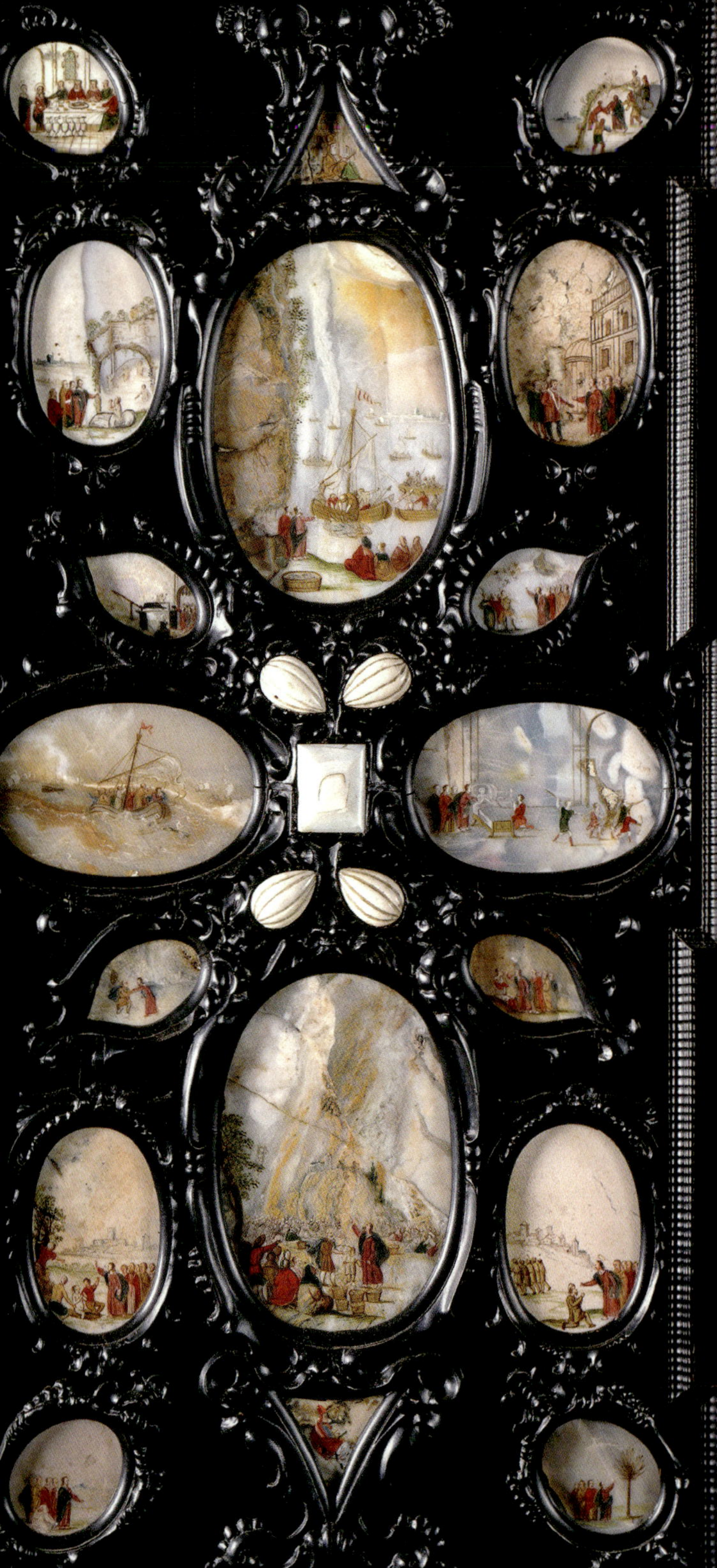

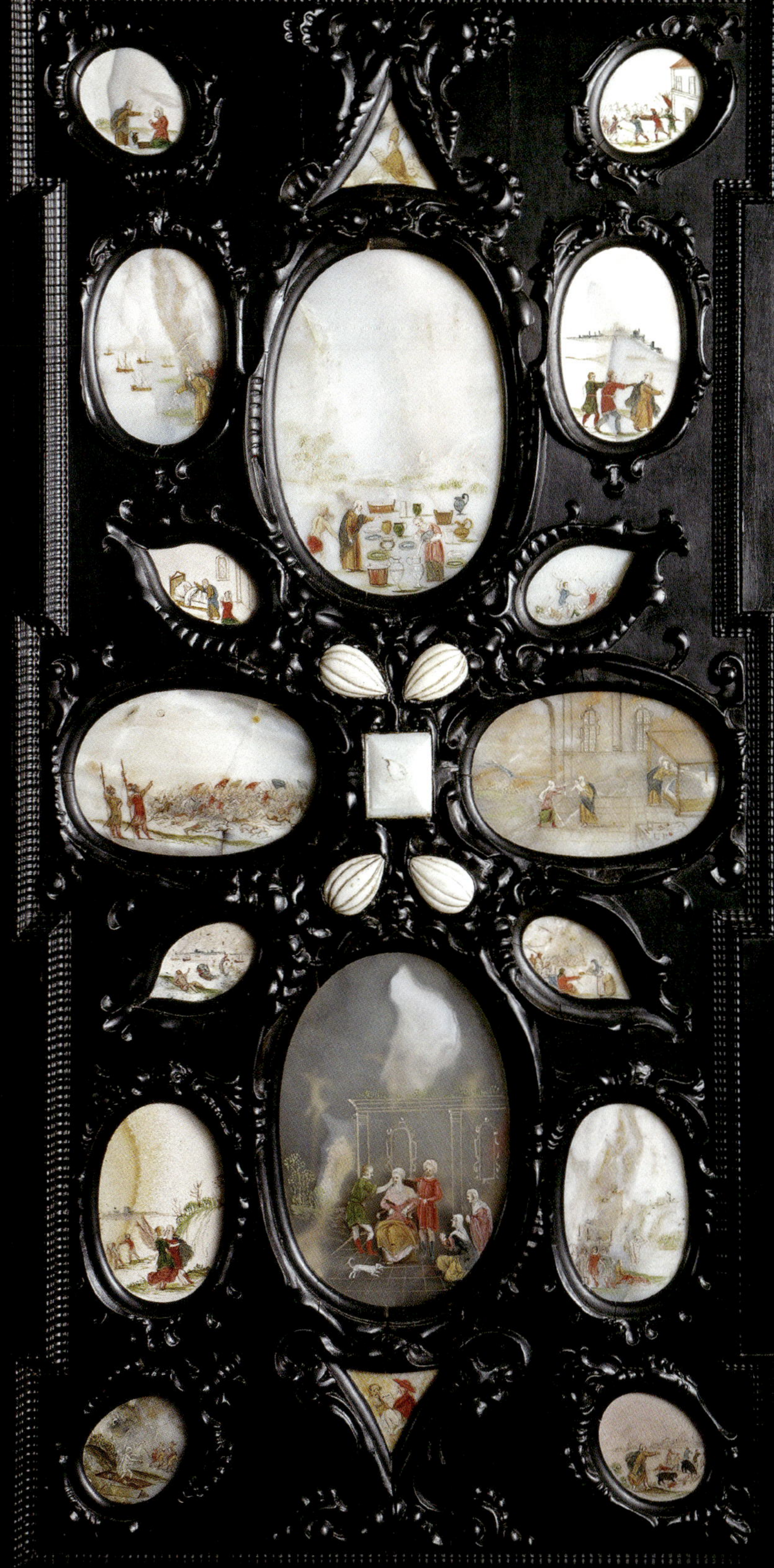

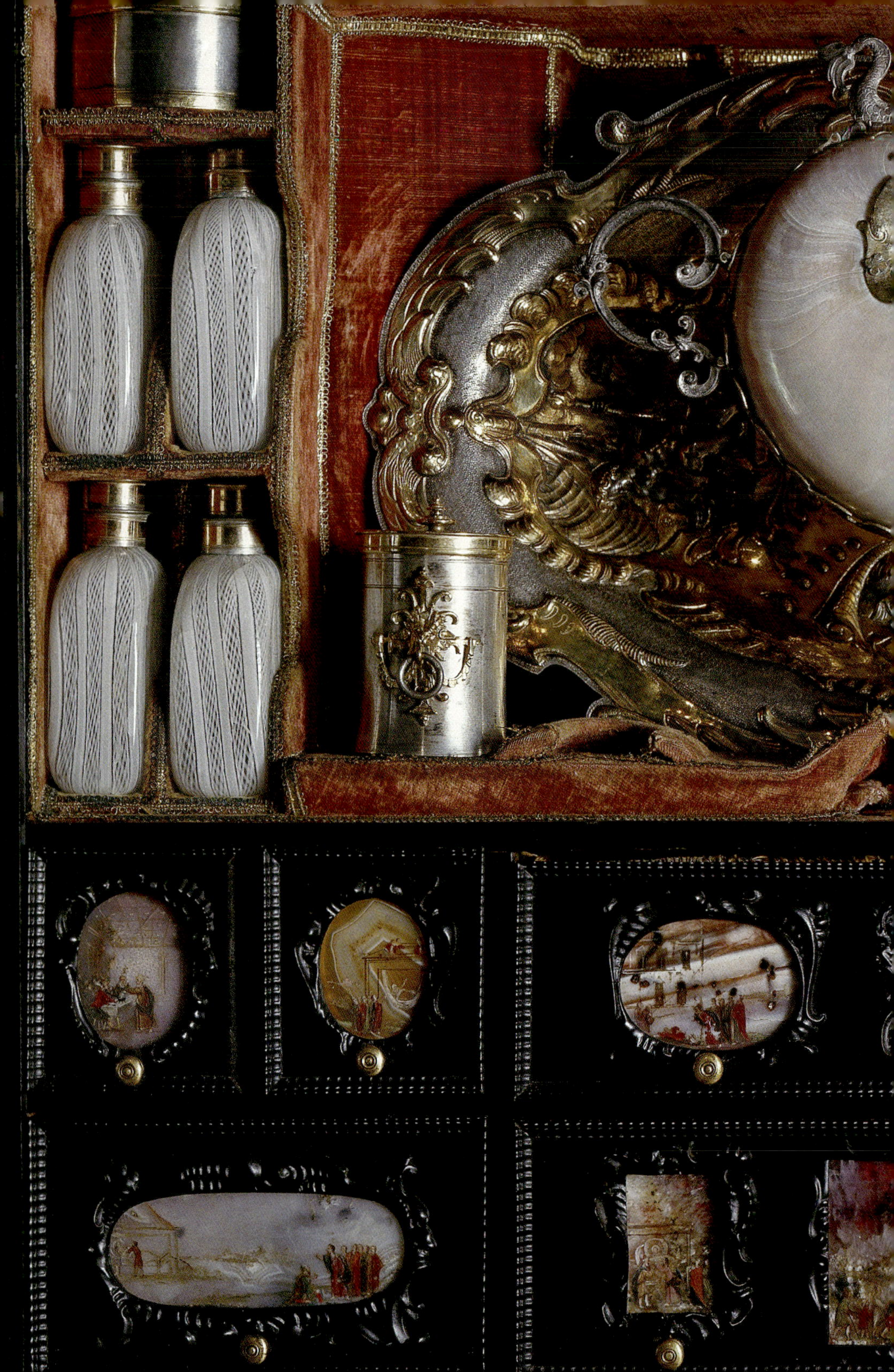

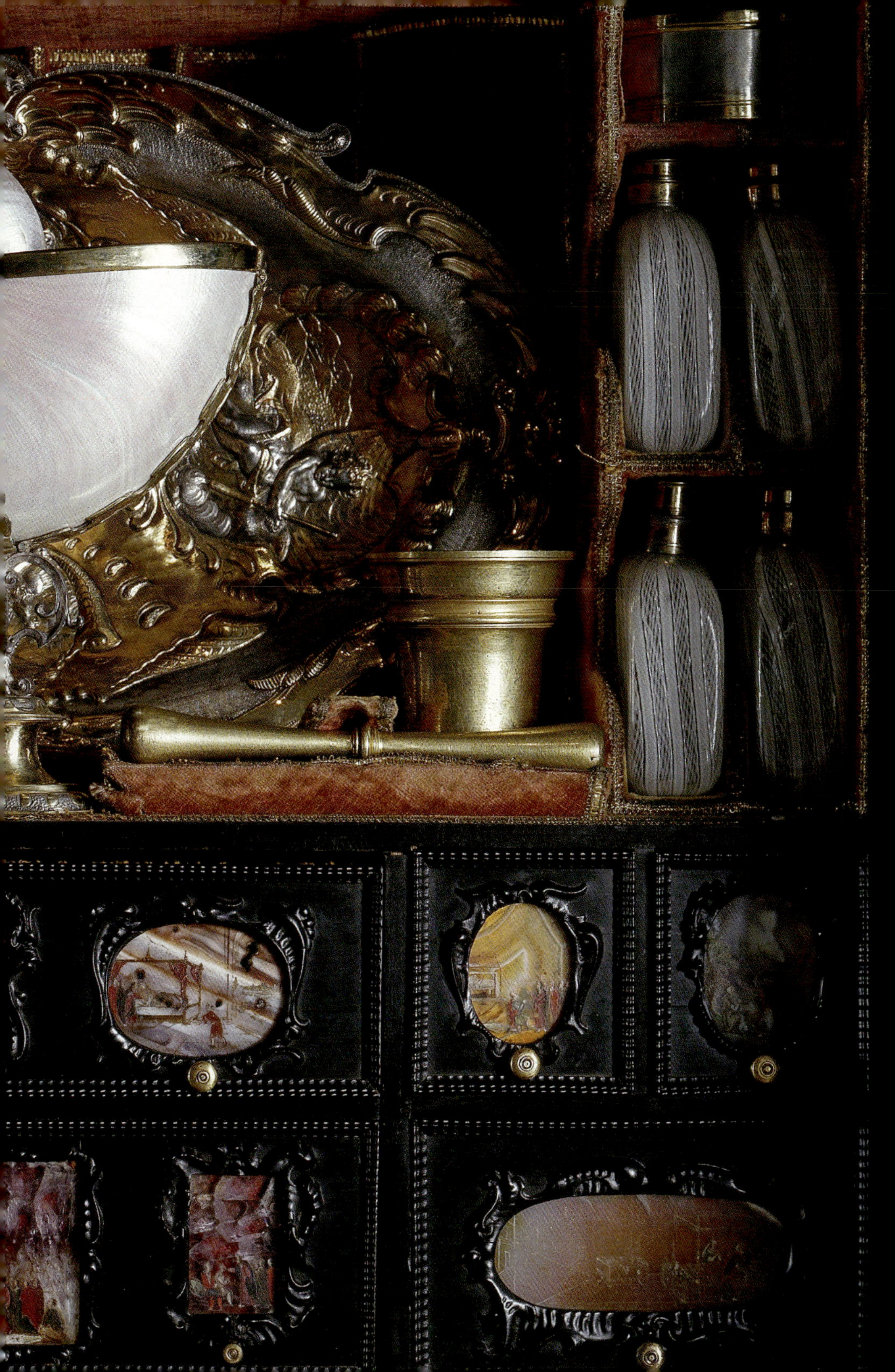

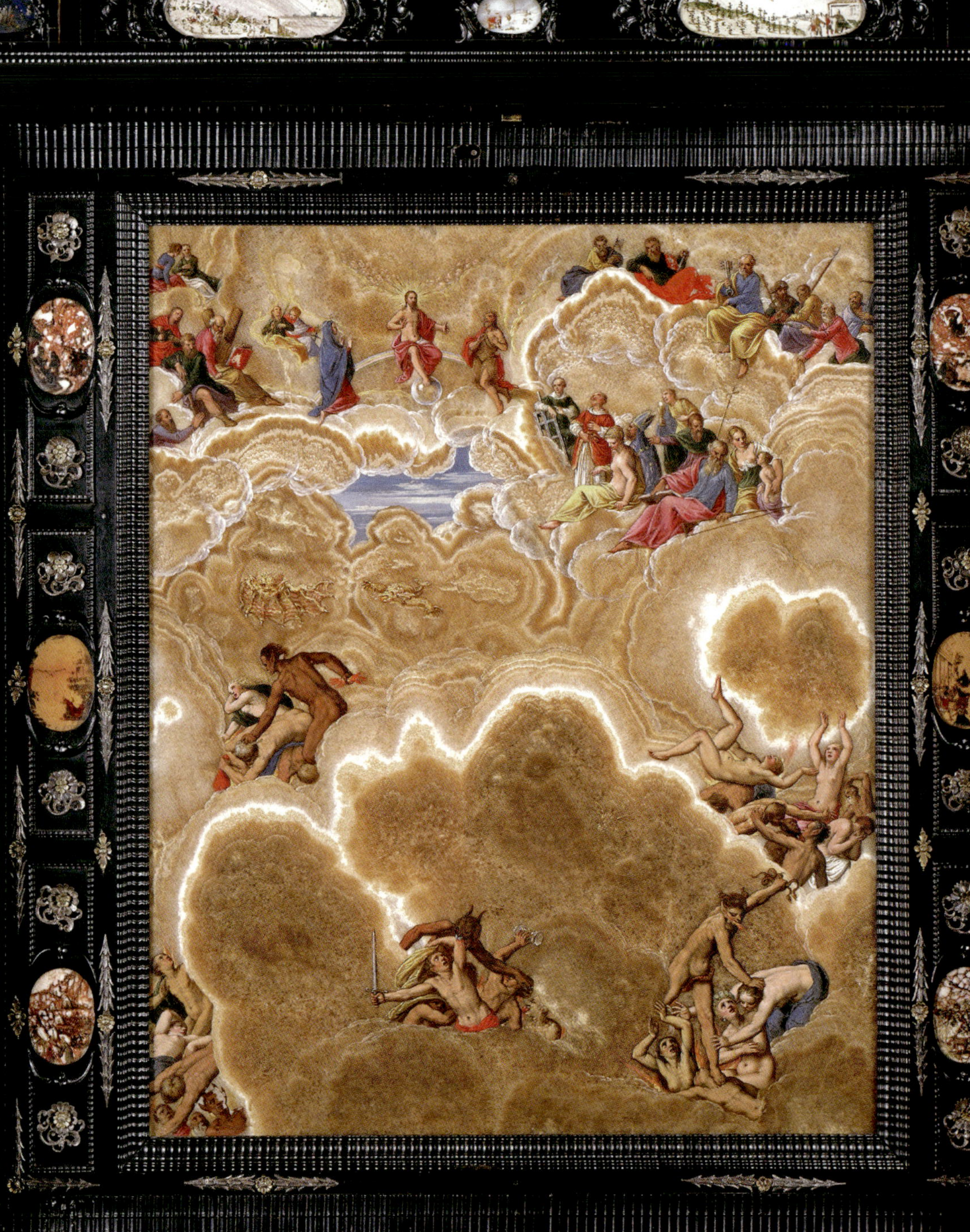

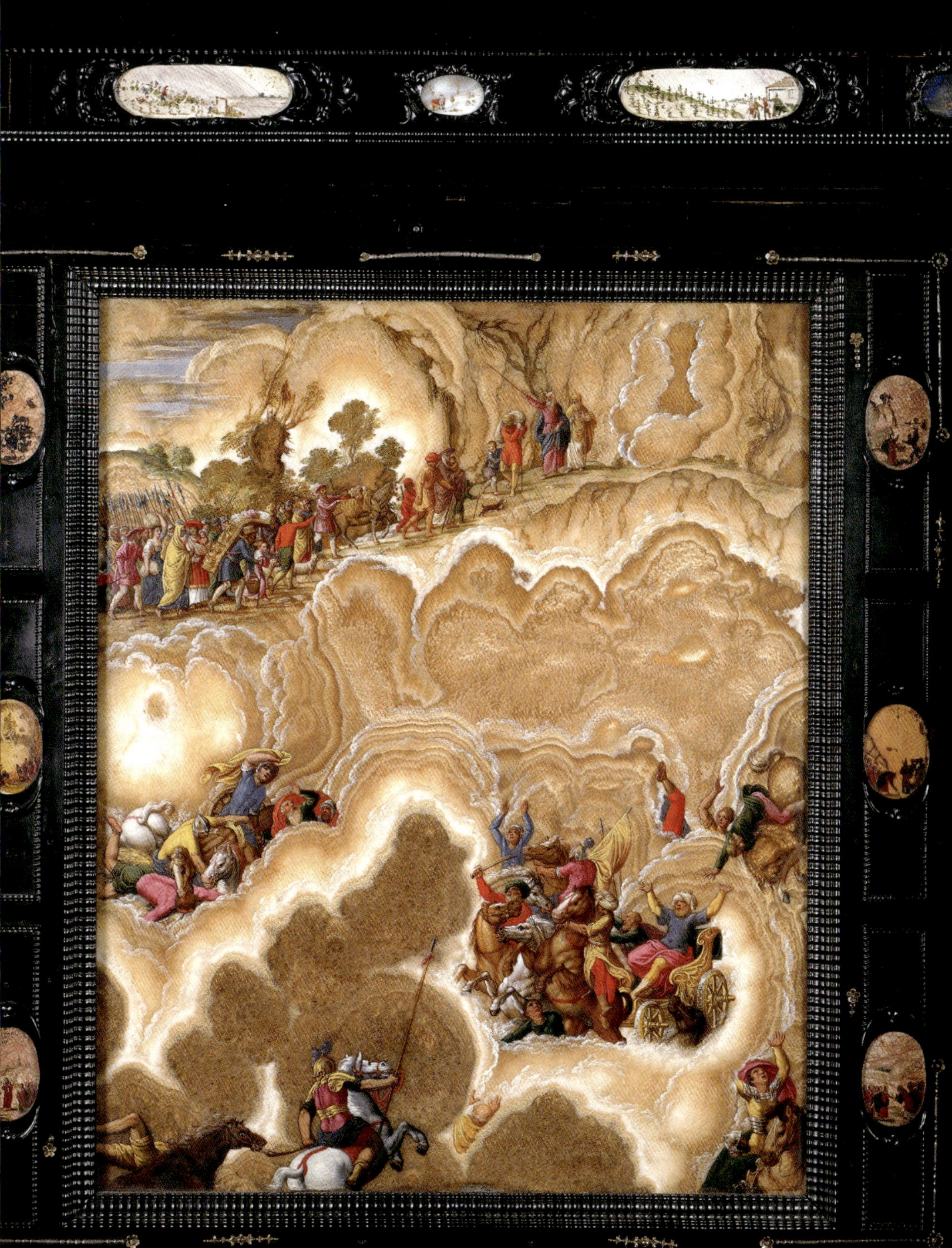

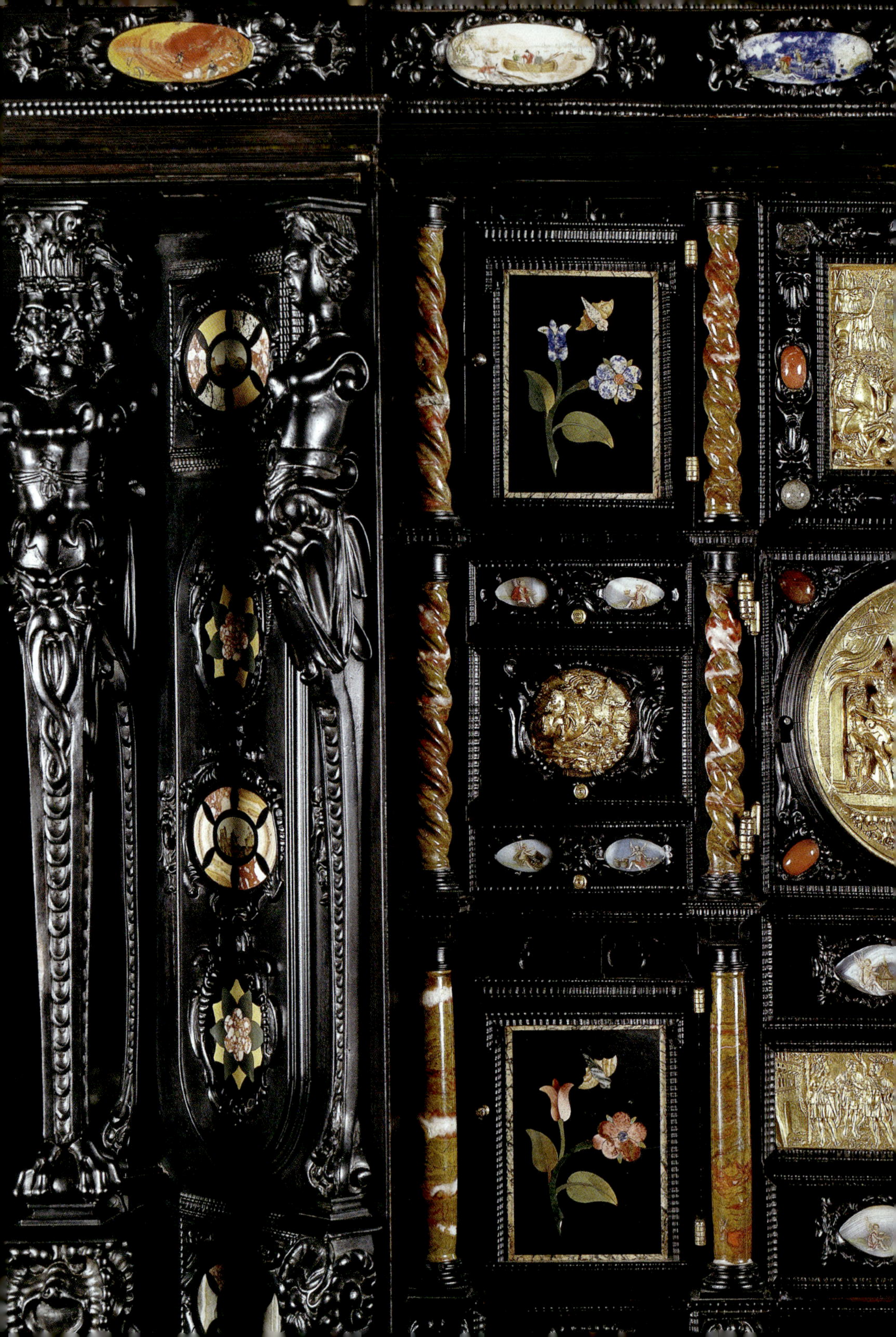

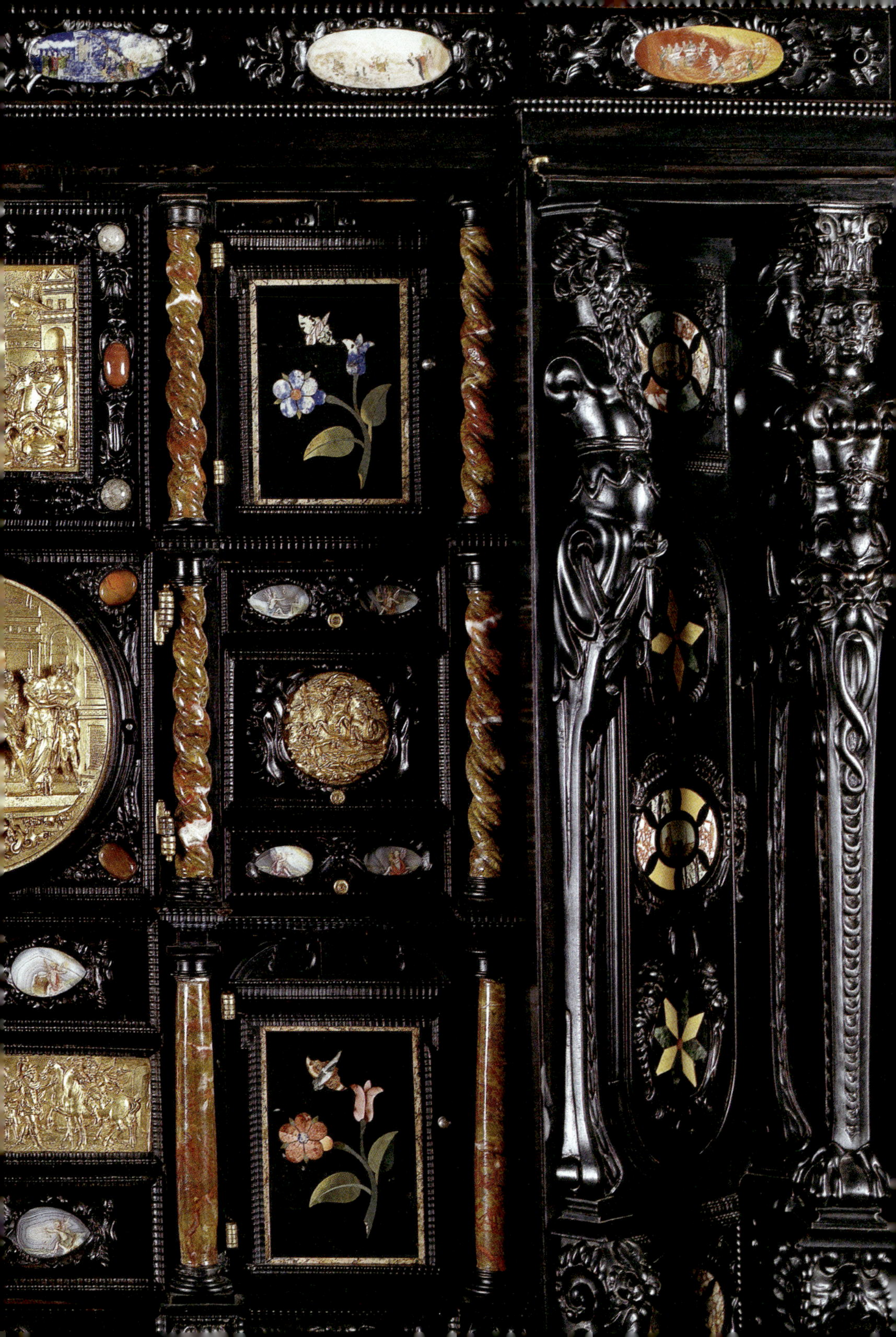

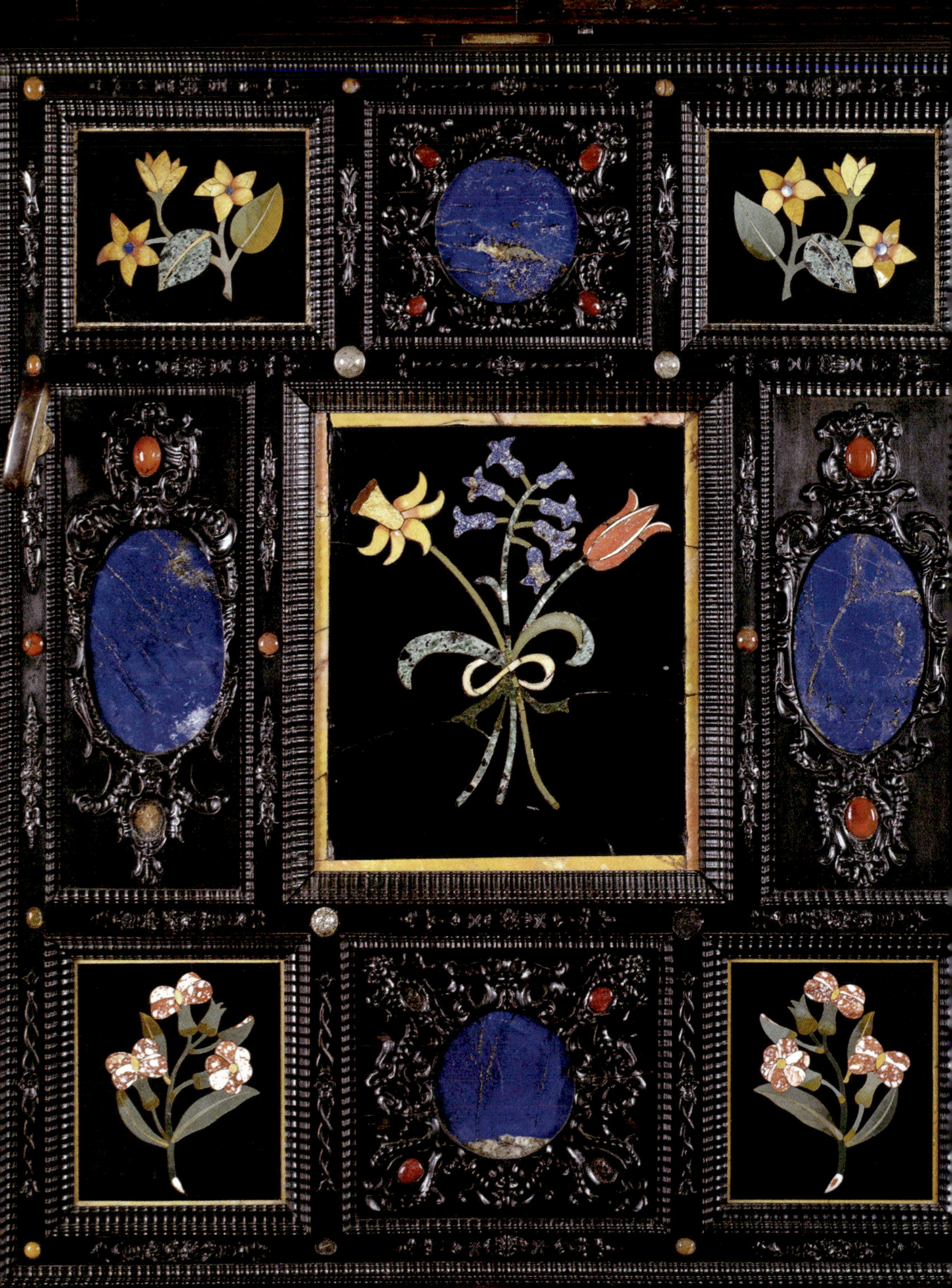

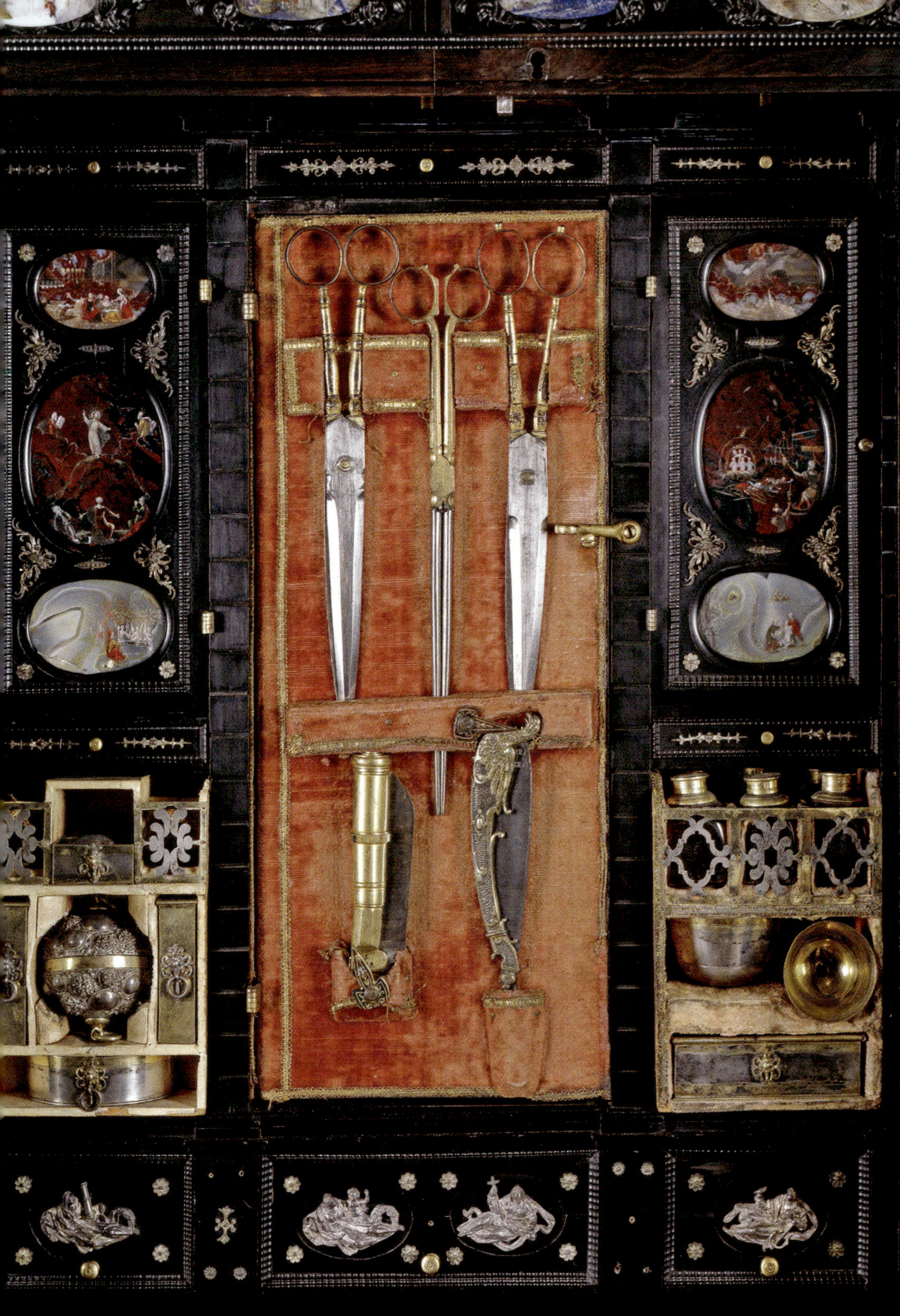

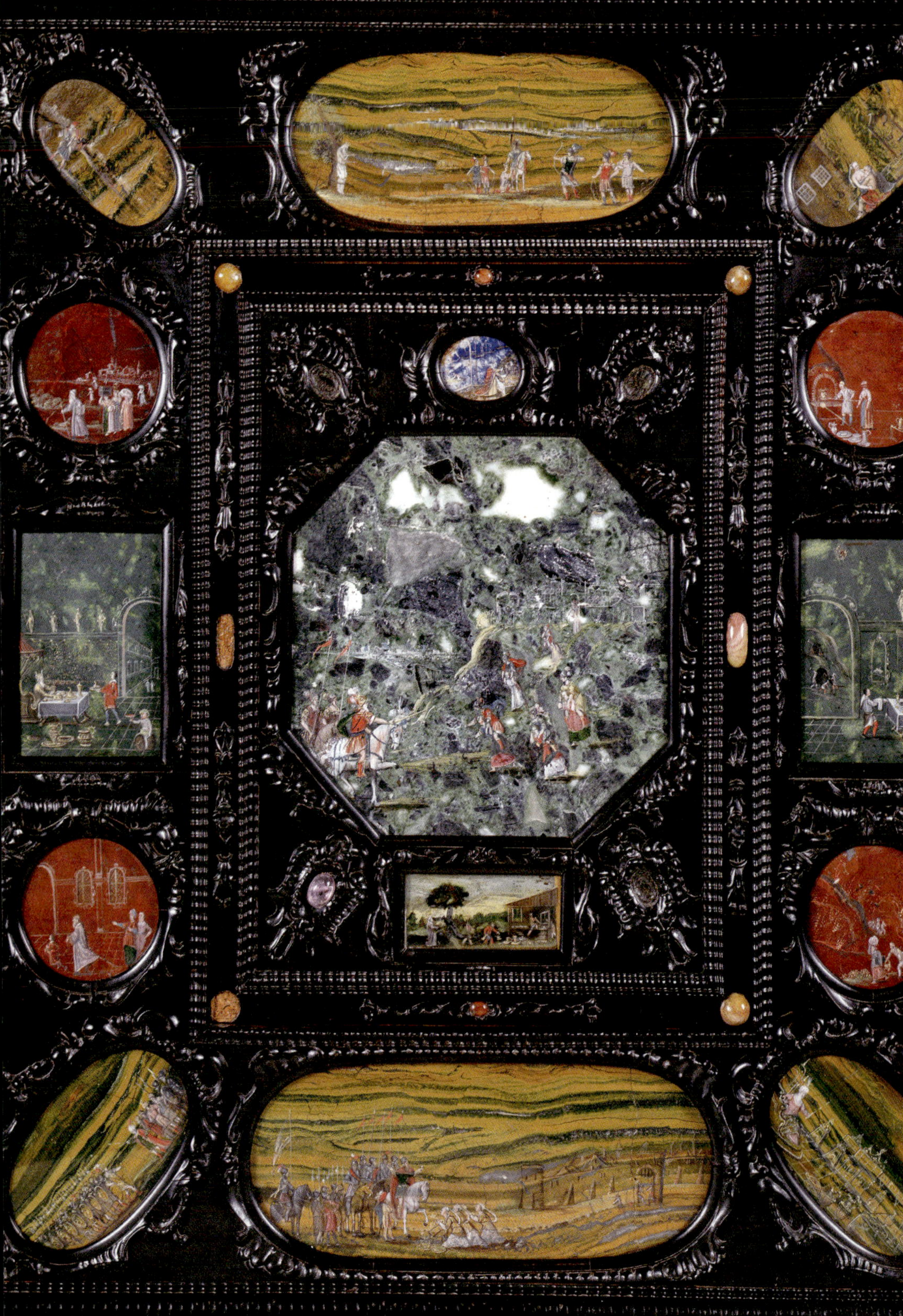

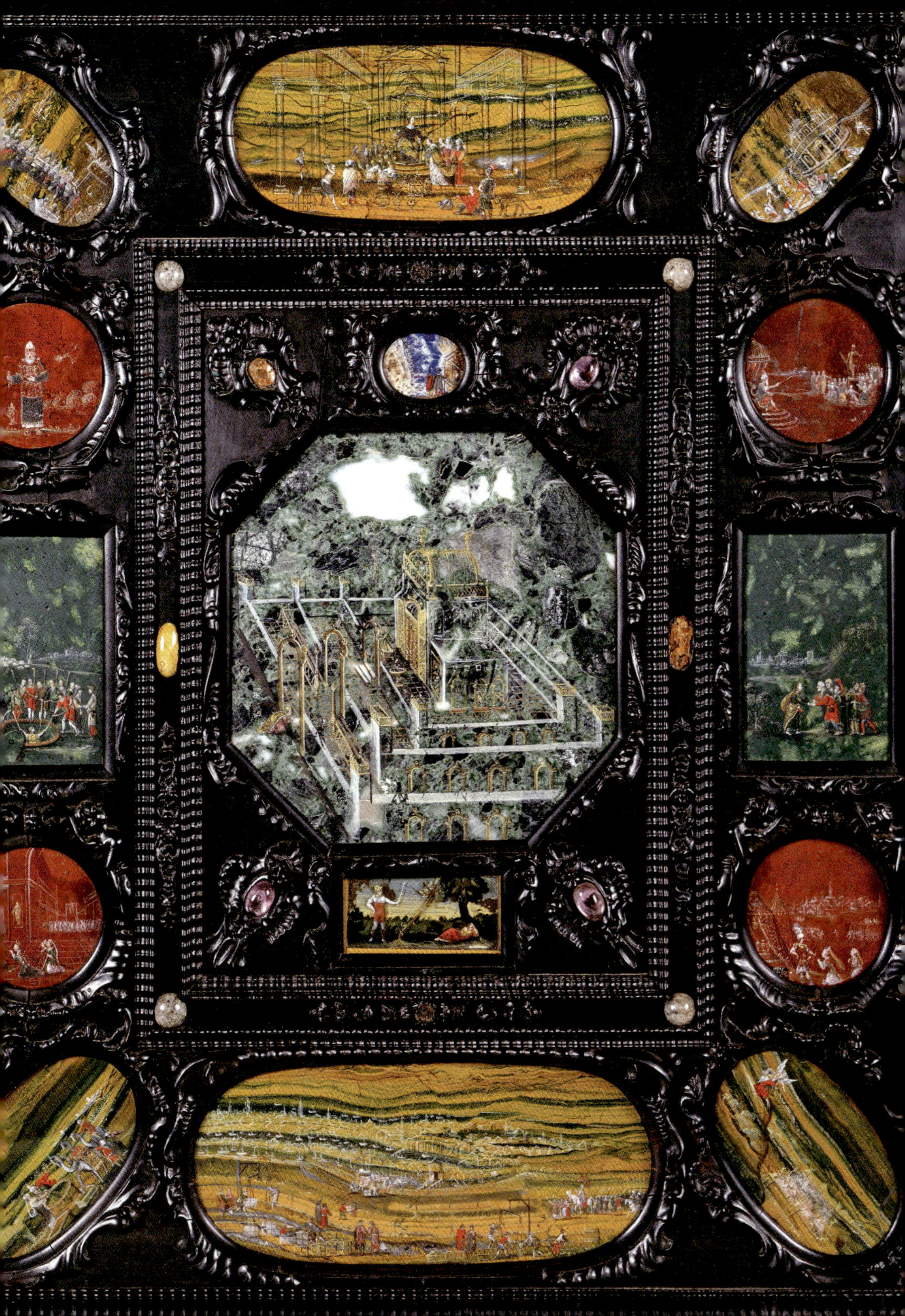

In 1632, shortly before he was killed in the Battle of Lützen which marked such a turning point in the Thirty Years' War, King Gustav II Adolf of Sweden (1594–1632) was given a gift truly fit for a king by the German town of Augsburg: a cabinet of curiosities designed by Philipp Hainhofer (1578–1647). This marvel of the cabinet-maker's art is a genuine "travel Wunderkammer", as its maker described it, and is the only example of its kind from this period to have survived with its original decorations intact; it now resides in the art collection of Uppsala University, part of the Museum Gustavianum.

As in other works by Hainhofer, the decoration of this cabinet illustrates the interplay between Nature and Art, a recurring theme in many of his designs which he managed to take to an exquisite level of sophistication by intertwining two different realms of reality so closely that they became indistinguishable. Furthermore, the use of unexpected shifts in scale caused by both miniaturisation and magnification subvert the usual points of reference an observer would expect to find and instead lead to feelings of wonder. While the Uppsala cabinet is in every respect unsurpassed in terms of its beauty, on a functional level it is also a masterpiece. Dubbed *Mehrzweckmöbel* (multi-purpose furniture) by the craftsmen of Augsburg, these pieces by Hainhofer were designed so that they could be transported like a sort of giant suitcase which, by means of an ingenious system of concealed drawers, sliding panels, foldable shutters and mirrors, provided a dressing-table, a travel pharmacy, various board-games, an altar and musical instruments. To put his designs into production Hainhofer relied on the skill of the master cabinet-maker Ulrich Baumgartner (*c.* 1580–1652), the one craftsman who had the ability to match different veneers of fragrant tropical wood, carve the ebony inlay-work, bring out the knots in the oak so they were more visible and even make use of the pine shavings. With the exception of the internal compartment at the back of the cabinet, within which a group of tiny drawers is decorated with inlaid designs featuring scenes of daily life, the rest of the ornamentation represents Biblical themes. The cabinet (240 cm high x 120 cm wide / 95 x 47 in.), which originally contained about 1,000 items, is set with ivory sculptures, enamels, cameos, precious stones and *Hinterglasmalerei* (reverse painting on glass), as well as paintings on slices of alabaster and pietra paesina (a type of limestone imported from Tuscany). The cabinet was intended to be both recreational and engaging, so that as well as having a chess-board and backgammon-board concealed behind its main façade, Hainhofer decorated some of the corners with anamorphoses, distorted images that could only be viewed correctly by using a conical or cylindrical mirror.

◈ ◈ ◈

Im Jahr 1632, kurz bevor er in der entscheidenden Schlacht des Dreißigjährigen Krieges bei Lützen fiel, erhielt der schwedische König Gustav II. Adolf (1594–1632) von der Stadt Augsburg ein wahrhaft königliches Geschenk: einen Kunstschrank von Philipp Hainhofer (1578–1647). Bei diesem Meisterwerk der Ebenholzverarbeitung handelt es sich um eine sogenannte „Reise-Wunderkammer", so die Definition des Erfinders. Der Schrank ist das einzige im Originalzustand erhaltene Exemplar seiner Art und kann im Museum Gustavianum der Universität Uppsala besichtigt werden.

Bei der äußeren Gestaltung beschäftigte sich Hainhofer wie in all seinen Entwürfen auch hier eingehend mit dem Thema der Wechselbeziehung von Natur und Kunst, einem Leitmotiv seines kreativen Schaffens, in dem er beide Bereiche auf unvergleichlich raffinierte Art untrennbar miteinander verband. Durch eine abrupte Veränderung der Größenverhältnisse, die durch Verkleinerungs- und Vergrößerungseffekte erzielt wurde, stellte er die gewohnte Sichtweise auf den Kopf und löste damit Staunen aus. Wenn der Augsburger Schrank schon in ästhetischer Hinsicht seinesgleichen sucht, so war er funktional ein Meisterwerk. Von den Augsburger Kunsthandwerkern als Mehrzweckmöbel bezeichnet, dienten die von Hainhofer entworfenen Schränke als eine Art Schrankkoffer, die man auf Reisen mitnahm: Aufgrund eines ausgeklügelten Systems aus Geheimschubladen, Schiebetüren, ausklappbaren Türchen und Klappspiegeln ließ sich der Schrank in einen Toilettentisch oder eine Apotheke verwandeln, beherbergte Gesellschaftsspiele, einen Altar und Musikinstrumente. Mit der Ausführung beauftragte Hainhofer den genialen Kunsttischler Ulrich Baumgartner (um 1580–1652), ein Spezialist, der sich wie kein anderer darauf verstand, mit den Maserungen tropischer Dufthölzer zu spielen und Ebenholz mit farbenprächtigen, fantasievollen Intarsien zu kombinieren. Mit Ausnahme eines Innenfachs an der Rückseite, auf dessen Minischubladen Szenen aus dem Alltagsleben dargestellt sind, besteht die Dekoration aus Bibelszenen. Außen ist der Schrank (240 cm hoch, 120 cm breit), der ungefähr tausend Teile enthielt, mit Einlegearbeiten aus Elfenbein, Email, Kameen, Pietra dura, Hinterglasmalerei, bemaltem Alabaster und Pietra paesina, einem besonderen, eigens aus der Toskana importierten Kalkstein, geschmückt. Da der Schrank auch zu Unterhaltung und Zeitvertreib gedacht war, fügte Hainhofer neben einem Schach- und einem Backgammonspiel, die sich hinter der Vordertür verbergen, an den angeschrägten Ecken einige Anamorphosen hinzu: Zerrbilder, die man nur mithilfe eines konisch oder zylindrisch gewölbten Spiegels entziffern konnte.

◈ ◈ ◈

En 1632, peu avant de trouver la mort lors de la bataille de Lützen qui marqua un tournant dans la guerre de Trente Ans, le roi Gustave II Adolphe de Suède (1594–1632) reçut de la Ville d'Augsbourg un don véritablement royal : un cabinet de Philipp Hainhofer (1578–1647). Sommet d'ingéniosité et prouesse d'ébénisterie, il s'agit d'un authentique « *Wunderkammer* de voyage » selon l'expression de son créateur. Seul et unique meuble du genre datant de cette époque, dont la décoration d'origine demeure intacte, le cabinet fait partie des collections d'art de l'université d'Uppsala et peut être admiré dans le Museum Gustavianum.

Comme pour tous les meubles de Hainhofer, la décoration éclaire la réciprocité de la relation entre la Nature et l'Art, thème fondamental des recherches de l'artiste en matière de création qui parviennent à un raffinement extrême en établissant des liens entre deux ordres de réalité devenus indissociables. Le brusque changement de dimensions résultant des effets de miniaturisation ou d'agrandissement donne lieu à un bouleversement des points de vue traditionnels familiers à l'observateur et suscite son émerveillement. Si le cabinet d'Uppsala est incomparable sur le plan esthétique, sur le plan fonctionnel il constitue un véritable chef-d'œuvre. Nommés *Mehrzweckmöbel* (meuble multi-usage) par les artisans d'Augsbourg, les cabinets de Hainhofer étaient conçus pour accompagner leurs propriétaires dans leurs déplacements, à l'instar d'une valise géante qui, grâce à un ingénieux système de tiroirs dissimulés, de portes coulissantes, de volets pliables et de miroirs rabattables, fournissait un nécessaire de toilette, une pharmacie portative, des jeux de société, un autel et des instruments de musique. Hainhofer fit appel à l'ingéniosité d'Ulrich Baumgartner (vers 1580–1652), seul et unique ébéniste capable de jouer avec les veines d'essences tropicales odorantes, de modeler les marqueteries de l'ébène, d'exalter les nœuds du chêne et de faire valoir les copeaux du pin. Hormis le compartiment interne postérieur composé de minuscules tiroirs rehaussés de marqueteries figurant des scènes de la vie quotidienne, la décoration du cabinet s'inspire de thèmes bibliques. Le meuble (h. 240 cm, l. 120 cm), qui comptait près de 1000 pièces, est incrusté de sculptures en ivoire, d'émaux, de camées, de pierres dures, de peintures sous verre, de peintures sur albâtre ou sur pietra paesina (variété de calcaire importé de Toscane). Distraire, divertir, telle était l'une des fonctions de ce cabinet ; aussi, aux jeux d'échecs et de trictrac dissimulés derrière la façade principale Hainhofer a-t-il adjoint dans les angles obliques du meuble quelques anamorphoses, ces images déformées dont seul un miroir conique ou cylindrique permet d'obtenir une vision correcte.

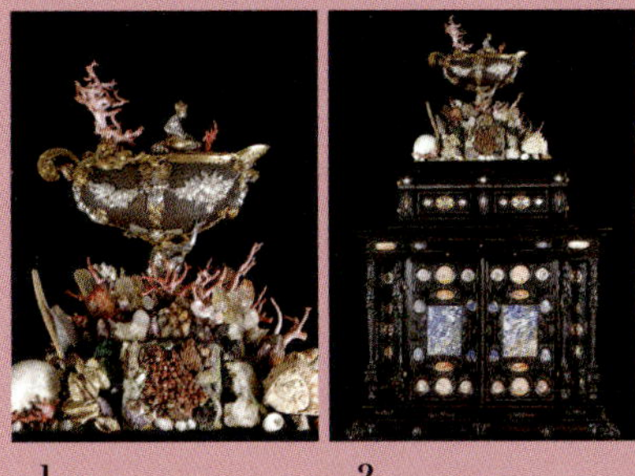

1

2

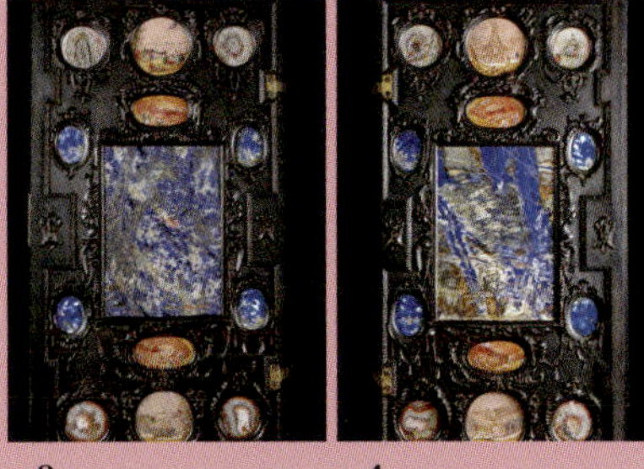

3

4

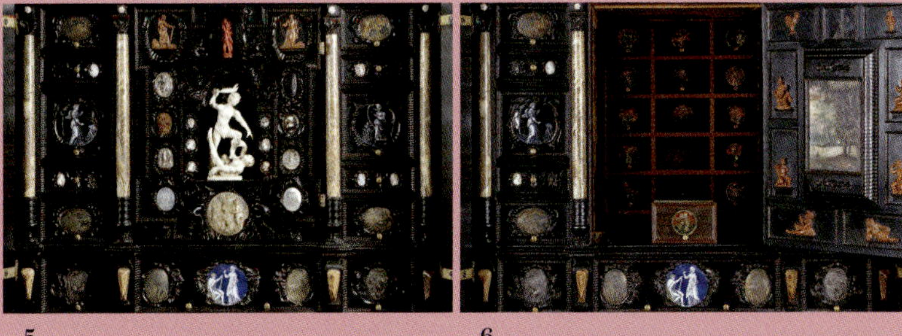

5

6

1 The cabinet is topped by a "mountain" made of material from the animal and mineral kingdoms, including rock crystal, malachite, amethyst and coral. On its summit sits a very rare Seychelles nut that functions as the cup of a drinking vessel, mounted in partially gilded silver and held aloft by Neptune.
Der Schrank wird von einem „Gipfel" bestehend aus Bergkristall, Malachit, Amethyst und Korallen bekrönt. Seine Spitze bildet ein Pokal mit einer seltenen Seychellennuss, die in teilweise vergoldetes Silber gefasst ist und von Neptun emporgestemmt wird.
Le Cabinet est couronné d'un « mont » constitué de matériaux issus des animal et minéral – cristal de roche, malachite, améthyste, corail. À son sommet se trouve une noix de Seychelles très rare fonctionnant comme la tasse d'un récipient, montée en partie sur vermeil et soulevée par Neptune.

2 Front view of the cabinet, sculpted and carved out of ebony and studded with pietra dura and cameos.
Vorderansicht des Kunstschranks, der aus Ebenholz geschnitzt und mit Pietra dura und Kameen verziert ist.
Face frontale du cabinet, sculpté et ciselé dans l'ébène et constellé de pietra dura et de camées.

3–4 The insides of the doors of the front part of the cabinet are decorated with scenes from the Old Testament painted on pietra dura.
Die Innenflügel sind mit Pietra dura geschmückt, wobei die Steine mit Szenen aus dem Alten Testament bemalt sind.
La face interne du vantail du cabinet vu de face, des scènes de l'Ancien Testament peintes sur pietra dura.

5 The central inner compartment of the front part of the cabinet features an ivory figure of Samson, surrounded by a series of cameos with various Pagan and Christian symbols.
Innenansicht des mittleren Fachs des Vorderteils des Kunstschranks: eine Elfenbeinfigur des Samson, umgeben von Kameen mit christlichen und heidnischen Symbolen.
Compartiment central intérieur du cabinet vu de face : une figure en ivoire de Samson, entourée de camées montrant des symboles païens et chrétiens.

6 Partial view of the inside of the front part of the cabinet, revealing the small drawers decorated with enamels, cameos and pietra dura.
Teilansicht der Innenseite des Vorderteils des Kunstschranks mit kleinen Schubladen, die mit Email, Kameen und Pietra dura verziert sind.
Vue partielle de l'intérieur du cabinet vu de face, montrant de petits tiroirs décorés d'émaux, de camées et de pietra dura.

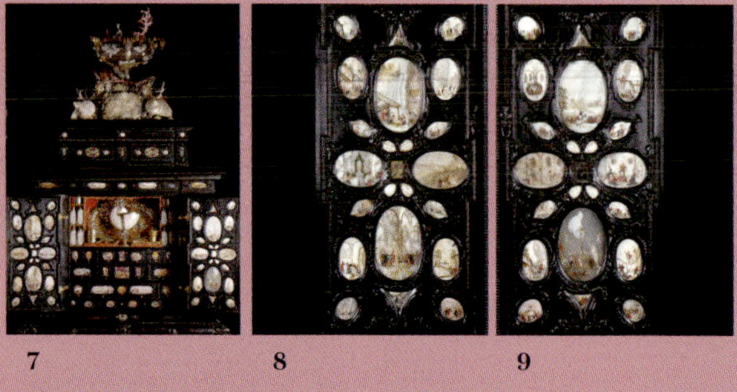

7 8 9

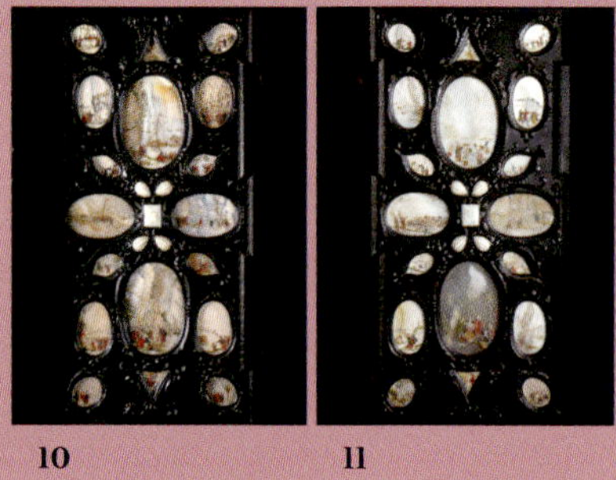

10 11

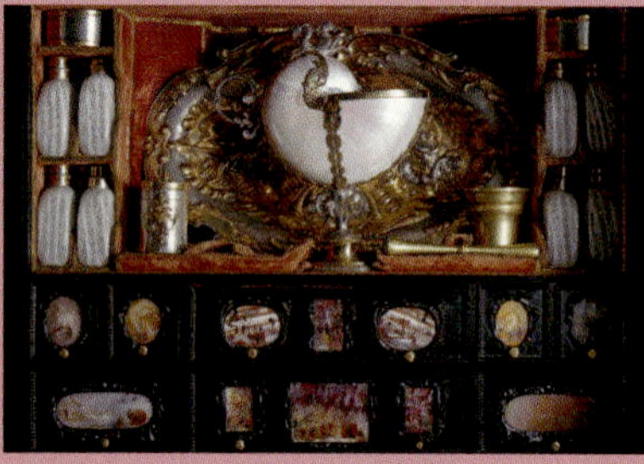

12

7 Rear view of the cabinet, with the doors open.
Rückansicht des Kunstschranks mit geöffneten Türen.
La face arrière du cabinet, portes ouvertes.

8–9 The outsides of the rear doors, showing scenes from the life of Christ painted on alabaster, from the Nativity through to the Crucifixion.
Außenansicht der Türen auf der Rückseite des Kunstschranks, die mit auf Alabaster ausgeführten Szenen aus dem Leben Christi von der Geburt bis zur Kreuzigung geschmückt sind.
Vue extérieure des portes de derrière avec des scènes de la vie du Christ peintes sur albâtre, de la Nativité à la Crucifixion.

10–11 The insides of the rear doors, showing scenes from the Old Testament painted on alabaster.

Innenansicht der rückwärtigen Türen, die mit auf Alabaster gemalten Szenen aus dem Alten Testament verziert sind.
Vue intérieure des portes de derrière avec des scènes de l'Ancien Testament peintes sur albâtre.

12 The central niche is dominated by a nautilus shell richly mounted in a gold and silver setting and surmounted by a prancing silver seahorse, with various toiletry accessories on either side. In the section underneath, a series of small drawers feature inlaid decorations depicting scenes of everyday life from the golden age of Augsburg.
Ein kostbar in Gold und Silber gefasster, von verschiedenen Toilettenartikeln umgebener und durch einen aufgerichteten Hippokampen bekrönter Nautilus dominiert die Mittelnische. Unten eine Reihe

kleiner Schubladen mit Einlegearbeiten, die Alltagszenen aus der Glanzzeit Augsburgs zeigen.
Le compartiment central est dominé par un nautile richement décoré d'or et d'argent, surmonté d'un cheval marin en argent et entouré de divers accessoires de toilette. Dans la partie inférieure, une série de petits tiroirs avec des décorations incrustées représentant des scènes de la vie quotidienne à Augsbourg durant son âge d'or.

13 This panel concealed inside the rear of the cabinet features a painting of the Last Judgement on a thin slice of alabaster.
Im Innern der Rückseite verborgene Tafel: Darstellung des Jüngsten Gerichts auf einer Alabasterplatte.
Panneau dissimulé à l'arrière du cabinet : une représentation du Jugement dernier peinte sur une plaque d'albâtre.

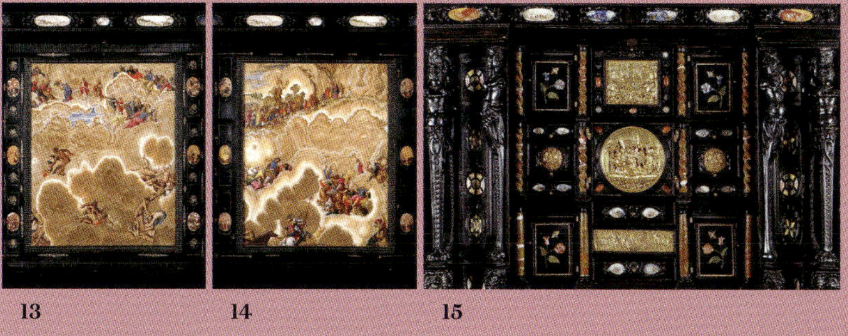

13   14   15

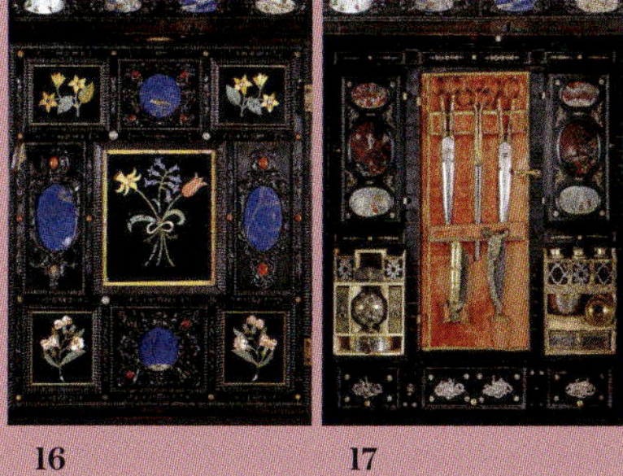

16   17

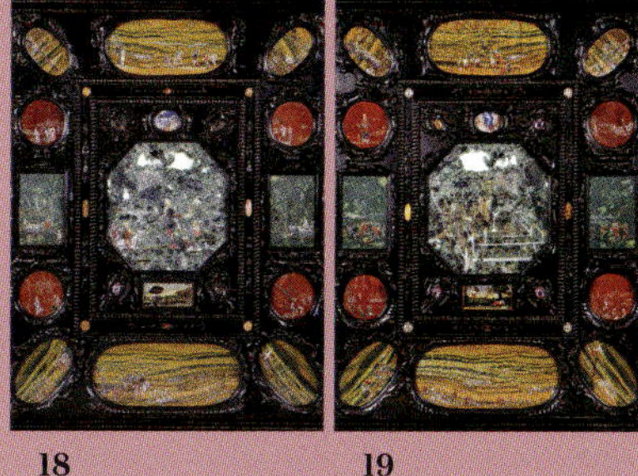

18   19

14 This concealed panel at the rear shows the crossing of the Red Sea, also painted on alabaster.
Im Innern der Rückseite Darstellung des Zugs der Israeliten durch das Rote Meer auf einer Alabasterplatte.
Panneau dissimulé à l'arrière avec une représentation de la Traversée de la mer Rouge peinte sur une plaque d'albâtre.

15 Inner compartment with pietra dura flowers and gold reliefs, showing scenes from the life of David.
Inneres Seitenfach mit Pietra-dura-Blumen und Goldreliefs mit Szenen aus dem Leben Davids.
Compartiment intérieur décoré de fleurs de pietra dura et de reliefs en or montrant des scènes de la vie de David.

16 Outer face of side door, with floral pietra dura decorations.
Äußere Seitentür mit Blumenmotiven in Pietra-dura-Technik.
Porte latérale extérieure décorée de fleurs en pietra dura.

17 Behind the central panel on the side are two pairs of scissors and a pair of tongs used for beard curling. Beneath these are two razors with steel blades and gilt-silver handles.
Hinter der seitlichen Mitteltafel: zwei Scheren und ein Bart-Frisierstab; darunter zwei Rasiermesser mit Klinge aus Stahl und Griff aus vergoldetem Silber.
Derrière le panneau central, sur le côté : deux paires de ciseaux et une pince à friser à barbe. Deux rasoirs en acier avec poignée en vermeil.

18 Inside of a side door showing stories from the life of Joseph painted on pietra dura.
Innenseite einer Seitentür mit gemalten Episoden aus dem Leben Josephs auf Pietra dura.
Porte latérale intérieure avec des scènes de la vie de Joseph peintes sur pietra dura.

19 Inside of a side door showing scenes depicting love in all its forms.
Innenseite einer Seitentür mit verschiedenen Liebesdarstellungen.
Porte latérale intérieure avec des scènes représentant l'amour sous toutes ses formes.

"Gli avori di Coburgo" e i nautili

Tesoro dei Granduchi, Firenze

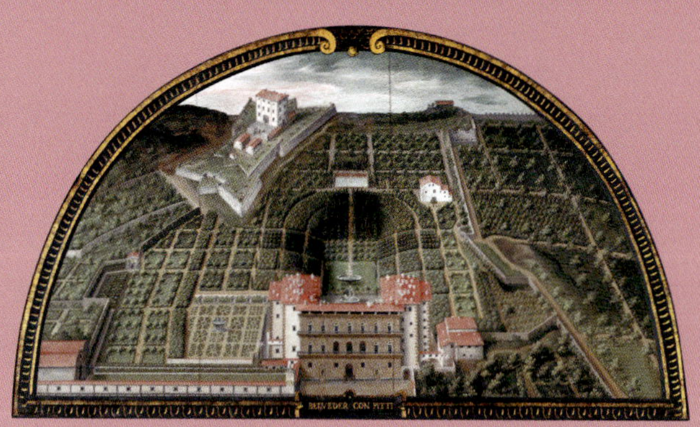

Founded 16th–17th century (ivories and nautilus shells)

Key item A 16th-century French cup composed of a nautilus shell engraved with scales and images of dragons in a Chinese style, mounted in gilt silver; the foot of the cup features three dolphins and the base is stamped.

Besonders sehenswert Ein französischer Pokal aus dem 16. Jahrhundert. Der Nautilus mit eingravierten chinesischen Drachen- und Schuppenmotiven hat eine Halterung aus vergoldetem Silber, einen Fuß mit drei Delfinen und einen Stempel auf der Unterseite.

À voir absolument Coupe du 16e siècle, art français : nautile gravé avec des motifs de dragon et d'écaille d'origine chinoise ; monture en argent doré ; pied constitué de trois dauphins et marqué d'un poinçon sur sa base.

Giusto Utens, *Palazzo Pitti and the Boboli Gardens in Florence. Lunette depicting the Medici villas*, 1599–1602. Oil on canvas, Florence, Villa La Petraia.

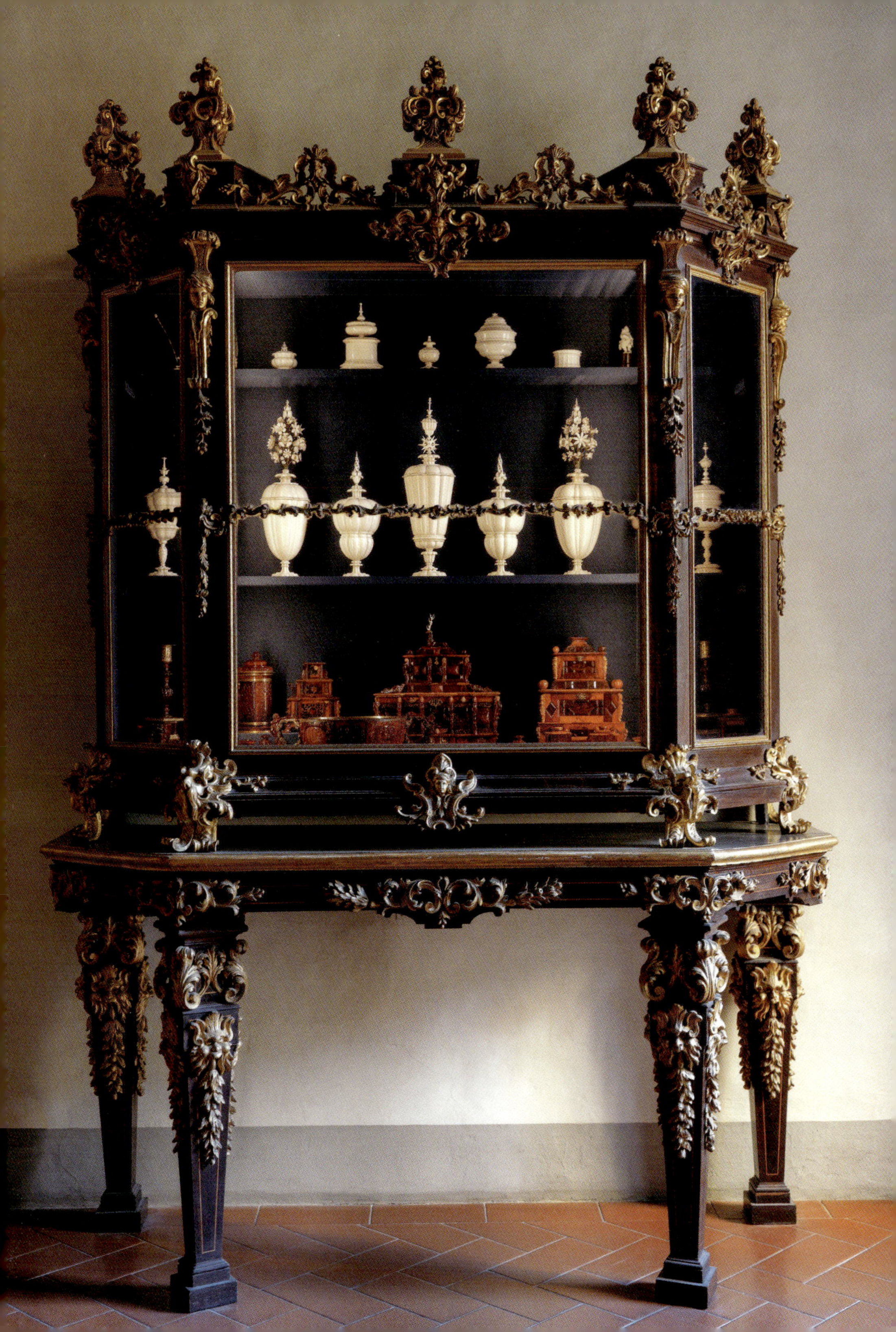

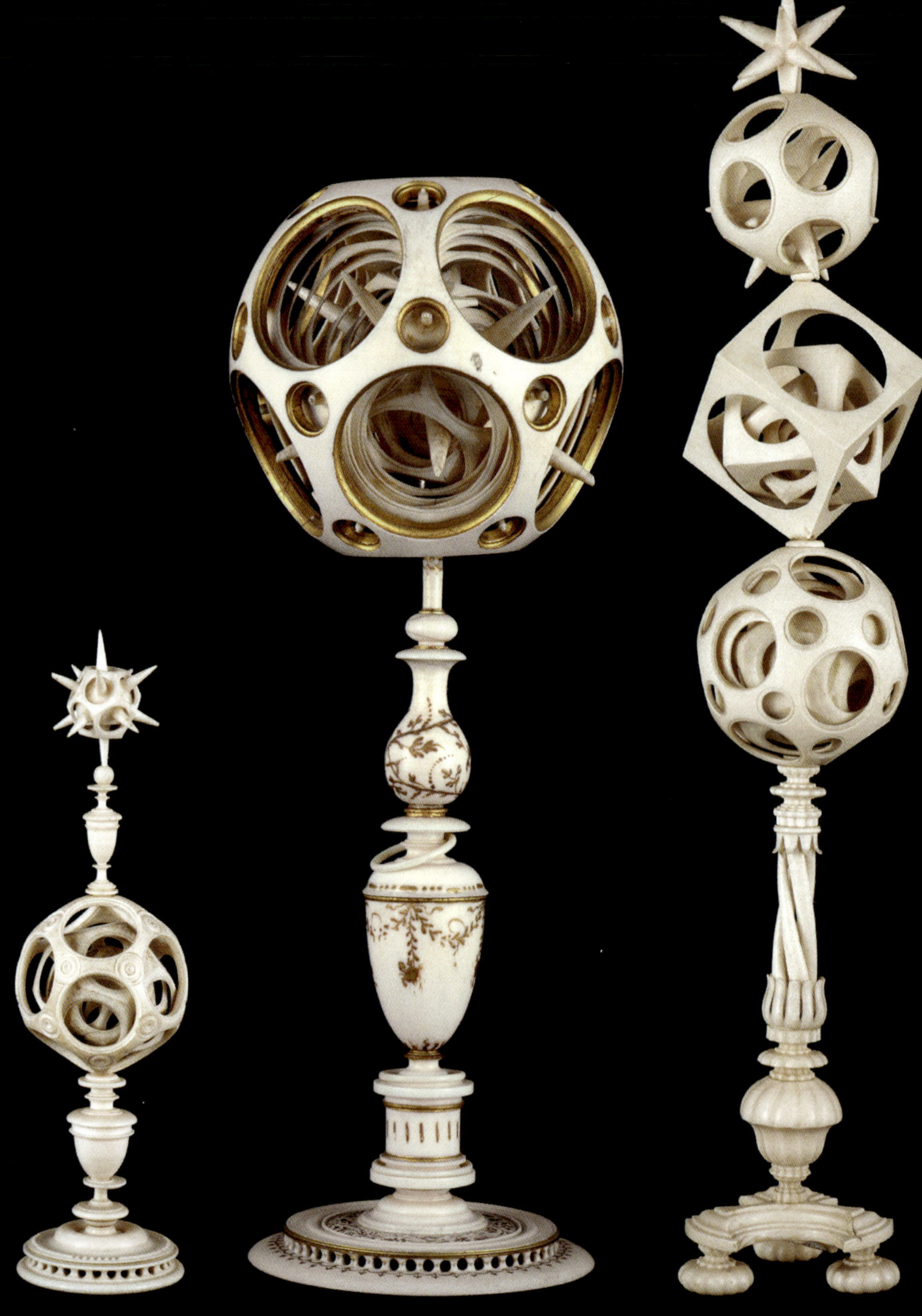

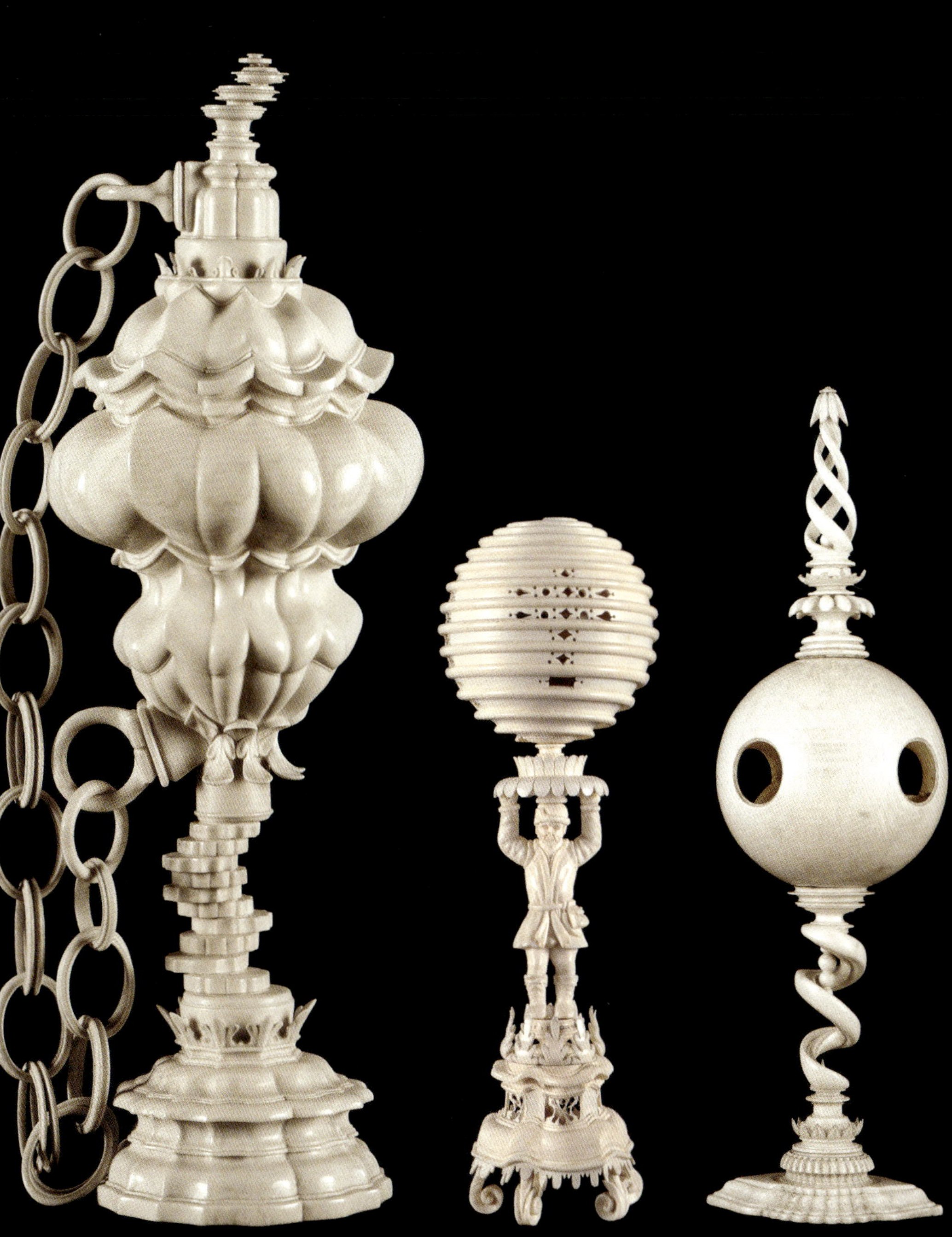

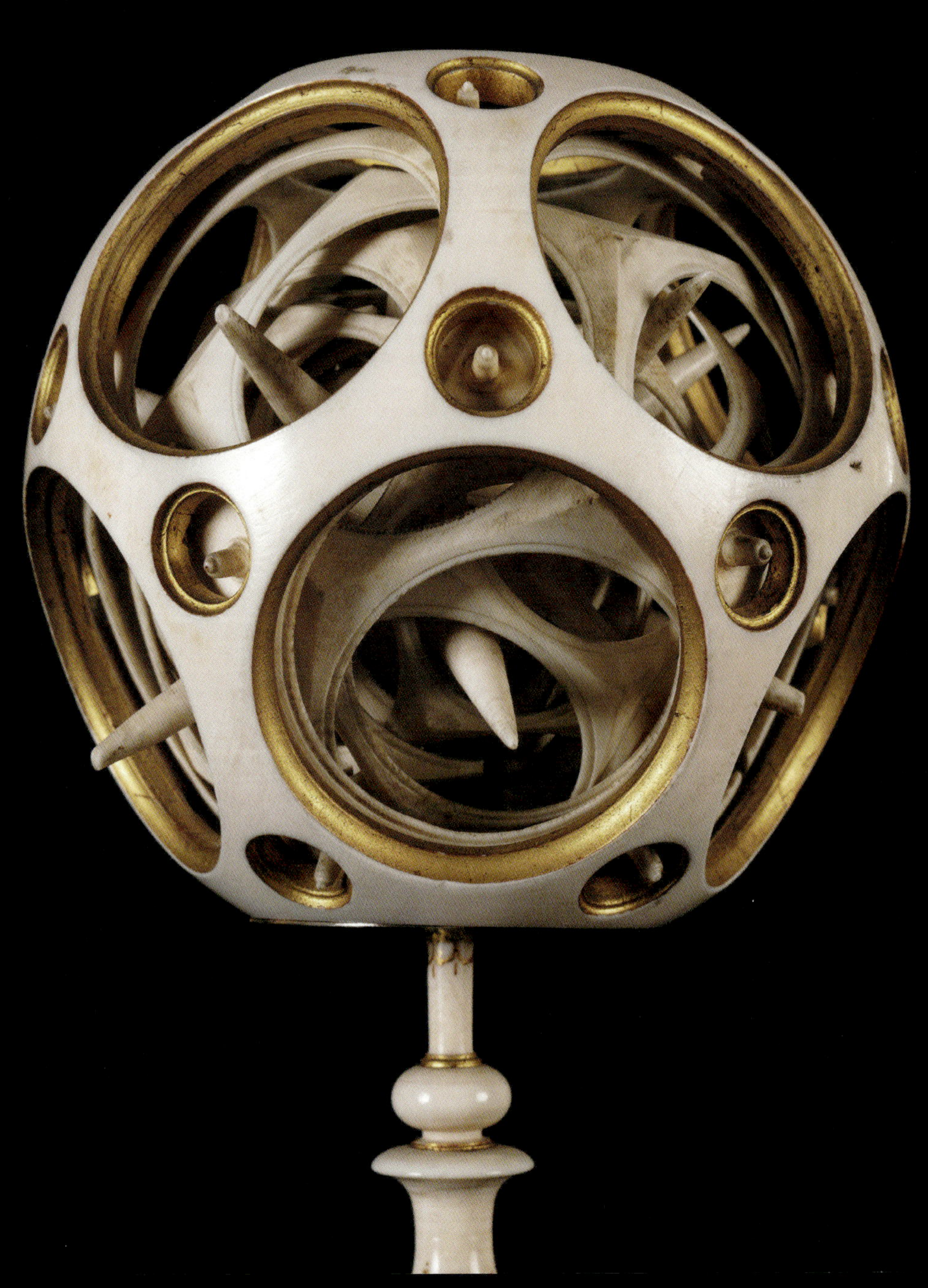

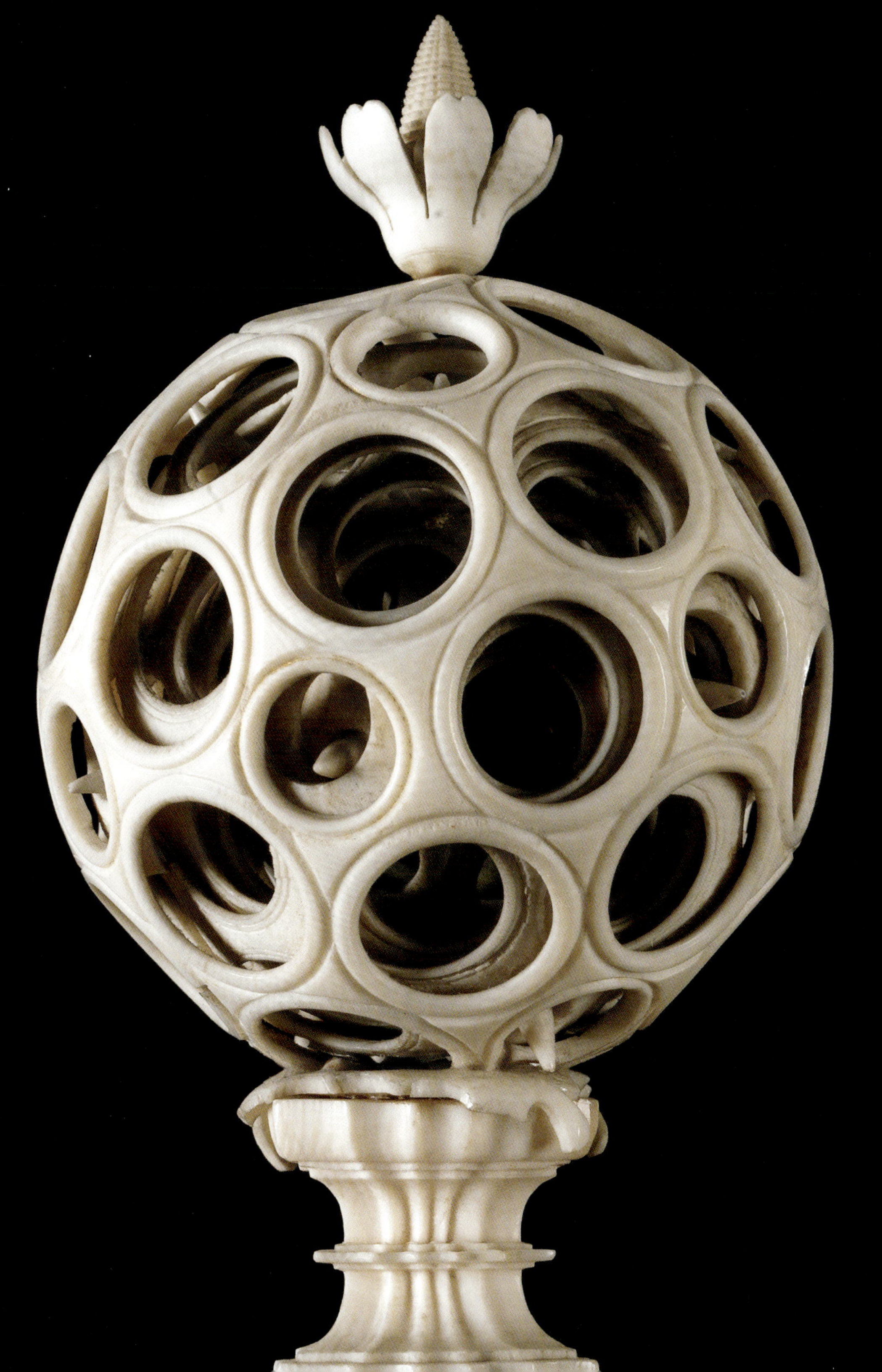

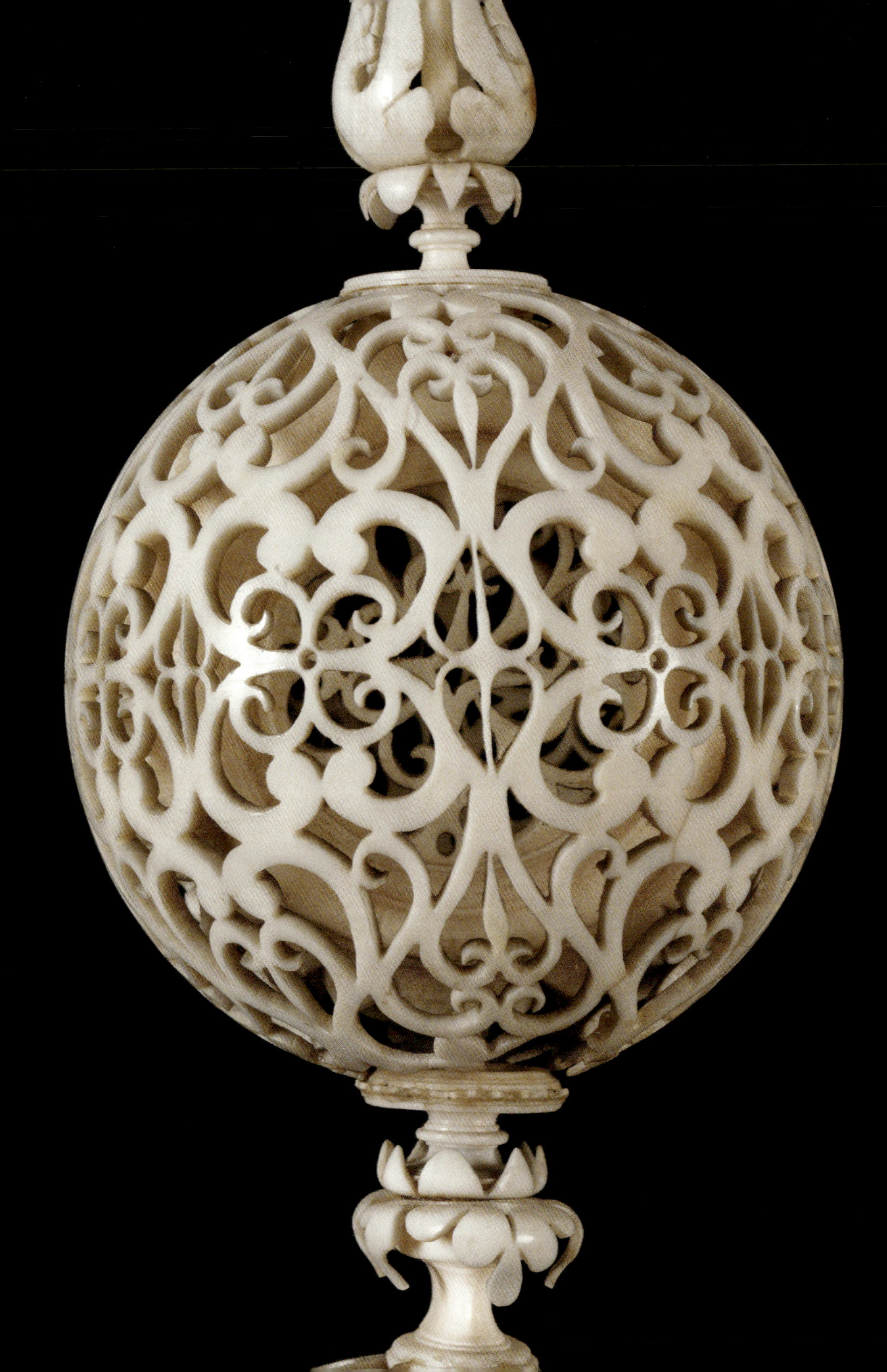

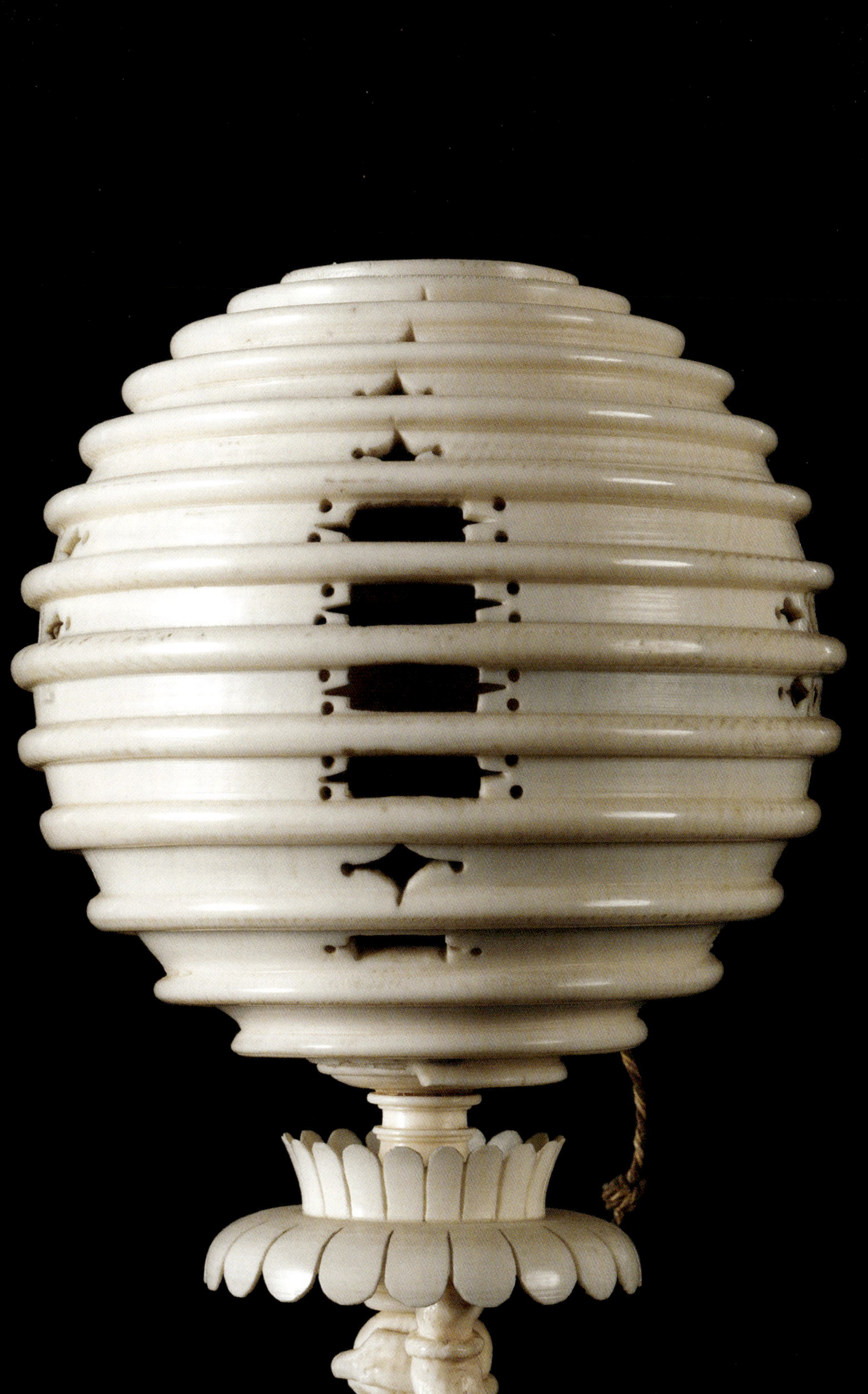

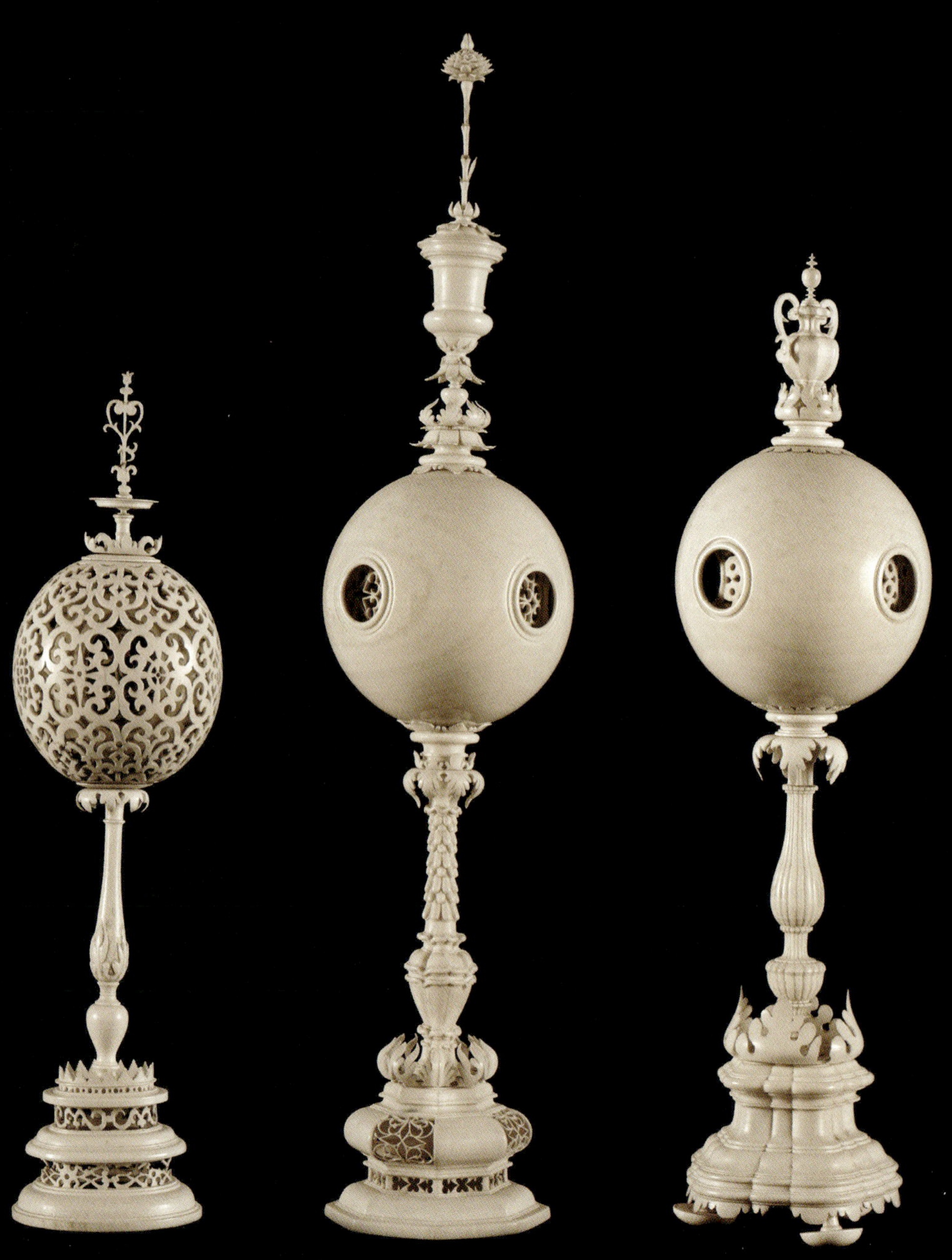

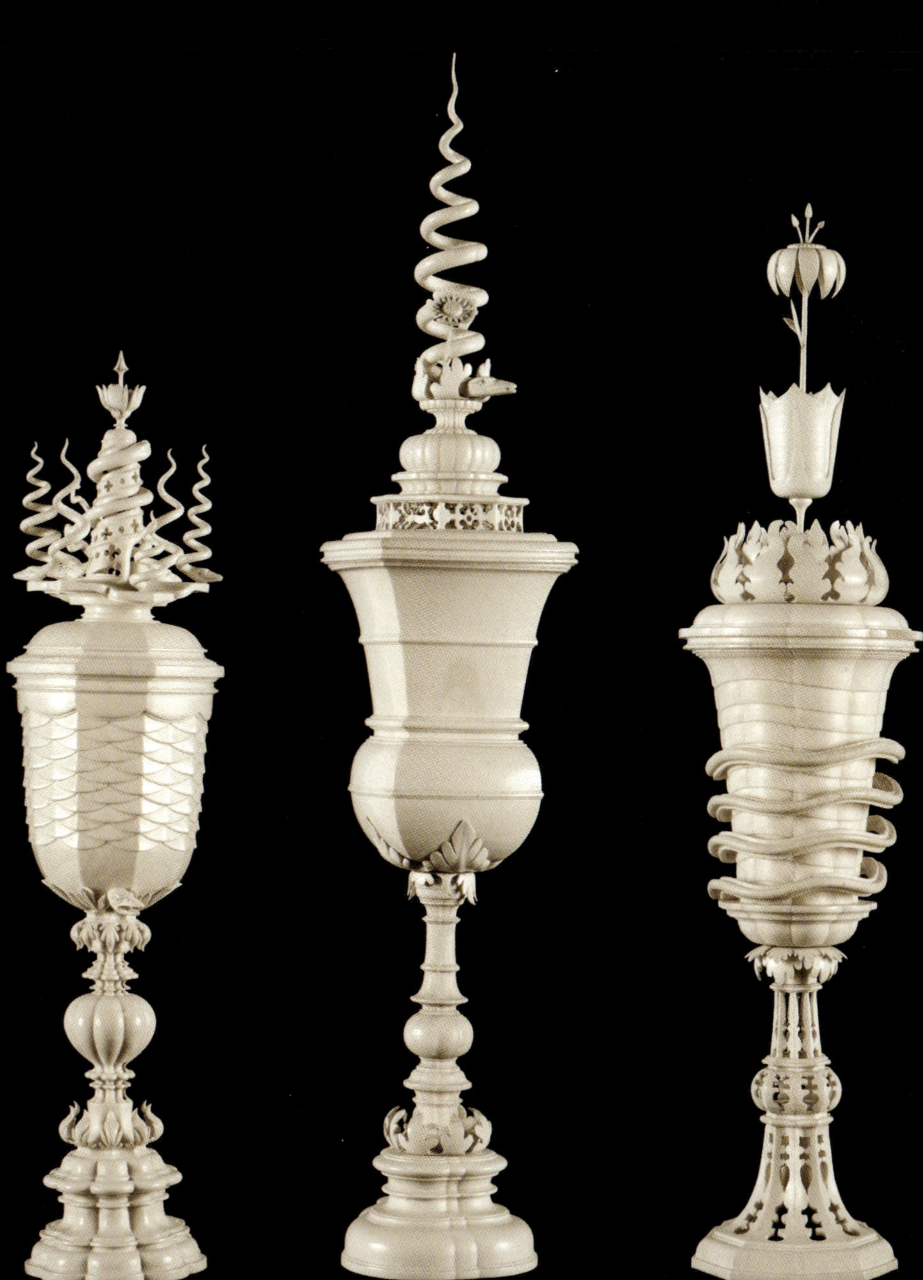

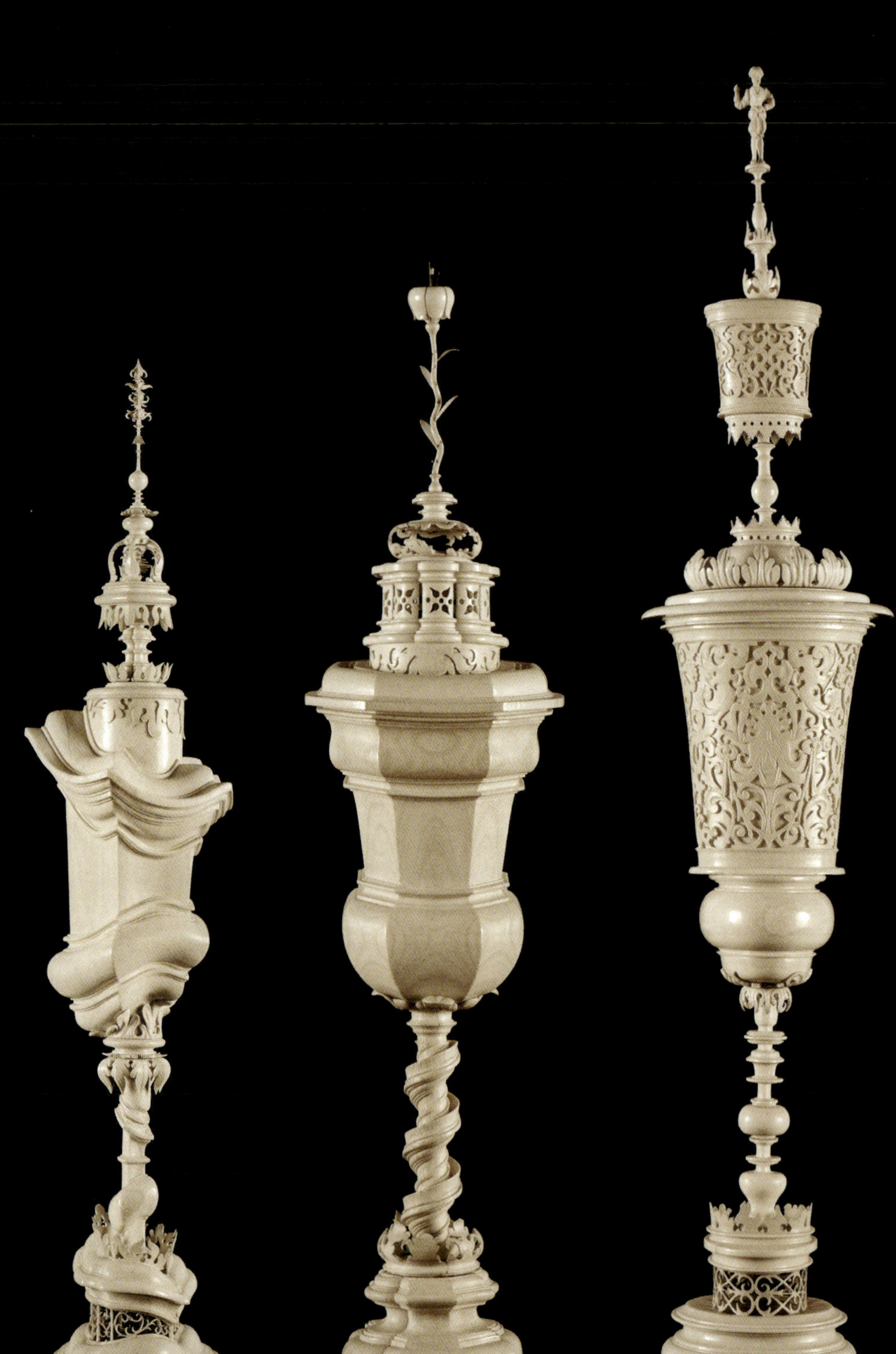

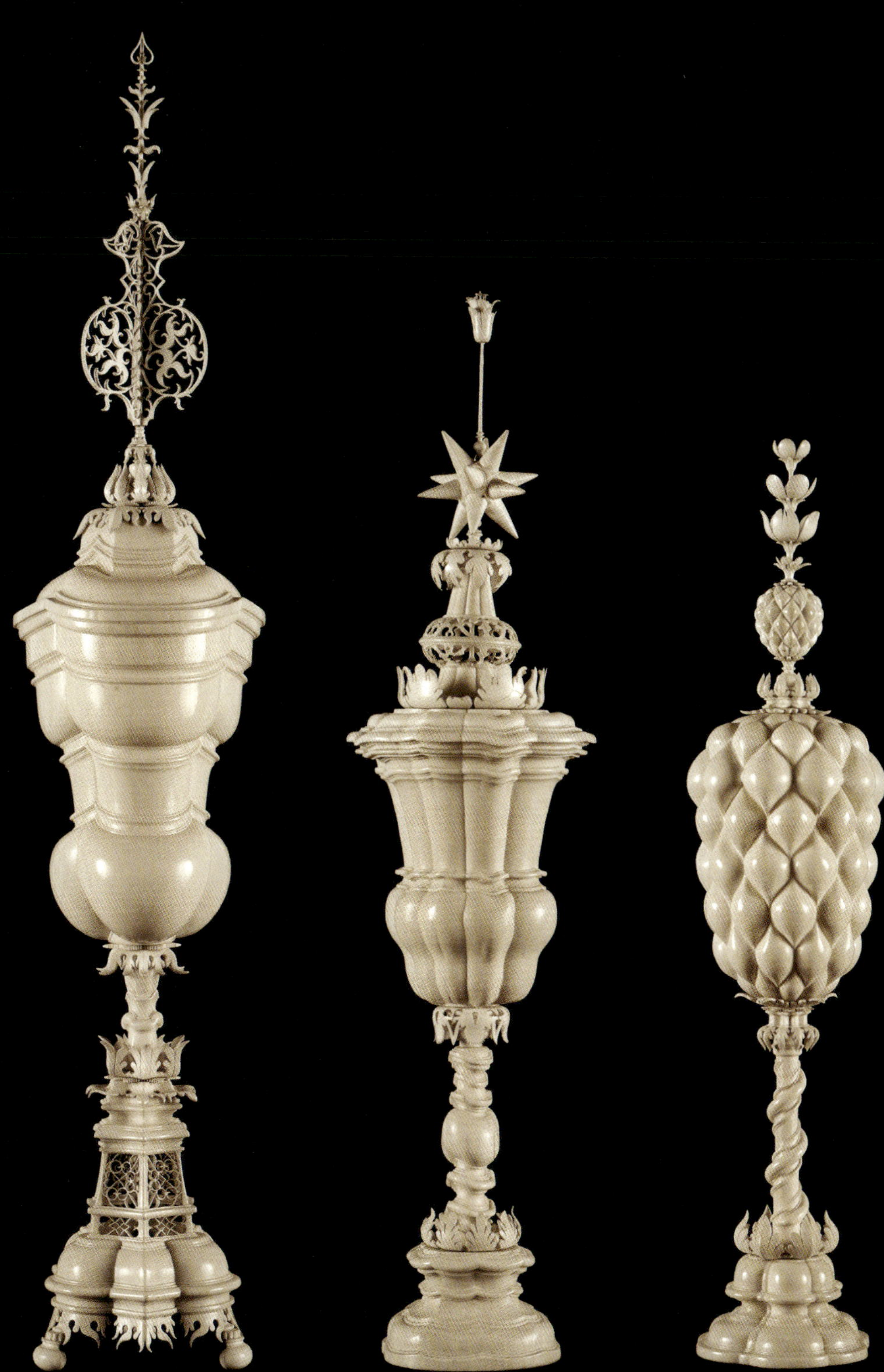

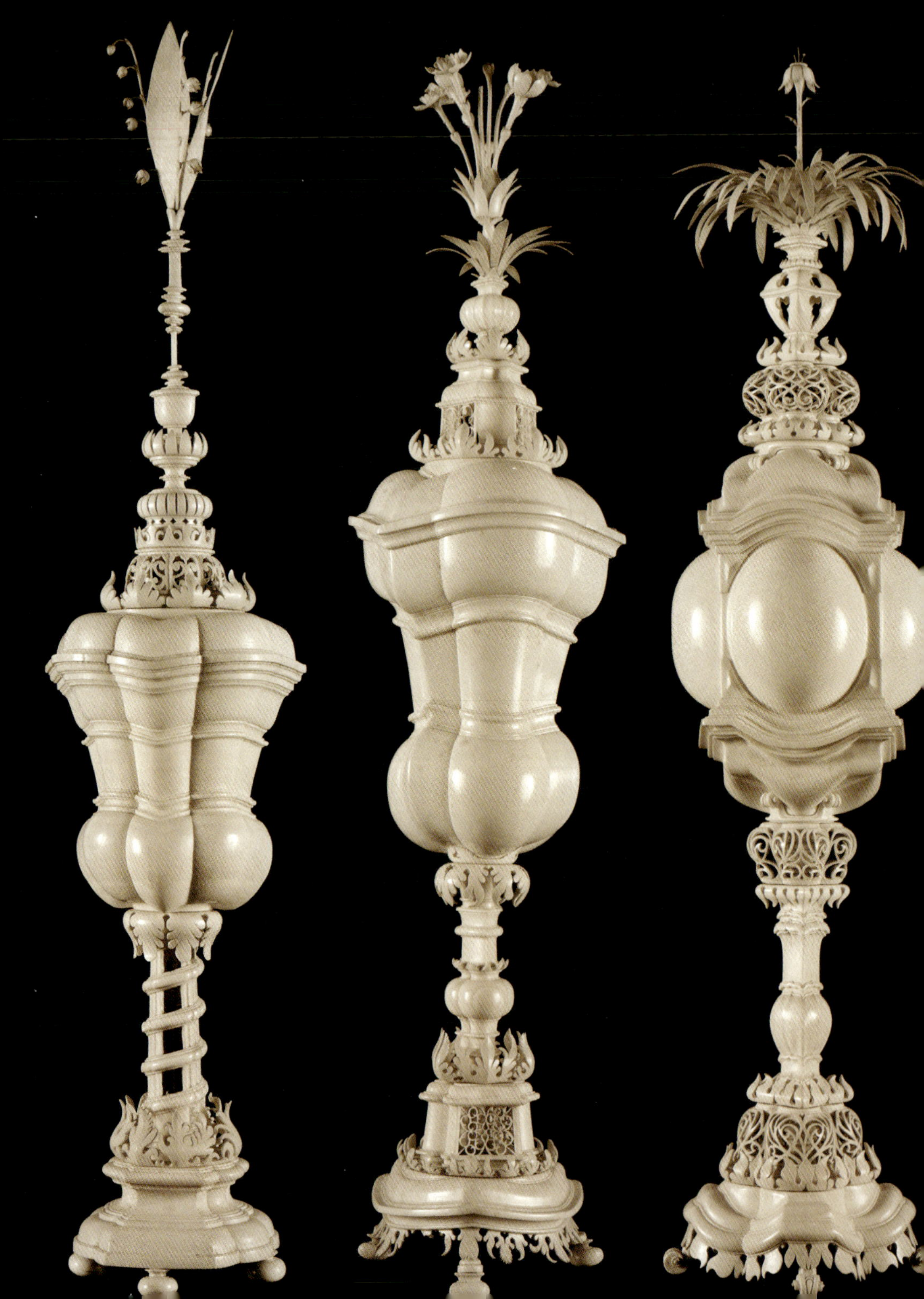

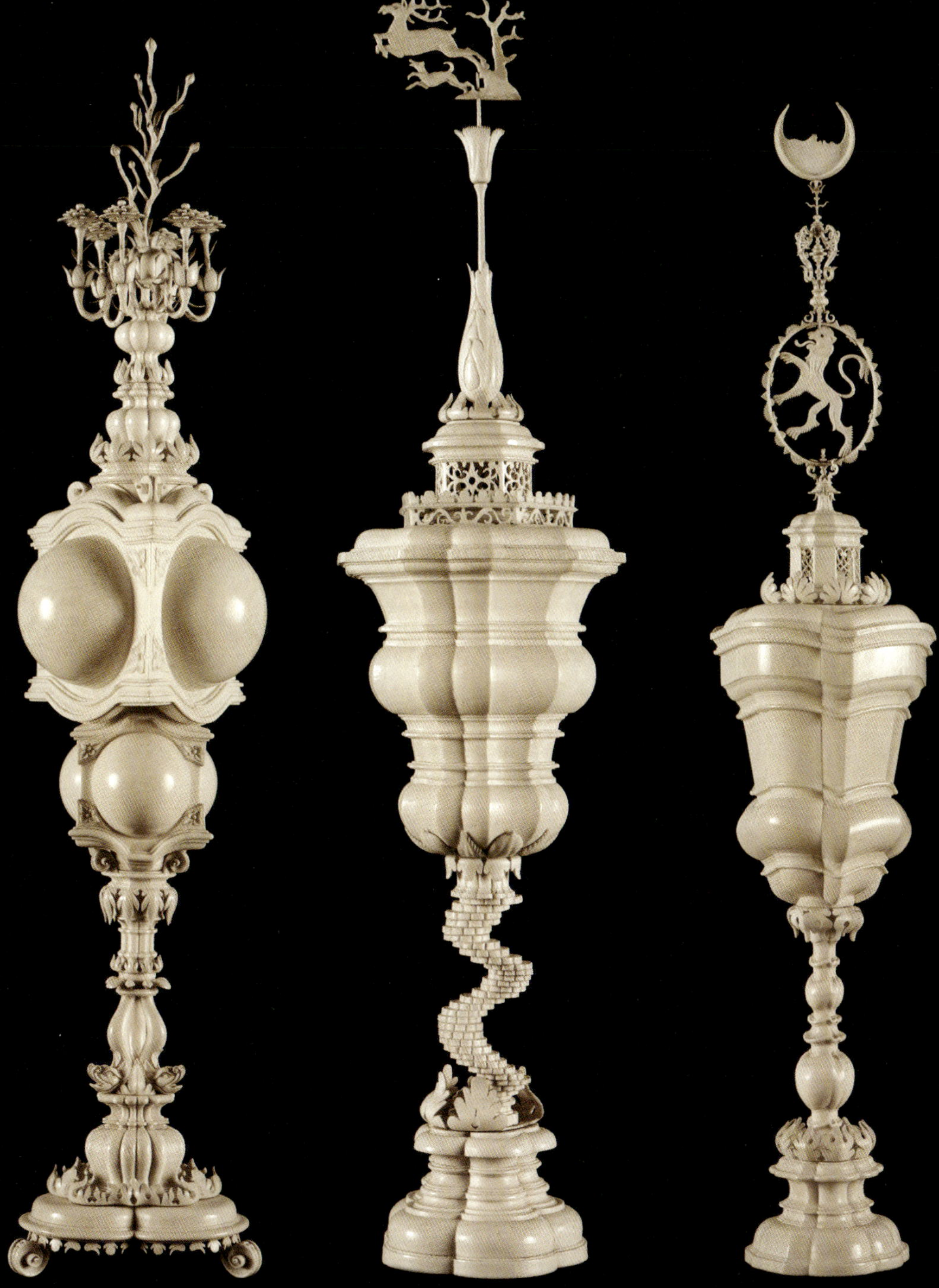

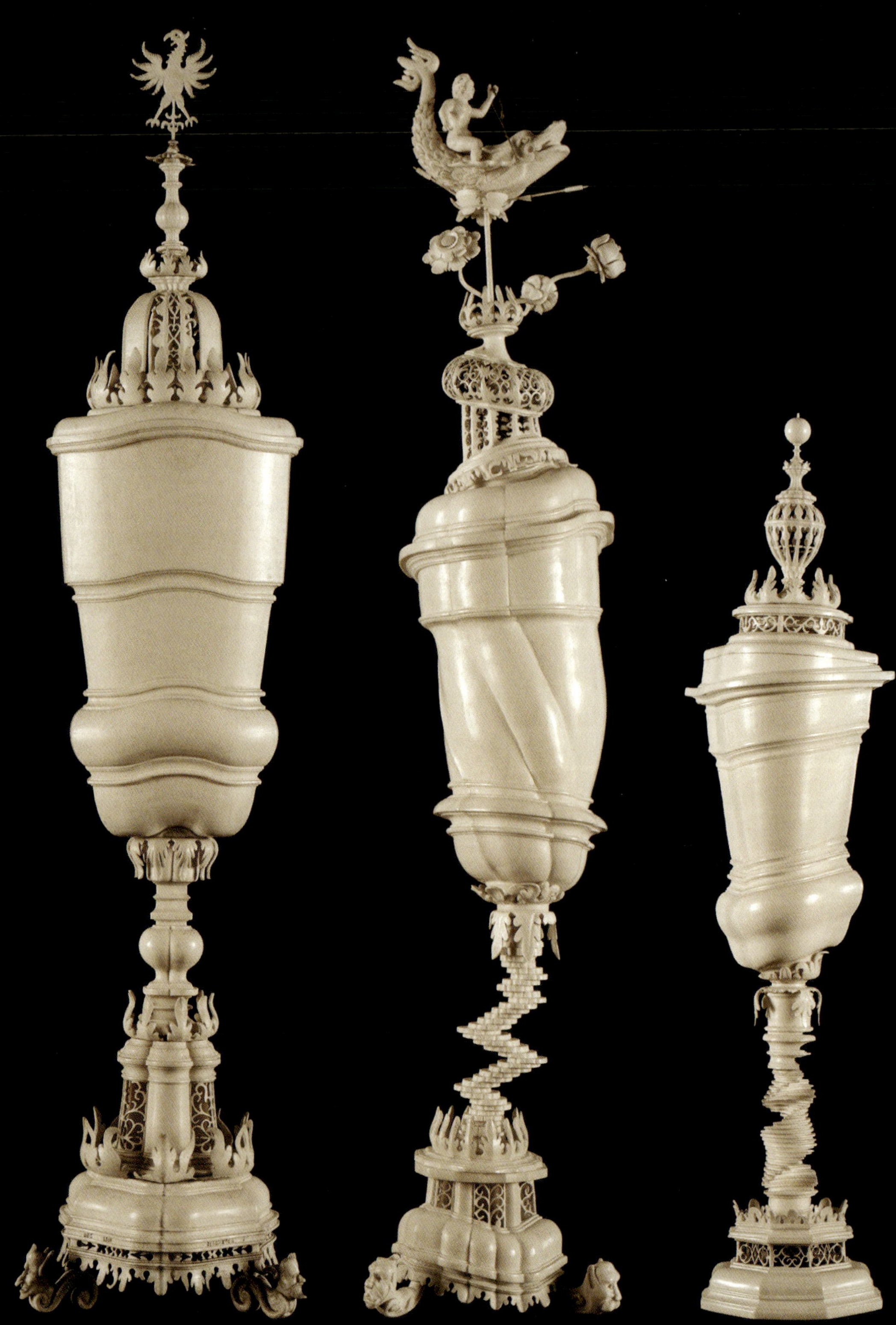

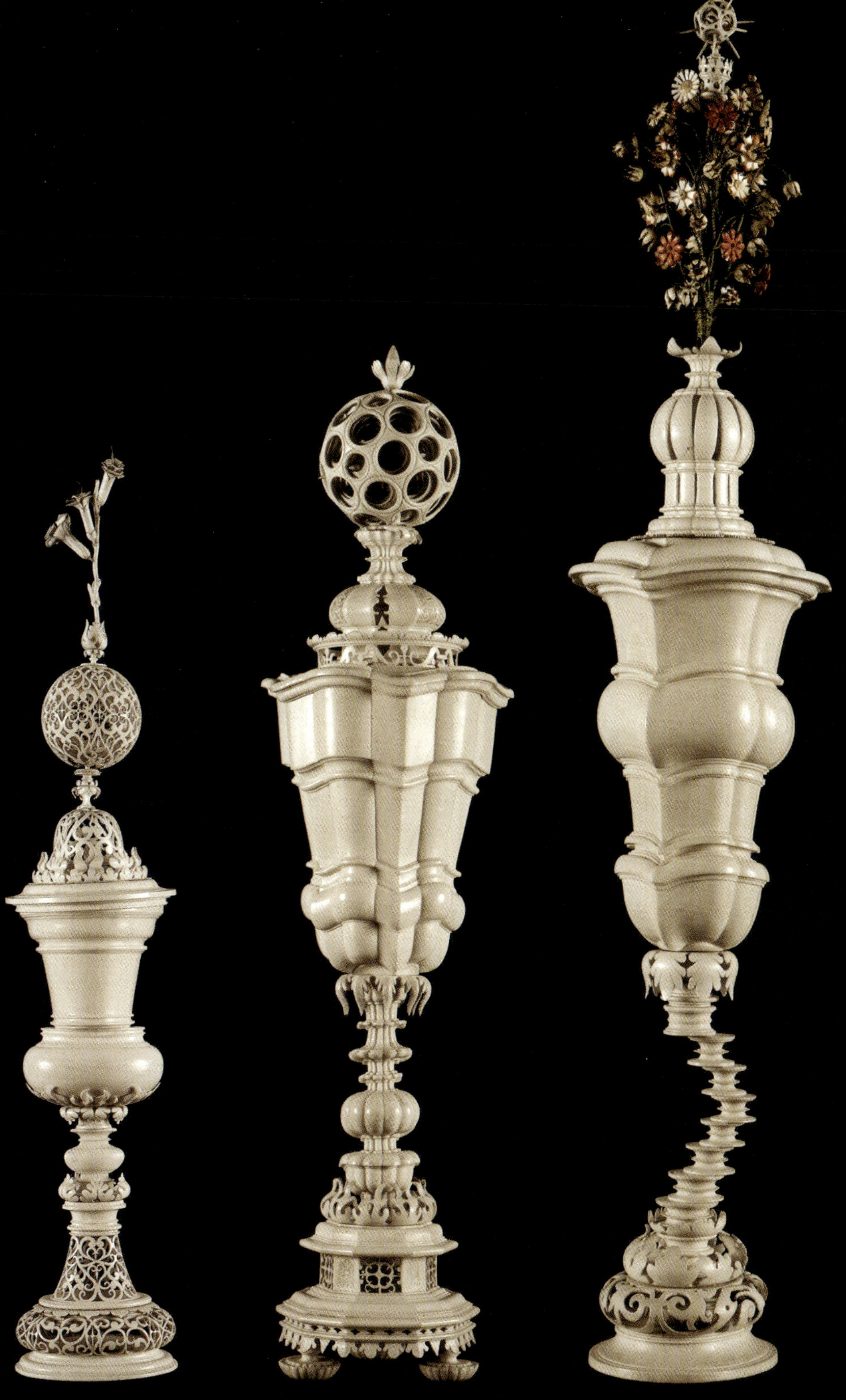

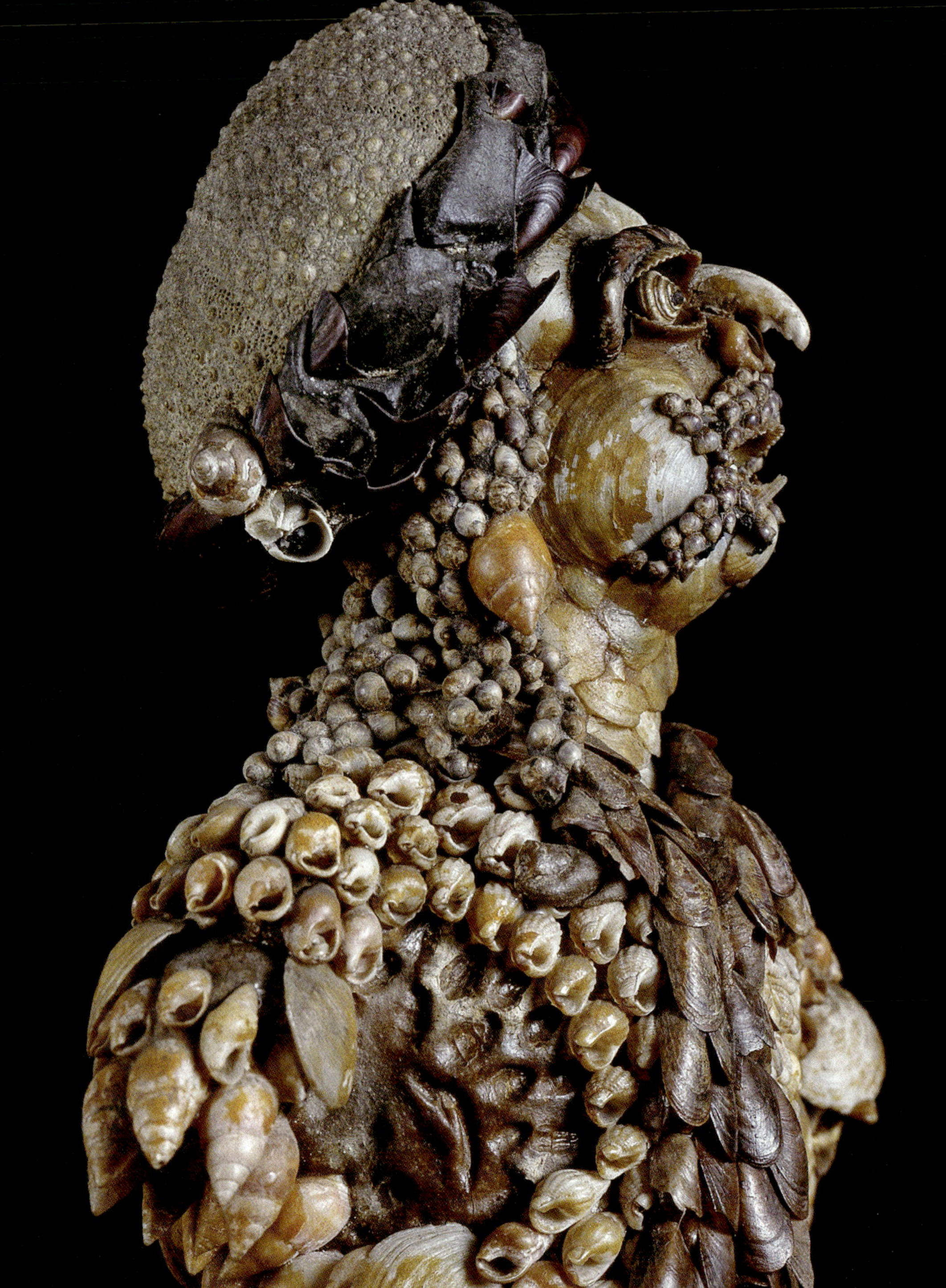

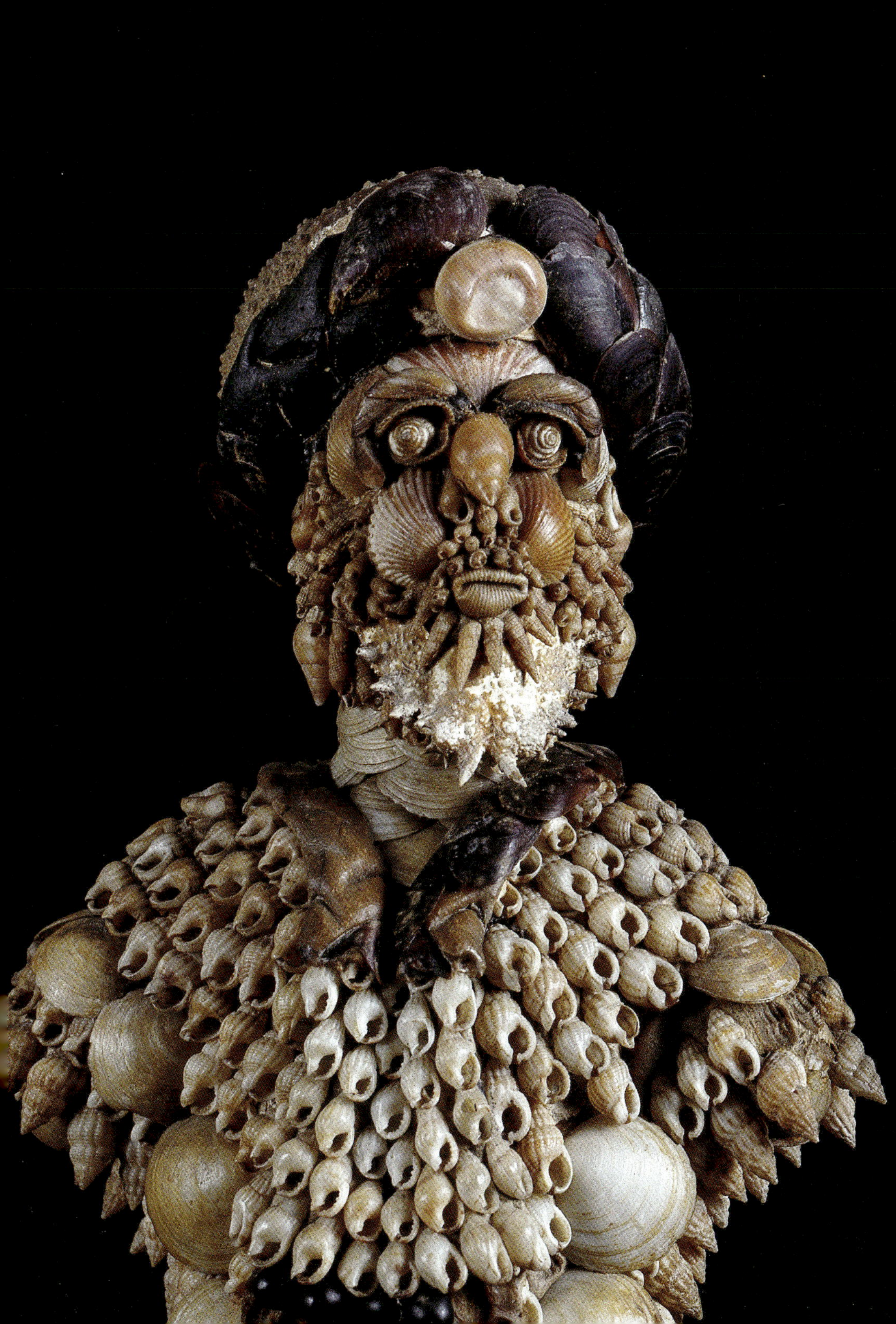

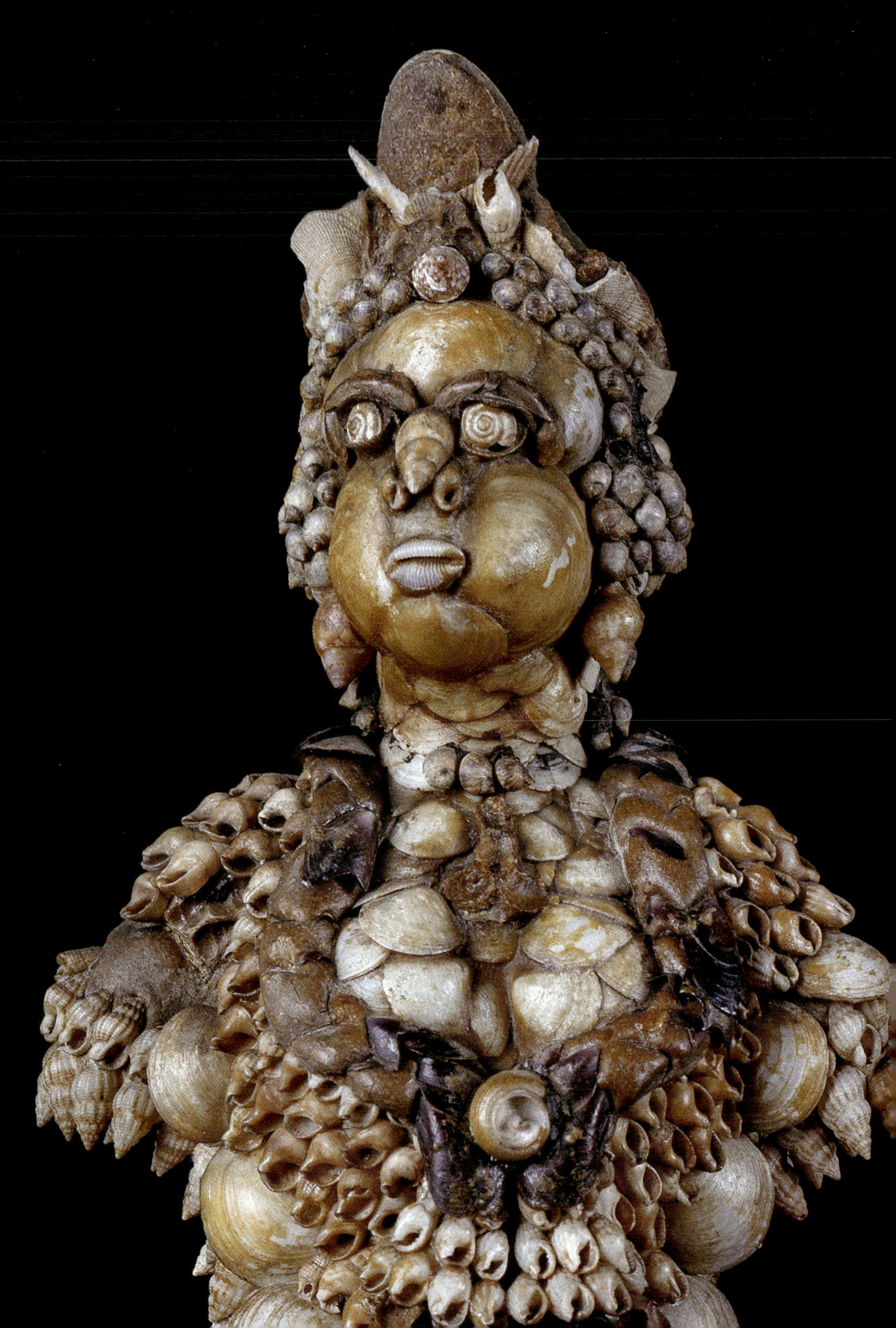

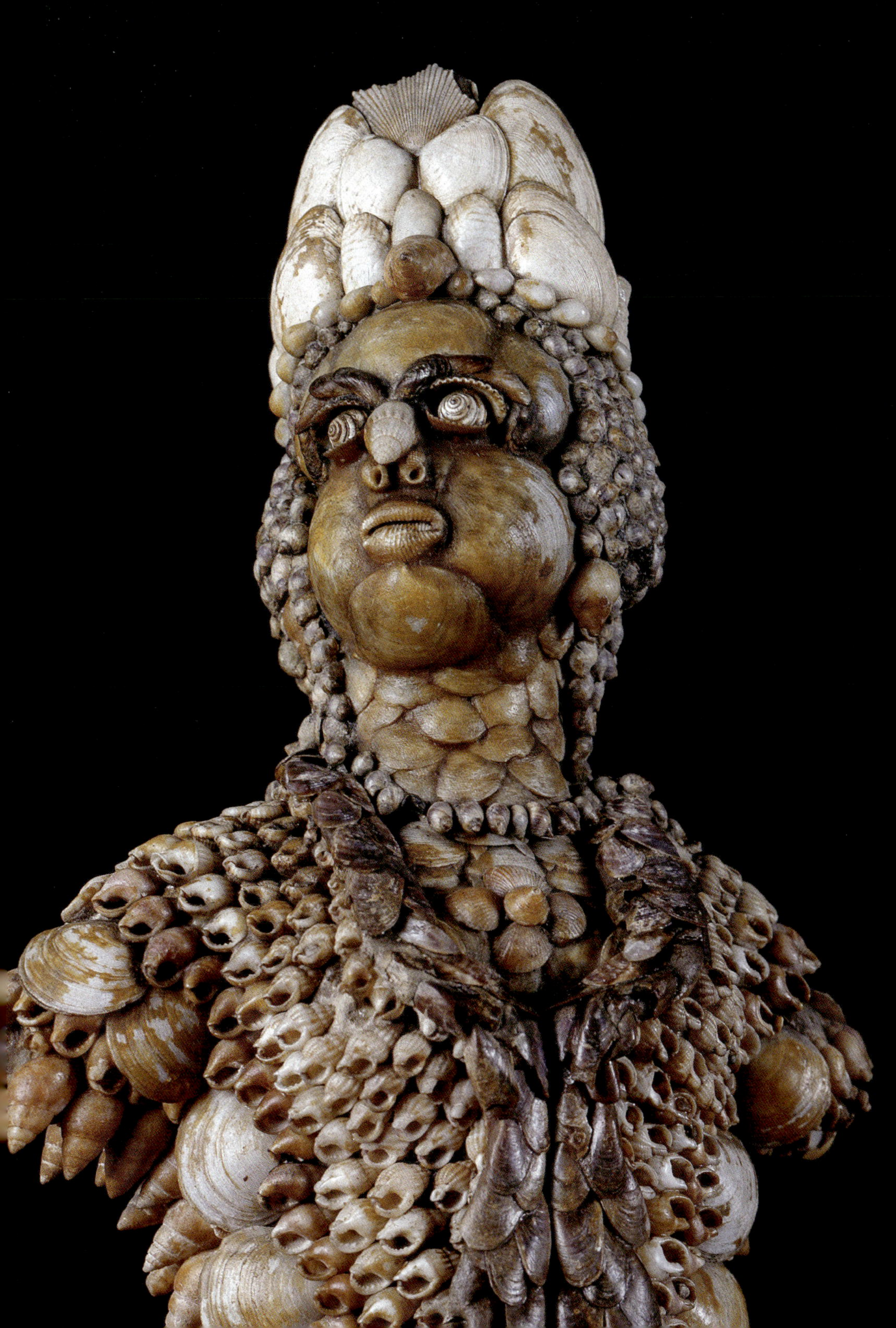

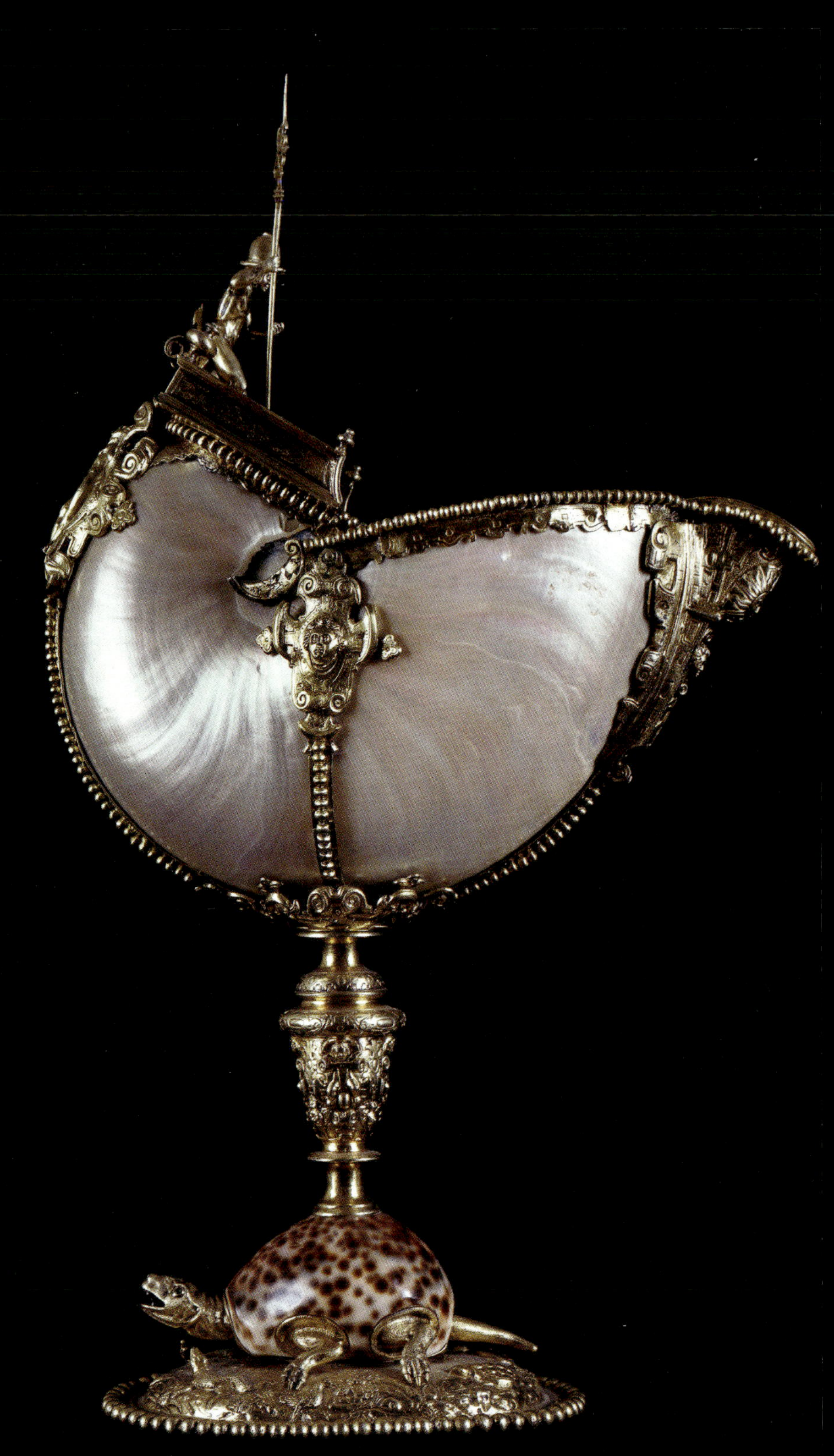

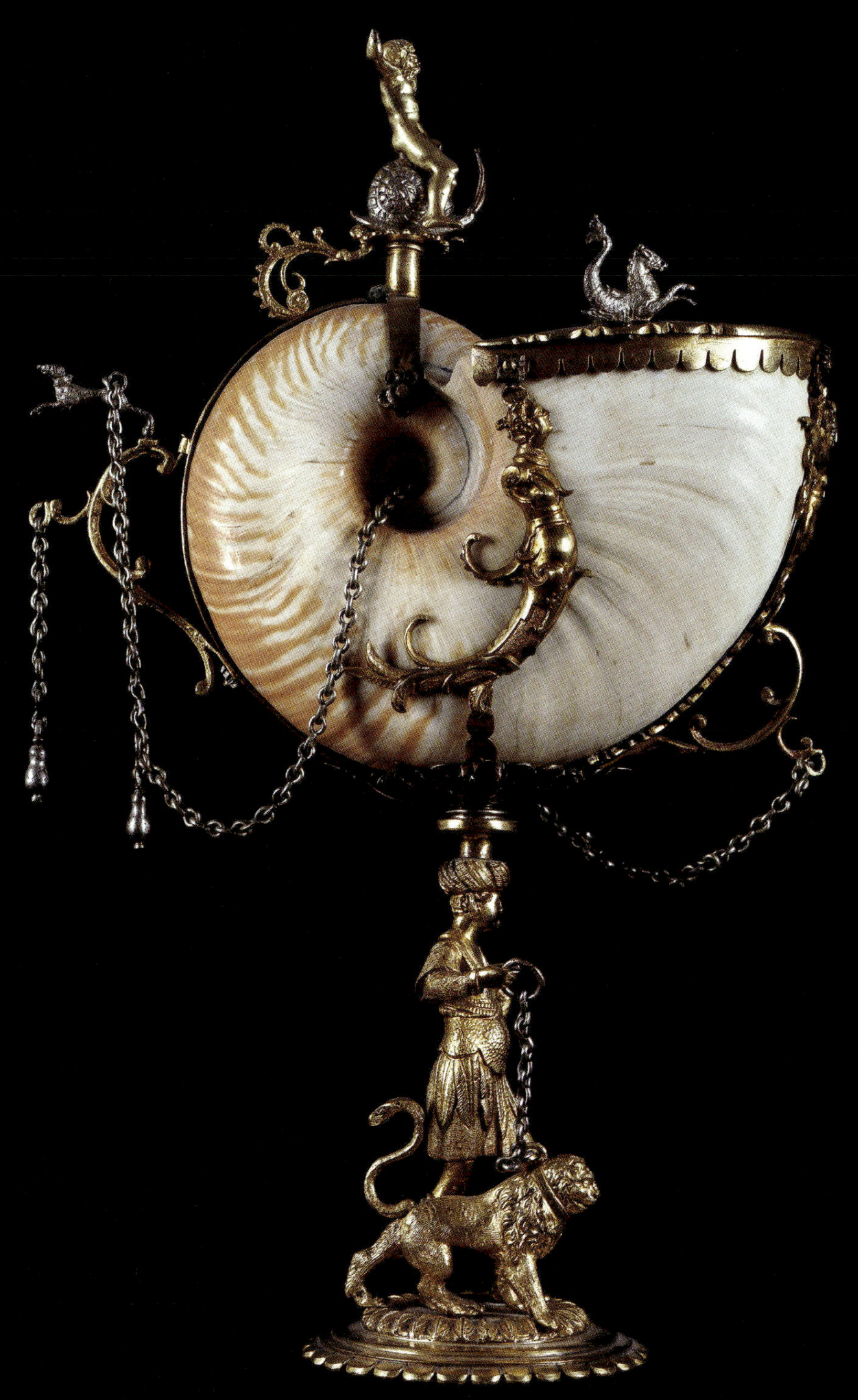

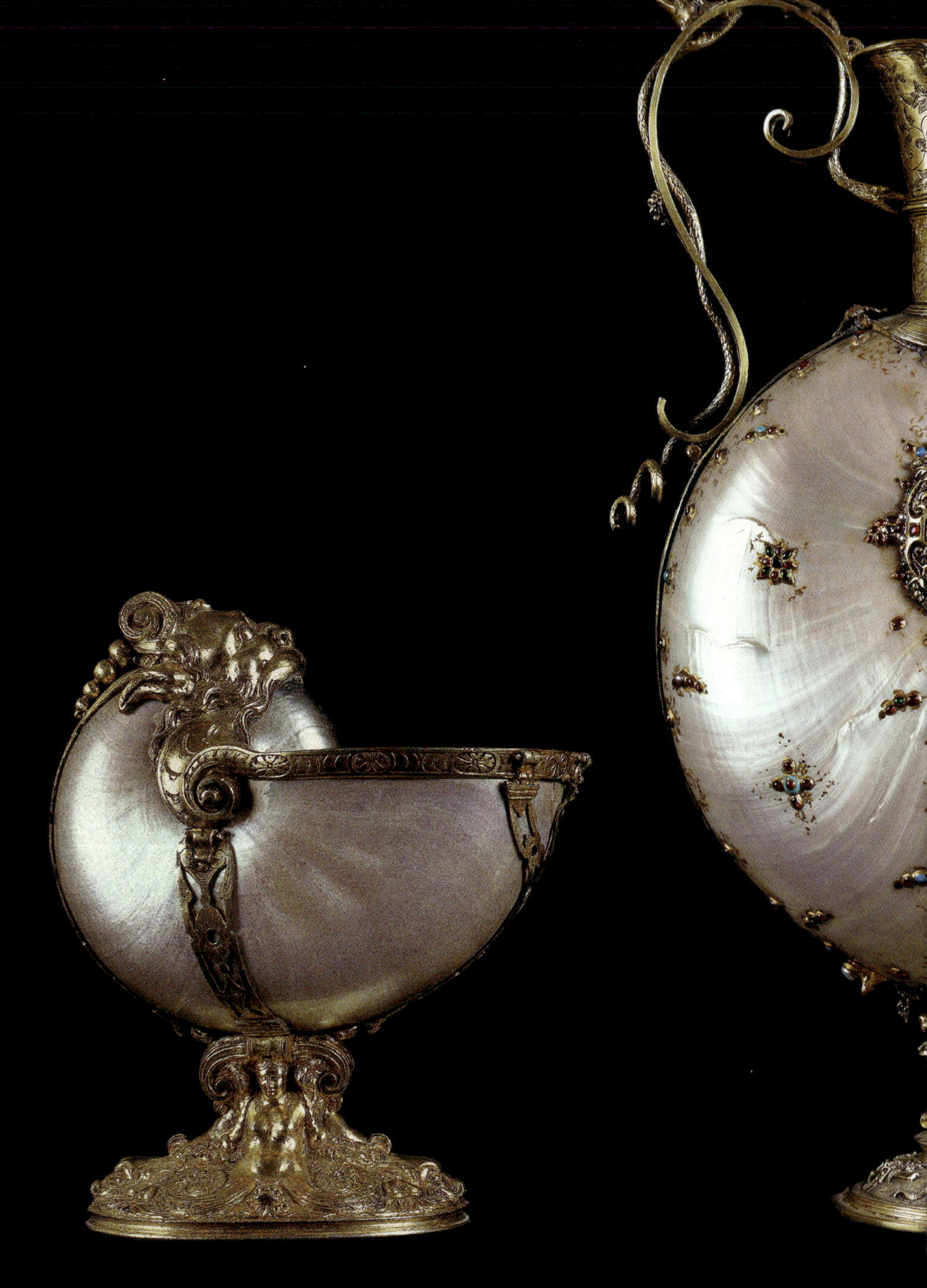

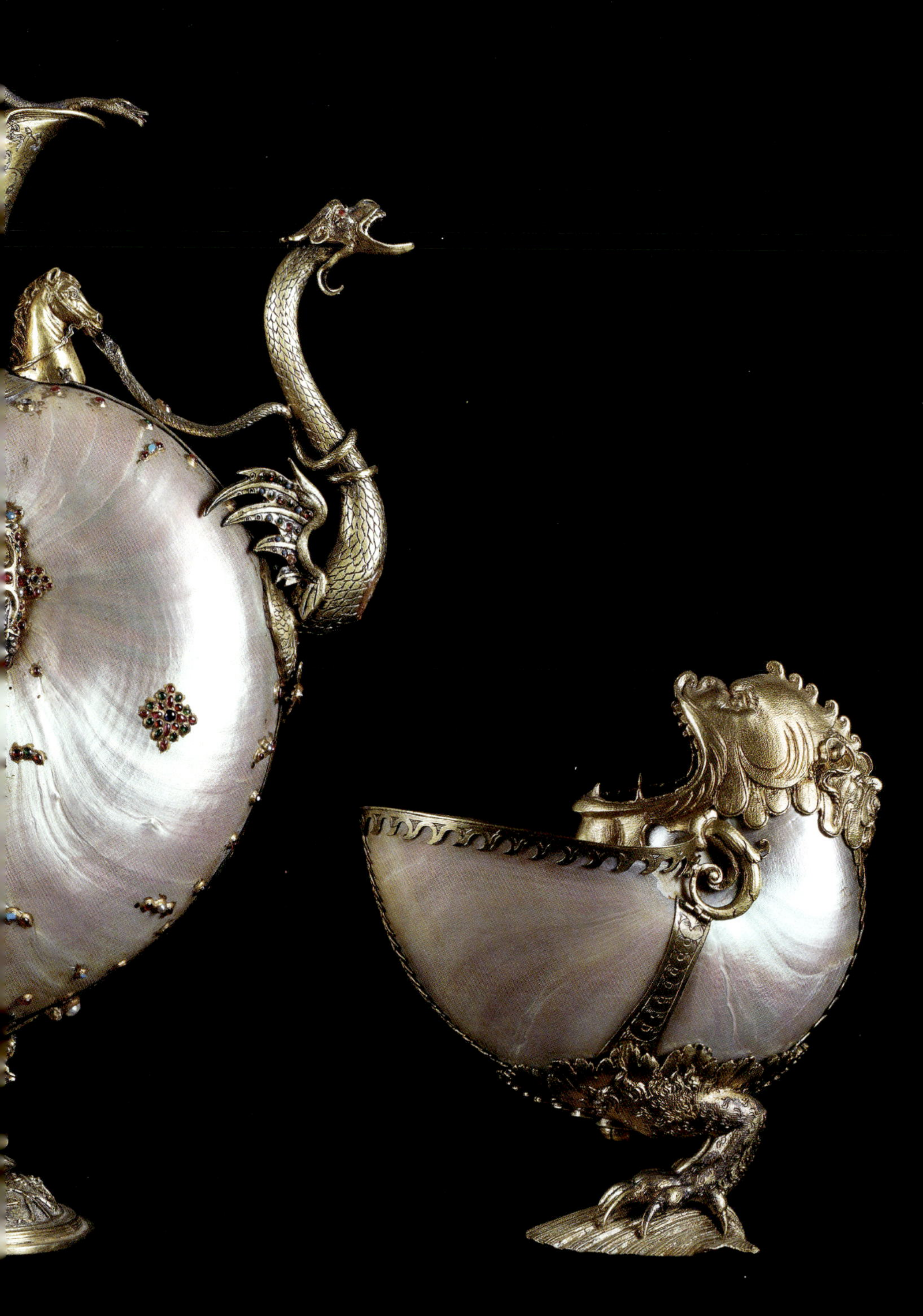

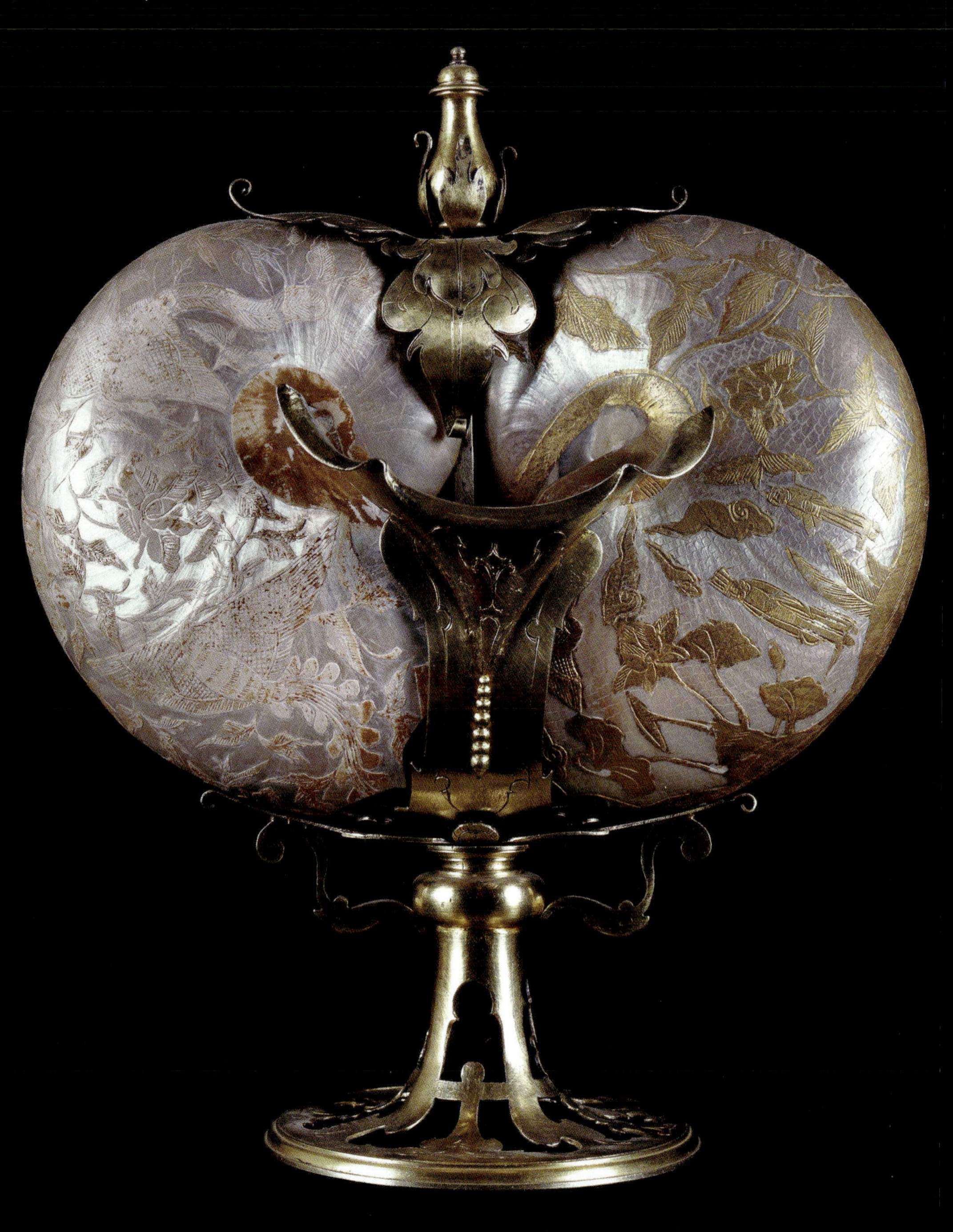

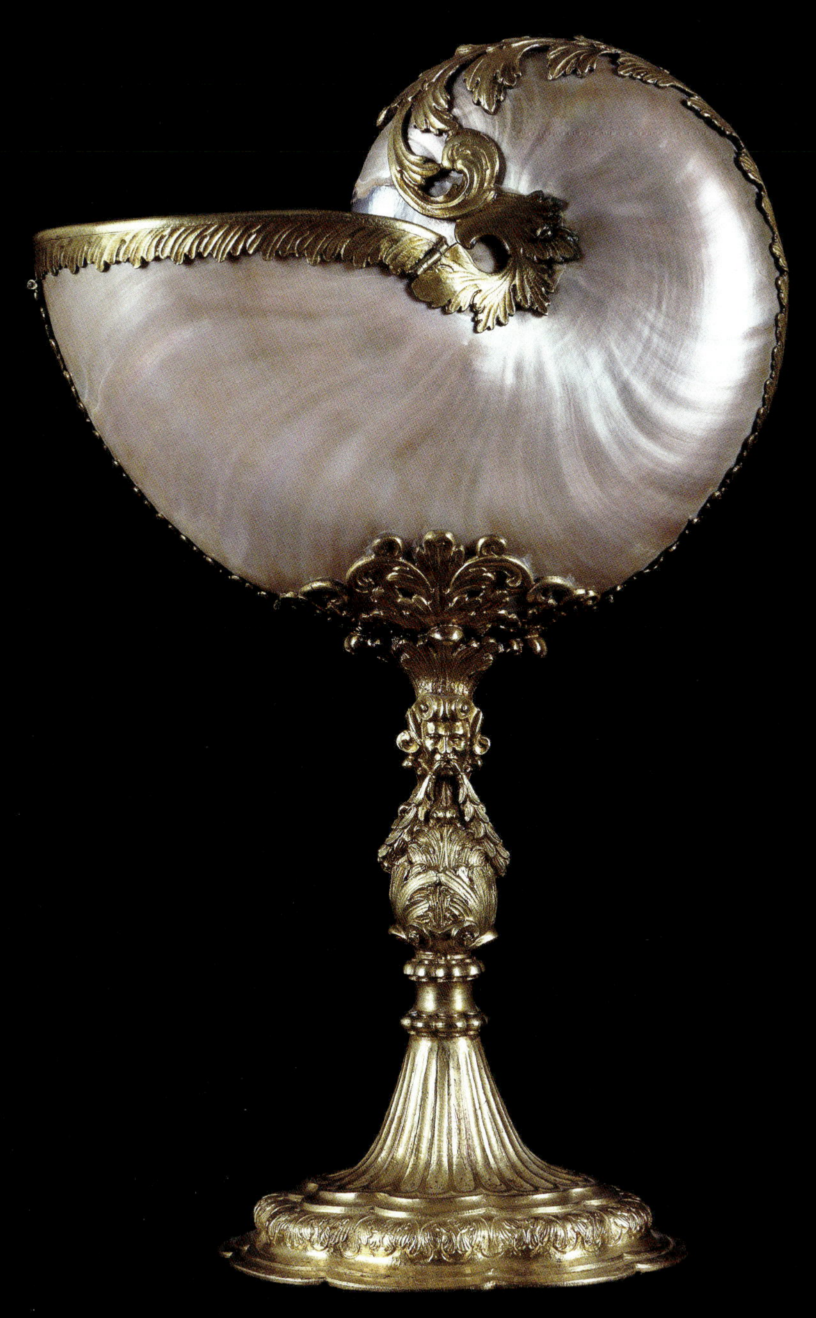

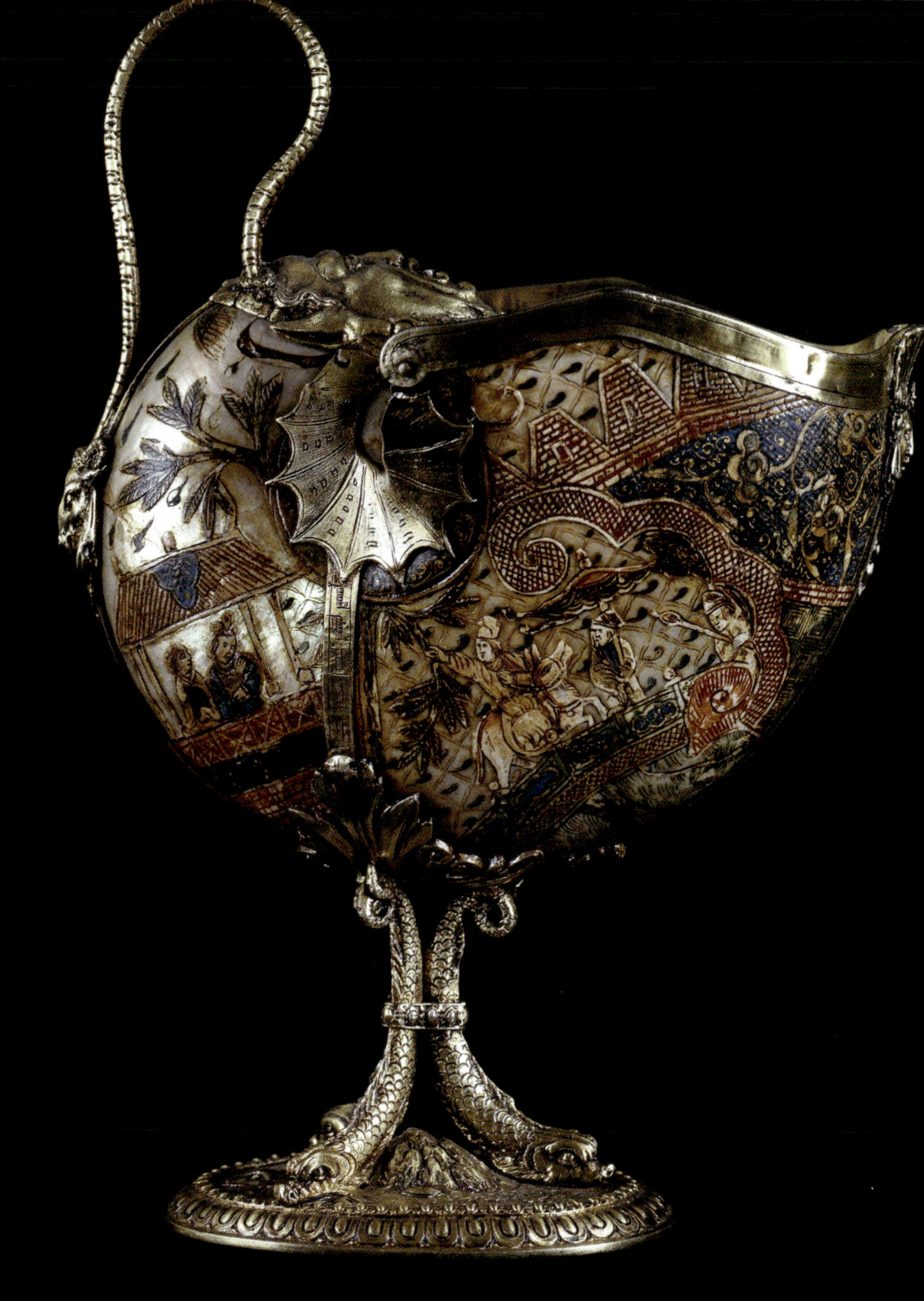

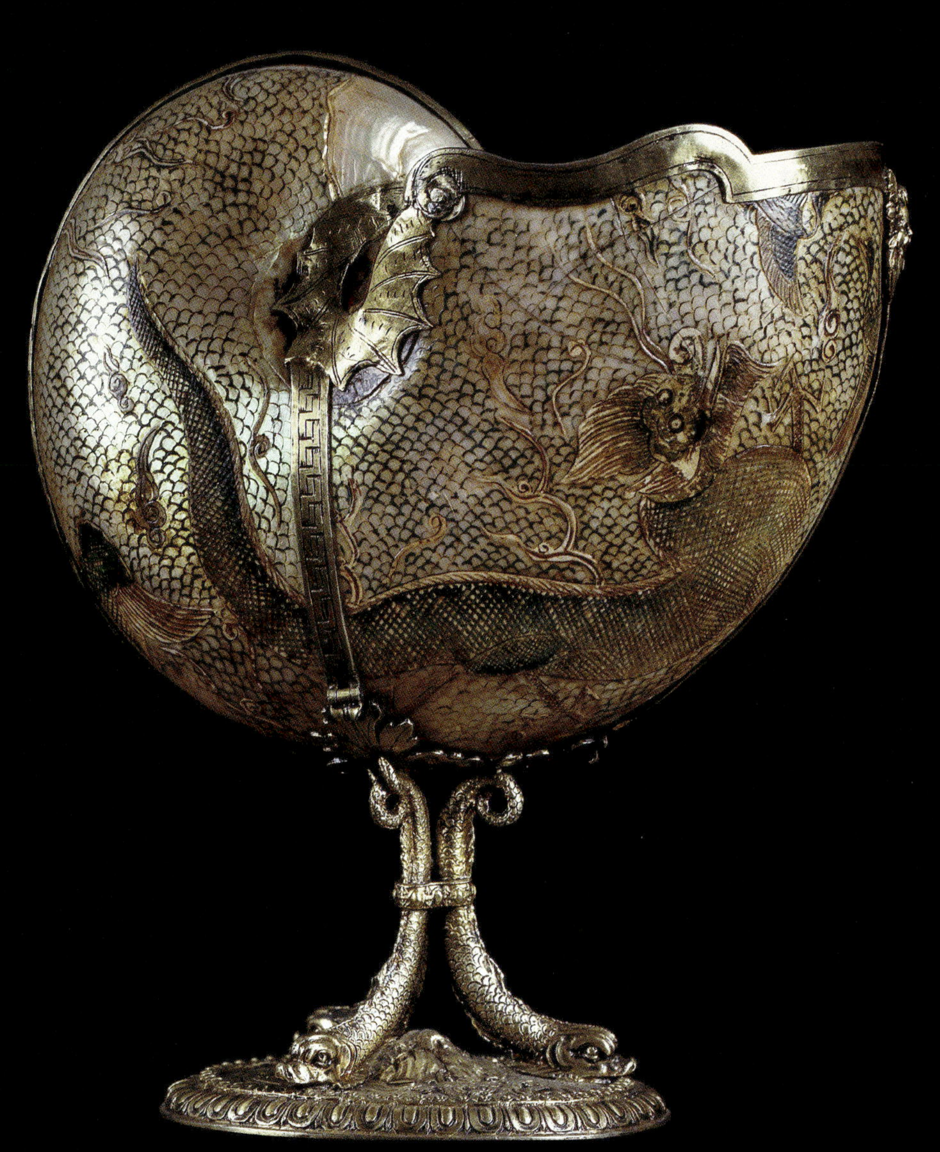

On crossing the threshold of the Museo degli Argenti in the Palazzo Pitti the viewer is surprised to discover that the collection does not consist mostly of silver objects. The origin of the museum's name instead dates back two centuries when the room, with frescoes by Giovanni da San Giovanni (1592–1636), was chosen to contain "the ancient silver" from Salzburg that was brought here in 1814 by Ferdinand III (1769–1824). Together with this initial nucleus, the museum today contains what remains of the treasure of the Medici Grand Dukes of Tuscany, the only surviving crown jewels in Italy. In 2019 it was thus renamed the Tesoro dei Granduchi.

The museum is a veritable treasure chest of marvels: it features cameos and jewels from the splendid collection of the Electress Anna Maria Luisa de' Medici (1667–1743), the last lineal descendant of the illustrious family; amber artefacts from the Baltic; pietra dura vases produced by master carvers in Milan; nautilus shells from the Pacific; and turned ivory sculptures collected by the Grand Dukes and by Leopoldo (1617–1675), the great Medici cardinal. Among the various curiosities, the most extraordinary objects, from a historical perspective, are undoubtedly the ivories and nautilus shells. This group of 27 fragile and fantastic vases, known as "the Coburg Ivories", was booty seized during the sack of Coburg on 28 September 1632, during the Thirty Years' War. With the exception of four globes mounted on stems, the others are lidded chalices. The main sections are extravagantly shaped, with off-centred discs, spirals, moulded and decorated columns, while their finials too are composed of highly complicated shapes: serpents, bunches of flowers, stars, and globes within globes. Produced between 1618 and 1631, some of them bear the signature of Marcus Heiden (active 1618–1664), known as the "master of fireworks and rifles". Their extraordinary shapes are a testimony to the artists' ability to accomplish feats of such virtuosity, achieved with the use of a precision lathe, and to the breadth of their knowledge: these craftsmen were equally assiduous in their study of geometry and the mechanical and natural sciences. In the 16th and 17th centuries a number of unusual shells were imported to Europe from remote south-east Asian seas by Portuguese and Dutch merchants. A colourful description of the Nautilus pompilius, a mollusc of the class of cephalopods, is found in the *Ricreazione dell'occhio e della mente* (Recreation of the Eye and the Mind, 1681) by the Jesuit father Filippo Buonanni (1638–1725), who wrote: "It is not a fish, but a shell provided with its own house, so beautiful that, when cleaned and mounted on a finely gilded metal foot, it becomes a cup fit to stand in the magnificent cupboards of great lords". It is fair to observe that, set within exquisite metal mountings and decorated by imaginative goldsmiths, the shells of these molluscs, at once *naturalia* and *mirabilia*, were transformed into unique and astonishing artefacts.

◎ ❖ ◎

Beim Betreten des Museo degli Argenti im Palazzo Pitti stellen Besucher immer wieder verblüfft fest, dass sich dort überhaupt kein Silberzeug befindet. Der Name entstand vor zweihundert Jahren, als man den von Giovanni da San Giovanni (1592–1636) ausgemalten

Saal als Standort für das „alte Silber" auswählte, das Ferdinand III. (1769–1824) im
Jahre 1814 aus Salzburg mitgebracht hatte. Ausgestellt sind die Überreste des Medici-
Schatzes, des einzigen Fürstenschatzes, der sich heute noch in Italien befindet. Seit
2019 heißt das Museum treffend Tesoro dei Granduchi.

Das Museum beherbergt wahre Schätze: Juwelen, Schmuck und Kameen aus der
sagenumwobenen Sammlung der Großherzogin Anna Maria Luisa de' Medici (1667–1743),
der letzten Vertreterin des Fürstengeschlechts; Bernsteinobjekte aus dem Baltikum;
Steingefäße aus den Werkstätten der Mailänder Steinschneider; Perlboote aus dem
Pazifik; Skulpturen aus Elfenbein, die von den Mitgliedern der Familie Medici und
Kardinal Leopoldo (1617–1675) zusammengetragen wurden. Zweifellos kommt den
Elfenbeinobjekten und den Perlbooten ästhetisch und historisch eine herausragende
Stellung zu. Bei den siebenundzwanzig auch als „Coburg-Elfenbein" bekannten, ebenso
fantasievollen wie zerbrechlichen Objekten handelt es sich um eine Kostbarkeit, die
im Dreißigjährigen Krieg bei der Plünderung Coburgs am 28. September 1632 durch
die kaiserliche Armee erbeutet wurde. Mit Ausnahme von vier Globen handelt es sich
um Deckelpokale mit bizarrer Stielgestalt: ovale Scheiben, Spiralen, modellierte und
bemalte Säulen; auch die Deckel sind aufwendig mit Schlangen, Blumen, Sternen und
ineinandergeschachtelten Globen dekoriert. Zwischen 1618 und 1631 entstanden, tragen
einige die Signatur von Marcus Heiden, der von 1618 bis 1664 tätig war und zunächst
als „Feuerwerker und Büchsenmacher" bekannt wurde. Die ausgefallene Form wie die
virtuose Ausführung verdanken sich der grenzenlosen Experimentierfreude der Künstler
sowie den technischen Möglichkeiten der Präzisionsdrehbank. Dieselbe Begeisterung
hegten diese Künstler für die Mechanik, die Geometrie und die Naturwissenschaften.
Aus den fernen Meeren Südostasiens hingegen stammen die erstaunlichen Gehäuse der
Perlboote, die durch portugiesische und holländische Kaufleute im 16. und 17. Jahrhundert
nach Europa gelangten. Eine farbige Beschreibung des Nautilus pompilius (Schiffsboot),
eines Kopffüßers aus der Familie der Cephalopoda, findet sich in dem Werk *Ricreazione
dell'occhio e della mente* (1681) des Jesuitenpaters Filippo Buonanni (1638–1725): „Es
ist kein Fisch, sondern ein Kopffüßer mit einem Gehäuse, das so wunderschön ist, dass
es, gesäubert und mit einem vergoldeten Metallfuß versehen, als Servierschüssel auf
jeder hochherrschaftlichen Tafel eine wahre Augenweide abgibt." Und er hat recht: In
Kombination mit raffinierten Halterungen und einfallsreicher Goldschmiedearbeit ent-
stehen aus diesen Gehäusen, *Naturalia* und *Mirabilia* zugleich, wundersame Kunstwerke.

◉ ❖ ◉

Une fois franchi le seuil du Museo degli Argenti du palais Pitti, quelle n'est pas la
surprise du visiteur en constatant que la présence de l'argenterie y est discrète. En réalité,
le musée reçut ce nom il y a deux siècles, lorsque la salle peinte à fresque par Giovanni
da San Giovanni (1592–1636) fut choisie pour accueillir l'« argenterie ancienne » provenant de Salzbourg que Ferdinand III (1769–1824) avait rapportée à Florence en 1814. Par

ailleurs, le musée abrite ce qui subsiste du Trésor des grands-ducs de Toscane, le seul Trésor princier demeuré en Italie. Depuis 2019, le musée est appelé avec justesse Tesoro dei Granduchi.

Véritable coffre aux merveilles, le musée conserve les camées et les bijoux de la fabuleuse collection de l'électrice Anne-Marie-Louise de Médicis (1667–1743), dernière descendante de l'illustre Maison, des objets en ambre de la Baltique, des vases en pierre dure sortis des ateliers d'artisans milanais, des nautiles du Pacifique, les sculptures en ivoire réunies par les grands-ducs et par Léopold de Médicis (1617–1675), cardinal et mécène. Au nombre des curiosités les plus extraordinaires par leur aspect et leur histoire, les ivoires et les nautiles occupent assurément une place de choix. Fragiles et pleins de fantaisie, les vingt-sept vases, dits « ivoires de Cobourg », sont un butin de guerre : ils furent pillés le 28 septembre 1632, lors du sac de Cobourg durant la guerre de Trente Ans. À l'exception de quatre globes montés sur tige, il s'agit de coupes avec couvercle. Leurs éléments principaux adoptent les formes les plus étranges : disques déformés, spirales, colonnes moulurées et historiées ; quant aux éléments terminaux, ils sont d'une facture très sophistiquée : serpents, bouquets de fleurs, étoiles, globes dans des globes. Réalisés entre 1618 et 1631, certains portent la signature de Marcus Heiden (actif entre 1618 et 1664), connu comme « maître des feux d'artifice et des fusils ». L'extravagance de leurs formes est le fruit de l'enthousiasme de leurs créateurs et de la virtuosité permise par l'utilisation d'un tour de précision – un égal enthousiasme les animait en matière de mécanique, de géométrie et de sciences naturelles. Quant aux stupéfiants coquillages pêchés dans les mers du Sud, ils furent rapportés en Europe aux 16e et 17e siècles par des marchands portugais et hollandais. Une savoureuse description du Nautilus pompilius, mollusque de la classe des céphalopodes, est fournie par la *Ricreazione dell'occhio e della mente* (1681) du père jésuite Filippo Buonanni (1638–1725) qui écrit : « Ce n'est pas un poisson, mais un coquillage pourvu d'une belle maison qui, nettoyée et fixée sur un beau pied de métal doré, fait habituellement office de coupe sur les tables des grands seigneurs. » Et de fait, enchâssées dans des montures de métal raffinées et décorées par des orfèvres imaginatifs, ces coquilles de mollusques, *naturalia* et *mirabilia* à la fois, se métamorphosent en d'originales et merveilleuses compositions.

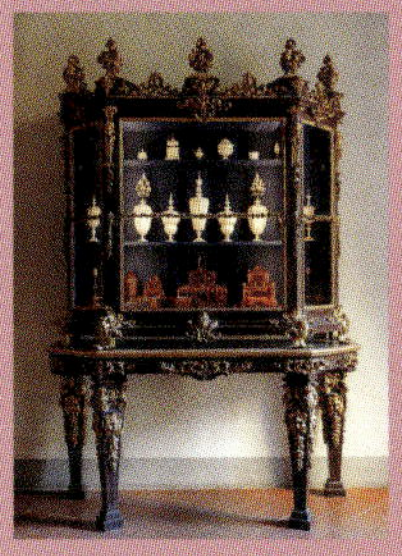

1

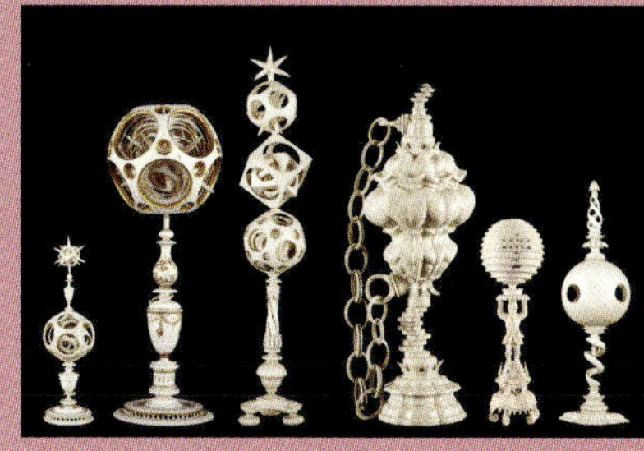

2

The lathe-turned ivories featured here are part of the Tesoro dei Granduchi (Treasury of the Grand Dukes), and are of German manufacture. The most famous among them are the so-called Coburg Ivories, a group of 27 goblets produced between 1618 and 1631 for the Duke of Coburg, subsequently seized by Mattias de' Medici in 1632 following the sack of that city.
Die hier gezeigten, in Deutschland hergestellten Drechselarbeiten aus Elfenbein gehören zur großherzoglichen Schatzkammer (Tesoro dei Granduchi). Die berühmtesten unter ihnen sind die sogenannten Coburger Elfenbeinarbeiten: eine Gruppe, bestehend aus 27 Pokalen, die zwischen 1618 und 1631 für den Herzog von Coburg geschaffen wurden und die Mattias de' Medici 1632 nach der Plünderung der Stadt erwarb.
Les ivoires tournés présentés ici font partie du Trésor des Grands-Ducs (Tesoro dei Granduchi), et sont de fabrication allemande. Les plus célèbres d'entre eux sont les dits ivoires de Cobourg, un ensemble de 27 vases exécutés entre 1618 et 1631 pour le duc de Cobourg, et acquis par Matthias de Médicis en 1632 après le sac de la ville.

1 *Scarabattola* (display case) in the Amber Room, containing ivory and amber objects from the Treasury of the Grand Dukes, constructed in Florence for the Grand Dukes, 1728.
Großherzogliche Florentiner Manufaktur, *Scarabattola* (Vitrine) im Bernsteinzimmer, in der Elfenbein- und Bernsteinarbeiten aus der großherzoglichen Sammlung ausgestellt sind, 1728.
Manufacture grand-ducale de Florence, *Scarabattola* (vitrine) dans la Salle d'ambre ; construite en 1728, elle contient des objets en ivoire et en ambre du Trésor des Grands-Ducs.

2a *Ornamental polyhedron*, Germany, c. 1600. Ivory, 16.8 cm / 6⅝ in. Chalice stem with planes displaced in relation to the vertical axis.
Polyeder, Deutschland, um 1600. Elfenbein, 16,8 cm. Schaft mit im Verhältnis zur vertikalen Achse verschobenen Ebenen.
Polyèdre ornemental, Allemagne, vers 1600. Ivoire, 16,8 cm. Tige de calice avec des plans décalés par rapport à l'axe vertical.

2b *Spheres with polyhedra*, Germany, late 16th/early 17th century. Ivory partly painted in gold, 28.6 cm / 11¼ in. Through the circular openings of the outer globe can be seen eight further globes nested inside each other and also polyhedra that similarly enclose a polyhedron with eight protruding points.
Contrefait-Kugel, Deutschland, Ende 16. / Anfang 17. Jh. Elfenbein teilweise mit Gold bemalt, 28,6 cm. Durch die runden Öffnungen der Kugel erkennt man im Inneren die anderen acht Polygone, die um eine Stachelkugel mit acht Spitzen angeordnet sind.
Sphères à polyèdres, Allemagne, fin du 16e siècle, début du 17e siècle. Ivoire en partie doré, 28,6 cm. À l'intérieur du globe montrant des ouvertures circulaires, huit autres globes et des polyèdres similaires entourent un polyèdre à huit pointes.

2c *Polyhedra, star and cubes*, Germany, c. 1600. Ivory, 34 cm / 13⅜ in.
Polyeder, Stern und Würfel, Deutschland, um 1600. Elfenbein, 34 cm.
Polyèdres, étoile et cubes, Allemagne, vers 1600. Ivoire, 34 cm.

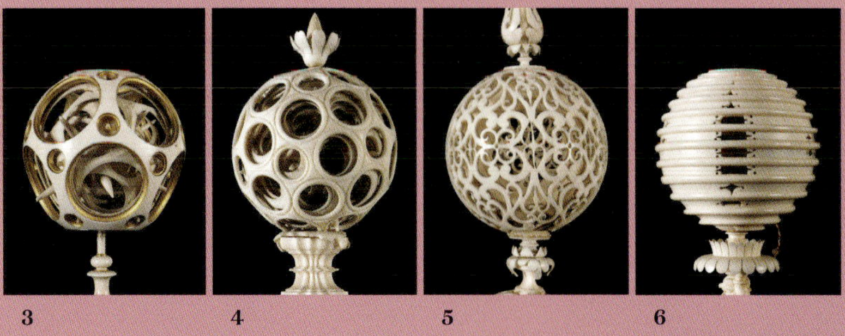

3   4   5   6

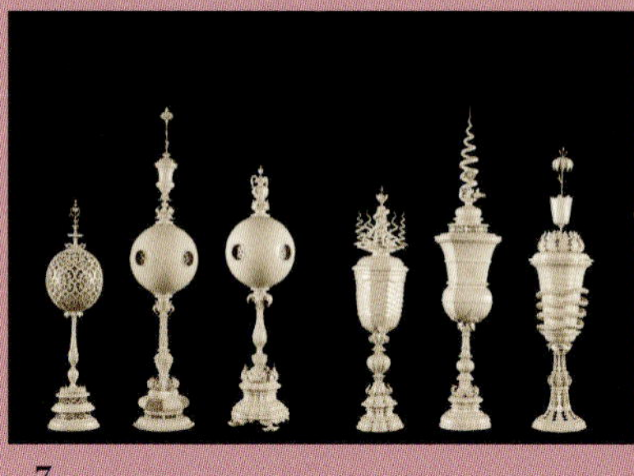

7

2d Johann Eisenberg, *Ornamental goblet with lid*, 1626. Ivory, 30.5 cm / 12 in. The lid is attached to the goblet with a chain made of 16 oval rings, plus two fixed rings that are part of the main structure.
Johann Eisenberg, *Deckelpokal*, 1626. Elfenbein, 30,5 cm. Der Pokal ist durch eine Kette aus 16 ovalen sowie zwei unbeweglichen Ringen fest mit seinem Deckel verbunden.
Johann Eisenberg, *Vase ornemental et son couvercle*, 1626. Ivoire, 30,5 cm. Le vase est attaché à son couvercle par une chaîne composée de 16 anneaux ovales et de deux anneaux fixes qui font partie de la structure principale.

2e Marcus Heiden, *Openwork globe supported by the figure of a hunter*, 1628. Ivory, signed and dated with engraved motto, 18.5 cm / 7¼ in.
Marcus Heiden, *Kunststück*, 1628. Elfenbein, signiert, datiert, mit graviertem Motto, 18,5 cm. Die durchbrochen gearbeitete Contrefait-Kugel wird von einem Jäger getragen.

Marcus Heiden, *Globe ajouré soutenu par la figure d'un chasseur*, 1628. Ivoire, signé et daté avec devise gravée, 18,5 cm.

2f *Sphere with portraits*, Nuremberg, 1618–1620. Ivory, 21.9 cm / 8⅝ in. Sphere with openings which reveal miniatures of the Grand Dukes Cosimo II and Ferdinand II. Spiral shaft and three-stemmed finial following a spiral movement.
Contrefait-Kugel, Nürnberg, 1618–1620, Elfenbein, 21,9 cm. Durch die Öffnungen sieht man im Inneren Miniaturporträts der Großherzöge Cosimo II. und Ferdinand II. Spiralförmiger Schaft und dreiteilige Bekrönung als Abschluss der Spiralbewegung.
Boule à portraits, Nuremberg, 1618–1620. Ivoire, 21,9 cm. Globe à ouvertures circulaires révélant les miniatures des grands ducs Côme II et Ferdinand II. Arbre spiralé et épi à trois tiges suivant un mouvement en spirale.

3 *Spheres with polyhedra* (detail of no. 2b), Germany, late 16th/early 17th century. Ivory, partly painted in gold, 28.6 cm / 11¼ in. Through the globe's circular openings can be seen eight further globes nested inside it, together with polyhedra that similarly enclose a polyhedron with eight protruding points.
Contrefait-Kugeln (Detail von Nr. 2b), Deutschland, Ende 16. Jh. / frühes 17. Jh., Elfenbein, teilweise mit Gold bemalt, 28,6 cm. Durch die runden Öffnungen erkennt man im Inneren weitere acht Polyeder, die um eine Stachelkugel mit acht Spitzen angeordnet sind.
Sphères avec polyèdres (détail du n° 2b), Allemagne, fin 16e siècle, début 17e siècle. Ivoire en partie doré, 28,6 cm. À l'intérieur du globe montrant des ouvertures circulaires, il y a huit autres globes et des polyèdres similaires qui entourent un polyèdre à huit pointes en saillie.

4 *Ornamental goblet with lid* (detail of no. 10e), Coburg, 1618–1631. Ivory, 47.5 cm / 18¾ in.
Dekorativer Deckelpokal (Detail von Nr. 10e), Coburg, 1618–1631. Elfenbein, 47,5 cm.

Vase ornemental et son couvercle (détail du n° 10e), Cobourg, 1618–1631. Ivoire, 47,5 cm.

5 Johann Casimir of Saxe-Coburg, *Goblet with lid* (detail of no. 10d), 1618–1631. Ivory, 42.9 cm / 16⅞ in. The lid features a double crown of leaves and a finely perforated cap that supports a sphere which in turn contains a medallion. At the very top is a small stem with four flowers, one of which has no petals.
Johann Casimir von Sachsen-Coburg, *Deckelpokal* (Detail von Nr. 10d), 1618–1631. Elfenbein, 42,9 cm. Ein doppelter Blätterkranz ziert den Deckel. Auf der fein gearbeiteten, durchbrochenen Kalotte ruht eine gedrechselte Contrefait-Kugel, die ein Medaillon umschließt. Den Abschluss bildet ein kleiner Ast mit vier Blüten, von denen eine keine Blätter hat.
Johann Casimir de Saxe-Cobourg, *Vase et son couvercle* (détail du n° 10d), 1618–1631. Ivoire, 42,9 cm. Le couvercle présente une double couronne de feuilles et un capuchon finement perforé qui soutient une sphère contenant un médaillon. Au sommet, il y a une petite branche avec quatre fleurs, dont l'une n'a pas de pétales.

6 Marcus Heiden, *Openwork globe supported by the figure of a hunter* (detail of no. 2e), 1628. Ivory, signed and dated with engraved motto, 18.5 cm / 7¼ in.
Marcus Heiden, *Kunststück* (Detail von Nr. 2e), 1628. Elfenbein, signiert, datiert, mit graviertem Motto, 18,5 cm. Die durchbrochen gearbeitete Contrefait-Kugel wird von einem Jäger getragen.
Marcus Heiden, *Globe ajouré soutenu par la figure d'un chasseur* (détail du n° 2e), 1628. Ivoire, signé et daté avec devise gravée, 18,5 cm.

7a *Globe*, Coburg, 1618–1631. Partly painted ivory, 35.6 cm / 14 in. The globe contains a moulded oval medallion featuring two miniature images depicting the Crucifixion and the Resurrection.
Contrefait-Kugel, Coburg, 1618–1631. Teilweise polychromes Elfenbein, 35,6 cm. Im Innern der Kugel befindet sich ein ovales Medaillon mit zwei Miniaturen, die die Kreuzigung und die Auferstehung zeigen.
Globe, Cobourg, 1618–1631. Ivoire en partie peint, 35,6 cm. Le globe contient un médaillon ovale moulé avec deux miniatures représentant la Crucifixion et la Résurrection.

7b *Globe, containing other globes*, Coburg, 1618–1631. Ivory, 50 cm / 19¾ in.
Mehrteilige Contrefait-Kugel, Coburg, 1618–1631. Elfenbein, 50 cm.
Globe, contenant d'autres globes, Cobourg, 1618–1631. Ivoire, 50 cm.

7c Johann Eisenberg, *Globe*, 1623. Ivory, 41 cm / 16⅛ in. The globe has four circular openings, through which seven further globes can be seen nested one inside the other, and at the centre is a polyhedron with protruding vertices.
Johann Eisenberg, *Contrefait-Kugel*, 1623. Elfenbein, 41 cm. Durch die vier Öffnungen der Kugel erkennt man sieben gegeneinander bewegliche, um eine Stachelkugel angeordnete Polygone.
Johann Eisenberg, *Globe*, 1623. Ivoire, 41 cm. Le globe présente quatre ouvertures circulaires permettant de voir sept autres globes, l'un à l'intérieur de l'autre, avec au centre un polyèdre aux sommets saillants.

7d Johann Eisenberg, *Chalice with lid and snake ornamentation*, 1625. Ivory, 38 cm / 15 in.
Johann Eisenberg, *Deckelkelch mit Schlangendekor*, 1625. Elfenbein, 38 cm.
Johann Eisenberg, *Calice et son couvercle orné d'un serpent*, 1625. Ivoire, 38 cm.

7e Marcus Heiden and Johann Eisenberg (attrib.), *Ornamental goblet with lid*, 1618–1631. Ivory, 50 cm / 19¾ in.
Marcus Heiden und Johann Eisenberg (zugeschrieben), *Deckelpokal*, 1618–1631. Elfenbein, 50 cm.
Marcus Heiden et Johann Eisenberg (attribué à), *Vase ornemental et son couvercle*, 1618–1631. Ivoire, 50 cm.

7f *Goblet with lid*, Coburg, 1618–1631. Ivory, 44 cm / 17⅜ in.
Deckelpokal, Coburg, 1618–1631. Elfenbein, 44 cm.
Vase et son couvercle, Cobourg, 1618–1631. Ivoire, 44 cm.

8a Johann Eisenberg, *Goblet with lid*, 1625. Ivory, 45.5 cm / 17⅞ in. The body features arched bands shaped to resemble architectural elements. The lid is carved in the shape of an arrowhead.
Johann Eisenberg, *Deckelpokal*, 1625. Elfenbein, 45,5 cm. Der Kelch ist mit umlaufenden bogenförmigen Bändern geschmückt. Der Deckel ist in Form einer Pfeilspitze geschnitzt.
Johann Eisenberg, *Vase et son couvercle*, 1625. Ivoire, 45,5 cm. Le corps est orné de bandes arquées qui ressemblent à des éléments architecturaux. Le couvercle est sculpté en forme de pointe de flèche.

8b Johann Casimir of Saxe-Coburg, *Ornamental goblet with lid*, 1618. Ivory, signed and dated, with coat of arms, about 50 cm / 19¾ in.
Johann Casimir von Sachsen-Coburg, *Deckelpokal*, 1618. Elfenbein, signiert, datiert, mit Wappen, ca. 50 cm.
Johann Casimir de Saxe-Cobourg, *Vase ornemental et son couvercle*, 1618. Ivoire, signé et daté, avec armoiries, environ 50 cm.

8c Marcus Heiden, *Goblet with lid*, 1625. Ivory, 58.8 cm / 23⅛ in.
Marcus Heiden, *Deckelpokal*, 1625. Elfenbein, 58,8 cm.
Marcus Heiden, *Vase et son couvercle*, 1625. Ivoire, 58,8 cm.

8d Johann Eisenberg, *Goblet with lid*, 1624. Ivory, 59.5 cm / 23⅜ in. Elaborate top, suggesting the shape of an arrow, adorned with arabesque openwork with vegetal elements.

Johann Eisenberg, *Deckelpokal*, 1624. Elfenbein, 59,5 cm. Aufwendiger Deckel, der an einen Pfeil erinnert, geschmückt mit durchbrochenen Arabesken und Pflanzenmotiven.
Johann Eisenberg, *Vase et son couvercle*, 1624. Ivoire, 59,5 cm. Partie supérieure élaborée, rappelant une flèche, ornée d'arabesques ajourées avec éléments végétaux.

8e *Goblet with lid*, Germany, 1618–1631. Ivory, 48 cm / 18⅞ in. The lid is surmounted by garlands of leaves curling sinuously at the ends. From the centre of the second garland rises a small column with a shaped stem, surmounted by a polyhedron with protruding points. On top of this is a slender stem ending in a bell-shaped flower.
Deckelpokal, Deutschland, 1618–1631. Elfenbein, 48 cm. Der Deckel ist mit geschwungenen Blättergirlanden geschmückt. Aus der Mitte der zweiten erhebt sich eine kleine Säule mit einer Stachelkugel auf modelliertem Stängel. Den Abschluss bildet ein zarter Stängel mit glockenförmiger Blume.
Vase et son couvercle, Allemagne, 1618–1631. Ivoire, 48 cm. Le couvercle est surmonté de guirlandes de feuilles aux extrémités ondoyantes. Du centre de la deuxième guirlande s'élève une petite colonne avec une tige, surmontée d'un polyèdre à pointes. Au sommet se trouve une tige élancée, terminée par une fleur en forme de clochette.

8f Johann Eisenberg, *Goblet with lid*, 1624. Ivory, 41.5 cm / 16⅜ in. The body is shaped like a fruit, inspired by the form of a *Traubenpokal* (a grape cup).
Johann Eisenberg, *Deckelpokal*, 1624, Elfenbein, 41,5 cm. Als Anregung dieser wie eine Frucht geformten Cuppa diente vermutlich ein Traubenpokal.
Johann Eisenberg, *Vase et son couvercle*, 1624. Ivoire, 41,5 cm. Le corps a la forme d'un fruit, inspiré d'une *Coupe aux raisins*.

9a *Goblet with lid*, Coburg, 1618–1631. Ivory, 62 cm / 24⅜ in.
Deckelpokal, Coburg, 1618–1631. Elfenbein, 62 cm.
Vase et son couvercle, Cobourg, 1618–1631. Ivoire, 62 cm.

9b Johann Eisenberg, *Goblet with lid*, 1623, signed and dated. Ivory, 60.4 cm / 23¾ in. Chalice with lid and decorative finishing.
Johann Eisenberg, *Deckelpokal*, 1623, signiert und datiert. Elfenbein, 60,4 cm. Deckelpokal mit dekorativen Details.
Johann Eisenberg, *Vase et son couvercle*, 1623, signé et daté. Ivoire, 60,4 cm. Calice à couvercle et finitions décoratives.

9c Johann Eisenberg, *Goblet with lid*, 1631. Ivory, 60.5 cm / 23⅞ in. Chalice with lid and decorative finishing, featuring the name and coat of arms of the Duke of Saxe-Coburg.
Johann Eisenberg, *Deckelpokal*, 1631. Elfenbein, 60,5 cm. Deckelpokal mit dekorativen Details sowie dem Namen des Herzogs von Sachsen-Coburg und seinem Wappen.
Johann Eisenberg, *Vase et son couvercle*, 1631. Ivoire, 60,5 cm. Calice à couvercle et finitions décoratives. Il porte le nom du duc de Saxe-Cobourg et ses armoiries.

9d Johann Eisenberg, *Goblet with lid*, 1628. Ivory, 54.5 cm / 21½ in. The lid supports a sumptuous crowning which ends in a six-armed flowered chandelier, at the centre of which is a small stem with flower buds and leaves.
Johann Eisenberg, *Deckelpokal*, 1628. Elfenbein, 54,5 cm. Den Deckel dieses Pokals bekrönt ein beeindruckender sechsarmiger Kronleuchter, in dessen Mitte man einen kleinen Zweig mit Knospen und Blättern erkennen kann.
Johann Eisenberg, *Vase et son couvercle*, 1628. Ivoire, 54,5 cm. Le couvercle est surmonté d'une somptueuse couronne au sommet de laquelle repose un lustre à six branches fleuries, au centre duquel se trouve une petite branche avec des boutons de fleurs et des feuilles.

9e *Goblet with lid*, Germany, 1618–1631. Ivory, 56.3 cm / 22⅛ in. The lid features a lantern with openwork mirrors and a long flower stem. On the pistil is a thin ivory plate, perforated and carved with the image of a deer leaping away to escape from a dog.
Deckelpokal, Deutschland, 1618–1631. Elfenbein, 56,3 cm. Den Deckel bekrönt eine Laterne mit durchbrochenen Spiegeln und langem Blütenstängel. Der Stempel ist mit einem zarten, durchbrochen gearbeiteten Elfenbeinplättchen besetzt, in das die Darstellung eines springenden Rehs, das vor einem Jagdhund flieht, geschnitzt ist.
Vase et son couvercle, Allemagne, 1618–1631. Ivoire, 56,3 cm. Le couvercle comporte une lanterne avec des miroirs ajourés et une longue tige de fleur. Sur le pistil est posée une fine plaque d'ivoire, perforée et sculptée, représentant un cerf sautant pour échapper à un chien.

9f *Goblet with lid*, Germany, 1618–1631. Ivory, 51.5 cm / 20¼ in. The lid features a lantern surmounted by a carved and openwork medallion depicting a prancing lion. The ensemble is crowned by a crescent moon with one eye and human features.
Deckelpokal, Deutschland, 1618–1631. Elfenbein, 51,5 cm. Der Deckel ist mit einem geschnitzten und durchbrochen gearbeiteten Medaillon mit aufsteigendem Löwen bekrönt. Den Abschluss bildet eine Mondsichel mit menschlichem Antlitz.
Vase et son couvercle, Allemagne, 1618–1631. Ivoire, 51,5 cm. Le couvercle est orné d'une lanterne surmontée d'un médaillon sculpté et ajouré représentant un lion rampant. L'ensemble est couronné d'un croissant de lune avec profil humain borgne.

10a Marcus Heiden, *Goblet with lid*, 1623/24. Ivory, 61.2 cm / 24⅛ in.
Marcus Heiden, *Deckelpokal*, 1623/24. Elfenbein, 61,2 cm.
Marcus Heiden, *Vase et son couvercle*, 1623/24. Ivoire, 61,2 cm.

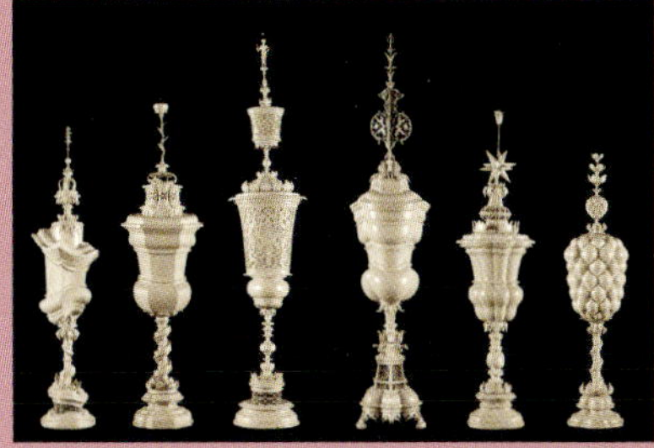

8

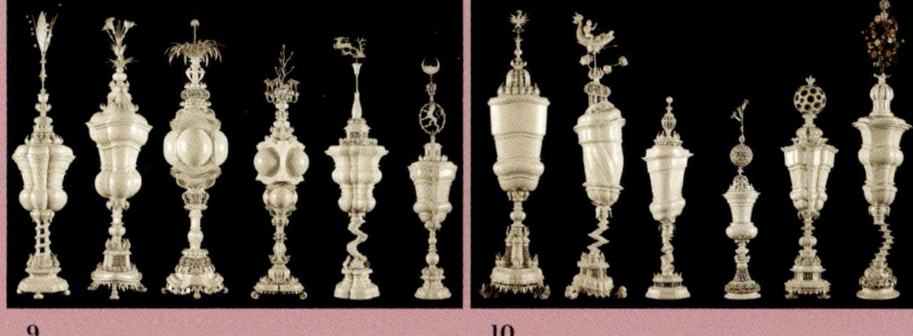

9   10

10b Marcus Heiden, *Goblet with lid*, 1626. Ivory, 60.8 cm / 24 in. Composed of a perforated open lantern surmounted by a putto riding a dolphin.
Marcus Heiden, *Deckelpokal*, 1626. Elfenbein, 60,8 cm. Deckelpokal mit durchbrochen gearbeiteter offener Laterne, bekrönt durch einen auf einem Delfin reitenden Putto.
Marcus Heiden, *Vase et son couvercle*, 1626. Ivoire, 60,8 cm. Composé d'une lanterne perforée surmontée d'un putto chevauchant un dauphin.

10c Marcus Heiden, *Ornamental goblet with lid*, 1627, signed and dated, with a poem by the Duke of Saxe-Coburg. Ivory, 43 cm / 16⅞ in.
Marcus Heiden, *Deckelpokal*, 1627, signiert und datiert, mit einem Gedicht des Herzogs von Sachsen-Coburg. Elfenbein, 43 cm.
Marcus Heiden, *Vase ornemental et son couvercle*, 1627, signé et daté, avec un poème du duc de Saxe-Cobourg. Ivoire et paint, 43 cm.

10d Johann Casimir of Saxe-Coburg, *Goblet with lid*, 1618–1631. Ivory, 42.9 cm / 16⅞ in. The lid features a double crown of leaves and a finely perforated cap that supports a sphere which in turn contains a medallion. At the very top is a small stem with four flowers, one of which has no petals.
Johann Casimir von Sachsen-Coburg, *Deckelpokal*, 1618–1631. Elfenbein, 42,9 cm. Ein doppelter Blätterkranz ziert den Deckel. Auf der fein gearbeiteten, durchbrochenen Kalotte ruht eine gedrechselte Contrefait-Kugel, die ein Medaillon umschließt. Den Abschluss bildet ein kleiner Ast mit vier Blüten, von denen eine keine Blätter hat.
Johann Casimir de Saxe-Cobourg, *Vase et son couvercle*, 1618–1631. Ivoire, 42,9 cm. Le couvercle présente une double couronne de feuilles et un capuchon finement perforé qui soutient une sphère contenant un médaillon. Au sommet, il y a une petite branche avec quatre fleurs, dont l'une n'a pas de pétales.

10e *Ornamental goblet with lid*, Coburg, 1618–1631. Ivory, 47.5 cm / 18¾ in.
Deckelpokal, Coburg, 1618–1631. Elfenbein, 47,5 cm.
Vase ornemental et son couvercle, Cobourg, 1618–1631. Ivoire, 47,5 cm.

10f *Goblet with lid*, Germany, 1618–1631. Ivory, metal and fabric, 64 cm / 25¼ in. The lid is crowned by a lantern with a segmented cover into which is inserted a posy of flowers with metal wire stems covered with fabric and partly painted ivory petals.
Deckelpokal, Deutschland, 1618–1631. Elfenbein, Metall und Stoff, 64 cm. Der Deckel wird durch eine Laterne mit einer gegliederten Abdeckung bekrönt, in die ein Blumenstrauß aus Metalldraht, bezogen mit Stoff und teils bemalten Elfenbeinblütenblättern, eingesetzt ist.
Vase et son couvercle, Allemagne, 1618–1631. Ivoire, métal et tissu, 64 cm. Le couvercle est surmonté d'une lanterne à partie supérieure

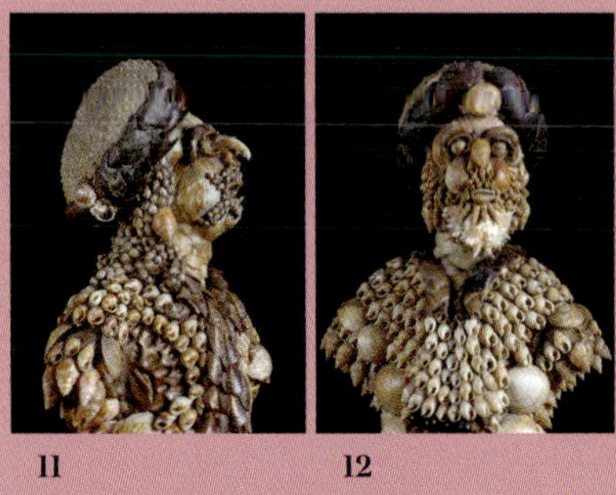

11   12

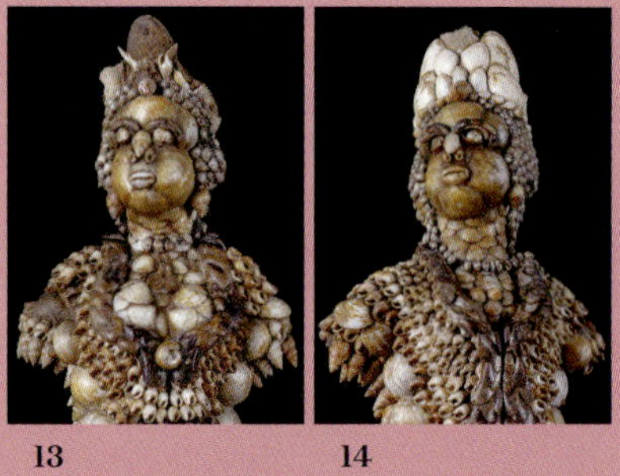

13   14

segmentée sur laquelle est inséré un bouquet de fleurs. Leurs tiges en fil de métal sont recouvertes de tissu, et les pétales en ivoire sont en partie peints.

11–14 *Arcimboldo figures*, Germany, 17th century. Wood covered with seashells. *Arcimboldeske Figuren*, Deutschland, 17. Jh. Holz mit Muscheln besetzt. *Figures arcimboldesques*, Allemagne, 17e siècle. Bois recouvert de coquillages.

15 *Ornamental cup*, Germany, c. 1600. Nautilus shell mounted as a boat with a man seated at the stern. The foot has a shell that forms the body of a turtle. Cantilever silver base, 35.5 cm / 14 in. *Pokal*, Deutschland, um 1600. Nautilus mit einer Fassung in Form eines Schiffes, an dessen Heck ein Mann sitzt. Der Fuß ist mit einer schildkrötenförmigen Muschel geschmückt; ausladender Silberfuß, 35,5 cm.

Coupe ornementale, Allemagne, vers 1600. Nautile en forme de nef avec un homme assis à l'arrière. Pied avec un coquillage monté en forme de tortue sur socle en argent, 35,5 cm.

16 *Ornamental cup*, Germany, c. 1640. Nautilus shell with a silver and gilt bronze setting featuring mermaids, sea-horses, chains and a man riding a snail. The foot consists of an oriental figure leading a lion on a leash, 33.5 cm / 13¼ in. *Pokal*, Deutschland, um 1640. Nautilus mit einer Fassung aus Silber, vergoldeter Bronze, mit Meerjungfrauen, Seepferdchen, Ketten und einem Mann, der auf einer Schnecke reitet. Der Fuß zeigt einen Orientalen, der einen Löwen an der Leine führt, 33,5 cm. *Coupe ornementale*, Allemagne, vers 1640. Nautile, monture en argent et bronze doré avec décor de sirènes, d'hippocampes, de chaînes, surmonté d'un homme chevauchant un escargot. Pied avec personnage oriental menant un lion en laisse, 33,5 cm.

17a *Cup*, Italy, 16th century. Nautilus shell with a gilt-silver setting in the shape of a lion's head. Foot with mermaids and dolphins, 17th century, 15.5 x 13 cm / 6⅛ x 5⅛ in. *Pokal*, Italien, 16. Jh. Nautilus mit einer Fassung aus vergoldetem Silber in Form eines Löwenkopfes. Der Fuß ist mit Meerjungfrauen und Delfinen verziert, 17. Jh., 15,5 x 13 cm. *Coupe*, Italie, 16e siècle. Nautile avec monture en vermeil en forme de tête de lion. Pied orné de sirènes et de dauphins, 17e siècle, 15,5 x 13 cm.

17b *Mesciroba* (pitcher), Flemish, 16th century. Double nautilus shell with engraved gilt-silver setting, encrusted with rubies and turquoises, 30 cm / 11¾ in. *Mesciroba (Krug)*, flämisch, 16. Jh. Doppelter Nautilus mit gravierter Silberfassung, mit Rubinen und Türkisen besetzt, 30 cm. *Mesciroba (cruche)*, flamand, 16e siècle. Nautile double avec monture en vermeil gravé et incrustations de rubis et de turquoises, 30 cm.

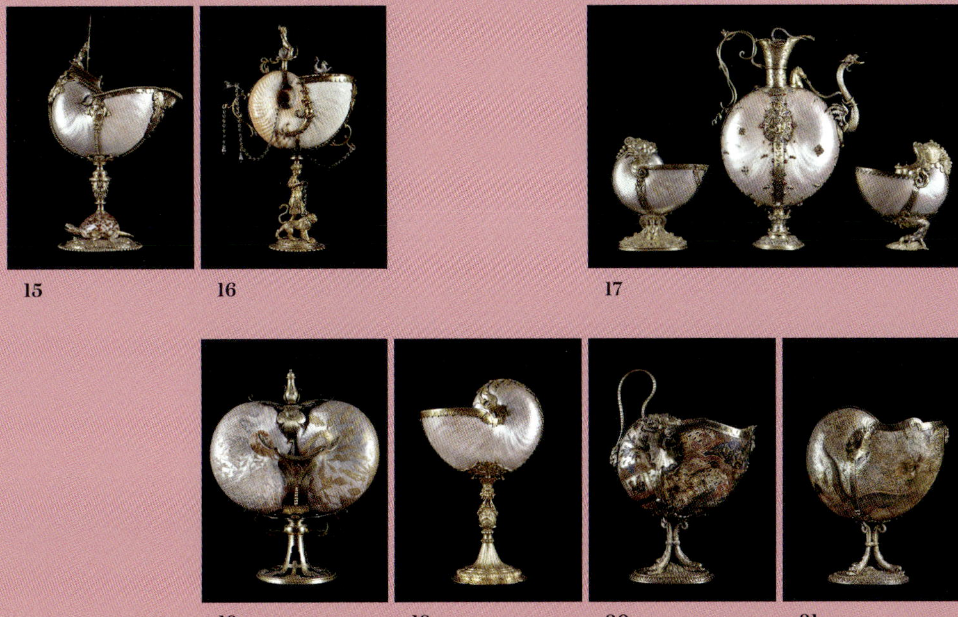

15   16   17

18   19   20   21

17c *Cup*, Germany, 16th century. Nautilus shell with silver-gilt setting in the shape of a lion's mouth. The eagle's foot rests on a gilt-bronze shell, 15 x 14 cm / 5⅞ x 5½ in.
Pokal, Deutschland, 16. Jh. Nautilus mit Fassung aus vergoldetem Silber in Form eines Löwenmauls. Der Adlerfuß ruht auf einer Muschel aus vergoldeter Bronze, 15 x 14 cm.
Coupe, Allemagne, 16ᵉ siècle. Nautile avec monture en vermeil en forme de gueule de lion. Pied d'un aigle reposant sur une coquille en bronze doré, 15 x 14 cm.

18 *Versatoio* (jug with spout), Flemish or German, first half of the 16th century. Double nautilus shell with floral gilt carvings of Chinese origin. Silver-gilt setting, 26 cm / 10¼ in.
Versatoio (Krug mit Ausguss), flämisch oder deutsch, erste Hälfte 16. Jh. Doppelter Nautilus mit chinesisch inspirierten, floralen Gravuren. Fassung aus vergoldetem Silber, 26 cm.

Versatoio (cruche à bec verseur), flamand ou allemand, première moitié du 16ᵉ siècle. Double nautile avec décor floral sculpté doré d'origine chinoise. Monture en vermeil, 26 cm.

19 *Cup*, Flemish, 17th century. Nautilus shell with gilt-bronze setting, 18th-century foot, 24.5 x 15 cm / 9¾ x 6 in.
Pokal, flämisch, 17. Jh. Nautilus mit Fassung aus vergoldeter Bronze, Fuß aus dem 18. Jh., 24,5 x 15 cm.
Coupe, flamande, 17ᵉ siècle. Nautile avec monture en bronze doré, pied du 18ᵉ siècle, 24,5 x 15 cm.

20 *Cup*, France, 16th century. Nautilus shell engraved with houses and trees, of Chinese origin. Gilt-silver setting, foot with three dolphins and with silver handle, 17 cm / 6¼ in.
Pokal, Frankreich, 16. Jh. Mit Häusern und Bäumen gravierter Nautilus, chinesisch inspiriert. Fassung aus vergoldetem Silber, Fuß mit drei Delfinen verziert, Silbergriff, 17 cm.

Coupe, France, 16ᵉ siècle. Nautile gravé de maisons et d'arbres, d'origine chinoise. Monture en vermeil. Pied formé de trois dauphins. Manche en argent, 17 cm.

21 *Cup*, France, 16th century. Nautilus shell engraved with dragons and scales, of Chinese origin. Gilt-silver setting, foot with three dolphins and with punch under the base, 17.5 cm / 6⅞ in.
Pokal, Frankreich, 16. Jh. Mit Drachen und Schuppen gravierter Nautilus, chinesisch inspiriert. Fassung aus vergoldetem Silber, Fuß mit drei Delfinen. Unter der Basis gestempelt, 17,5 cm.
Coupe, France, 16ᵉ siècle. Nautile gravé de dragons et d'écailles, d'origine chinoise. Monture en vermeil. Pied formé de trois dauphins. Poinçon sous le pied, 17,5 cm.

Collezione Lazzaro Spallanzani

Musei Civici di Reggio Emilia

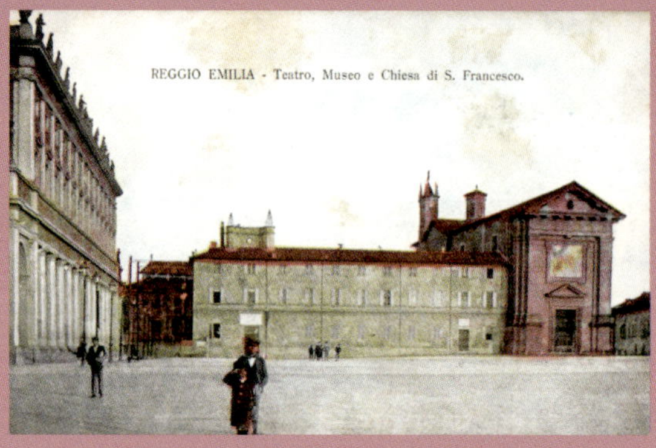

Founded *c.* 1775

Key item The collection of marine organisms—madrepores, sponges and corals.

Besonders sehenswert Die Sammlung von Meeresorganismen wie Steinkorallen, Schwämme und Korallen.

À voir absolument La collection des organismes marins, tels que les madrépores, éponges et les coraux.

Roberto Sevardi, *Reggio Emilia, Theatre, Museum and Church of San Francesco*, postcard, 9 x 14 cm (3⅝ x 5⅝ in.). Reggio Emilia, Biblioteca Panizzi.

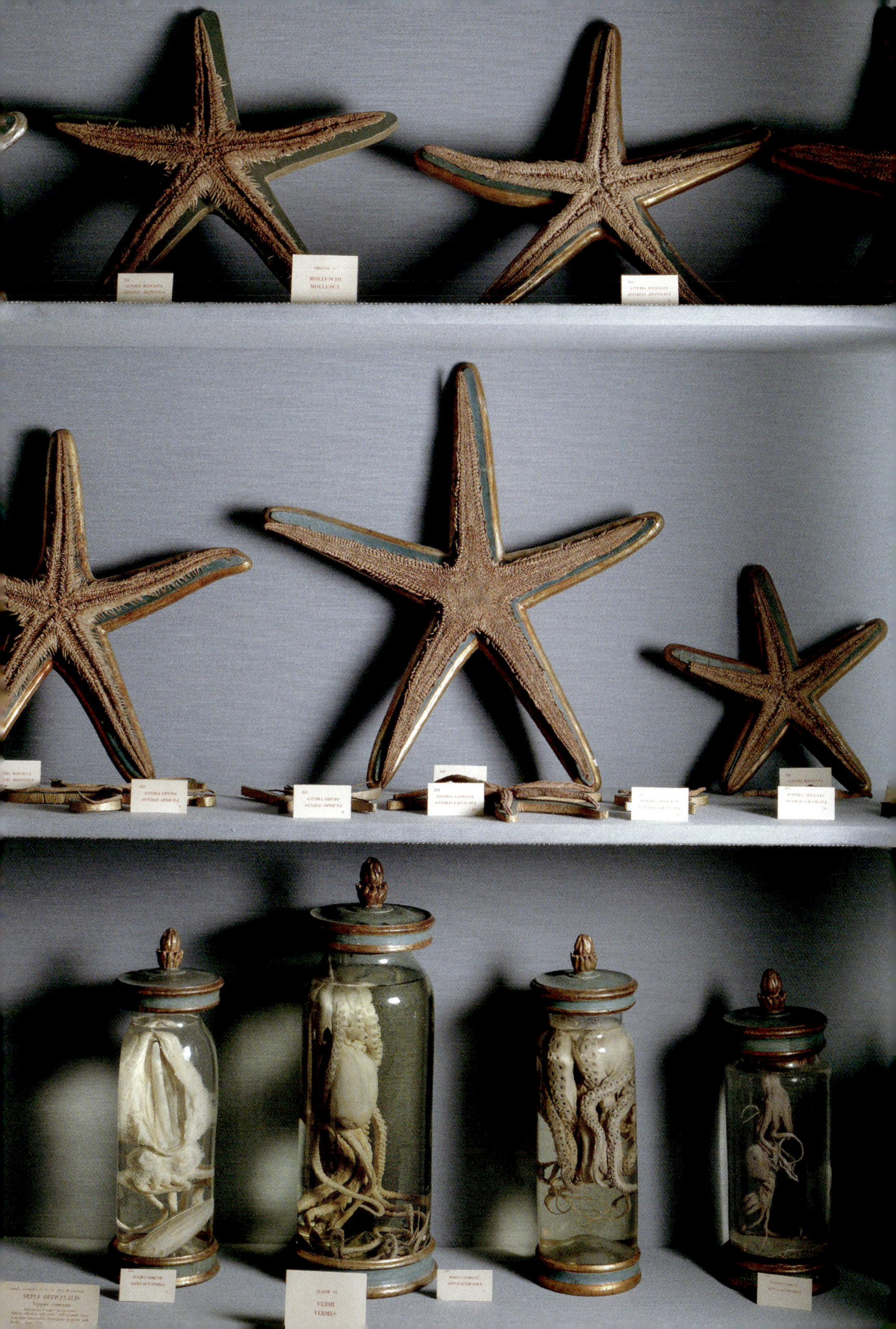

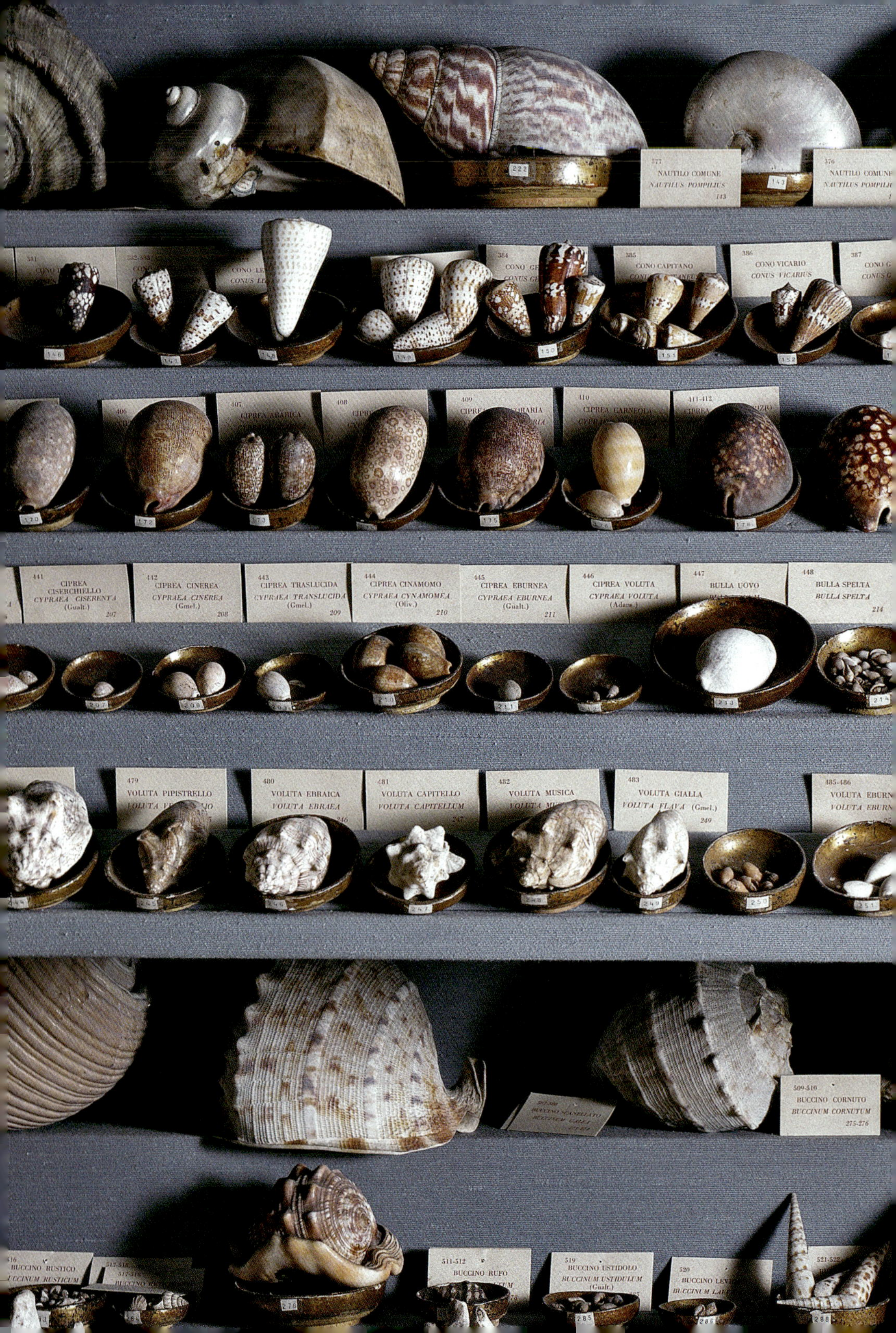

377 NAUTILO COMUNE NAUTILUS POMPILIUS 143
376 NAUTILO COMUNE NAUTILUS POMPILIU 1
381 CONO
382-383
CONO LE CONUS LE
384 CONO GE CONUS GE
385 CONO CAPITANO CONUS CTANEUS
386 CONO VICARIO CONUS VICARIUS
387 CONO G CONUS G
406
407 CIPREA ARABICA
408 CIPREA
409 CIPREA ORARIA RIA
410 CIPREA CARNEOLA CYPRAE
411-412 CIPREA IZIO
441 CIPREA CISERCHIELLO CYPRAEA CISERENTA (Gualt.) 207
442 CIPREA CINEREA CYPRAEA CINEREA (Gmel.) 208
443 CIPREA TRASLUCIDA CYPRAEA TRANSLUCIDA (Gmel.) 209
444 CIPREA CINAMOMO CYPRAEA CYNAMOMEA (Oliv.) 210
445 CIPREA EBURNEA CYPRAEA EBURNEA (Gualt.) 211
446 CIPREA VOLUTA CYPRAEA VOLUTA (Adans.)
447 BULLA UOVO BULLA
448 BULLA SPELTA BULLA SPELTA 214
479 VOLUTA PIPISTRELLO VOLUTA VE IO
480 VOLUTA EBRAICA VOLUTA EBRAEA 246
481 VOLUTA CAPITELLO VOLUTA CAPITELIUM 247
482 VOLUTA MUSICA VOLUTA MU
483 VOLUTA GIALLA VOLUTA FLAVA (Gmel.) 249
485-486 VOLUTA EBURN VOLUTA EBURN
509-510 BUCCINO CORNUTO BUCCINUM CORNUTUM 275-276
BUCCINO SCANELLATO BUCCINUM GALE
516 BUCCINO RUSTICO BUCCINUM RUSTICUM
517-518 BUCCINO RE
511-512 BUCCINO RUFO LTUM 278
519 BUCCINO USTIDOLO BUCCINUM USTIDULUM (Gualt.) 285
520 BUCCINO LEVE BUCCINUM LAE
521-522

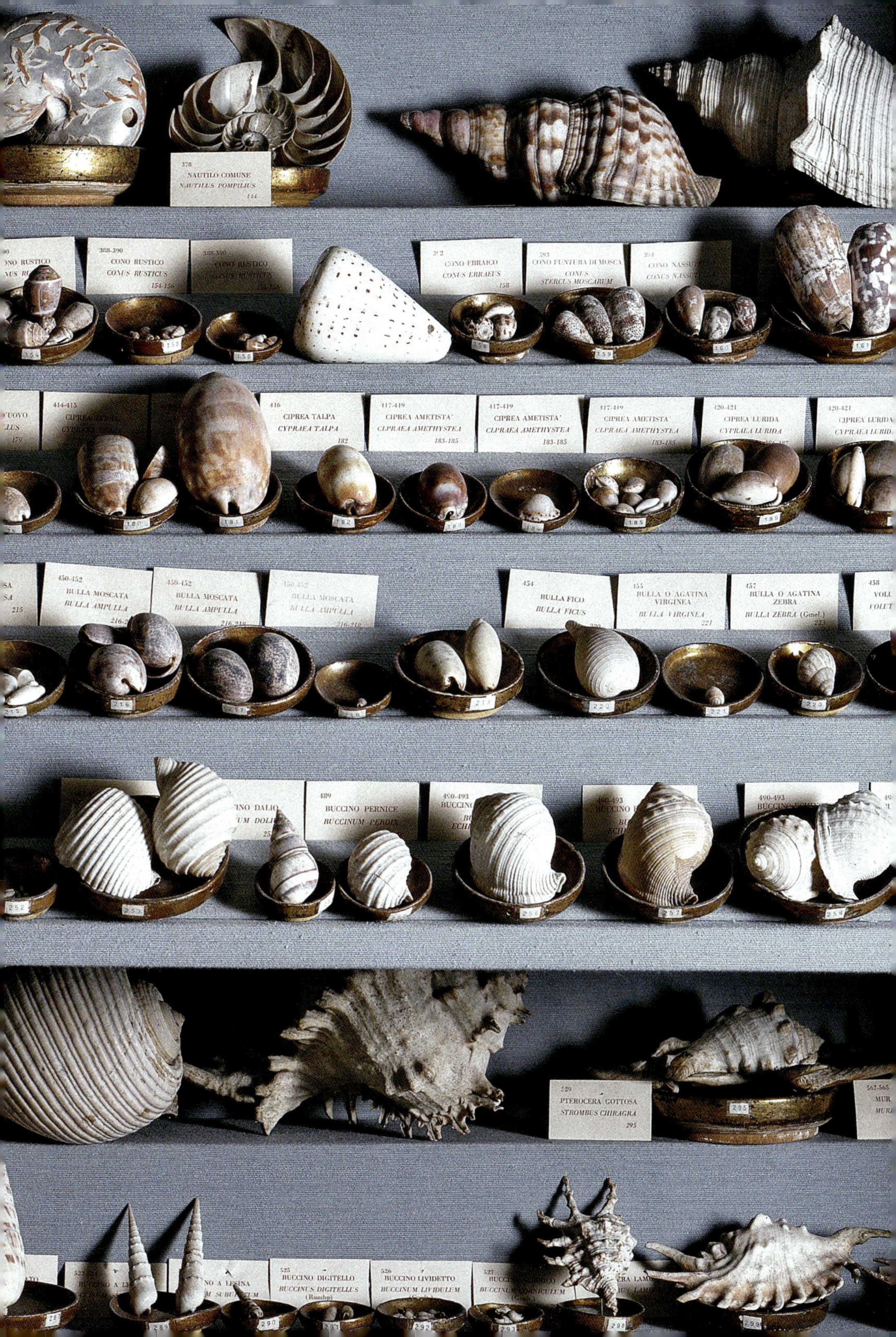

378
NAUTILO COMUNE
NAUTILUS POMPILIUS
144

CONO RUSTICO
CONUS RU...

388-390
CONO RUSTICO
CONUS RUSTICUS
154-156

388-390
CONO RUSTICO
CONUS RUSTICUS
154-156

3?2
CONO EBRAICO
CONUS EBRAEUS
158

393
CONO FUNTURA DI MOSCA
CONUS
STERCUS MOSCARUM
159

394
CONO NASSU...
CONUS N...

...UOVO
...US
179

414-415
CIPREA ...
CYPRAEA...

416
CIPREA TALPA
CYPRAEA TALPA
182

417-419
CIPREA AMETISTA'
CLPRAEA AMETHYSTEA
183-185

417-419
CIPREA AMETISTA'
CLPRAEA AMETHYSTEA
183-185

417-419
CIPREA AMETISTA
CLPRAEA AMETHYSTEA
183-185

420-421
CIPREA LURIDA
CYPRAEA LURIDA

420-421
CIPREA LURIDA
CYPRAEA LURID...

SA
215

450-452
BULLA MOSCATA
BULLA AMPULLA
216-2...

450-452
BULLA MOSCATA
BULLA AMPULLA
216-219

450-452
BULLA MOSCATA
BULLA AMPULLA
216-219

454
BULLA FICO
BULLA FICUS

455
BULLA O AGATINA
VIRGINEA
BULLA VIRGINEA
221

457
BULLA O AGATINA
ZEBRA
BULLA ZEBRA (Gmel.)
223

458
VOLU...
VOLUT...

...INO DALIO
...UM DOLI...

489
BUCCINO PERNICE
BUCCINUM PERDIX
25...

490-493
BUCCINO ...
ECHI...

490-493
BUCCINO ...
ECHI...

490-493
BUCCINO ...

529
PTEROCERA GOTTOSA
STROMBUS CHIRAGRA
295

562-565
MUR...
MUR...

523-524
BUCCINO A L...

...NO A LESINA
...M SUBULETUM

525
BUCCINO DIGITELLO
BUCCINUS DIGITELLUS
(Rumph)

526
BUCCINO LIVIDETTO
BUCCINUM LIVIDULUM

527
BUCCINO ...
BUCCINUM CORNICULUM

...ERA LAMB...
...US LAMB...

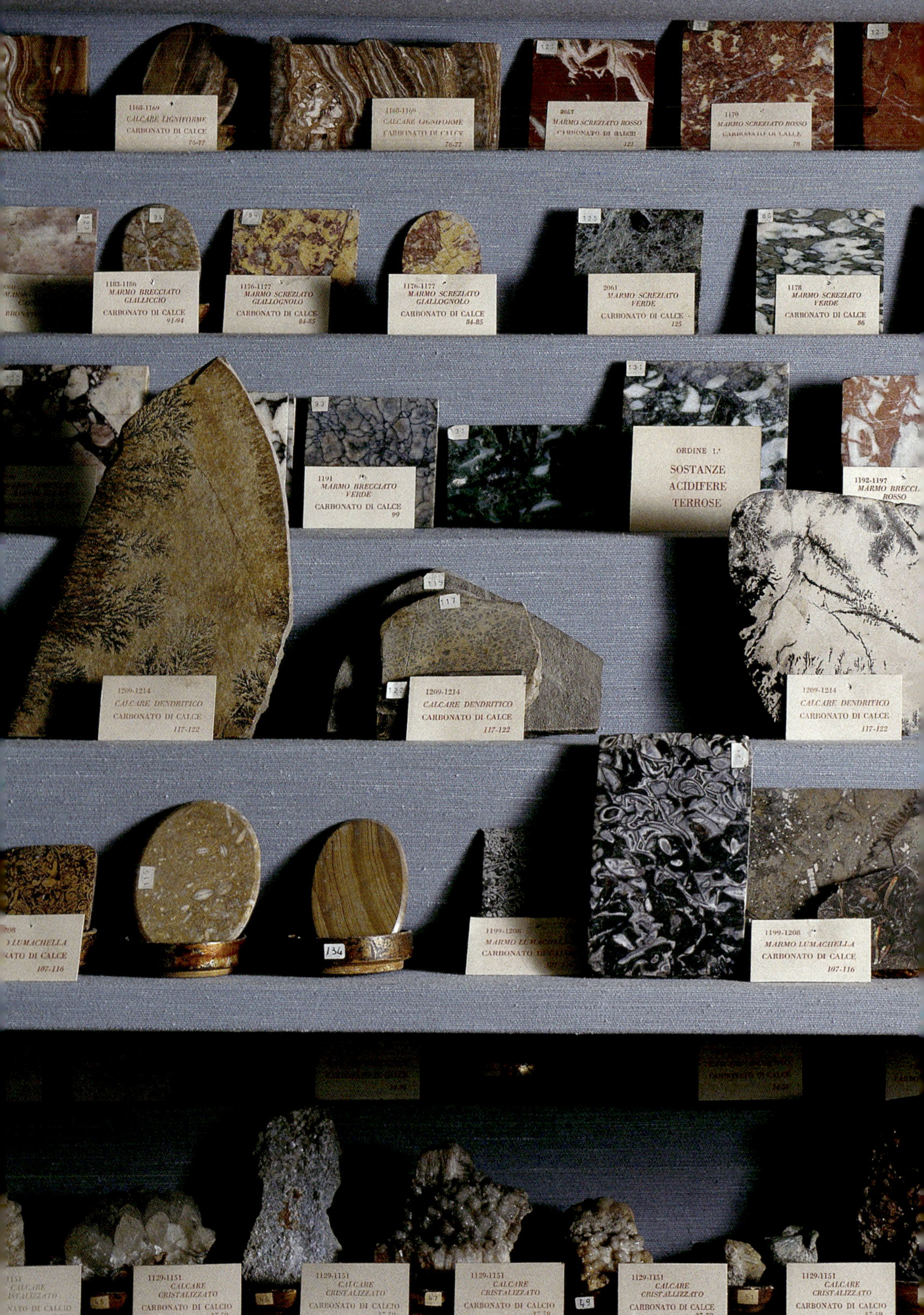

1168-1169
CALCARE LIGNIFORME
CARBONATO DI CALCE
76-77
1168-1169
CALCARE LIGNIFORME
CARBONATO DI CALCE
76-77
2057
MARMO SCREZIATO ROSSO
CARBONATO DI CALCE
121
1170
MARMO SCREZIATO ROSSO
CARBONATO DI CALCE
78
1183-1186
MARMO BRECCIATO
GIALLICCIO
CARBONATO DI CALCE
91-94
1176-1177
MARMO SCREZIATO
GIALLOGNOLO
CARBONATO DI CALCE
84-85
1176-1177
MARMO SCREZIATO
GIALLOGNOLO
CARBONATO DI CALCE
84-85
2061
MARMO SCREZIATO
VERDE
CARBONATO DI CALCE
125
1178
MARMO SCREZIATO
VERDE
CARBONATO DI CALCE
86
1191
MARMO BRECCIATO
VERDE
CARBONATO DI CALCE
99
ORDINE 1.º
SOSTANZE
ACIDIFERE
TERROSE
1192-1197
MARMO BRECC.
ROSSO
1209-1214
CALCARE DENDRITICO
CARBONATO DI CALCE
117-122
1209-1214
CALCARE DENDRITICO
CARBONATO DI CALCE
117-122
1209-1214
CALCARE DENDRITICO
CARBONATO DI CALCE
117-122
1199-1208
MARMO LUMACHELLA
CARBONATO DI CALCE
107-116
1199-1208
MARMO LUMACHELLA
CARBONATO DI CALCE
107-116
1199-1208
CALCARE LUMACHELLA
CARBONATO DI CALCE
107-116
1129-1151
CALCARE
CRISTALLIZZATO
CARBONATO DI CALCIO
37-59
1129-1151
CALCARE
CRISTALLIZZATO
CARBONATO DI CALCIO
37-59
1129-1151
CALCARE
CRISTALLIZZATO
CARBONATO DI CALCE
37-59
1129-1151
CALCARE
CRISTALLIZZATO
CARBONATO DI CALCE
37-59
1129-1151
CALCARE
CRISTALLIZZATO
CARBONATO DI CALCE
37-59

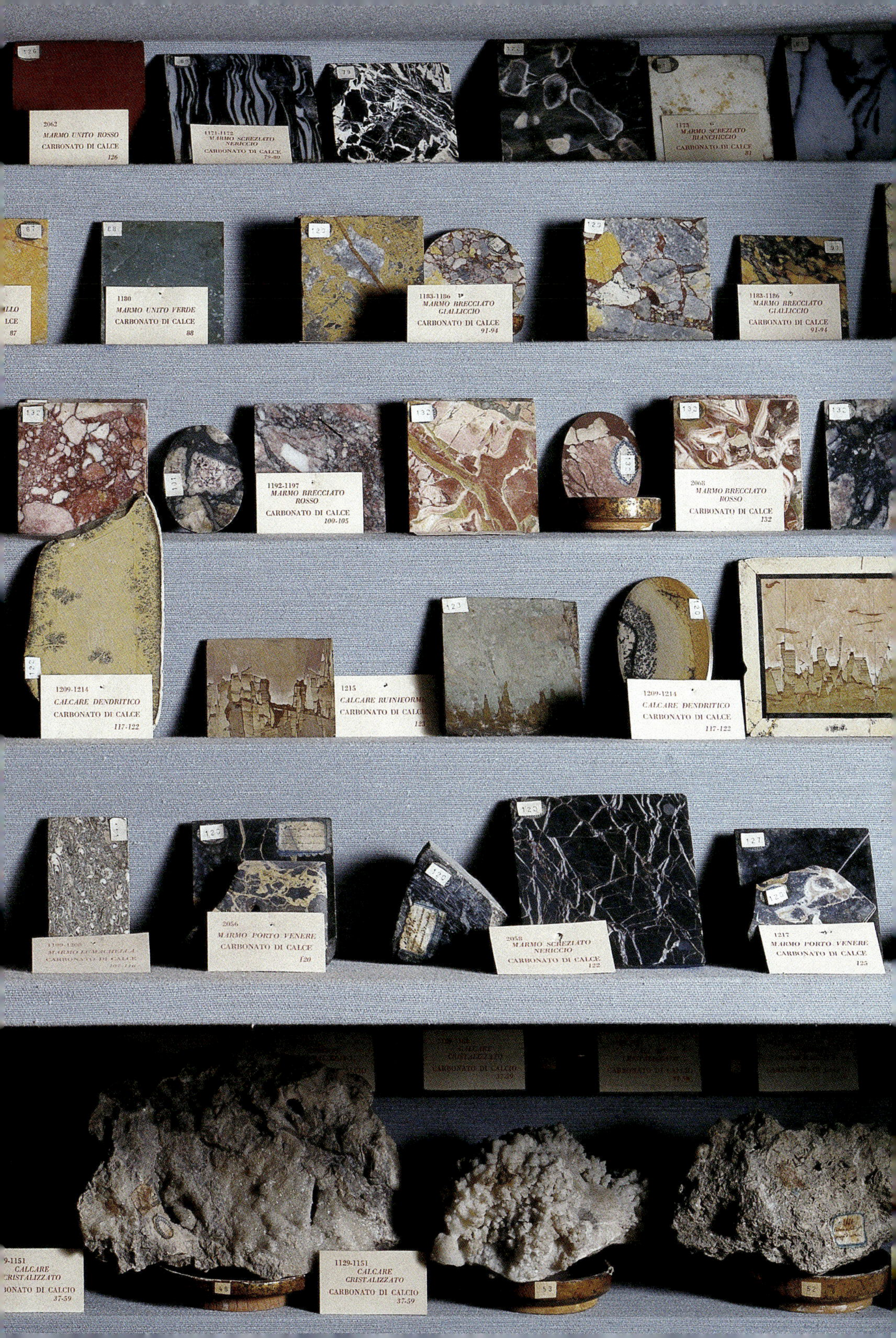

2062
MARMO UNITO ROSSO
CARBONATO DI CALCE
126

1121-1122
MARMO SCREZIATO NERICCIO
CARBONATO DI CALCE
79-80

1173
MARMO SCREZIATO BIANCHICCIO
CARBONATO DI CALCE
81

1180
MARMO UNITO VERDE
CARBONATO DI CALCE
88

1183-1186
MARMO BRECCIATO GIALLICCIO
CARBONATO DI CALCE
91-94

1183-1186
MARMO BRECCIATO GIALLICCIO
CARBONATO DI CALCE
91-94

1192-1197
MARMO BRECCIATO ROSSO
CARBONATO DI CALCE
100-105

2068
MARMO BRECCIATO ROSSO
CARBONATO DI CALCE
132

1209-1214
CALCARE DENDRITICO
CARBONATO DI CALCE
117-122

1215
CALCARE RUINIFORME
CARBONATO DI CALCE
123

1209-1214
CALCARE DENDRITICO
CARBONATO DI CALCE
117-122

1109-1108
MARMO LUMACHELLA
CARBONATO DI CALCE
107-116

2056
MARMO PORTO VENERE
CARBONATO DI CALCE
120

2058
MARMO SCREZIATO NERICCIO
CARBONATO DI CALCE
122

1217
MARMO PORTO VENERE
CARBONATO DI CALCE
125

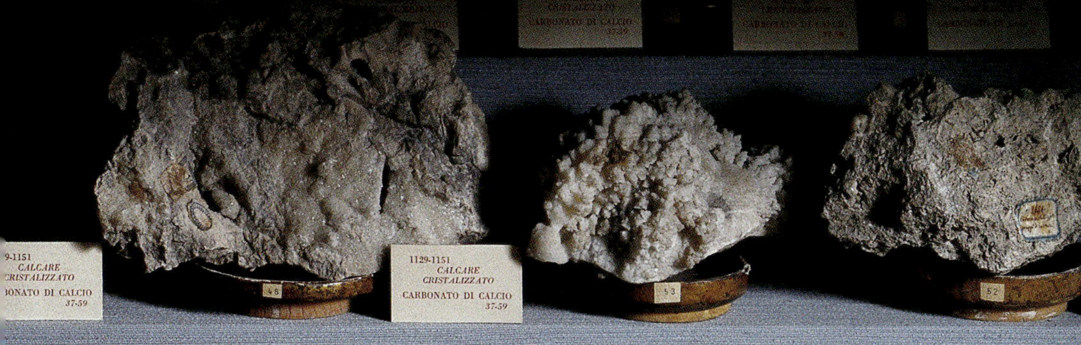
CALCARE CRISTALIZZATO
CARBONATO DI CALCIO
37-59

1129-1151
CALCARE CRISTALIZZATO
CARBONATO DI CALCIO
37-59

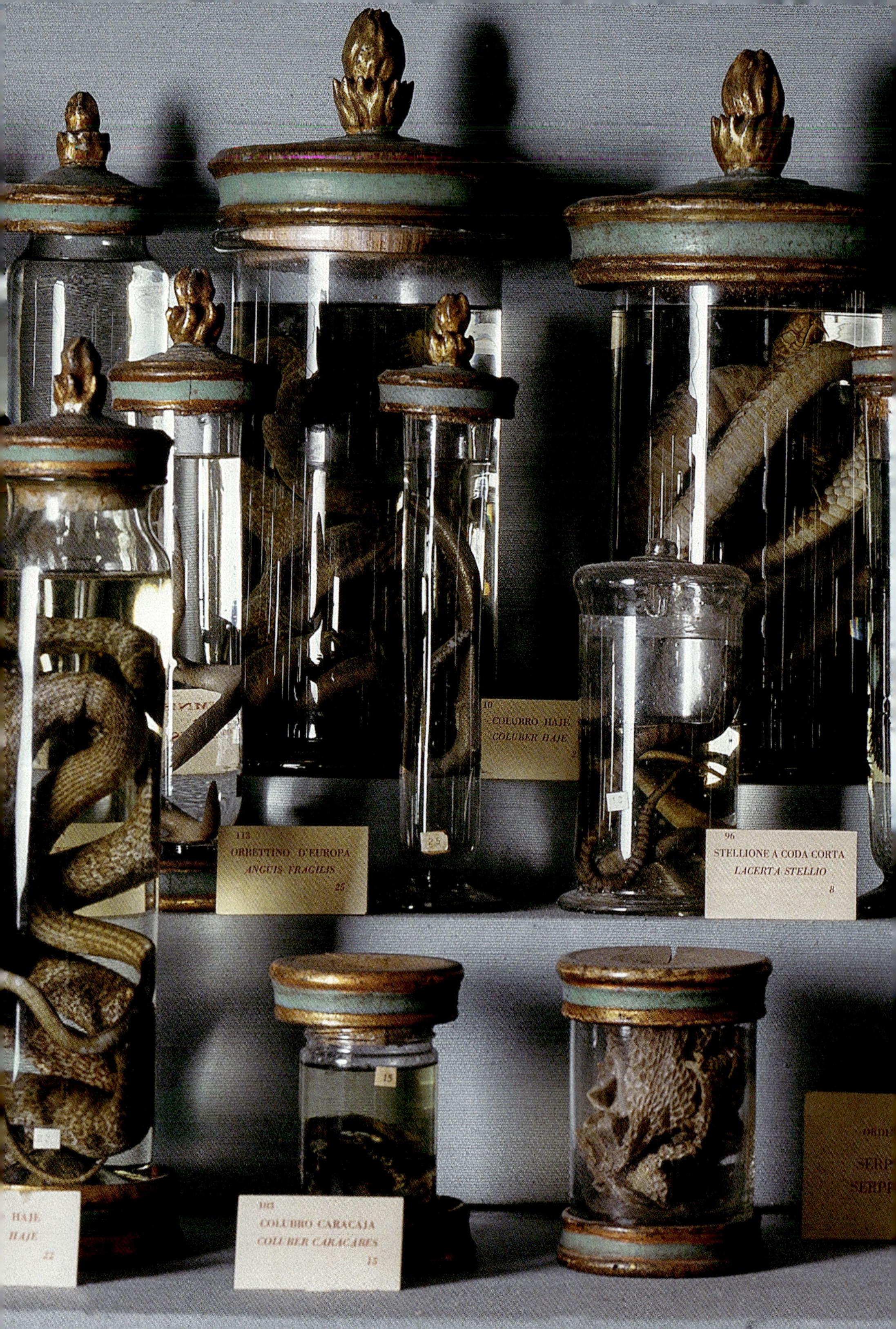
113
ORBETTINO D'EUROPA
ANGUIS FRAGILIS
25
10 COLUBRO HAJE
COLUBER HAJE
96
STELLIONE A CODA CORTA
LACERTA STELLIO
8
HAJE
HAJE
103
COLUBRO CARACAJA
COLUBER CARACARES
15
ORDI
SERP
SERP

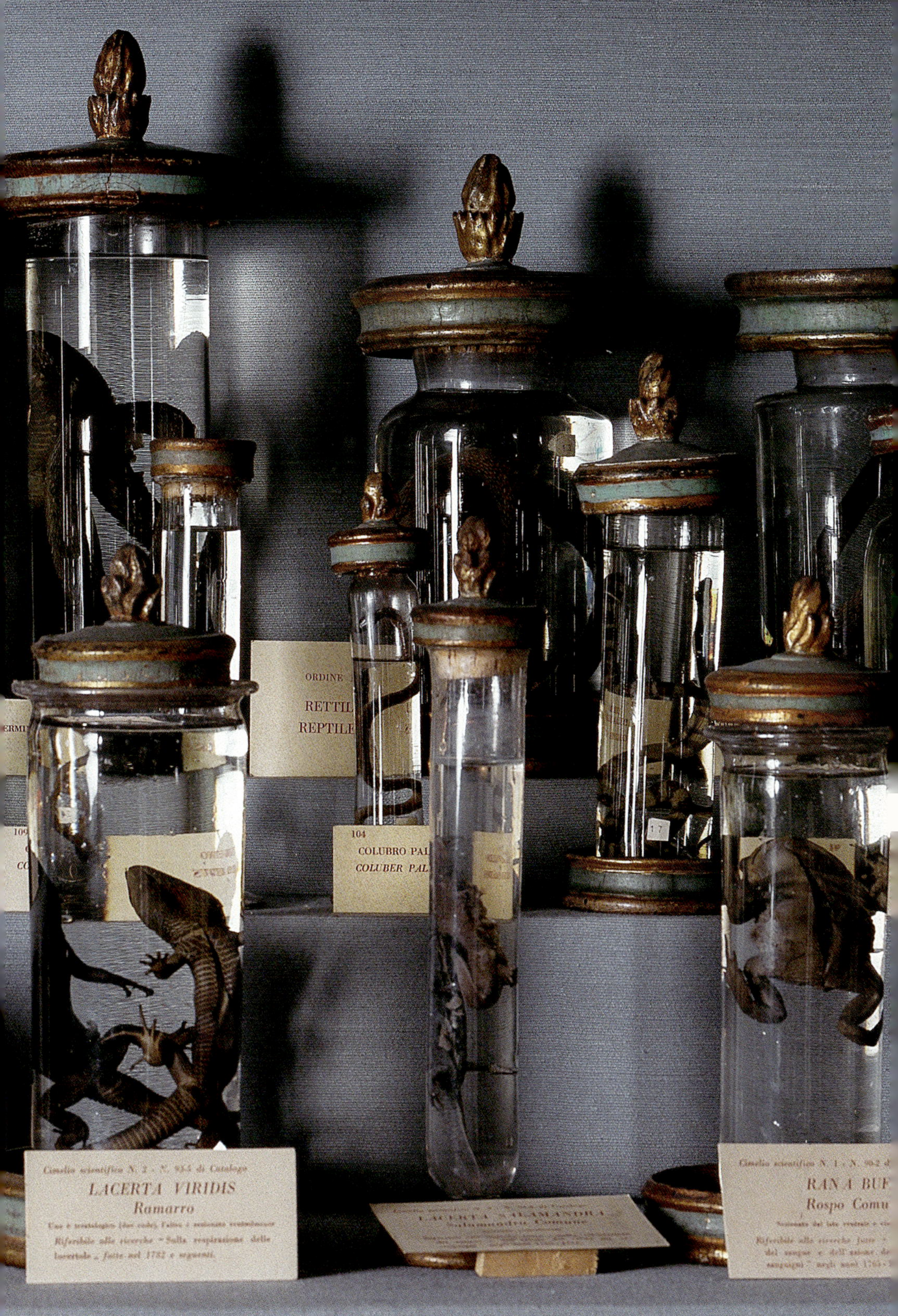

ORDINE
RETTILI
REPTILE
104
COLUBRO PAL
COLUBER PAL
LACERTA SALAMANDRA
Salamandra Comune
Cimelio scientifico N. 2 - N. 93-5 di Catalogo
LACERTA VIRIDIS
Ramarro
Riferibile alle ricerche " Sulla respirazione delle
lucertole ,, fatte nel 1782 e seguenti.
Cimelio scientifico N. 1 - N. 90-2 d
RANA BUF
Rospo Comu
Riferibile alle ricerche fatte
del sangue e dell'aria de
sangaigni ,, negli anni 1765

Lazzaro Spallanzani (1729–1799) figures prominently in the evolution of scientific thought and method which developed from "natural philosophy" into the beginnings of modern science, and is himself considered one of the founders of experimental biology and the father of modern science. Over the course of his life, and throughout his many travels and research expeditions, he also worked to establish a museum of natural history at the University of Pavia as well as enriching his own private cabinet of natural specimens, which included zoological, palaeontological, mineralogical, lithological and botanical finds, all organised according to a rigorous method.

After Spallanzani's death the Municipality of Reggio Emilia acquired the "small collection of natural productions" (in Spallanzani's scientific description) housed in his private residence in Scandiano; this constituted the historical nucleus around which the Musei Civici were formed. The collection, preserved intact in its 18th-century arrangement, was relocated to the rooms of the Palazzo dei Musei in 1830.

After a subsequent reorganisation between 1883 and 1885 the collection settled into the arrangement in which we see it today: the first room contains furnishings, souvenirs and artefacts (including a chequer-board made of amber with 100 squares), together with the large summary tables collated by Spallanzani when he compiled the numerous images for the zoological plates of the *Historiae naturalis* (1650–1653) by John Jonston (1603–1675); in the second room 21 armoires house the collection's 2,000 items, displayed according to the Linnaean system in use at the end of the 18th century. These cabinets present a small compendium of the animal kingdom, from mammals to amphibians, birds to fish, and insects to worms: many of the specimens are linked to the scientist's research on digestion, or investigations of the circulatory or respiratory systems. One fanciful section features a group of fish playfully created by combining natural and artificial parts, such as the *Cophanus concatenatus*. The case with the fossils stands between those relating to the animal and the vegetable kingdoms, while the sequence of cabinets ends with rocks and minerals, including stalactites, calcareous concretions, marble, crystals and salt. Alongside the strictly scientific specimens are certain attractive objects—such as *lumachelle*, pieces of limestone in which the oxidation of manganese has produced designs in the shape of trees, and pietre paesine, where multi-coloured oxides have created fantastical landscapes—with the aim of combining instruction with objects of beauty.

◎ ❖ ◎

In dem Prozess, der von der sogenannten Naturphilosophie zur Entstehung der modernen Naturwissenschaft führte, spielte Lazzaro Spallanzani (1729–1799) eine treibende Rolle und gilt daher zu Recht als Mitbegründer der modernen Physiologie und experimentellen Biologie. Die Ausbeute seiner zahlreichen Reisen und Forschungsexpeditionen verwendete er sowohl zum Aufbau des naturgeschichtlichen Museums an der Universität Pavia als auch für seine private Sammlung, in der er zoologische, paläontologische, mineralogische, lithologische und botanische Funde streng methodisch ordnete.

Nach seinem Tod erwarb die Gemeinde Reggio Emilia die von Spallanzani selbst als „kleine Sammlung von Naturprodukten" bezeichnete Kollektion, die er in seinem Haus in Scandiano zusammengestellt hatte, und legte damit den Grundstein für die Musei Civici. Seit 1830 ist die Sammlung in ihrer ursprünglichen Form im Palazzo dei Musei zu sehen.

Der aktuelle Ausstellungsaufbau geht auf eine Neuordnung zwischen 1883 und 1885 zurück. Im ersten Saal befinden sich Einrichtungsgegenstände, Souvenirs und Kunsthandwerk – darunter ein Damespiel aus Bernstein mit hundert zweifarbigen Feldern – zusammen mit den großen Synopsen, die Spallanzani selbst aus den zoologischen Tafeln der *Historiae naturalis* (1650–1653) von Johannes Jonston (1603–1675) zusammengestellt hat. Der zweite Saal beherbergt die Naturaliensammlung, bestehend aus über zweitausend Stücken, die in 21 Schränken nach dem seit Ende des 18. Jahrhundert gängigen Linné-System geordnet sind. Die Schränke enthalten ein kleines Kompendium der Tierwelt, von Säugetieren bis zu Amphibien, von Vögeln bis zu Fischen, von Insekten bis zu Würmern: Viele der Exponate haben einen direkten Bezug zu Spallanzanis eigenen Forschungen über den Verdauungsapparat, das Kreislaufsystem und das Atemsystem. Eine Kuriosität bilden Fische, die zum Scherz aus verschiedenen tierischen und künstlichen Teilen zusammengesetzt sind, wie beispielsweise der *Cophanus concatenatus*. Die Fossilien sind in der Ausstellung zwischen Tier- und Pflanzenreich zu finden und zuletzt die Mineralien und Steine, darunter Stalaktiten, Kalkablagerungen, Marmor, Kristalle und Salze. Neben Exponaten von streng wissenschaftlichem Interesse umfasst die Sammlung jedoch auch besonders dekorative Steine aus Muschelmarmor, sogenannte Lumachellen, auf denen durch Manganoxyd Figuren entstanden sind, und aus Pietre paesine, die aufgrund diverser Oxydationen fantastische Landschaften aufweisen.

◈ ❖ ◈

Lazzaro Spallanzani (1729–1799) est l'un des protagonistes de l'évolution de la pensée et de la méthode scientifiques qui ont conduit de la « philosophie naturelle » à la naissance des sciences modernes. Aussi est-il considéré comme l'un des fondateurs de la biologie expérimentale et le père de la science moderne. Au cours de ses nombreux voyages et expéditions scientifiques, il travailla à la constitution d'un musée d'histoire naturelle pour l'université de Pavie et à celle de son propre cabinet où il rassembla des échantillons zoologiques, paléontologiques, minéralogiques, lithologiques et botaniques qu'il classa avec méthode et rigueur.

À la mort de Spallanzani, la Municipalité de Reggio d'Émilie fit l'acquisition de ce que le savant appelait sa « petite collection de productions naturelles », qu'il avait installée dans les pièces de sa demeure à Scandiano et qui forme le noyau historique autour duquel se sont constitués les Musei Civici. La collection, dont la composition demeure inchangée depuis le 18ᵉ siècle, a trouvé place dans les salles du Palazzo dei Musei à partir de 1830.

Sa présentation actuelle est liée à la réorganisation effectuée entre 1883 et 1885 : dans la première salle se trouvent des éléments décoratifs, des souvenirs et des objets d'art – dont un damier d'ambre avec 100 compartiments aux nuances variées – et de grands tableaux synoptiques obtenus par Spallanzani en juxtaposant les nombreuses images contenues dans les tables zoologiques des *Historiae naturalis* (1650–1653) de John Jonston (1603–1675) ; la deuxième salle accueille la collection présentée dans vingt et une armoires pour un total de 2000 objets, en se conformant à la systématique linnéenne en vigueur à la fin du 18ᵉ siècle. Les armoires proposent un petit résumé du règne animal, des nouveau-nés aux amphibiens, des oiseaux aux poissons, des insectes aux vers : de nombreux exemplaires se rapportent aux recherches menées par le savant sur la digestion, ou à ses études sur les systèmes circulatoire et respiratoire. Objets de curiosité, telle est la présence de certains poissons résultent de l'amusant assemblage d'éléments animaux et artificiels, ainsi le *Cophanus concatenatus*. Selon l'agencement de la collection, la vitrine des fossiles se situe entre le règne animal et le règne végétal. En dernier lieu viennent les minéraux et les roches parmi lesquels figurent des stalactites, des concrétions calcaires, des marbres, des cristaux et des sels. Parallèlement à l'intérêt scientifique des exemplaires, la recherche de l'effet esthétique se traduit par la présence d'échantillons particuliers comme les lumachelles où les oxydes de manganèse dessinent des motifs arborescents ou bien comme les pietre paesine (variété de calcaire métamorphique d'Italie) où diverses oxydations composent des paysages fantastiques.

1 *The Cabinet of "Worms".* Collected here are starfish from the Venetian Lagoon and from Liguria, which were used to study their method of movement. The display also includes cuttlefish and octopuses, which were studied for the efficiency of their optical system. *Kabinett der „Würmer".* Ausgestellt sind Seesterne der venezianischen Lagune und Liguriens, deren besondere Fortbewegungsart studiert wurde. Weiter gibt es Tintenfische und Oktopusse, deren leistungsfähiges Sehsytem erforscht wurde. *Le Cabinet des « Vers ».* Les étoiles de mer ont été recueillies dans la lagune vénitienne et en Ligurie et utilisées pour étudier leur système de déambulation. La seiche et la pieuvre étaient étudiées à cause de leur système optique efficace.

2 Spallanzani purchased many of the pieces in this cabinet in Marseille. The small bowls together hold around 200 shells from the Mediterranean and also the distant South Seas. They include scallops, mussels, cockles and clams, but also elaborately carved nautilus shells. Lazzaro Spallanzani erwarb viele der in diesem Kabinett ausgestellten Objekte in Marseille. In kleinen Schalen werden ungefähr zweihundert Muscheln aufbewahrt, die sowohl aus dem Mittelmeer als auch aus der Südsee stammen – darunter Kamm-, Mies-, Tell- und Venusmuscheln –, zudem aufwendig gravierte Nautilusgehäuse. Dans ce cabinet, de nombreuses pièces proviennent d'achats effectués par Spallanzani à Marseille. Exposés dans des coupelles, on voit environ deux cents coquillages, provenant de la Méditerranée jusqu'aux mers tropicales lointaines. Il s'agit de pétoncles, de moules, de coques et de palourdes, mais aussi de spécimens de nautiles dont la coquille est artistiquement sculptée.

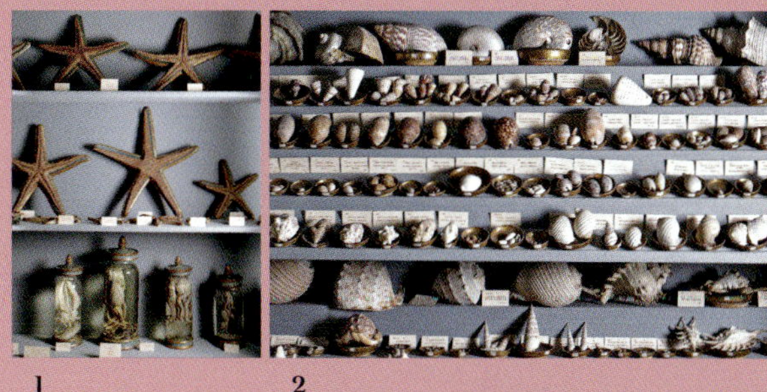

1   2

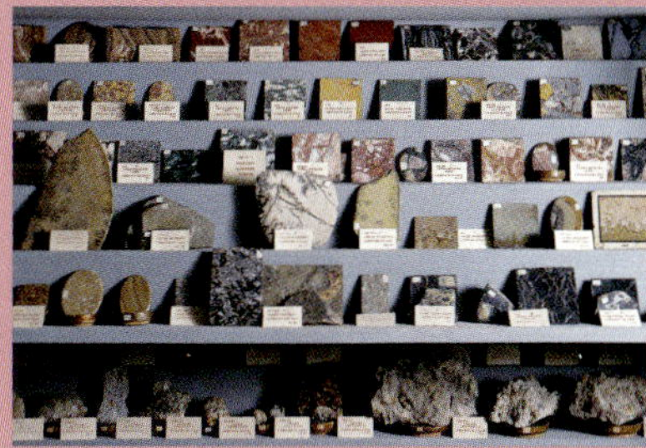

3

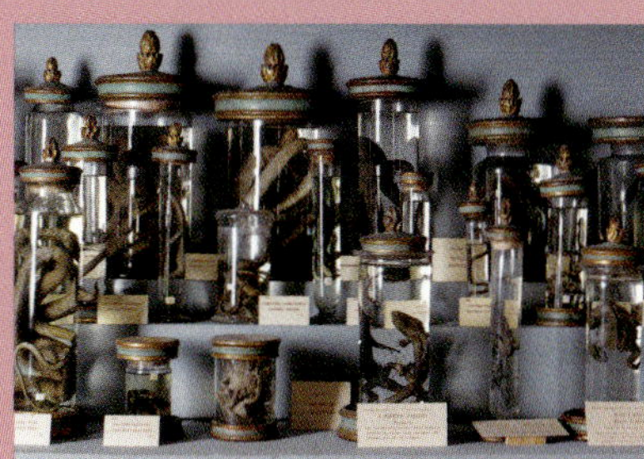

4

3 *The Cabinet of "Minerals".*
In this display case is a collection of various types of rare marble. On the lower shelf are examples of limestone, including dendrites, pietre paesine, ruin marble and *lumachelle.*
Kabinett der „Mineralien". In dieser Vitrine befindet sich eine Mustersammlung von seltenen Marmorsorten. Im unteren Regal sind Kalksteine, darunter Dendriten, Pietre paesine, sogenannter Ruinenmarmor, und Lumachelle ausgestellt.
Cabinet des « Minéraux ». Dans cette vitrine est exposée une collection de spécimens de marbres rares. Sur l'étagère inférieure se trouvent des calcaires, entre autres des dendrites, des pietre paesine, appelées marbre de ruine, et des lumachelles.

4 *The Cabinet of "Amphibians".* Displayed here are glass jars containing preserved specimens of toads, salamanders and newts, which Spallanzani experimented on as part of his research into artificial insemination. There are also several electric rays he used for experiments on their electrical discharge.
Kabinett der „Amphibien". Diese Vitrinen sind feuchtpräparierten Kröten, Salamandern und Molchen vorbehalten, die Spallanzani bei seinen Befruchtungsexperimenten verwandte. Außerdem gibt es mehrere Zitterrochen (Torpenidae), an denen er Stromexperimente durchführte.
Le Cabinet des « Amphibiens ». Ces vitrines présentent des bocaux contenant des crapauds, des salamandres et des tritons, que Spallanzani a utilisés pour ses recherches sur l'insémination artificielle. Il y a aussi plusieurs raies électriques (Torpenidae) utilisées pour des expérimentations sur leur puissance électrique.

Museo storico nazionale dell'arte sanitaria

Roma

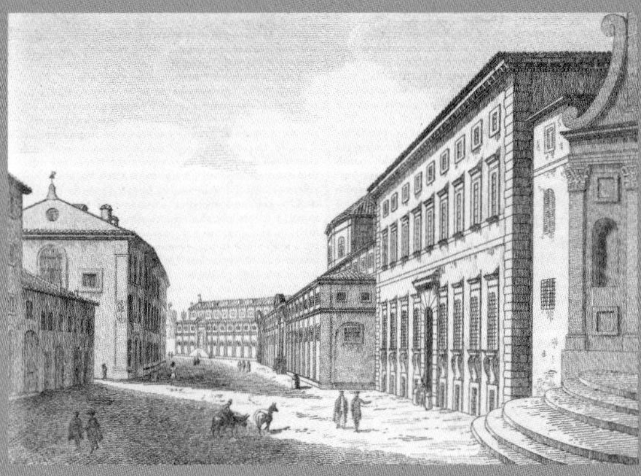

Founded 1933
(foundation of the museum)

Key item The alchemical
laboratory and the pathological
anatomical preparations.

Besonders sehenswert
Das alchemistische Labor und
pathologisch-anatomische
Präparate.

À voir absolument Le laboratoire
alchimique et préparations anatomiques pathologiques.

*General View of the Hospital of
Santo Spirito in Sassia, in L'album,
giornale letterario e di belle arti,
16 January 1841. Milan, Biblioteca
Ambrosiana.*

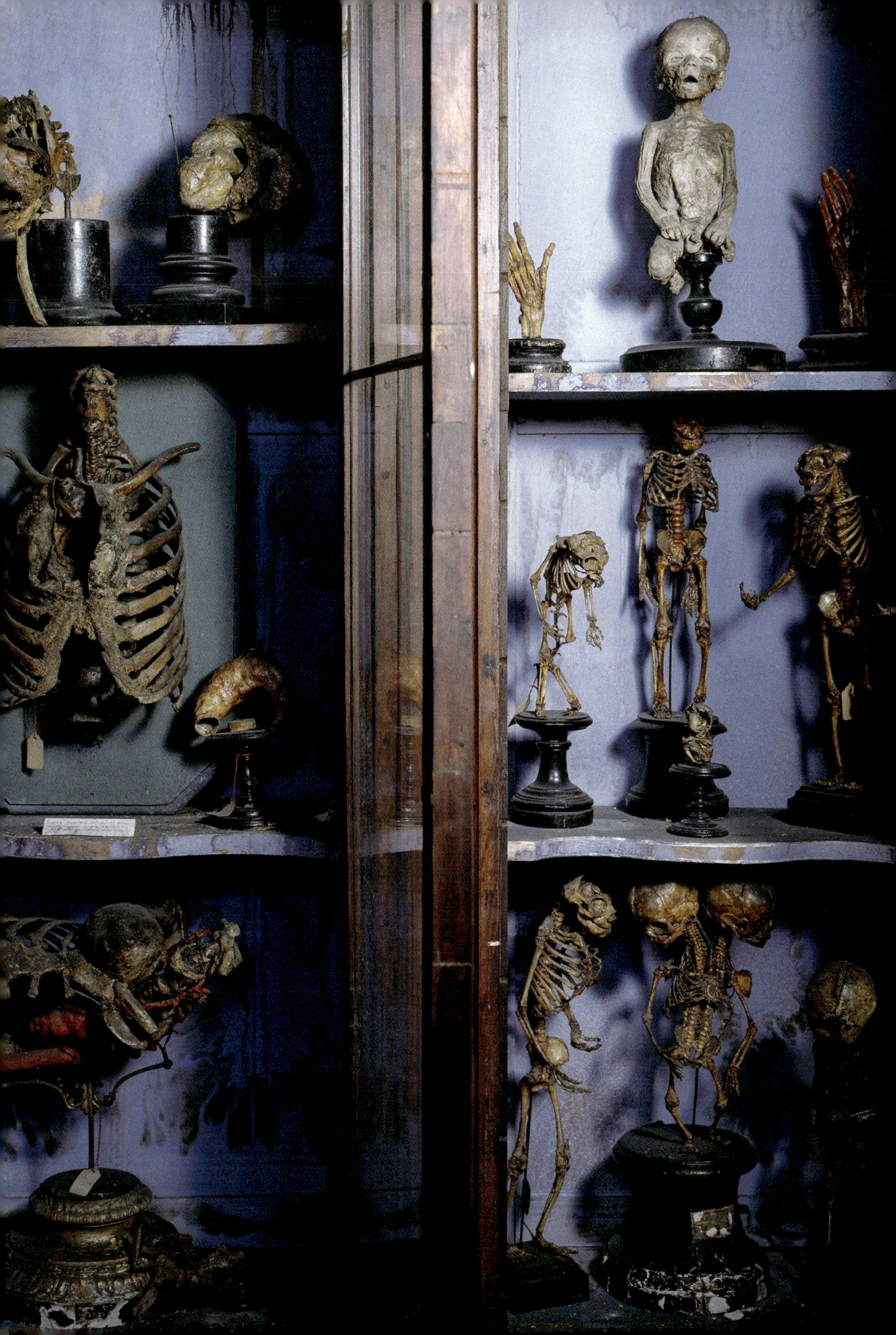

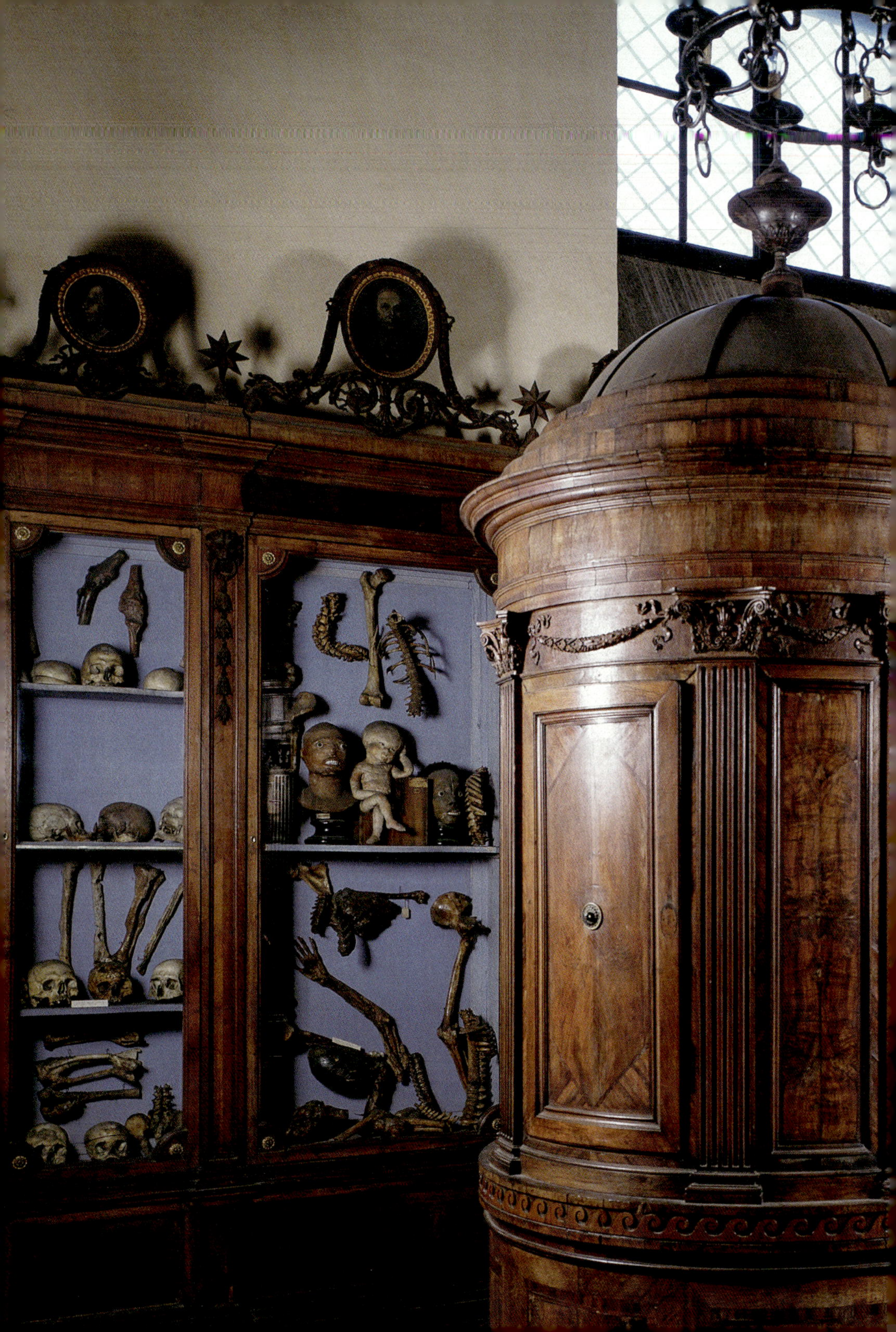

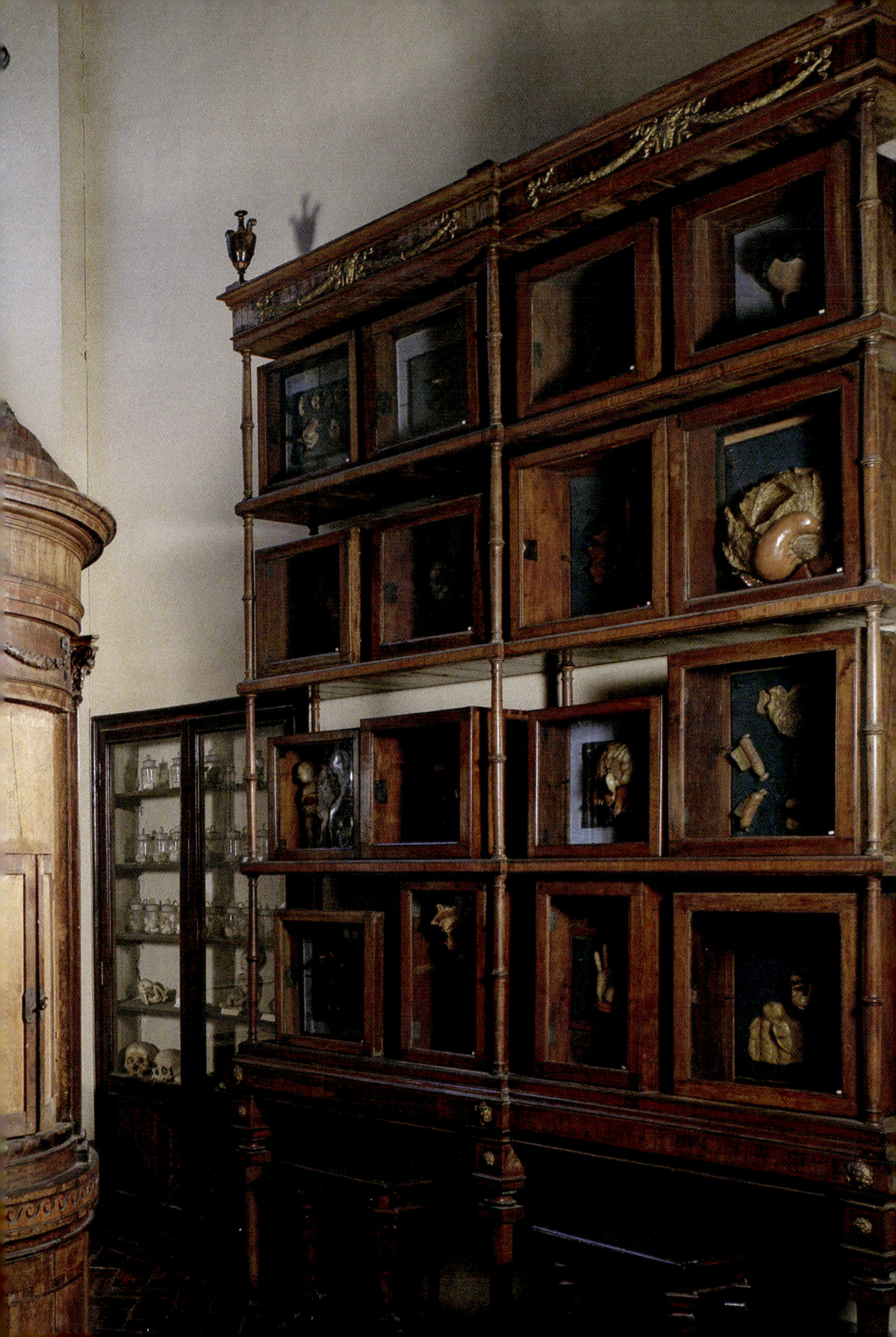

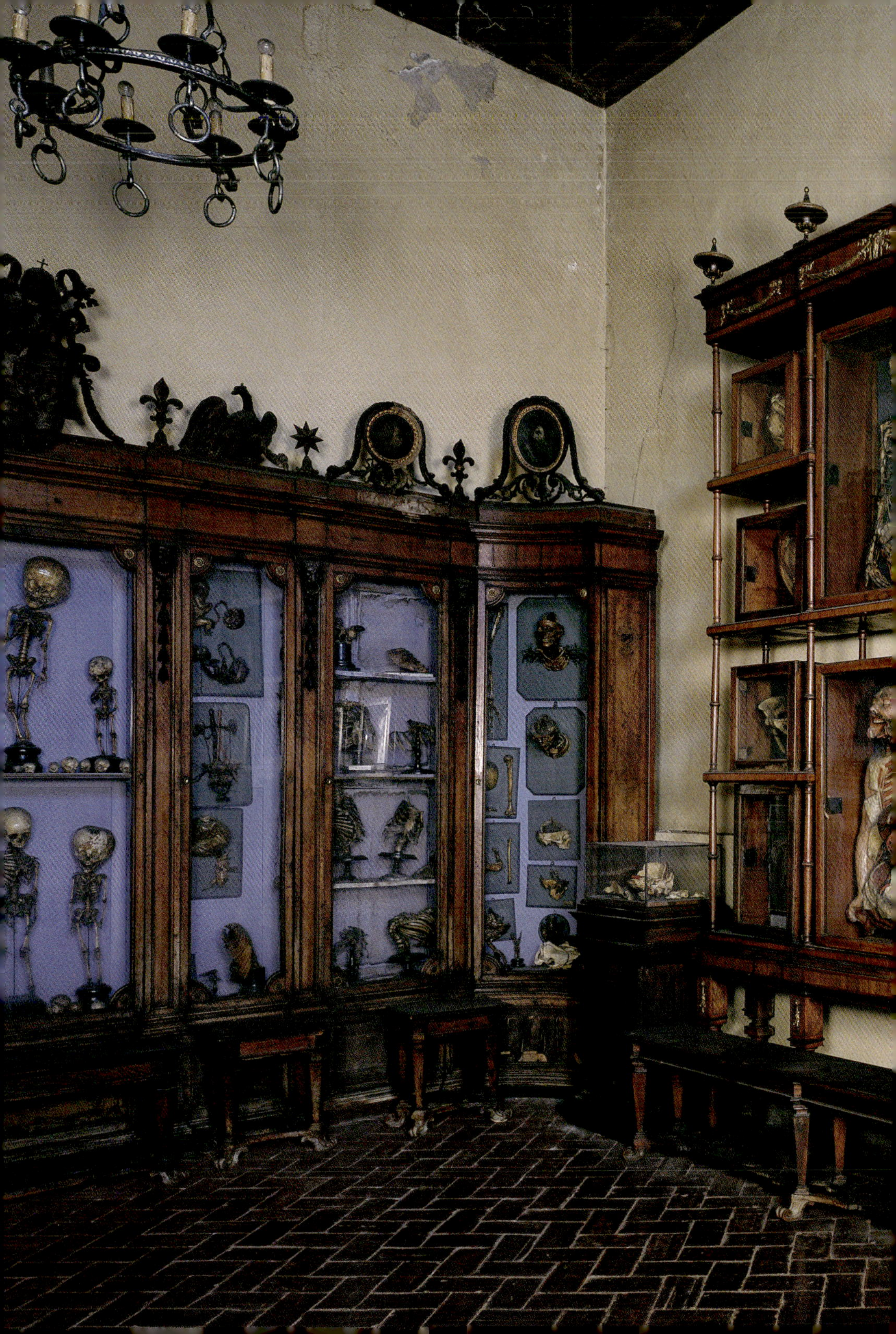

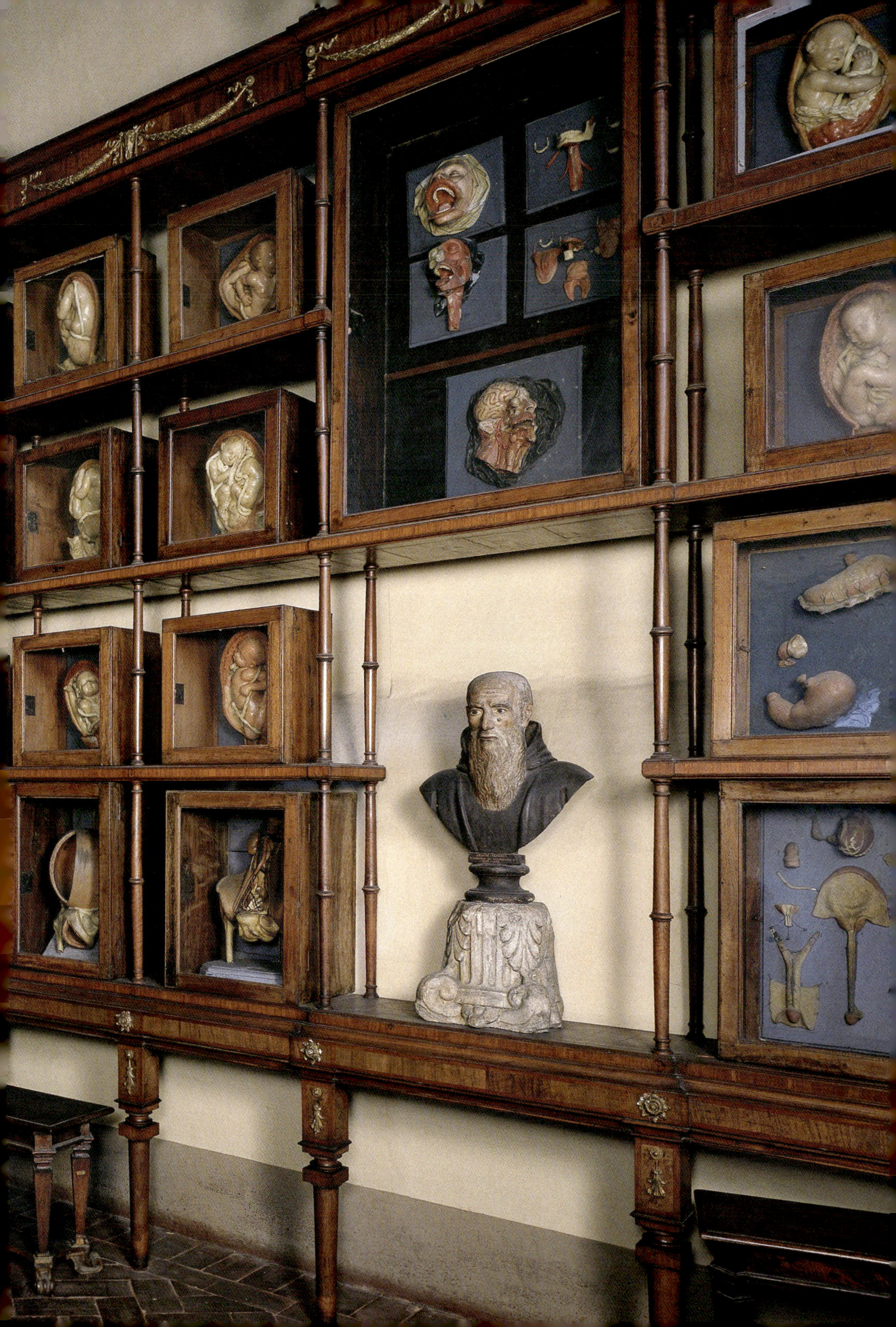

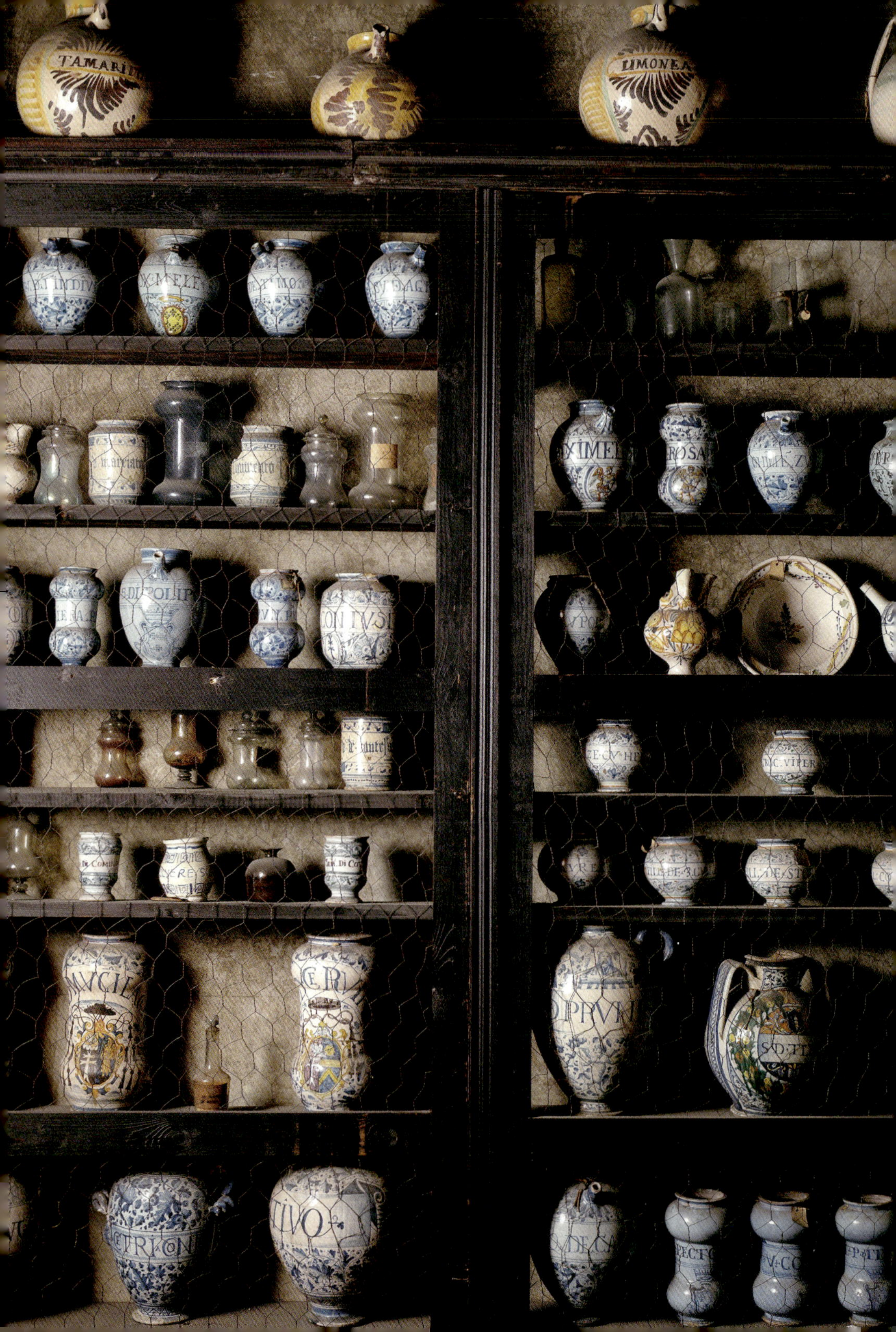

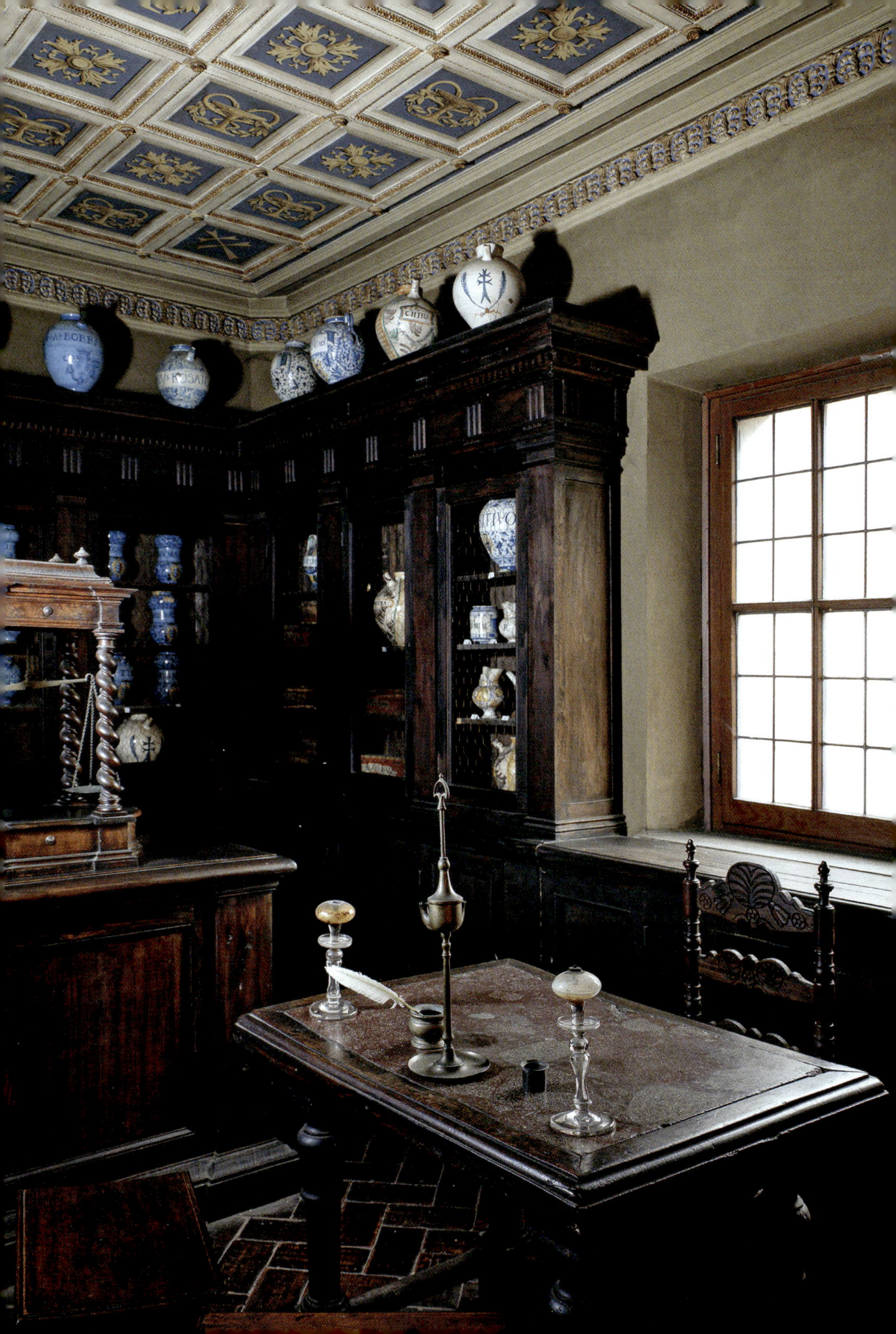

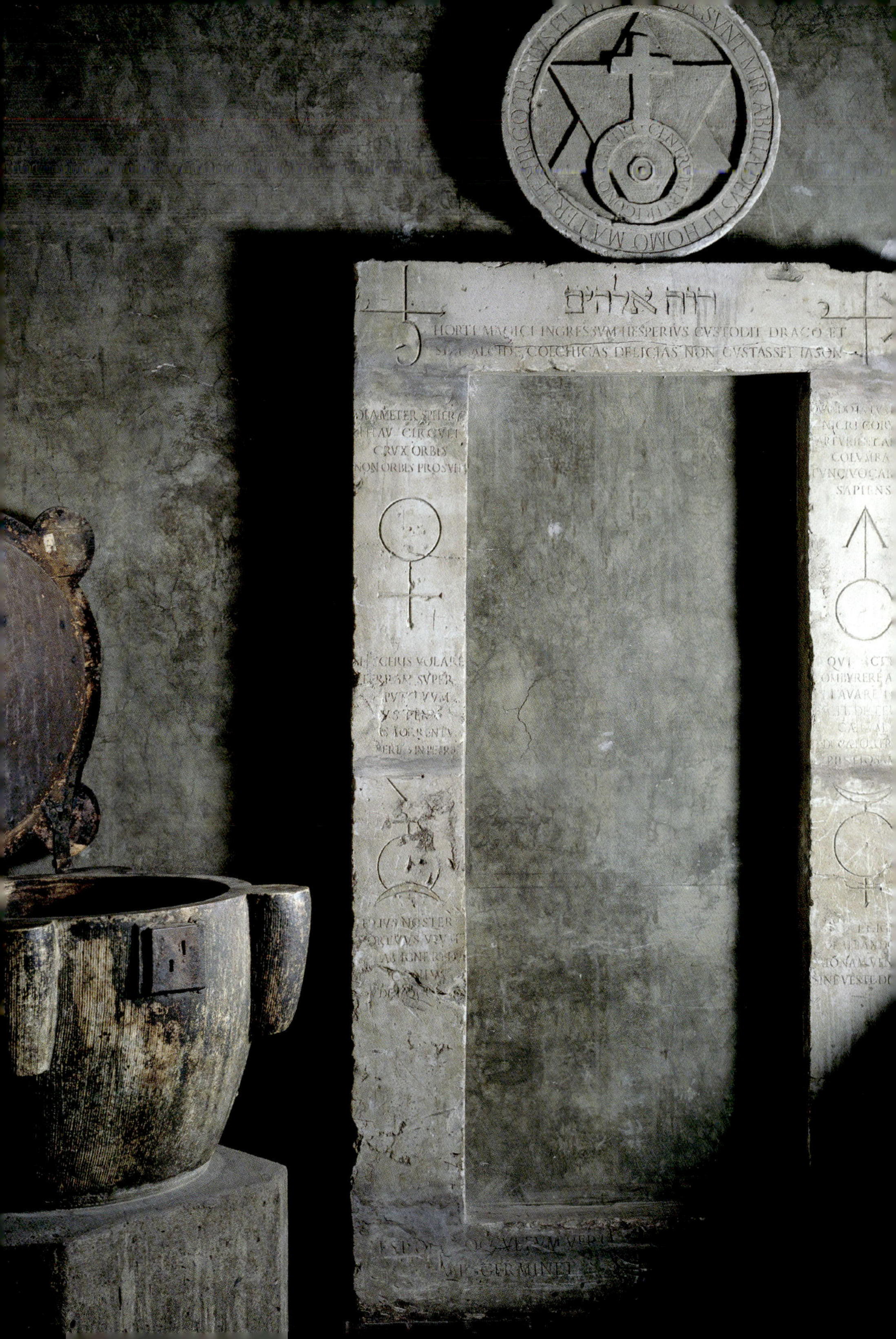
SVNT MIRABILIA DEVS ET HOMO MATER ET VIRGO
CENTRVM IN TRIGONO CENTRI
רוח אלהים
HORTI MAGICI INGRESSVM HESPERIVS CVSTODIT DRACO ET
SINE ALCIDE COLCHICAS DELICIAS NON GVSTASSET IASON
DIAMETER SPHERÆ
THAV CIRCVLI
CRVX ORBIS
NON ORBIS PROSVNT
SI FECERIS VOLARE
TERRAM SVPER
CAPVT TVVM
EIVS PENNIS
AQVAS TORRENTV
CONVERTES IN PETRAM
FILIVS NOSTER
MORTVVS VIVIT
REX AB IGNE REDIT
ET CONIVGIO
GAVDET
QVANDO IN TVA
DOMO NIGRI CORVI
PARTVRIENT ALBAM
COLVMBAM
TVNC VOCABERIS
SAPIENS
QVI SCIT
COMBVRERE AD
AQVAM LAVARE ET
FACIT DE TERRA
CÆLVM ET
DE CÆLO TERRAM
PRETIOSAM
EST OPVS
OCCVLTVM
SAPIENTVM
SINE VESTE DOCTA

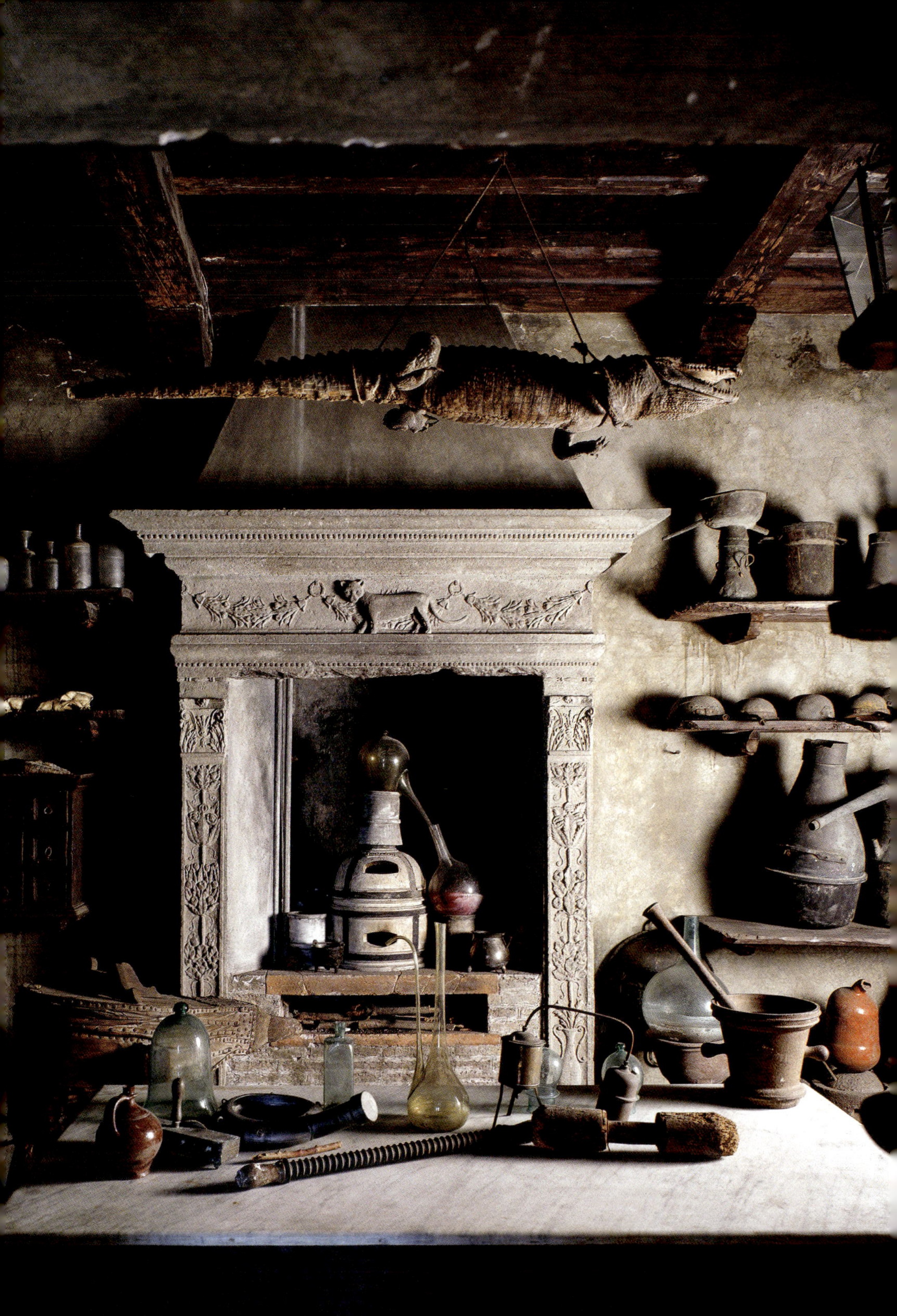

Opened in 1933, and administered by the Accademia di Storia dell'Arte Sanitaria, the museum is located in the 17th-century wing of the Hospital of Santo Spirito in Sassia, itself dating back to an even earlier period. According to the traditional account, in 1198 Pope Innocent III, following a nightmare he had in which an angel showed him the tiny bodies of unwanted babies that had been thrown into the river Tiber, founded a hospital to help the infirm, the poor and the "*proietti*" (illegitimate children abandoned by their mothers).

The old anatomical museum housed the anatomical theatre and the students' anatomy cabinet, used both for the dissection of corpses and for the pathological anatomical preparations now on display in the Sala Flajani. The original collection included the 18th-century wax models by Giovan Battista Manfredini (1742–1789), fashioned at the request of Cardinal Francesco Saverio de Zelada (1717–1801), who commissioned the first study of obstetrics based on more than 30 such anatomical models, as well as models of torsos, all with corresponding explanatory tables. The Capparoni and Carbonelli rooms house documents relating to the evolution and history of medicine from Antiquity through to the modern age: there are Etruscan, Roman, Greek and modern *ex-votos*, and examples of famous antidotes for poison or disease, such as a unicorn's horn—which is in fact a narwhal tusk—and a ball of bezoar, a calcareous substance produced by the bile and formed in the digestive tract of certain ruminants. There are, furthermore, some portable pharmacies dating from the 17th to the 19th century, used by chemists and physicians when out on call, or for urgent cases in which the patient could not be moved; a series of obstetrical and surgical instruments (drills, syringes and scalpels), including Mauriceau's syringe, a device used to baptise unborn foetuses that were in danger of dying while the mother was in labour; microscopes of different shapes and from various times, 16th- and 17th-century eye glasses; early 19th-century equipment used to induce anaesthesia; a Leyden jar (a prototype of the electric condenser invented in Leiden for experiments on electricity), an original device built by Avogadro and a 19th-century electrotherapy machine; as well as glass objects, vases, alembics, bottles, jars, apothecary jars, scales and mortars. There is also an extensive library containing over 10,000 works on the history of medicine.

◎ ◈ ◎

Das Museum wurde 1933 von der Akademie für die Geschichte des Gesundheitswesens gegründet und in einem aus dem 17. Jahrhundert stammenden Flügel des Ospedale di Santo Spirito in Sassia untergebracht, während das Krankenhaus selbst wesentlich älter ist. Der Legende nach soll Papst Innozenz III. 1198 infolge eines Albtraums, in dem ihm ein Engel die aus dem Tiber gefischten Leichen von unerwünschten Neugeborenen zeigte, ein Spital für Kranke, Arme und von ihren Müttern ausgesetzte Kinder gegründet haben.

Zu dem alten anatomischen Museum gehörten das anatomische Theater und der Anatomiesaal, die beide zu Sektionszwecken und der Herstellung von anatomisch-pathologischen Präparaten dienten, die heute in der Sala Flajani zu sehen sind. Zu den historischen Beständen zählen auch Modelle des Wachsmodellierers Giovan Battista Manfredini (1742–1789), die im Auftrag von Kardinal Francesco Saverio de Zelada (1717–1801) entstanden, der auch die erste, auf 30 solchen anatomischen Modellen beruhende Studie zur Geburtshilfe bestellte, ferner Wachsmodelle des menschlichen Rumpfes mit Erklärungstafeln. Die historische Entwicklung der Medizin von der Antike bis zur Neuzeit wird in den Sälen Capparoni und Carbonelli illustriert: Dort sind etruskische, römische, griechische und moderne Votivgaben zu sehen sowie berühmte Mittel gegen Vergiftungen und Krankheiten: etwa das Horn des Einhorns – in Wirklichkeit der Stoßzahn eines Narwals – und ein Bezoarstein, ein unverdaulicher Magenstein, der sich vor allem im Verdauungsapparat der Wiederkäuer findet. Außerdem werden diverse tragbare Apotheken aus dem 17. bis 19. Jahrhundert gezeigt, die von Apothekern und Ärzten auf Reisen oder bei Krankenbesuchen mitgeführt wurden, wenn der Patient nicht transportfähig war; darüber hinaus Instrumente aus der Geburtshilfe und der Chirurgie wie Bohrer, „Spritzen" und Skalpelle, darunter auch Kuriositäten wie die Spritze von Mauriceau, die dazu diente, den Fötus vor der Geburt zu taufen, wenn er vermutlich die Geburt nicht überlebte; Mikroskope unterschiedlichen Alters und verschiedener Form, Brillen aus dem 16. und 17. Jahrhundert, Anästhesiegeräte des frühen 19. Jahrhunderts, eine Leidener Flasche – Prototyp des Elektrokondensators – und ein Originalapparat von Avogadro, eine Maschine zur Elektrotherapie aus dem 19. Jahrhundert, sowie Glasgefäße, Destilliergeräte, Flaschen, Dosen, Albarelli, Waagen und Mörser. Darüber hinaus gibt es eine umfangreiche Bibliothek mit über zehntausend Publikationen zur Geschichte der Medizin.

◎ ◈ ◎

Inauguré en 1933 et administré par l'Accademia di storia dell'arte sanitaria, le musée est hébergé dans l'aile datant du 17ᵉ siècle de l'Ospedale Santo Spirito in Sassia d'origine bien plus ancienne. On raconte qu'en 1198, à la suite d'un cauchemar où un ange lui désignait les corps minuscules des nouveau-nés non désirés jetés dans le Tibre, le pape Innocent III fonda un hôpital destiné à prêter assistance aux infirmes, aux pauvres et aux enfants illégitimes abandonnés par leur mère.

L'ancien musée anatomique comprenait un théâtre anatomique et un cabinet d'anatomie fréquentés par les étudiants, tous deux affectés à la dissection des cadavres et aux préparations anatomiques pathologiques visibles dans la salle Flajani. Le fonds ancien inclut les cires réalisées au 18ᵉ siècle par le céroplasticien Giovan Battista Manfredini (1742–1789) à la demande du cardinal Francesco Saverio de Zelada (1717–1801) qui passa commande de la première étude d'obstétrique en plus de trente exemplaires : une collection de troncs anatomiques avec leurs planches explicatives. Dans les salles Capparoni et Carbonelli sont retracées l'évolution et l'histoire de la médecine de l'Antiquité à l'époque moderne : on y découvre des ex-voto étrusques, grecs, romains et modernes, des exemplaire d'antidotes célèbres comme une corne de licorne – une dent de narval en réalité – et une boule de bézoard, objet de nature calcaire d'origine biliaire qui se forme dans l'appareil digestif des ruminants. On y trouve encore plusieurs pharmacies portatives (17ᵉ–19ᵉ siècle), utilisées par les apothicaires et les médecins lors de leurs déplacements ou d'interventions d'urgence sur des malades intransportables ; une série d'instruments chirurgicaux (trépans, scalpels et seringues) et obstétricaux dont la seringue de Mauriceau employée pour baptiser *ante partum* les nouveau-nés dont la vie était en danger ; des microscopes de divers types et d'époques variées, des lunettes des 16ᵉ et 17ᵉ siècles, des appareils du début du 19ᵉ siècle utilisés en anesthésie, une bouteille de Leyde – prototype du condensateur électrique inventé à Leyde pour effectuer des expériences sur l'électricité – et l'appareil original d'Avogadro, une machine utilisée au 19ᵉ siècle en électrothérapie, sans oublier des alambics, des flacons, des bocaux, des albarelles, des balances et autres mortiers. Par ailleurs, les lieux abritent une riche bibliothèque où sont conservées plus de dix mille publications sur l'histoire de la médecine.

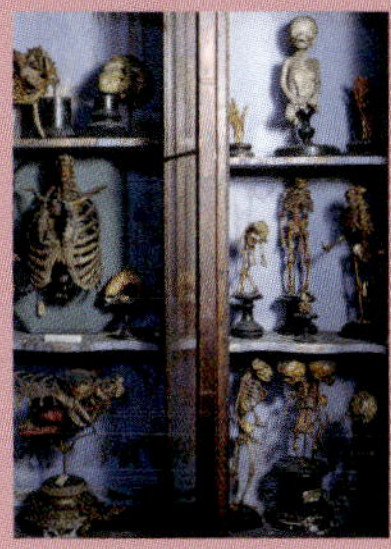

1

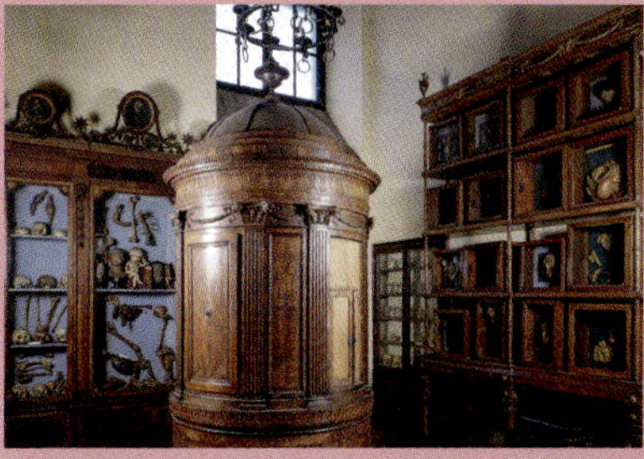

2

1 *The Sala Flajani.* This display case contains the specimens prepared for the study of pathological anatomy, based on anomalies of the skeleton or blood vessels.
Sala Flajani. In dieser Vitrine sind Präparate enthalten, die anatomische Auffälligkeiten des Skeletts und der Gefäße aufweisen.
La Salle Flajani. Cette vitrine contient les préparations anatomiques pathologiques montrant des anomalies du squelette et des vaisseaux sanguins.

2 *The Sala Flajani.* On the right-hand wall is a collection of stones removed from the livers, kidneys and bladders of patients operated on at Santo Spirito Hospital in the 19th century. In the centre of the room is a miniature temple in which a press was housed that was used to grind up cinchona bark. Constructed after a design by the Sienese Giovanni Battista Cipriani, it dates from the last quarter of the 18th century. The use of cinchona revolutionised the treatment of malaria, which had long affected Rome and the surrounding areas, claiming hundreds of victims every year.
Sala Flajani. Rechts an der Wand findet sich eine Sammlung von Leber-, Nieren- und Blasensteine aus dem 19. Jh., die von Patienten des Santo Spirito-Krankenhauses stammen. In der Raummitte steht ein Miniaturtempel, welcher eine Presse zur Pulverisierung von Chinarinde enthielt. Er stammt aus dem letzten Viertel des 18. Jhs. und wurde nach einem Entwurf Giovanni Battista Cipriani da Sienas gebaut. Chinarinde revolutionierte die Behandlung von Malaria, die in der Campagna Romana jährlich Hunderte Opfer fordete.
La Salle Flajani. Sur le mur de droite se trouve une collection des pierres trouvées dans le foie, les reins et la vessie des patients opérés à l'hôpital Santo Spirito au 19ᵉ siècle. Au centre de la pièce, le temple miniature qui contenait la meule avec laquelle l'écorce de quinquina était broyée et pulvérisée. Il date du dernier quart du 18ᵉ siècle et a été réalisée d'après un projet de Giovanni Battista Cipriani da Siena. La poudre de quinine a révolutionné le traitement du paludisme, une fièvre endémique qui touchait Rome et la région environnante, où elle faisait chaque année des centaines de victimes.

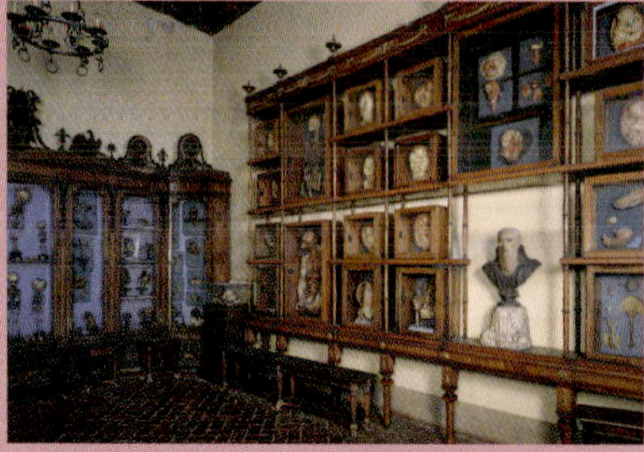

3

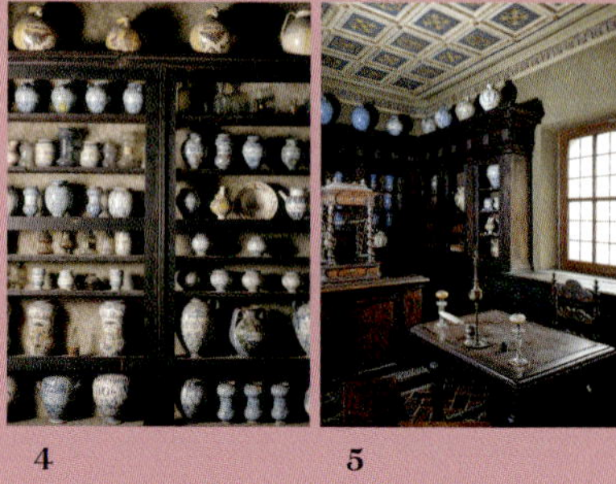

4   5

3 *The Sala Flajani*. The display cases on the right show anatomical wax models of different stages of pregnancy; they were made in the 18th century by the anatomist Mondini and the wax modeller Manfredini. On the left are anatomical torsos, for the study of the human body. All the wax models are in cases made of walnut wood.
Sala Flajani. In der rechten Vitrine befinden sich anatomische Wachsmodelle verschiedender Schwangerschaftsstadien. Sie wurden im 18. Jh. vom Anatom Mondini und dem Wachsmodellierer Manfedini geschaffen. Links davon sind anatomische Torsi für Anatomiestudien. Alle Modelle werden in Kisten aus Walnussholz aufbewahrt.
La Salle Flajani. La vitrine à droite abrite les modèles anatomiques en cire représentant les différentes étapes de la grossesse ; ils ont été réalisés au 18ᵉ siècle par l'anatomiste Mondini et par le modeleur de cire Manfredini. À gauche, les torses anatomiques pour l'étude du corps humain. Tous les modèles en cire sont stockés dans des caisses en noyer.

4 *The Pharmacy*. Arranged on the shelves that line the walls is a precious collection of apothecary jars used to contain various pharmaceutical substances and made between the 15th and 18th century.
Apotheke. Auf den Wandregalen aufgereiht steht eine kostbare Sammlung von Apothekergefäßen aus dem 15.–18. Jh., die verschiedene pharmazeutische Substanzen enthielten.
La Pharmacie. Sur les étagères qui recouvrent les murs, une précieuse collection de pots d'apothicaire fabriqués entre le 15ᵉ et le 18ᵉ siècle contiennent des substances médicinales.

5 *The Pharmacy*. A reconstruction of a 17th-century pharmacy with a terracotta-tiled floor and coffered ceiling. Facing the door into the room is a large bench of solid wood, while on the counter is a set of scales, used by the pharmacist to weigh out powders.
Apotheke. Rekonstruktion einer Apotheke aus dem 17. Jh. mit Terrakottaboden und Kassettendecke. Der Blick fällt auf eine große, schwere Holztheke. Darauf steht eine Waage, mit der Pulver abgewogen werden konnte.
La Pharmacie. Une reconstitution d'une officine du 17ᵉ siècle avec planchers en terre cuite et plafond à caissons. Un grand banc en bois massif fait face à la porte d'entrée. Sur le comptoir, il y a une balance utilisée par le pharmacien pour peser les poudres.

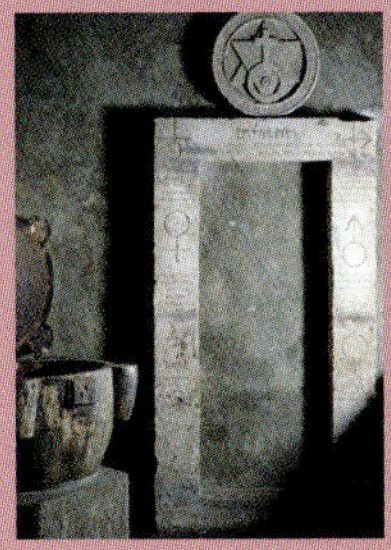 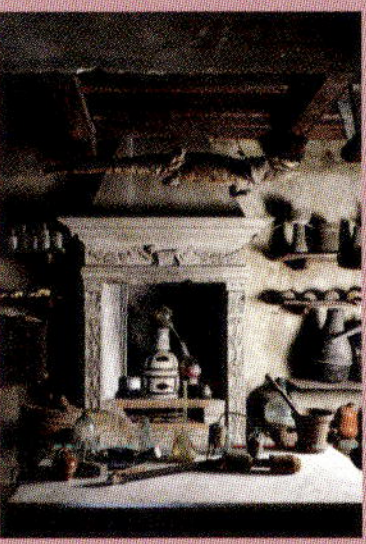

6   7

6 *The Alchemical Laboratory.* On the right is a cast of a famous hermetic doorway. It is said that the cabbalistic symbols engraved on the frame represent the formula for the philosophers' stone, which was supposed to have made it possible to turn base metals into gold. On the left is a large 17th-century stone vessel with a locking lid that was used to prepare theriac, a concoction believed to be a panacea against intoxications.
Alchemistisches Labor. Rechts erkennt man einen Abguss der berühmten hermetischen Tür. Die in die Tür geritzten Symbole sollten die Formel für den sogenannten Stein der Weisen ergeben, mit dessen Hilfe man unedle Metalle in Gold verwandeln wollte. Links steht ein großer, mit Deckel verschließbarer Steinbehälter des 17. Jhs. Darin wurde Theriak, eine

Art Allheilmittel, besonders gegen Vergiftungen, hergestellt.
Le Laboratoire d'alchimie. À droite, le moulage de la fameuse porte hermétique. On dit que les symboles obscurs et cabalistiques gravés sur la porte représentent la formule de la pierre philosophale, qui permettait de transformer les métaux communs en or. À gauche, un grand récipient en pierre du 17ᵉ siècle muni d'un couvercle et d'un verrou, utilisé pour préparer la thériaque, une sorte de remède contre les intoxications.

7 *The Alchemical Laboratory.* Partial view of the laboratory. A stuffed cayman hangs from the ceiling, and inside the Renaissance fireplace stands the athanor, a furnace used for alchemical transmutations; it sits on a brick stove, and is attached to an alembic.

Alchemistisches Labor. Eine Teilansicht des Labors. Von der Decke hängt ein präparierter Kaiman herab. Im Renaissancekamin steht auf dem Backsteinofen ein Athanor, ein Ofen, den Alchimisten für Transmutationen verwendeten. Er ist mit einem Destillierkolben verbunden.
Le Laboratoire d'alchimie. Une vue partielle du laboratoire. Un caïman empaillé est suspendu au plafond. À l'intérieur de la cheminée Renaissance du cabinet de l'alchimiste se trouve l'athanor, le fourneau utilisé pour toutes les transmutations ; il repose sur un poêle en brique et est équipé d'un alambic.

Collezione
Raniero Gnoli

Palazzo Patrizi,
Castel Giuliano, Bracciano

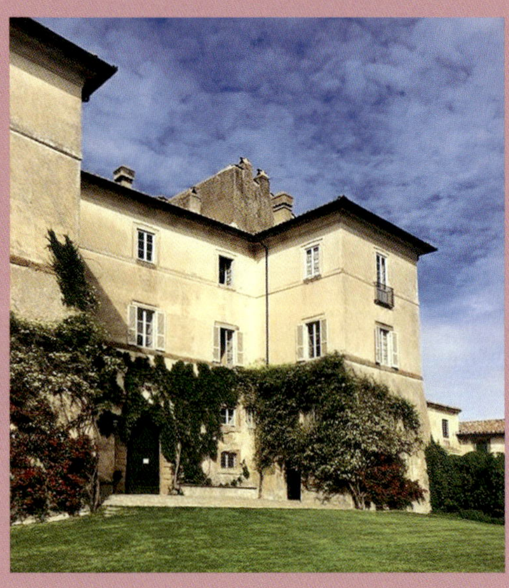

Founded 1940 (the year Count
Gnoli started his collection)

Key item The pyramid made
of oriental ebony, which contains
several fossilised marine creatures, including an extremely
rare "dwarf basilisk"; the gilded
bronzes are made in the 17th-
century Roman style.

Besonders sehenswert Eine
Pyramide aus orientalischem
Ebenholz mit Fossilien von Mee-
restieren, darunter ein äußerst
seltener „Zwergbasilisk", und
die vergoldeten Bronzearbeiten
im römischen Stil aus dem
17. Jahrhundert.

À voir absolument La pyramide
en ébène oriental qui contient
différents fossiles d'animaux marins dont un rarissime « basilique
nain » ; les bronzes dorés de style
romain du 17e siècle.

Massimo Listri, *View of Palazzo
Patrizi, Castel Giuliano*

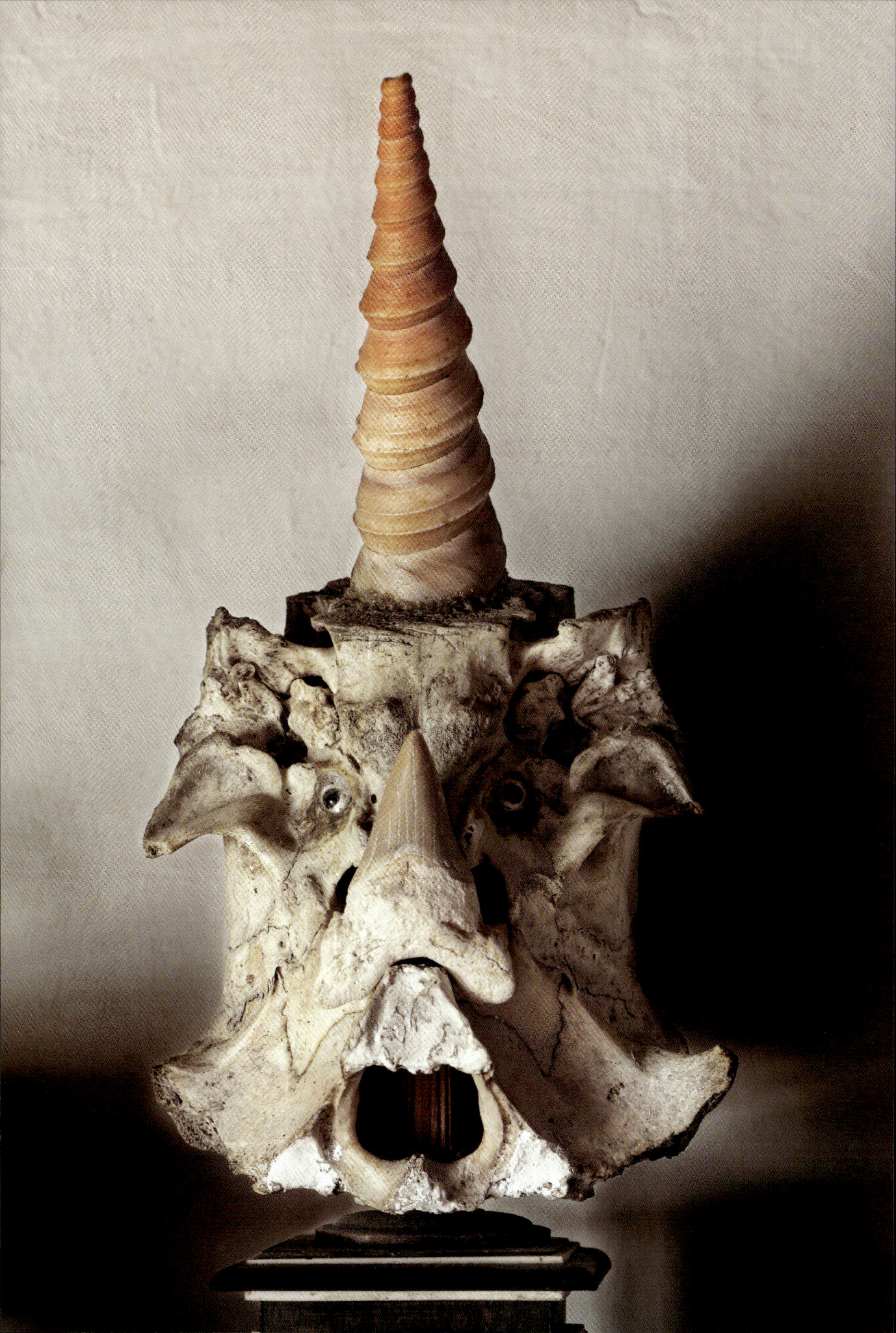

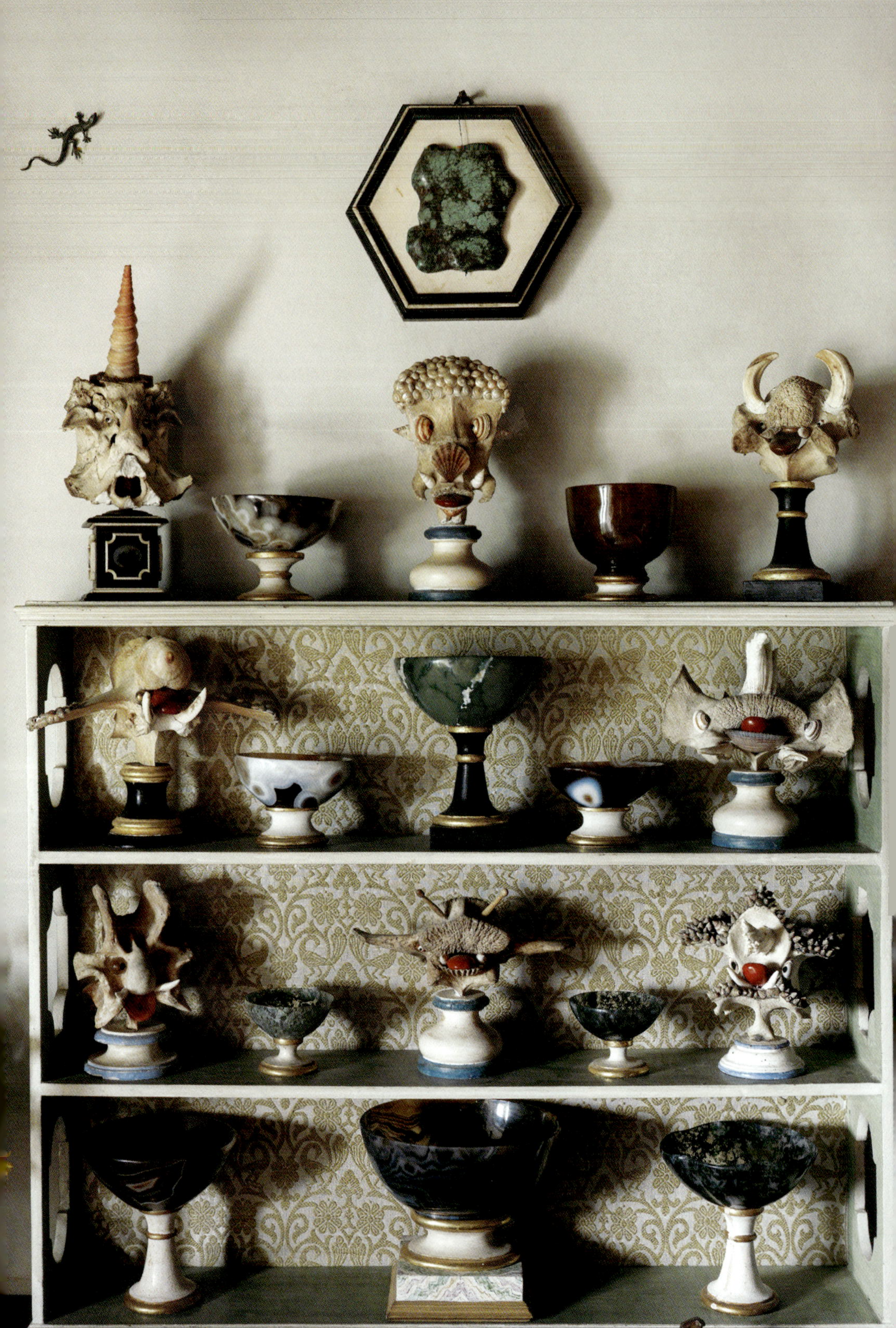

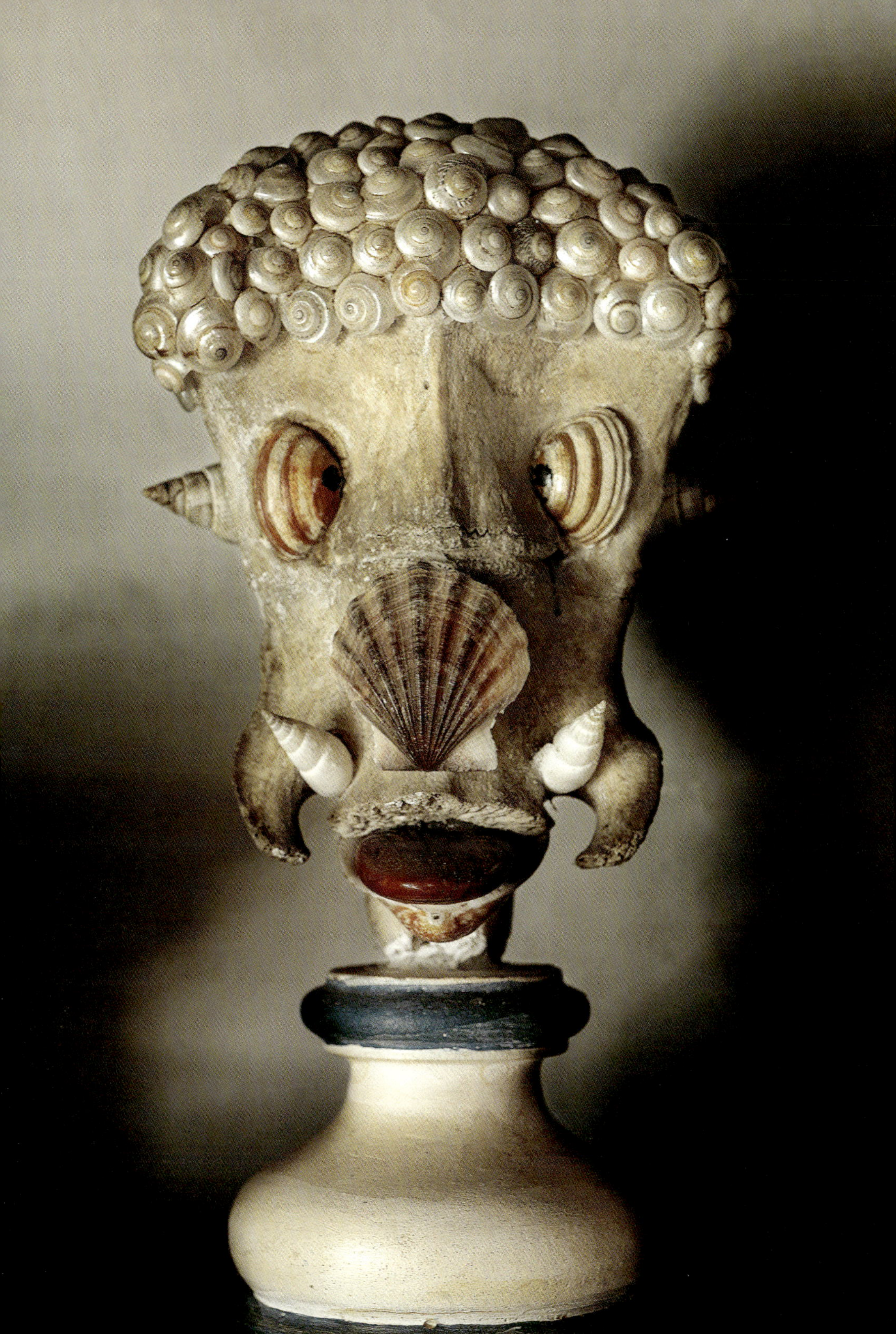

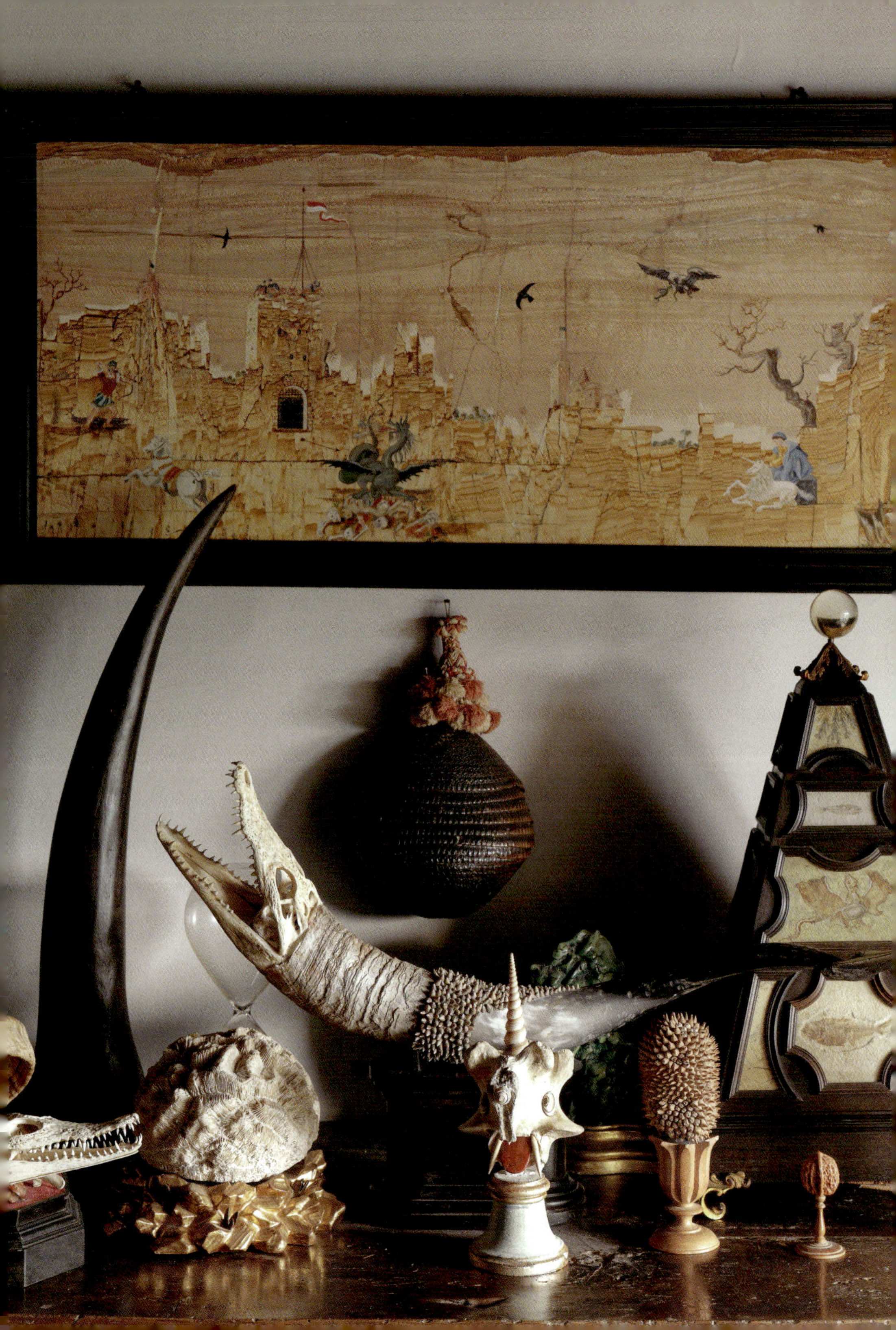

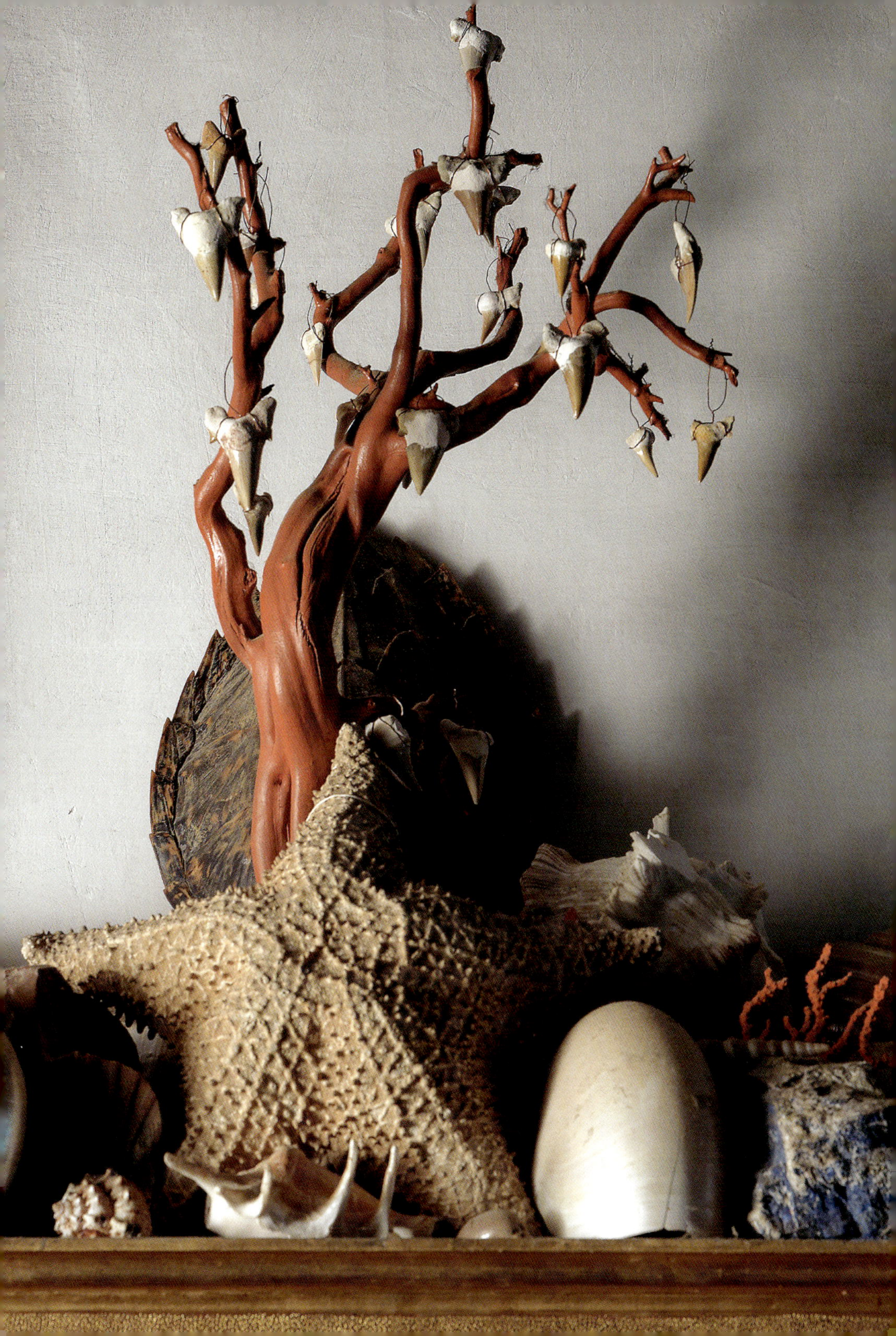

Raniero Gnoli is a world authority on the subject of antique marble, a distinguished Sanskrit scholar and head of the department of Oriental Studies at the Sapienza University of Rome. He is also a reader in Buddhist and Tantric philosophy, and among his many publications he translated the *Tantraloka* from Sanskrit, and edited *La rivelazione del Buddha*, an anthology of Indian Buddhist texts, published in the "I Meridiani" series. Gnoli is also a cabinet-maker, a restorer and collector of early textiles, a miniaturist and a painter of *chinoiseries*, as well as a designer of rock crystal chandeliers and armillary spheres.

When Count Gnoli visited Castel Giuliano in 1964, on the invitation of his friend the Marquis Innocenzo Patrizi Naro Montoro, the Palazzo Patrizi was in a state of total abandonment and the second floor of the castle was being used as an enormous henhouse. With the consent of the owner the henhouse was dismantled and removed, and careful restoration began to revive the ancient Roman country estate, something between an austere feudal fortress and a suburban villa—built over several years, but completed by the architect Sebastiano Cipriani (1660–1740).

During afternoon walks on the Palatine hill when he was still only five years old, Gnoli began, with a sense of profound commitment, to collect fragments of polychrome marble, the wonderful material that distinguished all the buildings of the Roman world between the first and the third centuries AD (his *Marmora romana* of 1971 is a monumental work on the subject). Gnoli's collection, now dispersed, consisted of about 1,500 pieces, including examples of his favourite marbles, the antique yellow marble of Numidia, Portasanta from Chios, africano from Teos, purple marble from Synnada and Egyptian red porphyry, found during his travels as he scoured the ancient quarries around the Mediterranean basin. However, the highlight of the various improvements made to his estate is a private cabinet of *naturalia* and curiosities. Suspended from one of the 17th-century roof beams are the gigantic egg of a prehistoric bird and the shell of an African tortoise, in a room which serves both as a gallery and as a living-room. Imaginary animals assembled with certain creative licence, narwhal tusks, an obelisk made from the eggs of different birds and a collection of prehistoric fossils are all displayed in cabinets and on shelves crowded with shells and rock crystal. A large globe with neither oceans nor continents, the count's own creation, dominates the centre of the room.

◦ ◈ ◦

Raniero Gnoli ist nicht nur ein weltweit anerkannter Experte für antiken Marmor, sondern auch Orientalist und Religionshistoriker, Dekan der Fakultät für Orientalistik an der Sapienza in Rom und Sanskrit-Gelehrter – so hat er unter anderem das *Tantraloka* übersetzt und *La rivelazione del Buddha* herausgegeben, eine Anthologie über den indischen Buddhismus, die in der Reihe „I Meridiani" erschien. Gnoli ist darüber hinaus Kunsttischler, restauriert, sammelt antike Stoffe, malt Miniaturen und Chinoiserien und baut Lampen aus Bergkristall sowie Armillarsphären.

Als er 1964 auf Einladung seines Freundes, des Grafen Innocenzo Patrizi Naro Montoro, zum ersten Mal nach Castel Giuliano kam, befand sich der Palazzo Patrizi in einem beklagenswerten Zustand, und im zweiten Stock hatten sich die Hühner eingenistet. Mit Zustimmung des Besitzers wurde der Hühnerstall ausquartiert und eine sorgfältige Restaurierung des alten Landsitzes in Angriff genommen, ein Gebäude zwischen strenger Feudalfestung und ländlicher Villa, das in mehreren Etappen erbaut und durch den Architekten Sebastiano Cipriani (1660–1740) vollendet wurde.

Schon im Alter von fünf Jahren begann Graf Gnoli damit, auf seinen nachmittäglichen Spaziergängen auf dem Palatin mit Hingabe polychrome Marmorfragmente zu sammeln, jenes herrliche Material, das man im alten Rom vom 1. bis zum 3. Jahrhundert als Baustoff verwendete: Sein 1971 publiziertes Buch *Marmora romana* wurde zum einschlägigen Standardwerk. Seine Sammlung, die inzwischen veräußert wurde, umfasste etwa 1500 Stücke, darunter Muster seiner Lieblingssorten (gelber Marmor aus Numidien in Nordafrika, Portasanta aus Chios, afrikanischer Marmor aus Teos Pavonazzetto aus Sinnada und roter Porphyr aus Ägypten), die er von Forschungsreisen zu den Steinbrüchen der Antike im Mittelmeerraum mitgebracht hatte. Das Glanzstück der Villa bildet zweifellos sein privates Naturalien- und Kuriositätenkabinett. In einem Raum, der zugleich als Galerie und Wohnzimmer dient, baumeln von den hohen Deckenbalken aus dem 17. Jahrhundert das Riesenei einer prähistorischen Vogelart und der Panzer einer afrikanischen Schildkröte. Überall sieht man kunstvoll geschaffene Tierwesen; Narwal-Stoßzähne, aus den Eiern verschiedener Vögel zusammengesetzte Obelisken und eine Sammlung prähistorischer Fossilien sind in Schränken und Regalen voller Muscheln und Bergkristall ausgestellt. Mitten im Raum steht ein großer Globus – ohne Meere und Kontinente –, den er selbst gebaut hat.

◉ ❖ ◉

Raniero Gnoli est l'un des plus grands spécialistes du monde en matière de marbres antiques, un sanscritiste réputé, l'ancien doyen de la faculté d'études orientales de l'université romaine de la Sapienza et un exégète de la pensée bouddhiste et tantrique – il a notamment traduit du sanscrit le *Tantraloka* et a dirigé l'édition de *La rivelazione del Buddha*, une anthologie de textes du bouddhisme indien publiée dans la collection des Meridiani. Par ailleurs, il est ébéniste, restaurateur et collectionneur de tissus anciens, peintre de miniatures et de chinoiseries, constructeur de lampadaires en cristal de roche et de sphères armillaires.

En 1964, lorsque le comte Gnoli se rendit à Castel Giuliano sur l'invitation du marquis Innocenzo Patrizi Naro Montoro, le palazzo Patrizi se trouvait dans un état d'abandon avancé, et le deuxième étage était un gigantesque poulailler. Avec le consentement du propriétaire, les poules furent expulsées et des travaux de restauration entrepris, qui ont redonné vie à l'ancienne propriété de la campagne romaine à mi-chemin entre sévère forteresse féodale et villa suburbaine – édifiée en plusieurs temps et achevée par l'architecte Sebastiano Cipriani (1660–1740).

C'est à l'âge tendre de cinq ans, au cours de ses promenades quotidiennes sur le mont Palatin, que le comte Gnoli commença à réunir avec passion des fragments de marbre polychromes, merveilleux matériau caractéristique de tous les édifices du monde romain entre le 1er et le 3e siècle, et thème de son monumental ouvrage intitulé *Marmora romana* (1971). Sa collection entre temps dispersée, comprenait près de 1500 pièces, dont certains exemplaires de ses marbres favoris, à savoir le jaune antique de Numidie, le marbre *portasanta* de Chios, le marbre africain de Téos, le pavonazzetto de Synnada et le porphyre rouge d'Égypte, collectés au cours de ses voyages sur la trace des anciennes carrières du bassin méditerranéen. L'apothéose de ses nombreux projets pour la demeure est un cabinet de *naturalia* et de curiosités. À l'une des poutres du 17e siècle présentes dans cet espace, qui est à la fois galerie et salle de séjour, sont suspendus un gigantesque œuf d'oiseau préhistorique et des carapaces de tortue africaine. Des animaux fantaisistes assemblés avec une grande liberté, des dents de narval, un obélisque composé d'œufs de différents animaux et des fossiles préhistoriques sont exposés dans des vitrines, armoires ou tables, débordant de coquillages et de cristaux de roche. Au nombre de ses créations, on signalera l'imposant globe sans océans ni continents qui occupe le centre de la pièce.

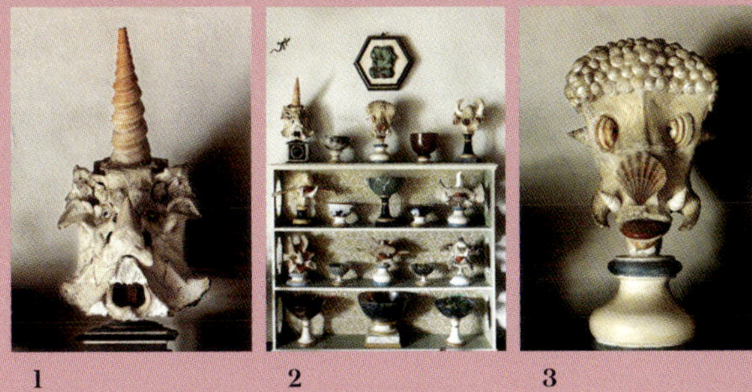

1   2   3

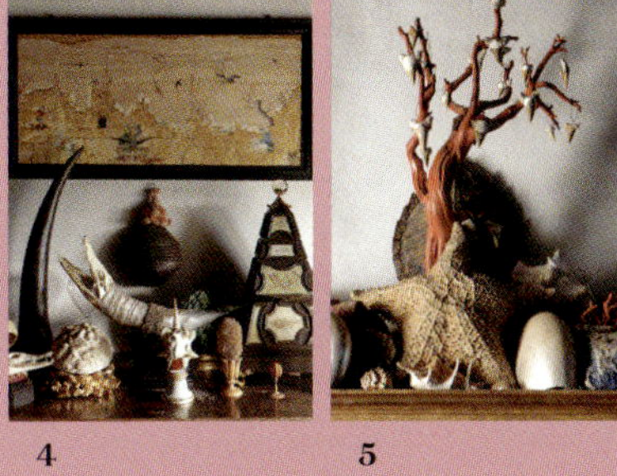

4   5

1 Head of a grotesque monstrous creature composed of animal bones and shells, with a fossilised shark's tooth on its nose; 18th-century base made of turned and painted wood, 20 cm / 7⅞ in.
Ein grotesk-monströses, aus Tierknochen und Muscheln zusammengesetztes Fantasiewesen mit einem versteinerten Haifischzahn auf der Nase; der Fuß aus gedrechseltem, polychromem Holz, 18. Jh., 20 cm.
Grotesque, créature monstrueuse composée d'os d'animaux, de coquillages et, sur le nez, d'une dent de requin fossilisée ; base du 18ᵉ siècle en bois tourné et peint, 20 cm.

2 Display case with various monsters made of *naturalia* and a series of agate cups; in the frame above, a large fragment of natural turquoise.
Regal mit aus verschiedenen Naturalien zusammengesetzten Fantasieobjekten sowie einer Reihe Achatpokale, darüber ein großes, gerahmtes Stück Türkis.
Étagère abritant divers monstres en éléments naturels et une série de tasses en agate ; en haut, un grand fragment de turquoise naturel.

3 Head of a grotesque monstrous creature composed of animal bones and shells, with a tongue of red jasper; 18th-century base made of turned and painted wood, 20 cm / 7⅞ in.
Grotesk-monströses, aus Tierknochen und Muscheln zusammengesetztes Fantasiewesen mit einer Zunge aus rotem Jaspis; der Fuß aus gedrechseltem, polychromem Holz stammt aus dem 18. Jh., 20 cm.
Grotesque, créature monstrueuse composée d'os d'animaux et de coquillages avec une langue en jaspe rouge ; base du 18ᵉ siècle en bois tourné et peint, 20 cm.

4 In the foreground is the grotesque monstrous head of a creature composed of various elements of *naturalia*; on the left, a rhinoceros horn; on the right, an ebony pyramid with fossil plaquettes; above, a pietra paesina, so-called ruin marble.
Im Vordergrund ein grotesk-monströses, aus verschiedenen Naturalien zusammengesetztes Fantasiewesen, links ein Rhinozeroshorn, rechts eine Ebenholzpyramide mit Fossilienplaketten, im Hintergrund Pietra paesina, sogenannter Ruinenmarmor.
Au premier plan, des créatures monstrueuses composées de divers éléments naturels ; à gauche, corne de rhinocéros ; à droite, pyramide d'ébène avec incrustations de fossiles ; sur le mur, une pietra paesina, appelée marbre de ruine.

5 Group of shells, madrepores, corals, fossilised starfish and a piece of lapis lazuli; in the background, the shell of a tortoise.
Arrangement aus Muscheln, Steinkorallen, Korallen, versteinerten Seesternen und Lapislazuli, im Hintergrund befindet sich ein Schildkrötenpanzer.
Groupe de coquillages, madrépores, coraux, une étoile de mer fossilisée et un spécimen de lapis-lazuli ; à l'arrière-plan, une carapace de tortue.

Collezione Alessandro Orsi

Villa Ca' Mera, Azzate (Varese)

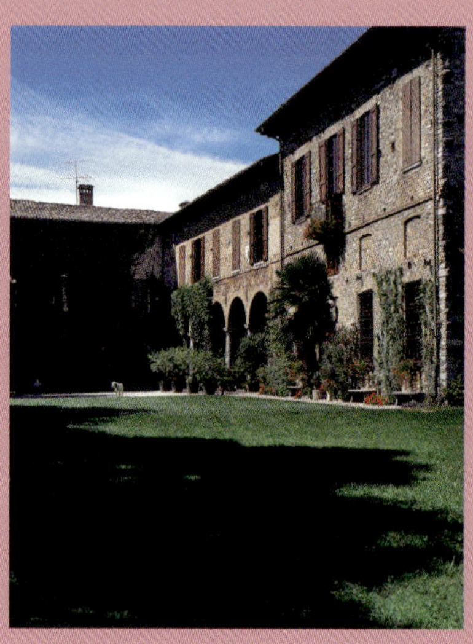

Founded The collection was established in the 20th century, the villa dates from the 16th century.

Key item The 19th-century globe showing all the countries known at the time and marked with the course of the three famous voyages of James Cook (1728–1779), undertaken to explore the extent of the South Seas and later in search of the north-west passage between the Atlantic Ocean and the Pacific.

Besonders sehenswert Ein Globus aus dem 19. Jh. mit kartografischer Darstellung der gesamten damals bekannten Erde und den Routen der drei sagenumwobenen Reisen, die Kapitän James Cook (1728–1779) unternahm, um die Südsee zu erforschen und später die berühmte Nordwestpassage zwischen Atlantik und Pazifik zu finden.

À voir absolument Mappemonde du 19e siècle avec la représentation cartographique de l'intégralité du monde connu jusqu'alors, et des trois voyages mythiques effectués par le capitaine James Cook (1728–1779) pour explorer les mers du Sud et découvrir le fameux passage du Nord-Ouest reliant l'océan Atlantique et l'océan Pacifique.

Massimo Listri, *View of the Villa Ca' Mera in Azzate, Varese*

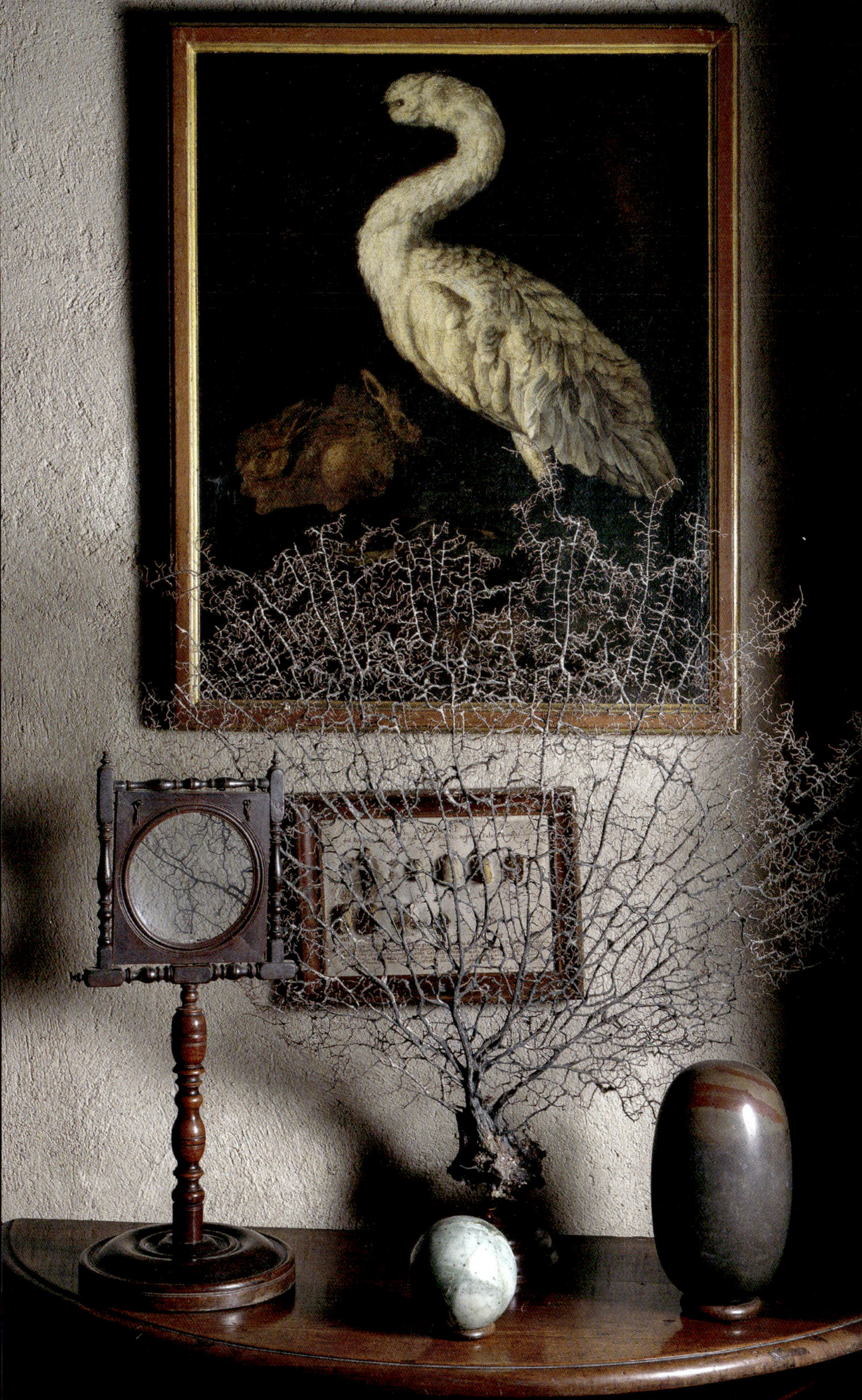

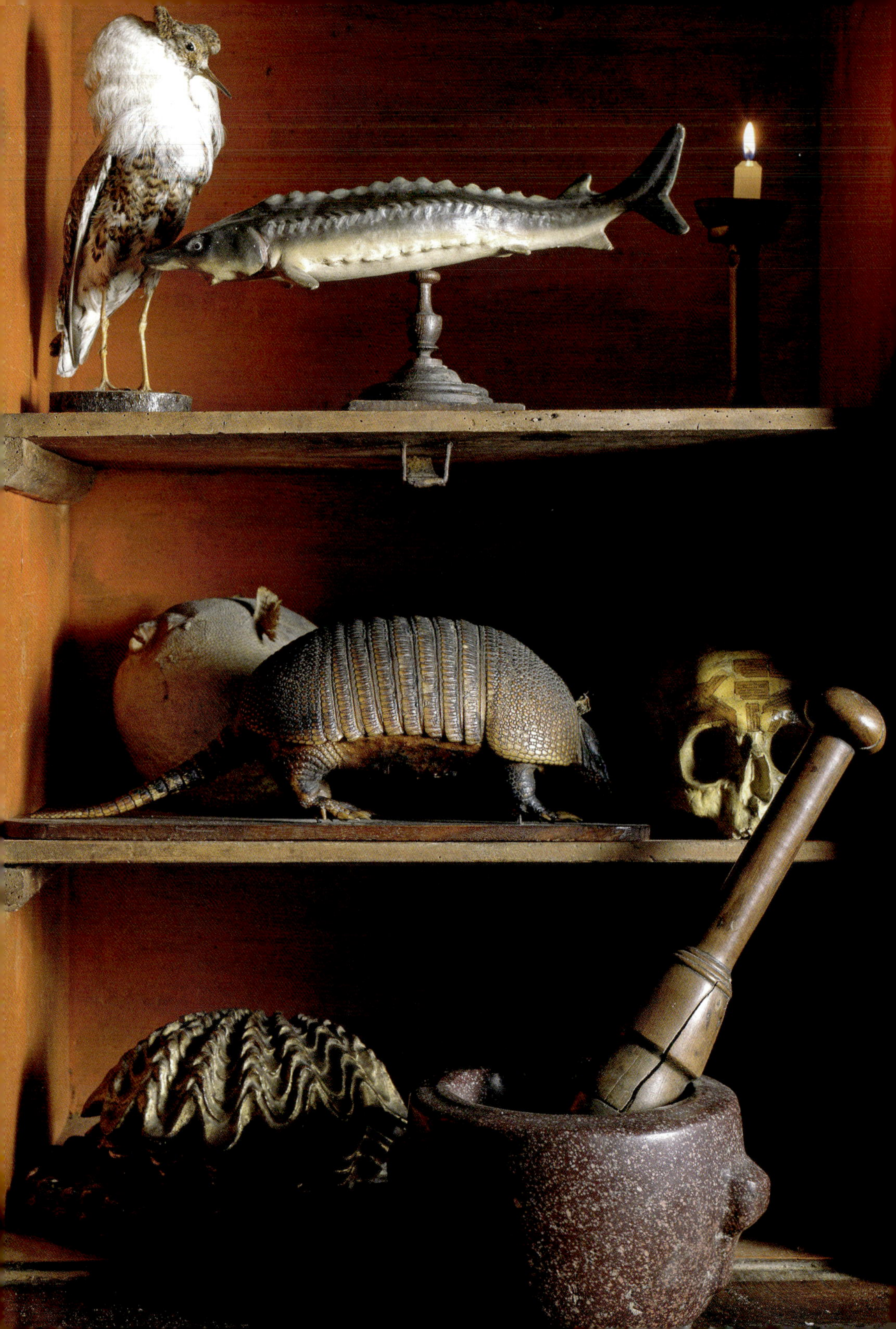

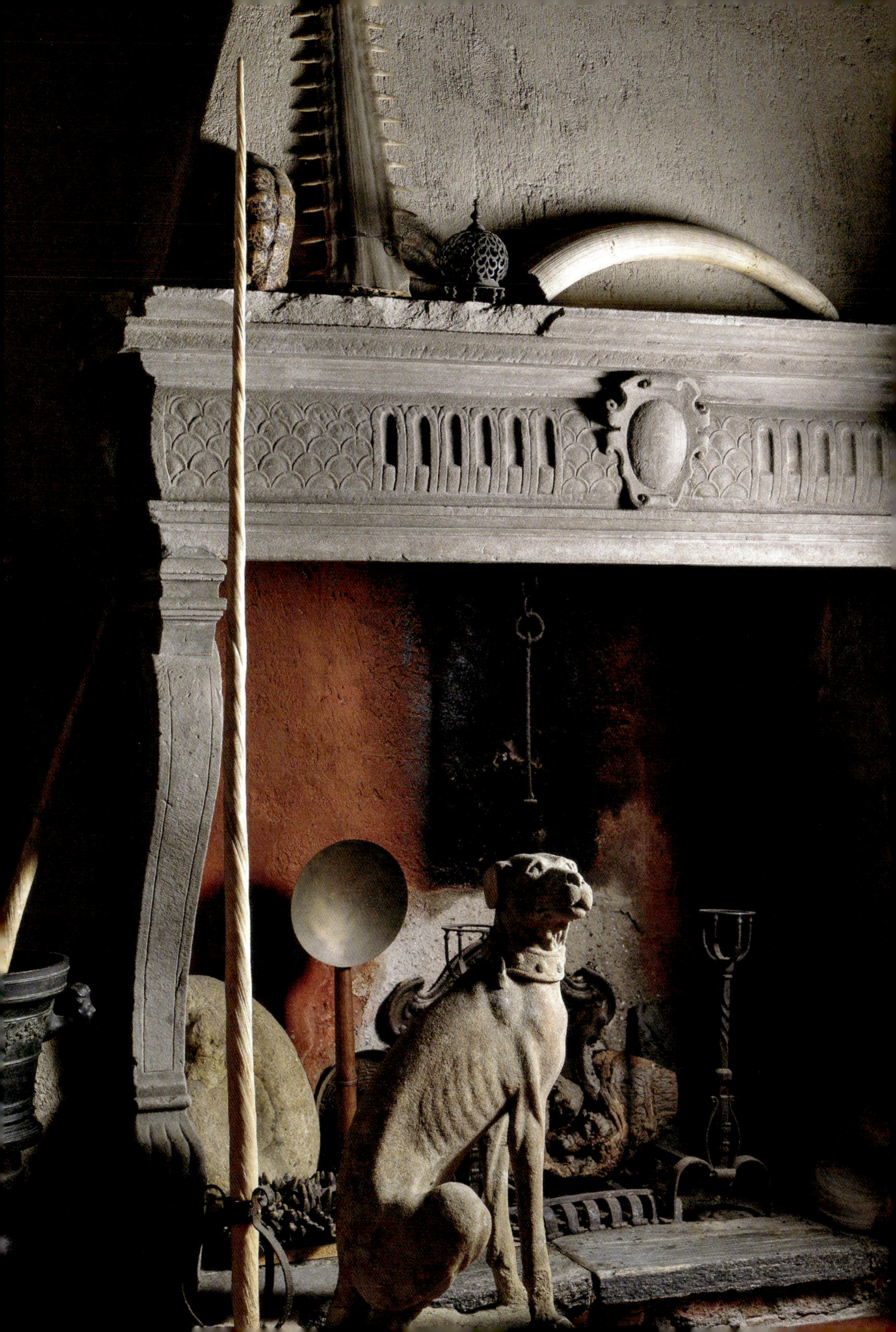

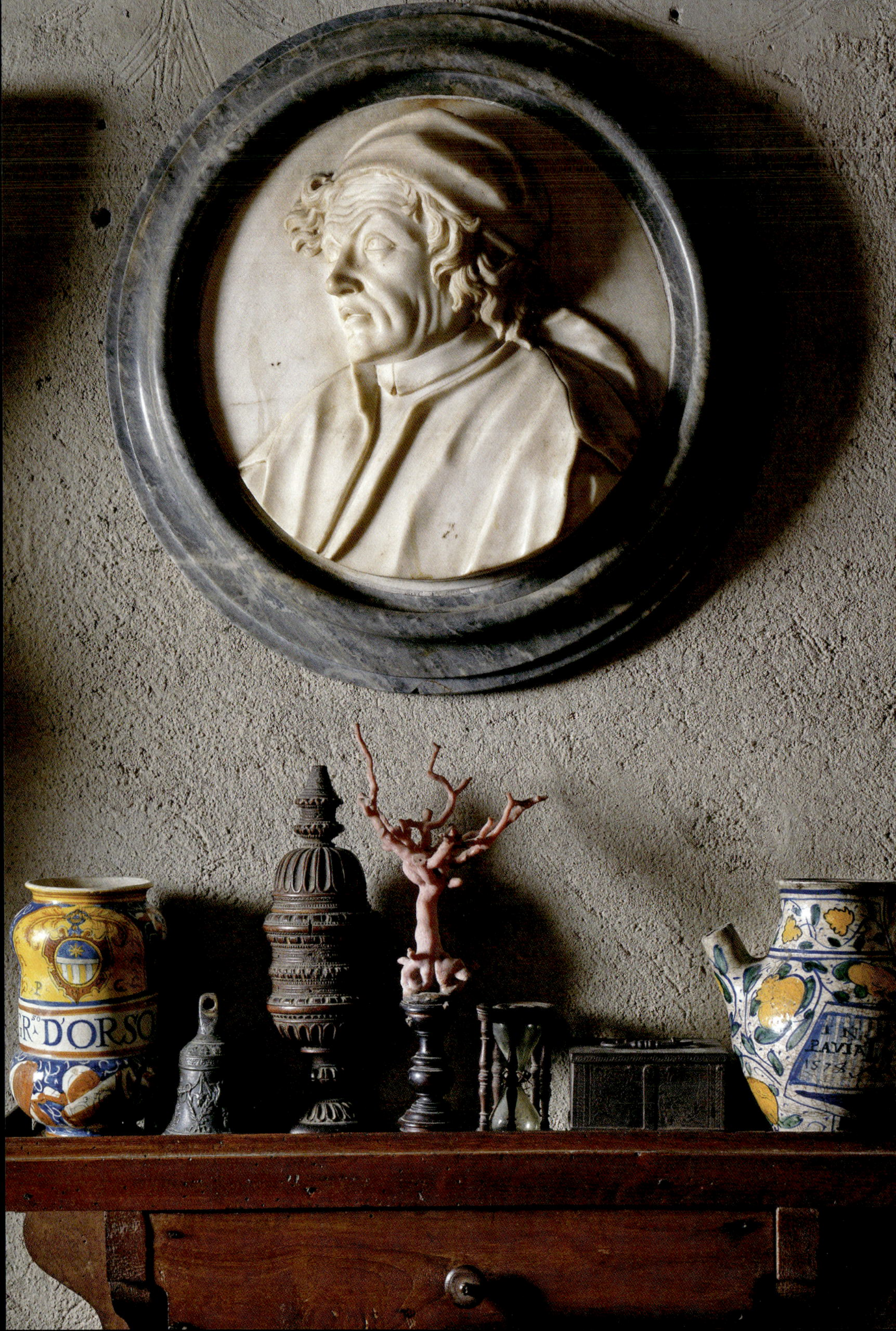
R.SO D'ORSO
IN PAVIA 1578

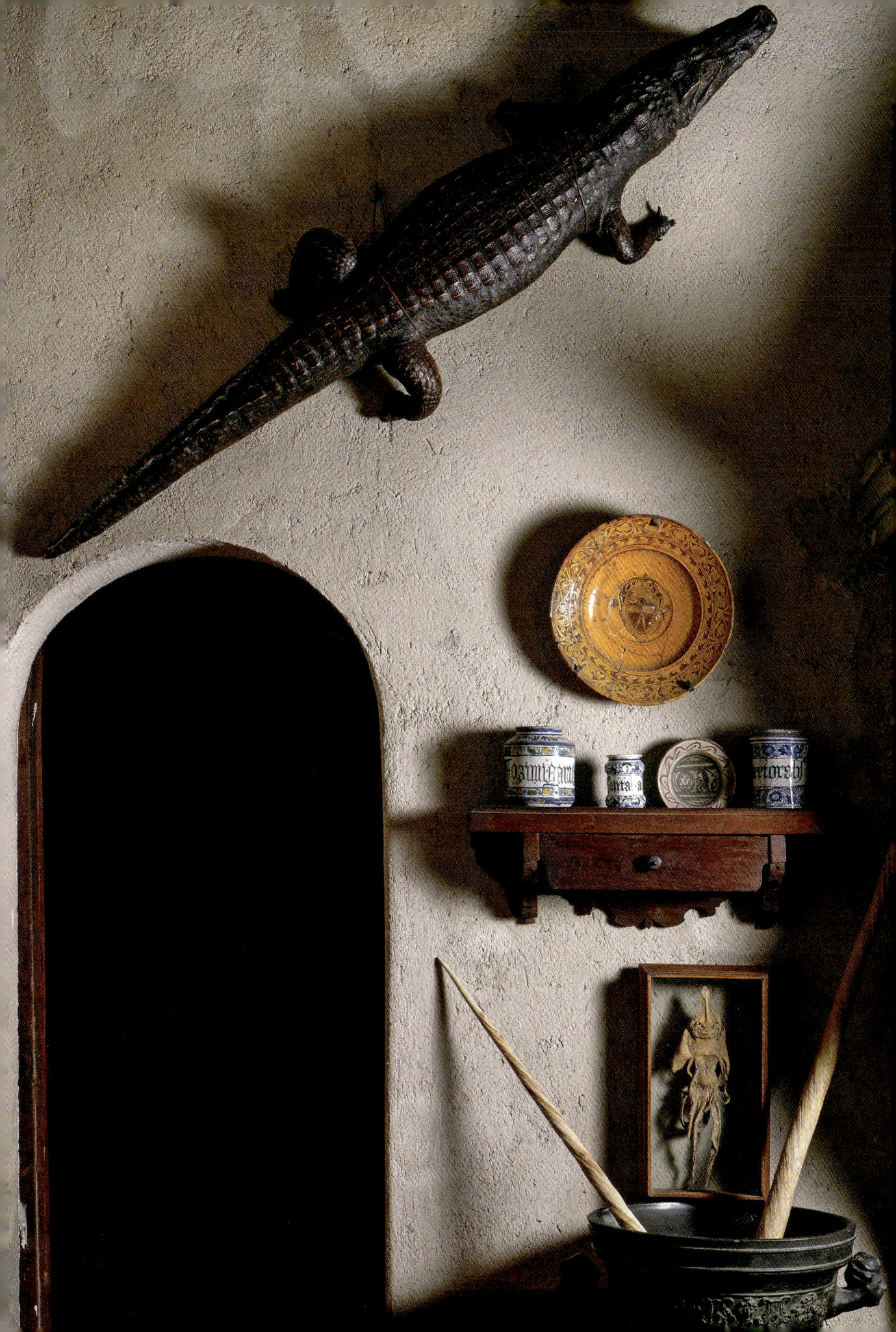

The Villa Ca' Mera, so called by Alessandro Orsi in honour of its previous owner, Canon Luigi Mera, was acquired in the late 1950s. At the time the original rooms were almost unrecognisable, since they had been divided up into 12 separate living spaces and workshops. The villa was restored to its original state following an intense programme of work, during which it was discovered that the building's foundations appeared to date back to the 16th century (as indicated by a date carved into one of the doors, and a graffito found on a beam of the coffered ceiling in the dining-room).

Over the course of the next few decades, the distinguished Milanese art-dealer and connoisseur extraordinaire Alessandro Orsi furnished this country house according to his personal vision, with a theatrical taste poised between the Renaissance and the Baroque and with a love for strange and rare objects, thus creating a veritable modern cabinet of curiosities. His collection includes precious objects dating from the 16th to the 19th century, and alongside the rarer pieces there are a number of fascinating and curious items, such as the large painting *Greyhound and Palazzo Chigi in Ariccia* by Michelangelo Pace, called di Campidoglio (1610–1670), a narwhal tusk, a globe illustrating Cook's famous voyages of exploration, a marble bust of Marsilio Ficino (1433–1499), together with pieces of quartz, a stuffed crocodile, a life-size wooden dromedary and a stuffed ostrich from the menagerie of the Villa Arconati in Bollate.

◎ ◆ ◎

Als Alessandro Orsi Ende der fünfziger Jahre des 20. Jahrhunderts die Villa erwarb, gab er ihr den Namen Ca' Mera, nach dem Vorbesitzer, dem Kanonikus Luigi Mera. Zu diesem Zeitpunkt war das eigentliche Haus kaum wiederzuerkennen, weil man die ursprünglichen Säle in zwölf Hauswirtschafts- und Laborräume unterteilt hatte. Bei einer umfangreichen Renovierung wurde der ursprüngliche Zustand wiederhergestellt. In Teilen stammt das Gebäude offenbar aus dem 16. Jahrhundert – Hinweise darauf liefern die eingeritzte Jahreszahl auf einer Tür sowie Ritzspuren an der Balken- und Kassettendecke, die bei der Restaurierung im Speisesaal zutage kam.

Mit einem Sinn fürs Theatralische, das zwischen Renaissance und Barock changiert, und einer Vorliebe für ausgefallene, bizarre Stücke hat es der Mailänder Antiquitätenhändler Alessandro Orsi, ein echter Connaisseur, im Laufe einiger Jahrzehnte verstanden, seinem Landsitz eine ganz besondere Note zu geben und eine moderne Wunderkammer aufzubauen. Die Sammlung umfasst viele wertvolle Stücke aus einem Zeitraum vom 16. bis zum 19. Jahrhundert sowie echte Kuriositäten: von dem Monumentalbild *Windhund und Palazzo Chigi in Ariccia* des Malers Michelangelo Pace, gen. di Campidoglio (1610–1670), dem Stoßzahn eines Narwals, dem Globus mit den Reiserouten von James Cook, einer Marmorbüste von Marsilio Ficino (1433–1499) bis hin zu den Quarzen, einem ausgestopften Krokodil, einem Holzdromedar in Lebensgröße und einem ausgestopften Strauß aus dem Serail der Villa Arconati in Bollate.

◎◈◎

La Ca' Mera, ainsi nommée par Alessandro Orsi en souvenir de son précédent propriétaire connu, le chanoine Luigi Mera, fut acquise à la fin des années 1950. À l'époque, les salles anciennes étaient quasiment méconnaissables, divisées en douze ateliers et pièces d'habitation. D'importants travaux de restauration ont permis à la villa de retrouver son état d'origine. La fondation de l'édifice remonte en partie au 16e siècle, comme en témoignent une date gravée sur une porte et les inscriptions figurant sur les poutres et les caissons du plafond mis au jour dans la salle à manger.

En l'espace de quelques décennies, Alessandro Orsi, antiquaire milanais raffiné et connaisseur hors pair, a su aménager la résidence de campagne dans un style tout à fait personnel alliant un goût théâtral à mi-chemin entre Renaissance et Baroque et un amour pour les objets bizarres et recherchés, et ainsi donner naissance à un véritable Cabinet des merveilles moderne. Si la collection inclut des pièces de grande valeur datées d'une période allant du 16e au 19e siècle, elle accueille aussi, outre certains objets rares, d'authentiques curiosités dont un grand tableau intitulé *Lévrier et palazzo Chigi à Ariccia*, œuvre de Michelangelo Pace, dit di Campidoglio (1610–1670), une dent de narval, une mappemonde où sont reportées les routes des voyages de James Cook, un buste en marbre de Marsile Ficin (1433–1499), sans oublier des quartz, un crocodile naturalisé, un dromadaire en bois grandeur nature et une autruche naturalisée provenant de la ménagerie de la villa Arconati de Bollate.

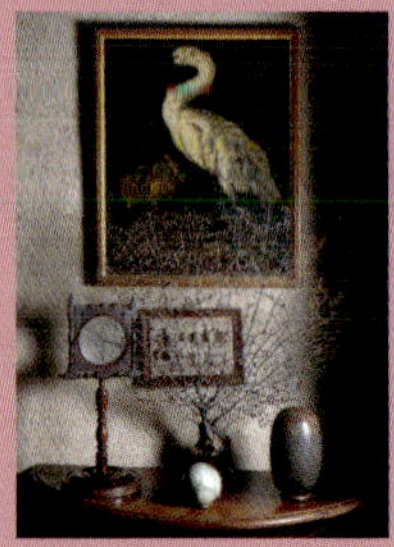

1

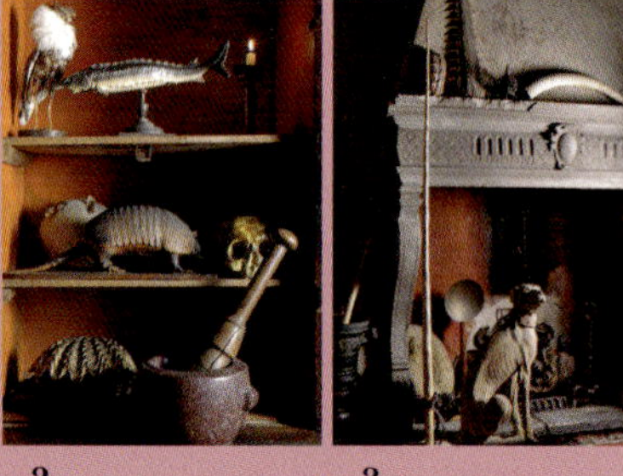

2   3

1 On the wall is a painting of a heron by an anonymous 18th-century artist; on the stand on the right is a lingam, a phallus which symbolises the potency of the Hindu deity Shiva; in the centre is a black coral.
An der Wand das Gemälde eines Reihers von einem unbekannten Malers aus dem 18. Jh. Auf der Konsole sind u. a. ein Lingam, d. h. ein Phallus, der die Zeugungskraft der hinduistischen Gottheit Schiwa symbolisiert, sowie eine schwarze Koralle ausgestellt.
Sur le mur, la représentation d'un héron par un artiste anonyme du 18ᵉ siècle ; sur l'étagère, un *lingam*, c'est-à-dire un phallus, qui symbolise la force de la procréation du dieu hindou Shiva, et un corail noir.

2 On the shelves are a number of stuffed animals, including an armadillo; in the foreground on the right can be seen a red porphyry mortar.
Im Regal findet sich eine Reihe präparierter Tiere, darunter ein Gürteltier; im Vordergrund rechts steht ein Mörser aus rotem Porphyr.
Sur les étagères, des animaux empaillés, dont un tatou ; au premier plan à droite, un mortier en porphyre rouge.

3 In the foreground is a narwhal tusk and a 17th-century sculpture of a dog carved from Tuscan stone; above the 17th-century fireplace are a tortoise shell, the beak of a sawfish and an elephant's tusk.
Im Vordergrund links steht ein Narwalstoßzahn neben einer Hundeskulptur, die im 17. Jh. aus toskanischem Stein gehauen wurde. Auf dem Kaminsims des 17. Jhs. liegen ein Schildkrötenpanzer, das Rostrum eines Schwertfisches sowie ein Elefantenstoßzahn.
Au premier plan, une dent de narval et une sculpture de chien en pierre de Toscane datant du 17ᵉ siècle ; sur la cheminée du 17ᵉ siècle, une carapace de tortue, le rostre d'un poisson-scie et une défense d'éléphant.

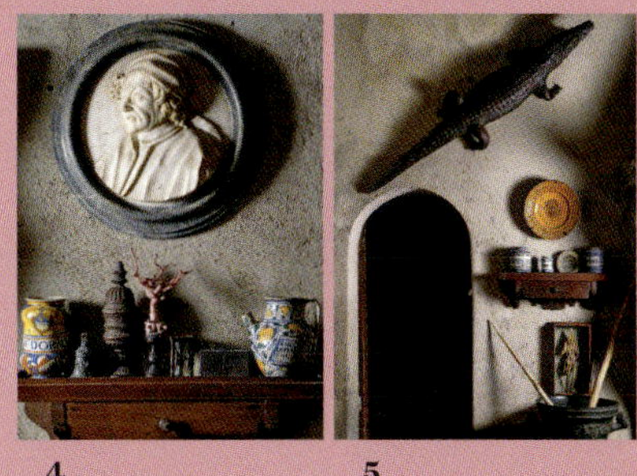

4   5

4 On the wall is a portrait in relief of Marsilio Ficino; on the table, two majolica jugs, a coral tree, an hour-glass and various other objects.
An der Wand hängt ein Reliefporträt Marsilio Ficinos; auf dem Tisch stehen zwei Majolikagefäße, ein Korallenbaum, eine Sanduhr und weitere Objekte.
Sur le mur, le portrait sculpté de Marsile Ficin ; sur la table, deux poteries en majolique, un corail, un sablier et divers autres objets.

5 Seen here at the top is a stuffed crocodile above a 16th-century dish from Pavia. Below are majolica pharmacy jars, and inside the display case is a Jenny Haniver: the mummified, mutilated carcass of a ray that was modified to resemble a monstrous, vaguely humanoid creature.
Oben ein präpariertes Krokodil über einem Teller aus Pavia aus dem 16. Jh. Unter diesem stehen Majolikagefäße für pharmazeutische Substanzen. Wiederum darunter in einem Schaukasten befindet sich eine sogenannte Jenny Haniver, ein Geigenrochen, der so präpariert ist, dass er an ein mumifiziertes, humanoides Meereswesen erinnert.
En haut, un crocodile empaillé et un plat de Pavie datant du 16e siècle. En bas, des pots de pharmacie en majolique et, à l'intérieur de la vitrine, une « Jenny Haniver », créature monstrueuse fabriquée à partir de la carcasse d'un poisson-guitare, qui est découpé, plié et mutilé pour lui donner l'aspect d'un être vaguement humanoïde.

Cabinet d'histoire naturelle de Clément Lafaille

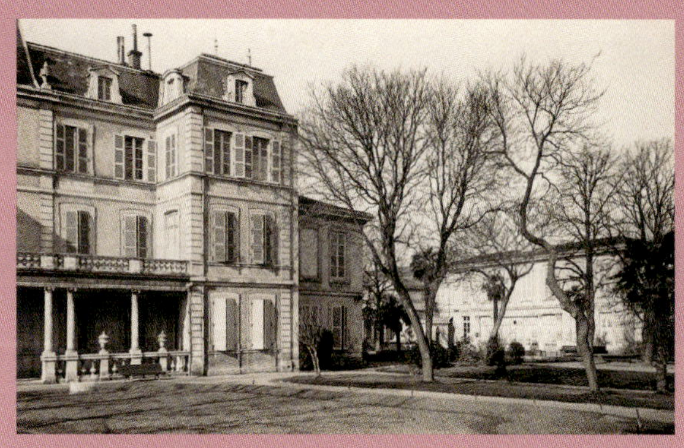

Founded 1776/1782

Key item The glass cases with starfish from the Atlantic, various types of crustaceans and the display of madrepores.

Besonders sehenswert Die Vitrinen, die Seesterne, Muscheln und Steinkorallen des Atlantiks beherbergen.

À voir absolument Les vitrines qui abritent les étoiles de mer de l'Atlantique, les crustacés et la collection-exposition de madrépores.

View from the garden of the Muséum d'Histoire Naturelle de La Rochelle. Photograph, Collection Bibliothèque Scientifique du Muséum de La Rochelle.

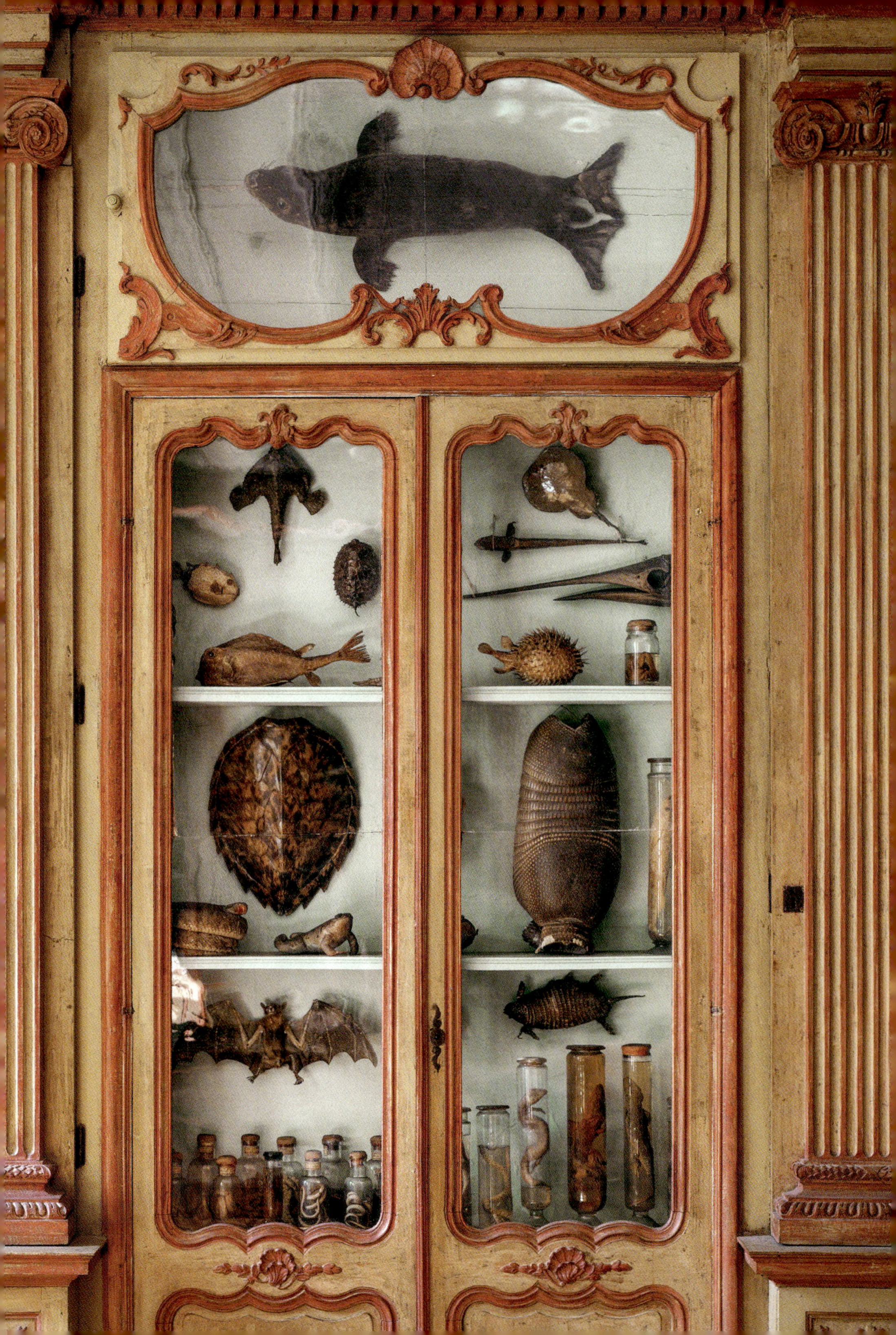

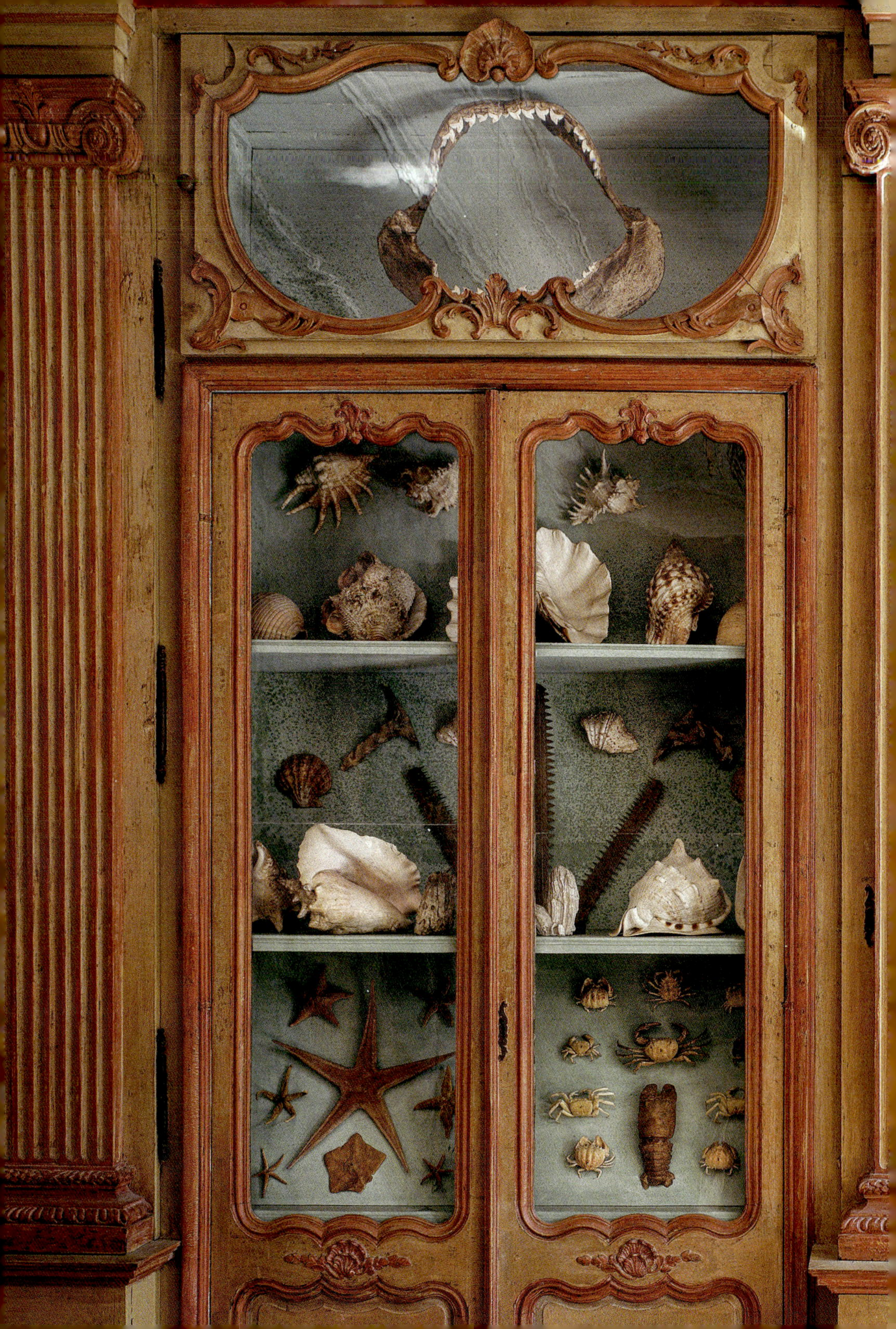

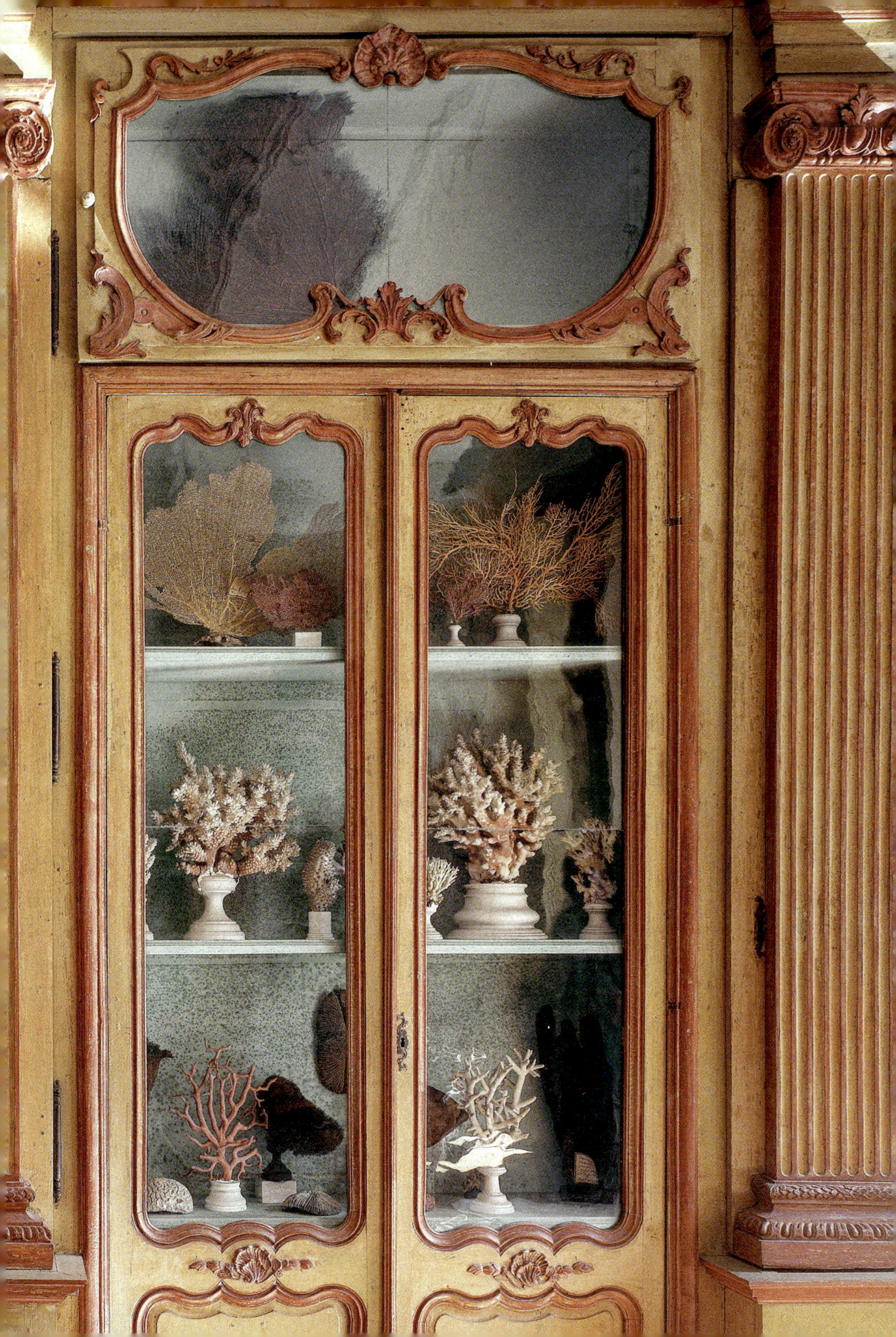

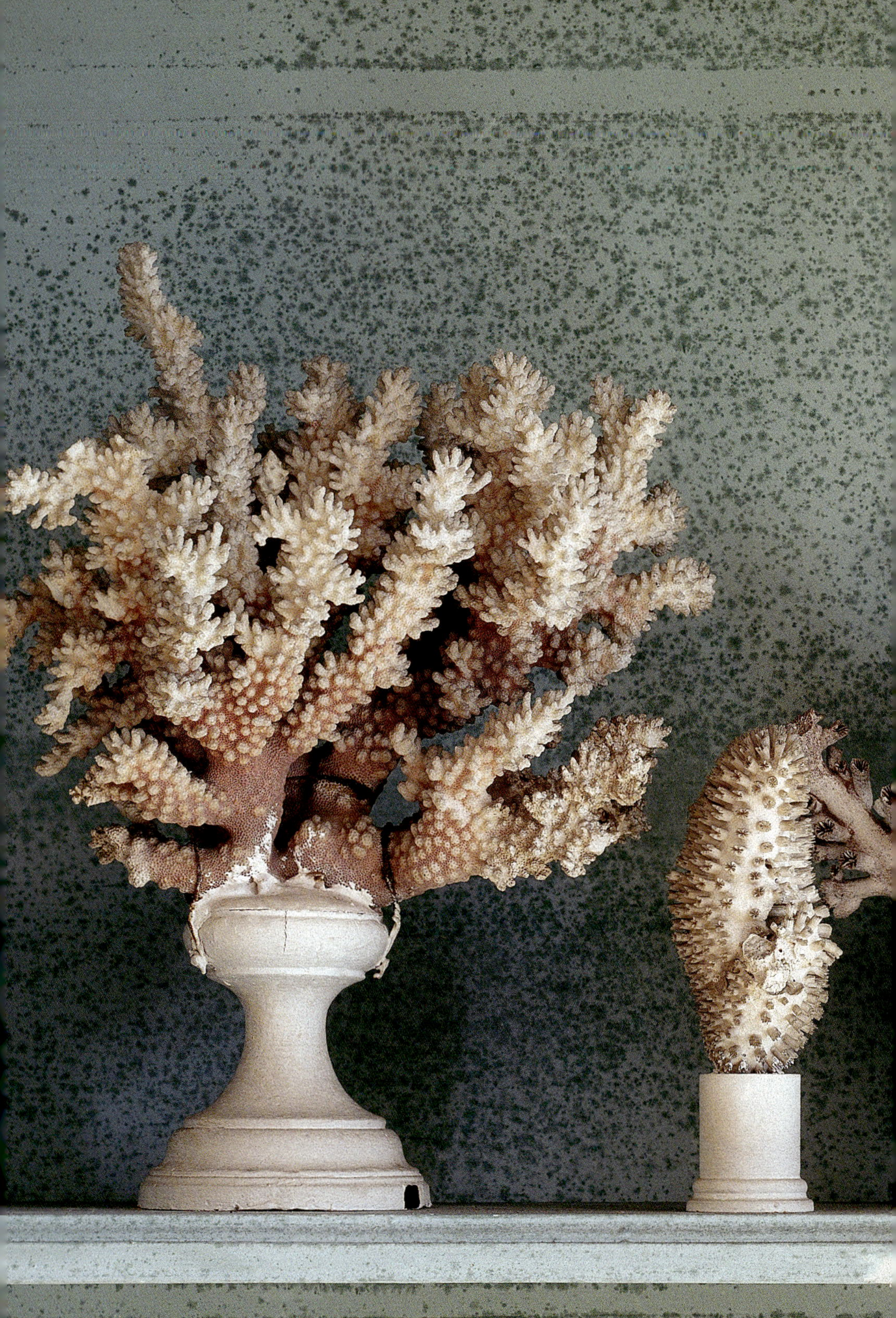

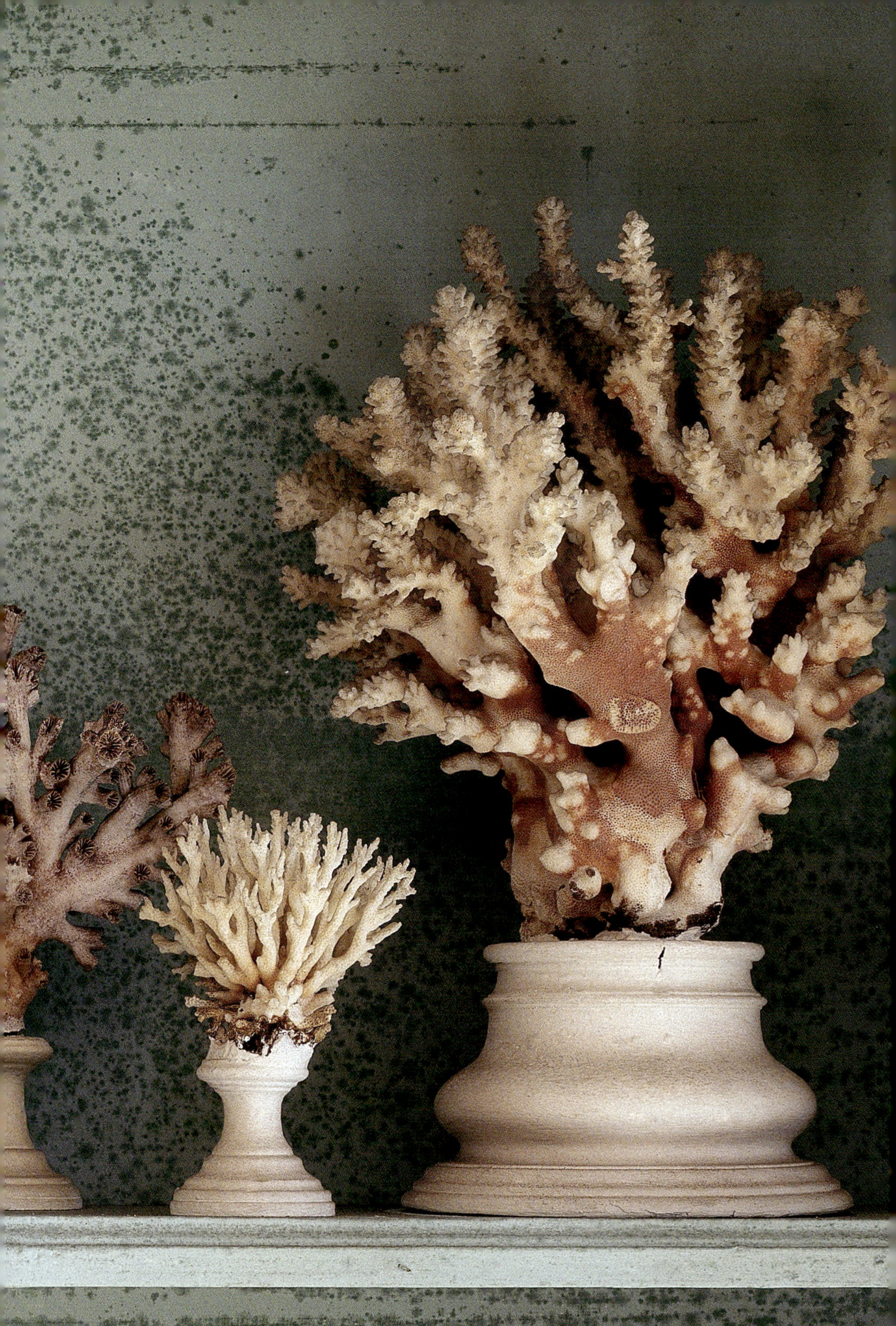

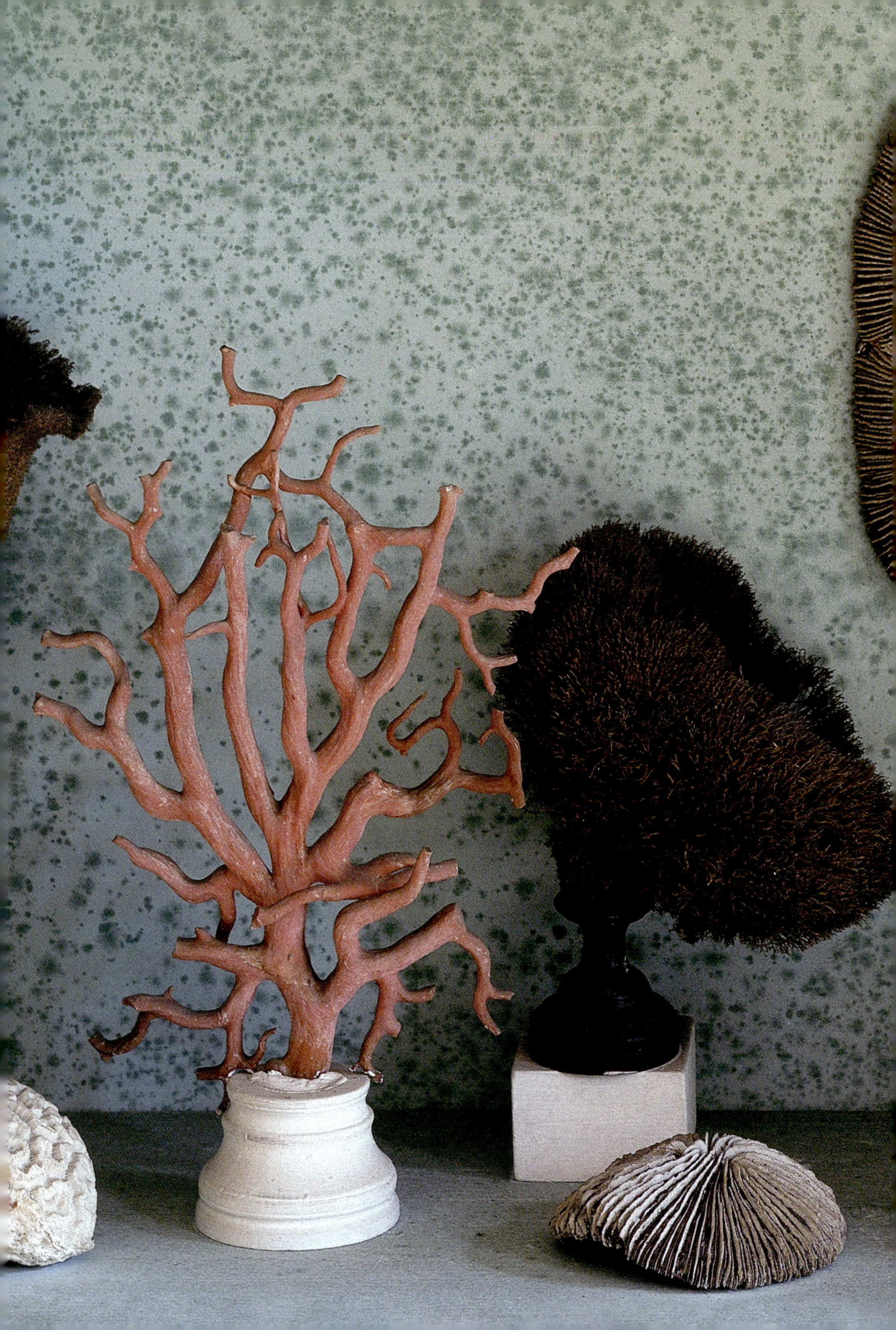

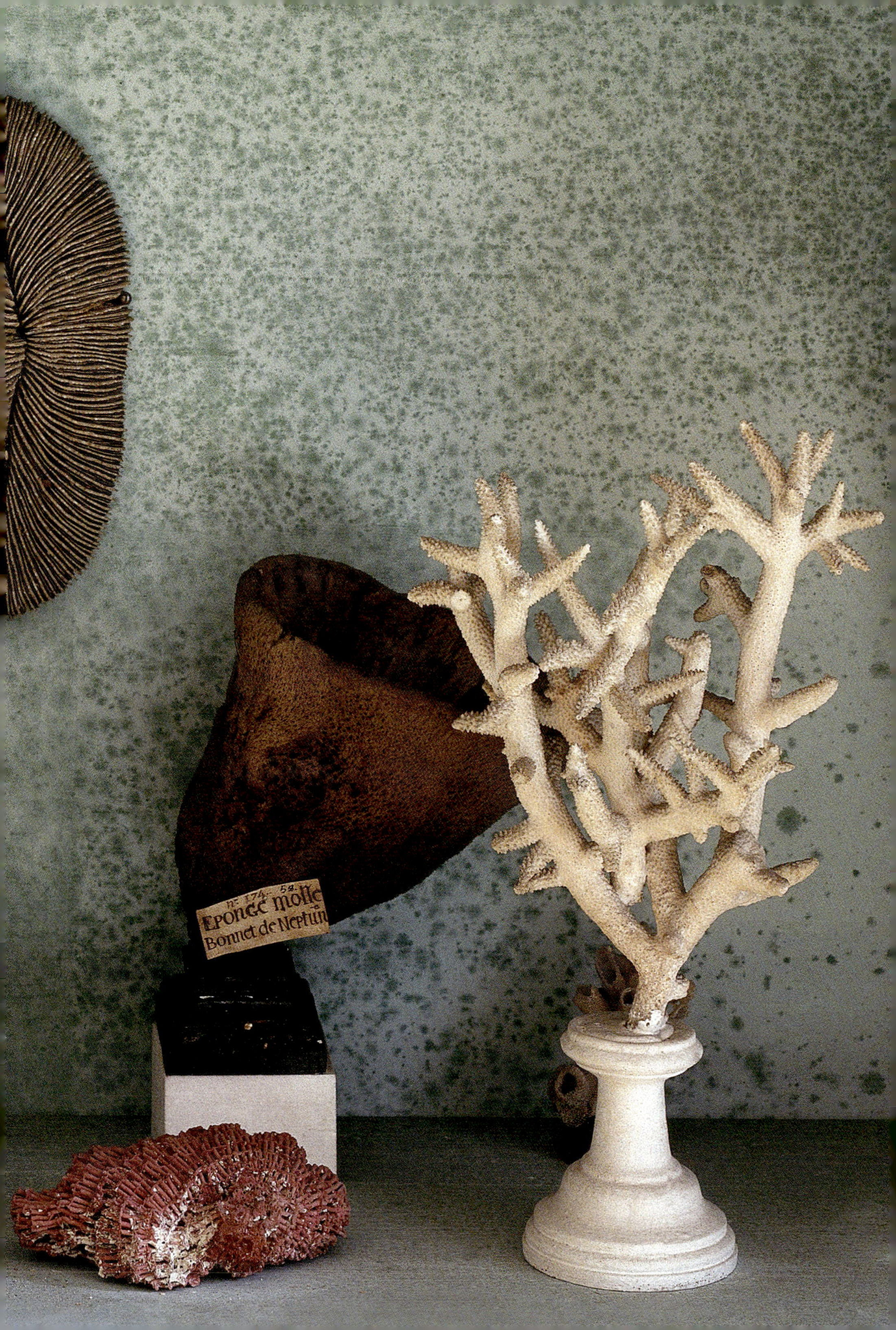
n° 174. 5g.
Eponge molle
Bonnet de Neptun

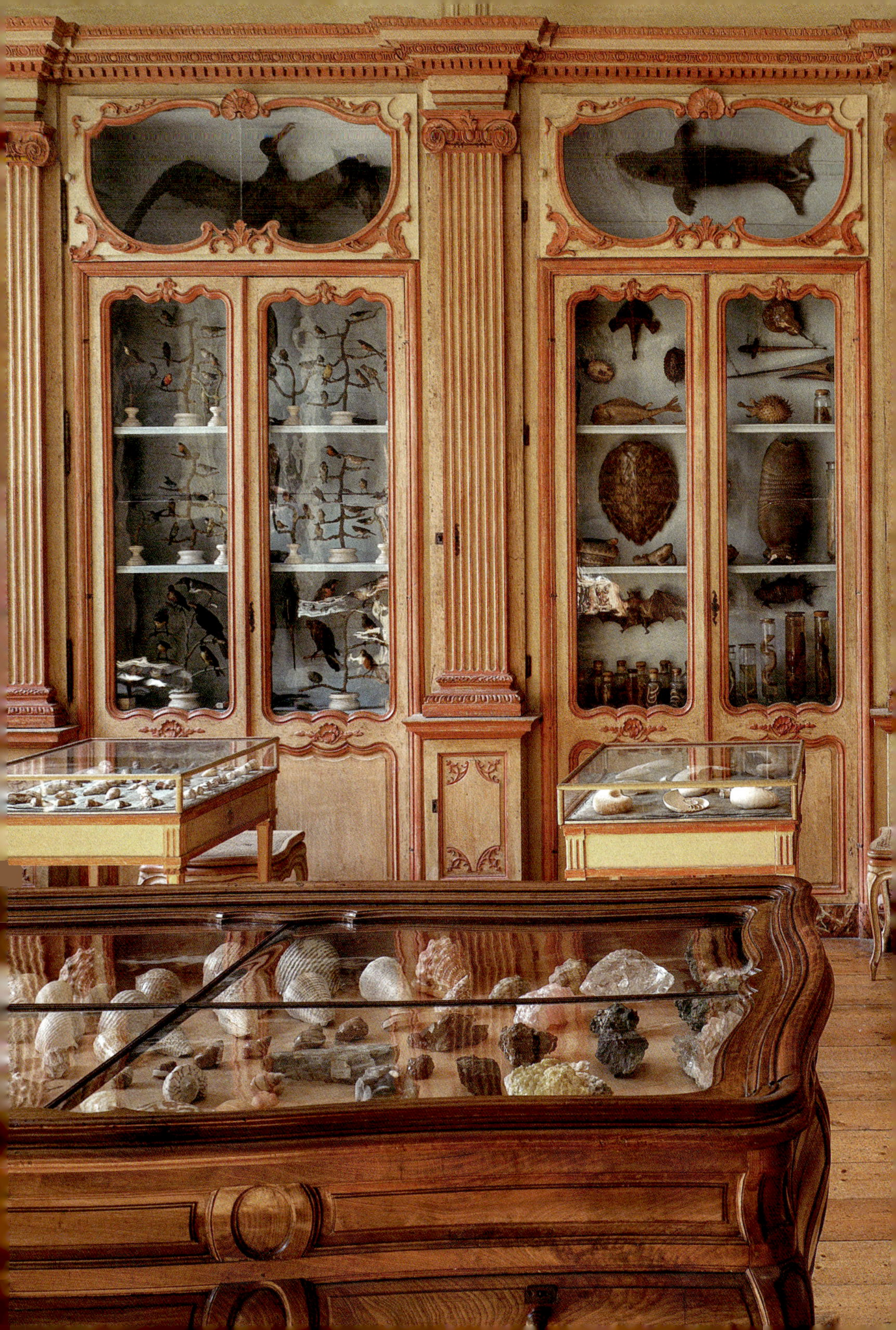

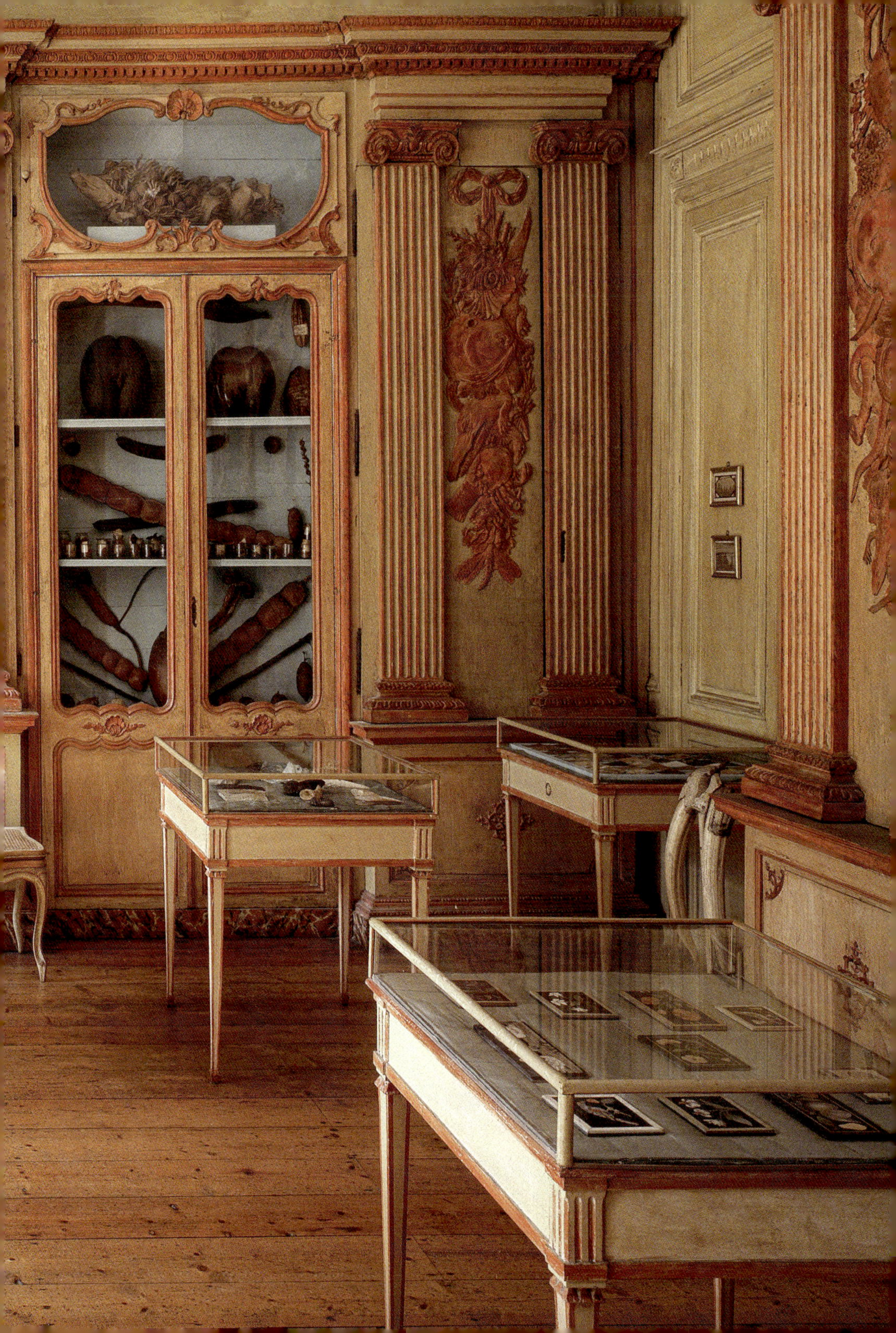

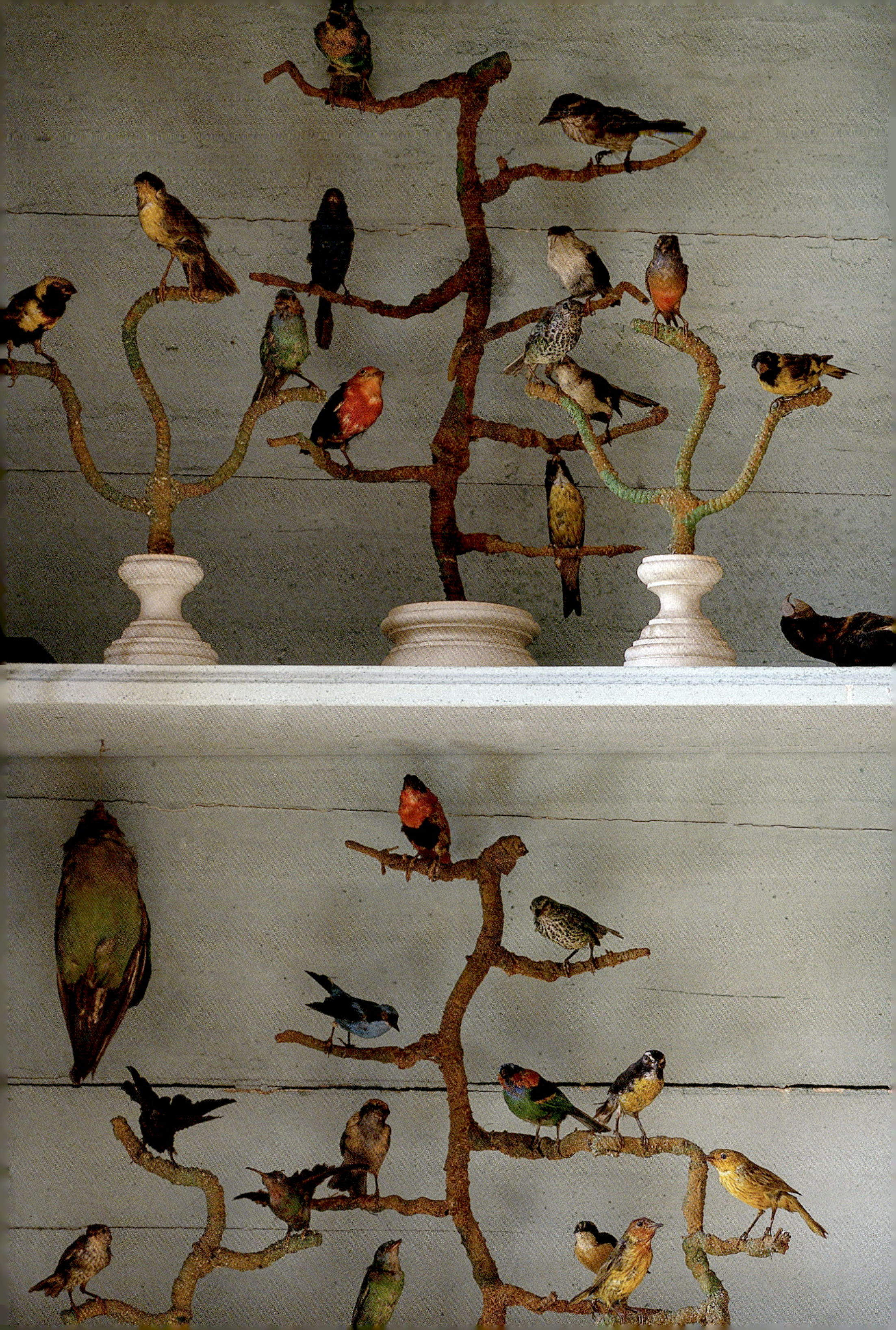

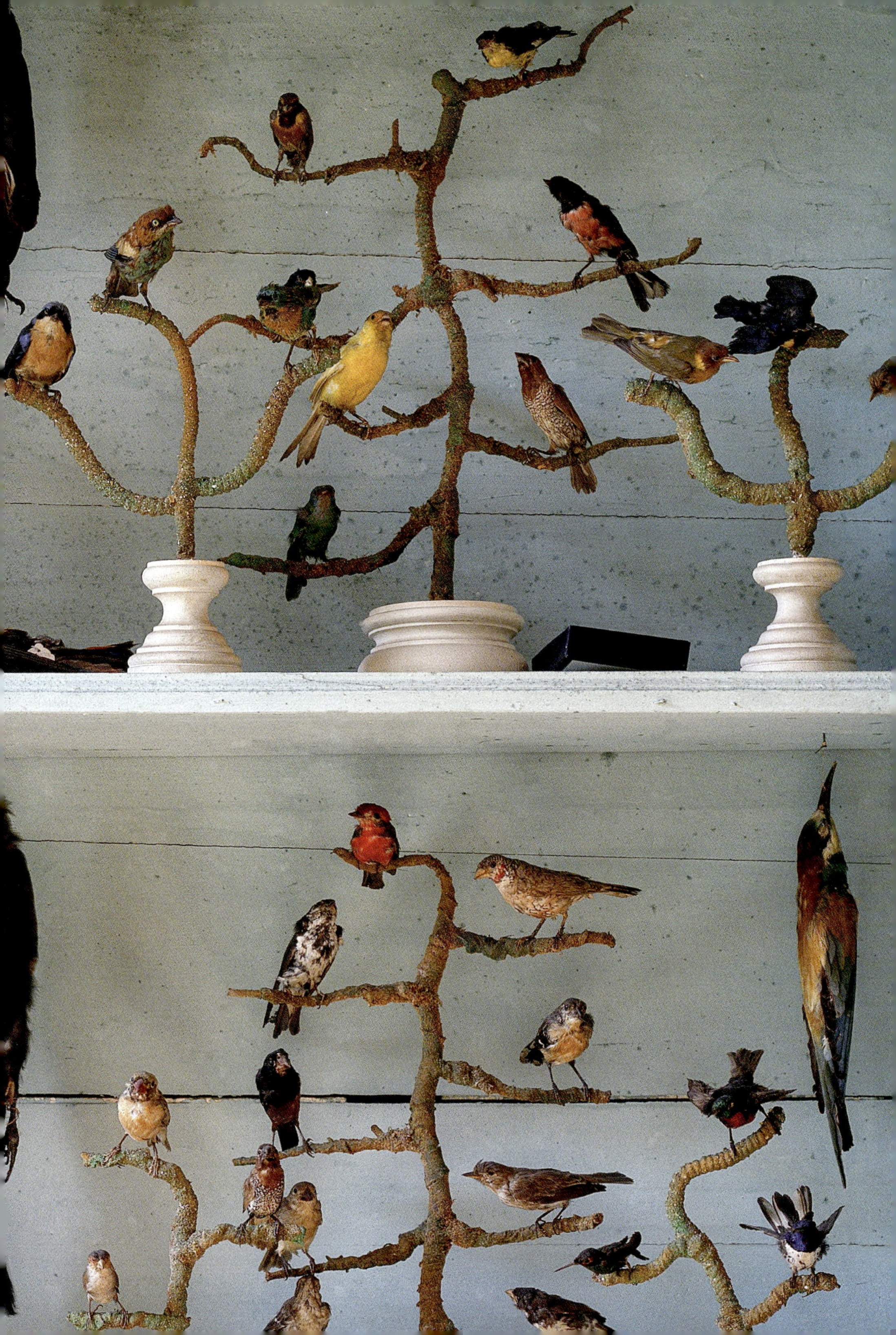

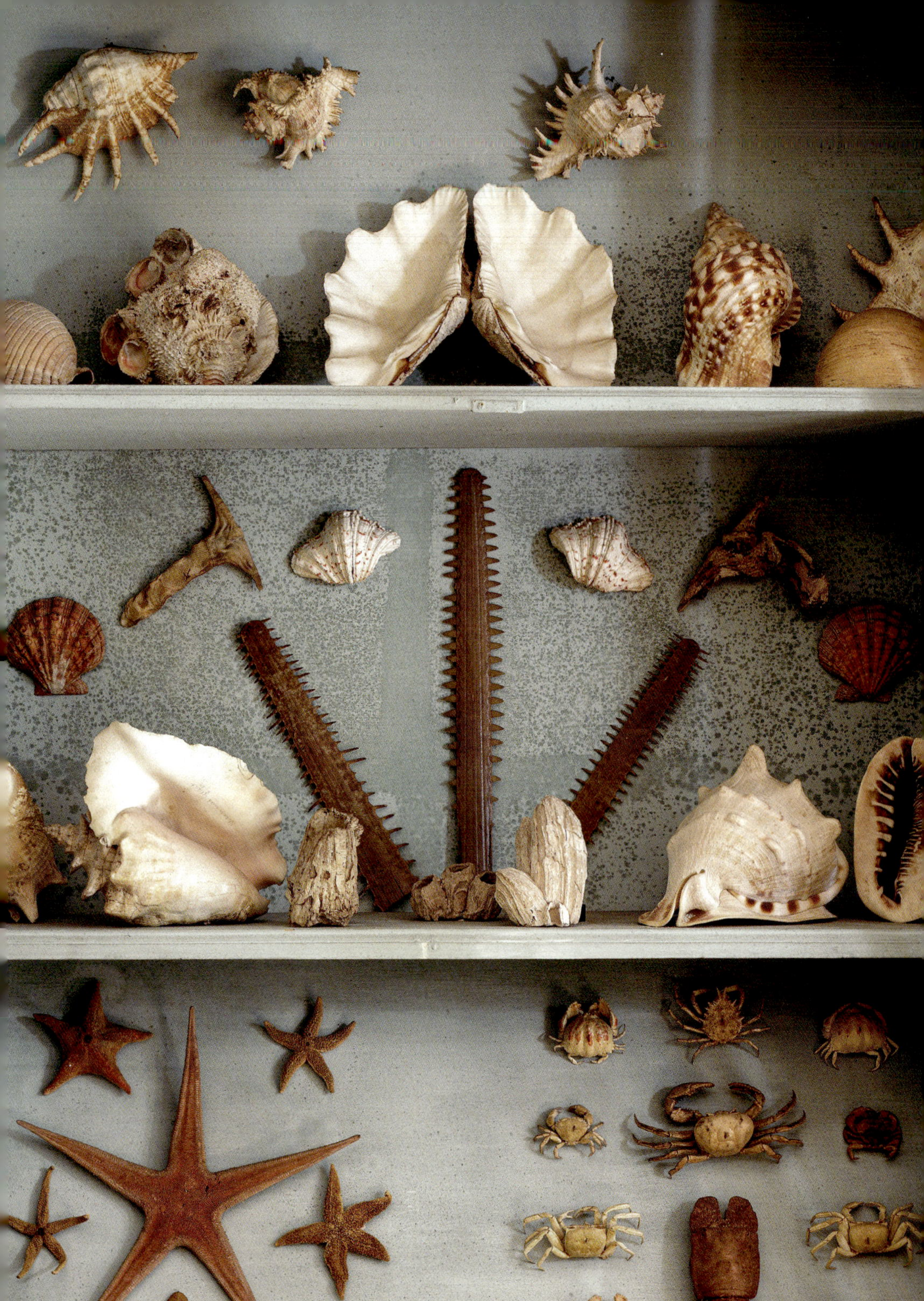

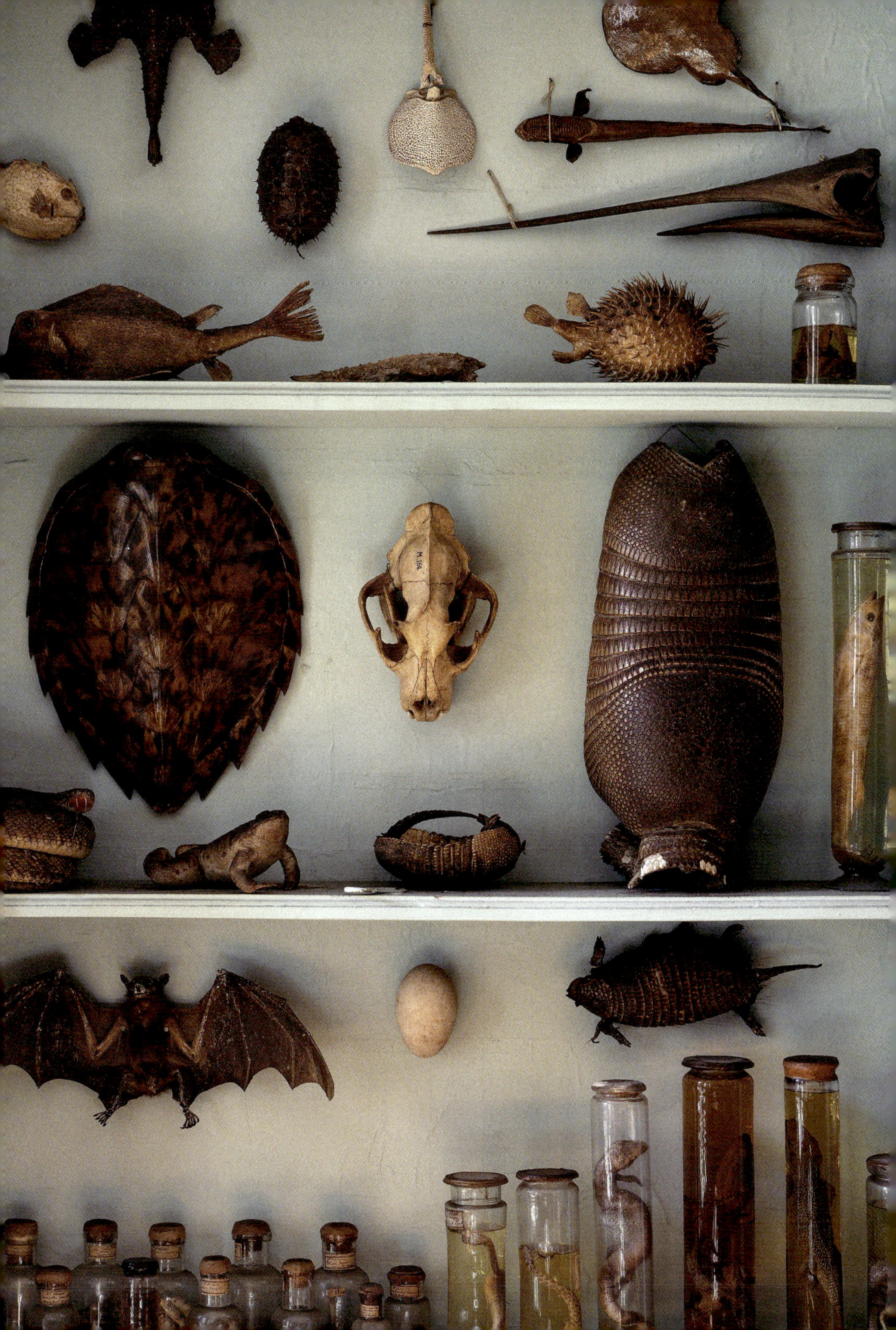

The magnificent French city of La Rochelle on the Atlantic coast was the main centre of Protestant resistance in France from the 16th to the 17th century. The city endured two terrible sieges—one of which was begun in October 1627 and ended a year later with occupation by the forces of Louis XIII—but in the 18th century La Rochelle became one of the country's most prosperous commercial ports. Its ships set sail for Cape Verde and the African mainland coast of Guinea, seeking slaves to trade in the Antilles in exchange for sugar, coffee and indigo dye, but also small treasure items and rare specimens from the natural world, such as unusual shells, the skins of exotic animals and skeletons of others that had almost become extinct.

Having been fascinated by the natural sciences since his childhood, Clément Lafaille (1718–1782) decided to create a "naturalistic cabinet" in which he collected, organised, classified and labelled the treasures that later came to form La Rochelle's cabinet of curiosities, now part of the Muséum d'Histoire Naturelle. While in past ages the obsession with wonders found expression through the accumulation, juxtaposition and constant addition of specimens, during the age of the Enlightenment there was a radical shift in attitude towards a universal vision of the world that was ordered hierarchically and based on a system of validity and reason. To support such a systematic organisation of Lafaille's collection the best cabinet-makers of the day were hired to fashion the coral-tinted boiserie within which the *naturalia* were to be housed, the various animal and mineral specimens. The tables were designed by the renowned furniture-maker Claude-Charles Saunier (1735–1807), while Mathieu Bauve (named "master" in 1754) created the unusual chairs in Louis XV style with folding backs which, with the weight of the person seated in the chair, enabled them to double up as a press for herbs, leaves and all kinds of plants.

Following his death, Lafaille's home and all its contents were left to the city of La Rochelle. The inventory, as compiled in 1780, lists rare and monstrous animals preserved in alcohol, petrified plants, dendritic crystals, crocodiles, as well as countless shells and dried starfish, stuffed hummingbirds in the most vivid colours, rare fish, trophy skulls of various mammals, the tanned hides of exotic animals, hippopotamus skulls and antelope antlers. Lafaille also provided substantial funds to increase the endowment of his library, on the condition that the cabinet remained open to the public.

◦ ◈ ◦

Die französische Stadt La Rochelle an der Atlantikküste war im 16. und 17. Jahrhundert Hochburg des Protestantismus in Frankreich. Nachdem die Stadt zwei schreckliche Belagerungen erlebt hatte, von der eine im Oktober 1627 begann und mit der Besatzung durch die Truppen Ludwigs XIII. ein Jahr später endete, mauserte sich die Stadt im 18. Jahrhundert zu einem florierenden Handelshafen. Von dort fuhr die Handelsflotte zunächst die afrikanische Küste entlang, wo man in Guinea und auf den Kapverden Station machte, um Sklaven an Bord zu nehmen, die dann über den Atlantik zu den Antillen verschifft wurden. Auf dem Rückweg transportierte man nicht nur Zucker, Kaffee und Indigo,

sondern auch seltene Naturschätze wie Muscheln, exotische Tierhäute und Skelette
fast ausgestorbener Tierarten.

Da er schon als Kind eine ausgeprägte Vorliebe für die Naturwissenschaften
hegte, legte Clément Lafaille (1718–1782) später ein eigenes Naturalienkabinett an, in
dem er die Schätze sammelte, kategorisierte, unterteilte und etikettierte, die später den
Grundstock für das Kuriositätenkabinett in La Rochelle bildeten und heute zum Muséum
d'Histoire Naturelle gehören. Ging es bei den Wunderkammern in erster Linie darum,
der Sammelleidenschaft zu frönen, möglichst viele Kuriositäten anzuhäufen und wahllos
nebeneinanderzustellen, so änderte sich das in der Aufklärung grundlegend. Nun ging
es um einen Universalanspruch, ein hierarchisches Weltbild und die Allgemeingültigkeit
der Vernunft. Um eine systematische Anordnung zu erleichtern, schufen die besten
Kunsttischler aufwendig furnierte, korallenfarbene Wandschränke, die dazu bestimmt
waren, *Naturalia*, Tierpräparate und Mineralien aufzunehmen. Die Schränke wurden von
dem bekannten Kunsttischler Claude-Charles Saunier (1735–1807) gefertigt, während
Mathieu Bauve (1754 zum „Meister" ernannt) die einzigartigen Louis-quinze-Stühle ent-
warf, hinter deren aufklappbaren Rückenlehnen sich eine Pflanzenpresse verbarg, sodass
der Hausherr mit seinem Körpergewicht beim Sitzen Blätter, Kräuter und Pflanzen jeder
Art pressen konnte.

Bei seinem Tod vermachte Monsieur Lafaille sein Haus mit allem, was darin war,
der Gemeinde La Rochelle. Das Inventar von 1780 umfasst seltene oder monströse Tiere
in Spiritus, versteinerte Pflanzen, Dendriten, Krokodile sowie zahllose Muscheln und
getrocknete Seesterne, farbenprächtige Kolibris, seltene Fische, Schädeltrophäen von
Säugetieren, gegerbte Häute von exotischen Tieren, Flusspferdschädel und Antilopen-
hörner. Außerdem hinterließ er eine nennenswerte Geldsumme, die er zum Ausbau
der Bibliothek bestimmte, alles unter der Bedingung, das Kabinett der Allgemeinheit
zugänglich zu machen.

◎ ❖ ◎

Cité de la côte atlantique au glorieux passé, La Rochelle fut un bastion de la résistance
protestante en terre de France aux 16e et 17e siècles, et connut deux redoutables sièges –
dont l'un commencé en octobre 1627 se conclut par l'occupation de la ville par les troupes
de Louis XIII un an plus tard–, avant de devenir l'un des ports commerciaux les plus floris-
sants de France au 18e siècle. Les navires négriers partaient d'ici et longeaient les côtes
africaines, s'approvisionnaient en esclaves en Guinée et au Cap-Vert, puis traversaient
l'Atlantique pour transférer leur chargement aux Antilles d'où ils ramenaient non seulement du sucre, du café et de l'indigo mais encore des trésors minuscules et des raretés
naturelles, parmi lesquels d'étranges coquillages, des peaux d'animaux exotiques et
des squelettes d'espèces en voie de disparition.

Attiré par les sciences naturelles dès son enfance, Clément Lafaille (1718–1782)
décida d'aménager un « cabinet naturaliste » où rassembler, classer et étiqueter les

trésors qui finirent par constituer le Cabinet de curiosités de La Rochelle, aujourd'hui partie intégrante du Muséum d'Histoire Naturelle. Si le culte des merveilles était accumulation, juxtaposition et addition à l'infini, au siècle des Lumières une attitude extrêmement différente opta pour l'universalité, une vision hiérarchisée du monde et la validité présumée des catégories générales de la raison. Pour faciliter le classement systématique de la collection, d'excellents ébénistes réalisèrent les vitrines couleur corail destinées à contenir les *naturalia*, animaux et minéraux. Si le célèbre Claude-Charles Saunier (1735–1807) était l'auteur des tables vitrines, Mathieu Bauve (nommé « maître » en 1754) était le créateur des étonnantes chaises Louis XV dotées d'un dossier rabattable qui, sous le poids de l'occupant du siège, devient une presse pour faire sécher herbes, feuilles et végétaux en tous genres.

À sa mort, Clément Lafaille légua à la Ville de La Rochelle sa demeure avec tout son contenu. Dressé en 1780, l'inventaire mentionne des animaux rares ou monstrueux conservés dans l'alcool, des plantes pétrifiées, des dendrites, des crocodiles et un grand nombre de coquillages et d'étoiles de mer séchées, des oiseaux-mouches naturalisés aux vives couleurs, des poissons rares, des crânes trophées de mammifères, des peaux d'animaux exotiques tannées, des crânes d'hippopotames, des cornes d'antilopes. À ces trésors il ajouta une somme conséquente destinée, notamment, à enrichir le fonds de la bibliothèque à la condition expresse que le cabinet fût ouvert au public.

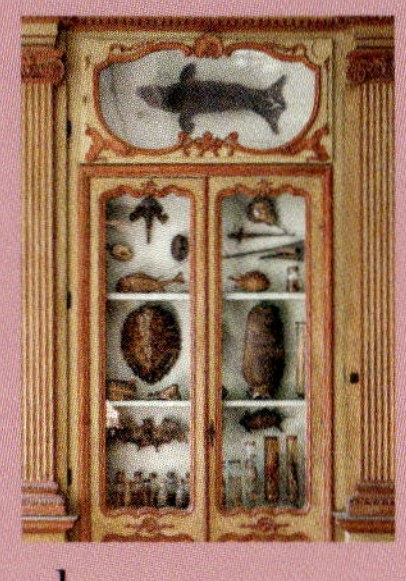

1

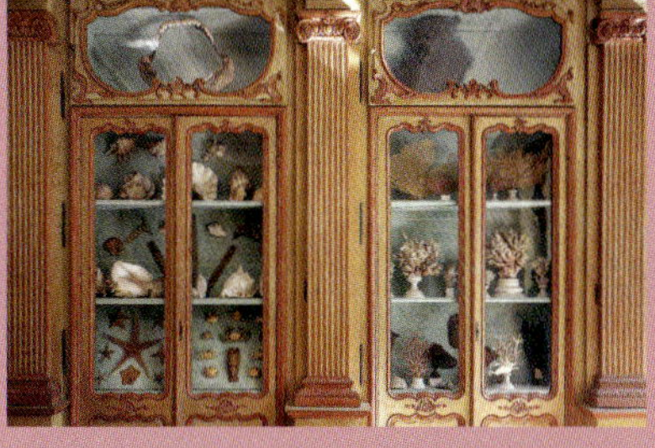

2

1 Display case featuring various specimens, including reptiles and amphibians, preserved in fluid or in their natural form.
Vitrine mit verschiedenen Präparaten, darunter trocken- und feuchtpräparierte Reptilien und Amphibien.
Vitrine présentant une sélection de spécimens, en outre des reptiles et des amphibiens naturalisés et conservés en fluide.

2 These two display cases in the cabinet present Atlantic starfish (Echinoderms), monovalve mollusc shells (Pecten) as well as bivalves, together with various specimens of crabs (Decapod crustaceans). In the right-hand display case are ancient corals and gorgonians.
In den zwei Vitrinen sind Seesterne (Echinoderme) des Atlantiks, Kammmuscheln (Pecten) und andere Muscheln (Bivalvia) sowie verschiedene Krabbenexemplare (Decapoda) ausgestellt. In der rechten lagern Korallen und Gorgonien.
Dans deux vitrines du cabinet, des étoiles de mer (Echinoderme) de l'Atlantique, des coquilles de mollusques univalves (Pecten) et bivalves, et divers spécimens de crabes (Decapoda). Dans la vitrine de droite sont disposés d'anciens coraux et des gorgones.

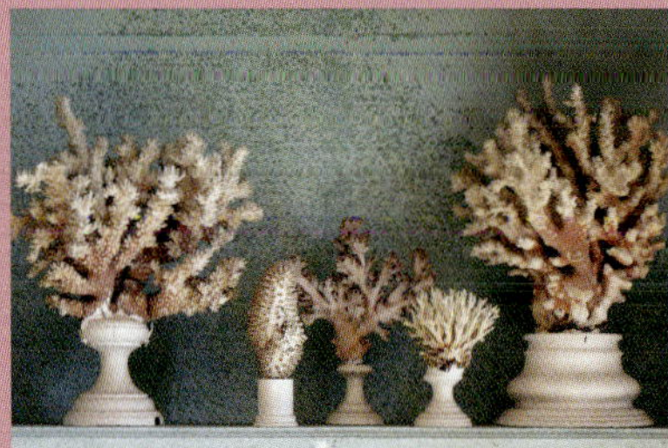

3

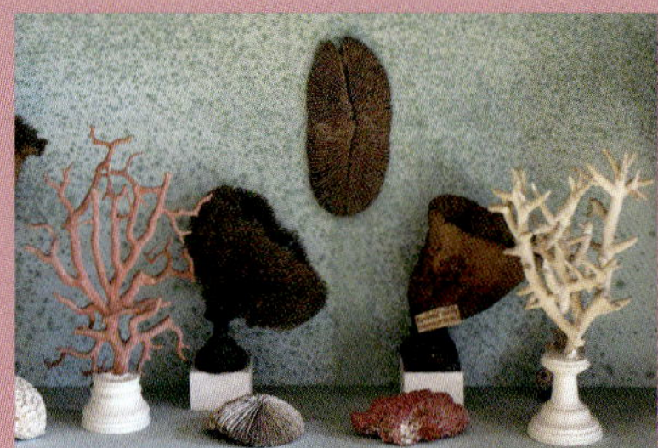

4

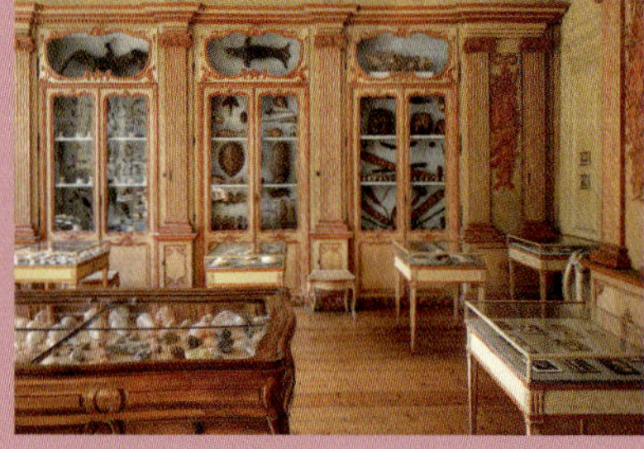

5

3–4 Views of the display case
containing the collection of
madrepores and corals.
Blick in eine Vitrine mit Madreporen und Korallen.
À l'intérieur de la vitrine, la collection de madrépores et de coraux.

5 Section of the cabinet of
natural history assembled by
Clément Lafaille; in the foreground,
a collection of shells. The display
case at the bottom right contains
examples of various kinds of
seeds, including giant pods from
Madagascar (Entada rheedii) and
the exotic fruit from the Seychelles
known as "coco de mer", fascinating objects that are believed to be
a powerful aphrodisiac.
Detailansicht des naturwissen-
schaftlichen Kabinetts Clément
Lafailles: Im Vordergrund ist eine
Muschelsammlung ausgestellt.
Die Vitrine hinten rechts enthält
Samen, u.a. Riesensamen aus
Madagaskar (Entada rheedii)
und Samen jener faszinierenden
exotischen Frucht, die Seychellennuss genannt wurde und die
man für ein starkes Aphrodisia-
kum hielt.
Détail du Cabinet d'histoire
naturelle de Clément Lafaille :
au premier plan une collection
de coquillages. En bas à droite,
la vitrine contient des exemplaires
de différentes sortes de graines,
dont des gousses géantes de
Madagascar (Entada rheedii) et
des fruits exotiques des Seychelles
appelés « cocos de mer », objets
fascinants considérés comme de
puissants aphrodisiaques.

6 View of the display case with
various families of birds including
hummingbirds and tropical birds
(Trochilidae family).
Blick in eine Vitrine, in der Vogel-
familien ausgestellt sind, darunter

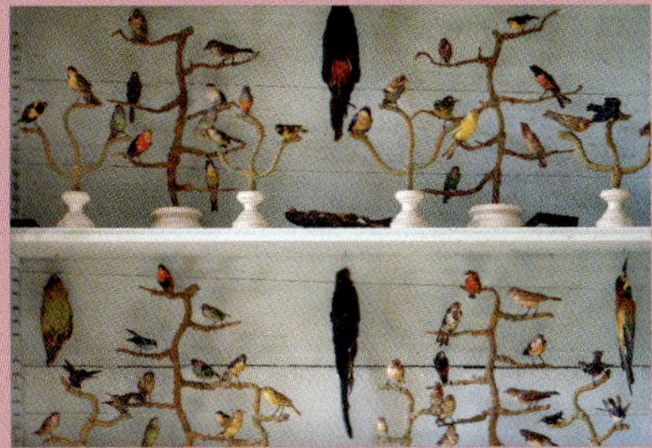

6

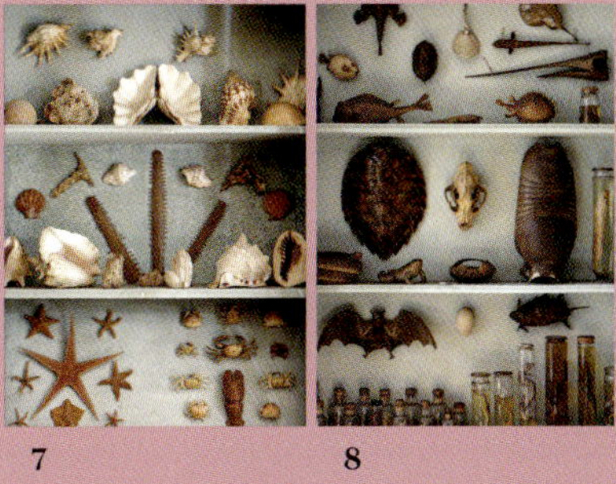

7 8

Kolibiris und tropische Vögel der Familie der Trochilidae.
À l'intérieur de la vitrine, des familles d'oiseaux, y compris les colibris, également connus sous le nom d'oiseaux-mouches (famille des trochilidés).

7 Detail of ill. 2: Atlantic starfish (Echinoderms), mono-valve mollusc shells (Pecten) and bivalves, and various specimens of crabs (Decapod crustaceans).
Detail von Abb. 2: Seesterne (Echinoderme) des Atlantiks, Kammmuscheln (Pecten) und andere Muscheln (Bivalvia) sowie verschiedene Krabbenarten (Decapoda).
Détail de l'ill. 2 : Étoiles de mer de l'Atlantique (Echinoderme), coquilles de mollusques univalves (Pecten) et bivalves, et divers spécimens de crabes (Crustacés décapodes).

8 Detail of ill. 1: Various preserved specimens: on the top shelf, marine creatures including puffer fish, porcupine fish and small species of rays; on the middle shelf, the carapace of an armadillo and the shell of a sea turtle; at the bottom, a bat.

Detail von Abb. 1: Feucht- wie Trockenpräparate, im oberen Fach marine Wesen, darunter aufgepumpte Kugel- und Igelfische sowie kleine Rochenarten; im mittleren Fach Gürteltier- und Meeresschild-krötenpanzer, im unteren Fach u. a. eine Fledermaus.
Détail de l'ill. 1 : Préparations humides et sèches, dans la partie supérieure des créatures marines, notamment des poissons-globes, des poissons-hérissons et des espèces de petites raies ; au centre, des carapaces de tatou et de tortue de mer, et en bas une chauve-souris.

Château de Dampierre

Dampierre-en-Yvelines

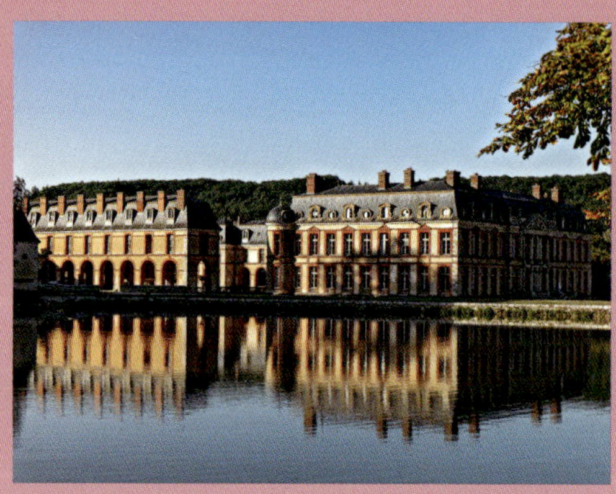

Founded The collection was established in the 19th century, the castle dates from the 16th century.

Key item In 1839, the Duke of Luynes commissioned Jean-Auguste-Dominique Ingres to create two mural paintings for his music room, *The Age of Gold* and *The Age of Iron*, although the work was left unfinished. The artist worked on these paintings from 1843 until 1849, when he eventually abandoned them.

Besonders sehenswert Im Jahre 1839 erteilte der Schlossherr, der Herzog von Luynes, Jean-Auguste-Dominique Ingres den Auftrag, den Festsaal mit zwei monumentalen Wandgemälden zum goldenen und ehernen Zeitalter zu dekorieren, die allerdings beide niemals fertiggestellt wurden. Der Künstler arbeitete ab 1843 daran, musste aber 1849 die Arbeit einstellen.

À voir absolument En 1839, le duc de Luynes passa commande à Jean-Auguste-Dominique Ingres de deux peintures murales pour le salon de musique, *L'Âge d'or* et *L'Âge de fer*, restées inachevées. L'artiste travailla à ces œuvres de 1843 à 1849, année où il dut renoncer à les mener à bien.

Massimo Listri, *View of the Château de Dampierre*

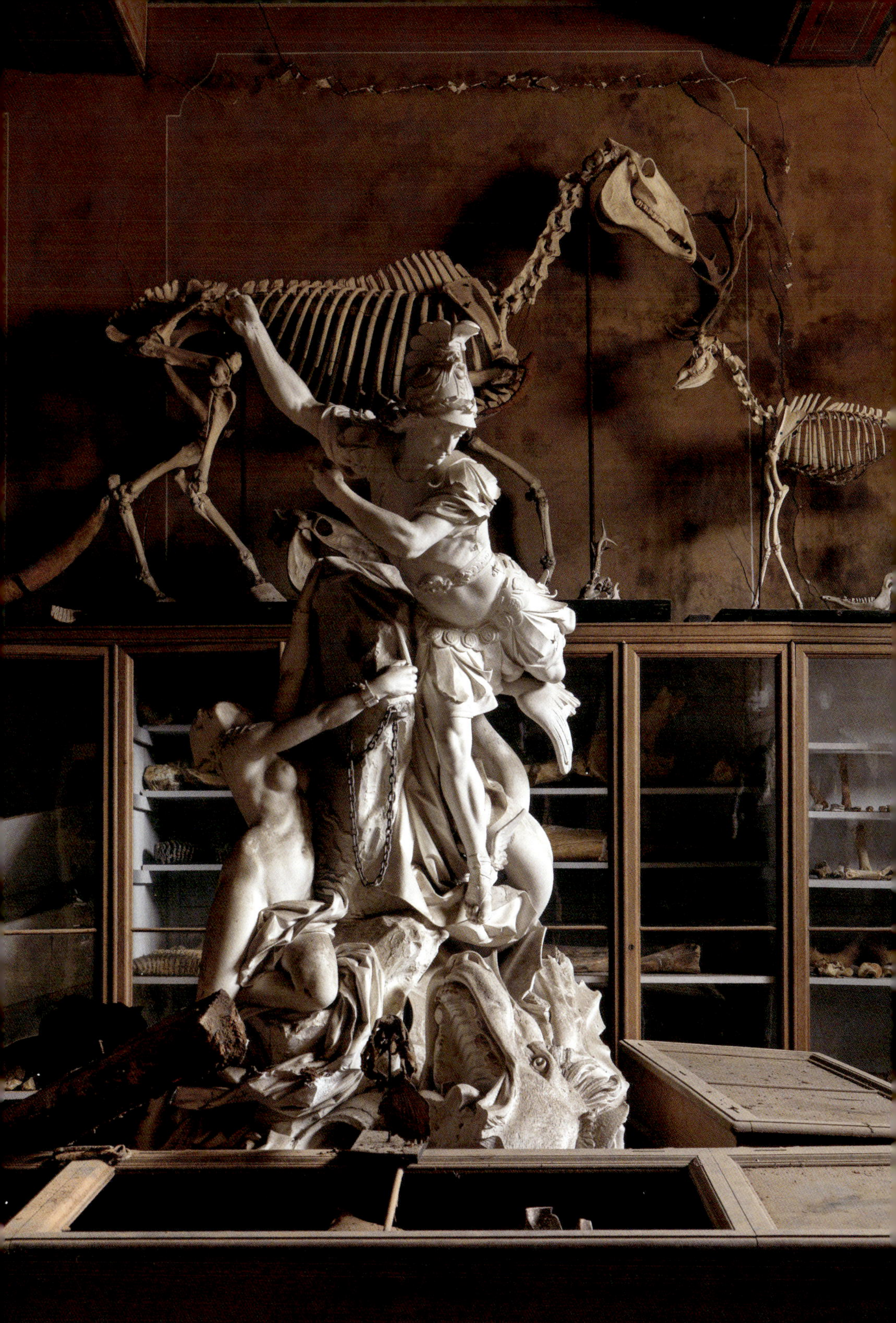

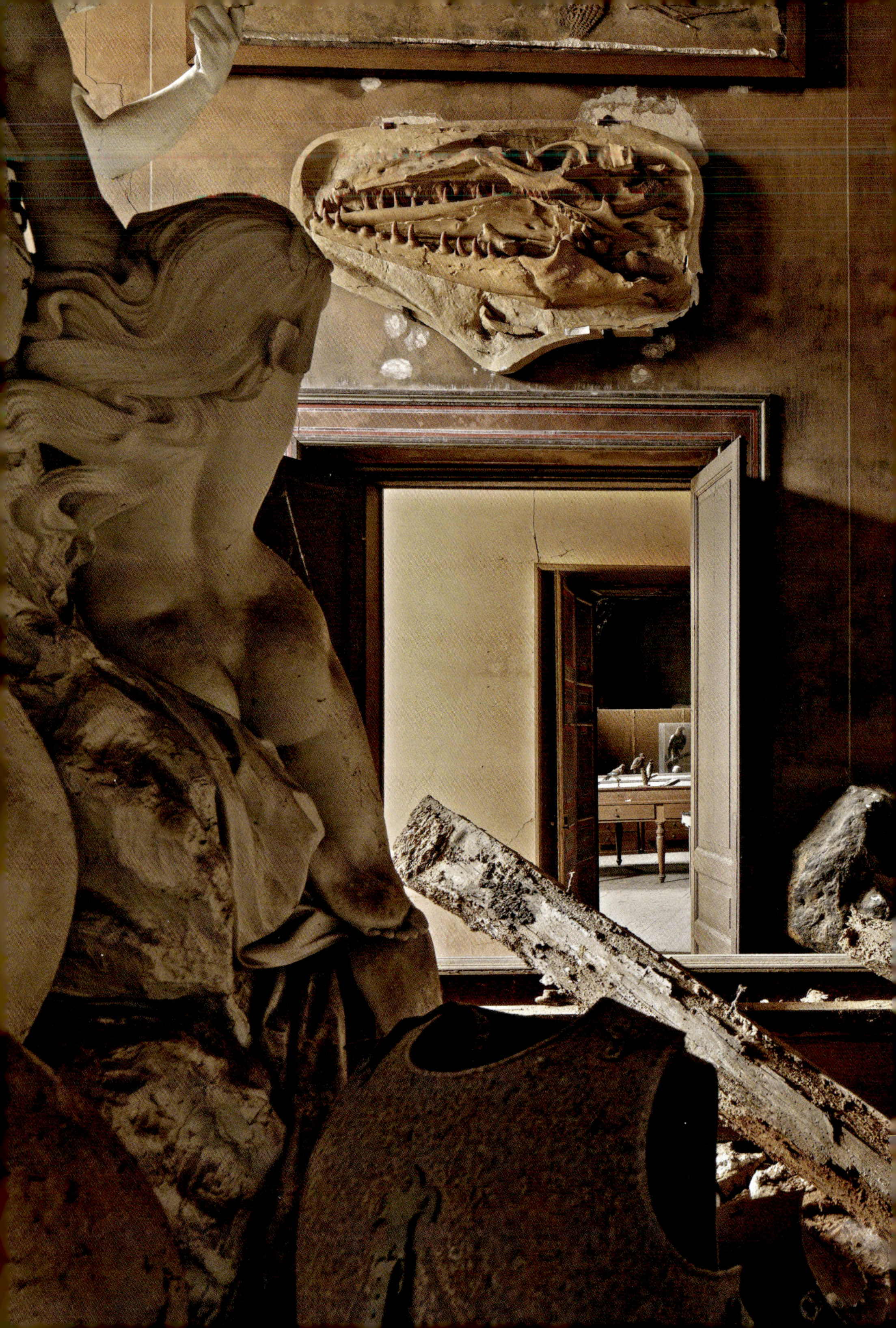

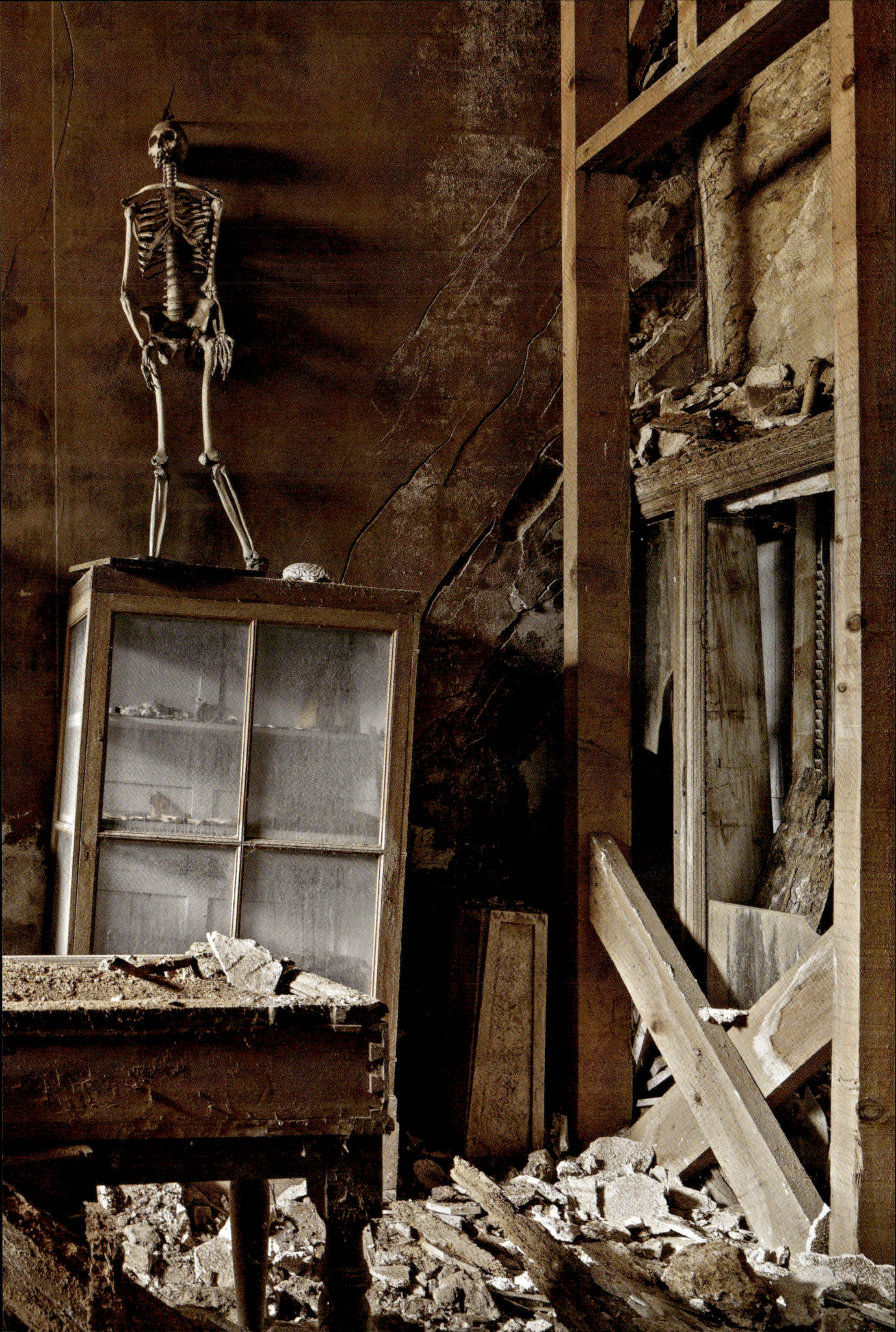

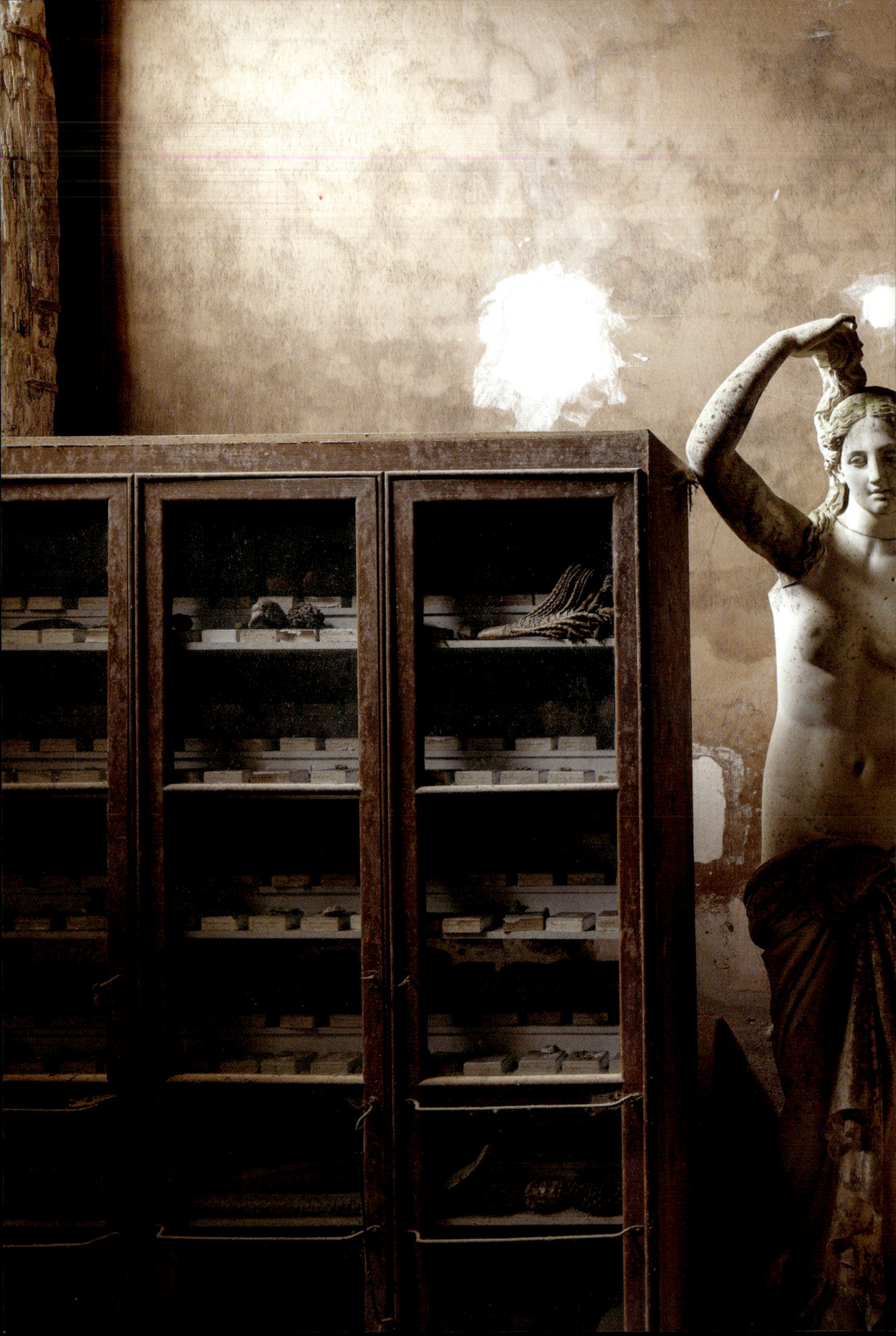

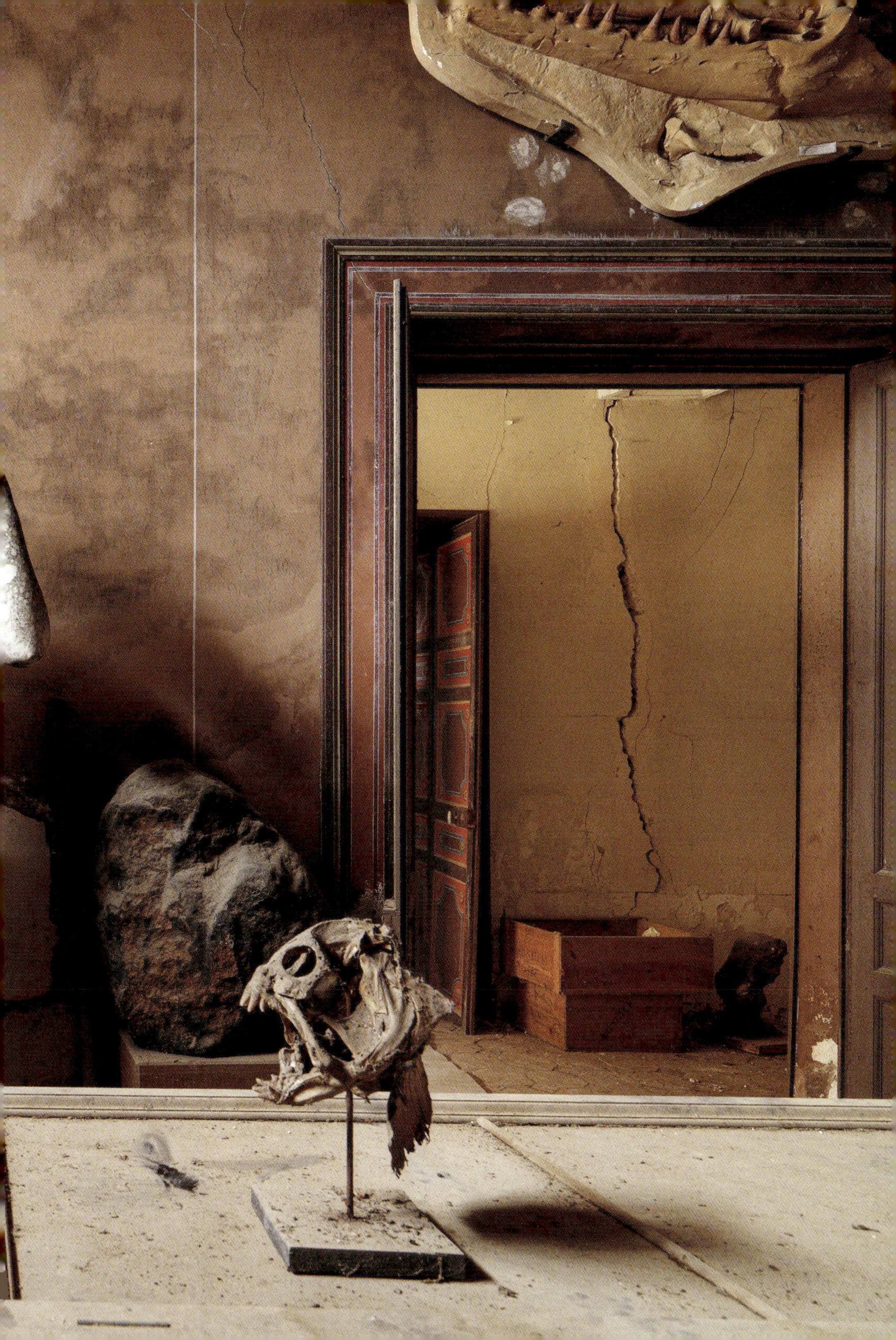

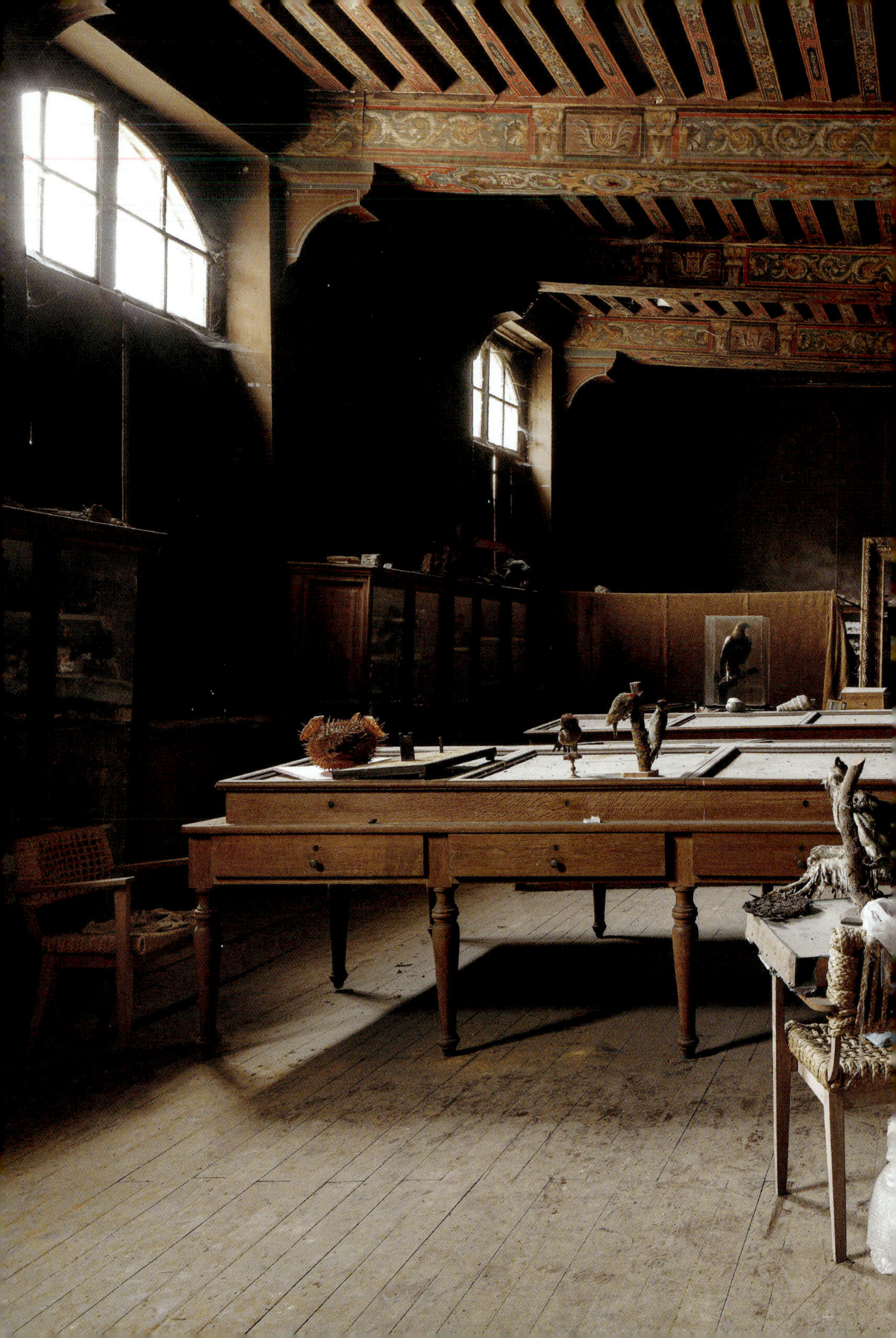

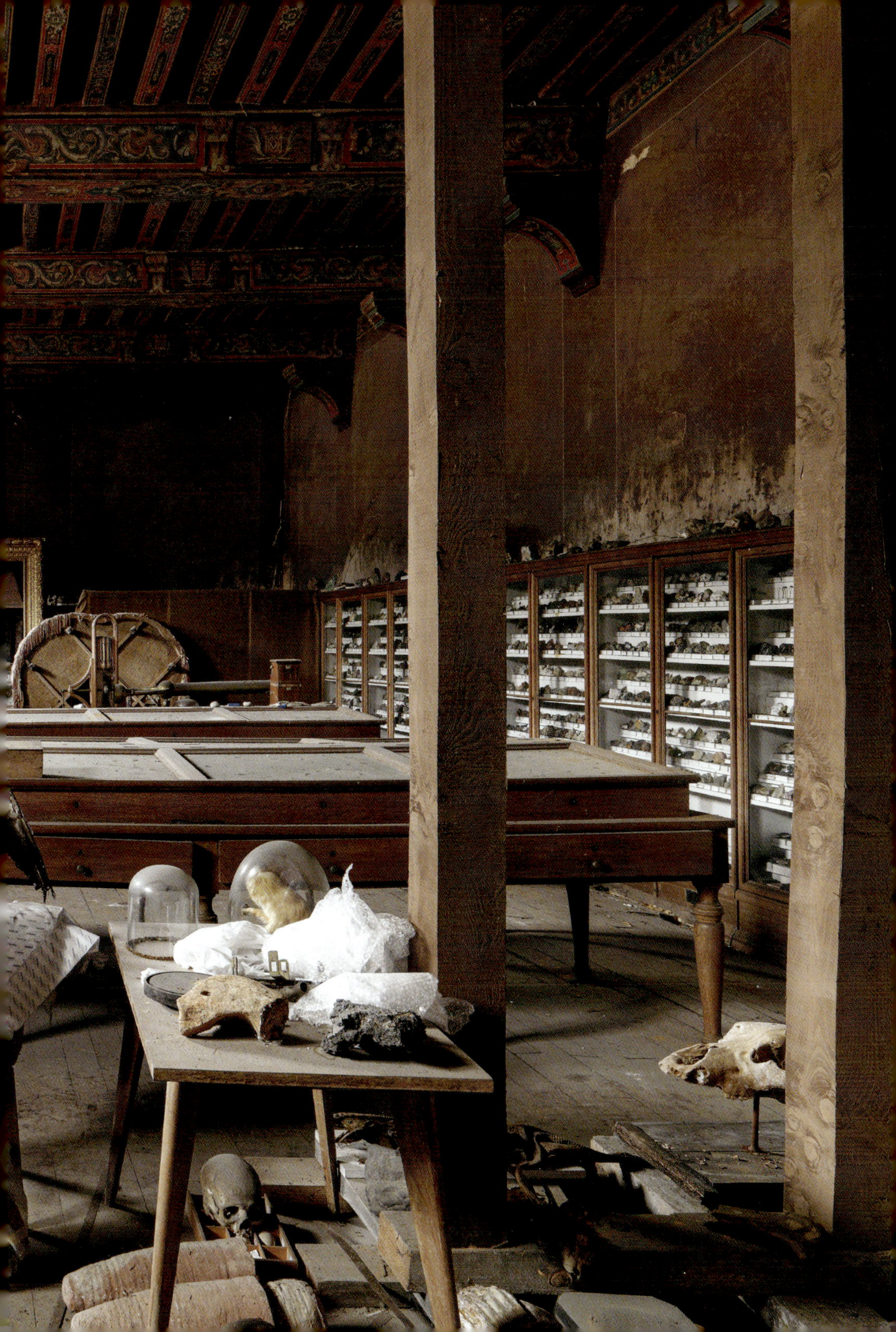

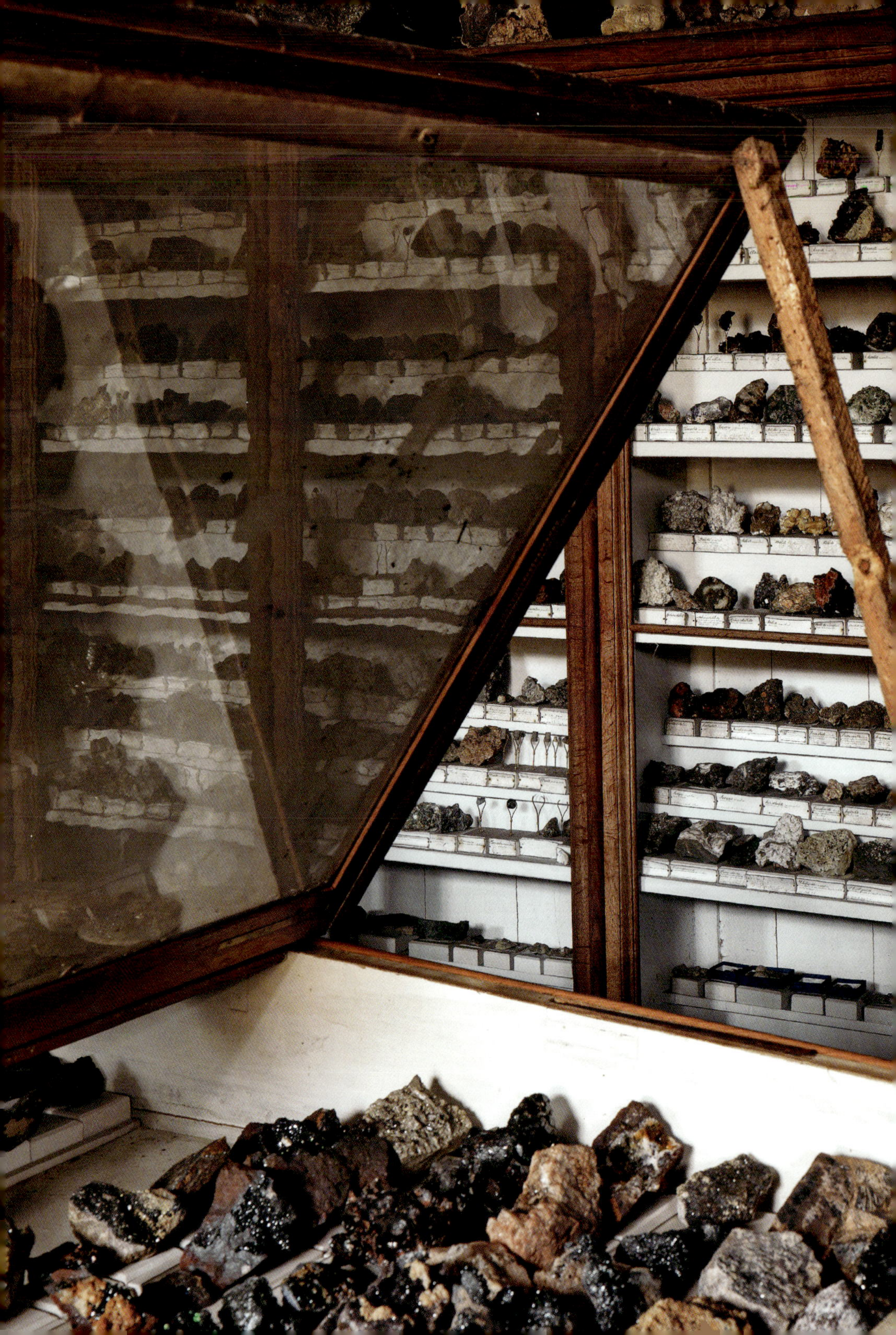

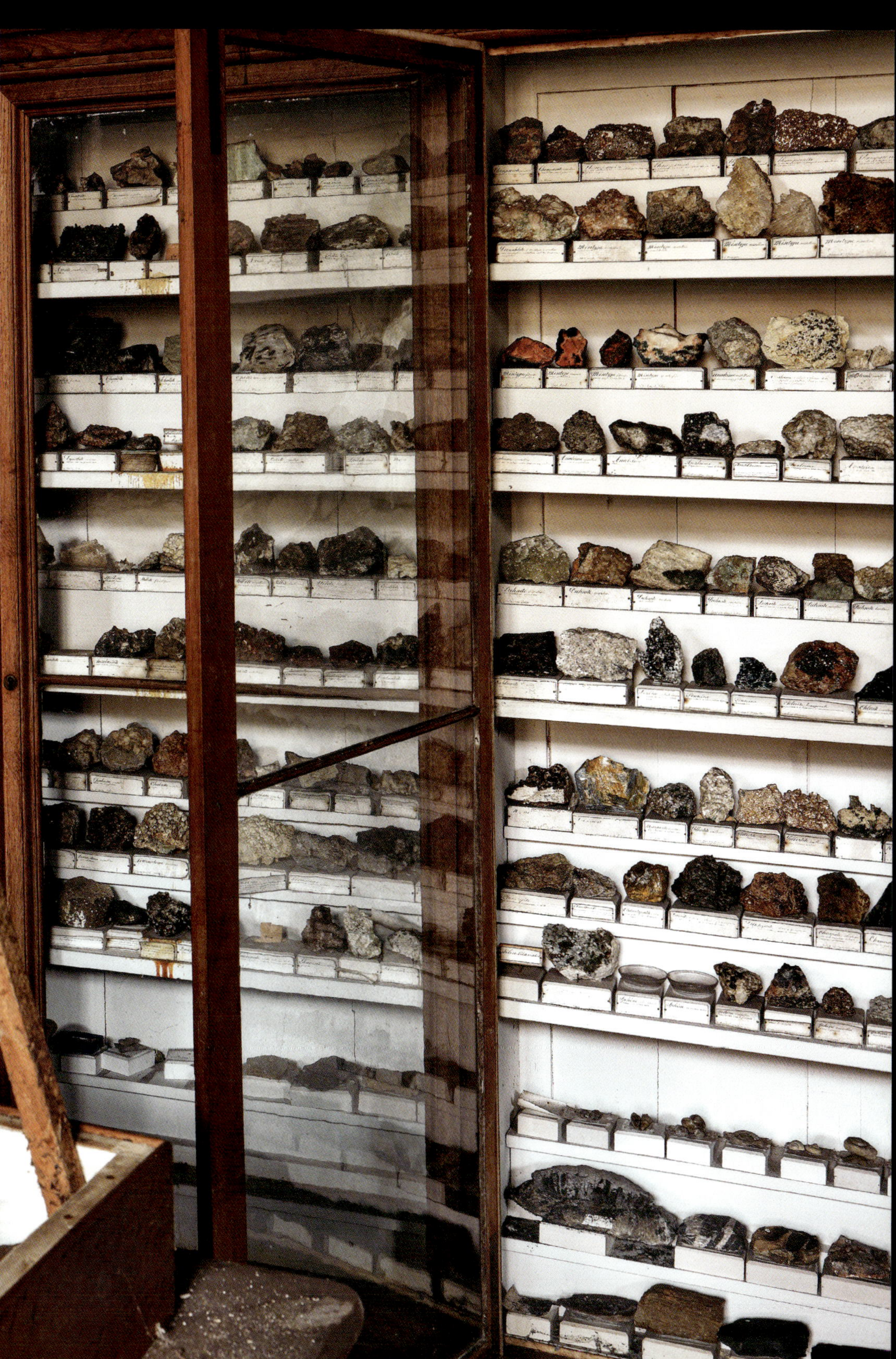

Nestled in the Chevreuse valley and a favourite destination for Parisians, the Château de Dampierre was built in the first half of the 16th century and in 1663 became the property of the aristocratic family of d'Albert de Luynes. Charles Honoré d'Albert de Luynes (1646–1712), the Duke of Chevreuse and son-in-law of the politician Jean-Baptiste Colbert, entrusted the reconstruction of the majestic castle and adjacent buildings to Jules-Hardouin Mansart (1646–1708), the First Architect to the King, and the transformation of the superb gardens to André Le Nôtre (1613–1700).

After surviving the French Revolution intact, the castle passed into the hands of Honoré Théodoric Paul Joseph d'Albert (1802–1867), Duke of Luynes, who was without question one of the greatest patrons of the arts in 19th-century France. He was an archaeologist as well as a scholar, and in 1839 commissioned Félix Duban to undertake an ambitious programme of renovation on the castle, which later became home to a number of notable masterpieces by Paul Hippolyte Flandrin, Charles Gleyre, François-Édouard Picot, Pierre-Charles Simart, Pierre-Jules Cavelier and François Rude, as well as a large library (since dispersed). Ingres was commissioned to produce mural paintings for the castle's hall, which was conceived to be a striking stage upon which to display the duke's collection of antiquities (7,000 coins and 1,000 ancient artefacts, including vases, jewels, carvings and engraved stones, together with Etruscan and Roman bronzes). Unfortunately, and perhaps because of a lack of adequate technical preparation, the project became an unmitigated failure and the duke's monumental designs were left unfinished.

At the Universal Exhibition of 1855 the Parisian public was deeply impressed by a remarkable quarter-sized reconstruction of the Classical gold and ivory statue of *Athena Parthenos* by Simart and Edmond Duponchel (later housed inside the castle). Created using marble, silver, gilt bronze, ivory and precious stones, it provoked an international debate on the question of the use of polychromy in the sculpture of Antiquity.

In his workshop in the castle, the duke (who was also a scientist with a particular interest in chemistry) investigated the methods used by artists in Antiquity in order to try and rediscover their techniques. Meanwhile, the intention behind his patronage was, above all, to inspire a renaissance of the arts during the Second French Empire, and because of these efforts goldsmiths such as Charles Wagner, François-Désiré Froment-Meurice and Edmond Duponchel, and workers in gems such as Jean-Valentin Morel, were able to contribute to a revival of the arts in precious stones and metals.

Starting in the 1840s, the duke's patriotism found concrete expression through a series of important gifts he made to the Louvre and the Cabinet des Médailles (Bibliothèque nationale de France), culminating in 1862 with the donation of his entire archaeological collection to the latter institution, in full confidence that he would be contributing to the development of modern archaeology.

After his death, the duke's art and natural history collection fell into oblivion, as Massimo Listri has compellingly documented in his photographs.

❖❖❖

Malerisch im Chevreuse-Tal gelegen und seit jeher ein beliebtes Ausflugsziel der Pariser, kam das in der ersten Hälfte des 16. Jahrhunderts errichtete Schloss Dampierre 1663 in den Besitz der Adelsfamilie von Albert de Luynes. Charles-Honoré d'Albert de Luynes (1646–1712), Herzog von Chevreuse und Schwiegersohn von Jean-Baptiste Colbert, ließ das majestätische Schloss sowie diverse Nebengebäude von Jules-Hardouin Mansart (1646–1708), Premier architecte du roi, umbauen und die herrlichen Gärten von André Le Nôtre (1613–1700) neugestalten.

Nachdem es die Französische Revolution unbeschadet überstanden hatte, ging das Schloss in den Besitz von Honoré Théodoric Paul Joseph d'Albert, Herzog von Luynes (1802–1867) über, zweifellos einer der bedeutendsten Kunstmäzene des 19. Jahrhunderts. 1839 wurde das Schloss nach Plänen von Félix Duban umfangreich restauriert und beherbergte danach zahllose berühmte Kunstwerke von Paul Hippolyte Flandrin, Charles Gleyre, François E. Picot, Pierre-Charles Simart, P. Jules Cavelier und François Rude sowie eine umfangreiche Bibliothek (nicht erhalten). Auf Wunsch des Herzogs sollte Jean-Auguste-Dominique Ingres den großen Festsaal im ersten Stock mit Wandgemälden ausmalen, die als prächtige Kulisse gedacht waren, um seine Antikensammlung gebührend in Szene zu setzen (7000 Münzen und 1000 antike Objekte, darunter Gefäße, Schmuck, Schnitzarbeiten, römische und etruskische Bronzen). Unglücklicherweise endete das Vorhaben für Ingres in einer absoluten Katastrophe, vielleicht weil ihm das technische Knowhow fehlte, und die monumentalen Werke blieben unvollendet.

Anlässlich der Weltausstellung 1855 war das Pariser Publikum zutiefst beeindruckt von einer verkleinerten Rekonstruktion (im Maßstab 1:4) der Chryselephantinskulptur der Athena Parthenos (später im Schloss aufgestellt) nach einem Entwurf von Charles Simart und Edmond Duponchel. Aus Marmor, versilberter und vergoldeter Bronze, Elfenbein und Edelstein gefertigt, rückte die Figur die internationale Diskussion um die Farbigkeit der antiken Skulpturen ins Zentrum des Interesses.

In seinem Labor unternahm der Herzog, Naturwissenschaftler und leidenschaftlicher Chemiker, zahllose Versuche, um die antiken Verfahren der Kunstproduktion zu erforschen. In seiner Tätigkeit als Mäzen zielte er vor allem darauf ab, die Kunst des Second Empire zu erneuern: Dank seiner Förderung konnten Goldschmiede wie Charles Wagner, François-Désiré Froment-Meurice oder Edmond Duponchel und Gemmenschneider wie Jean-Valentin Morel zur Erneuerung der Goldschmiedekunst beitragen.

Darüber hinaus äußerte sich seine patriotische Gesinnung auch darin, dass er dem Louvre und dem Cabinet des médailles (Bibliothèque nationale de France) ab den vierziger Jahren des 19. Jahrhunderts regelmäßig bedeutende Stücke aus seiner Sammlung stiftete, 1862 dann seine ganze archäologische Sammlung, weil er glaubte, damit dem wahren Fortschritt der modernen Archäologie am besten zu dienen.

Nach seinem Tod geriet seine Kunst- und Naturaliensammlung in Vergessenheit, was Massimo Listri in seinen Aufnahmen eindrücklich festgehalten hat.

❦

Niché dans la vallée de Chevreuse, destination fort appréciée des Parisiens depuis toujours, le château de Dampierre édifié dans la première moitié du 16ᵉ siècle devint possession de l'illustre famille d'Albert de Luynes en 1663. Charles-Honoré d'Albert de Luynes (1646–1712), duc de Chevreuse et gendre de Jean-Baptiste Colbert, confia les travaux de reconstruction du majestueux château et de ses divers corps de bâtiment à Jules-Hardouin Mansart (1646–1708), Premier architecte du roi, et l'aménagement des magnifiques jardins d'André Le Nôtre (1613–1700).

Après avoir traversé sans dommages la Révolution, le château échut à Honoré Théodoric Paul Joseph d'Albert (1802–1867), duc de Luynes, indéniablement l'un des plus grands mécènes français du 19ᵉ siècle. En 1839, le duc, archéologue et érudit, chargea Félix Duban de diriger d'importants travaux de restauration du château qui abrita dès lors des chefs-d'œuvre célèbres dus à Paul Hippolyte Flandrin, Charles Gleyre, François E. Picot, Pierre-Charles Simart, P. Jules Cavelier et François Rude, ainsi qu'une riche bibliothèque, dispersée aujourd'hui. Le duc proposa à Jean-Auguste-Dominique Ingres de peindre des peintures murales pour le salon de son château destiné à devenir l'éblouissant écrin de sa collection d'antiques, riche de 7000 monnaies et d'un millier d'objets au nombre desquels des vases, des bijoux, des intailles et des pierres gravées, des bronzes étrusques et romains. Malheureusement, l'entreprise se révéla être un échec retentissant pour Ingres, faute d'une préparation technique adéquate peut-être, et les monumentales compositions demeurèrent inachevées.

Lors de l'Exposition universelle de 1855, le public parisien fut impressionné par l'étonnante reconstitution à l'échelle 1: 4 de la statue chryséléphantine d'Athéna Parthénos (conservée ensuite au château) sur un projet de Charles Simart et d'Edmond Duponchel. Réalisée en marbre, argent, bronze doré, ivoire et pierres précieuses, elle plaçait au centre du débat international la question de la polychromie dans la sculpture antique.

Dans le laboratoire qu'abritait le château, le duc, scientifique passionné de chimie, explorait les procédés utilisés par les Anciens afin de retrouver leurs techniques de fabrication artistique. Le mécénat ducal avait pour but premier le renouveau des arts dans la France du Second Empire: il permit ainsi à des orfèvres comme Charles Wagner, François-Désiré Froment-Meurice ou Edmond Duponchel et à des gemmologues comme Jean-Valentin Morel de prendre part à la renaissance de l'orfèvrerie.

Le sentiment patriotique du duc s'exprima de façon manifeste dans les années 1840, par des donations régulières et importantes au Louvre et au Cabinet des médailles (Bibliothèque nationale de France) auquel il légua en 1862 la totalité de sa collection archéologique, mû par la conviction qu'il contribuerait à un véritable progrès de l'archéologie moderne.

Après sa mort, sa collection d'œuvres d'art et d'objets d'histoire naturelle est tombée dans l'oubli, ce que Massimo Listri a consigné de manière impressionnante dans ses photographies.

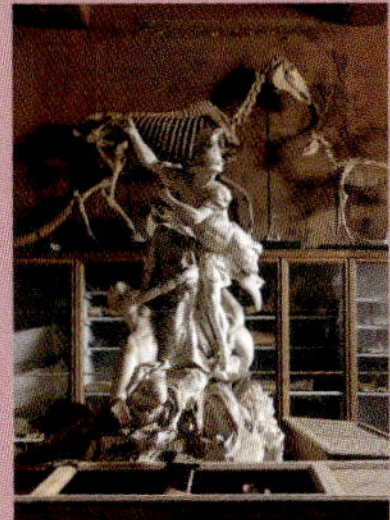

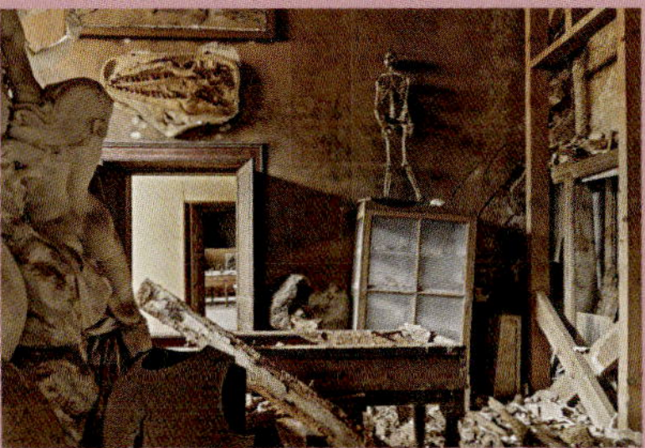

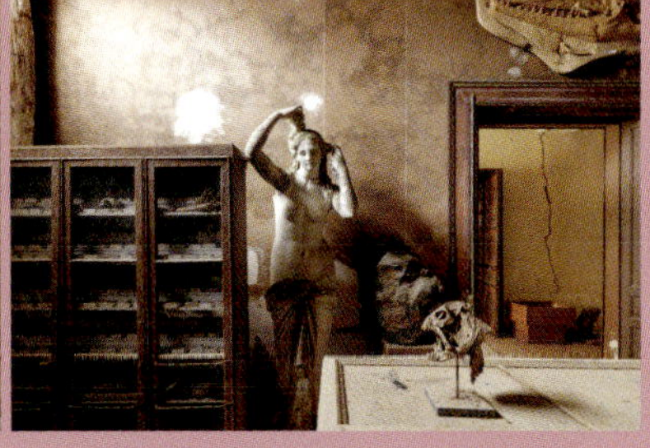

1

2

3

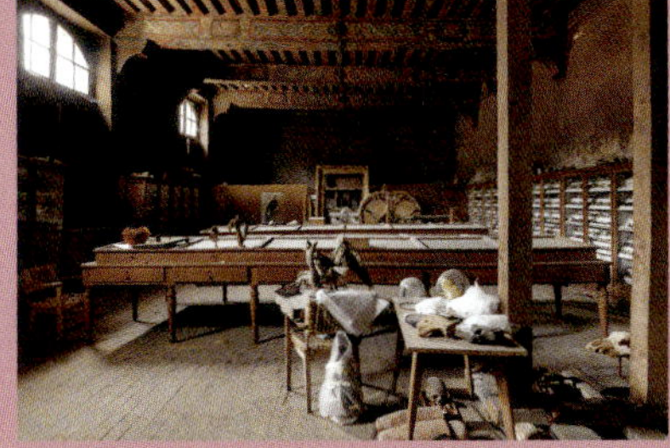

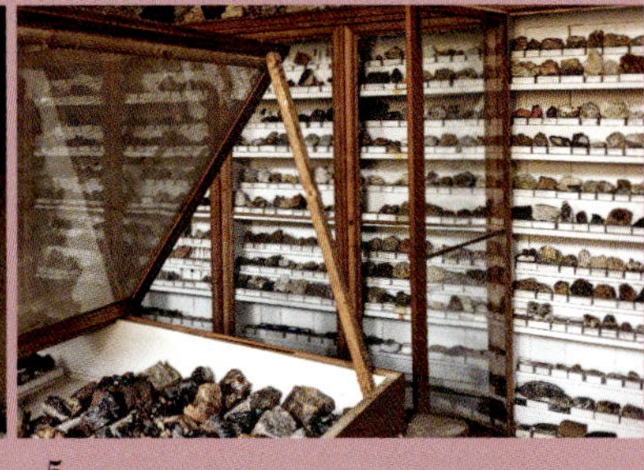

4

5

1 Very little is left in the large rooms that once housed the collections of the dukes who lived in the castle. In the centre of the room here stands a Baroque plaster group.
In den großen Sälen hat sich nur wenig aus der Sammlung der Herzöge erhalten, die hier einst residierten. In der Saalmitte steht eine barocke Gipsskulptur.
Il reste très peu de choses dans les vastes pièces qui abritaient autrefois les collections des ducs vivant dans le château. Au centre de la salle, un groupe baroque en gypse.

2 The remnants of the collections of *naturalia* and the rubble strewn about give a poetic dimension to this room.
Die Überreste der Naturaliensammlung inmitten des Schutts geben diesem Raum etwas Poetisches.
Les fragments des collections d'objets naturels et les gravats donnent une dimension poétique à cette pièce.

3 Skeletons, bones and animal skulls contribute to the theatrical dimension of these rooms, in which the statues seem to be watching over these deserted spaces.
Skelette, Knochen und Tierschädel tragen zur theatralischen Atmosphäre der Zimmer bei, in denen Statuen über die verlassenen Räume zu wachen scheinen.
Squelettes, os et crânes d'animaux contribuent à l'effet théâtral produit par ces salles, où les statues semblent veiller sur les espaces déserts.

4 One of the reception rooms where the original ceilings have been preserved. The display cases on the left contain stuffed birds and animals, and on the right is the collection of minerals. Birds, a puffer fish and parts of skeletons are scattered on the floor and tables.
Einer der Säle, in denen die Originaldecke erhalten ist. In den Vitrinen links lagern präparierte Vögel und andere Tiere, rechts befindet sich eine Mineraliensammlung. Vögel, ein Kugelfisch und Skelettteile sind über Boden und Tische verstreut.
Une des salles de réception avec ses plafonds d'origine. Les vitrines, à gauche, abritent des oiseaux empaillés et d'autres animaux, et, à droite, la collection de minéraux. Des oiseaux naturalisés, un tétraodon et d'autres squelettes sont dispersés sur le sol et sur les tables.

5 Cabinets containing hundreds of mineral specimens evoke the idea of the cabinet of curiosities.
Schränke mit Hunderten von Mineralien erinnern nur noch entfernt an die Idee der Wunderkammer.
Cabinets abritant des centaines de minéraux et évoquant vaguement un cabinet des merveilles.

Collection Guy Ladrière

Paris

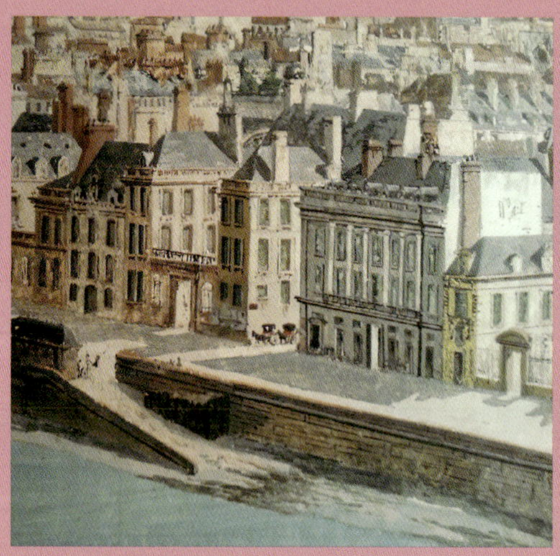

Founded The collection was put together in the 20th century.

Key item The carving depicting Queen Elizabeth I made invulnerable by the skin of the Nemean lion slain by Hercules, thus representing her as the one who can defeat the forces of evil.

Besonders sehenswert Eine Gemme mit der Darstellung Königin Elisabeths I., die wie Herkules das Fell des Nemeischen Löwen trägt, das sie unverwundbar macht, sodass sie das Böse besiegen kann.

À voir absolument L'intaille représentant la reine Élisabeth Iʳᵉ parée, comme Hercule, de la peau du lion de Némée, qui la rend invincible et fait d'elle celle qui triomphe du mal.

Jean-Jacques Prévost, *Project for the Quai de la Seine* (detail of the Quai Voltaire), 1810–1815. Watercolour. Courtesy Galerie Kugel.

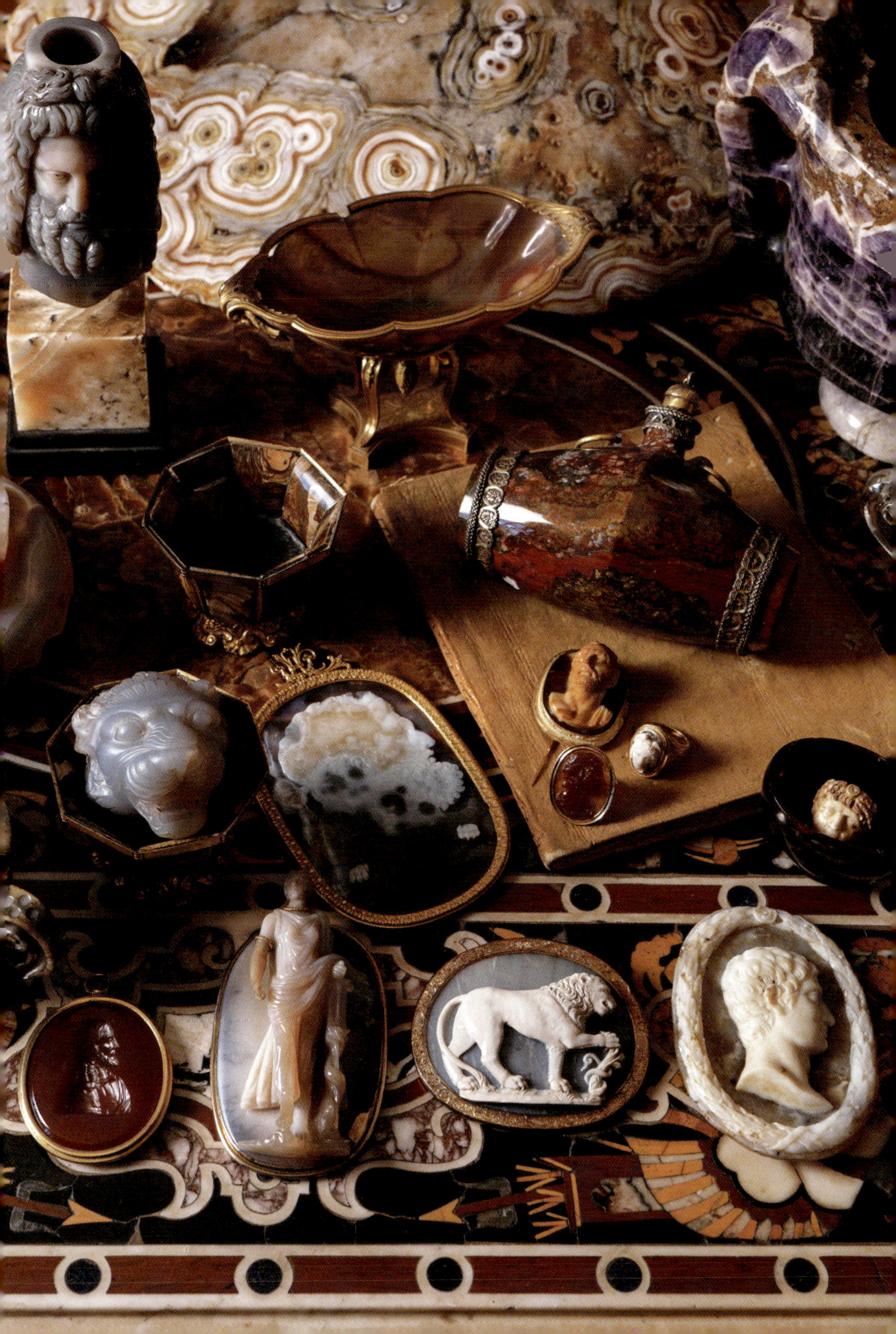

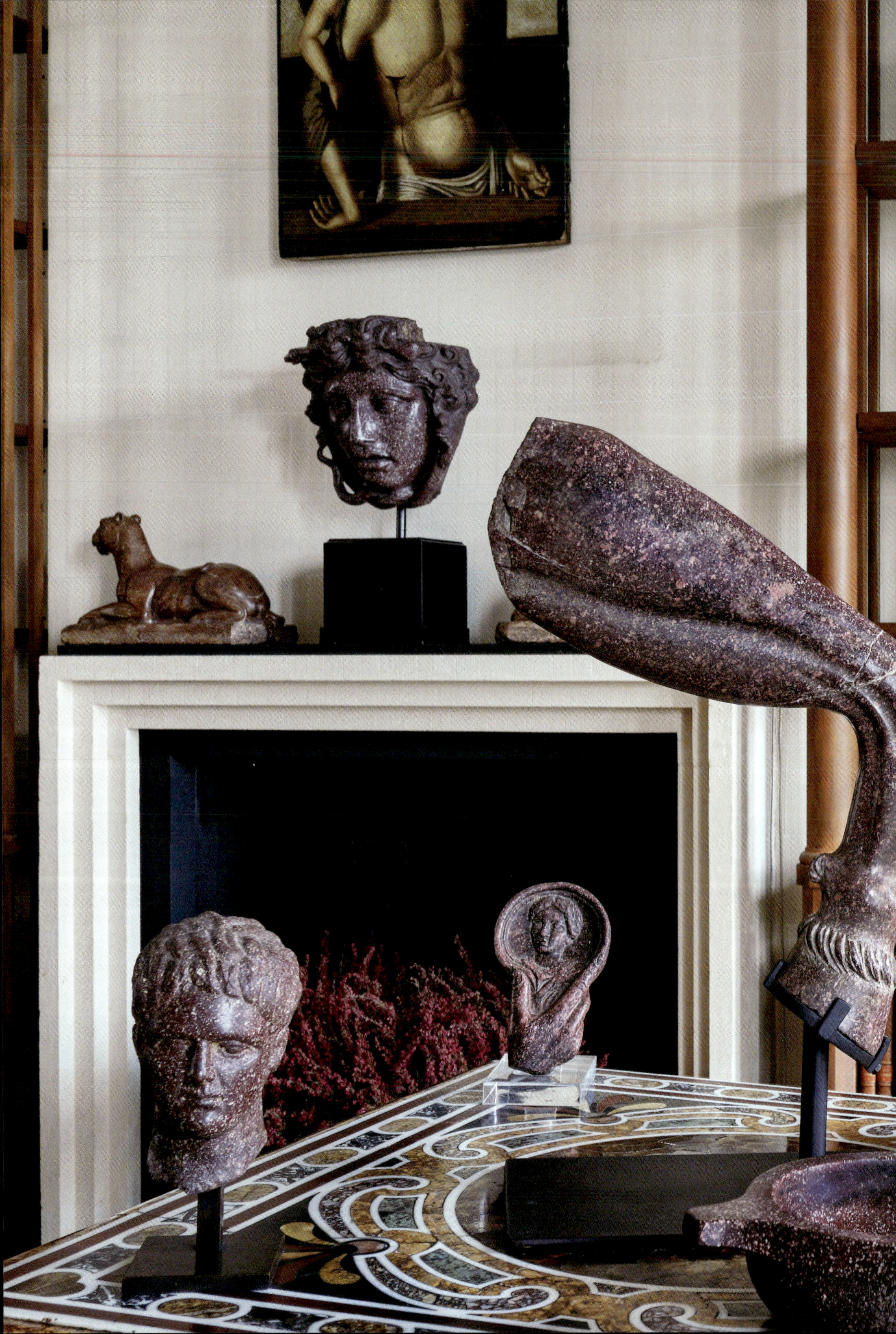

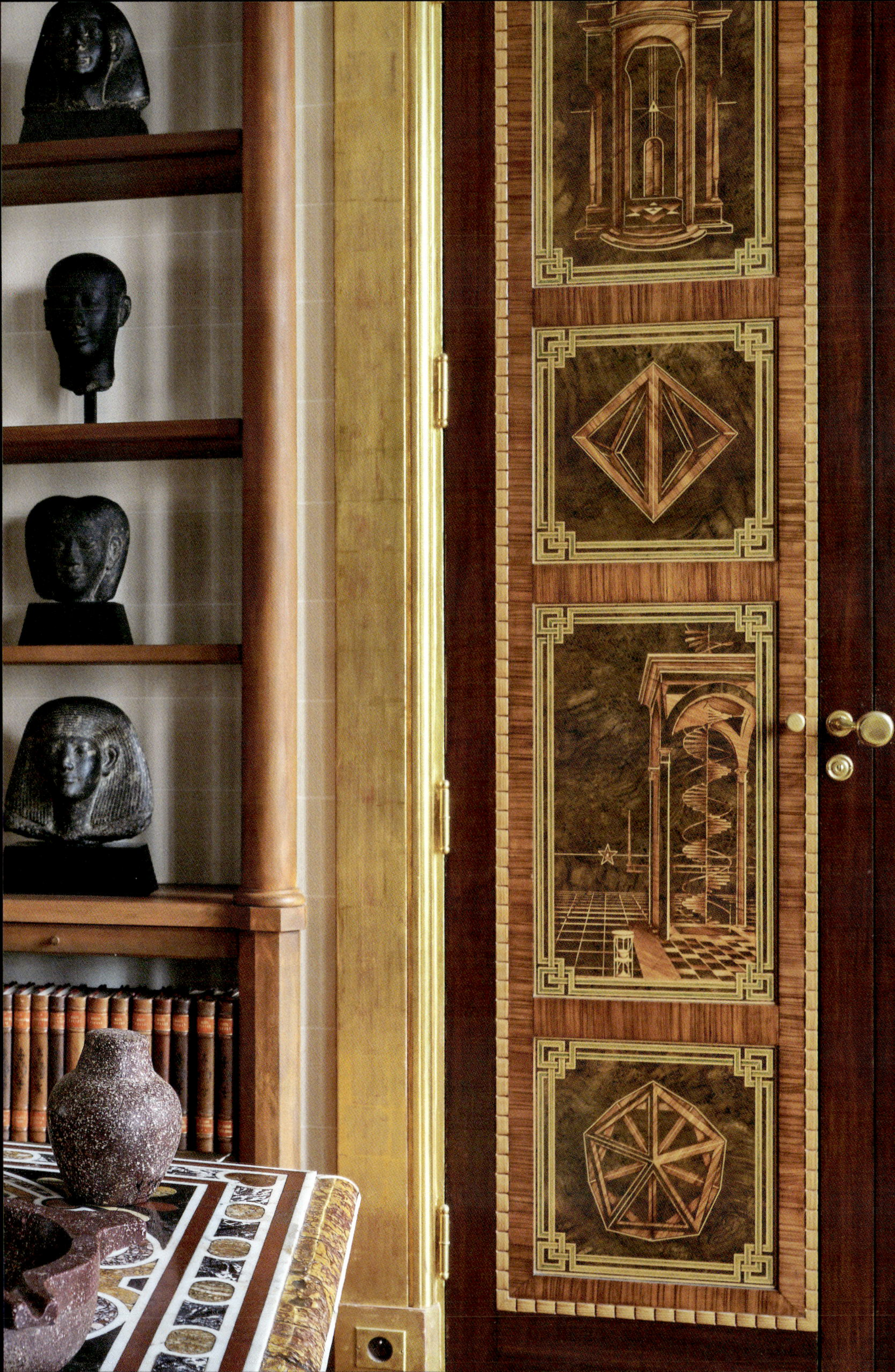

"Nothing fascinates me more than gems": these were the words of Peter Paul Rubens (1577–1640) when writing about his collection of carved and engraved precious stones, which both in quality and quantity rivalled those in the collections of kings. Like him, Guy Ladrière, a renowned Parisian art-dealer who has specialised in Old Master paintings and ancient sculptures, fell under the spell of such intaglio work, to the extent that over the years he has managed to assemble a veritable treasure trove. He has around 300 examples of this ancient art, which is now no longer practised but which for centuries was cultivated by the aristocratic élite of artists and art-dealers. Glyptic art, the art of carving pietra dura with an intaglio technique, gave rise to the production of cameos (positive carving, in relief) and gems (negative carving) where the decorative motif is cut into the surface, a technique used especially in the manufacture of seals.

The Ladrière collection is a survey of the history and development of the art of intaglio work in its many different syles, including sixth-century Etruscan scarabs and Classical and Hellenistic Greek pieces; objects produced in Imperial Rome as well as 10th-century Byzantine gems, where Christian iconography begins to appear; and Renaissance examples alongside a Neo-Classical onyx cameo depicting Theseus slaying the centaur, inspired by a sculpture by Antonio Canova (1757–1822). This valuable collection also includes gems from other celebrated private collections, such as those amassed by Cardinal Albani (1692–1779), the wealthy and acquisitive fourth Duke of Marlborough (1739–1817), the art-dealers Abraham van Goorle and John Evans and the gem-carver Ludwig Pichler (1773–1854). The rings, however, mostly come from the extraordinary collection of Ernest Guilhou (1844–1911), which was broken up and sold in 1937. The majority of the pieces are seals, which have been used since Antiquity to authenticate documents, letters and parcels and prevent them from being tampered with. Carved rings, from the Classical and Hellenistic period through to the Renaissance, depict mythological, historical and natural subjects, and are signifiers of the taste and cultural interests of their original owners.

◎ ❖ ◎

„Nichts kann mich mehr begeistern als Gemmen", schrieb schon Peter Paul Rubens (1577–1640) über seine Sammlung, die in Quantität und Qualität der eines Königs in nichts nachstand. Genau wie Rubens konnte auch Guy Ladrière, der große Pariser Antiquitätenhändler und Experte für Gemälde Alter Meister und Skulpturen, der Faszination der Gemmen nicht widerstehen und legte so mit der Zeit eine Sammlung an, die ein echter Schatz ist. Dazu gehören etwa dreihundert Stücke einer inzwischen fast ausgestorbenen Kunst, die jahrhundertelang von einer bestimmten Künstler- und Antiquitätenhändlerelite kultiviert wurde. Aus der Glyptik oder Steinschneidekunst, also der Bearbeitung von Schmuck- und Edelsteinen mit Schneide- und Schleifgeräten, hat sich die Produktion von Kameen entwickelt, einer Darstellung mit erhabenem Relief, und Gemmen, deren Gravur vertieft ist. Sie fanden vor allem als Siegel Verwendung.

Die Sammlung vollzieht die verschiedenen Entwicklungsstufen und Stile nach: vom etruskischen Skarabäus aus dem 6. Jahrhundert bis zu Exemplaren aus dem klassischen und hellenistischen Griechenland, von Stücken aus der römischen Kaiserzeit bis zu byzantinischen Gemmen des 10. Jahrhunderts, bei denen christliche Motive auftauchen, von der Renaissance bis zur neoklassizistischen Onyxkamee *Theseus besiegt den Kentauren* nach einem Werk von Antonio Canova (1757–1822). Manche Gemmen gehörten ursprünglich berühmten Sammlern wie Kardinal Albani (1692–1779) oder dem 4. Duke of Marlborough (1739–1817), Antiquitätenhändlern wie Abraham van Goorle und John Evans, oder dem Schnitzer Luigi Pichler (1773–1854). Die Ringe hingegen stammen zumeist aus der eindrucksvollen Sammlung von Ernest Guilhou (1844–1911), die 1937 aufgelöst wurde. Zumeist handelt es sich um Siegelringe, die seit der Antike benutzt wurden, um Dokumente, Briefe und andere Unterlagen vor Missbrauch zu schützen. Von der Antike bis zur Renaissance wurden Motive aus Mythologie, Geschichte und Natur verwendet, je nach Geschmack und Interesse des jeweiligen Besitzers.

◉ ◈ ◉

« Rien ne me passionne davantage que les pierreries », a écrit Pierre-Paul Rubens (1577–1640) à propos de sa collection d'intailles qui rivalisait en qualité et en quantité avec celle de maints souverains. Comme lui, Guy Ladrière, antiquaire parisien renommé, expert en peintures et en sculptures anciennes, éprouve pour les intailles une fascination qui l'a conduit à réunir une collection devenue un véritable trésor. Elle rassemble quelque trois cents pierres relevant de cet art ancien quasiment disparu, qui, des siècles durant, a été cultivé par une certaine élite aristocratique d'artistes et d'antiquaires. La glyptique ou l'art de graver les pierres fines a donné naissance à la production de camées (sculptures en relief) et d'intailles (taillées en creux) qui ont très souvent servi de sceau.

La collection de Guy Ladrière retrace l'évolution de la glyptique et en illustre les différents styles : du scarabée étrusque du 6e siècle aux exemplaires de la Grèce antique et hellénistique, puis de la Rome impériale aux pierres byzantines du 10e siècle à l'iconographie chrétienne, des pièces de la Renaissance au camée en onyx néo-classique montrant *Thésée tuant le centaure*, inspiré d'une œuvre d'Antonio Canova (1757–1822). La précieuse collection comprend des gemmes issues de collections particulières renommées dont celle du cardinal Albani (1692–1779), célèbre mécène, du riche et enthousiaste 4e duc de Marlborough (1739–1817), des antiquaires Abraham van Goorle et John Evans, et du graveur Luigi Pichler (1773–1854). Quant aux bagues, elles proviennent en majeure partie de l'extraordinaire collection d'Ernest Guilhou (1844–1911), qui fut dispersée en 1937. La plupart d'entre elles sont des sceaux, cachets utilisés depuis l'Antiquité pour authentifier lettres, plis et documents et en empêcher la falsification. Datées d'une période allant des époques classique et hellénistique à la Renaissance, ces bagues gravées s'ornent de motifs empruntés à la mythologie, à l'histoire et à la nature, emblèmes des goûts et des intérêts culturels de ceux qui se paraient de ces anneaux.

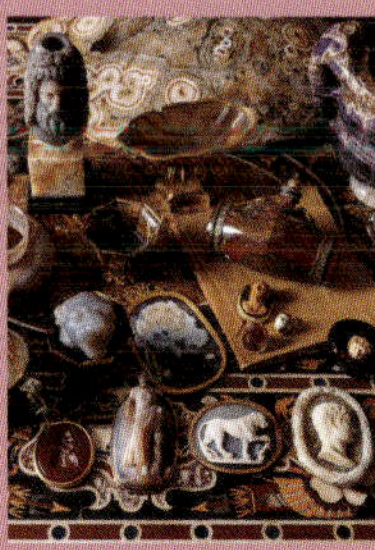

1

1 A table with various antiques.
Tisch mit antiken Stücken.
Table sur laquelle sont présentées
des pièces anciennes.
From left to right, and from top
to bottom:
Von links oben nach rechts unten:
De gauche à droite et de haut
en bas :

1a *Head of Harpocrates*, blue
agate, Roman, 1st–2nd century AD
Kopf des Harpokrates, blauer
Achat, römisch, 1.–2. Jh. n. Chr.
Tête d'Harpocrate, agate bleue,
romaine, 1er–2e siècle après J.-C.

1b *Cup*, chalcedony, Byzantine.
Mounted on gilt bronze,
17th century.
Pokal, Chalcedon, Byzanz. Fassung
aus vergoldeter Bronze, 17. Jh.
Coupe, calcédoine, Byzance.
Sertissage en bronze doré,
17e siècle.

1c *Large cup*, fluorite, Roman,
1st–2nd century AD
Großer Pokal, Fluorit, römisch,
1.–2. Jh. n. Chr.

Grande coupe, fluorite, romaine,
1er–2e siècle après J.-C.

1d *Goblet*, chalcedony,
14th century
Runde Vase, Chalcedon, 14. Jh
Vase rond, calcédoine, 14e siècle

1e *Octagonal salt cup*, agate.
Mounted on gilt bronze,
16th century.
Oktogonales Salzgefäß, Achat.
Fassung aus vergoldeter Bronze,
16. Jh.
Salière octogonale, agate.
Sertissage en bronze doré,
16e siècle.

1f *Keg*, agate. Mounted on gilt
silver, early 16th century.
Fässchen, Achat. Fassung aus
vergoldetem Silber, frühes 16. Jh.
Petit tonneau, agate. Sertissage en
argent doré, début 16e siècle.

1g *Octagonal salt cup*, agate.
Mounted on gilt bronze,
16th century. Inside, a lion's head
made from blue agate.
Oktogonales Salzgefäß, Achat.

Fassung aus vergoldeter Bronze,
16. Jh. In dem Gefäß ein Löwenkopf
aus blauem Achat.
Salière octogonale, agate. Sertissage en bronze doré, 16e siècle.
Dans la salière une tête de lion en
agate bleue.

1h *Hercules*, large cameo,
16th century, in an 18th-century
gold setting
Herkules, große Kamee, 16. Jh.
Goldfassung 18. Jh.
Hercule, grand camée, 16e siècle.
Sertissage en or, 18e siècle.

1i *Brooch with male portrait*,
agate, Roman, 1st–3rd century AD
Brosche mit männlichem Porträt,
Achat, römisch, 1.–3. Jh. n. Chr.
Broche avec portrait d'homme,
agate, romaine, 1er–3e siècle
après J.-C.

1j *Ring with a satyr*, carnelian,
early 19th century (Christine
Ladrière Collection)
Ring mit Satyr, Karneol,
Anfang 19. Jh. (Sammlung
Christine Ladrière)

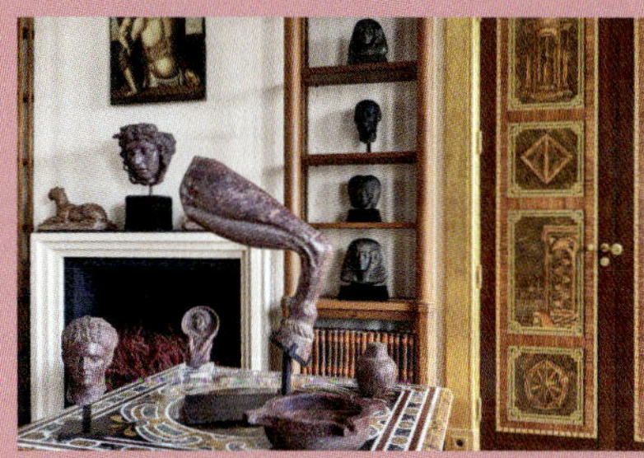
2

Bague avec satyre, cornaline, début 19ᵉ siècle (collection Christine Ladrière)

1k *Ring with Medusa* (codognato), agate, Roman, 1st–3rd century AD (Christine Ladrière Collection)
Ring mit Medusa (Codognato), Achat, römisch, 1.–3. Jh. n. Chr. (Sammlung Christine Ladrière)
Bague avec méduse (Codognato), agate, romaine, 1ᵉʳ–3ᵉ siècle après J.-C. (collection Christine Ladrière)

1l *Lachrymal vase*, garnet, Roman, 1st–2nd century AD. Inside the vase is a gold ring (codognato) adorned with the head of the emperor Constantine, agate, Roman, 1st century AD.
Tränenvase, Granat, römisch, 1.–2. Jh. n. Chr. Im Inneren der Vase befindet sich ein Goldener Ring (Codognato) mit einer Darstellung des Kopfes von Konstantin, Achat, römisch, 1. Jh. n. Chr.
Vase lacrymal, grenat, romain, 1ᵉʳ–2ᵉ siècle après J.-C. À l'intérieur du vase lacrymal se trouve un

anneau d'or (Codognato) avec une représentation de la tête de Constantin, agate, romaine, 1ᵉʳ siècle après J.-C.

1m *Bust of Christ*, carnelian cameo, 17th century
Christusbüste, Kamee aus Karneol, 17. Jh.
Buste du Christ, camée en cornaline, 17ᵉ siècle

1n *Female figure*, chalcedony cameo, Roman, 1st–2nd century AD
Weibliche Figur, Kamee aus Chalcedon, römisch, 1.–2. Jh. n. Chr.
Figure féminine, camée en calcédoine, romaine, 1ᵉʳ–2ᵉ siècle après J.-C.

1o *Striding lion*, cameo, 17th century
Schreitender Löwe, Kamee, 17. Jh.
Lion en marche, camée, 17ᵉ siècle

1p *Bust of emperor in profile*, large agate cameo, 16th century
Büste eines Kaisers im Profil, große Kamee aus Achat, 16. Jh.
Buste d'empereur en profil, grand camée en agate, 16ᵉ siècle

2 Among the oldest pieces in the collection is the series of Roman porphyry artefacts, including the ones shown here on a 17th-century pietra dura table.
Zum ältesten Bestand der Sammlung gehören eine Reihe römischer Porphyrobjekte. Einige davon sind hier auf einem Tisch aus Pietra dura aus dem 17. Jh. ausgebreitet.
Les objets les plus anciens de la collection incluent une série d'œuvres d'art romain en porphyre, dont les objets exposés sur une table en pietra dura du 17ᵉ siècle.

Collection Kugel

Galerie Kugel, Paris

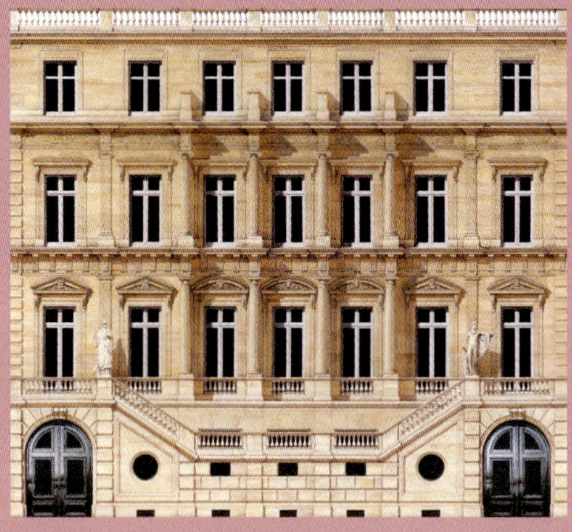

Founded The main collection was assembled in the 20th century, the ivories of the cabinet of curiosities date from the 16th to 17th centuries.

Key item The 16th- and 17th-century ivories, masterpieces of artistic virtuosity.

Besonders sehenswert Elfenbeinarbeiten aus dem 16. und 17. Jahrhundert. Meisterwerke künstlerischer Virtuosität.

À voir absolument Les ivoires des 16e et 17e siècles. Chefs-d'œuvre de virtuosité artistique.

Andrew Zega and Bernd Dams, *Galerie Kugel in Hôtel Collot*, 2004. Watercolour. Courtesy Galerie Kugel.

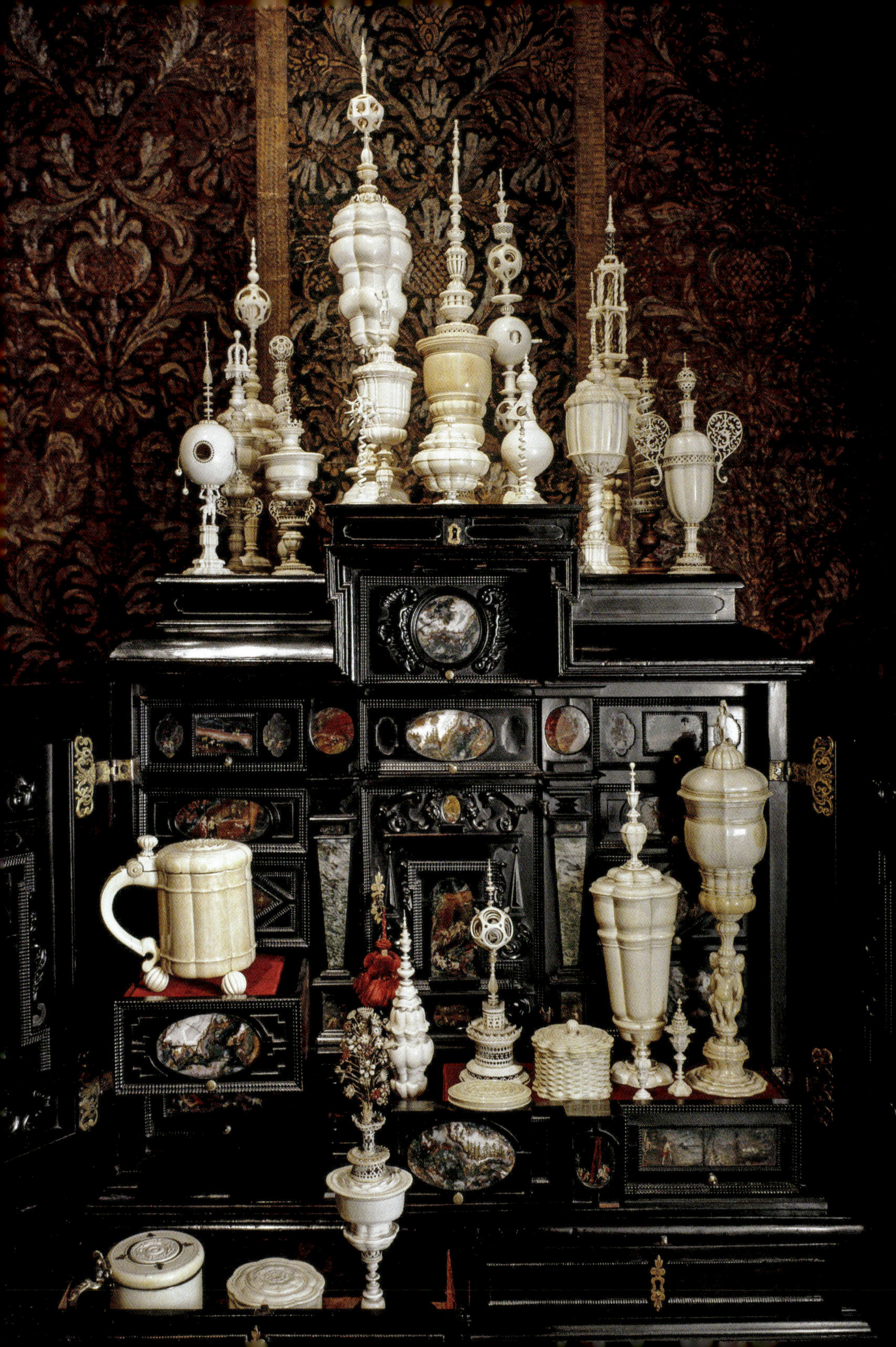

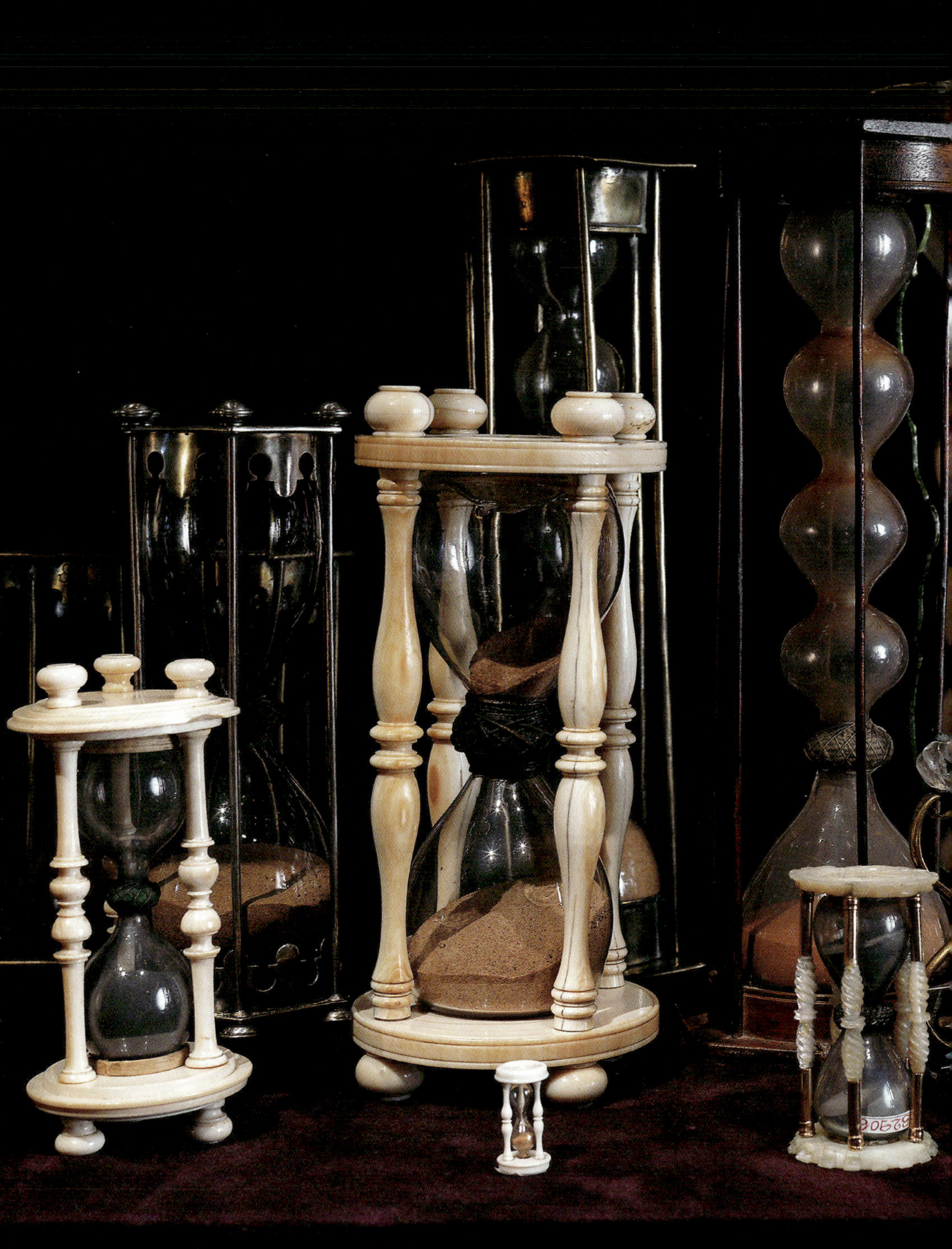

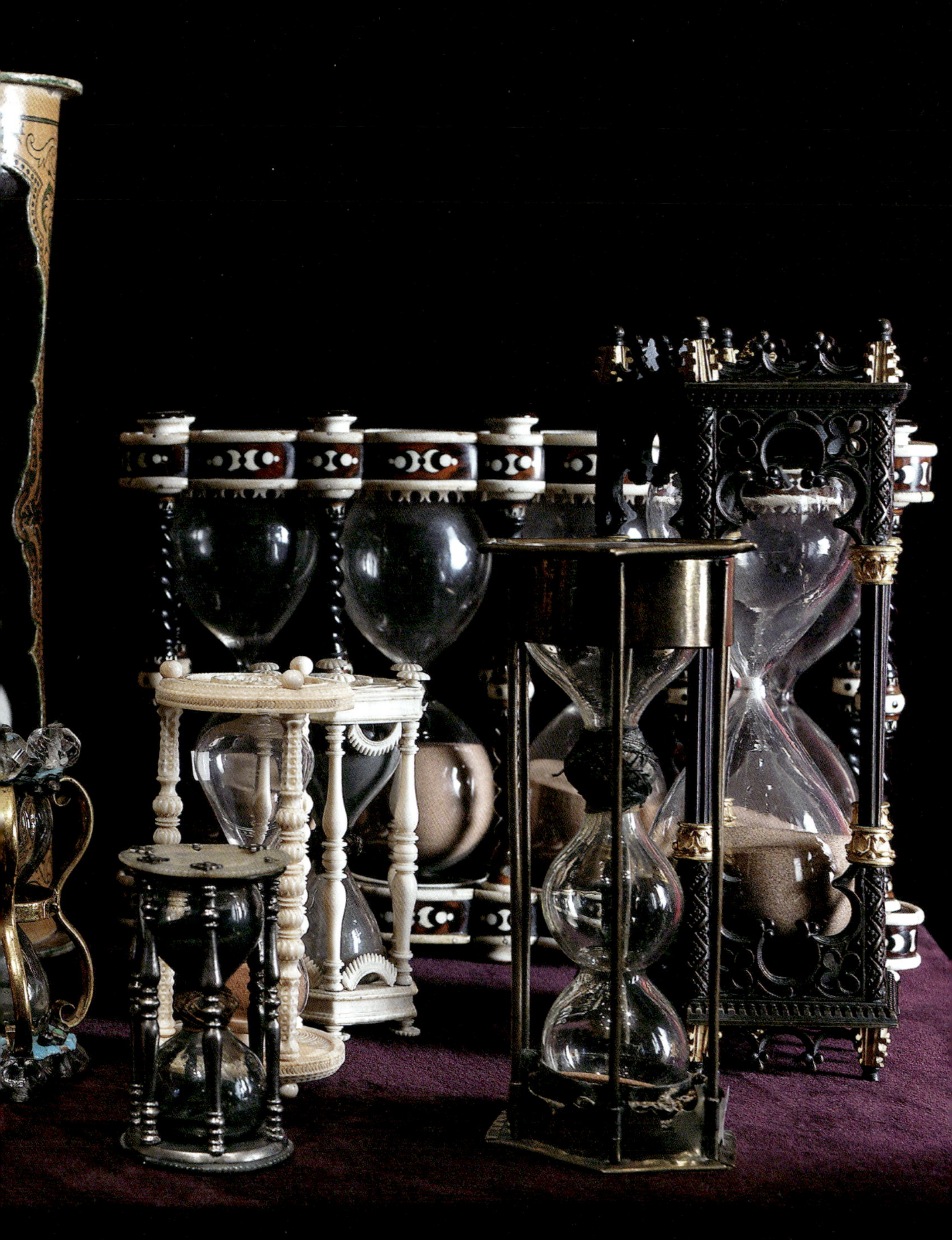

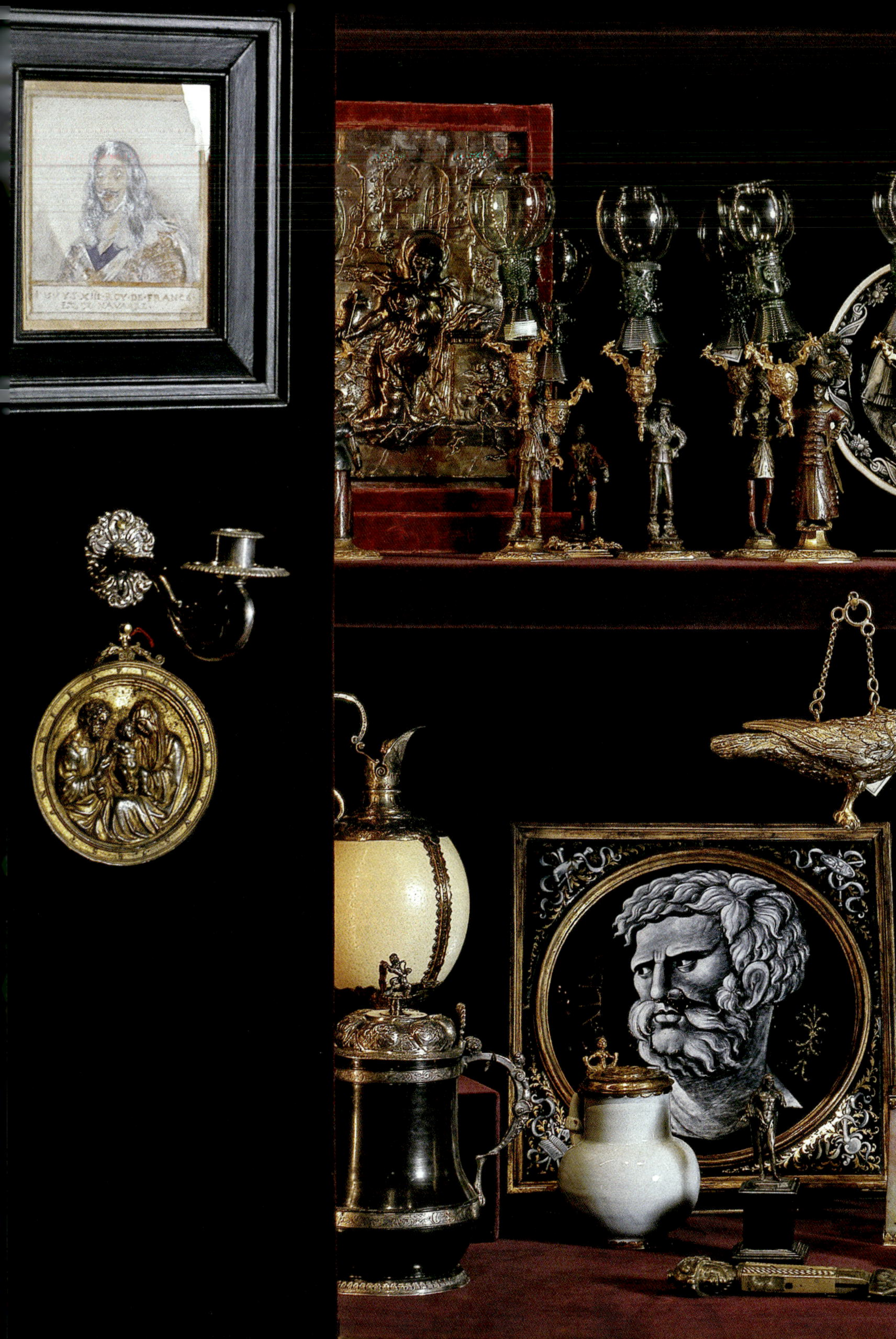

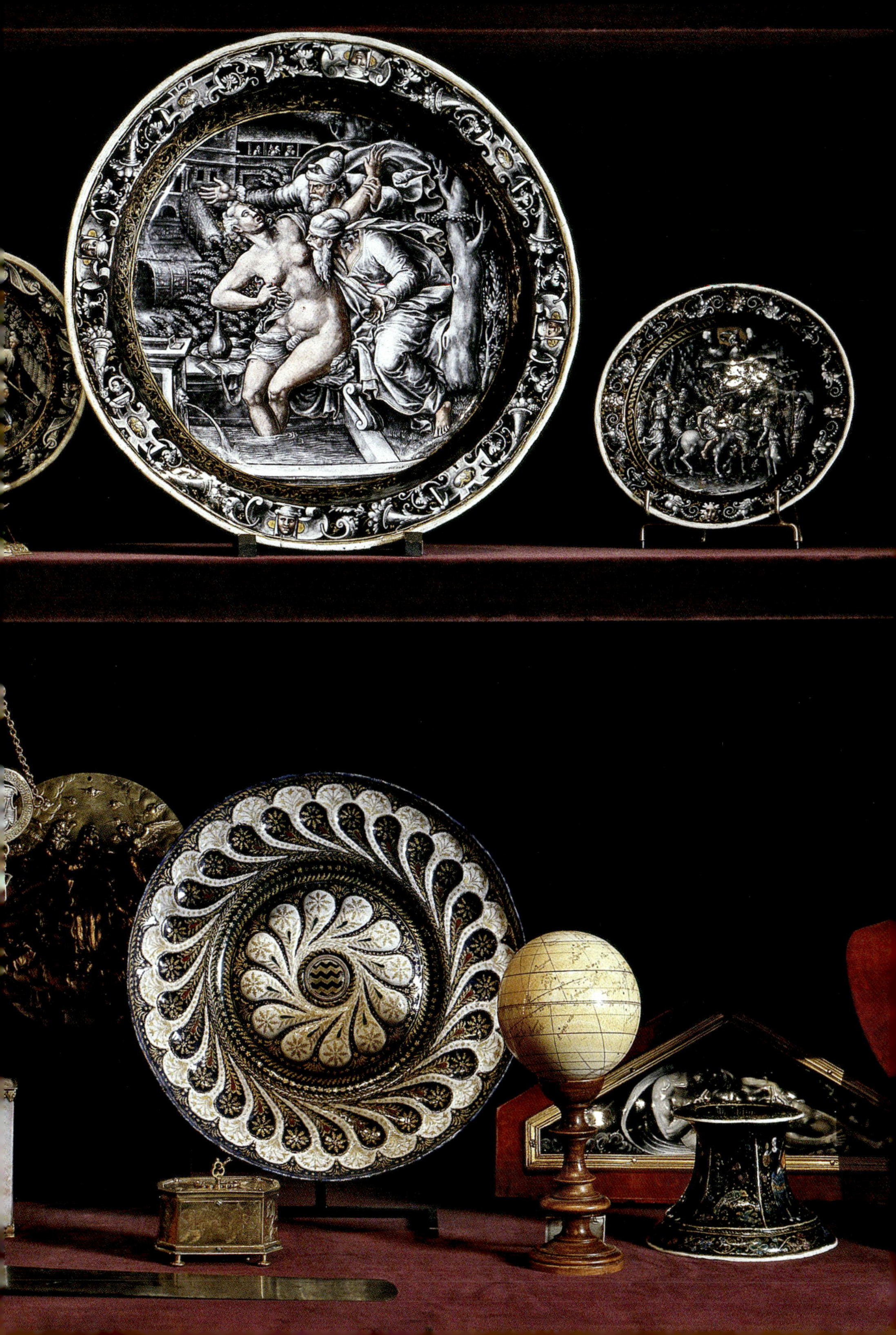

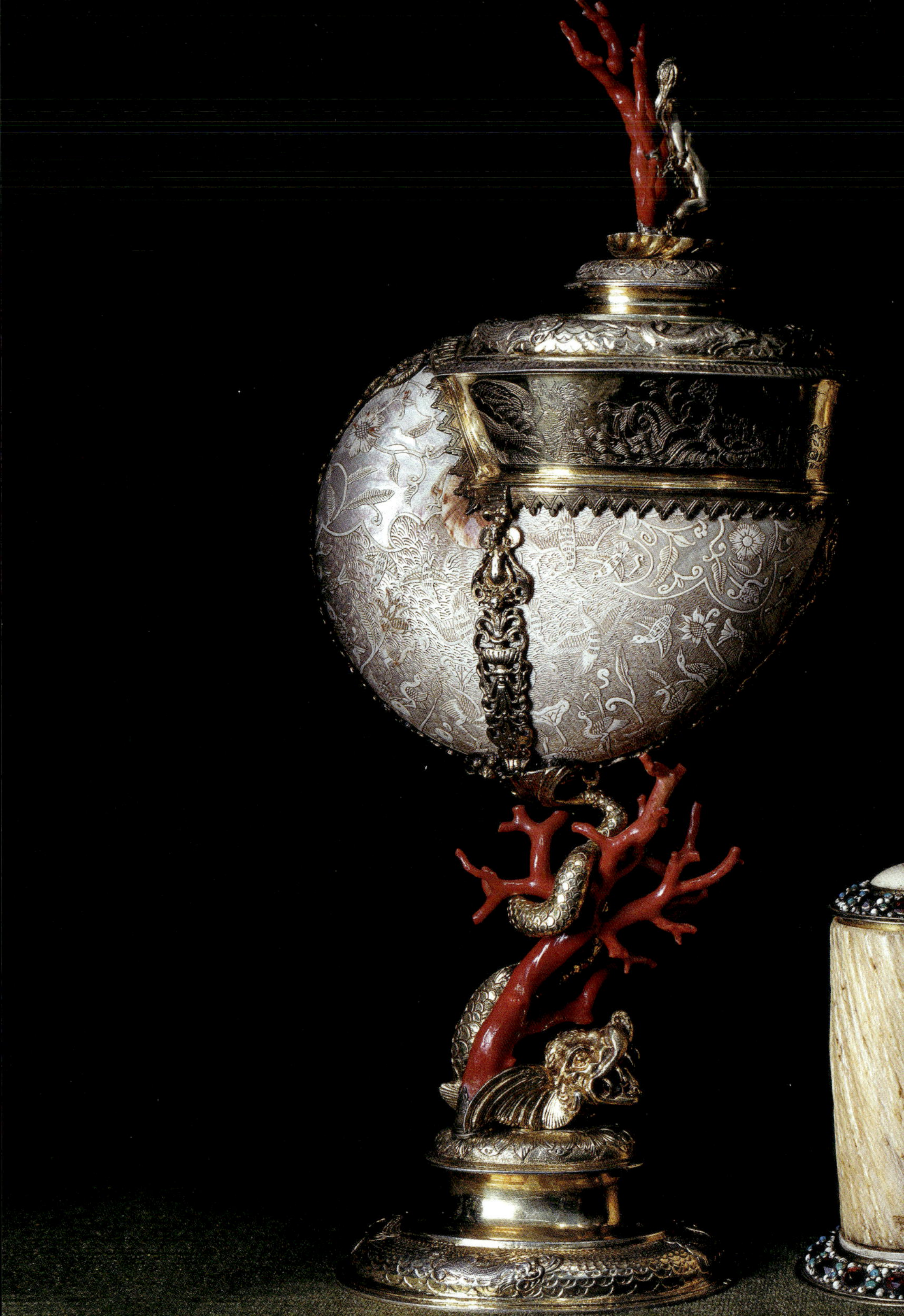

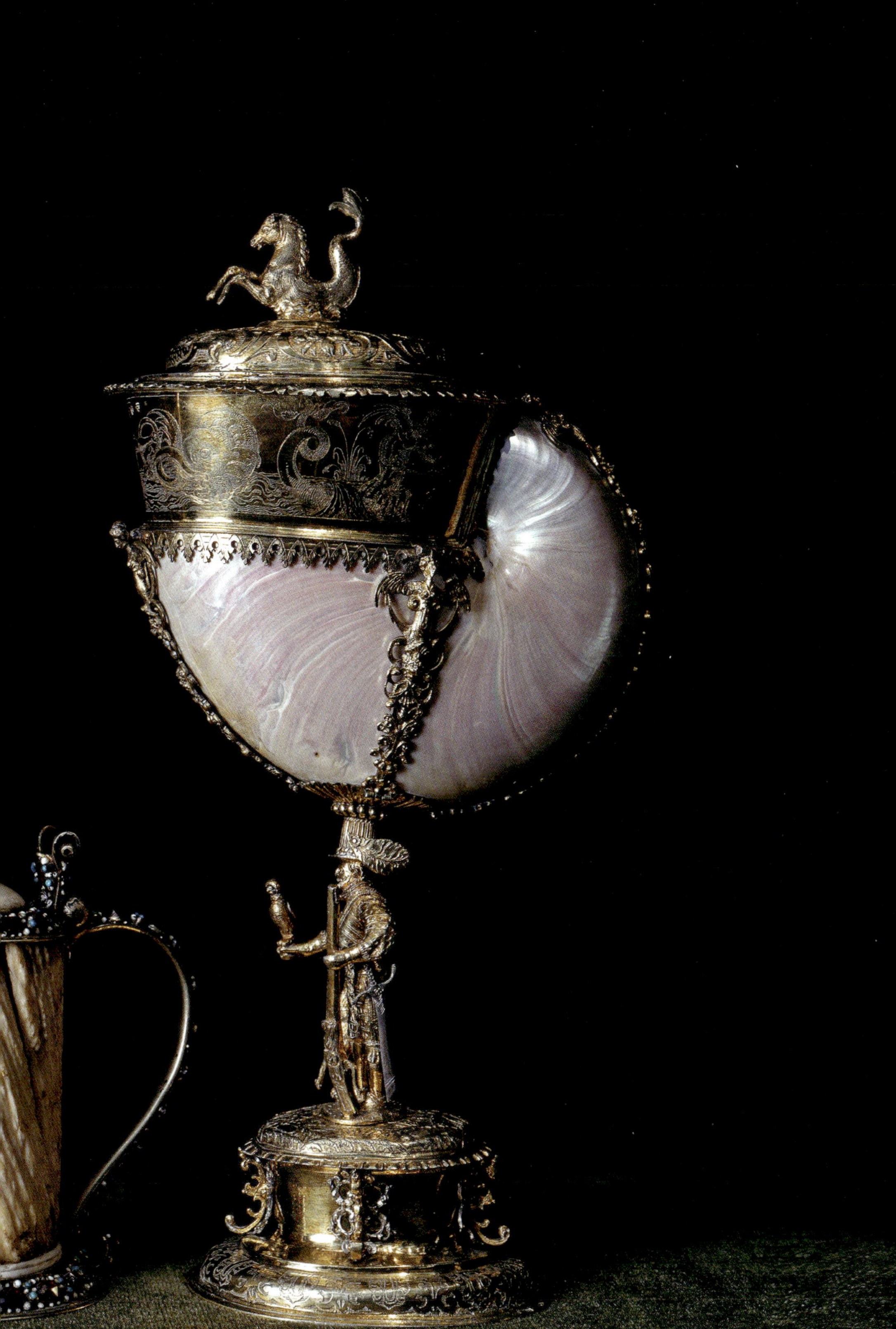

Nicolas and Alexis Kugel are fifth-generation art-dealers from a dynasty that originated in Minsk in White Russia in the late 18th century, where Elie Kugel began trading in clocks, gold objects and jewellery. In 1924, Elie's great grandson Jacques emigrated to Paris, and in 1958 opened his first shop there. Jacques Kugel was known for his discerning eye, and because of his reputation his gallery became an essential destination for international collectors; nowadays it is housed inside the Hôtel Collot, a building constructed in 1840 on the Quai Anatole France by the famous architect Louis Visconti (1791–1853) for the director of the French Mint, Jean-Pierre Collot.

All the objects in the collection—furniture, sculptures, silverware, ivories, rock crystal, enamels, snuffboxes and scientific instruments from different periods and places—are united by the same guiding principle, namely an extreme virtuosity in the use of materials and the obsessive pursuit of artistic excellence, qualities that were appreciated by a special kind of collector in the past, such as Lorenzo de' Medici, Cardinal Mazarin, William Beckford or Marie-Laure de Noailles, and in the present, Yves Saint Laurent or Pierre Bergé. Notable among the most extraordinary pieces are the 16th- and 17th-century ivories, genuine marvels of craftsmanship and design. As well as its undeniable appeal which results from its rare and exotic nature, ivory permitted those who worked with it to take their techniques of craftmanship to extremes bordering on the impossible. The vessels with their accompanying lids, or the bold compositions based on solid geometrical forms balanced on threadlike stems or asymmetrical miniature staircases, are all crafted from a single piece of precious African or Indian ivory; turned on a lathe on their insides as well as their outsides and worked until they are as thin as can possibly be, they are absolute miracles of technical virtuosity.

◦ ◈ ◦

Nicolas und Alexis Kugel verkörpern die fünfte Generation einer Dynastie von Antiquitätenhändlern, die ursprünglich aus dem weißrussischen Minsk stammt, wo ihr Vorfahre Elie Kugel im 18. Jahrhundert mit Uhren, Goldwaren und Schmuck zu handeln begann. Sein Urenkel Jacques emigrierte 1924 nach Paris und eröffnete dort 1958 eine Galerie. Jacques Kugel war bekannt für sein unbestechliches Auge, und dank seiner Reputation wurde die Galerie, heute im Hôtel Collot, das 1840 von dem berühmten Architekten Louis Visconti (1791–1853) für den Direktor der Münzprägeanstalt von Paris, Jean-Pierre Collot, am Quai Anatole France errichtet wurde, zu einem Pilgerziel der internationalen Sammlergemeinde.

Sämtliche Objekte der Sammlung – Möbel, Skulpturen, Arbeiten aus Silber, Elfenbein, Bergkristall und Email, Tabakdosen, wissenschaftliche Gerätschaften verschiedener Epochen und Herkunft – vereinen höchste künstlerische Qualität mit technischer Virtuosität, alles Eigenschaften, die besonders anspruchsvolle Sammler ansprechen, zu denen früher Lorenzo de' Medici, Kardinal Mazarin, William Thomas Beckford, Marie-Laure de Noailles gehörten und heute u.a. Yves Saint Laurent und Pierre Bergé.

Zu den Glanzstücken der Sammlung zählen zweifellos die Elfenbeinarbeiten des 16. und 17. Jahrhunderts, wahre Meisterwerke des menschlichen Erfindungsgeistes. Als Material war Elfenbein nicht nur wegen seiner exotischen Herkunft und seiner Seltenheit äußerst beliebt, sondern auch weil es sich ausnehmend gut für eine extreme, ans Unmögliche grenzende Bearbeitung eignete. Hier handelt es sich um Deckelgefäße oder gewagte geometrische Formen, die auf dünnen Stielen oder asymmetrischen Stufen zu schweben scheinen und aus einem Stück wertvollen afrikanischen oder indischen Elfenbeins gefertigt wurden. Hauchdünn, da sowohl innen wie außen gedrechselt, stellen sie ein Wunder an technischer Brillanz dar.

◉ ◈ ◉

Nicolas et Alexis Kugel représentent la cinquième génération d'une dynastie d'antiquaires qui vit le jour à la fin du 18e siècle dans la ville biélorusse de Minsk où Elie Kugel se lança dans le commerce des pendules, des objets d'orfèvrerie et des bijoux. En 1924, Jacques Kugel, arrière-petit-fils d'Elie, émigra à Paris où il ouvrit sa première galerie en 1958 et acquit une réputation internationale grâce à son œil infaillible. Aujourd'hui logée dans l'hôtel Collot édifié quai Anatole-France par Louis Visconti (1791–1853), l'architecte le plus en vue de son temps, pour Jean-Pierre Collot, directeur de la Monnaie, la galerie constitue une étape incontournable pour les collectionneurs du monde entier.

Tous les objets de la collection – meubles, sculptures, orfèvrerie, ivoires, cristaux de roche, émaux, tabatières, instruments scientifiques d'époques et de provenances diverses – ont en commun une même virtuosité dans l'utilisation des matériaux et une même recherche de la beauté, caractères distinctifs d'un type de collectionnisme représenté jadis par Laurent de Médicis, le cardinal Mazarin, William Thomas Beckford ou Marie-Laure de Noailles, aujourd'hui par Yves Saint Laurent et Pierre Bergé. Parmi les pièces les plus extraordinaires on citera les ivoires des 16e et 17e siècles, véritables miracles d'ingéniosité. Outre son indéniable fascination liée à sa rareté et son exotisme, l'ivoire avait l'avantage de permettre des techniques de travail extrêmes, à la limite de l'impossible, comme en témoignent les vases avec couvercle, ou les solides géométriques à la composition hardie, montés sur des tiges métalliques, ou encore les petits escaliers asymétriques réalisés dans une seule pièce de précieux ivoire africain ou indien. Tournés à l'intérieur comme à l'extérieur jusqu'à l'obtention d'une épaisseur infinitésimale, ces ivoires constituent de véritables prodiges de virtuosité technique.

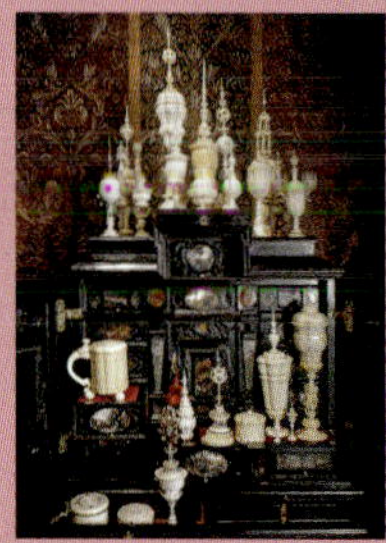

1

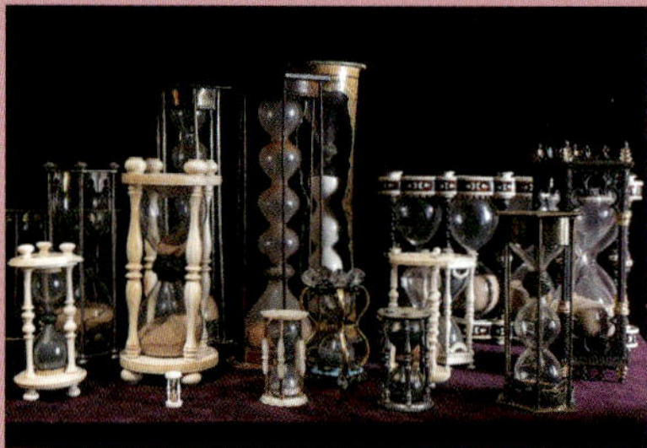

2

1 *Lathe-turned ivories* from the 16th and 17th centuries from this private collection displayed on an ebony and painted hardstone cupboard by Ulrich and Melchior Baumgartner, Augsburg, c. 1630–1640.
Gedrechselte Elfenbeinarbeiten, 16.–17. Jh. Aus der privaten Familiensammlung in einem Schrank aus Ebenholz mit bemalten Halbedelsteinen von Ulrich und Melchior Baumgartner, Augsburg, um 1630–1640.
Pièces en ivoire tourné des 16e et 17e siècles de la collection familiale privée, dans un cabinet en ébène orné de pierres semi-précieuses peintes, réalisé par Ulrich et Melchior Baumgartner, Augsbourg, vers 1630–1640.

2 *Collection of hour-glasses,* 16th–19th century, including examples in wrought brass, blown glass, ivory and wood. Considerably cheaper than clocks, hour-glasses also required no maintenance. These finely wrought examples, clearly destined for the top end of the market, were probably intended for use during private devotion. An hour-glass prompts its owner to reflect on the passing of time and the transience of life, while allowing him to time half-hour periods of prayer and meditation.
Sammlung von Sanduhren, 16.–19. Jh. aus getriebenem Messing, mundgeblasenem Glas sowie Elfenbein und Holz. Sanduhren waren wesentlich billiger als mechanische Uhren und bedurften keiner Wartung. Diese kunstvoll getriebenen Exemplare waren für das Luxussegment des Marktes bestimmt und wurden wahrscheinlich für religiöse Zwecke verwendet.

Eine solche Sanduhr regte seinen Besitzer nicht nur an, über die rasch verfliegende Zeit und die Vergänglichkeit des Lebens nachzudenken, sondern zeigte ihm auch an, wenn er bspw. eine halbe Stunde mit Gebet oder Meditation verbracht hatte.
Collection de sabliers, 16e–19e siècle. On y trouve des spécimens en laiton repoussé et en verre soufflé à la bouche ainsi qu'en ivoire et en bois. Les sabliers étaient beaucoup moins chers que les horloges et ne nécessitaient pas d'entretien. Ces exemplaires artistement travaillés étaient destinés au marché du luxe et probablement utilisés à des fins religieuses. Un tel sablier n'incitait pas seulement son propriétaire à penser au temps si vite enfui et au caractère éphémère de la vie, mais lui indiquait aussi quand il avait passé une demi-heure en prière ou en méditation.

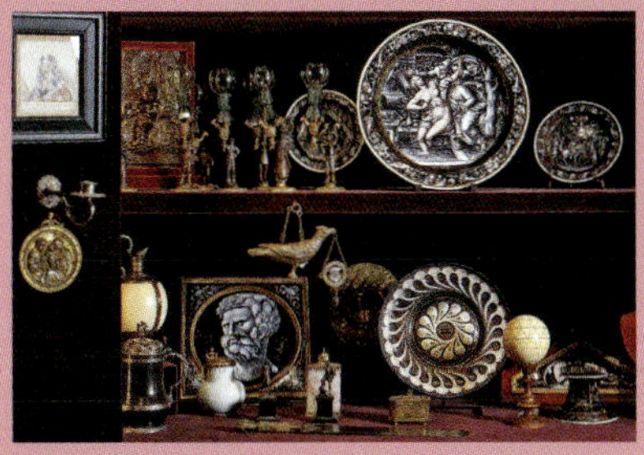

3

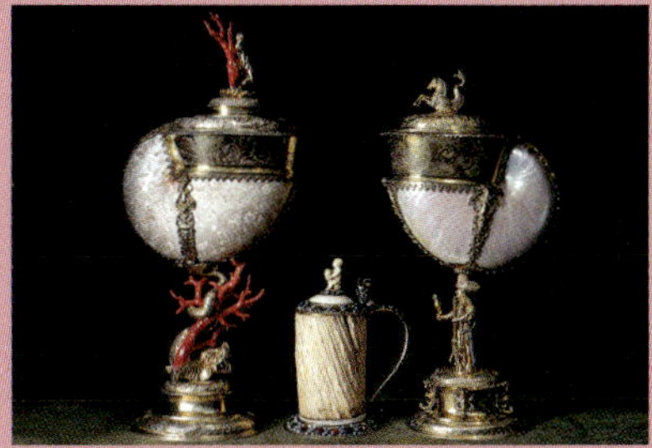

4

3 Some of the contents of the cabinet, including enamels from Limoges and Venice, mounted ostrich eggs and 17th-century glass holders.
In dem Kunstschrank werden Emailarbeiten aus Limoges und Venedig, gefasste Straußeneier und Glashalter aus dem 17. Jh. präsentiert.
Dans le Cabinet d'art sont présentés des émaux de Limoges et de Venise, des œufs d'autruche montés et des porte-verres du 17ᵉ siècle.

4a *Coppa*, Lauenburg, *c.* 1600. Silver-gilt mounted nautilus shell, set on a foot consisting of a dolphin entwined in coral, with the figure of Andromeda bound to a coral stem surmounting the lid, 42 cm / 16½ in.
Pokal, Lauenburg, um 1600. Nautilus, in vergoldetes Silber gefasst, gekrönt von der an eine Koralle gefesselten Andromeda; der Fuß besteht aus einem Delfin, der sich um eine Koralle windet, 42 cm.
Coupe, Lauenburg, vers 1600. Nautile surmonté d'Andromède enchaînée à une branche de corail, dans une monture en argent doré, dont le pied est orné d'un dauphin et d'une branche de corail, 42 cm.

4b *Narwhal tankard*, south Germany, *c.* 1670–1680. Silver-gilt mounting, 17 cm / 6¾ in.
Narwal-Humpen, süddeutsch, um 1670–1680. Fassung aus vergoldetem Silber, 17 cm.
Chope en dent de narval, sud de l'Allemagne, vers 1670–1680. Monture en argent doré, 17 cm.

4c *Coppa*, Nuremberg, *c.* 1600. Nautilus shell, mounted in gilt silver, featuring a composite sea creature, half horse and half fish. The foot consists of a hunter with rifle and falcon, 36 cm / 14⅛ in.
Pokal, Nürnberg, um 1600. Mit einem Fantasie-Meereswesen, halb Pferd und halb Fisch, dekorierter Nautilus in einer Fassung aus vergoldetem Silber. Der Fuß zeigt einen Jäger mit Gewehr und Falken, 36 cm.
Coupe, Nuremberg, vers 1600. Nautile orné d'un cheval marin, dans une monture en argent doré. Le pied montre un chasseur avec fusil et faucon, 36 cm.

407

Château de Bannes

Beaumont-du-Périgord

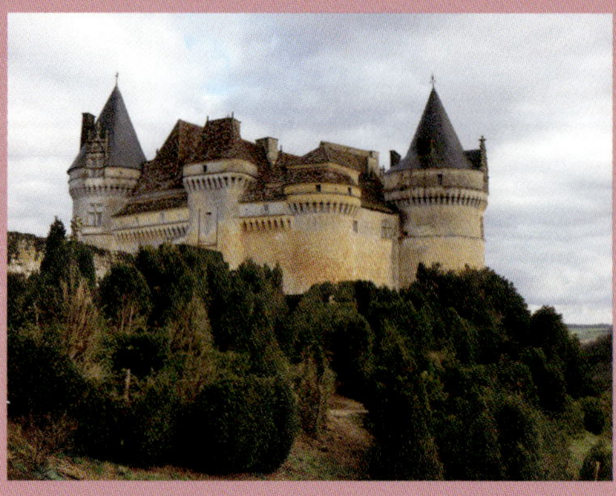

Founded The collection was established in the 21st century, the castle dates from the 16th century.

Key item The cabinet with the silver collection.

Besonders sehenswert Das Silberkabinett.

À voir absolument Le Cabinet d'argent.

Massimo Listri, *View of the Château de Bannes*

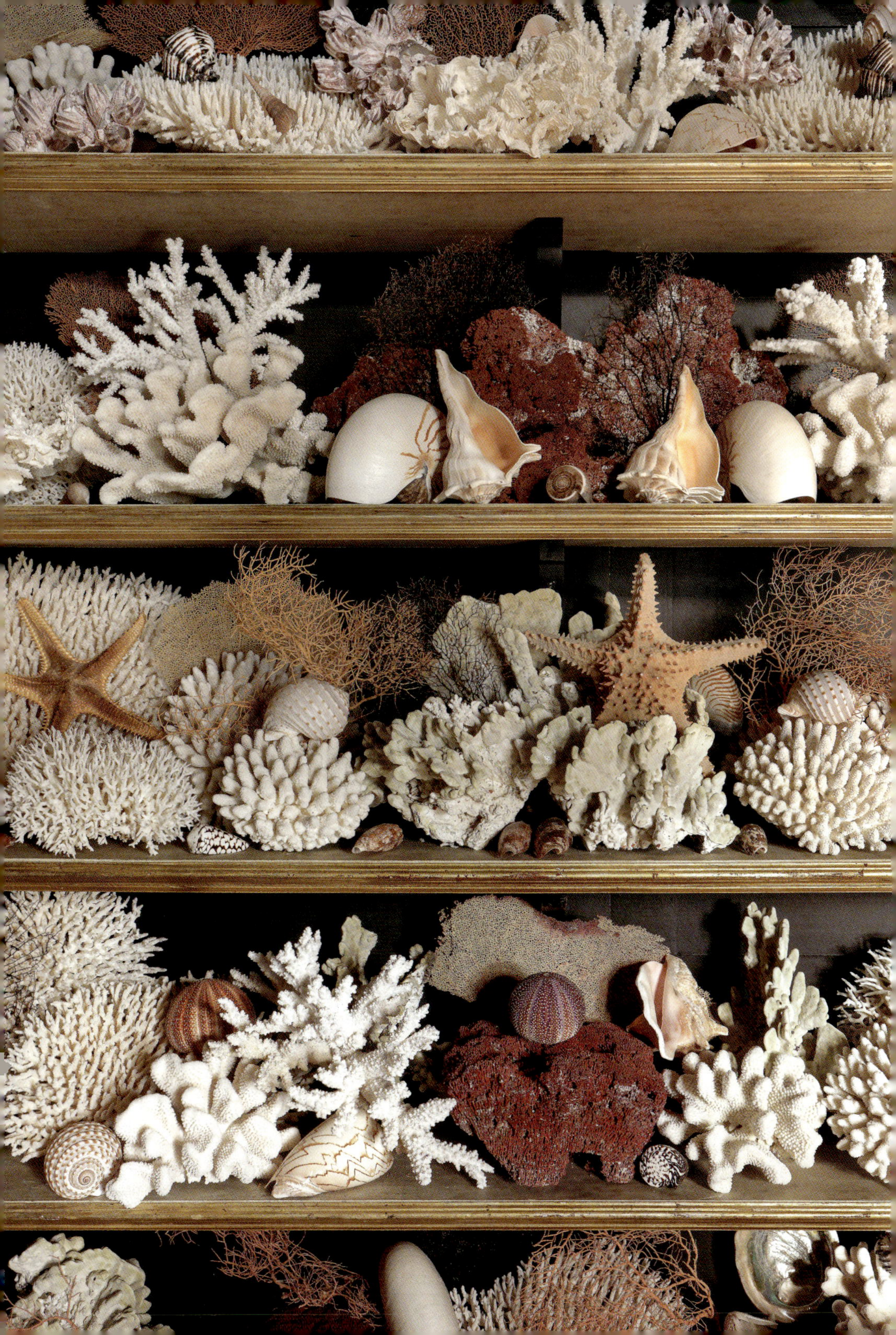

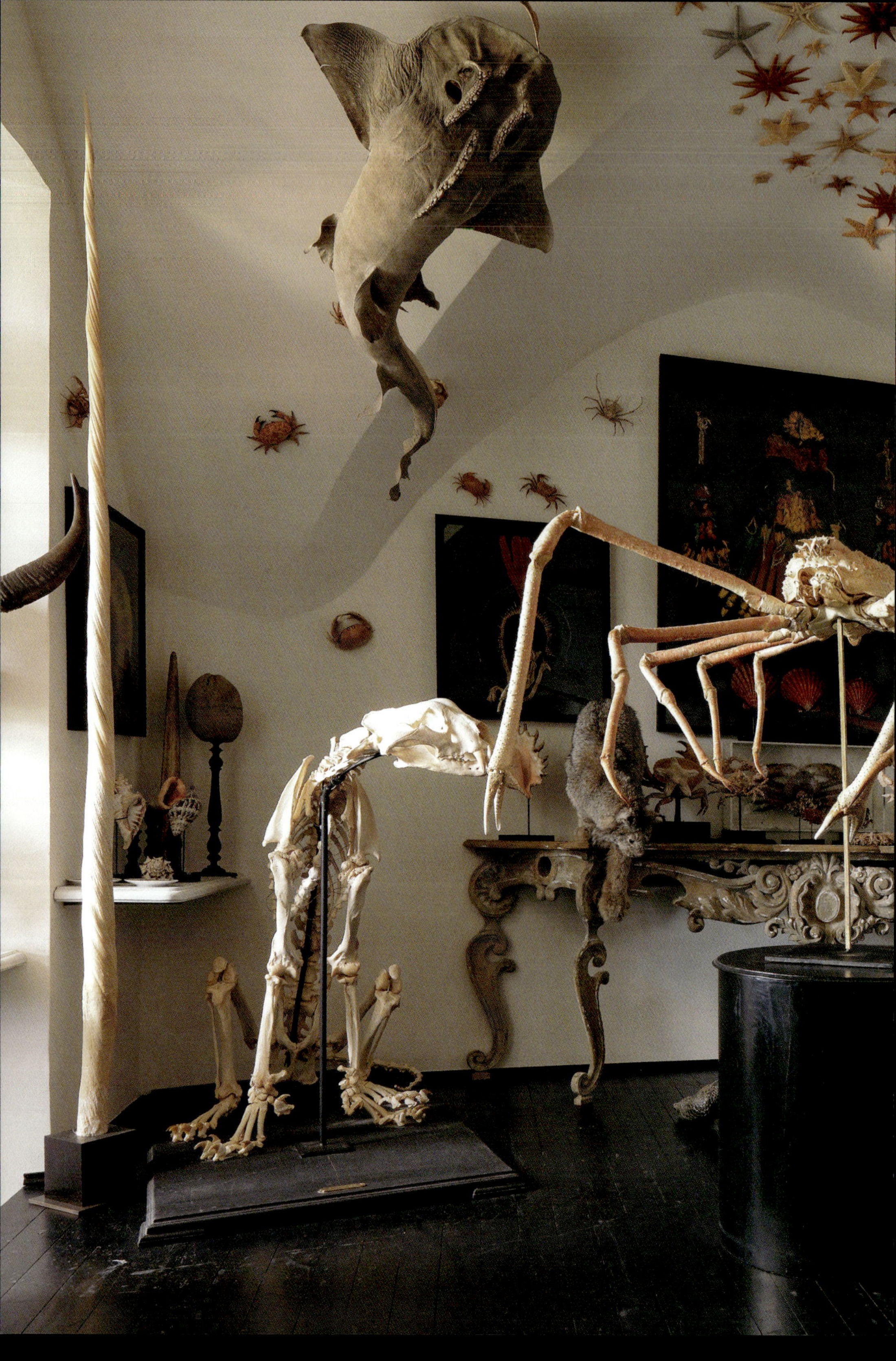

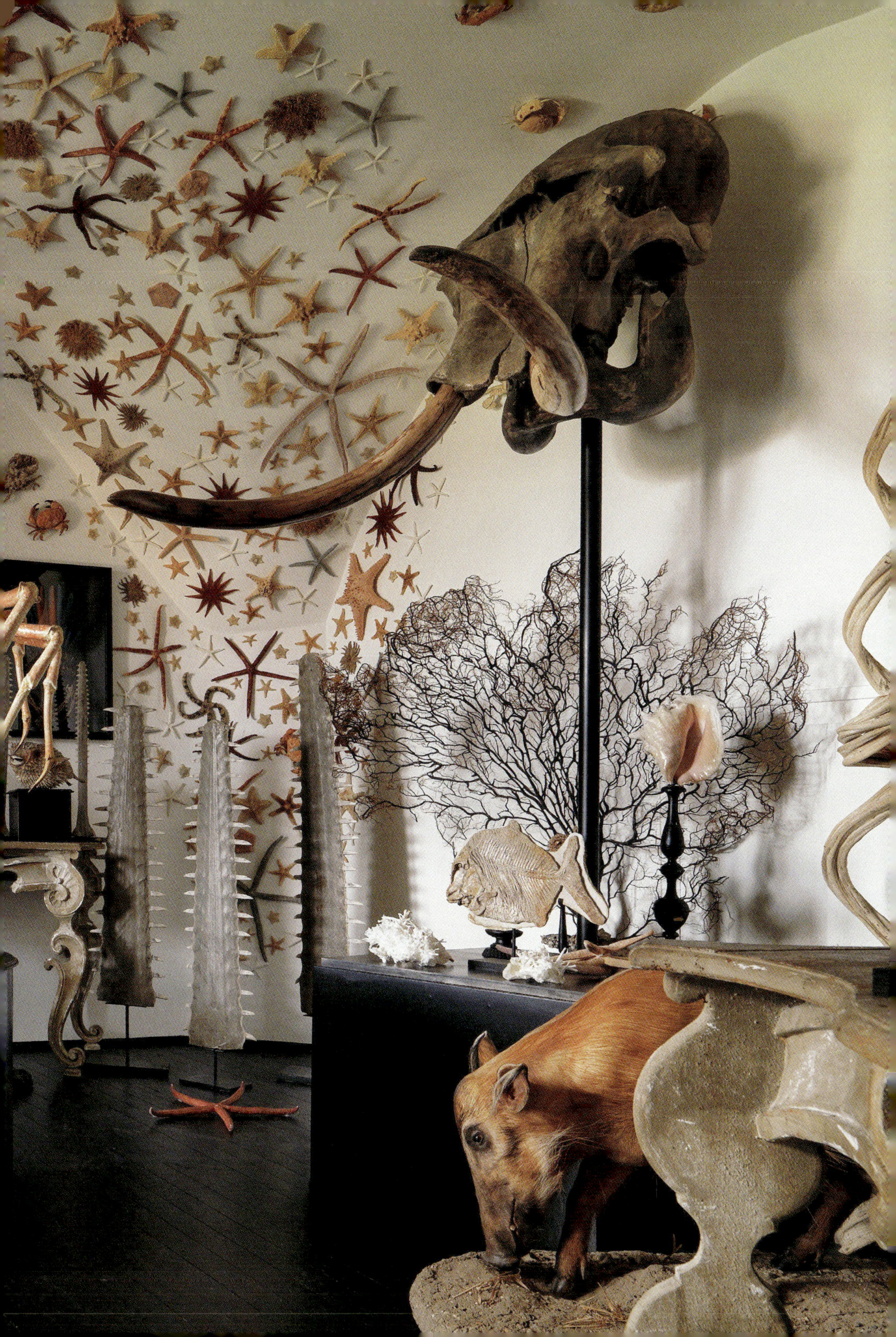

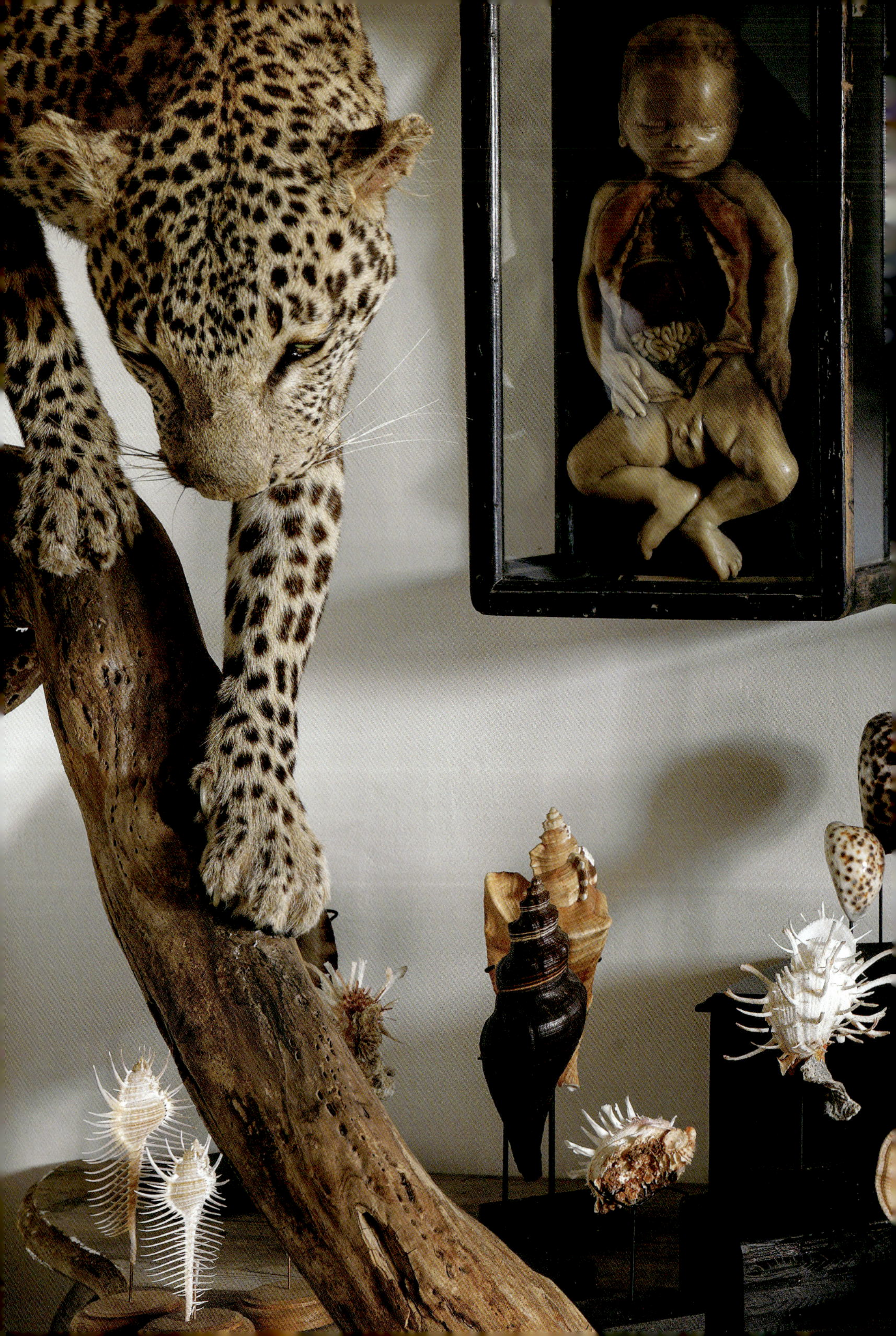

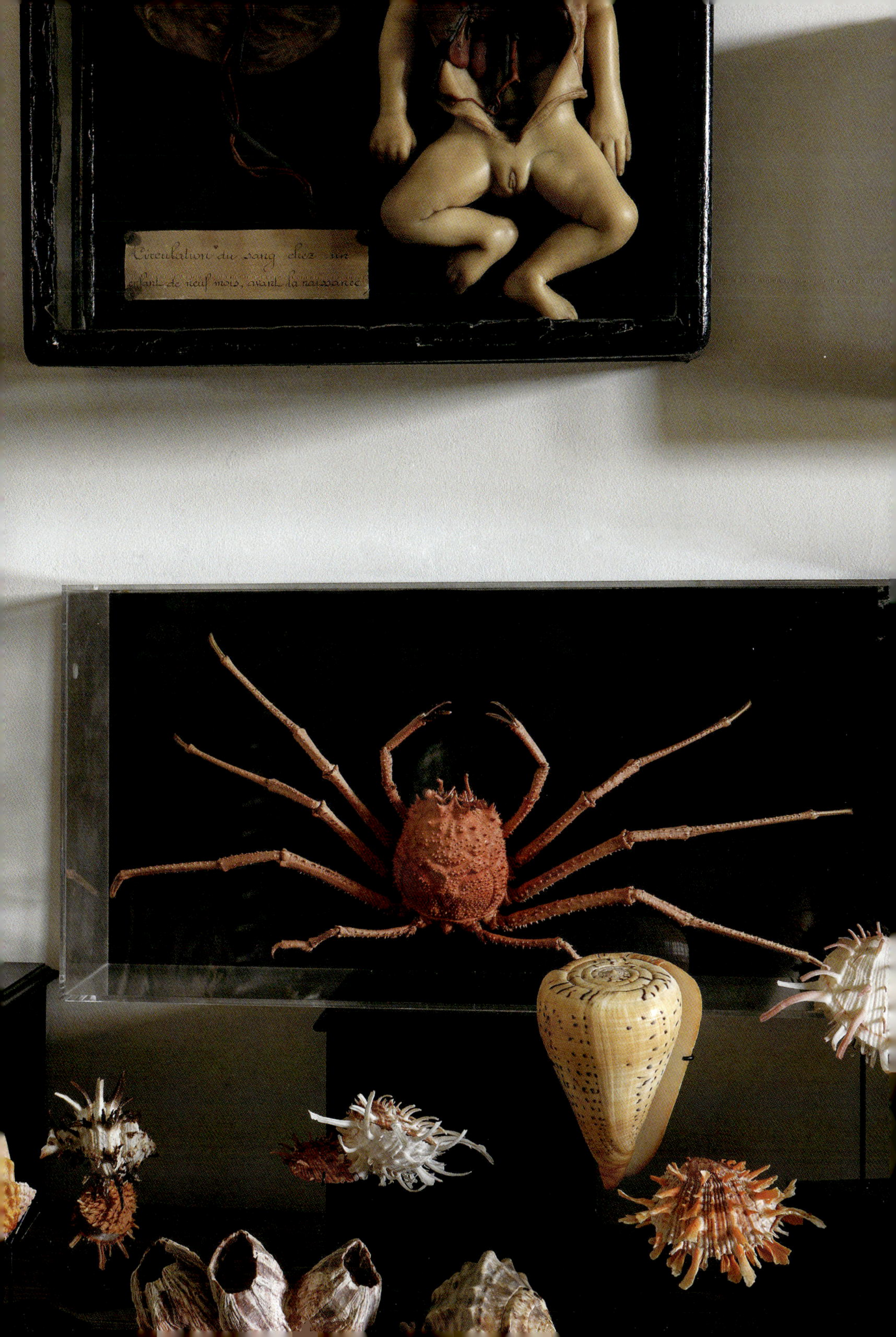
Circulation du sang chez un
enfant de neuf mois, avant la naissance

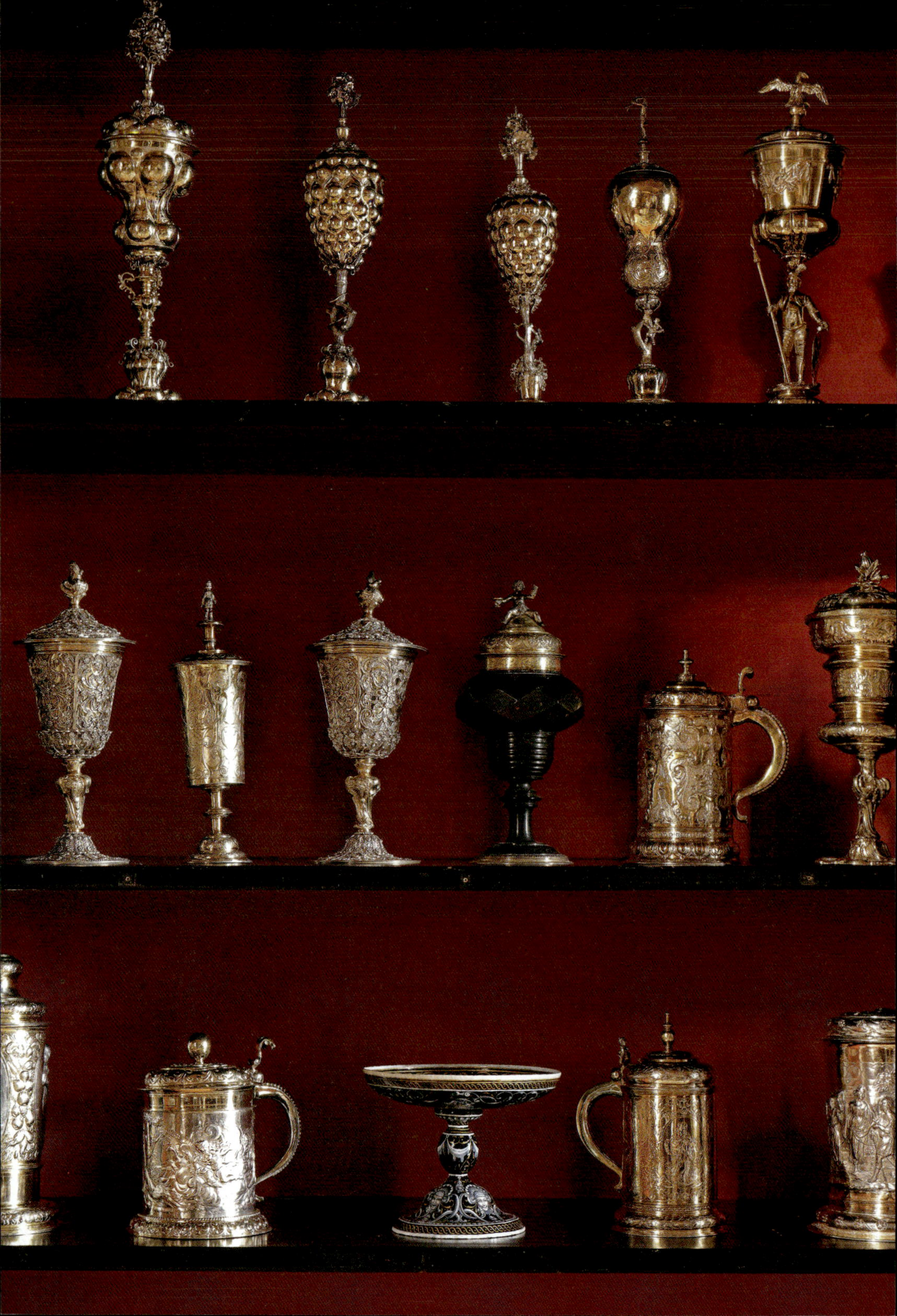

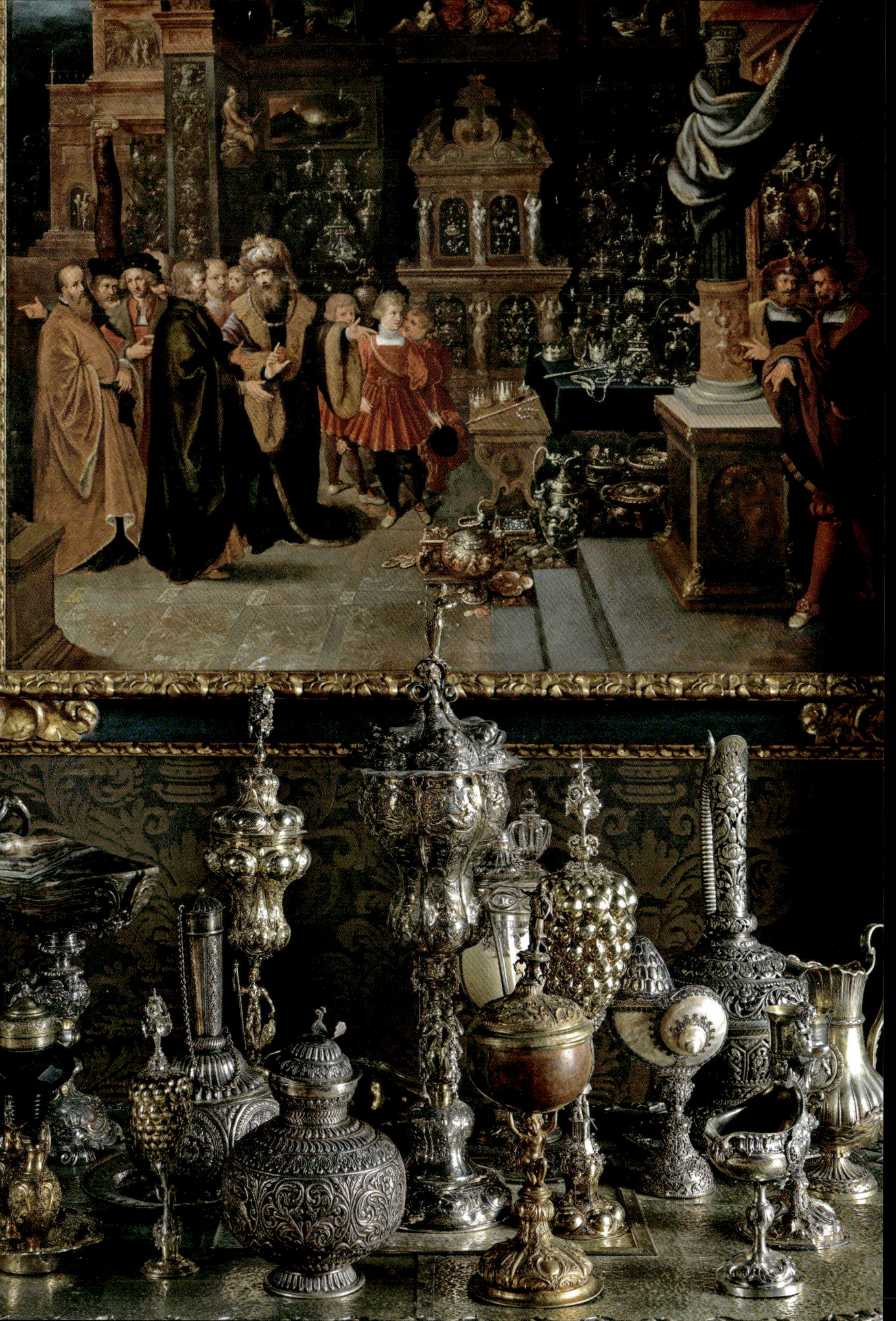

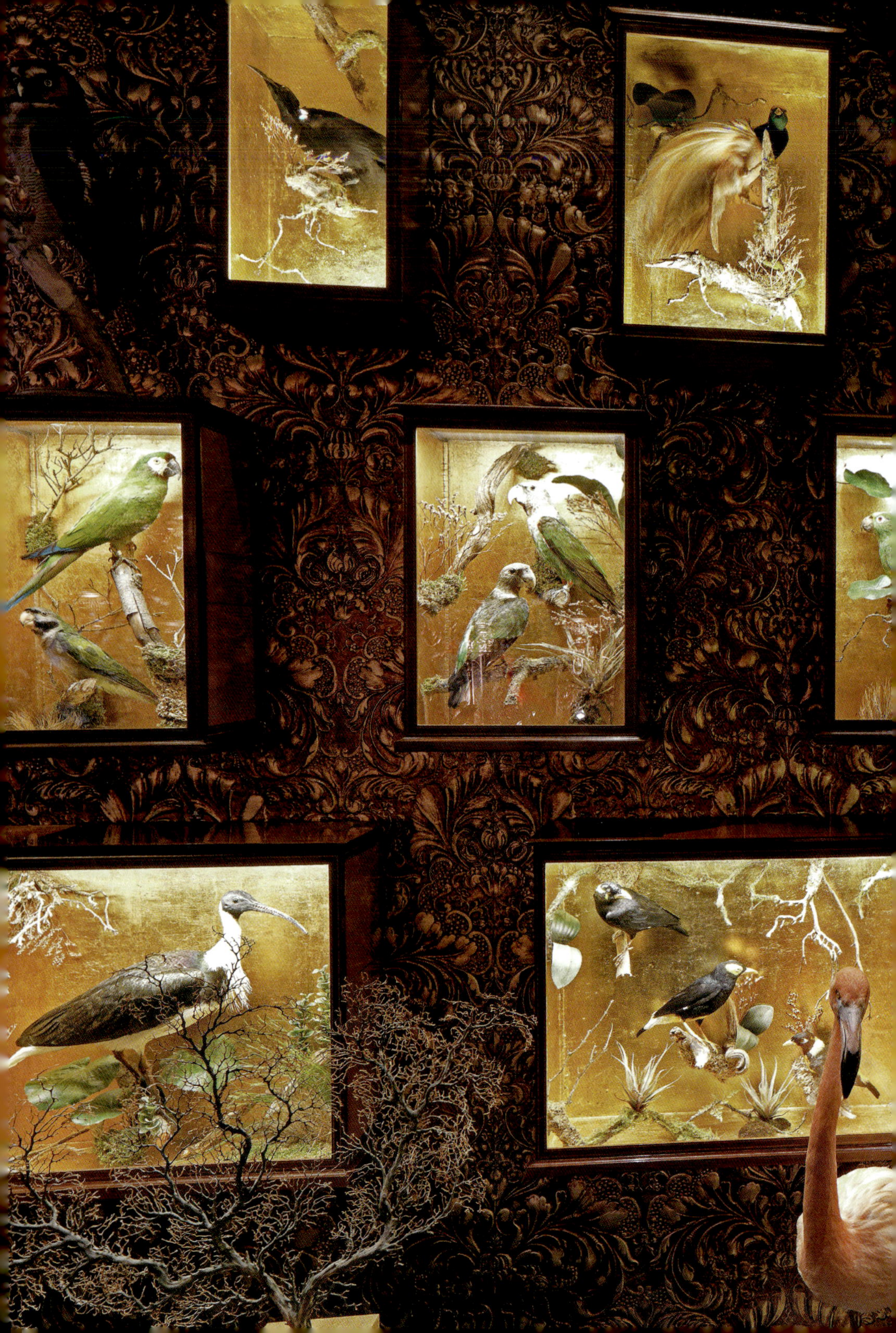

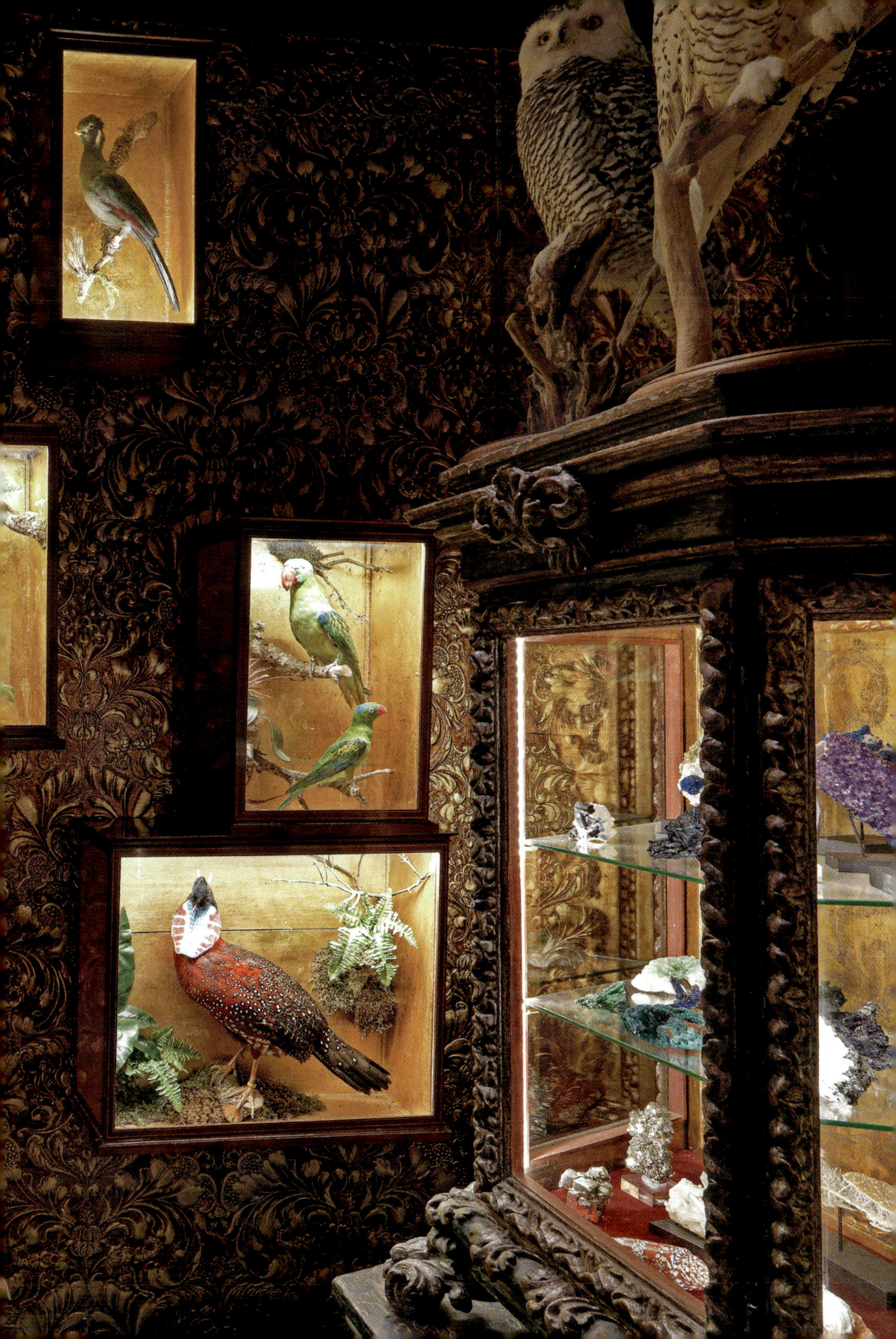

Some years ago Pierre Peyrolle, a noted visionary artist with a fascination for the Baroque, was asked by an important collector to restore a magnificent castle and turn it into a cabinet of curiosities. Set amidst lush greenery, this French castle stands imposingly on top of a rocky outcrop. The many mullioned windows scattered over its walls show that it was originally a place of residence rather than a fortress, although the drawbridge and the narrow embrasures sunk into the thick tower walls lend it a distinctly military appearance. Within the castle is a chapel, which dates from the time the main building was constructed around 1510, and also one of the most beautiful fireplaces in the whole of France.

Peyrolle's passion for extravagance and his taste which accords so closely with the Baroque have put his personal stamp on this project, giving a distinct sense of coherence to the rooms in which this extraordinary collection is housed. Sumptuous 17th-century furnishings are the backdrop for precious objects made of pietra dura, gold, amber and ivory, alongside rare archaeological finds, exotic animals and bronzes from the Renaissance and Baroque periods. Each piece of furniture, displayed in a theatrical setting, is itself a masterpiece, such as the chest with polychrome inlays signed BVRB, the monogram of Bernard van Risenburgh (1660–1738), the "remedies" case in ebony, pietra dura and gilt bronze by Giovanni Battista Foggini (1652–1725), the great inlaid bureau by André-Charles Boulle (1642–1732) and several other items. In the same way as in the collections of Rudolf II (1552–1612) and Athanasius Kircher (1602–1680), the accumulation of minerals, fossils, shells, skeletons of extinct animals, ancient masks, astronomical instruments, paintings and sculptures combine to give a powerful evocation of the spirit of the Baroque, while managing to overcome all chronological limitations.

◉ ◈ ◉

Vor einigen Jahren nahm der Maler Pierre Peyrolle, ein bekannter Vertreter des Phantastischen Realismus und Liebhaber des Barock, die Einladung eines Sammlers an, ein herrliches Schloss so zu restaurieren, dass es den rechten Rahmen für eine Wunderkammer abgibt. Umgeben von einer üppigen Vegetation thront das imposante Schloss oben auf einem Felsvorsprung. Die zahlreichen zweigeteilten Fenster, mit denen die Wände übersät sind, sprechen eher für einen Wohnsitz als für eine Festung, auch wenn das Anwesen mit Zugbrücke und Schießscharten in den Türmen eher militärisch wirkt. Im Inneren gibt es eine Kapelle aus der Gründungszeit, die auf 1510 datiert wird, und einen der schönsten Kamine ganz Frankreichs.

Peyrolles extravaganter Geschmack und seine Vorliebe für Barockes gaben dem Vorhaben eine ganz persönliche Note, sodass eine kohärente Flucht von Sälen entstand, in denen die Sammlung untergebracht ist. Eine prachtvolle, aus dem 17. Jahrhundert stammende Einrichtung bildet den Hintergrund für kostbare Gegenstände aus Gold, Bernstein und Elfenbein, seltene archäologische Fundstücke und exotische Tiere neben Bronzen aus der Renaissance und dem Barock. Jedes effektvoll in Szene gesetzte Möbelstück ist

selbst ein Meisterwerk: etwa ein mit mehrfarbigen Intarsien versehener Schrankkoffer
mit den Initialen BVRB, dem Monogramm von Bernard van Risenburgh (1660–1738), eine
Kassette für Heilmittel aus Ebenholz, Pietra dura und vergoldeter Bronze von Giovanni
Battista Foggini (1652–1725) oder ein großer Schreibtisch mit Intarsien von André-
Charles Boulle (1642–1732). Wie bei Rudolf II. von Habsburg (1552–1612) und Athanasius
Kircher (1602–1680) fühlt sich der Besucher angesichts der Anhäufung von Mineralien,
Fossilien, Muscheln, Skeletten ausgestorbener Tierarten, alten Masken, astronomischen
Instrumenten, Gemälden und Skulpturen in eine andere Zeit versetzt.

◎ ❖ ◎

Il y a quelques années, Pierre Peyrolle, artiste sophistiqué et visionnaire au style baroque,
accepta l'invitation d'un collectionneur à restaurer un magnifique château pour en faire
un Cabinet des merveilles. Entouré d'une végétation luxuriante, l'imposant édifice se
dresse au sommet d'un éperon rocheux. Les nombreuses fenêtres géminées dont ses
murs sont percés montrent qu'il était résidence plutôt que forteresse, même si, avec son
pont-levis et ses étroites meurtrières aménagées dans l'épaisseur des murs des tours,
son allure générale est éminemment militaire. À l'intérieur se trouvent une chapelle fondée à la même époque que le château, que l'on fait remonter à 1510, et l'une des plus
belles cheminées de France.

La passion de Pierre Peyrolle pour l'extravagance et son engouement pour le
style baroque ont marqué d'une empreinte des plus personnelles l'aménagement d'une
harmonieuse succession d'espaces abritant une extraordinaire collection. Un somptueux
mobilier du 17ᵉ siècle accueille de précieux objets en métal doré, en pierre dure, en ambre
et en ivoire ; des pièces archéologiques parmi les plus rares ; des animaux exotiques ; des
bronzes de la Renaissance et du Baroque. Chaque pièce de mobilier trouve place dans
un ensemble aménagé avec un goût pour la mise en scène et abrite un chef-d'œuvre : ainsi
la malle avec marqueteries polychromes signée BVRB, monogramme de Bernard van
Risenburgh (1660–1738), le coffret « à remèdes » en ébène, pierres dures et bronze doré de
Giovanni Battista Foggini (1652–1725), le grand bureau marqueté d'André-Charles Boulle
(1642–1732), notamment. Comme pour Rodolphe II de Habsbourg (1552–1612) et Athanase
Kirchner (1602–1680), l'accumulation de minéraux, fossiles, coquillages, squelettes d'animaux disparus, masques antiques, instruments d'astronomie, peintures et sculptures
incarne la réalisation d'un rêve : faire sentir avec force l'esprit d'une époque et franchir
les barrières temporelles.

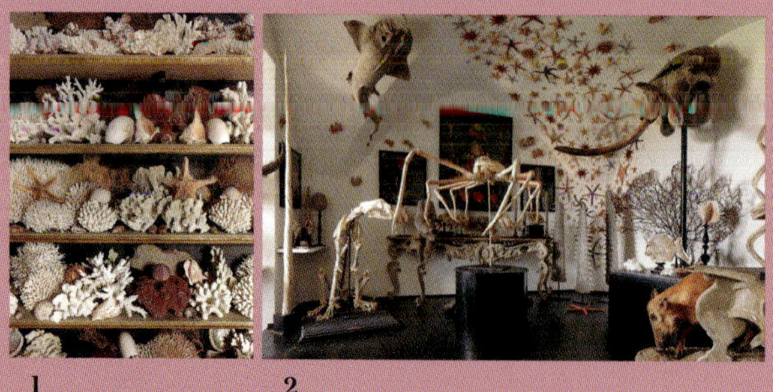

1   2

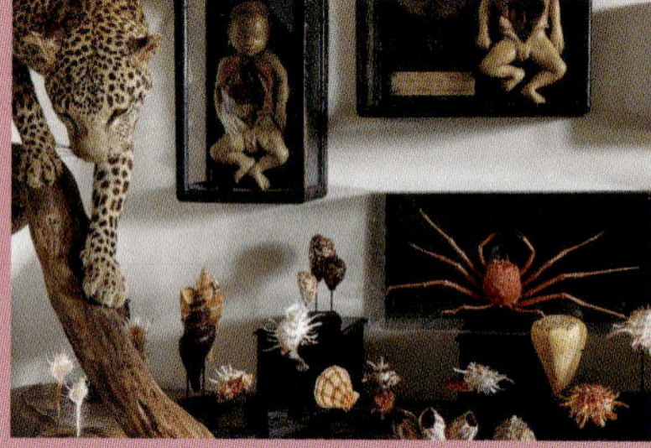

3

1 Shelves displaying a Nautilus repertus from Indonesia, a Balanus from the Philippines, various sea snails including a Murex nigritus from Mexico, queen conches (Strombus gigas) from the Bahamas, a Busycon whelk from the United States, a Tonna tessellata, starfish from the Philippines, corals from the Solomon Islands (Acropora, Pocillopora, Seriatopora, Tubipora), sea urchins (Echinus esculentus), madrepora, corals, sea fans (Gorgonia), Nautili and other shells.
Im Regal Nautilus repertus aus Indonesien, Seepocken (Balanus) von den Philippinen, Murex nigritus aus Mexiko, große Fechterschnecken (Stombus gigas) der Bahamas, Schnecken (Busycon) aus den USA, Tonna tessellata, Seesterne von den Philippinen,

Korallen von den Solomoninseln (Acropora, Pocillopora, Seriatopora, Tubipora), Seeigel (Echinus esculentus), Madreporen, Korallen, Gorgonien, Perlboote und Muscheln.
Une étagère avec diverses sortes de bivalves : comme Nautilus repertus d'Indonésie, Balanus des Philippines, Murex nigritus du Mexique, des mollusques (Strombus gigas) des Bahamas, Busycon des États-Unis, Tonna tessellata, étoiles des Philippines, coraux des îles Salomon (Acropora, Pocillopora, Seriatopora, Tubipora) oursins (Echinus esculentus), madrépores, coraux, oursins, gorgones (Gorgonia), nautiles et coquillages.

2 Above, a still-life that echoes Pierre Peyrolle's setting and acts as a metaphor for the confrontation between worldly goods and

wisdom, including a bowmouth guitarfish (Rhina ancylostoma) and starfish from the Philippines and the United States. Also displayed here are a mammoth skull, sawfish rostrums, a giant spider crab from Japan (Macrocheira kaempferi) and the skeleton of a tiger.
Oben ein Stillleben, das an Pierre Peyrolles Inszenierungen erinnert und als Metapher für die Gegenüberstellung von Weisheit und weltlichen Dingen dient: ein Rundkopf-Geigenrochen (Rhina ancylostoma), Seesterne von den Philippinen und den USA, ein Mammutschädel, Sägefischrostren, eine Riesenspinnenkrabbe aus Japan (Macrocheira kaempferi) und ein Tigerskelett.
Au-dessus une nature morte, qui rappelle les mises en scène de Pierre Peyrolle, écho de sa scénographie et métaphore

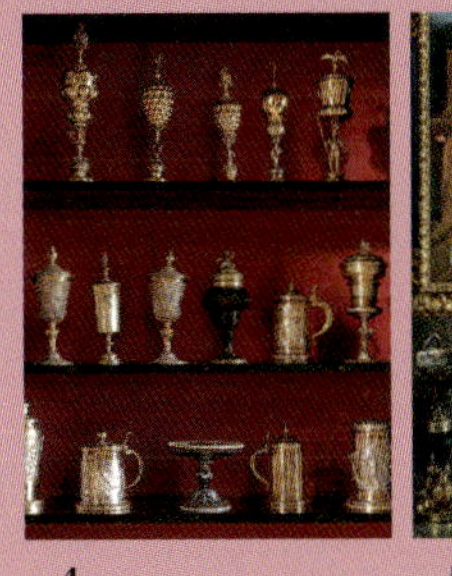

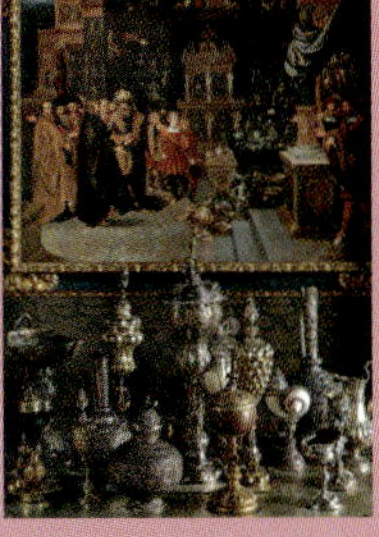

4   5

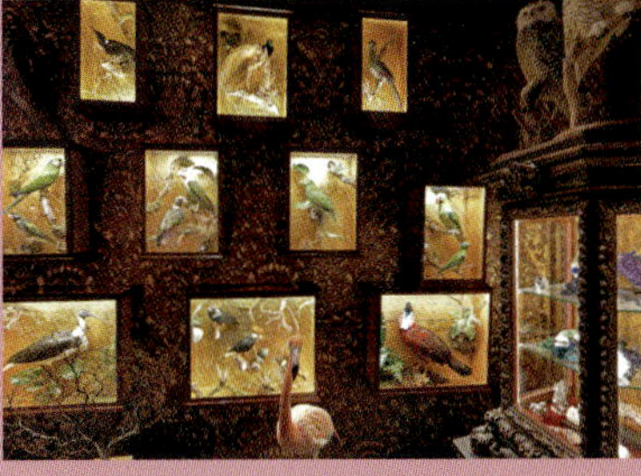

6

de la confrontation des biens de ce monde avec la sagesse. Requin du Vietnam (Rhina ancylostoma), étoiles de mer des Philippines, États-Unis. Crâne de mammouth, rostres de poisson-scie, crabe-araignée géant du Japon (Macrocheira kaempferi), squelette de tigre.

3 A leopard descends a branch in front of a wall featuring anatomical wax models, spiny oysters, scallops, cone shells and a spider crab.
Ein Leopard vor einer Wand mit anatomischen Wachsmodellen, Stachelaustern, Pecten und Kegelschnecken sowie einer Spinnenkrabbe.
Léopard devant un mur de cires anatomiques et des mollusques du genre Pecten, un cône et une araignée de mer.

4 A magnificent ensemble of objects from Augsburg with silver-gilt settings, including goblets and tankards.
Eine beeindruckende Sammlung von in Augsburg hergestellten Objekten aus vergoldetem Silber, darunter Pokale und Humpen.
Magnifique ensemble d'objets en vermeil d'Augsbourg avec, entre autres, des vases et des chopes.

5 On the table in the foreground is an ensemble of masterpieces from the silver collection: silver tankards, nautilus and coconut shells. On the wall is a painting by Frans Francken II, *Croesus Shows Solon His Treasures*, from 1610.
Auf dem Tisch im Vordergrund Meisterwerke der Silbersammlung: silberne Humpen, ein Nautilus- und ein Kokosnusspokal.

An der Wand ein Gemälde Frans Franckens II., *Krösus zeigt Solon seine Schätze*, 1610.
Sur la table au premier plan, une collection de chefs-d'œuvre du Cabinet d'argent : des chopes en argent, un nautile et une noix de coco. Sur le mur, un tableau de Frans Francken II *Crésus montre ses trésors à Solon*, 1610.

6 In the wall-mounted display cases are an emperor bird-of-paradise, an ibis, a horned pheasant, mynah birds and parrots.
In den Wandvitrinen ein Kaiserparadiesvogel, ein Tagopan, Mainas und Papageien.
Dans les vitrines sur le mur : un paradisier grand-émeraude, des tragopans, des mainates et des perroquets.

Malplaquet House

London

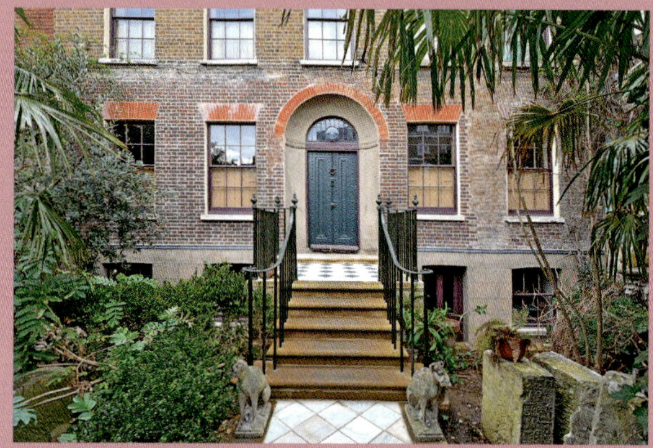

Founded The collection was established in the 20th century, the house dates from 1741.

Key item A glass case containing the enormous egg of a moa. Now extinct, this flightless bird was originally found in New Zealand, and according to archaeological finds a number of species lived on into the 17th century; it is thought that the Polynesian ancestors of the Maori destroyed their habitat and hunted them to extinction.

Besonders sehenswert Das Riesenei eines Moas, einer Vogelart ohne Flügel aus Neuseeland. Archäologische Funde belegen die Existenz einiger Moa-Arten bis 1600, danach wurden sie offenbar durch Jagd und Zerstörung ihres Habitats seitens der polynesischen Vorfahren der Maori ausgerottet.

À voir absolument La vitrine renfermant un gigantesque œuf de moa, oiseau dépourvu d'ailes, originaire de Nouvelle-Zélande. Certaines découvertes archéologiques laissent à penser que plusieurs espèces de moa ont existé jusqu'au 17e siècle avant d'être exterminées par les ancêtres polynésiens des Maoris, qui les ont chassées pour leur viande mais ont aussi détruit leur habitat.

Massimo Listri, *View of Malplaquet House*

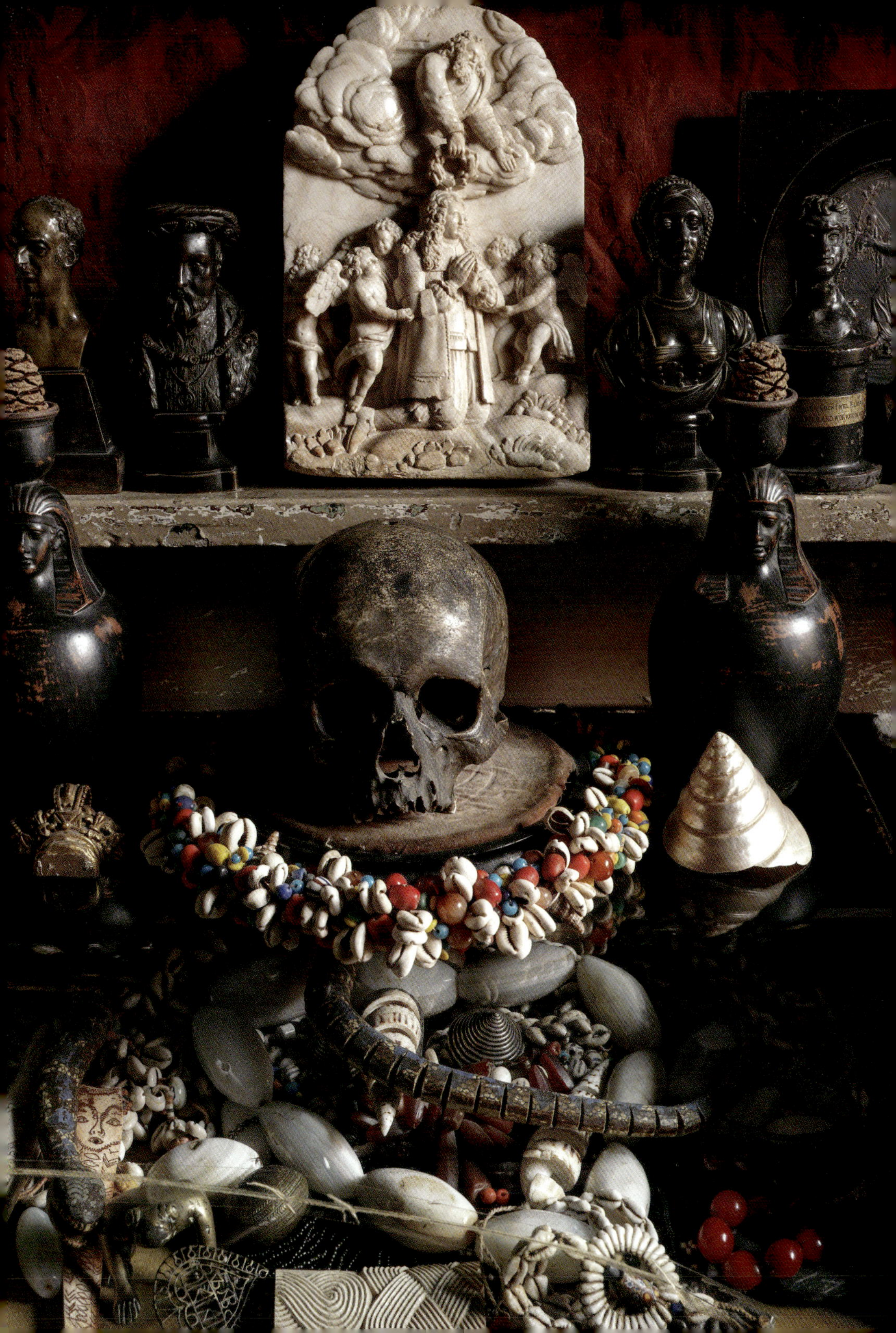

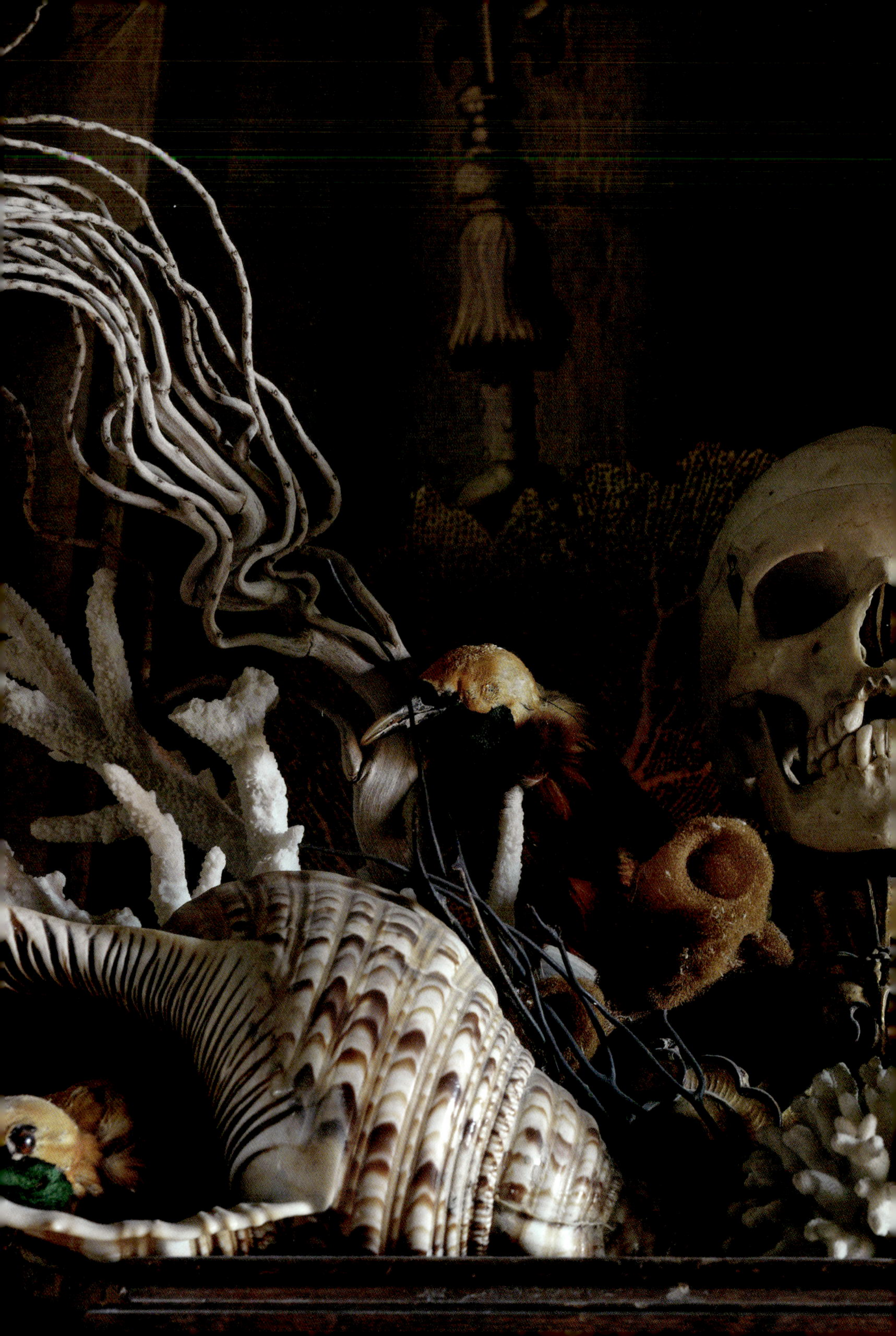

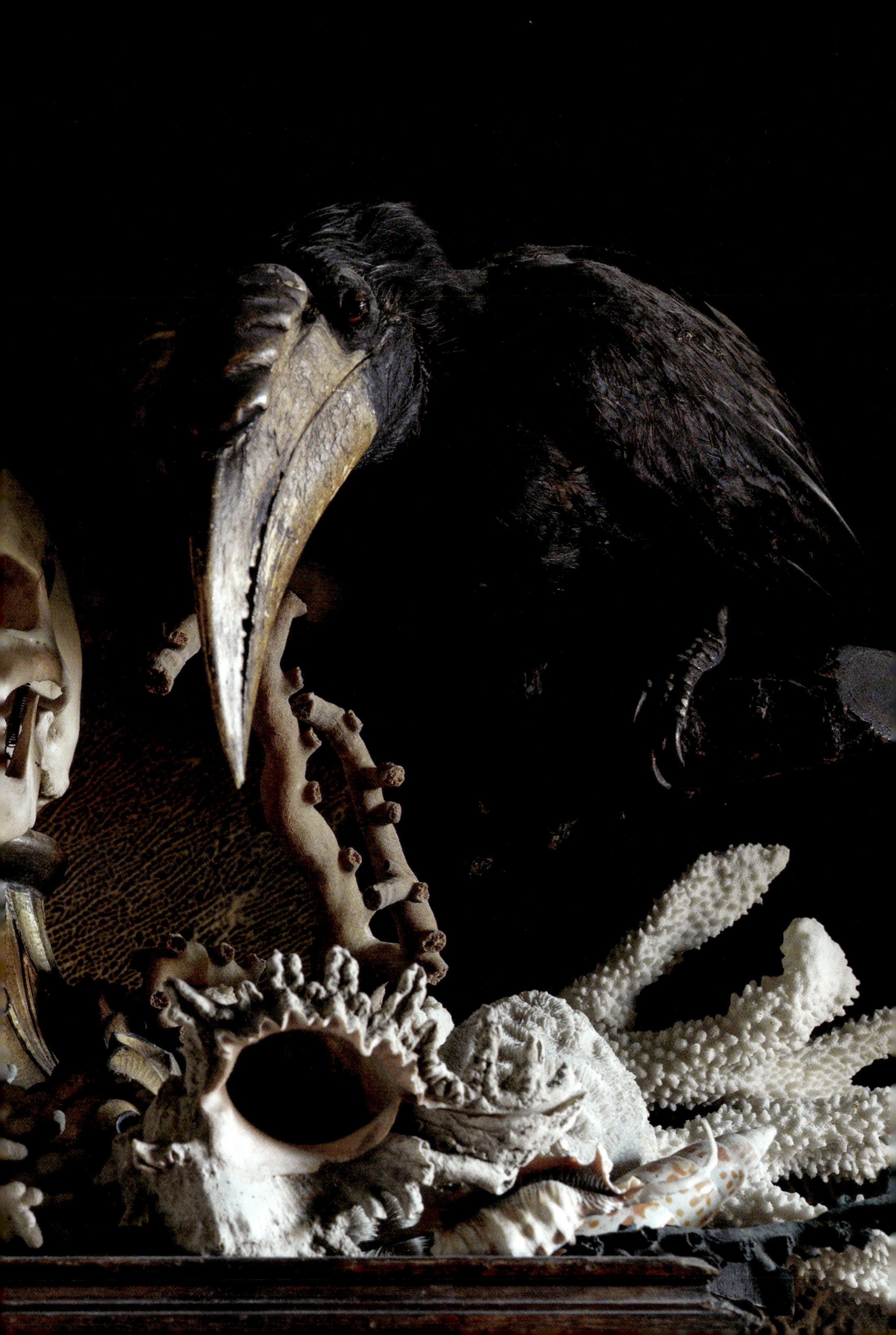

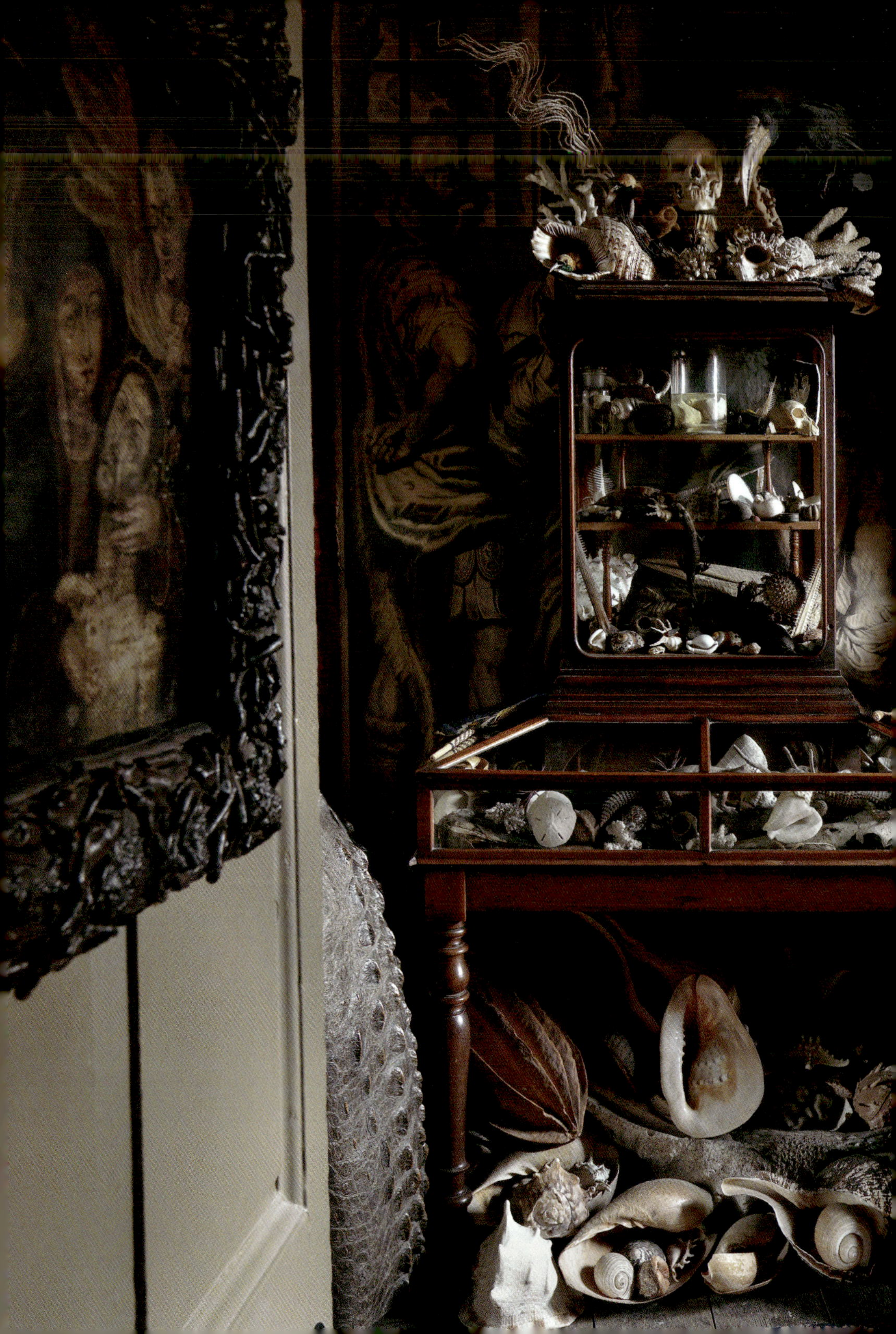

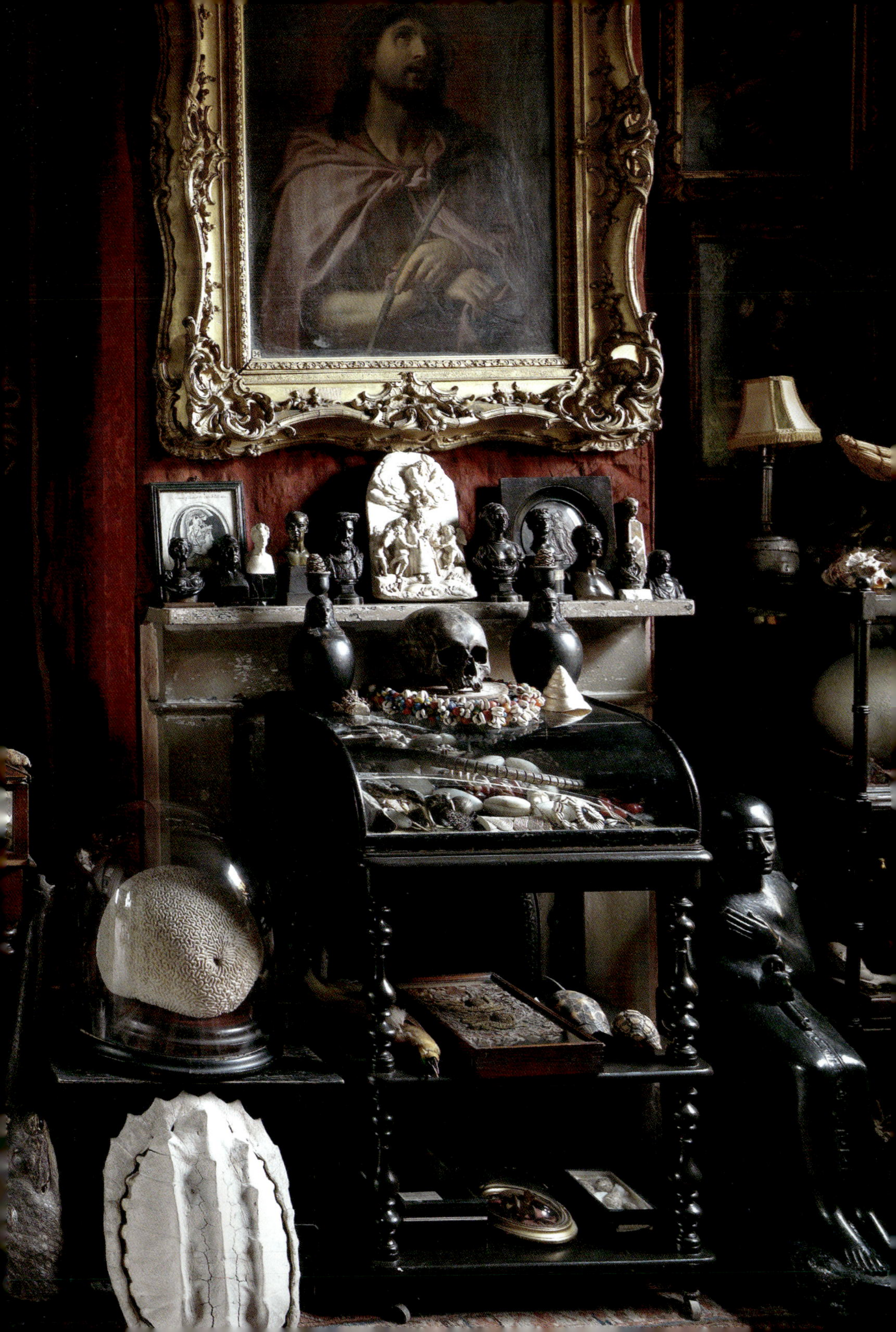

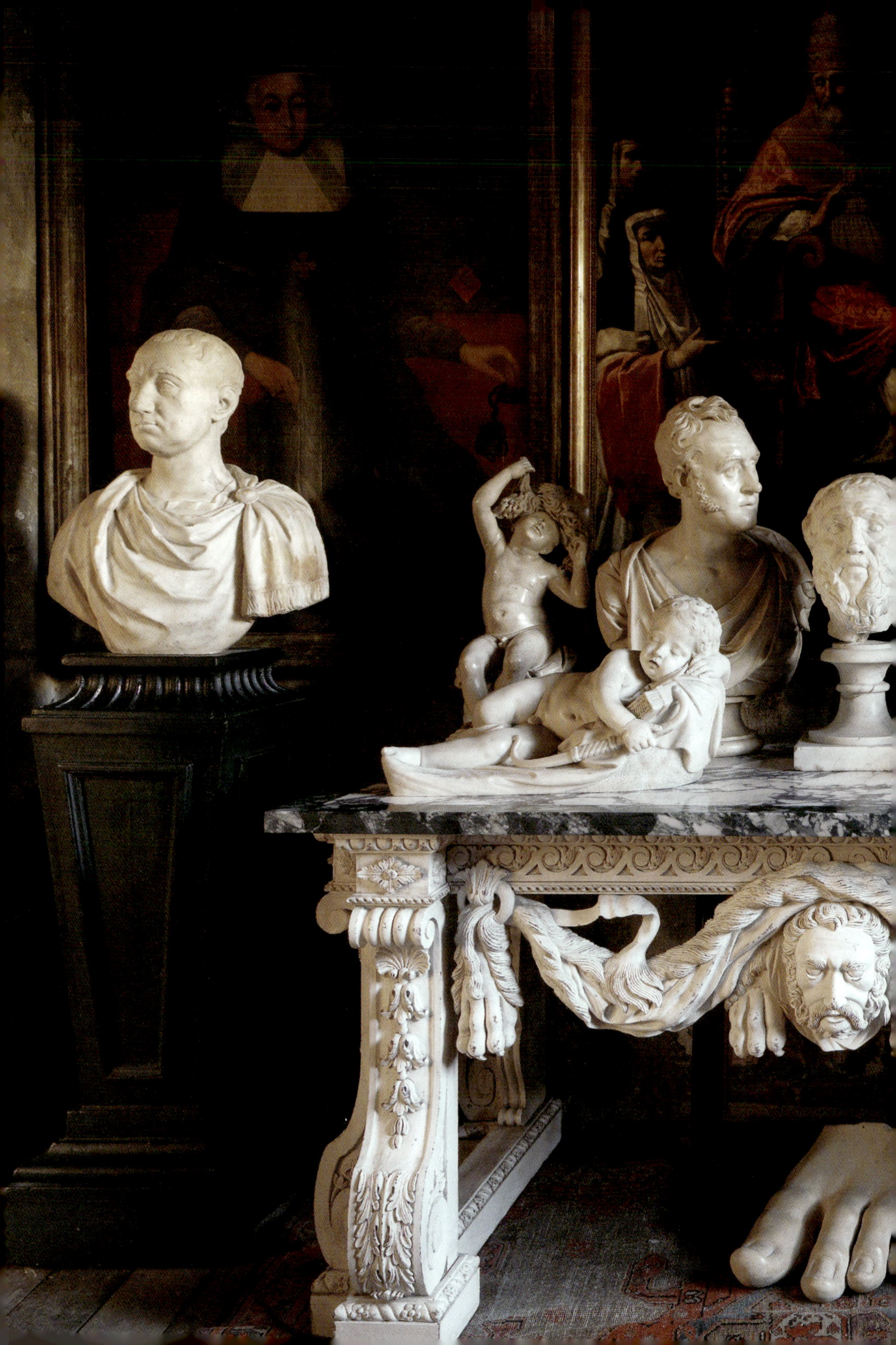

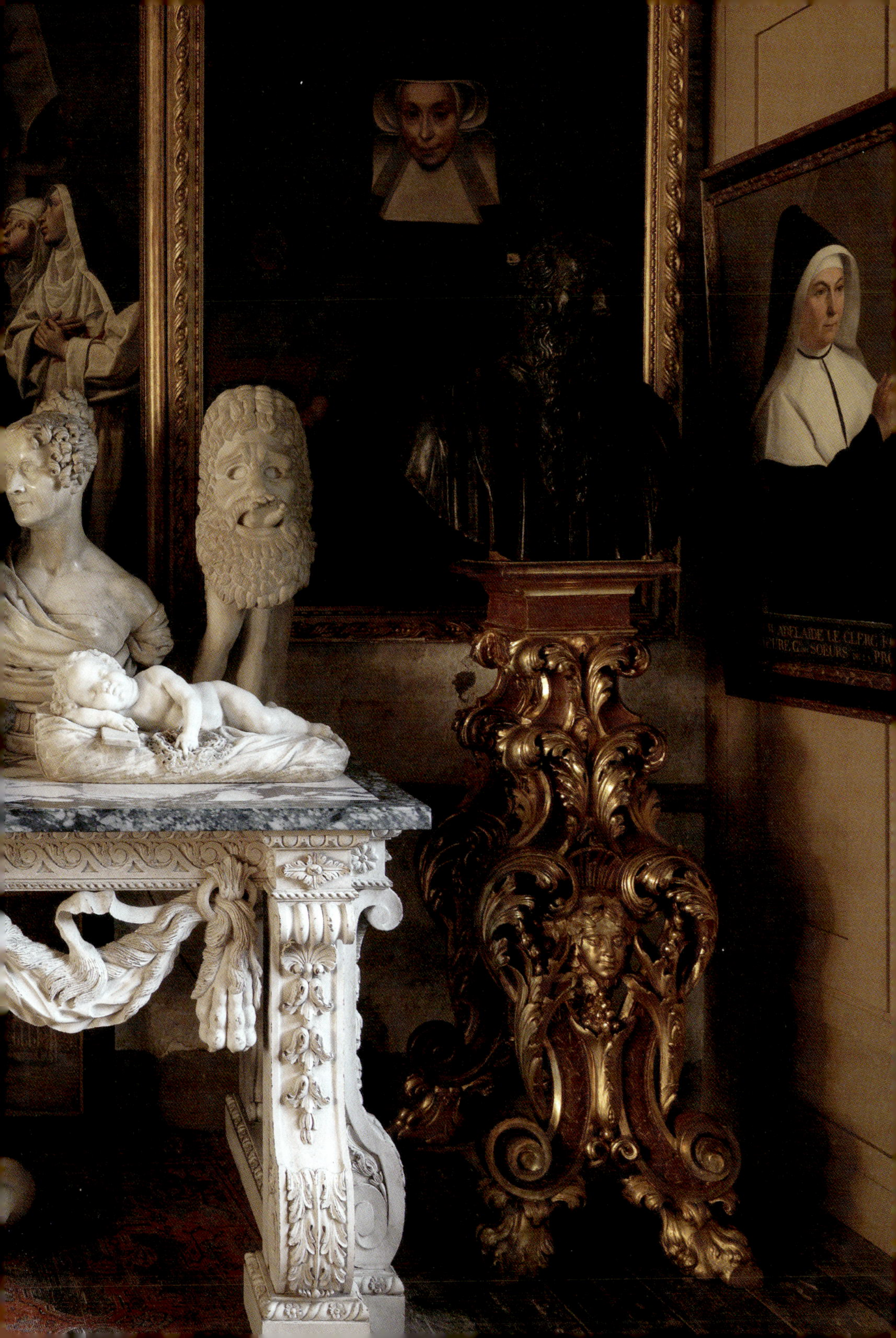

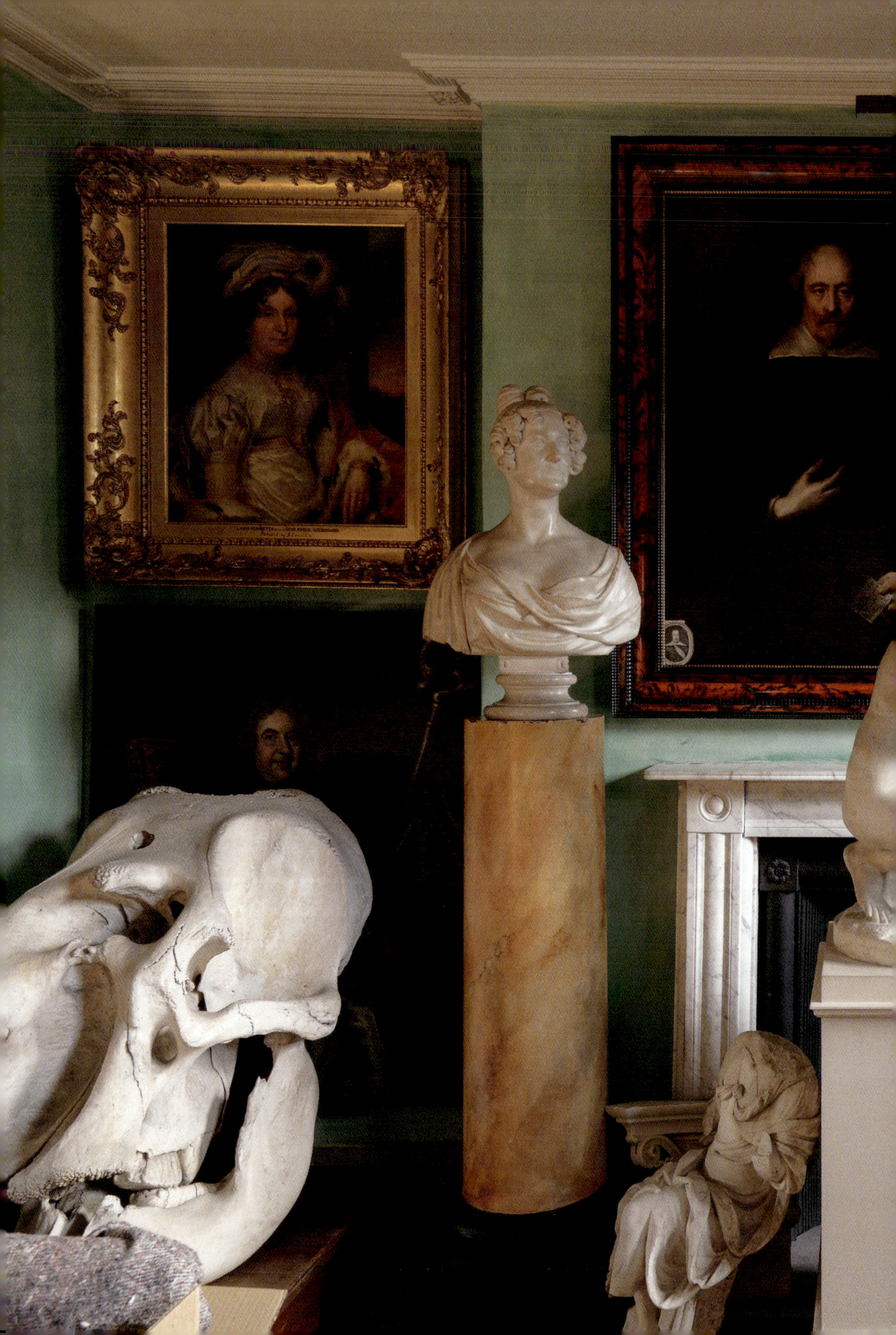

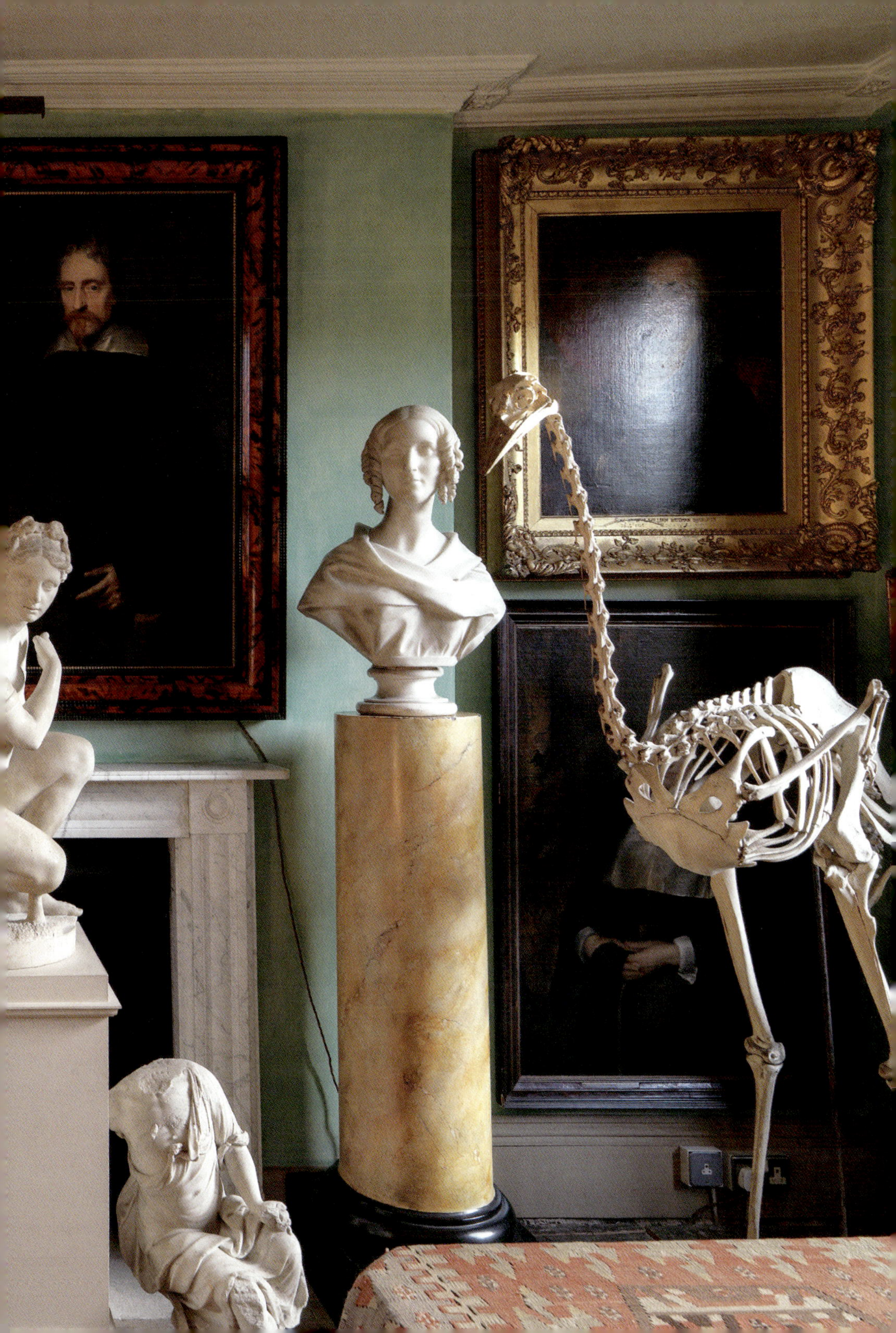

Situated in London's East End and surrounded by a lush garden, Malplaquet House was until recently the perfect example of a modern cabinet of curiosities (it was sold in 2016 and the collection relocated). The house is named after the Battle of Malplaquet, which took place on 11 September 1709 during the War of the Spanish Succession. It contains more than 20 rooms which were once filled with the private collection of the previous owners, Tim Knox, formerly director of Sir John Soane's Museum in London, and Todd Longstaffe-Gowan, a landscape designer behind some of the most celebrated gardens in England (including Hampton Court Palace, Kensington Palace Gardens and Waddesdon Manor).

The house was built in 1741/42 and transformed over time until 1998, when a monumental restoration took place. When the previous owners bought it the house had been unoccupied for over a century, and some of its rooms had been used by small businesses or as store-rooms which were all gradually dismantled. The complete restructuring of the house took five years with considerable work being required to restore the floors and windows, and to restore the original paint colours of the walls, particularly the dining-room's arsenic green. "Our philosophy," Knox said at the time, "was to try to keep the atmosphere and get it back to about 1800, its heyday under Harry Charrington (co-director of the nearby Charrington Brewery and who lived in the house until 1833)." Longstaffe-Gowan added: "It was not to be folky. We love the building so much and feel it's a miracle it's come down to us. We wanted to preserve it in that plain way. So many London houses lose their character by being too improved." The pair made Malplaquet House into a home for their collection of Old Master paintings, stuffed animals, religious art, marble busts, reliefs with hieroglyphic inscriptions, sketches, elephant and ostrich skeletons, hunting trophies, funerary masks, *mirabilia*, exotica and so many other objects accumulated over the years and bought at flea markets or auction houses. In the course of time they unearthed some extraordinary pieces which are now on display in various museums, such as a small bronze statue of *St. John the Baptist* commissioned from Michelozzo (1396–1472) by Piero di Cosimo de' Medici (1416–1469), now in the National Gallery of Scotland, and a relief by John Flaxman (1755–1826) showing the *Adoration of the Magi*, now in the Ashmolean Museum in Oxford. One of the most intimate and fascinating spaces in the house, however, was the cabinet of curiosities, in which Chinese and Egyptian relics filled the display cases alongside specimens of *naturalia*, in the form of shells and coral, all closely watched over by a human skull.

◎◈◎

Mitten im Londoner East End, umgeben von einem üppigen Garten, liegt das Malplaquet House, bis vor kurzem das perfekte Beispiel für eine moderne Wunderkammer (das Haus wurde 2016 verkauft und die Sammlung verlegt). Benannt wurde das Haus nach der Schlacht bei Malplaquet vom 11. September 1709, die im Rahmen des Spanischen Erbfolgekrieges stattfand. Es umfasst mehr als zwanzig Säle, in denen die Privatsammlung von Tim Knox und Todd Longstaffe-Gowan untergebracht war. Knox war Direktor des Sir John Soane's Museums in London, Longstaffe-Gowan einer der bekanntesten Gartenarchitekten (z.B. von Hampton Court Palace, Kensington Palace Gardens und Waddesdon Manor).

Das 1741/42 errichtete Gebäude erfuhr zahllose Umbauten, bis man 1998 mit einer umfangreichen Restaurierung begann. Zu dem Zeitpunkt, als die ehemaligen Besitzer es erwarben, hatte das Haus seit über einem Jahrhundert leer gestanden und war teilweise als Geschäfts- und Lagerraum genutzt worden, den man nun nach und nach abriss. Die Restaurierung nahm fünf Jahre in Anspruch, um Fußböden und Fenster in ihren ursprünglichen Zustand zurückzuversetzen, die Wände zu streichen und alte Farben, insbesondere das Arsengrün des Speisesaals, neu zu mischen. „Unser Ziel war", so Knox, „die ursprüngliche Anlage möglichst weitgehend zu erhalten, vor allem die Atmosphäre um 1800, der Blütezeit unter Harry Charrington (einer der Direktoren der nahegelegenen Charrington Brauerei, der bis 1833 in dem Haus lebte)." – „Dabei ging es nicht um Folklore: Uns gefiel das Haus einfach so sehr, dass wir möglichst nichts verändern wollten", ergänzte Todd Longstaffe-Gowan. Die beiden hatten daraus mit viel Liebe eine Sammlung Alter Meister, präparierter Tiere, religiöser Kunst, Marmorbüsten, Hieroglyphentafeln, Skizzen, Straußen- und Elefantenskelette, Jagdtrophäen, Totenmasken, *Mirabilia, Exotica* und vieles andere, was sie im Lauf der Jahre auf Flohmärkten oder Auktionen aufgestöbert haben, zusammen getragen. Darunter befanden sich auch so erstaunliche Stücke wie eine Bronzestatuette von Johannes dem Täufer, die Piero di Cosimo de' Medici (1416–1469) bei Michelozzo (1396–1472) in Auftrag gab, heute in der schottischen Nationalgalerie, oder ein Relief von John Flaxman (1755–1826) mit der *Anbetung der Heiligen Drei Könige*, heute im Ashmolean Museum in Oxford. Der intimste und faszinierendste Raum war die Wunderkammer, denn dort fanden sich neben *Naturalia* wie Muscheln und Korallen chinesische und ägyptische Fundstücke – in Sichtweite eines Totenschädels.

◎ ◈ ◎

Nichée dans un luxuriant jardin de l'East End londonien, Malplaquet House constituait récemment encore un parfait exemple de Cabinet des merveilles moderne (en 2016, la maison a été vendue, et la collection déplacée). La demeure tire son nom de la bataille de Malplaquet qui eut lieu le 11 septembre 1709 au cours de la guerre de Succession d'Espagne. Elle compte plus d'une vingtaine de pièces qui accueillaient la collection particulière de Tim Knox et Todd Longstaffe-Gowan. Le premier dirigeait le Sir John Soane's Museum de Londres, le second a aménagé de prestigieux jardins en Angleterre (Hampton Court Palace, Kensington Palace Gardens, Waddesdon Manor).

Construit en 1741/42, l'édifice a connu de nombreuses transformations jusqu'en 1998, date à laquelle d'importants travaux de restauration ont débuté. Lorsque ses anciens propriétaires en firent l'acquisition, la demeure était inhabitée depuis plus d'un siècle, et plusieurs de ses espaces étaient occupés par des magasins et des dépôts qui ont été progressivement démolis. Les travaux de remise en état se sont prolongés pendant cinq ans pour restaurer les sols et les fenêtres d'origine, blanchir les murs et retrouver leurs anciennes couleurs, notamment le vert arsenic de la salle à manger. « Notre but », disait Knox, « était de conserver autant que possible l'aménagement d'origine autour de 1800, période d'apogée sous la direction de Harry Charrington (l'un des patrons de la brasserie Charrington, qui vécut dans la maison jusqu'en 1833). » Todd Longstaffe-Gowan soulignait: « Non point par souci de folklore, mais parce que le bâtiment nous plaisait tellement que nous voulions y toucher le moins possible ». Ils avaient réussi à transformer Malplaquet House en un lieu où loger leurs collections qui rassemblaient tableaux anciens, animaux naturalisés, art religieux, bustes en marbre, reliefs gravés de hiéroglyphes, esquisses, squelettes d'autruche et d'éléphant, trophées de chasse, masques funéraires, *mirabilia*, *exotica* et maints autres objets accumulés au fil des ans, achetés sur les marchés aux puces ou dans des maisons de vente aux enchères. Des années de quête leur ont permis de dénicher certaines pièces stupéfiantes désormais exposées dans des musées ; tel est le cas d'une statuette de bronze de saint Jean-Baptiste conservée à la National Gallery d'Écosse, dont Piero di Cosimo de Médicis (1416–1469) passa commande à Michelozzo (1396–1472), ou d'un relief de John Flaxman (1755–1826) représentant l'*Adoration des Mages*, aujourd'hui à l'Ashmolean Museum d'Oxford. Pour autant, l'un des espaces les plus intimes et les plus fascinants de la demeure était le cabinet de curiosités où, à côté de vestiges égyptiens et chinois, s'amoncelaient des *naturalia* – coquillages et coraux – sur lesquels veillait un crâne.

1 A selection of curiosities: antiquities, minerals, relics and eggs. Above, a human skull flanked by a pair of canopic jars from Ancient Egypt.
Eine Raritätenauswahl: antike Objekte, Mineralien, Reliquien, Eier. Oben erkennt man einen menschlichen Schädel, den altägyptische Kanopen flankieren.
Une sélection d'objets rares : objets anciens, minéraux, reliques, œufs. En haut, on distingue un crâne humain flanqué de canopes égyptiens.

2 Detail of ill. 3: a human skull surrounded by shells, corals and stuffed birds.

Detail von Abb. 3: Menschlicher Schädel zwischen Muscheln, Korallen und ausgestopften Vögeln.
Détail de l'ill. 3 : Un crâne humain entourné de coquillages, de coraux et d'oiseaux naturalisés.

3 On the left is a mahogany cabinet, reserved for *naturalia*; in the background on the right is a reproduction of *The Derision of Christ* by Anthony van Dyck, 1620.
Der Mahagonischrank links ist für *Naturalia* reserviert; rechts im Hintergrund eine Reproduktion von Anton van Dycks *Verspottung Christi*, 1620.

Le cabinet en acajou à gauche est réservé aux éléments naturels ; à droite, à l'arrière-plan, une reproduction du *Couronnement d'épines* d'Antoine van Dyck, 1620.

4 A collection of marble statues, including a strange sculpture of a child playing with a Greek tragedy mask, a copy by Bartolomeo Cavaceppi, and a bust of Lady Thorold by Peter Rouw. Fragments of a Roman marble sculpture lie beneath a console sculpted in the early 18th-century style of Matthias Lock.
Eine Sammlung von Marmorstatuen darunter die ungewöhnliche Skulptur eines Kindes, das mit

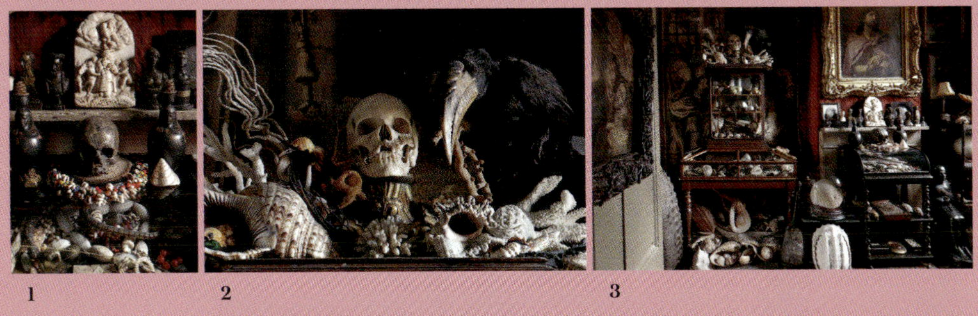

1   2   3

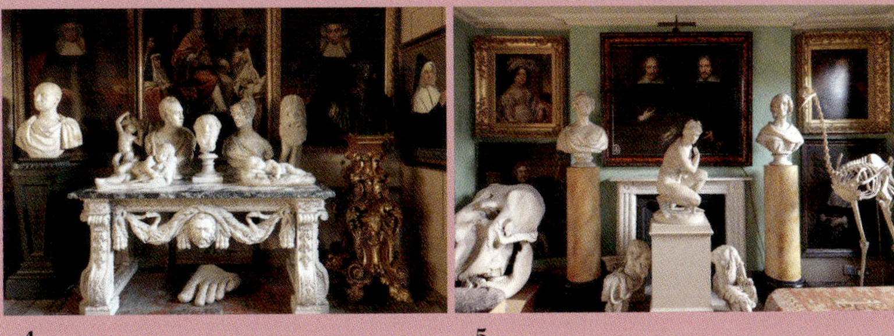

4   5

einer griechischen Tragödienmaske spielt – eine Kopie Bartolomeo Cavaceppis –, sowie Peter Rouws Büste von Lady Thorold. Unter der Konsole im Stil des Matthias Lock aus dem frühen 18. Jh. liegen Fragmente einer antiken römischen Skulptur.
Une collection de statues en marbre comprenant la représentation insolite d'un enfant jouant avec un masque de la tragédie grecque, une copie de Bartolomeo Cavaceppi, et le buste de Lady Thorold par Peter Rouw. Sous la console dans le style de Matthias Lock du début du 18e siècle, des fragments d'une sculpture romaine antique.

5 Ancestral busts and portraits flanked by selected items from natural history: the gigantic skull of an elephant and the skeleton of an ostrich. On the wall, Anthony van Dyck's double portrait of *Sir Arthur Hopton and His Brother, Sir Thomas Hopton*, begun in 1638 but never completed.
Büste und Ahnenporträts, umgeben von naturhistorischen Objekten: ein Elefantenschädel, ein Straußenskelett. An der Wand ein Doppelporträt von Anton van Dycks, das Sir Arthur Hopton und seinen Bruder Sir Thomas Hopton zeigt. Van Dyck hatte es 1638 begonnen, jedoch nie vollendet.

Bustes et portraits d'ancêtres entourés d'objets d'histoire naturelle : un gigantesque crâne d'éléphant, un squelette d'autruche. Sur le mur, un double portrait d'Antoine van Dyck, *Sir Arthur Hopton et son frère Sir Thomas Hopton*, tableau que le peintre a commencé en 1638 mais qu'il n'a jamais achevé.

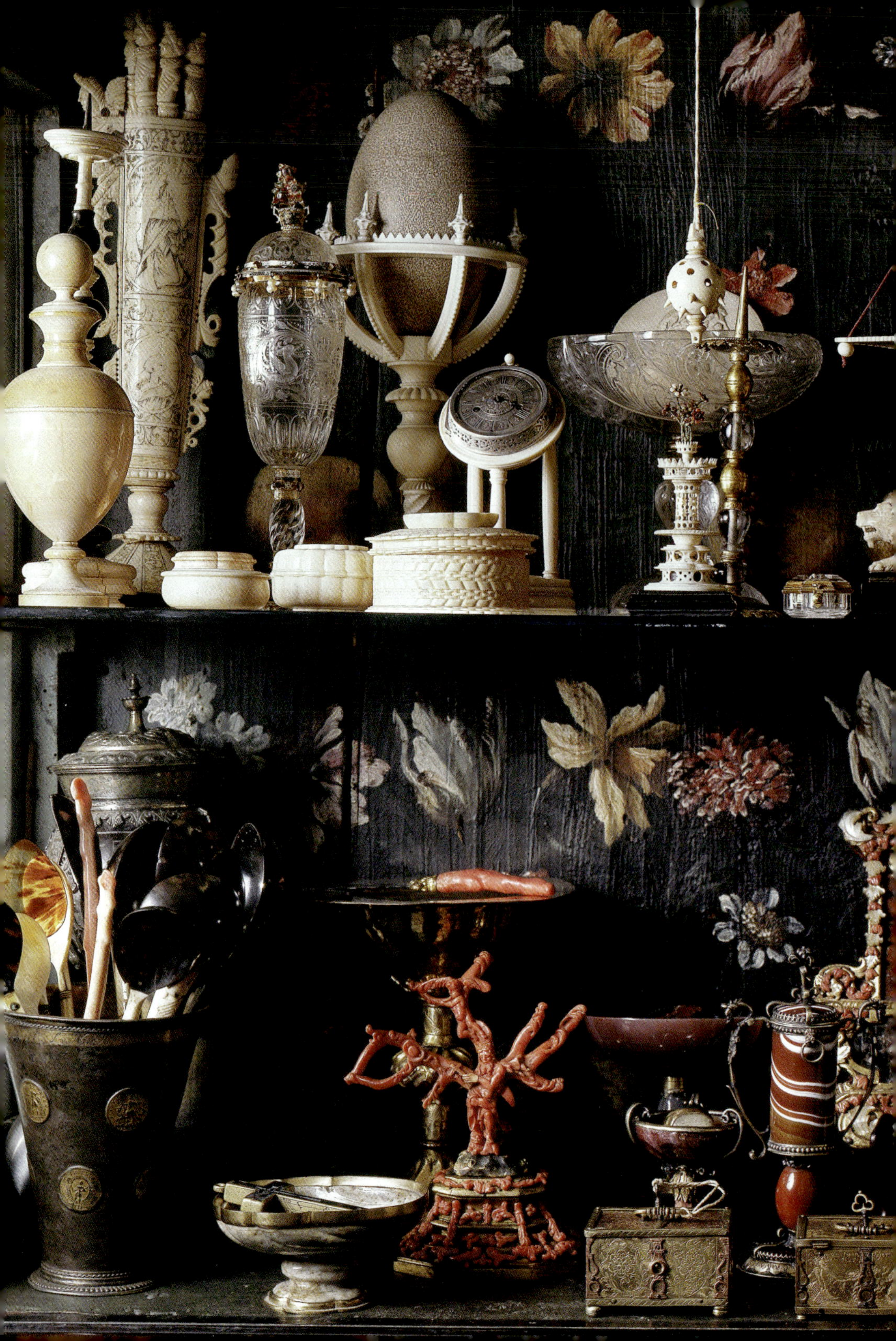

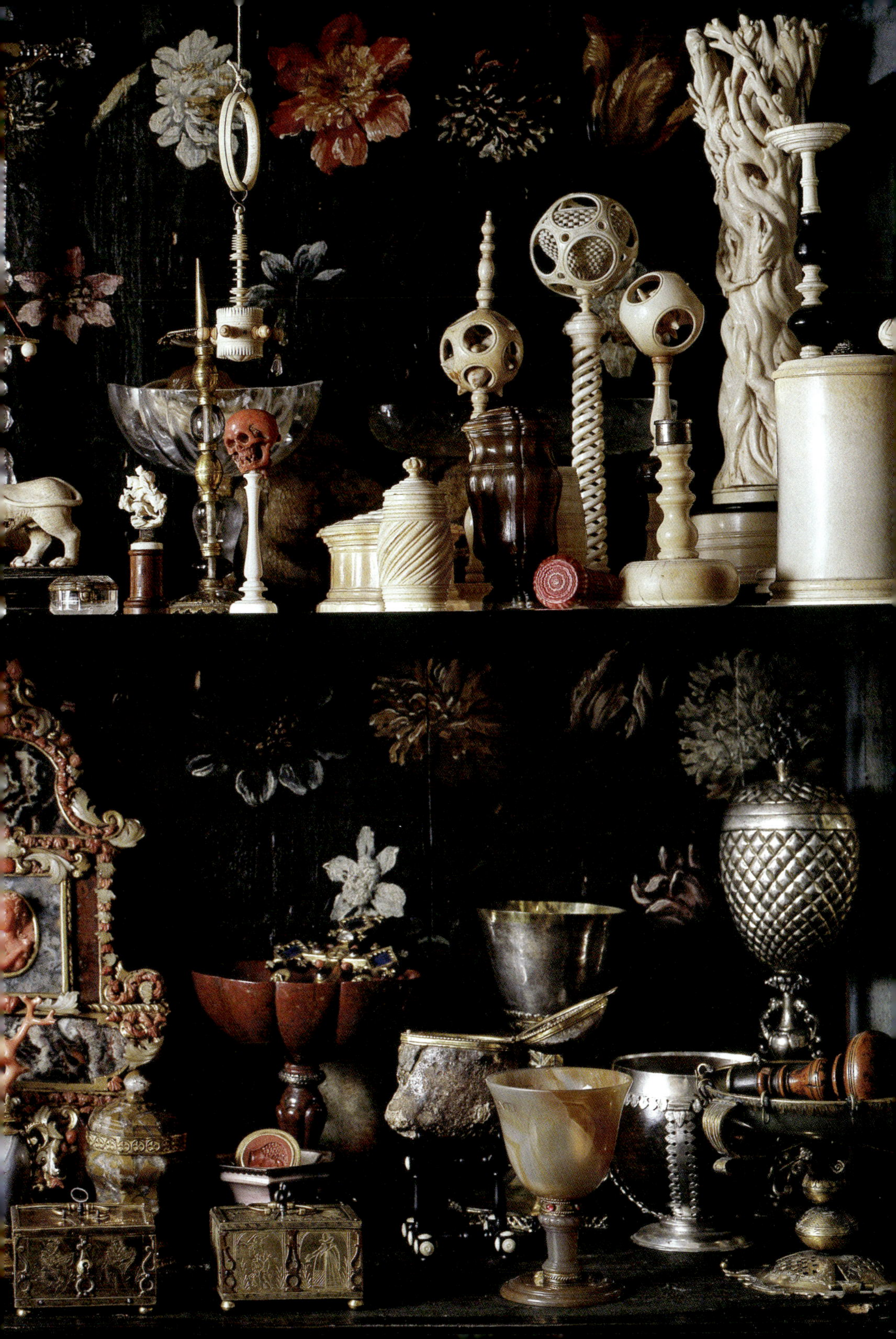

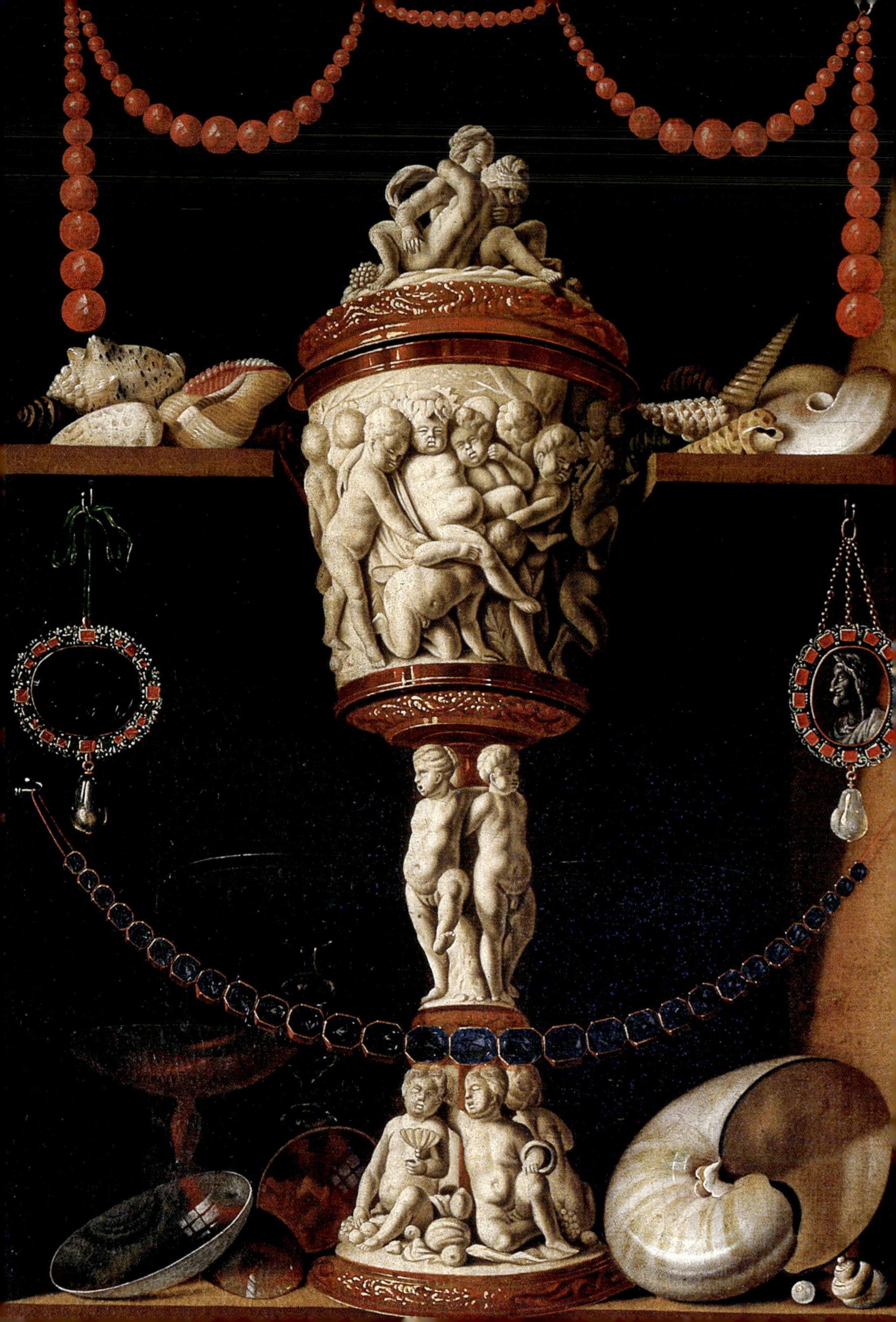

Addresses

AUSTRIA
Die Kunst- und Wunderkammer
Schloss Ambras
Schlossstraße 20
6020 Innsbruck
Tel.: +43 (0) 1 525 244802
info@schlossambras-innsbruck.at
www.schlossambras-innsbruck.at

Das Mineralienkabinett
Stift Seitenstetten
Am Klosterberg 1
3353 Seitenstetten
Tel.: +43 (0) 7477 423000
stift@stift-seitenstetten.at
www.stift-seitenstetten.at

Kunstkammer Wien
Kunsthistorisches Museum Wien
Maria-Theresien-Platz
1010 Vienna
Tel.: +43 (0) 1 525244409
info.kk@khm.at
www.khm.at

DENMARK
Rosenborg Slot
Øster Voldgade 4A
1350 Copenhagen
Tel.: +45 (0) 3315 3286
rosenborg@kosa.dk
www.kongernessamling.dk

ENGLAND
Malplaquet House
137–139 Mile End Road
London E1 4AW

FRANCE
Château de Bannes
24440 Beaumont-du-Périgord

Château de Dampierre
2, Grande Rue
78720 Dampierre-en-Yvelines

*Cabinet d'histoire naturelle
de Clément Lafaille*
Muséum d'Histoire Naturelle
de La Rochelle
28, rue Albert 1er
17000 La Rochelle
Tel.: +33 (0) 5 46411825
museum.info@ville-larochelle.fr
www.museum.larochelle.fr

Collection Kugel
Galerie Kugel
25, quai Anatole France
75007 Paris
Tel.: +33 (0) 1 42608623
galerie@galeriekugel.com
www.galeriekugel.com

Collection Guy Ladrière
Galerie Ratton-Ladrière
11, quai Voltaire
75007 Paris
Tel.: + 33 (0) 1 42612979
www.ratton-ladriere.com

GERMANY
Grünes Gewölbe
Staatliche Kunstsammlungen
Residenzschloss Dresden
Taschenberg 2
01067 Dresden
Tel.: +49 (0) 351 49142000
besucherservice@skd.museum
www.skd.museum

Schloss Friedenstein
Schlossplatz 1
99867 Gotha
Tel.: +49 (0) 3621 82340
service@stiftung-friedenstein.de
www.stiftungfriedenstein.de

Kunst- und Naturalienkammer
Franckesche Stiftungen
Franckeplatz 1
Haus 1
06110 Halle
Tel.: +49 (0) 345 2127450
oeffentlicÙeit@francke-halle.de
www.francke-halle.de

ITALY
Collezione Alessandro Orsi
Villa Ca' Mera
Piazza Cairoli, 32
21022 Azzate (Varese)

Collezione Raniero Gnoli
Palazzo Patrizi
Via della Mola
00062 Castel Giuliano,
Bracciano (Rome)
Tel.: +39 (06) 99802530
info@castelgiuliano.it
www.castel-giuliano.it

*"Gli avori di Coburgo" e i
nautili. Tesoro dei Granduchi*
Palazzo Pitti
Piazza Pitti 1
50125 Florence
Tel.: +39 (055) 294883
infouffizi@cultura.gov.it
www.uffizi.it/palazzo-pitti/
tesoro-dei-granduchi

Collezione Lazzaro Spallanzani
Musei Civici di Reggio Emilia
Palazzo dei Musei
Via Lazzaro Spallanzani, 1
42121 Reggio Emilia
Tel.: +39 (0522) 456477
musei@municipio.re.it

*Museo storico nazionale
dell'arte sanitaria*
Ospedale Santo Spirito
Lungotevere in Sassia 3
00193 Rome
Tel.: +39 (06) 68352748
segreteria@asas-accademia.it

SWEDEN
Det Augsburgska konstskåpet
The Uppsala University
Museum Gustavianum
Akademigatan 3
75310 Uppsala
Tel: +46 (0) 18 4717571
museum@gustavianum.uu.se
www.gustavianum.uu.se

Bibliography

Arnold, Ulli / Kappel, Jutta /
Syndram, Dirk, *Das Grüne
Gewölbe zu Dresden. Führer
durch seine Geschichte und
seine Sammlungen*, Munich/
Berlin 1997

Aschengreen Piacenti, Kirsten,
Il Museo degli Argenti a Firenze,
Florence 1967

Aschengreen Piacenti, Kirsten,
"Gli eburnei calici", in *FMR* 76,
Milan 1989, pp. 68–96

Berti, Luciano, *Il Principe dello
Studiolo. Francesco I dei Medici
e la fine del Rinascimento fiorentino*, Florence 1967

Bocchi, Francesco, *Le bellezze della
città di Firenze*, Florence 1591,
expanded edition by Giovanni
Cinelli, Florence 1677

Bredekamp, Horst,
*Antikensehnsucht und
Maschinenglauben: Die
Geschichte der Kunstkammer
und die Zukunft der Kunst-
geschichte*, Berlin 1993

Bredekamp, Horst / Brüning,
Jochen / Weber, Cornelia (ed.),
*Theater der Natur und Kunst:
Wunderkammern des Wissens*,
exh. cat. Martin-Gropius-Bau,
Berlin 2000

Cableri, Luca, *Theatrum Mundi*,
Arezzo 2015

Campanella, Tommaso, *La città
del Sole*, 1602, ed. A. Seroni,
Milan 1988

Campanella, Tommaso, "Sonnenstaat", in *Der utopische Staat*,
trans. and ed. Klaus J. Heinisch,
Reinbek 1983

Campanella, Tommaso, *La Cité
du Soleil*, trans. Arnaud Tripet,
Paris 2000

Clair, Jean, "La mélancolie du
savoir", in *Mélancolie. Génie et
folie en Occident*, Paris 2005,
pp. 202–208

Da Bisticci, Vespasiano, *Vite di
uomini illustri del secolo XV*
(c. 1482), Milan 1951

Daston, Lorraine J. / Park,
Katharine, *Wonders and the
Order of Nature 1150–1750*,
New York 1998

Davenne, Christine, *Cabinets of
Wonder*, New York 2012

De Benedictis, Cristina, *Per la storia
del collezionismo italiano. Fonti e
documenti*, Florence 1991

De Vecchi, Pier Luigi, "Il Museo
Gioviano e le 'Verae imagines'
degli uomini illustri", in *Omaggio
a Tiziano. La cultura milanese
nell'età di Carlo V*, Milan 1977,
pp. 87–93

Frey, Karl, *Der literarische Nachlass
Giorgio Vasaris*, Munich 1930

Haag, Sabine, *Capolavori delle
Collezioni del castello di Ambras*,
Vienna 2010

Haag, Sabine / Kirchweger, Franz,
*Treasures of the Habsburgs, at
the Kunsthistorisches Museum,
Vienna*, London 2013

Huber, Simone / Huber, Peter,
"Das Mineralienkabinett im
Stift Seitenstetten", in *Lapis* 13,
Munich 1988, pp. 15–21

Knox, Tim / Longstaffe-Gowan,
Todd, *Malplaquet House.
A Description*, Bristol 2008

Leithe-Jasper, Manfred /
Distelberger, Rudolf, *Il Kunsthistorisches Museum di Vienna:
il tesoro imperiale*, London 1998

Lugli, Adalgisa, *Naturalia et
Mirabilia. Il collezionismo enci-
clopedico nelle Wunderkammern
d'Europa*, Milan 1983

Lugli, Adalgisa, *Arte e scienza:
Wunderkammer*, Venice 1986

Lugli, Adalgisa, *Wunderkammer:
la stanza della meraviglia*,
Turin 1997

Marino, Giambattista, *La Galeria*,
Venice, 1620

Marino, Giambattista, *La Galeria*,
Italian-German ed., selected
and translated by Christiane
Kruse and Rainer Stillers,
Mainz 2009

Mauriès, Patrick, *Le stanze delle
meraviglie*, Milan 2002

Mazzotta, Martina, "Arte, scienza
e filosofia della natura nell'età
della meraviglia", in *Visioni del
fantastico e del meraviglioso.
Prima dei surrealisti*, Milan 2004,
pp. 11–18

Meloni, Stefano, *Lazzaro
Spallanzani e la collezione
naturalistica dei Musei Civici
di Reggio Emilia*, Reggio
Emilia 2013

Mosco, Marilena, "Le conchiglie
dei Medici", in *FMR* 134,
Milan 1999, pp. 37–68

Müller-Bahlke, Thomas,
*Die Wunderkammer der
Franckeschen Stiftungen.
2., überarbeitete und
erweiterte Auflage.*
Halle 2012, pp. 87–90

Paolucci, Antonio, "Lo sguardo
di Medusa", in Scritti d'arte,
Florence 2007, pp. 87–90

Rey, Daniel, "Il mobile infinito",
in *FMR* 138, Milan 2000,
pp. 29–50

Reynaud, Nicole / Ressort, Claudie,
"Les portraits d'hommes
illustres du Studiolo di Urbino
au Louvre par Juste de Gand
et Pedro Berruguete", in
Revue du Louvre, XLI, 1991,
pp. 82–114

Scarisbrick, Diana / Boardman,
Joy / Wagner, Claudia, *The Guy
Ladrière Collection of Gems and
Rings*, London 2016

Schäfer, Bernd, "Le pietre della
pace. Il castello di Friedenstein",
in *FMR* 135, Milan 1999,
pp. 19–44

Schlosser, Julius von, *Raccolte
d'arte e di meraviglie del tardo
Rinascimento*, Florence 1974

Schmidt, Eike D. / Sframeli, Maria,
*Diafane passioni, Avori barocchi
dalle corti europee*, exh. cat.,
Florence 2013

Syndram, Dirk / Kappel, Jutta /
Weinhold, Ulrike, *The Baroque
Treasury at the Grünes Gewölbe
Dresden*, Munich/Berlin 2006

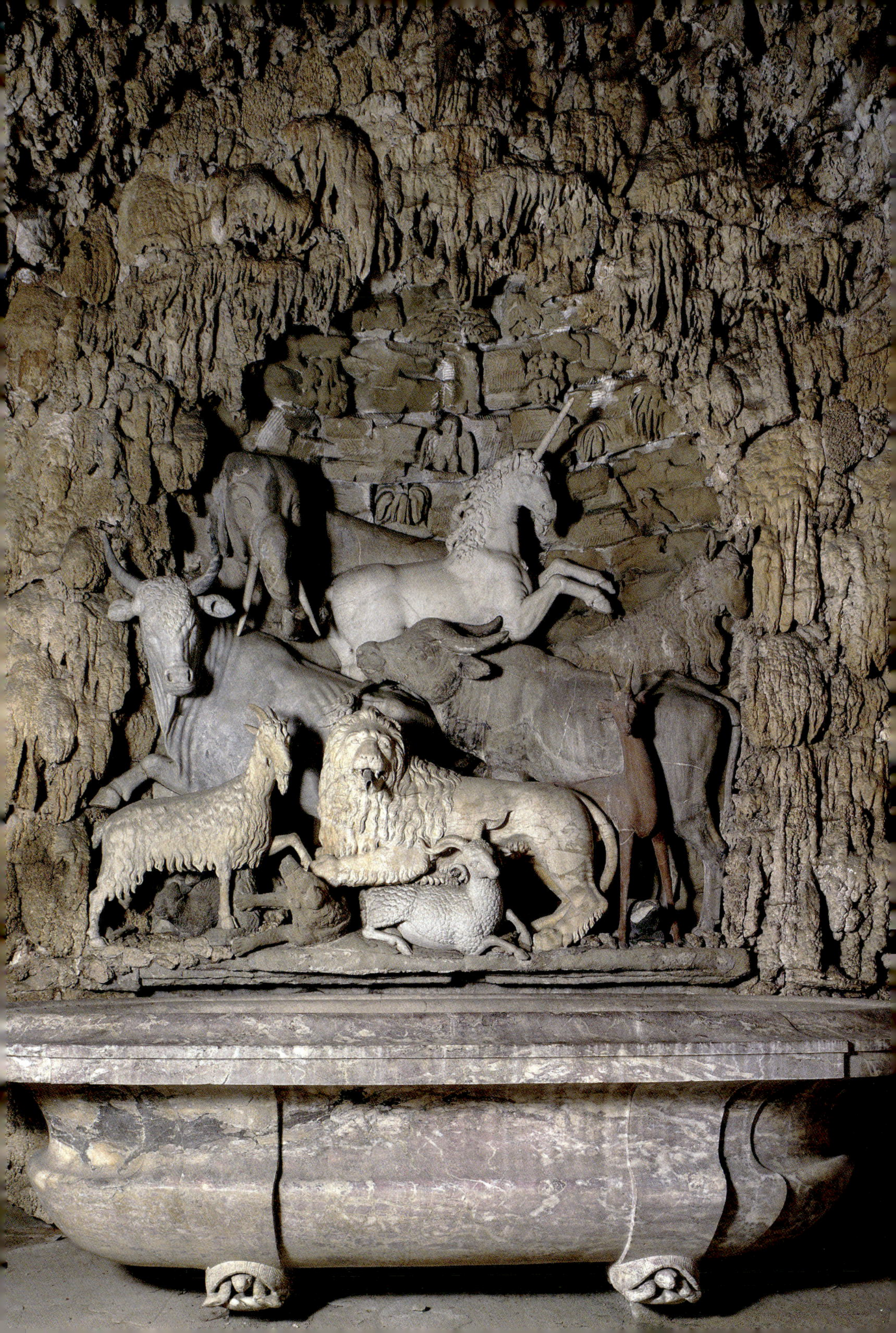

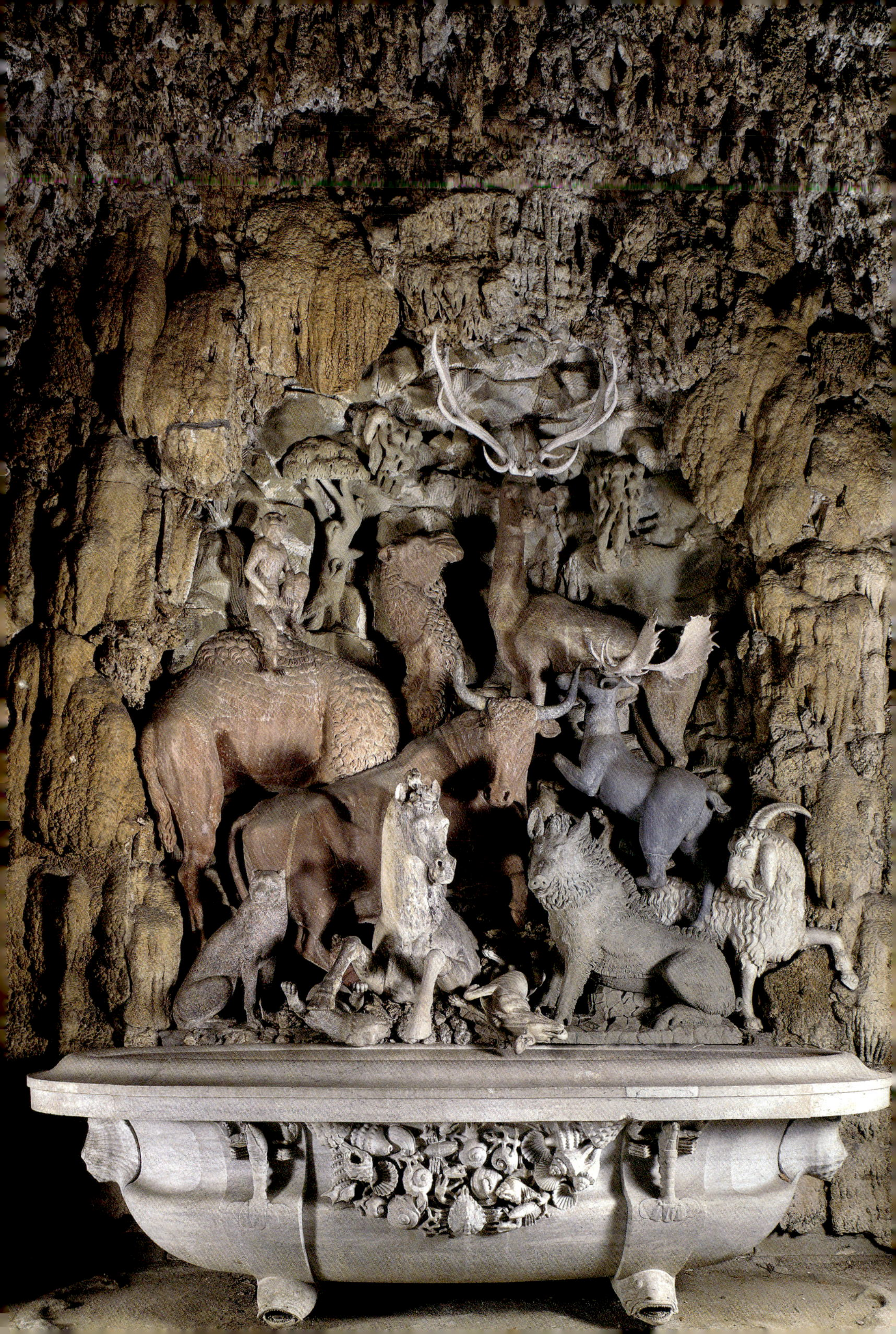

Photo Credits

All images © Massimo Listri
with the exception of:

Agenzia Photografica Scala,
  Antella, Florence © 2019 Photo
  Scala, Florence: pp. 11, 15, 21,
  268, 318.
Archiv der Franckeschen
  Stiftungen Bildarchiv,
  Halle: p. 126.
Bayerische Staatsbibliothek,
  Munich: p. 22.
Biblioteca Panizzi di Reggio
  Emilia: p. 306.
Bibliothèque scientifique du
  Muséum d'Histoire Naturelle
  de La Rochelle: p. 354.
Peter Böttcher, Allhartsberg:
  p. 182.
bpk / Kunstgewerbemuseum,
  SMB / Saturia Linke, Berlin:
  pp. 63, 101.
Bridgeman Images, Berlin:
  pp. 60–61.
Galerie Kugel, Paris:
  pp. 388, 396.
Kunsthistorisches Museum,
  Vienna: pp. 56, 144,
  166, 168–169.
Didier Loire, Paris: pp. 390–391.
Niedersächsische Staats- und
  Universitätsbibliothek,
  Göttingen: pp. 10, 18, 33, 38.
© SZ Photo / Scherl / Bridgeman
  Images: p. 66.
Ulmer Museen: p. 25.
Uppsala universitetsbibliotek:
  p. 236.
© Victoria and Albert Museum,
  London: p. 23.

Cover *Pediment with a mask in
the style of Arcimboldo / Schrankbekrönung mit einer Arcimbol-
desken Maske / Fronton de cabinet
avec masque arcimboldesque*, see
p. 132. Halle, Kunst- und Naturalienkammer, Francke Foundations,
cabinet II.B.

Back cover *Pediment with samples
of scripts / Schrankbekrönung mit
Schriftstücken / Fronton de cabinet
avec documents écrits*, see p. 130.
Halle, Kunst- und Naturalienkammer, Francke Foundations,
cabinet XVI.Q.

Front and back endpapers
*Pediment with articles of clothing /
Schrankbekrönung mit Kleidungs-
stücken / Fronton de cabinet avec
vêtements*, see p. 129. Halle, Kunst-
und Naturalienkammer, Francke
Foundations, cabinet XVI.O.

Page 1 *Pediment with a representation of a Malabar native /
Schrankbekrönung mit der Darstellung eines Malabaren / Fronton de
cabinet avec la représentation d'un
Malabar*, see p. 131. Halle, Kunst-
und Naturalienkammer, Francke
Foundations, cabinet XI.L.

Page 2 *Pediment with a mask in
the style of Arcimboldo / Schrankbekrönung mit einer Arcimbold-
esken Maske / Fronton de cabinet
avec masque arcimboldesque*,
see p. 133. Halle, Kunst- und
Naturalienkammer, Francke
Foundations, cabinet VI.F.

Pages 4–5 *Pediment with zoological ensemble / Schrankbekrönung
mit zoologischem Panoptikum /
Fronton de cabinet avec vue
d'ensemble des espèces animales*,
see page 127. Halle, Kunst- und
Naturalienkammer, Francke
Foundations, cabinet IV.D.

Pages 6–7 *Hall of the / Halle der /
Salle de la Galleria Mirabilia*. Rome,
Giano del Bufalo.

Pages 436–437
*Shelves with artefacts made of ivory,
rock crystal and horn, pietra dura
cups, Trapani corals and German
jewellery boxes / Wandregal mit
Objekten aus Elfenbein, Bergkristall,
Horn, Pietra dura, Korallen aus
Trapani und deutsche Schmuck-
kassetten / Étagère avec des objets
en ivoire, cristaux de roche, cornes,
tasses en pietra dura, coraux de
Trapani, boîtes à bijoux allemandes*,
16th–18th century. Milan,
private collection.

Page 438 Georg Heinz, *Cabinet of
Curiosities / Kunstkammerschrank
/ Le Cabinet des merveilles* (detail),
1666. Oil on canvas, 114.5 x 93.3 cm /
45⅛ x 36¾ in.

Pages 441, 442 Niccolò Tribolo,
*Grotto of the animals / Grotte
der Tiere / Grotte des animaux*,
1568–1580. Florence, Giardino
della Villa di Castello, Grotta
degli animali.

Pages 446–447 *Detail of
display case featuring various
specimens, including reptiles
and amphibians, preserved in
fluid or in their natural form /
Vitrine mit verschiedenen
Präparaten, darunter trocken-
und feuchtpräparierte Reptilien
und Amphibien / Vitrine
présentant une sélection de
spécimens, en outre des reptiles
et des amphibiens naturalisés
et conservés en fluide*. Cabinet
d'histoire naturelle de Clément
Lafaille, Muséum d'Histoire
Naturelle de La Rochelle.

Biographies

Antonio Paolucci (1939-2024)

After studying art history under Roberto Longhi, Paolucci began his career in cultural heritage and its administration. He was in charge of this work in Venice, Verona and Mantua before becoming director of the Opificio delle Pietre Dure in Florence, regional director for Cultural Heritage in Tuscany and, for almost 20 years, directing the Polo Museale Fiorentino. From January 1995 to May 1996 he served as minister of cultural and environmental heritage in the government of Lamberto Dini. Following the earthquake of 1997 Paolucci was appointed extraordinary commissioner for the restoration of the Basilica of St. Francis in Assisi. From 2007 to 2016 he was director of the Vatican Museums. A specialist in Italian Renaissance art, Paolucci authored several museum and exhibition catalogues, together with essays and monographs on Donatello, Piero della Francesca, Luca Signorelli, Antoniazzo Romano, Michelangelo, Raphael, Filippo Lippi, Cellini, Giorgione, Giovanni Bellini and Melozzo da Forlì, amongst many others.

◎ ◈ ◎

Giulia M.L. Carciotto

Carciotto graduated in art history from the Sapienza University in Rome before becoming a research fellow at the Warburg Institute in London, where she also worked for Christie's. She worked as editor-in-chief for the art publisher Franco Maria Ricci Editore in Milan, and now teaches at the Academy of Fine Arts in Palermo and at the Abadir Academy in Catania.

◎ ◈ ◎

Massimo Listri

Born in Florence in 1953, Massimo Listri began his professional career as a photographer at the young age of 17, working for art and architecture magazines. Thanks to publisher Franco Maria Ricci, he had the opportunity to produce the early great photo features for the magazine *FMR* dedicated to the most beautiful palaces, the most extraordinary villas and architecture, as well as memorable books of photographs. During the course of his career he has created over 70 books collaborating with the most prestigious European and international publishers. For the last few years he has devoted himself to exhibiting his art around the world. His most recent shows have taken place at the Morgan Library & Museum in New York, Palazzo del Quirinale in Rome, Museo de Arte Moderno in Buenos Aires, Benaki Museum in Athens, Kunsthistorisches Museum in Vienna, National Museum of San Carlos in Mexico City, National Central Library of Taipei, Schusev State Museum of Architecture in Moscow.

Acknowledgements

Publisher's Acknowledgements
We are much indebted to all the museums, institutions and collectors cited in the picture captions and in the photo credits for their kind assistance in the publication. Many curators and collectors have contributed decisively to the success of our undertaking. We should like to acknowledge: Lucille Bourroux (La Rochelle), Dario del Bufalo (Rome), Giano del Bufalo (Rome), Luca Cableri (Arezzo), Benoît Constensoux (Paris), Sabine Haag (Vienna), Peter Huber (Wiener Neustadt), Claudia Kryza-Gersch (Dresden), Nicolas and Alexis Kugel (Paris), Thomas Kuster (Innsbruck), Christine Ladrière (Paris), Marco Maria Melardi (Florence), Thomas Müller-Bahlke (Halle), Carlo and Francesco Orsi (Varese), Pierre Peyrolle (Paris), Paulus Rainer (Vienna), Camelia Ropotan (Florence), Veronika Sandbichler (Innsbruck), Maria Sframeli (Florence), Dirk Weber (Dresden).

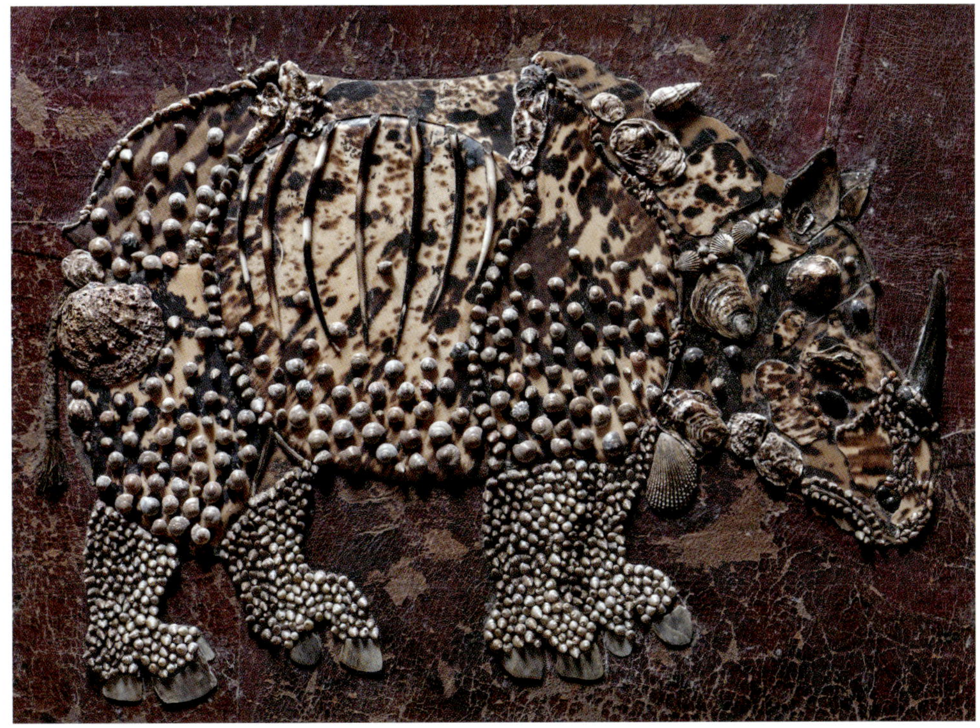

Rhinoceros / Nashorn / Rhinocéros,
German, end of the 17th century. Leather, shells,
38 x 53 cm / 15 x 20⅞ in. Private collection.

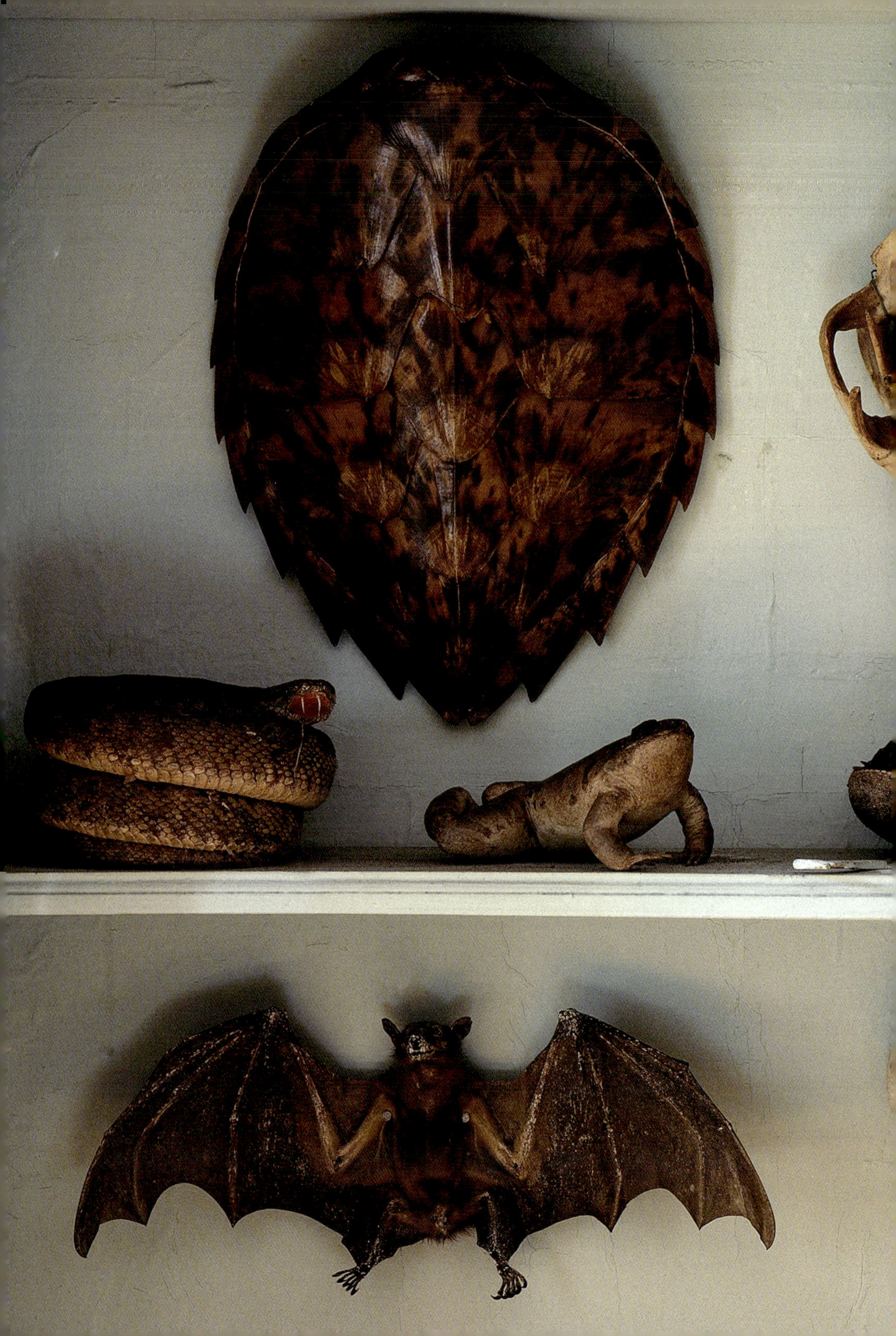

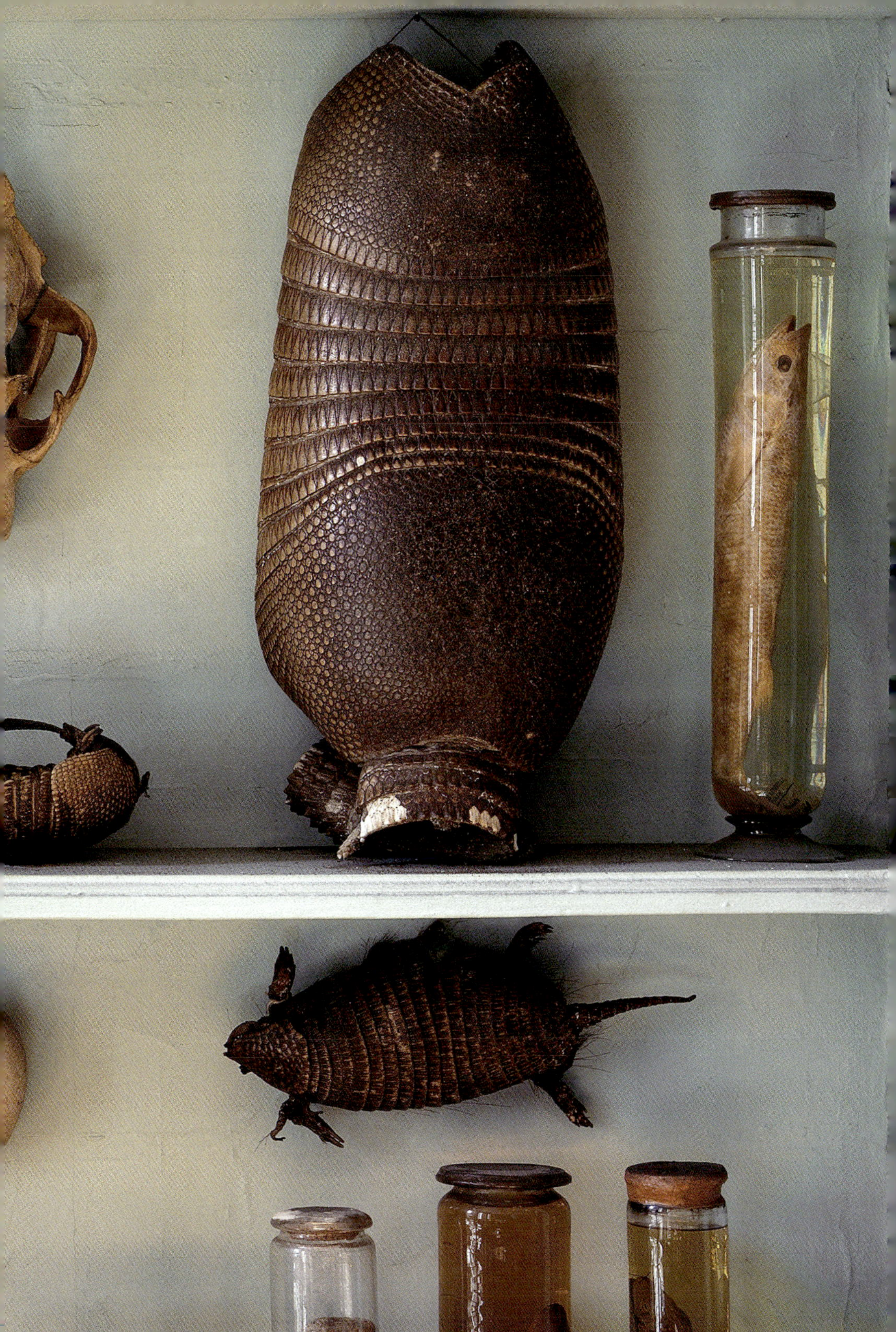

Imprint

EACH AND EVERY TASCHEN BOOK PLANTS A SEED!
TASCHEN is a carbon neutral publisher. Each year, we offset our annual carbon
emissions with carbon credits at the Instituto Terra, a reforestation program
in Minas Gerais, Brazil, founded by Lélia and Sebastião Salgado. To find out more
about this ecological partnership, please check: www.taschen.com/zerocarbon
Inspiration: unlimited. Carbon footprint: zero

Want to see more? Visit taschen.com to view our current publications, browse
our latest magazine, and subscribe to our newsletter.

© 2024 TASCHEN GmbH
Hohenzollernring 53, D–50672 Köln
www.taschen.com

English translation Antonia Reiner (Introduction by A. Paolucci, catalogue
entries by G. Carciotto), Toronto; Agnes Stillfried (plate captions), Cairo
German translation Petra Kaiser (Einführung von A. Paolucci, Katalogeinträge
von G. Carciotto), Berlin; Agnes Stillfried (Tafellegenden), Cairo
French translation Geneviève Lambert (introduction de A. Paolucci, textes
de catalogue de G. Carciotto), Fontenay-sous-Bois; Michèle Schreyer (légendes
des illustrations), Cologne

ISBN 978-3-8365-9378-6
Printed in Bosnia-Herzegovina